A GALLERY OF ROGUES

Portraits in True Crime

MICHAEL KURLAND

Prentice Hall General Reference
New York London Toronto Sydney Tokyo Singapore

ACKNOWLEDGEMENTS

I would like to thank Tom Ogden, Max Maven and Professor Marcello Truzzi for their advice and assistance, whether I took it or not, Tina Mascara for her technical aid, and Diana Kurland for her love and patience. I also thank the Research Unit of the Office of Public and Congressional Services of the F.B.I. for their courteous and prompt response to my requests for information and photographs. My editor, Deirdre Mullane, also deserves thanks for her patience, kindness and professionalism.

PRENTICE HALL GENERAL REFERENCE
15 Columbus Circle
New York, New York, 10023

Library of Congress Cataloging in Publication data
Kurland, Michael.
A gallery of rogues / Michael Kurland.
p. cm.
Includes bibliographical references and index.
ISBN 0-671-85011-3—ISBN 0-671-85032-6 (pbk.)
1. Crime—United States—Encyclopedias. 2. Criminals—United States—Biography—Dictionaries. I. Title.
HV6769.K87 1994
364.973—dc20 93-15171 CIP

Designed by Rhea Braunstein

Manufactured in the United States of America

10 9 8 7 6 5 4 3 2 1

First Edition

Contents

Introduction

People have an abiding fascination for things they can't have or shouldn't do. If that biblical fruit hadn't been forbidden, we'd still be in the Garden of Eden. Folk wisdom points out that the grass is always greener on the other side of the fence—and often "the fence" represents the boundaries of acceptable behavior. Most of us accept the legal and moral strictures on our behavior fairly well; partly through fear of being caught and punished, but perhaps largely because our religious or moral upbringing has taught us that certain actions are unacceptable, and that our peers will shun us if we commit them. Indeed people with a strong sense of morality sometimes willingly accept civil punishment when they find that the law is in conflict with their private probity. There is the story of Henry David Thoreau, who went to jail rather than pay a tax that he disagreed with. When Ralph Waldo Emerson went to visit him in the slammer, Emerson is reputed to have demanded, "Why are you here?"

"Why are you *not* here?" Thoreau replied.

We reasonably law-abiding citizens are fascinated by the acts we would not do, and by the people who do them. For in observing these people we often see ourselves; through a distorted and murky glass, but recognizably ourselves. And the crimes that interest us the most are not necessarily the most innately vicious or horrible, but the most disruptive of that public morality to which we subscribe.

There are murders, for example, that we concede are for the public good. A killing in defense of life or property is acceptable. The violent death of an enemy in wartime is not regarded as an infraction of the sixth commandment, even if the act was not directly in self-defense. The state executioner is performing a public service.

There are murders that do not shock us, although we do not condone them. The death of a mob boss in a gangland dispute is often treated humorously by the popular press. A gangster getting shot down in the street may horrify us or anger us, but unless there is something unique and compelling about it, it will cause no books to be written, no movies of the week to be shown. But even mob killings can get out of hand. The slaughter in a Chicago garage on St. Valentine's day, 1929, caused a popular revulsion that made gangsters unpopular at parties for the first time since the start of Prohibition. "Bugs" Moran, himself no tin angel, thought it excessive. "Only Capone kills like that," he told a reporter.

The murder of Andrew Borden and his wife in Fall River, Massachusetts, in 1892 has fascinated us for a century. His daughter Lizzie was the only logical suspect based on the facts, but for a churchgoing girl from a proper middle-class Victorian family to kill anyone, much less her parents, was just not done. It was so unthinkable that the jury was unable to come to grip with the facts of the case, and acquitted her. It was so unthinkable that it has become legendary, and is still remembered in a century in which much bloodier and more evil acts have been committed almost routinely.

Other crimes that have withstood the test of time are the 1924 Leopold & Loeb case, where two teenage boys from good families murdered a younger boy for the thrill of it; and the 1926 Hall-Mills case, where a minister and the choir singer who was his paramour were found murdered in a New Jersey orchard with their love letters strewn about the bodies. The kidnapping and subsequent murder of the Lindbergh baby (if, indeed, he was killed) in 1936 still holds a fascination for us over half a century later.

Today the public is fascinated by the grotesque, the bizarre, and the horrible, particularly when these qualities are combined in one mass murderer. And any number of serial killers have sprung up to satisfy this public thirst for blood: John Wayne Gacy, who performed as a clown and buried his victims under his house; Albert DeSalvo, the "Boston Strangler," who arranged his victims' bodies in obscene postures the police couldn't describe to the press; Jeffrey Dahmer, who left body parts from his victims around his apartment.

It may seem like the last quarter of the twentieth century has spawned an unseemly proliferation of mass killers, and that the United States can claim pride of place in the contest, but this is not so. The homicidal maniac has always been with us, appearing randomly on all parts of the globe, and some practitioners from the past could share top billing with any of today's crop. To cite some examples from beyond the scope of the present book: At the end of the last century Jack the Ripper terrorized London, and took body parts of his victim away as souvenirs. Peter Kürten, the "Vampire of Düsseldorf," who was apprehended in 1930 after killing a score of young girls and a few men, enjoyed drinking his victims' blood. Baron Gilles de Rais, who fought alongside Joan of Arc, was hanged in France in 1440 after confessing to the murder of at least 140 children, most of whom were raped, sodomized, and tortured to death in the Baron's castle.

We will concern ourselves in this book with the spectrum of crime, and look at murderers, gamblers, rum-runners, con-men, women of easy virtue, and politicians with sticky fingers. The study of crime is the study of law, for laws define and thus create crimes, and without law there would be no crime. As simplistic and obvious as that sounds, it is often overlooked in the creation of new laws, and the recasting of old ones. Laws are created by the society that enforces them, and crime is an offense against society. Those who believe that offenses against their particular deity or their particular morés or moral values are *per se* crimes, and would cast their country's laws to reflect this, should be sure that their views reflect the morés and values of a great majority within their society. Since laws create crimes, bad or unpopular laws can create a society of criminals.

It is also good to remember that human lawmakers cannot alter natural laws. The attempt of the legislature of Tennessee in 1910 to make π equal to 3 did not alter the ratio of the circumference of a circle to its diameter. The forbidding by many state legislatures in the 1920s of the teaching of evolution theory did not make the fossil evidence disappear.

The most obvious example of a law that went against the fabric of the society in which it was enacted, and created a nation of criminals, was Prohibition. The fact that the aims of the Women's Christian Temperance Union and other groups supporting the abolition of alcohol were noble, and that the evils they perceived were truly evil, did not make it possible to impose a workable ban on the consumption of alcohol. They saw drunkenness and dissipation, and the men of the lower classes spending their meager paychecks on alcohol and depriving their families of the necessities of life. It was an incessant theme of reformers in the 1890s. The melodramas *The Drunkard* and *Ten Nights in a Barroom* were ever-popular. But inebriation is a physiological condition, not a sin; and alcoholism is not a sin but a disease. The reformers tried neither to cure the disease of alcoholism or ameliorate the grinding poverty and unending toil that drove the underclass to drink, they merely removed the alcohol.

It didn't work.

What the reformers had ignored was that the middle class and the upper class also enjoyed their liquor, and saw no reason to give it up. And an overwhelming majority of the population saw no sin in an occasional glass of beer. Making it illegal merely added a little spice to the brew. Thus Prohibition became a joke among the drinking classes and a great source of revenue for organized crime. Indeed it turned organized crime from a minor nuisance into a major threat.

If you do not find your favorite criminal in here, I apologize. Crime is a popular pastime, and it would take a work of many volumes to list all the crimes of interest that occurred in this country in this century alone. I have tried to give a representative sample of the more popular sorts of crimes, along with a smattering of the unique, the bizarre, the implausible, and in a few cases the impossible.

I hope that you enjoy this book. The study of crime is fascinating and perfectly safe, as long as it is conducted in an easy chair from the pages of a book.

MICHAEL KURLAND

A

ABBANDANDO, Frank "The Dasher" (1910–1942)

A New York hoodlum active in the 1920s to 1940s, Frank Abbandando associated with Harry "Happy" Maione and ABE "KID TWIST" RELES. He and Maione were indicted for the particularly brutal murder of George "Whitey" Rudnick, a loan shark, who had been cut and stabbed 63 times with knives and an ice pick, as well as being strangled and having his head crushed. Reles turned state's evidence, and Maione and Abbandando, who failed to endear himself to the judge by threatening to kill him right in the courtroom, received the death penalty. They were executed in the electric chair at SING SING on February 19, 1942.

ABBOT, Burton W. "Bud" (1928–1957)

CONVICTED OF MURDER BY CIRCUMSTANTIAL EVIDENCE, ABBOT DIED IN CALIFORNIA'S GAS CHAMBER WHEN A STAY OF EXECUTION ARRIVED TOO LATE.

In one of the most talked-about cases of the 1950s, Burton Abbot was convicted and executed for the murder of Stephanie Bryan in 1957. Since the evidence against him was circumstantial, much of it was rebutted, and he seemed an unlikely murderer, doubt about his guilt continued past his execution. Yet the evidence against him, circumstantial though it was, was certainly damning.

At 3:30 in the afternoon of Thursday, April 28, 1955, 14-year-old Stephanie Bryan left Willard Junior High School, in Berkeley, California, and started home. She and a girl from her class stopped at a pet store to buy a book on parakeets, went to the public library to take out a couple of teen-age novels, and ended up at a doughnut shop. Afterwards, the two girls separated, and Stephanie cut through the tennis courts of the Claremont Hotel, a regular shortcut, to go home. She never arrived.

Stephanie was not a precocious child. She had always been painfully shy, a condition that was exacerbated by the onset of puberty and bad skin, the relic of a childhood eczema. Although she was an honor student, her teacher hesitated to call on her in class as the experience was so obviously distressing for her. Her reserve was so strong that it took six months for her to allow her piano teacher to drive her home after lessons.

The oldest of five children, Stephanie came from an overly protective family. Dr. Bryan, a radiologist in an Oakland hospital, drove his four daughters and one son to school every morning, and their mother told them the route to take home and watched for them, or sometimes went out to meet them in the evening. When Stephanie had not arrived by 4:15, her mother retraced the route Stephanie took home, going all the way back to the school, without meeting her. At 5:30, when Dr. Bryan arrived home, they began calling Stephanie's friends. At 6:15, they called the police. Stephanie was extremely punctual; if she was to be late for any reason she invariably called, and she would never go off with an acquaintance, much less a stranger. What in another child might be understandable tardiness was with Stephanie a sign that something was definitely wrong.

A week passed without a hint as to what had happened to the missing girl. The Bryans posted a $2,500 reward for information. Then, on May 5, a man in Contra Costa County, north of Berkeley, came to the police with a French textbook he had found in a field. It was Stephanie's. But there was no indication as to how it had come to that field.

For the next two months, the case was at a standstill. Then on Friday, July 15, it took off. Bud Abbot and his wife Georgia were at home entertaining two friends, Otto and Leona Dezman. Georgia worked for Leona, who ran a local beauty parlor. After dinner, Georgia went to the basement to sort through some old clothes, kept in a couple of cardboard cartons, trying to assemble a costume to use in an amateur theatrical. A short time later, she came upstairs with a red leather handbag she had found in one of the cartons. In it were identification papers, photographs, and an unfinished letter, all the property of Stephanie Bryan.

After some discussion, they agreed that the police should be called, and Dezman did so. Abbot's mother, Elsie, who lived with them, said that she had noticed the handbag in the basement in May and had tossed it into the carton. Apparently a staunchly uncurious woman, she had not opened it to see to whom it belonged. A police officer questioned them, and none of them could offer a guess as to how the handbag had arrived in the basement. The only idea, admittedly farfetched, that any of them could come up with was that in May their garage had been used as a polling place in a local election, and someone might possibly have wandered from the garage into the basement. No one knew why anyone would do such a thing. Bud Abbot seemed as puzzled as the rest of them and not in the slightest worried or alarmed.

The police obtained a search warrant for the Abbots' home and dug up the garden. The digging produced nothing, but hidden behind the dirt wall of the basement, they found Stephanie's schoolbooks, her eyeglasses, the two library books, and her brassiere.

Burton Abbot seemed an unlikely murderer, even to the police. He was small, skinny, and sickly. While in the service, he had contracted double pneumonia, which activated a latent tuberculosis. Doctors had removed one lung and five of his ribs. He had an infected abscess on his chest, which kept him in constant pain. He was so weak, according to his brother Mark, that he was unable to lift his four-year-old son. His alibi was that on the day of the murder he had driven up to a cabin the family had in Trinity County, in Northern California. The next day was the first day of the fishing season, and Bud was a fisherman. If he had arrived when he said he did, and could prove it, he had to be innocent.

The police searched the cabin and the surrounding area. On the night of July 20, two dogs that the police had borrowed from Harold Jackson, a local "bear and bobcat hunter," homed in on a shallow grave up a steep hillside, 335 feet from the cabin. In the grave were the badly decomposed remains of Stephanie Bryan. She had been bludgeoned to death by repeated blows to the head, and her panties were tied loosely around her neck.

Abbot was arrested and indicted for Stephanie's murder. His trial began on November 7, 1955, a little more than five months after the murder. Alameda County District Attorney J. Fred Coakley handled the prosecution, while two experienced defense attorneys, Stanley Whitney and Harold Hove, appeared for the defense. The trial judge, Charles Wade Snook, handled what proved to be a difficult case with equity and skill. Abbot's guilt was not evident, but with the preponderance of evidence, it became inescapable. On the other hand, for almost every point that the prosecution made, the defense found someone to deny or refute it.

The prosecution brought in witnesses who had seen Abbot in Berkeley on the afternoon of April 28—the day of Stephanie's disappearance. Leona Dezman, Georgia Abbot's employer, was one of them. There was no dispute, however, that Bud was at his cabin the following day. The police testified as to the discovery of the body near the cabin and to the discovery of the girl's handbag and belongings in the Abbots' basement. Dr. Paul L. Kirk, a criminologist from the University of California, testified that microscopic samples of fibers and hairs taken from Abbot's car matched samples taken from Stephanie's sweater and two hairs from her head. Soil and gravel and clay from the grave site matched samples taken from Abbot's boots. Pinpoints of blood were found in Abbot's car, but they were too small to be typed beyond the fact that they were human in origin.

The defense brought in witnesses to show that Abbot had been miles away from Berkeley on the day of the kidnapping. They tried to establish that he had visited a tavern near the cabin on the night of the kidnapping, and then again the next day. He had, indeed, been there the next day, but the day of the murder was left in doubt. Unfortunately for Abbot's alibi, nobody would swear that he had not been there, but nobody would swear that he *had*, either. One man heard Delbert Cox, the tavern owner, greet Abbot the next morning with "Why, Bud Abbot, what the hell are you doing here this time of year?" Cox could not remember one way or the other. Besides, Abbot might have been there the night before, and Cox, who was very busy that night, might merely not have noticed.

The most disturbing testimony came from three different people who said that, on April 28, on a road in Berkeley, they had seen a man in a car struggling with a girl. None of them could identify the man, the car, or the girl. Each of them had a reason for not notifying the police at the time.

The defense brought in an expert witness of their own: Lowell Bradford, head of the crime laboratory of Santa Clara County. He testified that the soil and fibers and hair could all have come from other sources. He said that one of the two hairs was coated with dye, and Stephanie had never dyed her hair.

Abbot took the stand and protested his own innocence. It was all a horrible coincidence. Abbot had attempted to be readmitted to the veterans' hospital, probably to reinforce the belief that he was far too weak to have committed such a crime. The doctors who examined him found that his physical condition was "almost that of a normal non-tuberculous man." This weakened considerably the defense's contention that Abbot was physically incapable of having committed the crime.

It took the jury six days to reach a verdict. Seven men and five women found Abbot guilty of kidnapping and murder. There was no recommendation of mercy, and Abbot was sentenced to death in California's gas chamber.

Abbot's new attorney, Leo Sullivan, handled the automatic appeal to the California Supreme Court. He suggested that the physical evidence had been tainted. Perhaps the soil, fibers and hairs had fallen off the policemen's uniforms when they were bending over the trunk of the car. The appeal was turned down. Judge Snook fixed the date of execution for March 15, 1957.

A series of appeals were filed and denied before the execution date. On the morning of the last day, Abbot's newest attorney, George T. Davis, reached the governor of California, Goodwin J. Knight, on board a U.S. Navy ship he was visiting. Davis made one final argument for a postponement, citing a possible lack of due process. Governor Knight agreed to call his secretary for pardons and reprieves, Joseph Babich, for an opinion. At 11:15 A.M. Babich called Warden Teets of San Quentin. "Too late," the warden told him, "the gas has been applied."

This ended the life, and the story, of Burton W. Abbot, but it left a few lingering questions. It would be stretching the bounds of credulity to suggest that some unknown second party buried the girl outside Burton's cabin in Trinity County and concealed the girl's belongings in Burton's basement in Alameda County, and that Burton knew nothing about it. But it would be hard to suggest a reason why Burton would bury poor Stephanie 200 miles from home and then bring back her handbag, books, and brassiere and hide them in the basement. Also, how did the French book get into a field in Contra Costa County? Perhaps Abbot had begun to distribute the girl's belongings about the countryside and never got around to finishing it.

The failed attempt to grant Abbot a stay of execution raises the one unsolvable dilemma about CAPITAL PUNISHMENT: No matter how richly deserved, there is always the chance of making a mistake. And, no matter what new evidence is discovered at a later date, the decision cannot be reversed.

ABEL, Colonel Rudolf Ivanovich (1902–1972)

THE SOVIET UNION'S MASTER SPY LIVED UNDETECTED IN A LOFT IN BROOKLYN FOR NINE YEARS

The man authorities eventually knew as Colonel Rudolf Abel of the NKVD, one of the Soviet Union's top spymasters, entered the United States through Canada in 1948 under the name and passport of Andrew Kayotis. This was apparently the real passport of a naturalized American citizen who had returned to Lithuania in 1947 to visit relatives and had died there. Once in the United States, the pseudo-Kayotis disappeared, and by 1954, Abel was living as Emil R. Goldfus in a top-floor studio apartment at 252 Fulton Street in Brooklyn Heights, New York. The Goldfus identity was also based on reality: Emil Robert Goldfus was born on August 2, 1902, in New York but died in infancy. Since birth and death records were not correlated, it was a simple matter to obtain a certified copy of the dead baby Goldfus's birth certificate and become the man he might have been, a method often used by spies and criminals as the first step in creating an identity that can withstand at least superficial investigation.

In 1952, Goldfus was joined in New York by Eugene Maki, the American-born son of a Finnish father who had emigrated back to Finland in the mid-1920s, and his Finnish wife Hanna. There was no one within 3,000 miles of New York to tell the immigration authorities that the real Maki had disappeared during the war and that an NKVD agent named Reino Hayhanen had taken his place.

At that time, the Brooklyn Heights area was Brooklyn's version of Greenwich Village—full of artists, poets, writers, and others with artistic goals and little money. The shy, retiring Goldfus, a photographer with a certain amount of talent, made friends in the neighborhood, blending in easily with the artists and other mildly bohemian types that lived around him. His alter ego, Colonel Abel, masterminded a spy ring that extended beyond the borders of the United States into Mexico, Latin America, and Canada. During his nine years of spying in the United States, Abel passed atomic and military information of great value to his NKVD bosses.

Abel made one slight slip in 1953, but it accomplished nothing except to present a fascinating puzzle to the FBI and CIA. A 14-year-old Brooklyn newspaper boy named James Bozart happened to drop a nickel, which he had been given. When the nickel hit the ground it split open, revealing a tiny sliver of film. Bozart took the nickel and the film to the police, who turned it over to the FBI. The film turned out to be a reduced photograph of rows of numbers, undoubtedly a cipher key. And there the story ended for four years.

On April 26, 1957, a man named Reino Hayhanen staggered into the U.S. Embassy in Paris

Colonel Rudolf Abel (on the right) being flown from Houston, where he was held for questioning, to his espionage trial in New York. (*Associated Press*.)

and demanded to see the ambassador. He was a Soviet agent, he said, and he wanted to defect. Convinced that he was either a drunk or a crank, the official who saw him was prepared to escort him to the door, when, to illustrate a point in the elaborate tale of espionage he was spinning, he took a nickel from his pocket and carefully split it open. A thin sliver of microfilm rested inside.

Abel had found Hayhanen, whom the NKVD had foisted on him as an assistant, to be totally unreliable, dangerously unstable, and an advanced alcoholic. After complaining about him for a while, he finally received permission to send his drunken assistant home. He directed Hayhanen to fly to Paris and make contact with Soviet intelligence there. Hayhanen did so, but when it became clear that the NKVD was going to send him back to Moscow, he panicked. Being sent home in disgrace was not a good career move for an NKVD officer. He promptly, and wisely, decided to make a change of employment. By May 3, he was back in New York and safe in the arms of the FBI. Convinced that only the FBI could keep him alive, as the NKVD had a long reach and a longer memory, Hayhanen was happy to cooperate with his new friends.

Abel, possibly warned by his handler that Hayhanen had never shown up in the Soviet Union, dropped out of sight before Hayhanen began his interview with the FBI. Now calling himself Martin Collins, and with a birth certificate to match, Abel moved down to the Plaza Hotel in Daytona Beach, Florida. On May 7, for some reason that is still unknown, he returned to New York and, still using the name Martin Collins, checked into the Latham Hotel on East 28th Street, just off Fifth Avenue.

With the security within security that intelligence agencies are so fond of, Hayhanen knew Abel only as "Mark" (Hayhanen had been "Vic"), and he had no idea where Abel lived. But once, Hayhanen recalled, he had gone with "Mark" to a room somewhere on Fulton Street, Brooklyn. The FBI staked out the neighborhood, armed with a detailed description of "Mark," and waited patiently.

Abel made the mistake of violating his own security rules, possibly to pick up some equipment he could not easily replace. One night in June, a man who resembled Hayhanen's description of "Mark" visited the Fulton Street apartment and was then followed back to the Latham. The agents quickly discovered that he was registered in room 839 under the name of Martin Collins.

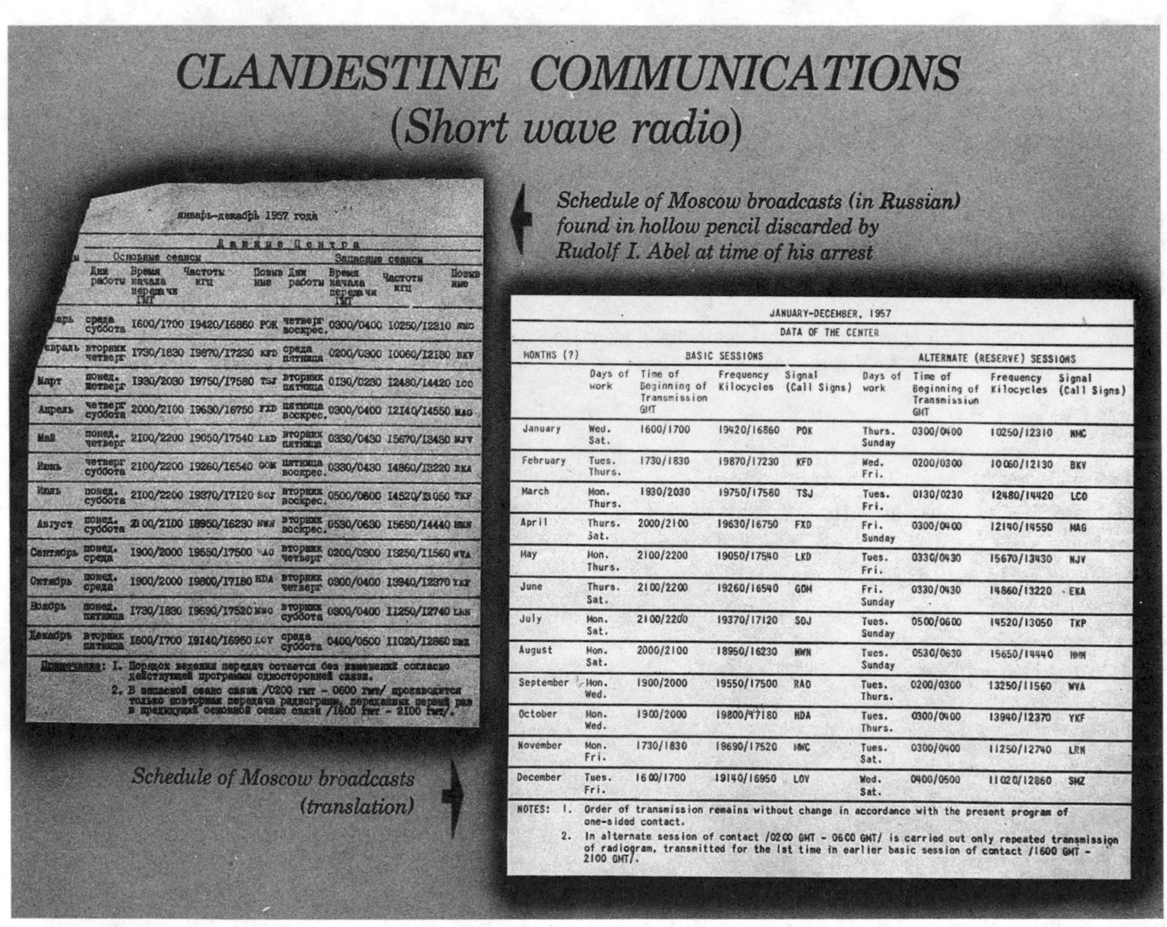

JANUARY-DECEMBER, 1957

DATA OF THE CENTER

MONTHS (?)	BASIC SESSIONS				ALTERNATE (RESERVE) SESSIONS			
	Days of work	Time of Beginning of Transmission GMT	Frequency Kilocycles	Signal (Call Signs)	Days of work	Time of Beginning of Transmission GMT	Frequency Kilocycles	Signal (Call Signs)
January	Wed. Sat.	1600/1700	19420/16860	POK	Thurs. Sunday	0300/0400	10250/12310	NMC
February	Tues. Thurs.	1730/1830	19870/17230	KFD	Wed. Fri.	0200/0300	10060/12130	BKV
March	Mon. Thurs.	1930/2030	19750/17580	TSJ	Tues. Fri.	0130/0230	12480/14420	LCO
April	Thurs. Sat.	2000/2100	19630/16750	FXD	Fri. Sunday	0300/0400	12140/14550	MAG
May	Mon. Thurs.	2100/2200	19050/17540	LKD	Tues. Fri.	0330/0430	15670/13430	NJV
June	Thurs. Sat.	2100/2200	19260/16540	GOM	Fri. Sunday	0330/0430	14860/13220	EKA
July	Mon. Sat.	2100/2200	19370/17120	SOJ	Tues. Sunday	0500/0600	14520/13050	TKP
August	Mon. Sat.	2000/2100	18950/16230	NWN	Tues. Sunday	0530/0630	15650/14440	HMM
September	Mon. Wed.	1900/2000	19550/17500	RAO	Tues. Thurs.	0200/0300	13250/11560	WYA
October	Mon. Wed.	1900/2000	19800/17180	HDA	Tues. Thurs.	0300/0400	13940/12370	YKF
November	Mon. Fri.	1730/1830	19690/17520	MMC	Tues. Sat.	0300/0400	11250/12740	LRN
December	Tues. Fri.	1600/1700	19140/16950	LOV	Wed. Sat.	0400/0500	11020/12860	SMZ

NOTES: 1. Order of transmission remains without change in accordance with the present program of one-sided contact.

2. In alternate session of contact /0200 GMT - 0600 GMT/ is carried out only repeated transmission of radiogram, transmitted for the 1st time in earlier basic session of contact /1600 GMT - 2100 GMT/.

FBI record of transmissions between Abel and his Soviet controller. (*Federal Bureau of Investigation*.)

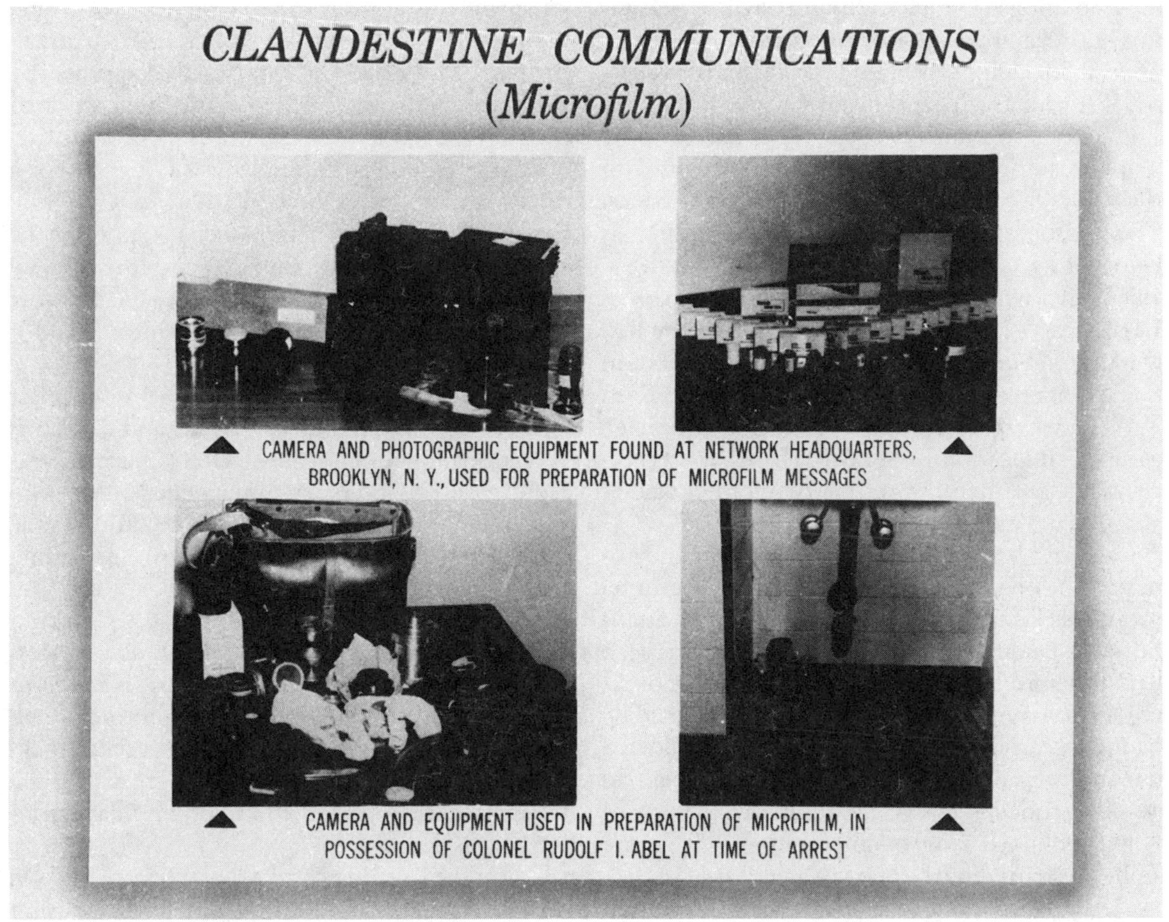

Exhibits prepared for Abel's trial by the FBI, illustrating surveillance equipment found in Abel's possession. (*Federal Bureau of Investigation*.)

On June 21, 1957, at seven o'clock in the morning, Special Agent Edward F. Gamber of the FBI, along with two of his colleagues and three men from the Immigration and Naturalization Service, knocked on the door of room 839. They heard a padding noise within the room, and then a toilet flushing, and then the door was cautiously opened. A naked man (Abel slept in the nude) peered at them from around the door.

The three FBI men pushed into the room, waving their identification cards at Abel. For five minutes they talked to him, urging him to cooperate, telling him things could go very hard for him if he refused. When they paused, he asked them if it would be all right if he put his pants on, and they agreed.

"Collins" was arrested by the immigration officers as an illegal alien. He chose to stand mute, refusing to answer any but the most innocuous questions, and watched silently while the platoon of federal agents searched his room and examined his belongings. The agents found birth certificates for both Emil R. Goldfus and Martin Collins, $6,500 in cash, a bankbook with a balance of $1,386, and a safe deposit box key.

They also found two snapshots tucked away in a bureau drawer, of a man and a woman, with the names *Morris* and *Shirley* written on the backs. The photographs were subsequently identified as being of MORRIS AND LEONA COHEN, two Soviet agents who had been in the same network as ETHEL AND JULIUS ROSENBERG, until they fled the United States in 1950. They later resurfaced in Great Britain under the names of Peter and Helen Kroger, where they were arrested for espionage along with Gordon Lonsdale. Why Abel was carrying ancient snapshots of his two former associates was never explained.

After Abel was taken into custody by the immigration officers and removed to jail, the hotel room was given a thorough search. Special attention was paid to the few items that Abel was seen to throw into the wastebasket, while he was packing a small suitcase to take with him. A pencil he had so discarded was found to have been hollowed out and contained microfilm. A scrap of paper had a partly coded message on it. A small block of wood contained a tiny onetime pad—a very secure cipher system—in its hollowed core.

Abel was moved to the Federal Detention Camp for Aliens in McAllen, Texas, while the FBI prepared its case against him. He was interrogated almost continuously. His FBI questioners told him that if he would cooperate they would get him food, liquor, an air-conditioned room in a hotel, and a 10,000-dollar-a-year job with another, unspecified government agency. He chose not to talk.

By the time he came to trial, he had admitted that he was a Russian citizen. He declared that his name was Rudolf Ivanovich Abel, that he had smuggled himself into the United States with a forged U.S. passport purchased in Denmark, using a large sum of American money that he had somehow found in a ruined blockhouse somewhere in Russia. Ridiculous as the story was, ridiculous as he must have felt telling it, particularly in the face of the hollowed-out pencils and other spy paraphernalia found in his room, Abel stuck to that story.

The temper of the times was not good for a Soviet spy caught in the United States. On October 5, 1957, the Soviets launched Sputnik, the world's first artificial satellite, and the United States suddenly felt very vulnerable. On October 14, 1957, Colonel Rudolf Abel went on trial for espionage.

Abel's lawyer, appointed by the Brooklyn Bar Association, was James Donovan, and Abel was very lucky to get him. An ex–OSS (Office of Strategic Services) and Naval Intelligence officer who had served as an associate prosecutor at the Nuremberg trials, Donovan was an outstanding trial lawyer who tempered his dislike of communism with an abiding affection for the Constitution of the United States and its due process clause. Any man, even a Communist, is innocent until proven guilty. Besides, as a former intelligence officer, Donovan could appreciate Abel's professionalism. It was not as though Abel was a traitor. He was a Soviet citizen, doing a dangerous job for his country.

But the law did not take that into account. On the principal charge, "conspiracy to transmit atomic and military information to Soviet Russia," Abel could face the death penalty. In Donovan's interviews with Abel, and during the trial, Donovan found his client to be an intelligent and likable man.

The government's chief witness was Hayhanen, and despite the alcoholic haze that enveloped him, there was no doubt that he was telling the truth. In three days on the witness stand, he told his version of what it was like to be a Soviet agent in the United States. He told of leaving messages in hollow trees and nickels with microfilm in the middle and coding and decoding messages and transmitting them in the dead of night.

On October 25, despite Donovan's summation, in which he pointed out to the jury that, although Abel was certainly a spy, there was no evidence presented that he had ever transmitted atomic or military secrets to anyone, Colonel Abel was found guilty on all counts. Sentencing was set for November 15.

Donovan presented arguments against imposing the death penalty on Abel. "It is absurd," he said, "to believe that the execution of this man would deter the Russian military." He pointed out that it was possible that Abel would choose to cooperate sometime in the future, if he were alive to do so. And, Donovan said, it was possible that "in the foreseeable future an American of equivalent rank will be captured by Soviet Russia or an ally—at such time an exchange of prisoners through diplomatic channels could be considered to be in the best interests of the United States." Abel was sentenced to 30 years in prison and was put in the federal penitentiary in Atlanta.

On May 1, 1960, a U-2 spyplane piloted by Francis Gary Powers was shot down while flying deep inside Soviet territory. In February 1962, after serving nearly five years in prison, Colonel Abel walked across the Glienicker Bridge, which connected East and West Berlin. He was walking from West to East. Francis Gary Powers, going from East to West, passed him in the middle. The exchange was largely arranged by James Donovan, who was doing his best for his client.

The defector, Reino Hayhanen, was killed in a mysterious auto accident on the Pennsylvania Turnpike in late 1961.

In 1965, Rudolf Abel was awarded the Order of Lenin, the Soviet Union's highest award.

ACCARDO, Anthony Joseph "Big Tuna" (1906–1992)

An enforcer in the Chicago organization of AL CAPONE in the 1920s, Anthony Joseph Accardo, who was born and grew up in Chicago's Little Italy, is reputed to have invented the practice of carrying his machine gun in a violin case during the early days of Prohibition. His preference for using a baseball bat as an enforcement tool brought him the nickname of "Joe Batters." There is strong reason to believe that he was one of the five pseudo-policemen who machine-gunned seven members of the Bugs Moran organization in the 1929 SAINT VALENTINE'S DAY MASSACRE. By 1931, he had earned a listing by the Chicago Crime Commission as a public enemy, and he is suspected of being involved in the 1945 kidnapping of JAKE "GREASY THUMB" GUZIK, who reportedly paid $75,000 for his own release.

Accardo quickly rose through the ranks of Chicago's MAFIA, becoming one of the triumvirate running the Chicago Syndicate when Capone was put away. Accardo was in charge of enforcement, Jake Guzik, who apparently did not hold a grudge, took administration and FRANK NITTI took operations. By 1943, when Nitti committed suicide, Accardo and Paul Ricca were the bosses. According to one of his associates, Accardo "had more brains before breakfast than Al Capone had all day."

Accardo had a reputation of being fair but stern with his troops, but if he was crossed, he was deadly. When one of his collectors in a loan sharking operation, a gentleman known as William "Action" Jackson, was found to be letting more than his share of the profits stick to his fingers, he was beaten to death. Pictures of his bruised and battered corpse were distributed among the remaining collectors to encourage loyalty and prudence.

Accardo was constantly in trouble with the law but was never convicted of anything but tax evasion, and that 1960 conviction was overturned on appeal. He appeared several times before the Senate Investigations Subcommittee, but took the Fifth Amendment each time. He went into semiretirement by the late 1970s. In 1984, during his last appearance before the Senate subcommittee, he declared, "I have no control over anybody. I've never been a boss."

ADLER, Polly (1900–1962)

New York City's premier madam from the early 1930s until she retired in 1944, Polly Adler kept a stable of beautiful, agreeable play-for-pay girls in some of Manhattan's most fashionable East Side apartments. Her customers came, as she said, "not only from *Who's Who* and the *Social Register*, but from *Burke's Peerage* and the *Almanach de Gotha*." They also came from the Broadway crowd: a motley assortment of gangsters, newspaper men, policemen, politicians, and theatrical celebrities. She kept a well-stocked bar and buffet for her guests. Newspaper columnists used to regularly drop in on Polly's "house" for refreshments and gossip, since Polly knew more about what was going on in Gotham than anybody else. Among her clients were some of the biggest mobsters of the 1930s, including DUTCH SCHULTZ, CHARLES "LUCKY" LUCIANO and FRANK COSTELLO.

Polly was often seen about town in the most fashionable nightclubs, at the theater, and at other social gatherings, escorting a pride of her most beautiful girls. Her entourage got her into the gossip columns, which was, she judged, the most effective advertising she could do. Her establishments were raided several times, but on the whole, she had as good a relationship with the authorities as is possible for someone in an illicit business.

In 1953, she published her autobiography, *A House Is Not a Home,* which told of her adventures and something of her personal philosophy. She comes across as someone who would have been interesting to know. Those who knew her agreed, including such diverse people as Damon Runyon, Robert Benchley, and Dr. Alfred Kinsey.

ADONIS, Joe (1902–1972)

A major figure in the American MAFIA, Joe Adonis was born Joseph Doto in Montemarano, Italy (although he always claimed to have been born in the United States). Adonis was one of the mass of illegal Italian immigrants to come to New York shortly after the turn of the century. He became Joe Adonis, or simply Joey A., supposedly because of his good looks, early in his career running with street gangs in lower Manhattan. Judging by his photographs, we must assume that he gave himself the nickname. The gang of his youth included such future notables as ALBERT ANASTASIA, VITO GENOVESE and CHARLES "LUCKY" LUCIANO. In the mid-1920s, he was pretty much in control of the Broadway Mob, which dominated the distribution of bootleg liquor over much of midtown Manhattan. With this background and training, it was only natural for Joey A. to rise to the top of gangdom in the 1930s.

After Brooklyn Mafia boss FRANKIE YALE died in a feud with the AL CAPONE mob, Adonis took over much of Yale's territory. He was involved in the assassination of JOE "THE BOSS" MASSERIA in 1931 as part of Lucky Luciano's destruction of the "MUSTACHE PETES," as the older, traditional Mafiosi crime bosses were called. Adonis, who combined loyalty with ruthless efficiency, became one of Lucky Luciano's trusted lieutenants. When New York prosecutor THOMAS E. DEWEY put Luciano in prison, Adonis found himself in charge of the business of the New York crime combine, under the guiding hand of MEYER LANSKY.

With the end of Prohibition, Adonis and the Mob moved into waterfront unions and took a slice of the gambling operations in New York and New Jersey. Intelligent and not dangerously ambitious, Adonis worked his way up in the national organization until he is said to have become a member of the national board of directors. In 1951, Adonis pled guilty to a violation of the gambling laws in New Jersey and was sentenced to two years in prison. In 1956, Adonis, faced with federal perjury laws, accepted deportation as an agreeable substitute. He lived out his life as a wealthy returnee in Milan, Italy.

ADVERTISING CONS

There are many who feel that all advertising is a form of CONFIDENCE GAME, but we will limit our discussion here to only those come-ons that are frowned upon by district attorneys' offices or postal authorities.

From the 1880s until the postal inspectors began cracking down on them in the 1930s, there were a certain subset of newspaper advertisements that had a whimsical charm. One of them read: "Guaranteed insect killer—Works every time on any sort of insect—send $1.00." The earnest or curious who replied to the advertisement would receive two blocks of wood in the mail, labeled "A" and "B," with instructions reading: *Place insect on Block A. . . .*

Another tempter to the credulous in the early decades of the twentieth century read:

> *HOUSEHOLD ARTICLES*
>
> We have a limited number of all-metal household articles, which we are disposing of in assorted lots of one dozen. Not more than three lots sold to one buyer. Send only $1.00 for a dozen articles. We pay the postage.
>
> US BUNCOS, Nowhere, MW

When the expectant householder sent for the all-metal articles, he or she would receive a dozen assorted needles.

Perhaps the classic was the gentleman who supported himself for many years, until the Post Office actively discouraged him, with an ad that read merely: "This is your last chance to send in one dollar," followed by his P.O. box number.

Despite its inherent visibility, the advertising con has proved extremely difficult to control. The line between legitimate advertising and a swindle is a narrow one and hard to police. The letter you receive telling you that you have won a prize in a contest you never entered could be a confidence game or it could merely be a way to get you to examine a time-sharing vacation home or some overpriced jewelry—misleading but not yet illegal. The basic rule is to beware of all unsolicited offers; if it seems too good to be true, it probably is. *See also:* SHORT CONS

AGAINST THE WALL

See: SHORT CONS

AGEUCI, Albert (–1961)
AGEUCI, Vito

Albert and Vito Ageuci emigrated from Sicily to Canada in the early 1950s. There they ran a bakery in Toronto that fronted for a drug ring led by New York mobster STEFANO MAGADDINO, which smuggled drugs from Italy to Canada. On July 20, 1961, the brothers were picked up on a narcotics charge in New York City. When Magaddino failed to bail them out or provide legal assistance, Al felt it was a violation of their agreement and vowed to get even. He was murdered at Magaddino's behest, if not by Magaddino himself, on November 23, 1961. He had been tortured and his body, burned almost beyond recognition, was found in a field outside of Rochester, New York. Vito was convicted on the narcotics charge and sent to the federal penitentiary in Atlanta.

In Atlanta, Vito met JOSEPH VALACHI, a button man for the New York City crime family led by VITO GENOVESE. Vito asked Valachi to arrange a meeting with Genovese, who was also in the prison facility. Genovese refused to meet with Ageuci, apparently afraid that Vito was trying to avenge his brother's death. It is not clear how

Genovese was involved with Al Ageuci's murder.

Valachi found himself in the middle and became convinced that both sides were out to get him. As a result he murdered the wrong man in self-defense, which pushed him into seeking government protection and led to his revelations about MAFIA crime families at the MCCLELLAN crime hearings.

AGNEW, Spiro Theodore (1918–)

Vice President of the United States under Richard M. Nixon, Spiro Agnew resigned his office on October 10, 1973, 10 months before Nixon. The second vice president to resign (the first was John C. Calhoun, who left Andrew Jackson's administration in 1832 for political reasons), and the only one forced out of office, Agnew pled "no contest" to a charge of evading income tax on illegal kickbacks made by contractors while he was governor of Maryland. He accepted the plea bargain in return for the prosecutor agreeing not to file bribery charges.

AIELLO, Joseph (1891–1930)

Head of a MAFIA family in Chicago in the 1920s, Joe Aiello and his brothers Antonio, Andrew, and Dominick, along with BUGS MORAN and his mob, were in open warfare with the forces of AL CAPONE for control of the Chicago rackets. More subtle than most of his compatriots, Aiello tried to have Capone killed by bribing the chef at the Bella Napoli Cafe, Capone's favorite restaurant, to poison Capone's pasta. When the chef refused to get involved, Aiello put out the word that he was offering $50,000 for Capone's head. Big Al was not amused. Aiello died in a hail of gunfire one day as he left his apartment on North Kolmar Avenue. The autopsy surgeon took 59 bullets, weighing more than a pound, out of his body.

ALCATRAZ

An island in the middle of San Francisco Bay, Alcatraz, from the Indian "island of the pelicans," was first used as the site for a prison in 1868, when the U.S. War Department set up a prison for deserters and other military prisoners. In 1933, the federal government built a prison for incorrigibles on the island. Called a "superprison for supercriminals," it was quickly dubbed "the Rock" and was supposed to be escape proof. Even if the prisoners could somehow get through the prison walls, the authorities told the nervous citizens of San Francisco, they could never make the swim to shore; the undertow would carry them out to sea and certain death. Shortly before the prison was scheduled to open, a bevy of bathing beauties swam from the island to the mainland without any trouble, but this did not stop the opening of the Alcatraz Federal Penitentiary on January 1, 1934.

Alcatraz operated under punitive regulations, a harsh version of the Auburn system named for the prison in Auburn, New York, where it was first tried, which did not allow the prisoners to speak and kept them locked up at least 14 hours a day, every day. With a ratio of one guard for every three prisoners, much higher than any other prison, the prisoners were guarded to excess, but since they were regarded as incorrigible, no attempt at rehabilitation was made. Most prisons used a trustee system or a system of special privileges to encourage prisoners to behave; Alcatraz used punishment, including water hoses, handcuffing to cell bars with especially painful handcuffs, a strait jacket that was regarded as particularly cruel by those who suffered it, and the "hole" of solitary confinement.

The stars of the federal penal system went to Alcatraz, including AL CAPONE, GEORGE "MACHINE GUN" KELLY, ARTHUR "DOCK" BARKER, and ALVIN "CREEPY" KARPIS. Some of them were indeed incorrigible, but some of them were merely notorious; however, they all received the same harsh treatment. One man became famous while he

The view of the Alcatraz federal prison first seen by prisoners aboard the launch as they were escorted to the island. (International Newsreel Photo.)

was in Alcatraz. Robert Stroud, in Leavenworth and then Alcatraz for murder, became an expert on bird diseases, writing two highly respected books. He became known as the "Birdman of Alcatraz," and a book and a movie documented his life.

Many attempts were made to escape from Alcatraz. The prisoners had nothing else to do but plot escapes. One nearly succeeded. In 1946, a 46-year-old bank robber named Bernie Coy masterminded a plan in which he and a few confederates overpowered nine guards and took over the gun gallery, where the weapons were kept. They let most of the convicts out of their cells and planned to cross the yard in the confusion. But one of the keys needed to open the doors was not where it was supposed to be, and they could not get out.

The released prisoners rioted, and the prison authorities called in the Marines. Most of the ringleaders were killed, including Coy. In the ensuing investigation, the authorities zeroed in on the harsh conditions in the prison, including finding one man who had been in solitary confinement for the previous seven years.

By the time the federal prison on Alcatraz was closed in 1963, the facility was already starting to crumble.

ANASTASIA, Albert (1903–1957)

Five Anastasia brothers immigrated to the United States around 1920. One became a priest and returned to Italy; the other four became members of the Mangano crime family and went to work on the Brooklyn docks. The Manganos controlled the longshoremen's union without the formality of union meetings, elections, or records. When a longshoreman named Peter Panto protested, and over 1,000 of his fellow longshoremen rallied behind him, Albert Anastasia (who had changed the "o" ending his surname to an "a" while in his teens for unknown reasons) and two assistants were detailed to take Panto for a ride. The story is that they took him to New Jersey, strangled him, and buried his body in a lime pit. Anastasia was tried for the crime and convicted, but after a year and a half in SING SING waiting to be executed, he was granted a new trial. This time his friends took no chances, and the four principal witnesses against him failed to show up at the trial. Anastasia was freed. The four were never seen again.

Anastasia developed a reputation for using murder as an answer to any problem. He enjoyed killing. When MURDER, INCORPORATED was formed in Brownsville, Brooklyn, in the 1930s, it was only natural that CHARLES "LUCKY" LUCIANO would think of Anastasia for an executive position in the organization. LOUIS "LEPKE" BUCHALTER was the boss, but Anastasia was the liaison between the Brownsville mob and the big bosses of the national combination. Several times the various police agencies thought they had developed a case against Anastasio, but somehow the principal witnesses would always disappear at the last minute.

After Luciano was deported to Italy in 1946, Anastasia took control of the Luciano crime family. His penchant for killing increased. In one of the more bizarre incidents, Anastasia was watching television when a news program showed that a young man named ARNOLD SCHUSTER had recognized bank robber WILLIE "THE ACTOR" SUTTON on the street and called the police. Anastasia had a fit. Screaming that he could not stand squealers, he ordered Schuster murdered. The killing remained a mystery until JOSEPH VALACHI mentioned it in the MCCLELLAN COMMITTEE hearings in the U.S. Senate as an example of Anastasia's instability.

Anastasia's habit of casual death made others in the Syndicate hate and fear him, and after Luciano left, FRANK COSTELLO was one of his few remaining friends among the top bosses. On October 25, 1957, two men entered the barbershop in New York's Park Sheraton Hotel while Anastasia was relaxing in the chair and his bodyguard was parking the car in the underground garage. A few seconds later, Anastasia was dead, his body full of bullets. The killing has never been officially solved, but most authorities put the blame on VITO GENOVESE, who was trying to take over the Luciano crime family.

ANTHROPOMETRY

See: ALPHONSE BERTILLON

APALACHIN CONFERENCE

On November 14, 1957, over 60 bosses of the various crime syndicates, organizations, arms, and other manifestations of the American MAFIA gathered for a secret conclave at the 58-acre Apalachin, New York, estate of mobster JOSEPH BARBARA. Believed to have been called by VITO GENOVESE so that he could claim the long-vacant title of "Boss of Bosses," it was broken up by the New York State Police when an officer wondered what all the limousines were doing going up a country road. The state police went to investigate and found the well-dressed hoods piling out of windows and into the woods.

Fifty-eight gangster chieftains were rounded up and booked, and five more were shown to have been there, although they escaped the police net. The total, including those who fled through the woods in their Italian loafers and silk suits, was probably close to 100. Over $300,000 in cash was found among those apprehended. This appeared suspicious to the police, but mobsters like carrying around a lot of cash, so it was probably just pocket money.

There is a theory that the break-up of the meeting was not an accident, that some of the bosses who did not want Genovese to succeed with his plans for domination arranged for the interruption. But Genovese would not have lasted long anyway—within two years he was in prison.
See also: FRANK COSTELLO

ARIZONA RANGERS

Formed in 1901 at the direction of Arizona Governor Nathan O. Murphy, and placed under the leadership of CAPTAIN BURTON C. MOSSMAN, the Arizona Rangers, along with the older TEXAS RANGERS and the New Mexico Rangers, fought for law and order in the western United States. The reason for their formation was the predations of such outlaws as Augustine Chacon, a Mexican bandit who was said to have murdered over 30 men. This was the last eruption of an outlaw era that was already ending when the Rangers came into existence, but they aided local authorities in capturing or killing many desperadoes before they were disbanded in 1910.

ARNSTEIN, Nicky (1878–)

GAMBLER, CON MAN, HUSBAND OF "FUNNY GIRL" FANNY BRICE, HE WENT TO PRISON FOR A CRIME HE PROBABLY DID NOT COMMIT

A tall, lean, aristocratic-looking con man and professional gambler who worked the ocean liners, Jules W. Arndt Stein, who preferred to be known as Nicky Arnstein, was known for his intelligence, charm, and wit, attributes that helped him fleece the highest class of victim.

In 1910, Arnstein crossed the ocean with Ohio Columbus Barbour, head of the Ohio Match Company, and J. R. Graves, a friend of Barbour and builder of the Polk Street railroad station in Chicago. Barbour was going to Europe in search of art, and Nicky Arnstein, who could talk art like a professional, was going to help him find it. On the way, the three of them and another passenger they met on the boat, Harry Holland, played a few friendly games of poker. Holland, who looked like a typical midwestern grocer who has made his pile and is in search of "culture," was one of the leading card mechanics (professional card manipulators) of the day. ARNOLD ROTHSTEIN, who was on the boat, looked the situation over and offered Arnstein $10,000 for the privilege of sitting in on the games. He was refused. Arnstein and Holland took Barbour and Graves for over $100,000.

Even after Arnstein became known, he had no trouble getting people to play cards with him. New York City Police Inspector John J. Sullivan, who happened to be making an Atlantic crossing, once tried to warn a sucker away from Arnstein, telling him, "Don't you know he's a card sharp?"

"Of course I know it," the man told him, "but he's better company than the honest men on board this ship."

Arnstein was involved in a BIG STORE operation run by the Gondorf brothers, who invented that particular swindle, before World War I—an exercise that earned him thousands of dollars and his first prison sentence.

By 1920, Arnstein was married to vaudeville star Fanny Brice, of Ziegfeld Follies fame. "I never liked chiselers," she said. But she married him anyway and spent the next few years unsuccessfully trying to reform him.

For about 18 months, culminating in February 1920, Wall Street brokerage houses in New York were being robbed on a regular basis of negotiable securities, mostly highly liquid Liberty Bonds. The messengers, who regularly carried negotiable securities between the houses in manila envelopes, were being held up and relieved of their envelopes. Although this had been going on for a year and a half, none of the brokerage houses changed its method of securities delivery.

Nicky Arnstein in Los Angeles in 1947. (Dept. of Special Collections, Research Library, UCLA.)

Despite the simplicity of the method, and the stupidity of the houses in not changing their system, the fact that over four million dollars in securities had vanished convinced the police that the robberies were the work of a "mastermind." And the name that kept occurring to them was Arnold Rothstein; by this time a major gambler and believed to be masterminding much of New York's crooked activity. Although no proof was forthcoming, and he had denied it, it was widely believed that Rothstein had arranged the fixing of the WORLD SERIES OF 1919, only a year before.

On February 6, 1920, seven men were arrested for the robbery of a Parrish and Company messenger. One of them was a small-time hood named Joe Gluck. Joe sat in the Tombs, New York City's prison, for 10 days, waiting for his lawyer to come and spring him. But the lawyer never showed up. On the eleventh day, Gluck asked to talk to the district attorney. He claimed that there was, indeed, a mastermind, known only as "Mr. Arnold." He had never actually met this big boss, but he had seen the man who roped him into the deal, one Nick Cohn, talking to "Mr. Arnold" once in a restaurant. He and several of the other boys had needed this convincer before coming into the scheme. And the appearance of "Mr. Arnold" had been enough to convince them: tall and aristocratic looking, he was every inch the embodiment of their image of the master criminal.

The district attorney was convinced that he would shortly be arresting Arnold Rothstein, but it was not to be. Gluck identified a photograph of Nicky Arnstein as the man he had seen.

Rothstein heard what was happening through his police contacts and called Nicky. Arnstein remembered the meeting with Cohn. He thought it strange at the time. Cohn had arranged to meet him at a restaurant, claiming he had a proposition to discuss. But he had never come to the point. And Nicky remembered seeing a half-dozen young punks staring in through the window at him. Now the whole thing made sense.

There was no use protesting his innocence. The district attorney was not interested in whether he was guilty or not, but in whether he could build a case. Rothstein advised Arnstein to get out of town until the whole thing blew over. Arnstein took his advice and fled to Cleveland, Ohio, known in those days as a "safe" town. The advice turned out to be good. The district attorney identified Arnstein to the newspapers as the "mastermind" and issued a warrant against him. They had eyewitnesses, and Arnstein had been in prison once already. What more did they need to convict? Fanny Brice was asked by a reporter what she thought of the accusation. "Mastermind!" she laughed. "Nicky couldn't mastermind an electric light bulb into a socket."

When it was clear that the district attorney was going to pursue his indictment, Arnstein arranged his return to New York. He met his wife and his attorney, William Fallon, in Westchester, and they drove together into the city to surrender Nicky. On the way, they got caught in the annual police parade and drove down Fifth Avenue surrounded by New York's finest.

Rothstein paid for Arnstein's defense. As Leo Katcher explains in his book *The Big Bankroll* (1958):

> "It was not friendship that caused Rothstein to aid Nicky, but self-preservation. Rothstein told his wife, "They're not after Nicky, they're after me. A lot of people would like to tie me into this and some of them think they can get Arnstein to say something that would lead them to me."
>
> A lot of people did think so. When Arnstein was questioned by detectives and members of the District Attorney's office, he was told repeatedly that if he would tell the full story of the bond thefts and name the man behind them he would be treated most leniently. Time after time he was asked directly what he knew of Rothstein's connections with the bond thefts.
>
> "I know nothing," Nicky said, "of any relevance about any thefts of any kind. I am an innocent man."

Fallon had the case moved to federal court, since the federal penalties were lighter. He also invented a much-copied technique to avoid answering questions: To counter the prosecution's wish to bring Arnstein's past and his questionable friends into the trial, Fallon advised Arnstein to use the Fifth Amendment provision against self-incrimination; the first time that had been done. Arnstein was held in contempt of court for this, and Fallon had the chance to argue his premise before the Supreme Court. He maintained that Arnstein did not have to give answers that "might tend to incriminate or degrade" him. The Court agreed.

Arnstein's first trial resulted in a hung jury. He was found guilty in a second trial and sentenced to Leavenworth. Fanny Brice wrote "My Man" as a tribute to her absent husband, which became a hit song. When Arnstein got out, after 20 months, Brice divorced him.

Arnstein moved to California and spent his golden years out of the limelight. The Liberty Bonds turned up for years afterward, paying for booze during PROHIBITION and later for narcotics. Who actually masterminded the thefts has never been established.

ASHLEY, Leslie

A female impersonator, Leslie Ashley was tried for the murder of a Houston real estate agent in 1961. Committed to a mental hospital, he escaped in 1964 and was put on the FBI's TEN MOST WANTED list, the second known cross-dresser to achieve that distinction. (The first was Isale Beausoleil, a Canadian who came south to commit murder. Beausoleil was caught in 1953 after 14 years at large. The last couple of years he had spent in women's clothes.) After about two weeks on the list, Ashley was captured by the FBI at an Atlanta carnival, where he had been working as Bobo the Clown.

ASSASSINATIONS

The word *assassin* comes from the Arabic *hash'shashin,* "hashish-eaters." The original assassins were followers of Hasan Al-Sabah, "The Old Man of the Mountains," a political and religious leader of eleventh-century Persia, and his successors. Although few in number, the *hash'shashin* terrorized the Middle East for two centuries by the threat of secret murder. They were utterly fearless and devoted to their master; both assets could be attributed to hashish-induced dreams, during which the Old Man and his successors took them into wonderful gardens replete with beautiful, attentive women. When they awoke, he told them that they had been privileged to visit the paradise that they would enter if they died in his service.

The term *assassination* entered the English language meaning "murder for political reasons," or "murder of the socially or politically prominent." The first recorded assassination attempt in this country occurred during the colonial period. In New York City in 1774, a Tory attempted to murder George Washington by feeding him a stew made with tomatoes, which were then called love apples, that were believed to be poisonous.

Political assassinations have been a popular sport in various countries over the past two centuries. In India in the last century, the Thuggies, who prayed to the goddess Kali and killed their victims with a silken noose, terrorized the countryside until a major effort was made to eliminate them. In Japan prior to World War II, various secret societies eliminated their political enemies at such a rate that from 1910 to 1930 over one-third of all Japanese officeholders had been assassinated.

Assassinations take on greater meaning by demonstrating how fragile life is and how easy it is to kill someone, no matter how important or well protected he or she is. This is what makes the shock of the murder of a beloved leader reverberate so long, and encourages conspiracy theories to abound regardless of the evidence. This is also what causes insane people to think that murdering a celebrity is a way to ensure their own immortality.

Following is a list of the most prominent political assassinations or attempted assassinations in the United States.

March 30, 1981—Ronald Reagan, 40th president of the United States, is shot at by JOHN W. HINCKLEY, JR. as he leaves the Washington Hilton Hotel. The president is wounded but recovers. Three other people, including James Brady, the president's press secretary, were also hit, Brady the most seriously.

September 22, 1975—As Gerald Ford, the 38th president of the United States, leaves the St. Francis Hotel in San Francisco, he is shot at by Sarah Jane Moore, who misses because a bystander knocks her arm up as she fires.

September 5, 1975—Lynette "Squeeky" Fromme points a gun at President Gerald Ford in Sacramento, California, but is seized before she can fire. She is a member of CHARLES MANSON's murder cult.

May 15, 1972—Alabama governor and possible presidential candidate George C. Wallace is shot at a campaign stop in Laurel, Maryland, by janitor's assistant Arthur Herman Bremer. Hit by four bullets and paralyzed for life, he is forced out of the presidential campaign.

June 5, 1968—Robert F. Kennedy, U.S. senator from New York and brother of assassinated president John F. Kennedy, is shot by Sirhan Sirhan in a Los Angeles hotel immediately after winning the California presidential primary. He died the next day.

April 4, 1968—Martin Luther King, Jr., civil rights leader, is shot in a motel in Memphis, Tennessee, by James Earl Ray. His assassination prompted widespread civil unrest in numerous cities.

February 21, 1965—MALCOLM X, disaffected Black Muslim leader, is shot and killed by three Black Muslims before he is to deliver a speech in New York City.

November 22, 1963—John F. Kennedy, 35th president of the United States, is shot and killed in Dallas, Texas, by LEE HARVEY OSWALD. His death seemed particularly difficult for Americans to accept, and 30 years later, theories that his death was a result of government conspiracy still abound.

November 1, 1950—Harry Truman, 33rd president of the United States, is assaulted by Puerto Rican nationalists GRISELIO TORRESOLA and Oscar Collazo at Blair House, a Washington, D.C., residence he is using while the White House is being renovated. A White House guard, Leslie Coffelt, is killed, and two guards are wounded defending the president. Torresola is killed and Collazo wounded by the guards. The president is unhurt. Collazo is sentenced to life in prison.

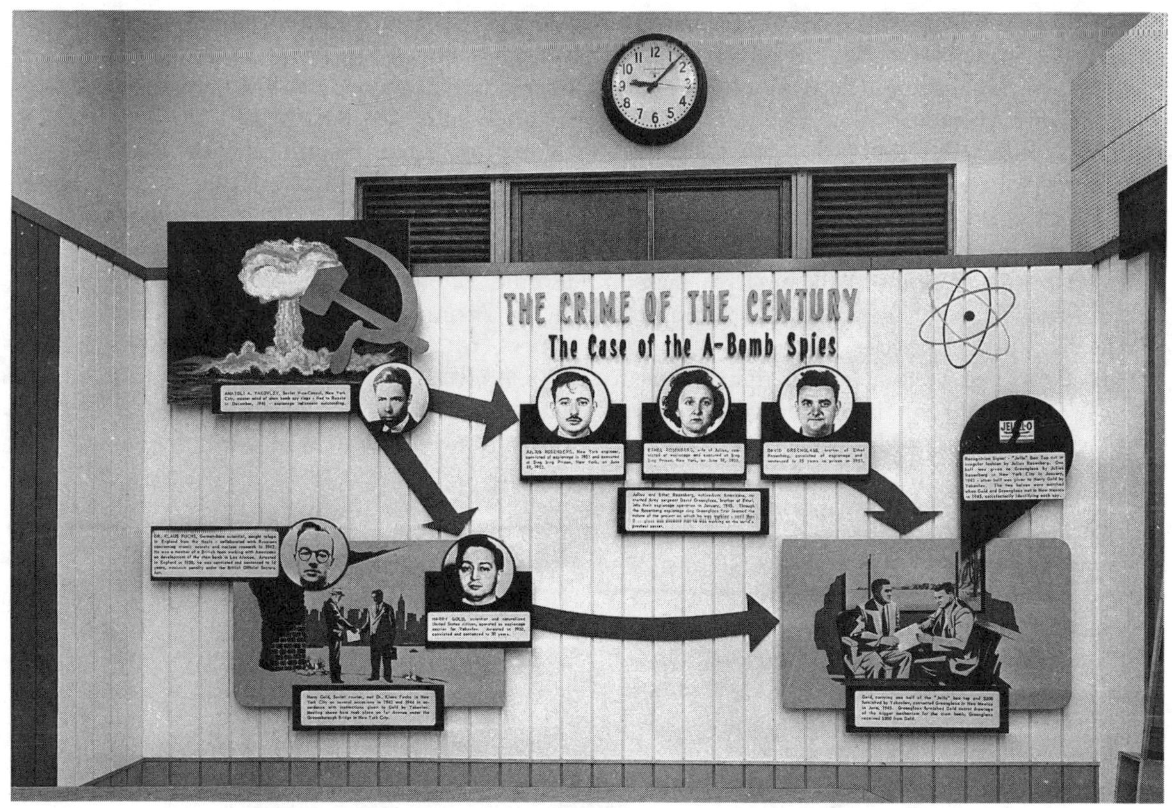

FBI exhibit of the relationship between the most important of the Atom bomb spies, the members of the Rosenberg ring (See Atomic Spy Ring, page 20). (Federal Bureau of Investigation.)

September 8, 1935—Huey P. Long, U.S. senator from Louisiana, is shot by Dr. Carl A. Weiss. He died two days later.

February 15, 1933—Anton Cermak, mayor of Chicago, is shot in Miami, Florida, by Joseph Zangara, who was aiming at Franklin D. Roosevelt, the president-elect, who was riding in the car with Cermak.

September 10, 1913—Mayor William J. Gaynor of New York City dies from a bullet wound suffered three years before, when he was shot by James J. Gallagher, a discontented employee of the Dock Department, on the deck of the steamship *Kaiser Wilhelm* as he was about to sail for Europe.

October 14, 1912—Former President Theodore Roosevelt is shot in a hotel in Milwaukee, Wisconsin, by the insane John Schrank. Roosevelt lives but carries the bullet with him for the rest of his life.

September 6, 1901—25th President of the United States William McKinley is shot by Leon Czolgosz, who claimed to be an anarchist, in a reception line in Buffalo, New York. McKinley died on September 14.

July 2, 1881—James A. Garfield, 20th president of the United States, is shot by Charles Julius Guiteau, a religious fanatic who wanted to be appointed ambassador to Paris. He died on September 19.

April 14, 1865—Abraham Lincoln, 16th president of the United States, is shot by Confederate sympathizer and actor JOHN WILKES BOOTH in Ford's Theater in Washington, D.C.

January 3, 1835—Andrew Jackson, 7th president of the United States, when attending a funeral in the Capitol building rotunda, is attacked by housepainter Richard Lawrence, who fired two pistols at point-blank range as Jackson left the House of Representatives chamber. Both pistols misfired. Lawrence, who professed to believe that he was rightful heir to the English throne, is committed to a lunatic asylum. When tested by the police, the pistols fired flawlessly time after time. Experts found that the odds of both weapons misfiring at the same time were something like 100,000 to 1.

ATOMIC SPY RING

With the defection of a Soviet code clerk in Ottawa, Canada, at the end of World War II came the sudden shocking realization that there was a network of Soviet spies operating in the United States, Canada and Great Britain, which had been in place since the mid-1930s. This marked the beginning of a great spy hunt in the United States. After an intensive investigation the FBI apprehended the members of a loosely connected group that was responsible for stealing military and atomic secrets, which collectively became known as the Atomic Spy Ring. They included, among others, MORRIS AND LEONA COHEN, HARRY GOLD, ETHEL AND JULIUS ROSENBERG, and Klaus Fuchs. The master spy COLONEL RUDOLF IVANOVICH ABEL was also associated with the group.

AXIS SALLY

See: MILDRED GILLARS

B

BADGER GAME

One of the classic CONFIDENCE GAMES practiced in this country since before the Civil War, the badger game preys on two basic human emotions: lust and fear. In its simplest form, an attractive woman invites a man up to her hotel room with the implicit promise of shared sexual favors. She proceeds to disrobe and helps him take some of his clothes off. At this point, a man bursts into the room. He asserts that he is the hotel detective, the woman's husband or a private detective gathering divorce information against the woman. In the last case, he has a camera with which he takes pictures of the couple before they have a chance to disengage.

Depending on the circumstances, the "detective" threatens to tell the police or the man's wife, or use the man as correspondent in a divorce action. The man pays whatever money he has on him, and usually quite a bit more, to get out of the situation. Even if he realizes he is being conned, the threat of exposure is usually enough to ensure compliance. *See also:* PANEL THIEF; SHORT CONS

BAG MAN

In gangland parlance, the person who collects money is a bag man. This can be the person who collects money for the Mob, a BUTTON MAN who goes around to tithe neighborhood shopkeepers weekly in a shakedown racket or the person who receives money from the Mob to distribute it to judges, politicians and police officials to pay for protection in a bought town. In NEW YORK CITY in the 1930s, James J. "Jimmy" Hines, a TAMMANY HALL ward boss, received money from DUTCH SCHULTZ and other mobsters and distributed it among Tammany leaders, judges and police precinct captains to win forbearance for their little peccadillos, such as bootlegging, loan sharking and running the numbers racket.

BAKER ESTATE

In 1839, Colonel Jacob Baker died in Philadelphia, Pennsylvania. Twenty-seven years later a gang of con men based in Ontario, Canada, devised the scheme that Colonel Baker had an undistributed estate, which comprised over 2,000 acres of land encompassing most of downtown Philadelphia. According to these gentlemen, the heirs to the Baker estate were entitled to the land on which stands the Liberty Bell, Independence Hall, the Pennsylvania Railroad Station and numerous hotels, office buildings and other property. For only a small investment, citizens in Pennsylvania or nearby states named Baker or Barker or Becker, or similar permutations, could invest in the estate, which would pay off a thousand to one when the estate was settled. The proposition did not lack for investors.

Like OSCAR HARTZELL's scheme with the heirs of Sir Francis Drake, the con men had hit on a popular chord and collected millions of dollars until the vein of Bakers ran out. Every few decades, as new generations of Bakers or Barkers or Beckers grew up, the con would be revived. In 1936, three con rings, operating out of Altoona, Johnstown, and Pittsburgh had more than 3,000 people investing in the Baker estate when their activities were interrupted by the postal authorities. Twenty-eight Baker operators were rounded up in the 1936 bust, including 70-year-old William Cameron Morrow Smith, who had made millions of dollars over the last 30 years recruiting the heirs of Colonel Baker. *See also:* CONFIDENCE GAMES

BALL, Joe (1894–1938)

The Sociable Inn, Joe Ball's spacious tavern outside of San Antonio, Texas, was a favorite of the local wealthy drinking class in the late 1930s. It had two attractions that kept the customers coming: the five pet alligators kept in a pond behind the establishment, and the 30 or so waitresses in skimpy costumes inside. One of the high points of the evening was going in back to watch Joe feed the " 'gators." Sometimes, as a crowd-pleaser, he would toss the reptiles a live stray dog or cat.

In 1937, the family of one of his girls, Minnie Mae Gotthardt, complained to the police that Minnie had been out of touch for a long time. Ball told them that she had left to take another job—he did not know where. Another girl, Julia Turner, had also left, so quickly that she had not packed. Ball explained that he had loaned her $500 to get away after she had a fight with her roommate.

Over a period of time, the TEXAS RANGERS received a number of reports about disappearing waitresses from the Sociable Inn. Hazel Brown, who told her banker that she was going to marry Joe, was nowhere to be found. Ball denied the betrothal and claimed that she had just wandered off, as so many of his waitresses did. It was very difficult to keep good help. "They come, they go," he told the Rangers. Refusing to be placated by this explanation, the Rangers looked into Ball's affairs. They found that he had been banking large amounts of money and hypothesized that he had been murdering the missing waitresses for their life savings after promising to marry them.

Amazingly, witnesses to Ball's behavior toward his missing waitresses were not lacking. They had just been afraid to come forward. "I just happened to stumble into Joe cutting up a couple of bodies one night," one of them testified. "He was feeding the pieces to the alligators, heads and all. Well, he saw me and threatened me. He said he'd kill me and feed me to the alligators, too, if I didn't leave town. So I left town."

On September 24, 1938, Rangers went to the tavern to arrest Ball. They were still not sure they had a case, but he took the problem out of their hands by pulling a revolver out of his cash register and shooting himself in the head.

The investigation by the Texas Rangers turned up some of the missing girls, who had indeed left for better jobs, but at least 20 of the waitresses were never found.

BALLEM, Francis Xavier (1926–)

The high point of Francis Ballem's life was the impulsive murder of a drunken acquaintance. Everything that came before led up to that act, and everything that came after was anticlimax.

Ballem grew up in a suburb of Philadelphia, the only child of middle-aged, overly protective parents from whom he was unable to break free while they were alive. He was an oversized dumpy child, clumsy, self-centered and friendless. He considered himself a genius, and he was actually quite bright. However, since he refused to study anything that did not interest him, and very little did, his actual sphere of knowledge was quite small. As Miriam Allen deFord said in her essay, "Rejection's Child" (from her book *Murderers Sane and Mad* [1965]), "Only one thing worried Francis Ballem as an adolescent—other boys apparently developed impulses that led them to an interest in girls; he felt no such impulse. He brooded over the possibility that he was a 'queer.' But he wasn't attracted to men, either. He wasn't attracted to anyone but his own superior self. He was the perfect narcissist."

At 24, possibly to break free of his parents, Ballem married a girl he met in a dance hall. When she got pregnant and insisted that she would not give the child up for adoption, he felt betrayed as he had told her he didn't want children. By then she had had enough of his petty tyrannies; when he started hitting her, she left. He moved back in with his parents.

In 1953, both of Ballem's parents died of cancer, leaving him the house and a little money. The bank insisted that Ballem must sell the house to satisfy the mortgage, which would force him out into the world. He resisted this bitterly and irrationally and he began roaming the slums of Philadelphia. As his paranoia crept up on him, he became convinced that the world was out to kill him and began stockpiling weapons to keep the world away. He went out searching for victims, but none were suitable. He shot his own dog, leaving its body in the house to rot.

A drunken part-time dishwasher named John Dopirak became his constant companion in his travels through the Philadelphia slums. He invited Dopirak to his house one evening after they had made the rounds of the bars. Dopirak went home with him and never left. Ballem took his guest into the living room, gave him something to drink and went upstairs. A minute later he came back downstairs and shot Dopirak in the stomach. Ballem had originally intended to transport the drunken Dopirak to New York City and leave him stranded, but at the last minute, that was too much trouble, so he just shot him. While Dopirak was lying, groaning, on the living room floor, bleeding to death, Ballem went up to his bedroom and took a nap. When Ballem came downstairs, Dopirak was dead.

Ballem suddenly realized that he had a body to dispose of. He tried burning it with a blowtorch, but that was counterproductive. So he cut the body into many small pieces, spread powdered lime on them, wrapped them in cloth and stored them in various places around the house. Three days later, he went to a taxi stand and brought the taxi back to the house. He had the driver help him put a footlocker in the cab and together they took it to the bus station. When the cab left, Ballem looked at magazines for a while and then went home, leaving the footlocker in the middle of the bus station.

The next day, tired of looking at the foot-locker, bus station employees took it aside and opened it. There were two packages inside. Inside one package was a man's upper trunk. In the other were the man's arms, hands, and head. They shut the foot locker and called the police.

When the police began their investigations, they sought for questioning everyone who had been to the station that day. The cab driver who had brought Ballem to the station remembered his fare and took the police to his house. The police broke in. They found parts of Dopirak scattered around the house. In the refrigerator, on a plate, they found the man's sex organs. Ballem, who they found crouching in a closet in the basement, apologized to them for not cleaning the house before they arrived.

Ballem was found guilty and sentenced to death. His sentence was at first stayed and then, in November 1958, commuted, as it became unquestionable that he was insane. He was confined to a mental hospital, where he soon became catatonic.

BANK ROBBERY

Robbing banks has been a popular sport among the more lawless elements of our society in several periods of American history. During the decades after the Civil War, when organized gangs of criminals prowled the West, some of the bank-robbing gangs, such as the DALTON BROTHERS, the YOUNGER BROTHERS and the JAMES BROTHERS, achieved a high level of notoriety. With the cleanup of the West in the 1880s, these groups were either captured or killed, or they went into some other line of work.

The next wave of bank robberies came with the Depression, when jobless workers and landless farmers searched for an acceptable alternative to starvation. Very few actually turned to bank robbery, but those who did, such as JOHN DILLINGER, "PRETTY BOY" FLOYD, "BABY FACE" NELSON and the BARKER-KARPIS GANG, were popular heroes. Dillinger, perhaps the most accomplished at this craft, learned his skills from followers of HERMAN "BARON" LAMM, who left the Prussian Army to come to the United States and rob banks. By 1934, with the entrance of the FBI into the continuing game of cops and robbers, the wave of bank robberies by organized gangs subsided.

Some of the specialties within the bank-robbing fraternity were the jug marker, the stick-man, and the wheelman. The jug marker picked the bank, "cased" it, noted the peculiarities of its alarm system, found out what day the most money would be on hand and sometimes developed dossiers on the bank manager and assistant manager if it would be useful to the plan.

The stickmen—there were usually two or three—actually entered the bank. They were crowd psychologists, who knew how to use enough force to cow the bank employees and customers so that no one would try to be a hero, and yet not so much that the victims were rendered incapable of motion through fear, which might well botch the job. In a good bank job, nobody got hurt.

The wheelman drove the getaway car and planned the escape route. He knew where the police would put up roadblocks and how to get around them. He was responsible for hiding a second car, so they could switch cars unobserved.

Bank robbery is becoming endemic again today, under the combined influences of drug addiction and a serious recession. But today's bank robber is a loner, who sticks up the teller at one window. Sometimes he has a gun, sometimes just a note. Depending on the instructions, tellers usually hand over money without argument. Banks are developing defenses against these lone bandits, including silent alarms, bullet-proof teller windows, money bundles that spit indelible dye and television camera surveillance. The most recent twist is robbing people as they withdraw money from automatic teller machines. No adequate defenses have been developed against this except care and the buddy system for using ATMs, especially at night.

BARBARA, Joseph (1905–1959)

A minor MAFIA figure, Joseph Barbara's name became prominent when his estate at Apalachin, New York, was picked as the site of a meeting of the nation's crime bosses. The state police interrupted what became known as the APALACHIN CONFERENCE but could get little information from the assembled gangster bosses, all of whom insisted that they had come to pay their respects to Barbara, who was suffering from a heart condition. It was mere coincidence, they claimed, that they had all arrived on the same day. Barbara insisted that he was too sick to testify because of his heart condition, so the State Investigation Commission had him examined by a specialist, who pronounced him fit. But before he could testify, he had a heart attack and died.

BARKER-KARPIS GANG

THE FBI'S CAPTURE OF THOSE BANK ROBBERS AND VICIOUS KILLERS MADE J. EDGAR HOOVER'S REPUTATION AS A FEARLESS LAWMAN

The four sons of MA BARKER, Herman (1894–1927), Lloyd (1896–1949), Arthur "Dock" (1899–1939), and Fred (1902–1935), and their companion, Alvin "Creepy" Karpis, formed what was one of the toughest, most vicious gangs of bank robbers, kidnappers and murderers to roam the Midwest in the 1920s. The legend has grown that Ma Barker controlled her boys and directed their operations, but this is exaggerated and possibly false.

The boys began their life of crime early. Arthur, known as "Dock," went to the Oklahoma State Penitentiary at McAlester in 1922, sentenced to life for robbing a bank and murdering the night watchman. It is possible that he was innocent of this crime, for a man in California later confessed to it. In the same year, Lloyd went to Leavenworth for robbing the mails. The next year, Fred went to a reformatory for theft. He got out on parole five years later and promptly was arrested for robbing a bank. He jumped a $10,000 bail bond put up by his mother and stayed free for a while. During this hiatus from prison, he set about robbing enough to pay Ma back. On May 31, 1931, he got out of prison officially and, two months later, was joined by his prison buddy Alvin Karpis.

Karpis, born Francis Albin Karpaviecz, was a Canadian of Lithuanian descent. His family moved to Topeka, Kansas, where he became city marbles champion. In 1926, he went to Kansas Reformatory for robbery, escaping from that institution in 1929. In 1931, he ended up in the penitentiary at Lansing, where he met Freddie Barker. On June 17, 1932, Fred and Alvin and five associates robbed the Fort Scott (Kansas) Bank of $47,000.

On September 10, 1932, Dock was paroled and returned to his brothers on the condition that he leave Oklahoma forever. By that time, Herman was already dead, having killed himself rather than surrender to the police after being severely wounded in a gun battle following a robbery in 1927.

The Barker-Karpis Gang spent a year in the St. Paul–Minneapolis area, robbing banks. On December 16, 1932, the Barker-Karpis Gang robbed the Third Northwestern Bank of Minneapolis of $20,000, killing two lawmen in making their escape. On August 15, 1933, they robbed the Swift Company payroll in St. Paul, Minnesota, of $30,000. On August 22, they hit a mail truck in Chicago, killing policeman Miles A. Cunningham in the process, but got only cancelled checks. On June 15, 1933, branching out into a new crime, they kidnapped William A. Hamm, Jr., of the brewery Hamms, and collected a $100,000 ransom. They released Hamm unharmed. On January 17, 1934, the gang kidnapped Edward G. Bremer, a millionaire banker, and held him for a $200,000 ransom. When the money was paid, they released Bremer.

On January 8, 1935, Dock Barker was captured by FBI agents on the way out of his apartment. "Where's your gun?" one of the agents asked, frisking him. "Home," he replied. "Ain't that a hell of a place for it?" Dock was tried for the two kidnappings and sentenced to life on Alcatraz. On June 13, 1939, he was killed trying to escape.

On April 25, 1935, Alvin Karpis and three non-Barker associates took the $70,000 payroll of the Youngstown Sheet & Tube Plant in Youngstown, Ohio. Two months later, a slightly different mix of Karpis associates robbed a mail train in Warren, Ohio, making off with $34,000.

On May 1, 1936, Alvin Karpis and Fred Hunter, an associate, were located by the FBI in New Orleans. J. Edgar Hoover flew down to be in on the capture. Karpis was surrounded and captured as he went for his car. "Put the cuffs on him," Hoover snapped.

As an interesting aside, the FBI's version of the story at the time had Hoover grabbing Karpis before he could get at a rifle in his back seat. The problem with this story is that Karpis's car, a 1936 Plymouth coupe, had no back seat. Karpis claimed in his memoirs that Hoover stayed in hiding until others had safely subdued Karpis. "I made Hoover's reputation as a fearless lawman," Karpis wrote. "It's a reputation he doesn't deserve."

Karpis was sentenced to life imprisonment and went to Alcatraz. In 1962, he was transferred to the McNeil Island Penitentiary in Washington state. In 1969, he was released on parole and deported to Canada. He published *The Alvin Karpis Story* in 1971.

The Barkers are buried side-by-side in a graveyard near Welch, Oklahoma.

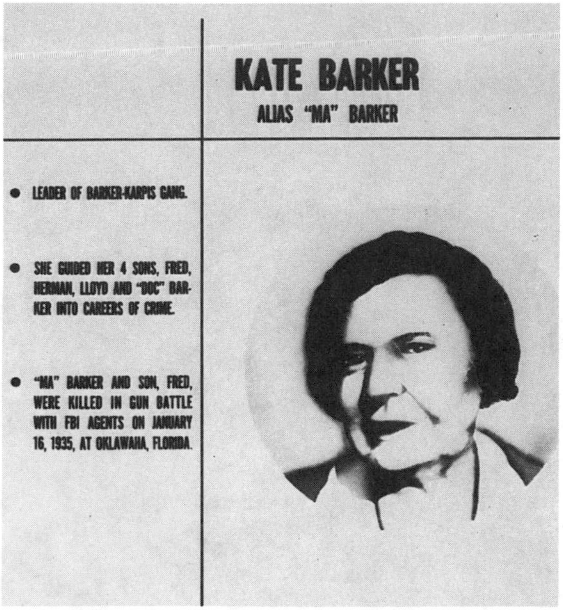

KATE BARKER
ALIAS "MA" BARKER

- LEADER OF BARKER-KARPIS GANG.
- SHE GUIDED HER 4 SONS, FRED, HERMAN, LLOYD AND "DOC" BARKER INTO CAREERS OF CRIME.
- "MA" BARKER AND SON, FRED, WERE KILLED IN GUN BATTLE WITH FBI AGENTS ON JANUARY 16, 1935, AT OKLAWAHA, FLORIDA.

Information sheet prepared by the FBI on Kate (alias "Ma") Barker, the so-called the "leader" of the Barker-Karpis Gang. (Federal Bureau of Investigation.)

BARKER, Ma (1870?–1935)

Ma Barker's given name at birth was Arizona Clark, a name she soon changed to the more practical "Kate." She grew up in the Ozark Mountains and married George Barker, a farm laborer with no ambitions to rise above that station. But over the years, Kate developed plans for herself and her four boys, Herman, Lloyd, Arthur, and Freddie. She saw that the only way out of the grinding poverty that was their lives would be to develop some skill or occupation that paid well and that was within their intellectual and educational limits. After some experimentation with lesser crimes, she and her brood turned to bank robbery.

There are two versions of the career of the Barker family. The official version, encouraged by J. EDGAR HOOVER and the FBI's active but unof-

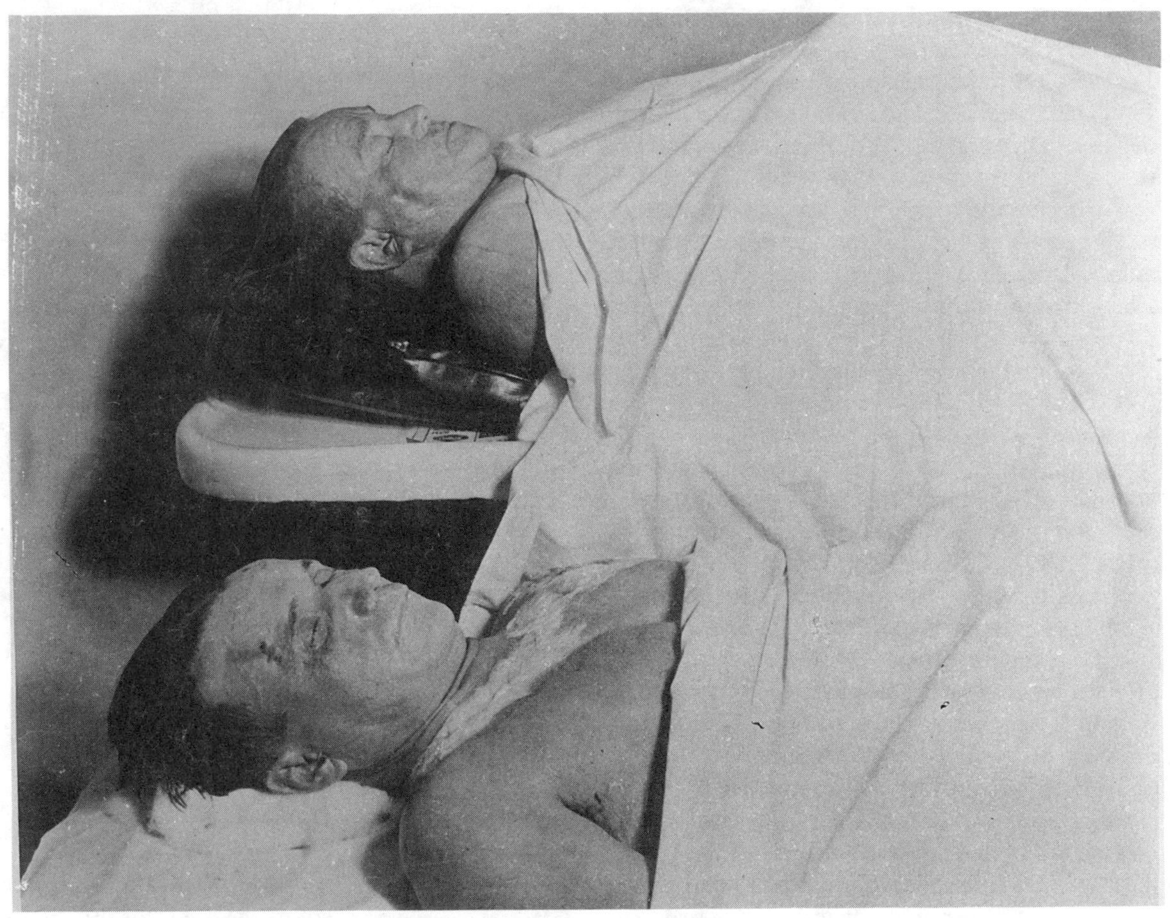

Ma Barker, killed in a shootout with federal officials. (Federal Bureau of Investigation.)

ficial public relations division, was that Ma was the mastermind of the gang, plotting the robberies, personally going over the escape routes, and controlling her sons' lives with an iron hand. This is probably nonsense. Many of the other outlaws who worked with the Barker boys, including Frank Nash, Ray Terrill and Alvin Karpis, would not have allowed her to take control. In his memoirs, Karpis described what was probably Barker's true role:

It's no insult to Ma's memory that she just didn't have the brains or know-how to direct us on a robbery. It wouldn't have occurred to her to get involved in our business, and we always made a point of only discussing our scores when Ma wasn't around. We'd leave her at home when we were arranging a job, or we'd send her to a movie. Ma saw a lot of movies.

In 1927, Herman Barker was killed in a gunfight with police. On January 26, 1935, Ma and Freddie were killed at their hideout at Lake Weir, Florida. It was after this that Hoover built up the legend of "Ma Barker," vicious killer and brains of the Barker gang. That image may have been created to explain why the FBI and local police machine gunned a little old lady to death in a Florida cottage. *See also:* BARKER-KARPIS GANG

BARROW, Clyde

See: BONNIE AND CLYDE

BECKER, Charles (1869–1915)

Lieutenant Charles Becker of the New York Police Department was the personal assistant to Commissioner Rhinelander Waldo, as well as head of the Police Special Crimes Squad. Unknown to Waldo, who thought he was cleaning up the department, Becker was the chief bag man for TAMMANY HALL boss Tim Sullivan and used the Special Crimes Squad as his personal enforcement division.

When gambler Herman "Beansie" Rosenthal refused to pay the customary kickback, Becker decided to make an example of him. Becker sent men to intimidate Rosenthal to bring him into line, but they succeeded too well. Rosenthal, now frightened to death, decided that his only safety lay in telling all to District Attorney Charles S. Whitman and *New York World* reporter Herbert Bayard Swope.

Afraid that things could get out of hand, and suffering from overweening pride, Becker decided to have Rosenthal removed. He let his underworld associate Big Jack Zelig, whom he had released from jail for the occasion, make the arrangements. Zelig lined up Gyp the Blood (born Harry Horowitz), Dago Frank Cirofici, Whitey Lewis (born Jacob Siedenshner), and Lefty Louis Rosenberg to do the job. On July 15, 1912, Beansie Rosenthal was called to the door of the restaurant he was dining in at the Hotel Metropole and was met by a fusillade of gunfire from his four assailants.

Becker was put in charge of the investigation. He did his best to obfuscate the evidence, even ordering the police to "lose" the license number of the hit car. One of the witnesses, "Billiard Ball" Jack Rose, managed to get to District Attorney Whitman before Becker could get to him.

Whitman assembled the evidence and tried the four gunmen for murder and Becker for being the instigator. They were all convicted. Becker was granted a second trial and was convicted for a second time. On July 7, 1915, he was electrocuted in Sing Sing prison, his four hirelings having preceded him by many months.

BERKOWITZ, David R. (1953–)

THE "SON OF SAM" KILLER—AN OBSESSED LONER WHO KEPT NEW YORK CITY IN TERROR FOR A YEAR

The adopted son of Nat and Pearl Berkowitz, David Berkowitz was a troubled and troublesome child. He alternated between docility and anger, studiousness and truancy. When Pearl died in 1967, David cut off the few friends he had and withdrew into himself. He enlisted in the army in 1971, served a tour in Korea, and sometime during this period left the Jewish faith of his adoptive parents to become a Baptist. He finished his service obligation at Fort Knox, Kentucky, and returned to New York. When his father moved to Florida a few months later David moved into his own apartment, and began to be plagued by demon-dogs that howled at him through the night.

David came to believe that the dogs were relaying messages to him—orders from "Sam," the six-thousand-year-old Prince of Darkness, to commit crimes. "Sam" was personified by either a neighbor named Sam Carr, or Carr's black Labrador. At first the dogs ordered him to set fires, and by the account in his diary he set more than 1,500 fires in 1975. And then the howling of the dogs told him that Sam wanted blood.

Berkowitz first tried to appease his private demons on Christmas Eve, 1975. He drove through the streets of the Bronx until he found a girl walking alone. Quickly parking his car, he ran up to her and stabbed her in the back with a hunting knife. She screamed. David had not expected her to scream. "I wasn't going to rob her, or touch her, or rape her," he explained to police after he was caught, "I just wanted to kill her." The girl, a Hispanic, never came forward. Police speculate that she was afraid to because she was an illegal immigrant.

The demon inside of him was not satisfied, and Berkowitz wandered the streets until he came upon 15-year-old Michelle Forman. He stabbed her repeatedly in the head and back until her screaming drove him away.

In their book, *Mass Murder: America's Growing Menace* [1985], sociologist Jack Levin and criminologist James Alan Fox explain:

> Berkowitz was surprised at how messy and difficult stabbing could be; it always seemed easy on television. He even found the encounters distasteful, repulsed by his victims' screaming and struggling. For David, unlike a number of other mass murderers, physical contact with the victim was not an important form of gratification. Instead, killing was but a means toward an end. If David obeyed dutifully Sam's command to kill, he would get his reward: a strong, satisfying orgasm. So David switched to a gun, a light .44 caliber Bulldog pistol he purchased while in Texas that would be very effective at close range.

In March, 1976, Berkowitz moved into an apartment overlooking the Hudson River. Convinced that someone was watching him from outside, he nailed blankets over all the windows. Early in the morning of July 29, 1976, David responded once more to his voices, this time taking the .44 caliber handgun instead of the hunting knife. He drove through the streets of the Bronx until he came upon a double-parked car with two girls in it. Jody Valenti, a 19-year-old student nurse, and Donna Lauria, an 18-year-old medical technician, were sitting in Donna's car talking when Berkowitz approached. He emptied his gun through the window, killing Donna with a bullet through the neck and wounding Jody with a bullet in the thigh. Jody began screaming and fell onto the car horn; the noise sent Berkowitz scurrying away.

On October 19, David emptied his gun at two figures sitting in a parked car in Flushing, New York. He missed the girl, Queens College student Rosemary Keenan, but hit her companion, 20-year-old Carl Denaro, in the head. Denaro was seriously injured, but recovered after surgery. On November 26, David followed 18-year-old Joanne Lomino and her friend 16-year-old Donna DeMasi as they got off a bus in Queens and headed home. As they frantically tried to open the door to Joanne's house to escape the following footsteps, David emptied his gun at them, wounding them both. The two girls recovered, but Joanne, with a bullet in her spine, was paralyzed for life.

In December David killed a German shepherd near his home in an attempt to silence his demons, but it merely made them angry. On January 29, 1977, he went to Forest Hills, Queens, and found a couple in a car. He walked up to the passenger window and put two bullets into the girl, 26-year-old Christine Freund. She died in the hospital two hours later. On March 2, he returned to Forest Hills and killed 21-year-old Virginia Voskerichian, a Columbia University student, with one bullet to the head.

By now the police realized that they had a serial killer on their hands, having determined that the bullets in several of the victims had been fired from the same .44 caliber handgun. The press promptly dubbed him the ".44 caliber killer."

The police set up a special task force, "Operation Omega," headed by Captain Joseph Borelli of the Queens Homicide Squad, to hunt the killer. Borelli gave the obligatory interview to the newspapers to try to ease the growing hysteria among the citizens of New York. In it he said that the .44 caliber killer must surely hate women. David enjoyed the notoriety, but felt that he must correct Captain Borelli about his motive.

On April 17, he went hunting again. Curiously, a policeman stopped him while he was driving around and gave him a ticket for driving without auto insurance. At about three in the morning he found his targets on a Bronx street: 18-year-old Valentina Suriani and her boyfriend, Alexander Esau, two years older. Having just returned from an evening in Manhattan, they were embracing in his car when David put four shots through the window, killing them both. David left a block-printed, quaintly spelled explanatory letter for the police on the street next to the car:

> Dear Captain Joseph Borelli:
>
> I am deeply hurt by your calling me a women hater. I am not. But I am a monster.
>
> I am the "Son of Sam." I am a little "Brat." . . .
>
> I feel like an outsider. I am on a different wavelength then everybody else—programmed too kill.
>
> However, to stop me you must kill me. Attention all police: Shoot me first—shoot to kill or else keep out of my way or you will die! . . .
>
> I am the "monster"—"Beelzebub"—the chubby behemouth. . . .

The newspapers took him at his word, and he promptly became the "Son of Sam." In looking for a pattern to his killings, it was noted that he went after young women with long brown hair. Thousands of New York women promptly cut their hair short and died it blond.

Columnist Jimmy Breslin of the New York *Daily News* suggested in his column that the Son of Sam should surrender. Berkowitz replied with a long letter, containing the ominous phrase, "Don't think that because you haven't heard from me for a while that I went to sleep." On June 25 he emptied his gun into a red Cadillac parked in front of a disco in Bayside. Sal Lupo was hit in the arm, and the girl he was driving home, Judy Placido, was hit in the head, neck, and back. Both of them survived and recovered.

On July 30 David drove through the streets of Brooklyn, looking for a victim who would satisfy his demons. He parked his car in front of a fire hydrant at two in the morning and strolled toward a local lovers' lane. While he was picking out his victim, a policeman ticketed the car.

Bobby Volante and Stacy Moskowitz, both twenty, and on their first date, pulled into a space in the lovers' lane and parked. They got out to play on nearby swings, and then returned to the car. The Son of Sam stepped forward and emptied his gun through the window. Stacy died from a bullet in the head. Bobby, hit twice in the face, lost the vision in one eye and most of the vision in the other.

The police finally found a substantial lead. In checking the cars that had been ticketed in the area of the lovers' lane that night, they found that one of the owners, David Berkowitz, was on a list of suspects for dog killing in Yonkers. Two detectives sent to investigate spotted his car and discovered a machine gun in the back seat. That in itself was cause enough to arrest him. They staked out his car. At ten o'clock in the evening of August 10, David Berkowitz approached his car carrying a brown paper bag. When he got in the car, the detectives arrested him. In the bag was a .44 caliber handgun. New York City's long nights of terror were over.

Despite Berkowitz's insistence that he was getting his murderous instructions from the howling of dogs, and a history of psychopathic behavior, he was adjudged sane enough to stand trial. Public opinion would not admit of anything else, and perhaps public opinion was right. If he was found insane under New York law he could have been released in a year. He almost certainly would not have been, but more assurance than that was needed.

Berkowitz pled guilty to murder, and was sentenced to a total of 547 years in prison. From prison he wrote to Dr. David Abrahamsen, the forensic psychiatrist who had examined him for the state, and the doctor began a correspondence and a series of interviews that resulted in Abrahamsen's book, *Confessions of Son of Sam* (1985). In it Abrahamsen discusses the sexual pathology that led to and reinforced Berkowitz's psychopathic personality. But he still concludes that the Son of Sam killed with "clear-headed cunning."

BERMAN, Otto "Abbadabba" (1880–1935)

Otto Beiderman was a dumpy little man whose sense of humor would have made him the clown prince of the DUTCH SCHULTZ gang were it not for his other, more useful skills. Otto had been nicknamed "Avisack" by famed "sporting man" ARNOLD ROTHSTEIN, after one of his favorite horses, but he preferred the moniker "Abbadabba Berman," given him by his gangster pals, because he thought it sounded more sinister. One of Schultz's most trusted aides, Abbadabba was a skilled racetrack handicapper as well as a lightning calculator. Schultz, who had taken over New York City's NUMBERS RACKET from its Harlem operators, used Berman's skills to increase his profits by an estimated 10 percent. This made Berman easily worth the estimated $10,000 a week that Schultz paid him.

The numbers game paid off on the last three digits of the total parimutuel handle of a racetrack—the total amount wagered during the course of one racing day. On any given day, certain numbers would be heavily played—perhaps the day's date; perhaps a happening of the day that could be reduced to three digits. Berman's job was to place bets at the last possible minute to swing the total away from any heavily played numbers. In tracks where the Mob had an in with the officials, the bet could be placed after the last race was run. As long as it was on a horse that ran out of the money, it benefited the track.

Berman had the misfortune to be with Dutch Schultz at the Palace Chop House in Newark, New Jersey, on Wednesday, October 23, 1935, the day the Dutchman was assassinated by a trio of killers sent by the Organization. Schultz wanted to put out a contract on THOMAS E. DEWEY, a racket-busting special prosecutor, but the other mob bosses violently disagreed. They had a sitdown, but Schultz was adamant. Berman and two other men who happened to be with Schultz at the table were also gunned down.

Earlier that evening Berman had brought Schultz the figures for the last six weeks' numbers handle. The total amount bet had come to $827,253.43. The players' winnings had come to only $313,711.99, leaving the Schultz organization with a gross profit of $513,541.44, or 62 percent. The difference between this and the 40 percent average take of an "honest" game was Berman's contribution to Dutch Schultz's bankroll.

BERTILLON, Alphonse (1853–1914)

The founder of the *Service de l'Identité Judiciaire*, the Criminal Identification Bureau of the Paris Police Department (1889), Alphonse Bertillon devised a system of anthropological measurements, known as *bertillonage* or "anthropometry," which was adopted for criminal identification by police departments all over the world in the 1880s until it was replaced in the 1920s by fingerprinting.

Bertillon's theory of anthropometry was based on the following observations:

1. The human skeleton is unchangeable after the age of 20. The thigh bones continue to grow somewhat, but this is compensated for by the curvature of the spine, which happens at about the same rate.

2. The bones of no two human beings will be alike.

3. The necessary measurements can be taken easily using simple instruments.

The measurements taken were height, sitting height, width of outstretched arms, length and breadth and diameter of head, length of right ear, length of left arm from the elbow to the tip of the outstretched middle finger, length of left middle and little fingers and length of left foot.

At first the system was successful. In 1882, anthropometry identified 49 criminals giving false names. By 1892, the number had risen to 680. Unfortunately for anthropometry, it proved impossible to make uniform measurements from police department to police department, or even from time to time in the same police department. Also, despite Bertillon's second postulate, occasionally two people would turn up with essentially the same measurements. In 1903, in the federal prison at Leavenworth, Kansas, were two prisoners named West; one was Willie West, and the other William West, and to compound the confusion, the pair had exactly the same Bertillon measurements. Their fingerprints, however, were not the same. This began the decline of the use of Bertillon measurements in this country. Although no longer in use in the United States, anthropometry is still used in some police departments throughout the world as an adjunct to fingerprinting, but it is recognized as less than completely dependable.

Bertillon also devised the *PORTRAIT PARLÉ*, a uniform method of describing a person, and the standards for photographing criminals that are essentially used today.

THE BIG CON, THE BIG STORE

THE ACME OF CONFIDENCE GAMES, PRACTICED BY THE MASTER CON MEN

Begun in the 1840s, and perfected in the years after the Civil War, the big con, more properly called the big store, was the elite of CONFIDENCE GAMES, and its practitioners were the nobility of confidence men. Charley Gondorf and his brother Fred were masters of the game in turn-of-the-century New York. In 1920s Denver, Lou Blonger ran a big store in Denver for a decade, and just about ran the town. The game changed through the years, but its elements remain the same.

First, a mark (victim) is selected by the "outside man" or "steerer," who cultivates him and then takes him to the "inside man," or "roper," who "tells him the tale." Then he is taken to the "big store," and, after at least one "convincer," relieved of his money. Finally the "blowoff" convinces the mark that he should just go home and lick his wounds without complaining to the police.

Many victims of big store swindles, as with most confidence games, are so ashamed of being taken that they seldom complain to their own families, much less the police. They are usually successful businessmen who pride themselves on their knowledge of human nature and the pitfalls of life, and when they find that they did not know as much as they thought, their egos prevent them from talking about it.

Let us walk through one fictitious example in detail. We will set it in the past, but if it reminds you of something that happened to you, step back and examine your situation.

It is 1932, and John Goodman, a "butter and egg man" (wholesale grocer) from Big Falls, Kansas, has to go to the Big City (e.g., New York) on business. On the train, he meets Bill, a respectable-looking gentleman of similar interests. They strike up a casual friendship. Bill, who spends a lot of time in New York, tells Goodman of the delights of the city and, by adroit questioning, establishes Goodman's status in the community and his net worth, to the nearest dollar. Bill, the "outside man," has now done his job, and will get a percentage of any profits the gang makes from their association with Mr. Goodman.

When they arrive in New York, Bill invites John Goodman to dinner, where they meet Bill's friend Tom. Tom, the "roper," now tells the tale. There are several tales to tell; this one is the "Golden Wire." Tom asks Bill if John is all right, if he is to be trusted. Bill reassures Tom, who then tells them that he now works for a very exclusive betting parlor, and invites them to visit it. Goodman, so pleased at being judged trustworthy, does not stop to reflect that he just met Bill on the train and knows nothing about him. Besides, it is not Bill but Tom who is telling the tale, and Bill's vouching for Goodman worked in reverse to reassure Goodman about Tom.

Goodman is taken to the betting parlor and is impressed with its opulence and the evident wealth of the customers. Now comes the end of the tale—the part with the hook. A little while later Tom comes to Goodman with an offer. If Goodman will return to the betting parlor and put down a bet—using Tom's money—Tom will give him a percentage of the winnings. Goodman is naturally curious. Tom explains. A friend of Tom's works at Western Union on the "Golden Wire," the special wire that is used to send the race results to the betting parlors. They have decided to make a big killing at the parlor Tom works at—the owner has been mistreating Tom—and will reward Goodman for his help.

Tom's friend will withhold the racing tape on a certain race until after it is actually run and will phone the name of the winner to Goodman, who will place the bet. Tom cannot do it himself since he works there, and if any of his friends do it, the hated owner will get suspicious. If Goodman agrees, they will try it once with a small sum of money to make sure it works, and then they will do it once more with a lot of money and make a killing. Tom is arranging to get the required stake for the big bet.

They go through it once and it works perfectly. Goodman is given a share of the take. This is the convincer. The honest grocer from Kansas sees that it works, and he wants his share.

The psychology of the con is carefully thought out. First of all, the mark is not on his home grounds. If they were trying to take somebody from New York City, they'd probably play him in Kansas. The mark sees the big store—the swell gambling parlor—which looks like it has been there forever. He sees the quality of the people gambling in there. It never crosses his mind for an instant that the whole thing is phoney; the wall of chalk boards, the cashiers' cages, and the comfortable furniture have all been put there for his benefit. It never occurs to him that the score of men in tuxedos and women in evening gowns, the girls in skimpy costumes giving out drinks, the earnest-looking tellers in the cashiers' cages, the excited voice calling the races over a loudspeaker, have all been hired as stage dressing for his benefit. How could it? Such a thing is entirely outside of his experience. And the constant talk of big money is disarming and counterconditioning. His new friends are taking him to expensive restaurants and they insist on paying. They throw money around like it really is meaningless. And Mr. Goodman does not want to appear a piker. A man who worries about paying a quarter for a meal when he is at home is among people who put down a dollar as a tip. Without his awareness, his values have been changed.

Now the big day approaches, but Tom is having trouble raising the money he needs. He has $50,000, but the friend with the other $50,000 has been called away, and they cannot wait any longer. His boss is getting suspicious. And it has to be done all at once, because Tom's friend at the telegraph company is being promoted and won't be on the golden wire much longer.

"Say!" Goodman says, suddenly getting a

bright idea. "Why don't I put up the other 50,000?" He feels like a sport. He feels like a big spender. And, after all, the money will never leave his hands—he's the one putting the bet down.

"I couldn't ask you to do that," Tom tells him. But Tom allows himself to be convinced, and Goodman wires home for the money. From this point on Goodman is going to be secretly shadowed by another member of the gang to make sure he does not suddenly wise up and go to the police. But that seldom happens.

"Are you sure you know what you're doing?" Tom asks him anxiously.

"Of course I do," Goodman replies.

"Are you sure you understand horse racing?"

Goodman is offended. With that same masculine ego that forbids a male motorist from asking directions, he assures Tom that he knows everything there is to know about horse racing.

The big moment arrives. Goodman is waiting by a telephone with $100,000 in his bag—half his and half his good friend Tom's. The phone rings. "Place the money on Hambone in the third at Pimlico," the voice tells him. "Did you get that—place the money on Hambone in the third race at Pimlico."

"I understand," Goodman says. He races across the street to the betting parlor and gets on line at the betting window. The suspense is awful. The line moves so slowly. But finally he is in front, and he shoves the money through the window. "Hambone in the third at Pimlico," he says, "to win."

The teller is unimpressed with the size of the bet, and hands Goodman his ticket.

The race is called. Hambone comes in second. Mr. Goodman sits there looking dazed. Tom comes over, looking pleased. "Well, we did it," he whispers.

"What do you mean, 'we did it'?" Goodman asked. "Hambone came in second."

"That's right," Tom agrees. "He *placed*. And you were told to place the money on Hambone. Don't tell me . . ."

"I bet him to win," Goodman admits dejectedly. It is clearly all his fault.

"And I thought you knew about racing," Tom whispers scornfully. He sighs. "Well, nothing for it but to try it again."

If they think the mark is good for it, and he is well and truly hooked, they may actually try it again and find some other excuse to lose. More often the "boss" will suddenly come storming up to Tom and accuse him of being in collusion with Goodman. "You're fired!" he yells at Tom. "Get out of here!"

Now Goodman really feels bad. He has lost his money and Tom's money and gotten Tom fired in the bargain. Now they will never get the money back. And he is to blame.

On the train back to Kansas, as Goodman ponders what happened, the aura usually falls away, the story unravels in his mind, and he realizes he has been taken. He vows vengeance. But usually, by the time the train pulls into Topeka, Goodman has decided not to admit what a fool he has been, and he chalks the whole thing up to experience. Probably the most exciting experience he has had since World War I.

BILL OF RIGHTS

The Bill of Rights, which is made up of the first 10 amendments to the Constitution of the United States, is an amazingly compact document (for what it does). Before the federal Constitution was adopted, many of the states had bills of rights, which were designed to protect the rights of individuals from the power of the state, written into their own constitutions. Their experience with the autocracies of Europe and the absentee monarchy of George III in England had given them the incentive and had given them a good idea of what rights most needed protecting.

Six of the 10 amendments relate directly to criminal law, protecting in one way or another the rights of the accused in criminal cases or providing a defense for actions that the government might otherwise deem criminal. The United States is still one of the few countries in the world to have codified in law and custom the rights of the individual over those of the state.

The First Amendment assures freedom of religion, speech, and the press and the right of peaceful assembly. It is, perhaps, the most challenged, by administrations that feel that their secrets are more important than the people's right to know, and by transient public opinion that feels that any group can assemble and speak except the group it dislikes.

The Second Amendment presents interesting problems in interpretation: "A well-regulated Militia, being necessary to the security of a free State, the right of the people to keep and bear Arms shall not be infringed." The National Rifle Association takes the extreme view that this is an absolute mandate for any citizen to own any weapons he or she chooses at any time. On the other side is the unorganized but substantial minority that feels that the Second Amendment was meant for an earlier age and is inappropriate today and that private citizens have no business possessing guns. A more moderate view, based on the word *militia* in the amendment, holds that private citizens should be able to own weapons, but that the state has the right to regulate that ownership for the protection of others.

The FOURTH AMENDMENT prevents the government from conducting random or unwarranted searches or seizures.

The FIFTH AMENDMENT prevents a defendant from being forced to testify against himself or herself. It also, in the so-called double jeopardy phrase, prevents a defendant from being tried twice for the same charge.

The Sixth Amendment assures a criminal defendant a speedy and public trial, states that the defendant must be informed of the charges against him or her and be allowed to confront the witnesses against him or her and have witnesses in his or her favor and assures the defendant of the right to counsel. The right of counsel was expanded in the *Gideon v. Wainwright* decision of 1963 to a necessity. Today if the defendant cannot afford a lawyer, then the state must provide one.

The Eighth Amendment prohibits excessive bail and cruel and unusual punishments. It is this amendment that is used by those opposing CAPITAL PUNISHMENT, who feel that any death sentence is cruel, and as other countries give up the death penalty, it is becoming increasingly unusual.

See: MIRANDA RULE; RELIGIOUS RIGHTS

BILLY THE KID

See: WILLIAM H. BONNEY

BLACK HAND

In the United States, from 1890 to 1920, Italian immigrant families suffered from a wave of extortion demands from the criminal element among their fellow immigrants. Some of the perpetrators were MAFIA, some were CAMORRA, and some were free-lance extortionists. They would send a demand for money to shopkeepers, bankers and other businessmen, threatening to destroy merchandise, burn down the shop, or kidnap the victim's children, signing the note with a crudely drawn black hand. The victim, afraid to fight back and afraid to go to the police, would usually pay up.

One of the most famous Black Hand victims was tenor Enrico Caruso, a world-renowned Italian opera star. While playing at the Metropolitan Opera House in New York City in 1916, he received an extortion demand for $2,000, which he paid. Shortly thereafter he received a second demand, this time for $15,000. Not liking the direction of this trend, Caruso notified the police, who set a trap for the extortionists. They had Caruso comply with the note, leaving a package at the specified drop-off point. When the extortionists appeared, they were arrested. The two, who turned out to be respected Italian businessmen, were tried and convicted and sentenced to prison.

This was one of the few successful terminations to a case of Black Hand extortion. The lure of easy money at the expense of their hard-working countrymen was one that many Italian gangsters found hard to resist. The practice became so widespread that New York City and other large cities with Italian populations founded Italian squads principally to fight the Black Hand extortionists.

In May 1921, Giuseppi Verotta, five years old, was kidnapped from the street in front of his Lower East Side apartment house by Black Handers. The kidnappers demanded a $2,500 ransom from his father, an Italian pushcart merchant. They threatened to drown the child, kill the rest of the family and burn down the house if the ransom was not paid. With the aid of the father, who captured one of the extortionists, the police arrested five suspects. The whereabouts of the child remained a mystery until his body washed up on an island in the Hudson River. He had been strangled before being tossed in the river.

This was the first recorded case in the United States where kidnappers were known to have carried out their threat to kill the victim. The five were tried for kidnapping, which carried a sentence of 10 to 50 years in prison, and first-degree murder, which carried the death penalty. The jury took seven hours to find the first defendant guilty, and he was sentenced to death. In return for a reprieve from the governor, he turned state's evidence and implicated 40 people in the crime. One after another, the perpetrators were tried and sentenced to either death or life imprisonment. All of the death sentences were eventually commuted to life imprisonment.

After this incident, Black Hand kidnappings became quite rare.

See also: KIDNAPPING

BLACK MARIA

A nineteenth century term used to describe a police or sheriff's van used for transporting prisoners. Legend has it that the term comes from Maria Lee, a black lady of exceptional size and strength, who ran a sailors' boarding house in Boston before the Civil War. When the police had trouble subduing a drunk and rambunctious sailor in the neighborhood, they would send for "Black Maria" [*ma-rye-ah*], who would easily overpower the troublemaker and take him back to her boarding house if he was one of her guests, or to the lockup if he was not. You may believe that if you like.

BLACK SOX SCANDAL

See: WORLD SERIES OF 1919

BLACKBEARD

See: TEACH, EDWARD

BOLIN, Patty (1936–1976)

On Thanksgiving Day, 1976, Patty Bolin, wife of Ronald Bolin of Columbus, Ohio, purchased a .22-caliber pistol. Two weeks later, on December 8, she used it. First she shot her husband. Then she shot her 12-year-old daughter Pamela Jean. Her 9-year-old son ran out of the house screaming, "She's shooting everyone! She's shooting up the place!" He got his neighbors to call the police and then returned to the house, hoping to help his sisters. Patty shot him dead in the kitchen. Having no idea anything was wrong, Alicia Ann, Patty's 15-year-old daughter, came into the house. Patty pointed the gun at her and clicked the trigger three times, but the gun failed to fire. "Alicia," she said firmly, "go to your room!" As she attempted to reload the pistol, Alicia ran screaming from the house, almost tripping over her brother's body on the way.

The first policeman arrived and peered through the window. When Patty pointed the pistol at him, he ducked. Before he could do anything else, Patty Bolin turned the gun on herself and fired. Her death removed the possibility of discovering the motives for her shooting spree.

BONNEY, William H. (1859–1881)

Known as "Billy the Kid" during his brief career as a Western outlaw, William Bonney was born in Brooklyn, New York. He was involved with a gang of cattle rustlers in New Mexico in his teens and became known for his tendency to shoot people with little provocation. He is apocryphally reputed to have killed his first man at the age of 12 for insulting his mother, and to have run up a string of 21 murders by the time he died at 21. Billy became involved in a bitter power struggle in the New Mexico Territory in the 1870s that became known as the Lincoln County War. On one side were cattlemen John Chisum, of Chisum Trail fame, and Alexander McSween, and on the other businessmen James Dolan, James Riley and Lawrence Murphy. When his mentor, an Englishman named John Tunstall, was murdered in 1878 by a gunman allied to the Dolan-Riley-Murphy faction, Billy vowed to get revenge. He went on a spree, killing an unknown number of the opposition.

When the war ended Billy went back to cattle rustling and murder. His gang roamed the countryside until Sheriff Pat Garrett and others wiped them out, one at a time. Finally, in 1881, Garrett caught up with Bonney at Fort Sumner, New Mexico, and gunned him down. Despite the myths that have grown up around him since his death, the consensus among those who knew him, including some who rode with him, was that he was a cold-blooded, psychopathic killer.

BONNIE AND CLYDE

SHE WROTE POETRY, HE PLAYED THE SAXOPHONE; THEY ROBBED BANKS

Their names were Clyde Chestnut Barrow (1909–1934) and Bonnie Parker (1911–1934) and they robbed banks. In the depression many people, especially in the Midwest, considered this an admirable thing to do, since farmers were losing their land and tradesmen were losing their businesses as the banks foreclosed. Of course, there was more to it than that, but in times of crisis, people tend to simplify and to look for a villain. If the banks were the villain, then bank robbers must be heroes. The Barrow Gang, as Bonnie and Clyde liked to call themselves, also robbed grocery stores, luncheonettes and filling stations, which were perhaps not as deserving targets, and they had a habit of brutally murdering anyone who stood in their way, but that was overlooked by their romanticizing public. After all, they did rob banks.

Bonnie Parker was small as a child and grew up to be a small woman, less than five feet tall and weighing comfortably under 100 pounds. A red-headed child with bright blue eyes, she was bright, impetuous, and had a knack for drawing attention to herself, sometimes with startling results. When she was three she was asked to sing a solo hymn in her Baptist Sunday School. She took the stage and, in her piercingly clear soprano, belted out a song named "He's a Devil in His Own Home Town." She seemed pleased at the ensuing bedlam.

Her father died in 1914, when she was four, leaving her mother with three small children and no money. Mrs. Parker was forced to move back in with her mother, Bonnie's grandmother, in Cement City, Texas. Bonnie attended elementary school and possibly high school in Cement City. Her mother always insisted that Bonnie had graduated from high school, but since she married her boyfriend, Roy Thornton, when she was fifteen—and he two years older—it seems doubtful. The young couple lived a few blocks from Bonnie's mother for a while, and then moved in with Mrs. Parker both to save money and because Bonnie found it hard to be without her mother. Roy evidently suffered mother-in-law problems, as he soon took to staying away from home for long periods of time. One day Bonnie decided that she had had it with his absences, and told him not to bother to come back. A few months after, Roy got arrested for robbery and went to prison for five

Bonnie Parker poses in back of one of the gang's getaway cars. (Federal Bureau of Investigation.)

Clyde Barrow in front of the same car. (Federal Bureau of Investigation.)

years. Bonnie never bothered getting a divorce, although she went back to using her maiden name.

Clyde Barrow grew up in West Dallas, Texas. He and a group of his fellow youths, who called themselves the "Root Gang," were known as petty thieves and general troublemakers in their neighborhood. He developed a love for music as a young man, and became fairly proficient on the saxophone. His older brother Marvin "Buck" Barrow was in constant trouble with the law, and the local police soon developed the habit of running Clyde in with his brother. Although often justified, this experience developed in Clyde a strong distaste for the law. It was during this period that he formed the habit of running away promptly whenever there was the slightest hint of trouble. Once, when Clyde had parked a rented car outside the house of friends, a police car stopped at the house on a routine check to see why a rental car was being held for an extra day; Clyde was off through the fields before the two policemen reached the house. The policemen, assuming he was a fleeing felon, fired two shots at him as he departed, which didn't help. He didn't return until the next morning.

Clyde had two loves in his life before he met Bonnie: Anne, whose parents finally forbade her meeting him, and Gladys, who moved in with him briefly under a false facade of marriage. When Gladys left him, he moved in with a petty crook named Frank Clause, and he, his brother Buck, and Frank began a series of robberies and safe burglaries. In October, 1929, they took the safe from a garage in Denton, Texas, and put it in the back seat of their car, planning to open it in a location and time of their own choosing. The police took out after them and Clyde, who was driving, ran the car into a curb and broke its front axle. He was out of the car in a flash and racing away. Buck was shot, receiving a minor wound, and captured. Buck was sentenced to five years in prison, and Clyde, arrested on other charges, pled guilty to auto theft and burglary and received a reduced sentence of two years in return for his plea.

On March 7, 1930, Buck broke out of jail by simply walking off the prison farm—he had been a model prisoner. On March 10, he managed to pass a hacksaw to Clyde, and Clyde and two other prisoners sawed their way to freedom. Buck meanwhile married a girl named Blanche Caldwell.

Bonnie Parker met Clyde Barrow in 1930 in Dallas. There are several different versions of how they met, as befits folk heroes, but they were certainly close friends by the time the police picked up Clyde on several outstanding warrants. Bonnie visited him every day in jail and finally smuggled him a gun which he and another prisoner used to escape. He was captured in Middletown, Ohio, after robbing an office of the Baltimore & Ohio Railroad and returned to Waco, Texas, where he began serving time in the Texas State Penitentiary at Huntsville.

On February 2, 1932, Texas Governor "Ma" Ferguson pardoned a group of prisoners including Clyde and brother Buck, who had returned voluntarily to finish serving out his term at the instigation of Blanche, who didn't want to spend her life on the run. By the time Clyde was paroled he had learned, but not mastered, the principles of armed robbery in prison. He would never master them, but he would certainly keep trying.

Buck swore he would go straight, and for a while he tried. It is even possible that Clyde tried. But the times were against them. As Miriam Allen deFord put it in *The Real Bonnie & Clyde* (1968): "The United States was deep in the big Depression. Ruined tycoons were still jumping out of their skyscraper office windows; jobless men were selling apples on the streets; the popular song was 'Brother Can You Spare a Dime?' Hoover was still president, and the Bonus Army had been rousted out of Washington . . .

"The hardest way to make money was to earn it. Robbery had become a competitive profession, and the underpaid, overworked officers of the law, Federal, State, County, and local, were finding it increasingly difficult to cope with the wave of crime . . . It was partly incredible luck, partly the timidity and stupidity of some of the officers of the law, but also partly the repercussions of the Depression that protected Bonnie and Clyde so long from their inevitable end."

Bonnie, Clyde, and Buck began a series of small and unimpressive robberies, gradually working their way up to more daring escapades. A young man named Ray Hamilton was with them through much of 1932; it was he and Clyde who killed Sheriff G. G. Maxwell and Undersheriff Eugene Moore when the two lawmen stopped their car in Atoka, Oklahoma, while Bonnie was in jail briefly for car theft. Hamilton stayed with the gang until he went to visit his father in Michigan, got blind drunk, talked too much and was arrested and expedited back to Texas. He was tried for a string of robberies and for a murder he probably did not commit and was sentenced to a total of 263 years in the penitentiary at Huntsville.

In December 1932, 16-year-old William Daniel Jones drifted into the Barrow Gang in Dallas. At first eager to join, he soon became frightened by the gang's activities and kept trying to run away. When he finally succeeded, he dictated a 28-page confession, claiming that he had been Bonnie Parker's sex slave and begging the authorities to keep him safe from her.

This is the foundation of the legend that Parker was a nymphomaniac and that Barrow was a homosexual who could not satisfy her. The truth of this cannot be known, but it is known that when Clyde heard of Jones's allegations, he broke up laughing. Bonnie probably did have a healthy appetite for men, and Clyde was away much of the time. And what we today would consider normal sexual desires for a woman would in 1932 have been considered nymphomania—especially in Texas.

As they continued their predations, the newspaper accounts were slowly creating the "Bonnie and Clyde" legend. Even though their robberies continued to be minor, and their murder toll mounted, they became popular heroes. Bonnie wrote bad, maudlin doggerel verse, which she sent to newspapers who published it.

The authorities began to get serious about catching the Barrow Gang as their notoriety increased. Even though their predations were not as serious as those of AL CAPONE in Chicago or "LUCKY" LUCIANO in New York by several orders of magnitude, their popular acclaim was bad for public order and they had developed a nasty habit of killing lawmen.

On January 6, 1933, Bonnie and Clyde barely evaded a police trap in Dallas, shooting Deputy Sheriff Malcolm Davis as they made their escape. On April 13, 1933, they aroused the curiosity of the police in Joplin, Missouri, when a neighbor reported strange goings-on in the apartment the gang had rented. When the police came in force to investigate, possibly suspecting who they would find in the apartment, Clyde and Buck and Bonnie and Blanche and Billie Jones made their escape, crashing their car through a garage door and a barricade of police cars. Policemen J. Wes Harryman and Harry L. McGinnis died in that encounter.

Over the next few months, they went on an ineffectual robbery spree, robbing the Lucerne State Bank in Lucerne, Indiana, of $300; the First State Bank of Okabena, Minnesota, of $1,500; and three gas stations in Fort Dodge, Iowa, of less than $100. JOHN DILLINGER is reported to have said, on reading of the Barrow Gang's exploits, "They're punks—they're giving bank robbing a bad name."

On July 22, 1933, the police located and surrounded the gang in a tourist park six miles outside of Platte City, Missouri. They escaped in a running gun battle, which severely wounded Buck, only to fall into an ambush at a deserted amusement park outside of Dexter, Iowa. The entire gang was wounded in the ensuing gun battle, and Buck and Blanche were captured. Buck died six days later, and Blanche went to prison for 10 years.

Bonnie and Clyde went through several other shoot-outs with the law until, on May 23, 1934, they were led into a police trap near Gibsland, Louisiana, informed on by former gang member Henry Methvin. Their car was riddled with gunfire from rifles, shotguns, machine guns and one Browning Automatic Rifle. They both died instantly. The autopsies showed that Clyde had been hit by 25 bullets, and Bonnie by 23.

One of Bonnie's poems told her version of the story of Bonnie and Clyde and is worth reading, if not for the verse, then for the maudlin self-justification and what it reveals of Bonnie's thought processes.

THE STORY OF BONNIE AND CLYDE
by Bonnie Parker

You've read the story of Jessie James—
Of how he lived and died.
If you're still in need of something to read,
Here's the story of Bonnie and Clyde.

Now Bonnie and Clyde are the Barrow gang.
I'm sure you all have read
How they rob and steal, and those who squeal
Are usually found dying or dead.

There's lots of untruths in these write-ups;
They're not so ruthless as that.
Their nature is raw, they hate all the law—
The stool pigeons, spotters and rats.

They call them cold-blooded killers,
They say they are heartless and mean,

But I say this with pride, that I once knew Clyde
When he was honest, upright and clean.

But the law fooled around, kept taking him down
And locking him up in a cell,
Till he said to me, "I'll never be free.
So I'll meet a few of them in hell."

The road was so dimly lighted;
There were no highway signs to guide;
But they made up their minds, if all roads were blind,
They wouldn't give up till they died.

The road gets dimmer and dimmer;
Sometimes you can hardly see;
But it's fight man to man, and do all you can,
For they know they can never be free.

From heartbreak some people have suffered;
From weariness some people have died;
But take it all in all, our troubles are small,
Till we get like Bonnie and Clyde.

If a policeman is killed in Dallas
And they have no clew or guide,
And they can't find a fiend, they just wipe their slate clean
And hang it on Bonnie and Clyde.

There's two crimes committed in America
Not accredited to the Barrow mob;
They had no hand in the kidnap demand[1]
Nor the Kansas City Depot job.

A newsboy once said to his buddy,
"I wish old Clyde would get jumped;
In these awful hard times we'd make a few dimes
If five or six cops would get bumped."

The police haven't got the report yet,
But Clyde called me up today;

[1] Probably a reference to the kidnapping of Charley Urschel by GEORGE "MACHINE GUN" KELLY.

He said, "Don't start any fights—we aren't working nights—
We're joining the N.R.A."

From Irving to West Dallas Viaduct
Is known as the Great Divide,
Where the women are kin, and the men are men,
And they wont "stool" on Bonnie and Clyde.

If they try to act like citizens
And rent them a nice little flat,
About the third night they're invited to fight
By a sub-gun's rat-tat-tat.

They don't think they're too smart or desperate,
They know that the law always wins;
They've been shot at before, but they do not ignore
That death is the wages of sin.

Some day they'll go down together;
They'll bury them side by side;
To few it'll be grief—to the law a relief—
But it's death for Bonnie and Clyde.

BOOSTER

A booster is a thief of new merchandise. A good booster will take orders for goods, including size and style of clothing, and guarantee delivery within a week.

BOOTH, John Wilkes (1838–1865)

THE MAN WHO KILLED PRESIDENT LINCOLN CAUSED AMERICA'S FIRST MAJOR CONSPIRACY THEORY

The son of Junius Brutus Booth and brother of Edwin Booth, both noted Shakespearean actors in their day, American actor John Wilkes Booth was a rabid Southern sympathizer during the Civil War. When General Lee surrendered at Appomattox,

John Wilkes Booth, the actor who assassinated President Abraham Lincoln. (Collection of the author.)

Booth and his cronies spent their time sitting around a Washington, D.C., rooming house owned by Mrs. Mary Surratt and devising all sorts of mad schemes to get revenge on the North, and on their particular villain, President Abraham Lincoln.

One scheme was to kidnap Lincoln and convey him in chains to Richmond, Virginia, where he would be held hostage until the Union Army laid down its arms. The schemers actually lay in wait one night late in March 1865 for the president's carriage to pass by, planning to jump out of ambush and seize Mr. Lincoln. Their plan was thwarted when the president took another route.

A new plan was drawn up, calling for Booth to assassinate President Lincoln while other conspirators struck at Vice President Andrew Johnson, Secretary of State William Seward and other members of the Cabinet. Three weeks later, on the night of April 14, 1865, Booth was in attendance at Ford's Theater in Washington, D.C., when the president and his wife arrived and settled into box seats to watch a performance of *Our American Cousin*, a popular comedy by English dramatist Tom Taylor. Booth pulled aside the curtain to the box and fired his Derringer into the president's head. Dropping his one-shot pistol, he pulled a dagger and slashed at an Army officer who tried to grab him. Striking a pose, he yelled "*Sic Semper Tyrannis*" ("Thus Ever with Tyrants," the motto of the state of Virginia), and made a leap for the stage. In an ironic accident, the spur on his boot caught on an American flag outside the box, and he fell heavily, fracturing his leg. When he reached the stage he yelled, "The South is avenged!" to a startled audience and staggered out the stage door. The President was taken to a nearby hotel, where he died some hours later.

Booth and fellow plotter David Herold, who had tried for Seward and failed, met in Maryland, and Herold helped Booth to a doctor named Samuel Mudd to have his leg set. Then the pair left, heading south. On April 26, they were cornered by Union troops in a tobacco shed on a farm outside of Port Royal, Virginia. Herold surrendered, but Booth rejected the notion. The shed was set afire to drive Booth out, but before it had succeeded there was a shot, and Booth fell. It is not clear whether Booth shot himself, or was shot by an over-zealous Union soldier. Soldiers rescued Booth from the burning barn, and one of them took down his dying words: "Tell my mother—I died—for my country. I thought I did for the best. Useless! Useless!"

Eight other people were believed to be involved in the conspiracy. One of them—John Surratt—eluded capture. The other seven, including John's mother Mary Surratt, were tried before a military tribunal. Four, including Mrs. Surratt, were sentenced to be hanged, while the others received jail sentences. Up until the last minute, it was expected that Mary Surratt's sentence would be commuted, since her only offense was owning the rooming house where the plotters had assembled. Several of the admitted plotters even swore that Mary Surratt had known nothing of the plot, but it did not save her. The public was in the mood for a hanging, and she was hanged with the other three on July 7, 1865.

In 1867, John Surratt was captured in Italy, where he had joined the Swiss Guard. He was brought back to stand trial, but the people's blood-furor had died, and he was released when the jury couldn't agree on a verdict. In 1869, the imprisoned group, including Dr. Mudd, who had been guilty only of setting Booth's leg, were pardoned by President Andrew Johnson.

BORDEN, Lizzie Andrew (1860–1927)

THE PROPER VICTORIAN GIRL WHO WAS FOUND INNOCENT OF CHOPPING HER PARENTS TO DEATH WITH AN AXE—BUT WHO ELSE COULD HAVE?

Lizzie Borden took an axe
And gave her mother forty whacks.
When she saw what she had done,
She gave her father forty-one.
—*Anonymous*

One of the most famous women in American crime, and the subject of what is certainly the most famous stanza in American crime verse, Lizzie Borden was indicted and tried for the murder of her father and stepmother in Fall River, Massachusetts, in 1892. She was acquitted. The murder has never officially been solved.

Over the past century, the apparent parricide has been the subject of innumerable magazine articles and books, as well as a couple of plays, an opera, a ballet, several movies and television shows and a musical comedy sketch that included the memorable song, "You Can't Chop Your Poppa Up in Massachusetts."

Andrew Jackson Borden was one of the leading citizens of Fall River, a mill town and seaport that had been important in the Commonwealth of Massachusetts since the Revolution. The Borden clan had been among the most important, influential citizens of Fall River for longer than that. During the past 20 years, with the success of the cotton mills, the population of the town had more than doubled, growing from just under 50,000 to just over 100,000. The town's leading citizens, Andrew Borden among them, had prospered.

Andrew lived with his second wife, née Abby Durfee Gray, and the two surviving daughters of his first marriage, Emma and Lizzie, in a two-and-a-half-story frame house at 92 Second Street. The house was ill-planned and ill-favored, and the neighborhood was shabby genteel. Both daughters thought their home below their station in life and had urged their father to move to a nicer house in a better neighborhood. Andrew, being a frugal man unconcerned with appearances, refused to consider it.

On Thursday, August 4, 1892, the date of the "Fall River Tragedy," Andrew Borden was 70 years old; his wife was 64; Emma was 41 and Lizzie was 32. As nearly as can be reconstructed, the events of the tragedy unfolded like this:

Emma was not home that day, having left a few days before to visit friends in Fairhaven, a nearby seaside town. But the girls' Uncle John had arrived the day before, Wednesday, for an unannounced visit. John Vinnicum Morse, the 60-year-old brother of Andrew Borden's first wife, was a regular guest at the Borden house, coming from his home in Dartmouth, Massachusetts, several times a year to visit relatives, conduct bits of business and gossip with the Bordens.

The first person awake in the Borden household on that Thursday morning, as on most mornings, was Bridget Sullivan, the maid, a respectable Irish girl, whom Emma and Lizzie persisted in calling "Maggie," after a previous servant, although the older Bordens seemed able to remember her name. She came down from her attic room at about six o'clock to build the fire in the kitchen stove and start preparing breakfast. At about seven, the older Bordens and Mr. Morse came down and chatted around the breakfast table. Lizzie slept late and did not join them.

The breakfast has attracted most students of the Borden murders. Uncle John remembered that on this hot August morning he sat down to mutton, bread, "sugar cakes," bananas and coffee. Bridget denied the bananas. Her recollection was mutton broth, mutton, johnny cakes, coffee and cookies. It is the mutton and mutton broth that seems to have fascinated the observers. Edmund Pearson, a noted student of murder, says in his commentary on the Borden Case (in *Studies in Murder*, Macmillan, 1924) that "for a hot morning in mid-summer it was a breakfast well adopted to set the stage for a tragedy."

At about a quarter to eight, Mr. Morse left the house to take a trolley car to visit a niece and nephew. Mr. Borden locked the screen door behind him. It was the custom in the Borden house to keep most of the doors locked. Even the doors between certain of the rooms upstairs were usually locked. Lizzie came down a short while later, but she wasn't hungry. She had coffee and a cookie or two. There was perhaps a mild touch of some stomach disorder going around, as Bridget felt the need to go out in the backyard and throw up sometime after breakfast. Of course, it could have been the mutton soup. Two days before, the elder Bordens had been quite ill during the night, both of them having fits of vomiting. Presumably it was not food poisoning, since nobody else in the house was similarly affected. It might have been the onset of the stomach illness, or something more sinister.

Andrew Borden left to go downtown at a quarter past nine, and Abby Borden went upstairs to make the bed in the guest bedroom, where Uncle John was staying. She asked Bridget to wash the windows. At about nine-thirty she came downstairs briefly, and then went back up, remarking that she had to put pillowcases on the pillows in the guest bedroom.

Bridget went about her chores, collecting the necessary window-washing paraphernalia from about the house and pails of water from the barn, pausing to talk to the hired girl next door over the fence. She had finished the outside at about ten-thirty and began on the inside. Fifteen minutes later Mr. Borden returned home. Bridget let him in, and Lizzie came downstairs. "Mrs. Borden has gone out—she had a note from somebody who was sick," she told her father. She always called her stepmother "Mrs. Borden" these days; the relations between Abby and the two girls, especially Lizzie, were rather strained.

Mr. Borden took the key to his bedroom off a shelf and went up the back stairs. The access to his bedroom was by the back stairs; there was no hallway, and the front stairs gave access to only Lizzie's room and the guest bedroom (Emma's bedroom was reached through Lizzie's room). There were connecting doors between Lizzie's room and her parents' bedroom, but they were normally kept locked.

He only stayed upstairs for a few moments, before coming back down and settling in the sitting room. Lizzie began to heat up an iron to press some handkerchiefs. "Are you going out this afternoon, Maggie?" she asked Bridget according to the maid's testimony at the trial. "There is a cheap sale of dress goods at Sargent's this afternoon, at eight cents a yard."

But Bridget, overcome by her work in the heat of the day, and her recent illness, resisted this tempting suggestion and went up the back stairs to her room in the attic to take a nap. This was shortly before eleven o'clock.

At about a quarter past eleven Lizzie yelled upstairs to her from the foot of the stairs: "Maggie, come down!"

Bridget got up. "What is the matter?" she called.

"Come down quick! Father is dead. Somebody came in and killed him!"

Bridget rushed downstairs. Lizzie stopped her from going into the sitting room and sent her running for the doctor.

Dr. Bowen, a family friend, lived across the street. Bridget ran across and gave Mrs. Bowen the message. The doctor was out, so Bridget ran back home. "Where were you when this thing happened?" she asked Lizzie.

"I was out in the yard, and I heard a groan, and came in and the screen door was wide open."

By now the neighbors were starting to assemble, and somebody called for the police. Mrs. Churchill, a next-door neighbor, came over and held Lizzie's arm. "Oh Lizzie!" she said. "Where is your father?"

"In the sitting room."

"Where were you when it happened?"

"I went to the barn to get a piece of iron."

"Where is your mother?"

"I don't know. She had a note to go see someone who is sick, but I don't know but that she is killed too, for I thought I heard her come in. . . . Father must have an enemy, for we have all been sick, and we think the milk has been poisoned."

Dr. Bowen had returned by this time, and he hurried to the house and entered the sitting room. Andrew Borden was lying on the sofa. He had been attacked with a sharp object, presumably an axe, and so much damage had been done to his head and face that Dr. Bowen, his medical advisor and friend, could not at first positively identify him. "Physician that I am," Bowen testified, "and accustomed to all kinds of horrible sights, it sickened me to look upon the dead man's face." As there were no signs of a struggle, Dr. Bowen concluded that Borden had been killed in his sleep, probably by the first of the many blows that had struck him.

It was perhaps ten or fifteen minutes before anyone thought of going upstairs to see if Abby Borden had come home. Bridget was afraid to go alone, so Mrs. Churchill went up with her. They went up the front stairs. Mrs. Churchill was the first to see the body. "As I went upstairs," she said later, "I turned my head to the left, and as I got up so that my eyes were on the level with the front hall, I could see across the front hall and across the floor of the spare room. At the far side on the north side of the room I saw something that looked like the form of a person."

Bridget went in the guest room for an instant to take a look, and then they both ran back downstairs. There was something about Mrs. Churchill's appearance that told the story. "Is there another?" a neighbor asked.

"Yes," Mrs. Churchill said. "She is up there."

Abby Borden was lying on the floor on the far side of the bed in the guest room, in a pool of blood.

By one of the little ironies that Fate is so fond of sprinkling in life's path, on the day that put Fall River on the map of American Crime with an incredible double murder, the Fall River Police department was off to Rocky Point on its yearly picnic. The only policeman sent to answer the initial call was Officer Allen, the committing officer at the police station. He immediately ran back to the station house to inform the City Marshal of the events, leaving nobody in charge. In his absence, neighbors overran the house, comforting Lizzie, peering at the horrible sights and trampling on and destroying any clues that might have been present. There is no way to know what memento some curious onlooker might have walked off with during the next confused few hours.

Uncle John Morse came home about an hour after the murders were discovered. He walked up the street without noting the small group of neighbors gathered by the front of the house, turned into the yard and picked a couple of pears from the tree at the rear of the house. He entered at the side door, munching the pears, still unaware that anything unusual had occurred. When he asked the neighbors in the hall what they were doing there, they told him.

A county medical examiner named Dr. Dolan passed the house by chance at a quarter to twelve. He looked in and was pressed into service by Dr. Bowen. He examined the bodies and the condition and contents of their clothing. Andrew Borden had his wallet and watch and $81.56 in cash. Hearing that the family had been sick two days before, and that Lizzie suspected the milk, he took samples of it. Later that afternoon he had the bodies photographed and then removed the stomachs and sent them, along with the milk, to Harvard Medical School for analysis.

The police were reluctant to suspect Lizzie of the double murder. Indeed, it went against the perceived social understanding of the later Victorian era to even consider the possibility that a proper lady of the upper middle class could commit such a heinous crime, and to further consider that she could have done it to her own parents was impossible. But as other solutions were advanced, they had to be discarded as even more impossible. At first Uncle John was a suspect, but his alibi checked out in every detail, and that idea had to be dropped. Edwin Porter, a journalist for *The Fall River Globe*, considered the possibility of an outside killer in his book *The Fall River Tragedy*, a compilation of his newspaper stories issued a year after the crime:

> To those who stop to contemplate the circumstances surrounding the double murder, it was marvelous to reflect how fortune had favored the assassin. Not once in a million times would fate have paved such a way for him. He had to deal with a family of six persons in an unpretentious two-and-a-half story house, the rooms of which were all connected and in which it would have been a difficult matter to stifle sound. He must catch Mr. Borden alone and either asleep, or off his guard, and kill him with one fell blow. The faintest outcry would have sounded an alarm. He must also encounter Mrs. Borden alone and fell her, a heavy woman, noiselessly. To do this he must either make his way from the sitting room on the ground floor to the spare bedroom above the parlor and avoid five persons in the passage, or he must conceal himself in one of the rooms upstairs and make the descent under the same conditions. The murdered woman must not lisp a syllable at the first attack, and her fall must not attract attention. He must then conceal the dripping implement of death and depart in broad daylight by a much frequented street. . . . In making his escape there must be no blood stains upon his clothing; for such tell-tale marks might have betrayed him. . . .
>
> It was a wonderful chain of circumstances which conspired to clear the way for the murderer; so wonderful that its links baffled men's understanding.

It was even more wonderful than Porter realized at the time. Abby Borden was killed at least an hour, and possibly as much as two hours, before her husband. The killer, if it was anyone but Lizzie or Bridget, must have concealed himself in the house for that length of time waiting patiently for Andrew Borden's return, risking one of the two women residents glancing into the guest room and seeing Abby's body at any moment.

On the day after the crime, the Borden sisters put the following advertisement in the newspapers:

> *FIVE THOUSAND DOLLARS REWARD*
>
> The above reward will be paid to any one who may secure the arrest and conviction of the person or persons, who occasioned the death of Andrew J. Borden and his wife.
>
> Signed,
>
> Emma L. Borden and Lizzie A. Borden

There were a profusion of clues in the next couple of days, all of which went nowhere. A boy reported seeing a man jump over the back fence of the Borden property. Two policemen found a man matching the boy's description. His name was Bearsley S. Cooper, and he was chief of a nomadic horse-dealers' camp. But, unfortunately, he had an unbreakable alibi for the time in question. A bloody hatchet was found on the Sylvia farm in South Somerset, and the police raced out to make an arrest. But it proved to be chicken blood, and they went back empty-handed. As Pearson put it in *Studies in Murder*: "The usual crop of 'strange,'

'Wild' and 'crazy' men, of tramps and vagrants, of 'foreigners,' and other guilty-looking persons was more prolific than ever. There was a suspected Portuguese, who was called a Portuguese because he was a Swede; and there were miscreants who turned up in lonely places, days and weeks after the murders, still brandishing axes or hatchets dripping with gore."

For a while the police concentrated on Bridget. But her good character and her complete lack of motive, combined with Lizzie's account of her movements, which put Bridget in the wrong place to have committed the crimes, caused them to lose interest in her as a suspect.

There was a six-day hearing, at which the evidence was examined, and the inevitable conclusion was reached. An indictment was issued against Lizzie Borden for the murder of her father. For some reason, Mrs. Borden was not mentioned in the indictment. Perhaps they felt that the murder of one parent was quite enough. Lizzie was arraigned and pled not guilty.

The evidence, all circumstantial, was weighty. First of all the history: Lizzie and her father and stepmother had been living what one observer called "an armed truce" for some time. The condition had been exacerbated when Andrew Borden gave his wife some bank stock in 1887. The daughters protested, feeling that they should get a gift of equal value. The witnesses, relatives and friends, indicated politely that it was Lizzie who did most of the protesting. Emma was a quiet lady who disliked conflict. It was then that Lizzie ceased calling her stepmother "mother," and began calling her "Mrs. Borden."

To keep peace in his family, Andrew deeded his daughters a rental property: "the homestead on Ferry Street, an estate of 120 rods of land, with a house and a barn, all valued at $3,000." The girls didn't think that was enough, so he added 10 shares of stock for each of them. It was in the Crystal Spring Bleachery Company, and Andrew had paid $100 a share for them. They sold the stock soon after for less than $40 a share. Andrew gave his daughters other shares of stock and gifts of money over the years, but they remained unsatisfied, and the scrabbling continued.

The conflict was not an unusual one within families; Andrew was tight-fisted and disliked parting with money for things he considered unimportant or frivolous. Lizzie and Emma, but especially Lizzie, felt the need to live up to the social position of their friends and associates. This is the sort of dispute that, although serious to those concerned, rarely results in murder, especially considering that the social position that Lizzie occupied included Sunday school teacher and secretary of the Christian Endeavor Society.

Lizzie's actions and statements in the days immediately preceding the crime had also attracted the attention of the investigators. She had told her friend Alice Russell that "I feel as if something were hanging over me that I cannot throw off" and added that her father had enemies, and she was afraid something was going to happen to the family. She was not clear as to what or who the enemies were. She also had attempted to purchase some prussic acid from a local drugstore for the purpose of "killing moths in a sealskin coat." The druggist had refused to sell it to her.

The story of a burglary of the Borden household, which took place a year before the murders, was used by both Lizzie's supporters and her detractors to support their cases. It happened in June 1891. In response to Andrew Borden's complaint that his residence had been burglarized, a police captain inspected the premises. He found that Mr. Borden's desk in a small room on the second floor had been broken into. Over a hundred dollars was taken, along with Andrew Borden's watch and chain, some assorted small items and a stack of street-car tickets. The puzzle was how a stranger could have gotten in and out of the house unseen, and it was never satisfactorily answered, although Lizzie offered the fact that the cellar door was open. Neighbors on both sides of the street were questioned, and none of them had noticed a stranger at the time. According to the police captain, Andrew Borden several times said to him: "I am afraid the police will not be able to find the real thief." Exactly what he meant by that statement will never be known.

On October 10, while Lizzie was awaiting trial, a long article appeared in the *Boston Globe* purporting to give in detail the Commonwealth's case against Miss Borden. A detective named Edwin D. McHenry had supplied Henry G. Tricky, a reporter for the *Globe*, with the information. One witness, the article stated, would testify to seeing Lizzie in her stepmother's room while passing in the street below; another, also in the street, had heard a scream and seen a woman wearing some sort of rubber hood inside the Borden house. And several incriminating conversations between Lizzie and her father and between Lizzie and her Uncle John Morse were to be testified to by Bridget and others. It was quite a sensation.

The next day, the *Globe* printed a partial retraction. The day after, the *Globe* printed a full retraction, admitting that it had been "grievously misled" and that the whole story was a hoax. The aptly named Tricky was indicted by a grand jury for his part in the affair and fled to Canada, where he was killed in a railroad accident in November.

The trial of Lizzie Andrew Borden for the murder of her father, Andrew Borden, and her stepmother, Abby Durfee Borden (who had been added to the indictment by the grand jury), began in the New Bedford Court House, on June 5, 1893. News of the trial filled the front pages of every major newspaper in the country, and between 30 and 40 reporters from the Boston and New York papers and the wire services were in the courtroom every day. They covered the trial, the town of New Bedford, the costume of the defendant ("a new dress of black mohair, cut in the latest style, with leg-of-mutton sleeves") and each other.

The commonwealth, represented by District Attorneys Hosea M. Knowlton, who had been with the case since the beginning, and William H. Moody, who had been appointed to aid him in his disagreeable task, slowly and painstakingly built its case. It was not an easy thing to bring a capital charge against a sober, middle class, church-going lady, known for her charity work, but they did their best.

To convict someone of a crime in the absence of a believable confession or credible eyewitnesses, it is necessary to show some combination of motive or intent, means, capacity and opportunity. Perhaps not all five in every case, but the prosecutor should come as close to this ideal as possible. It is also helpful to show guilty knowledge. The commonwealth had to show that Lizzie had a reason or desire to kill her parents, that she was capable of obtaining and wielding the axe and that she was in the right place at the right time. They also attempted to show guilty knowledge by means of her words and actions both before and after the crime.

Motive was established with a gaggle of witnesses who testified to Lizzie's dislike of her stepmother and animosity toward her father. Means and opportunity were shown by the defendant's presence in the house during both murders—in the barn during her father's death, if she was to be believed, getting lead for sinkers. But the barn loft was the hottest place on the property on that hot day, and she had shown no interest in fishing for many years prior to this. Her statements as to her exact location were also contradictory and evolved over the three days after the murders. Indisputably she was there, and she could have committed the murders. And, the prosecutors maintained, it was hard to see how anyone else could have.

The specific means—the murder weapon—was never positively located. There was an axe head without a handle in the cellar that could have been the weapon, if it had a handle. No trace of blood was found on it, but it could have been wiped clean, presumably at the same time as the handle was removed.

Lizzie's friend Alice Russell testified—reluctantly, it would seem, since she had not offered this testimony at the police investigation or the inquest—that she had seen Lizzie standing with Emma, burning a dress in the stove three days after the crime. To Emma's question as to what she was doing, Lizzie had replied, "I am going to burn this old thing up, it is covered with paint." Neither Emma nor Miss Russell had attempted to stop her at the time, although Alice had commented, according to her testimony, "I wouldn't let anybody see me do that, Lizzie."

This offered a possible solution to one of the questions that had been plaguing the prosecution: if Lizzie had committed the murders, why was there no trace of blood on her or her clothing? It would be unlikely to hit someone repeatedly in the head with an axe and not get heavily splattered with blood; it would be highly improbable to do it twice; and it would be impossible to plan on doing it. Several theories were advanced to explain Lizzie's lack of blood: the smock worn over other garments theory, and the naked Lizzie theory. But the smock would have been badly bloodstained itself, and she would have had to hide it somewhere. And the mores of the Victorian age were such that, although it is conceivable that Lizzie took an axe to her father, it is inconceivable that she should appear before him naked, even to kill him.

But the burned dress offered an explanation: Lizzie simply changed her dress. Against this was the fact that Alice Russell testified that she had seen no blood on the dress being burned. Lizzie claimed that the dress was paint stained, and perhaps this was so. It was customary in the Borden household to burn worn, stained and useless clothing, and if it were blood instead of paint, it would have been odd of Lizzie to keep the garment for three days after the murders. Also, the murders were at least an hour apart. Had she worn the blood-spattered dress between the two killings? Surely Bridget would have noticed. Had she changed into it twice? This shows a level of rationality not consistent with the frenzied attack on the two elder Bordens.

On the seventh day of the trial, Moody attempted to offer Lizzie's own testimony at the inquest as evidence. Lizzie's defense team, headed by George D. Robinson, a man known for his intelligence and probity and who had once been governor of Massachusetts, objected strenuously, and the jury was withdrawn so the lawyers could fight it out in their absence. Moody averred that, while a confession might not be admissible, Miss Borden's statements were all denials, and that it was in the nature and inconsistency of those denials that evidence of guilt was to be found. Governor Robinson claimed that, as Lizzie had been the prime suspect at the time, and that a warrant for her arrest had been drawn up but not executed, she should have been advised of her rights. Since she had not been and had not had the advice of counsel, any statements she made at the time could not be used against her. He ended his oration: "If that is freedom, God save the Commonwealth of Massachusetts!"

Moody pointed out that it was not common to have counsel at a hearing, but that Lizzie had counsel before the hearing, who was free to have told her whatever he thought she should know. The three-judge panel went off to confer. When they returned, they excluded the testimony and called back the jury. The defense won that round, as it had won earlier when it had excluded the testimony of the druggist identifying Lizzie as the woman who had tried to buy prussic acid.

Several medical witnesses, including Dr. Dolan, who had been at the scene, were called by the prosecution. A macabre note was added when one of them produced the skull of Andrew Borden to demonstrate how the blows were struck. Edmund Pearson didn't understand the fuss:

> The Mawkish and sentimental newspapers—and this included three-quarters of them at this stage—made great play with this fact, and dwelt upon how it affected the poor prisoner. The newspapers were few which did not act as if the deaths of Mr. and Mrs. Borden ought to have been forgotten long ago; that the officers of the law were little better than brutes to have prosecuted anybody; and

> that the sole concern of mankind was to rescue, from her grievous position, the "unfortunate girl," and send her home amid a shower of roses.

Pearson had an opinion. And he wrote this in 1924, when Lizzie was still alive, and he could be sued for libel. A more moderate view might be that, whether Lizzie were guilty or innocent, there was no need to bring her father's skull into the courtroom. The facts attesting to the manner of his death were not in dispute, only who had wielded the axe.

The defense took advantage of the prosecution's medical witnesses to establish one of the strongest points in Lizzie's favor: that, as mentioned above, whoever committed the murder would have to have been splattered with blood.

When the prosecution rested, the defense put on witnesses offering a variety of corroboration and alternate possibilities. An ice cream peddler had seen a woman, presumably Lizzie, coming out of the barn, thus bolstering her story that she had been there. A pair of neighbors had heard a loud thump the night before. Two children claimed to have been playing in the barn loft that afternoon and found it cool and comfortable. A passerby had seen a "wild-eyed man." And Mr. Joseph Lemay had been walking in a deep wood some miles from the city 12 days after the murders, when he heard someone saying, "Poor Mrs. Borden! Poor Mrs. Borden! Poor Mrs. Borden!" He had looked over a conveniently placed wall, where he had spied a man sitting on the ground. The man, who had blood spots on his shirt, picked up a hatchet and shook it at him, and then leaped over the wall and disappeared into the wood.

The defense did not feel the need to demolish the prosecution's case. The most damaging bits of evidence had been excluded, and popular sentiment was clearly on the side of the defendant. They just needed to introduce enough reasonable doubt to give the jury a plausible excuse for voting to acquit. Lizzie chose not to testify in her own defense.

The trial lasted 13 days, and the jury was out for little more than an hour. They found Lizzie not guilty. Public opinion by that time was unanimously of the sentiment that Lizzie had been persecuted by the police and the courts quite enough.

Emma and Lizzie, who henceforth called herself "Lizbeth," moved into a large house about a mile and a half from their old home. Some years later, Emma separated from her sister and moved to Fairhaven, and the two ceased talking to each other. Rumors about sensational revelations regarding the murders persisted for years, but no such revelations were ever forthcoming. Lizbeth died in June 1927, one week before her sister. They were both buried in the family plot in Fall River, next to their father, mother and stepmother. In Lizzie's will, she left $500 for the perpetual care of her father's grave.

BOSTON POLICE STRIKE

THE POLICE WENT ON STRIKE, THE PEOPLE RIOTED, AND THE CITY OFFICIALS PROCRASTINATED

Out of the 3,253 strikes in the United States in 1919, the one that struck fear into the hearts of Americans was the police strike in Boston that September. Strikes were a comparatively new phenomenon on the American scene, the results of the first attempts of labor to organize trade unions. It was a time when workers were thought of as a commodity by the bosses and treated with little regard for their needs or desires. Still, the press reported that strikes were the result of alien agitators and creeping Bolshevism and that the workers should be grateful for what they had.

When the Boston police tried to unionize and affiliate with the American Federation of Labor, Mayor Andrew J. Peters and a citizens' committee headed by James J. Storrow negotiated with them and reached a settlement. But the Commissioner of Police, who for some reason was appointed by the governor, suspended the 19 "ringleaders" and refused to honor the negotiations. Peters and Storrow asked Governor Calvin Coolidge to intercede, but "Silent Cal" did not take immediate action.

The officers, who earned $1,100 a year, out of which they were expected to buy their own uniforms and equipment, voted to strike. On September 9, at 5:45 P.M. all but 400 of the city's 1,544 police officers turned in their badges and walked off the job.

For the first few hours things remained orderly, but as the night wore on, the lawless element began to emerge. "Boston never had such a night," said the *Boston Globe*. "Utterly without police, in the hands of wanton hoodlums, a proud city fell into pointless, meaningless disorder. Store fronts were smashed and goods of all sorts were stolen by the roughs, absolutely at will."

This scene, so alien in 1919, has been repeated in many American cities as the century progressed. As the *Globe* described it:

> Shortly after midnight, a crowd of about 300 young men, with several girls in their midst, started up Washington Street from Milk Street. They smashed window after window, robbing the place each time. A single policeman remonstrated with them, but they laughed at him. Opposite Macullar Parker Company's store two sailors held up a man in real movie fashion, and went through his pockets with 500 persons looking on.
>
> The downtown crowd, although good-natured enough, was soon engaged in deliberate robbery. Men walked along the street with shirts or neckties, shoes, jewelry and haberdashery, openly trading shirts for shoes or jewelry for either.

The president of Harvard University offered to send 1,000 students into the city to maintain order. The proposition intrigued many Bostonians who stayed at their windows to watch for the influx of Harvard students. The sporting element made book on how long the Harvard boys would last. But the offer was either not taken seriously or it got lost in the excitement, and the students never showed up.

Then Governor Coolidge decided to act and uttered the comment that wafted him into the vice presidency, and thence into the White House. "The wrong of leaving the city unguarded furnished the opportunity, the criminal element furnished the action," he said, "There is no right to strike against the public safety by anybody, anywhere, at any time." The words rang out with a noble air. He refrained from mentioning, and no one pointed out to him, that had he acted when Mayor Peters asked him to there would have been neither strike nor riot.

Coolidge called out the National Guard and 6,000 troops were in the city by the night of the tenth. Untrained for police duties, unprepared, and badly led, they came to the job as to a war. They took up skirmish formation and advanced toward a mob in South Boston. When the mob failed to disburse, they fired no warning shots but put a volley directly into the people massed before them. The crowd melted away, leaving a dozen men behind on the pavement. Two were dead. Nine were wounded, four seriously. Infantrymen with fixed bayonets marched down the downtown streets, and cavalrymen rode their horses into the crowds. Despite, or perhaps because of, this action, the rioting was general, much worse than the night before, and large sections of the city were looted.

Somehow all of this was understood to be the fault of the absent police, not of the city officials that refused to pay them a decent wage, nor the commissioner who refused to negotiate, nor the governor who was totally unprepared for the consequences of his own nonactions. The country's newspapers came out heavily against the actions of the police. The questions of a living wage or tolerable working conditions were not addressed. The event was couched in terms of "bolshevism," "anarchy," and "the radical element." The Philadelphia *Evening Public Ledger* gave its moderate view:

> Bolshevism in the United States is no longer a specter. Boston in its chaos revealed its sinister substance. In their reckless defiance of the fundamentals of morality, in their bullying affront to the structure of civilization, wherein do the police of the New England metropolis differ from the mad minority which overthrew Kerensky and ruined Russia? Only an arrant casuist, a fatuous hairsplitter, can proclaim a shade of contrast. The nation has chosen. If ever it was vague in its conception of the Bolshevist horror, its vision is clean-cut now. So is the issue. Defiled Boston has seen to that.

The striking policemen were replaced. And, strangely, their replacements were given the increased pay—$1,400 a year to start—and better working conditions than the strikers had originally asked for.

The country was given a foretaste of big-city rioting that would become all too common over the course of the century. "Uncle Dudley" of the *Boston Globe* raised an issue that has not yet been settled:

> That such a thing should happen at all raises all sorts of questions—questions which, in the normal course of events, we would never think of asking at all. Where does this wanton spirit of destruction come from? Does society live on a crust as thin as this would seem to indicate? Is the mere disappearance of a thousand-odd bluecoats from our streets the signal for the crust to cave in under us? Does the peace of our streets depend on a policeman's club, or the instincts of decency in average humanity? Is it true, then, that modern society rests on a basis of organized force? If so, by whom and for whom is that force organized? If it is relaxed ever so little (as for a few hours in the city of Boston), must we expect looting as the consequence? If this is the way the children behave the instant teacher steps out of the room, is there something wrong with our principles of discipline?

BOSTON STRANGLER

See: ALBERT DESALVO

BROWN, John (1800–1859)

Born in Torrington, Connecticut, John Brown was a radical abolitionist at a time when the question of whether Kansas and other new states entering the Union would be slaveholding or free was answered in blood. His belief in the evil of slavery led him and his followers to increasingly violent acts, when it seemed that nothing less would serve. Brown led a raid on a proslavery settlement at Pottawatamie Creek, Kansas, in 1856, killing five of the settlers. On October 16, 1859, he and his followers captured the federal arsenal at Harpers Ferry, Virginia, planning to use the captured arms to start a slave revolt in the South.

A detachment of U.S. Marines, led by Colonel Robert E. Lee, captured Brown, and he was tried for murder and treason against the state of Virginia. Convicted, he was hanged on December 2, 1859. In death, he became a martyr to the abolitionist cause, and the song "John Brown's Body," sung by Union troops during the Civil War, made him a legend. Julia Ward Howe later set the "Battle Hymn of the Republic" to the tune of "John Brown's Body."

BROWN v. MISSISSIPPI

A 1936 U.S. SUPREME COURT decision emphasizing the constitutional right against self-incrimination enumerated in the FIFTH AMENDMENT, *Brown v. Mississippi* was the first step on a road that led to the MIRANDA RULE 30 years later.

The case originated when three black men were arrested for murder. One of them was hanged twice to force him to confess, and when that did not work, he was tied to a tree and whipped. On his way to jail, the deputy sheriff stopped the car several times to further whip the suspect, telling him that the whipping would continue until he confessed. The deputy dictated the statement the suspect was to confess to, and the suspect was whipped until he signed it.

The next day, the other two suspects were similarly treated. In the words of the Supreme Court: "They were likewise made by the same deputy definitely to understand that the whipping would be continued unless and until they confessed, and not only confessed, but confessed in every matter of detail as demanded by those present; and in this manner the defendants confessed the crime, and as the whippings progressed and were repeated, they changed or adjusted their confession in all particulars of detail so as to conform to the demands of their torturers."

At the trial, there was no other evidence against the defendants except their confessions. The whippings were freely admitted to by the deputy, and the marks of the hanging were still visible on the neck of the first defendant. They were found guilty and sentenced to death. The Supreme Court of Mississippi upheld the convictions.

The U.S. Supreme Court, in reversing the decision, said:

> Because a State may dispense with a jury trial, it does not follow that it may substitute trial by ordeal. The rack and torture chamber may not be substituted for the witness stand.
>
> . . . It would be difficult to conceive of methods more revolting to the sense of justice than those taken to procure the confessions of these petitioners, and the use of the confessions thus obtained as the basis for conviction and sentence was a clear denial of due process.

BUCHALTER, Louis "Lepke" (1897–1944)

THE GANGLORD WHO HEADED BROOKLYN'S INFAMOUS "MURDER, INCORPORATED"

Louis "Lepke" Buchalter had the distinction of being called by J. EDGAR HOOVER, "the most dangerous criminal in the United States." He grew up on the Lower East Side of New York, and quit school in the eighth grade to work as a three-dollar-a-week delivery boy. When his father died, the family moved in stages to Colorado, except for Lepke, who stayed in New York.

Louis "Lepke" Buchalter (on the right) being tried in a New York courtroom for the murder of candy store owner Joseph Rosen. (International News Photo.)

Lepke soon found that robbing pushcarts and picking pockets paid a better wage than delivering groceries, and by the time he was 20, he was a small-time hoodlum. The next year, he was sent to Cheshire Reformatory for a short stay. In 1920, he was convicted of larceny and spent two years in prison.

After release, he attempted to take over the labor union rackets in the New York area. While other mobsters fought over PROHIBITION's lucrative liquor concessions, Lepke and his associate Jake "Gurrah" Shapiro consolidated their hold on

New York City's garment workers, furriers, and bakers. For a fee, their goons would intimidate employers for union kickbacks, while keeping the workers in line for the bosses. A small gang in Brownsville, Brooklyn, that Lepke used for enforcement, soon took over that duty for the Syndicate nationwide and became infamously known as MURDER, INCORPORATED.

In his book *Treasury Agent* (1958), Andrew Tully describes Lepke at the height of his power:

> Lepke was probably the greatest criminal in the nation's history, a tycoon who bossed a veritable General Motors of crime. For years he was undisputed ruler of the fur, garment and baking industries in the New York City area, a role which enabled him to extort from these businesses at least $50,000,000. He was the director of at least 250 criminal enterprises with 300 so-called "foremen," and a herd of accountants, bookkeepers, professional killers and industrial wrecking crews. As chairman of the board of Murder, Inc., he ordered the deaths of between sixty and eighty persons [we know now that, counting contract killings for other crime bosses, the number was closer to 1,000]. He was a silent partner in a dope-smuggling ring which between October 1935 and February 1937 smuggled into the United States more than $10,000,000 worth of narcotics.

Lepke's scheme for smuggling drugs into the country was elegantly simple. He arranged to bribe U.S. Customs inspectors in New York to pass on to the gang a supply of Customs stamps. The stamps were issued in eight different colors and were used in random rotation, which was kept secret until the morning of the day they were to be used. For a flat fee of $1,000, Lepke's men bought the appropriate stamps the morning their ship came in and fastened them to the luggage lined up on the dock. The Customs men never opened trunks that had already been stamped.

In the fall of 1937, Lepke's empire began to fall apart. He was under separate indictments for extortion, labor racketeering, and narcotics violations. He went into hiding, moving around constantly, while trying to keep law enforcement at bay. New York Prosecutor THOMAS E. DEWEY, who had already put CHARLEY "LUCKY" LUCIANO behind bars, was determined to get Lepke. Lepke intended to use the instrument he had created, Murder, Incorporated, to save himself. Deciding to stay in hiding until the heat was off, Lepke gave a list of people who might testify against him to ALBERT ANASTASIA, paymaster to the gang. Contracts went out on at least a dozen people, most of them fellow gangsters, and all of them were killed in a very short time. But the heat did not disappear, it merely intensified.

Lepke realized that if this continued, he would become a dangerous liability to the Organization. And, as he had reason to know, someone who was dangerous to the Organization usually did not stay around very long. Lucky Luciano and MEYER LANSKY, on behalf of the National Commission, decided that Lepke had to either come in out of the cold or go out permanently. They passed word to Lepke through Moe "Dimples" Wolensky, a trusted underling, that a deal had been worked out with J. EDGAR HOOVER for Lepke's surrender. He was to be tried only on a federal narcotics charge and get no more than five years. The state charges would be dropped.

Through New York newspaper columnist Walter Winchell, Lepke arranged to surrender directly to Hoover. On August 24, 1939, Anastasia drove Lepke from his Brooklyn hideout to Fifth Avenue and 28th Street and pulled up behind a parked car with two men in it. Lepke got out and walked over to the car. Winchell opened the door. "Mr. Hoover, this is Lepke," he said.

Lepke then discovered that he had been lied to—there was no deal. The federal authorities gave him 14 years for the narcotics charge, and then Dewey went after him, and Lepke drew a sentence of 30 years to life for labor racketeering. Three years later, "Dimples," the man who helped arrange the deal, and who probably believed it himself, suffered the usual fate of the messenger: He was cut down by a shotgun blast on a New York street.

Lepke's situation continued to get worse. ABE "KID TWIST" RELES, one of the principals in Murder, Incorporated, began talking to the authorities. In 1936, Lepke had ordered the murder of Joe Rosen, who owned a candy store in Brooklyn. Rosen had threatened to talk to the district attorney about Lepke's extortion, and Lepke had responded in his usual way. It was a minor killing as such things went; Lepke might not even have remembered it. But Reles turned out to have an astounding memory for details. He described how six men including Mendy Weiss, Louis Capone and PITTSBURGH PHIL Strauss had put 10 bullets in Rosen, four of them after he was lying dead on the floor.

Pittsburgh Phil was already sentenced to death for another killing, but Lepke, Weiss, and Capone were executed for the Rosen murder on March 4, 1944.

BUCKET MEN

In New York City around the turn of the twentieth century, as in other big cities, gambling and prostitution were so prevalent and so well protected that almost every dance hall had a "gambling den" in the back room or upstairs, and there were certain avenues where the ladies of the evening would show their wares from the windows of their rooming houses. Once a week a policeman would come around to collect the pay-off money. The amounts were not large, between $100 and $200 a dance hall, but there were so many places to visit that, it was said, he carried a bucket.

BUNCO; BUNKO

A term for SHORT CONS, now more common with law enforcement authorities than with the practitioners.

BUNDY, Theodore Robert (1946–1989)

THE CLEAN-CUT YOUNG LAW STUDENT WHO KILLED AT LEAST 30 WOMEN IN FIVE STATES

Ted Bundy was the unwanted child of a brief illicit affair his mother, Louise Cowell, had with a passing sailor. He never knew his father, indeed his father was never spoken of. He grew up in Philadelphia with a mother who didn't want him and didn't care for him and a grandfather, Sam Cowell, who was subject to violent rages and kept the family in constant terror. This combination was psychologically unfortunate. At an early age he showed the sort of bizarre behavior that is a sign of

Theodore "Ted" Bundy, the handsome law student and serial killer. (Federal Bureau of Investigation.)

deep emotional disturbance. When he was about three and a half years old his mother's younger sister Julia, then a teenager, woke up in the middle of the night to find Ted standing by her bed and carefully arraying all the sharp kitchen knives in the house under the blankets next to her. According to Dr. Dorothy Lewis, who worked with Bundy in prison, as quoted by Jean F. Blashfield in *Why They Killed* (1990), this sort of behavior is seen "only in very seriously traumatized children who have either themselves been the victims of extraordinary abuse or who have witnessed extreme violence among family members."

Shortly after that incident Ted and his mother moved to Tacoma, Washington, where the neighbors wouldn't know them, and where some pretense could be made that Ted was not illegitimate. They changed their family name to Nelson, a name Louise picked at random, and then to Bundy when Louise married Johnnie Culpepper Bundy, an army cook. Ted refused to accept his olive-green-collar stepfather as a role model, instead fixating on his great-uncle Jack Cowell, a college professor who was well-educated, cultured, and fairly well-to-do. Bundy became fascinated by stories of murders and murderers, and read everything he could find on the subject.

When he entered his teens, Bundy became morose, withdrawn, and actively rebellious against his parents, especially his stepfather. This might have been partly because he had discovered that he was illegitimate, but he probably was headed in that direction anyway. It was then that he discovered sex, pornography, and masturbation. His junior high school friends remember him for his habit of surreptitious masturbation in the school bathrooms, and even in closets. His taste in pornography ran toward the sado-masochistic; especially showing extreme violence toward women. Combined with his already developed fascination with murder, it did not augur well.

Sometime in his teens Bundy developed a taste for voyeurism, wandering about at night and peering through bedroom windows. He also began stealing, and soon became quite proficient at it. He stole a complete set of skiing gear and became a competent skier, using forged lift tickets on the slopes.

In 1966 Bundy enrolled in the University of Puget Sound, in Tacoma, to which he commuted in his aged Volkswagen. A year later he transferred to the University of Washington in Seattle and moved into a coed dorm. A rather handsome young man, he had a brief relationship there with the sort of girl he had always dreamed about: a beautiful, sophisticated young lady from an upper-class family. When they broke up in the summer of 1968, Bundy was devastated. He dropped out of school, took on a variety of odd jobs, and traveled across the country and back in a series of stops punctuated by visiting relatives, signing up for college courses at Temple University, leaving in midterm, and visiting his ex-girl in San Francisco long enough for her to reject him again.

Bundy returned to Seattle, rented a room in a private home, and reenrolled in school. He majored in psychology, and became an honors student. By now he was living a complex double life; his time with a new girlfriend and at school, where he was sophisticated, charming, and a perfect gentleman, completely divorced from the nights when he prowled the streets peering into bedroom windows and stealing whatever attracted him. Most of the furnishings in his room were acquired by theft.

Bundy went to work for the Seattle Crisis Clinic on their crisis telephone hot line in the fall of 1971, after taking a 40-hour crisis-prevention course. In 1972 he graduated from college with a BA in Psychology and tried to enroll in law school. Although his professors wrote him impressive recommendations, his law aptitude test scores were not as impressive, and he was not accepted. Bundy took a variety of jobs over the next year, including working as a volunteer for the reelection campaign of Daniel J. Evans, the Republican governor. When Evans was reelected, he wrote Bundy a glowing letter of recommendation, and Bundy was subsequently accepted at the University of Utah law school.

Bundy's darker side now began to take a powerful hold on him. Peering through windows to catch women undressing was no longer satisfactory. He began to follow women as they walked home. He fantasized about hitting them with blunt objects. One night he actually attacked a woman as she was getting into her car, but he ran off when she screamed.

He decided to switch to the University of Puget Sound law school in Tacoma, but realized that he had made a mistake shortly after classes started. The rest of the students weren't up to Bundy's image of himself. He was a young Republican, clean cut, well scrubbed, handsome, destined for success. He reapplied to the University of Utah.

But even while his facade glowed with all the virtues of an Eagle scout, under the mask his soul was beginning to disintegrate. On January 4, 1974, he followed Susan Clarke, an 18-year-old college student, home and attacked her in her basement bedroom. He beat her with a metal rod taken from the frame of her own bed, and ended by shoving it up her vagina. She lay in a coma for several weeks, and awoke to remember nothing of the episode, but with permanent brain damage.

On January 31, 21-year-old Lynda Ann Healy, a ski reporter for a Seattle radio station, vanished from her basement bedroom and was never seen again. The sheets on her bed were bloody, and a blood-stained nightgown was found hanging in her closet.

Now the Bundy nightmare began in earnest. On March 12, Donna Gail Manson, a 19-year-old music student at the Evergreen State College at Olympia, disappeared while walking to a jazz concert. Five weeks later on April 17, and 120 miles from Seattle, freshman student Susan Rancourt vanished from the campus of Central Washington State College in Ellensburg. She had been on her way to see a German language film. On May 6, coed Roberta Parks disappeared from the campus of Oregon State University in Corvallis, over 200 miles from Seattle. On June 1, Brenda Ball, a student at the community college in Burien, left a local tavern with a strange man and was last seen talking to him in the parking lot. On the night of June 11, 18-year-old Georgeann Hawkins disappeared while crossing the 15 yards from a fraternity house to the sorority house she lived in. A young man with crutches and his leg in a cast was seen in the area.

It took the police a while to connect the disappearances; first because no bodies had yet been found, which made them missing persons rather than homicides, and second because of the geographical spread of the victims. Several police forces were involved, and it wasn't until July 3, that representatives from the various forces came together to pool information on the strange disappearances of an otherwise unrelated group of attractive young ladies with long brown or black hair, worn parted in the middle.

On July 14 Janice Ann Ott disappeared from Washington's Lake Sammamish State Park. A probation caseworker, she was visiting the park with friends while her husband was away. Later that same afternoon 19-year-old Denise Naslund left her boyfriend to go to the public bathroom and never returned. When the police questioned people who had been at the park that day, several of them remembered seeing Janice Ott talking to a man who had his arm in a sling. One of them remembered him introducing himself as "Ted." A couple of the women were able to fill in the story. They had themselves been approached by the friendly, likable "Ted," with his arm in a sling, and asked for help in getting his boat to the water. When they went to the parking lot, his Volkswagen had no boat attached. Ted's tale was that it was at a nearby house up the hill, and he asked them to go with him to help hitch it up. Luckily for them, they refused.

A short while later Bundy traveled up to Vancouver, Washington, and a young lady named Carol Valenzuela disappeared.

The police now knew what Ted looked like, and what kind of car he drove, but when Bundy's name came up in the investigation, he was rejected as a suspect out-of-hand. By this time the public had reported their suspicions, implicating thousands of their neighbors, and with Bundy's respectable background his name just didn't stand out. His public persona still successfully disguised his private vice.

On September 7, two months after they disappeared, the remains of Janice Ott and Denise Naslund were found by a hunter in a shallow grave in the woods a few miles from Lake Sammamish. There was part of a third corpse, but it had been reduced to a skeleton, and beyond the fact that it was female it could not be identified.

In September Bundy went to Salt Lake City, Utah, to start law school. On October 2, Salt Lake City high school student Nancy Wilcox disappeared from the street. On October 18, Melissa Smith disappeared from nearby Midvale.

Meanwhile, on October 12, a hunter in Clark County, south of Olympia, Washington, had stumbled across the skeletal remains of two more women. One was identified as Carol Valenzuela; the other was never identified.

On October 31, in Orem, Utah, Laura Aime, another high school student, disappeared while in costume walking back to her home from a Halloween party.

Carol DaRonch, 18, an attractive recent high school graduate, was looking for a birthday gift for her cousin in a Walden book shop in Murray, Utah, on November 8, when "Officer Roseland" of the police department approached her. He was wearing a sports jacket and green slacks, and an assertive but friendly manner. He asked her to come outside and check her car in the parking lot, as someone had been caught stealing things from the parked cars. Then he asked her to come with him to the central police station. It didn't make sense to her, but she had been brought up to obey authority. She did ask him for identification, and allowed herself to be satisfied by the gold badge he flashed. She did wonder a bit about the old, beat-up Volkswagen he was driving.

Luckily for Carol she was already a bit apprehensive when "Officer Roseland" suddenly tried to handcuff her. When she resisted, with the handcuffs already around one of her wrists, he picked up a crowbar and swung it at her head. She was just able to intercept the blow with her arm, and she jumped from the car and ran off, to be rescued by a passing motorist. While she was telling her story to the police, Bundy, his murderous need still unfulfilled, picked up 17-year-old Debra Kent from the parking lot at Viewmont High School in Salt Lake City.

The new year brought new atrocities. To recuperate from the strains of law school—his grades were only mediocre—Bundy went on a skiing vacation in Colorado during the winter break. On January 12, 1975, Caryn Campbell vanished from the Wildwood Inn at Snowmass, near Aspen, shortly after leaving her fiancé and his two children to return to her room. On February 17, her body was found; she had been savagely beaten and raped.

On March 1, a human skull was found on Taylor Mountain in the Cascades. After a search the remains of at least four girls were unearthed; women who had been reported missing in Washington and Oregon. The local press speculated that the area was the site of ritual killings by Satan worshiping cults.

On March 15, Julie Cunningham was on her way to a local bar in Vail, but she never arrived. On April 15, Melanie Cooley disappeared while on a bicycle ride in Nederland. Her body was discovered a week later; her pants pulled down and her skull crushed. In Golden, Colorado, on July 1, Shelly Robertson disappeared. Her body was found in a mine shaft on August 23.

On August 16, Bundy was arrested for erratic driving and attempting to flee from the police car that was trying to pull him over. The arresting officer searched Bundy's Volkswagen and found a pair of handcuffs, an ice pick, a crowbar, rope, wire, a ski mask, and a mask cut out of a pair of panty hose. At first the items were thought of as burglary tools, and Bundy was held for resisting arrest to give the police a chance to investigate and see what else he might be charged with.

Slowly the story unfolded. Those who spoke to the handsome, articulate Bundy found it hard to believe him guilty of any crime, but careful and painstaking police work began to tie him to the bizarre homicides that had plagued the area. Carol DaRonch picked Bundy's photograph out of a group as the man who had attacked and attempted to handcuff her. An analysis of gasoline credit card receipt records put Bundy at the scene of several of the abductions.

On February 23, 1976, Bundy was tried for the attempted kidnapping of Carol DaRonch while authorities in Washington, Oregon, and Utah attempted to make cases against him for some of the killings. He was found guilty after a four-day trial, and sentenced to one to fifteen years in the Utah state prison, which would have made him eligible for parole after eighteen months. By November the police thought they could make a strong enough case for conviction in the murder of Caryn Campbell, and he was charged. On June 7, while en route to the courthouse for a hearing, Bundy escaped custody. He was recaptured after six days, and moved to a more secure prison. On December 31, he escaped from the prison by crawling through a small hole he had cut in the ceiling. Bundy had spent the last five months losing weight so he could fit through the hole.

By January 8, 1978, Bundy was in Tallahassee, Florida. He took a room near the Florida State University campus under the name Chris M. Hagen and began prowling the streets at night, stealing credit cards and items to furnish his room. He used the credit cards to eat at some of Tallahassee's finest restaurants.

Late in the night of January 15, Bundy crept into the Chi Omega sorority house with a club and attacked four girls, killing two of them, Margaret Bowman and Lisa Levy. The bite marks he left in Lisa Levy's buttock, whom he had raped and sodomized while she was either unconscious or dead, would eventually help convict him of the murder. After leaving the sorority he continued on to a house three blocks away, where he clubbed dance student Cheryl Thomas in her bed. She would survive, but the beating had so impaired her hearing and her equilibrium that she could no longer expect to have a career as a dancer.

On February 9, Bundy intercepted 12-year-old Kimberly Leach as she was going to a class at her junior high school in Lake City, near Jacksonville. Her body was found two months later in Suwanee State Park.

Bundy was caught driving a stolen car on February 15 in Pensacola, Florida. He was not extradited, as Florida authorities had murders of their own to try him for. He was convicted for the murders of the two Chi Omega sorority girls and, in July 1979, sentenced to death. While awaiting execution he was further convicted for the murder of Kimberly Leach. It took the appeals process ten years to run out and, on January 24, 1989, Theodore Robert Bundy died in Florida's electric chair.

BURGER, Warren Earl (1907–)

Born in St. Paul, Minnesota, Warren Burger was a justice of the United States Court of Appeals from 1956 to 1969. He was appointed fifteenth Chief Justice of the United States Supreme Court by President Richard Nixon in 1969 to replace the retiring Earl Warren. Chosen because of his conservative views, Burger surprised critics with a series of liberal decisions, including favoring busing to end school segregation in *Brown v. Board of Education at Topeka, Kansas,* in 1971, and overturning state laws restricting abortion during the first two trimesters of pregnancy in the landmark *Roe v. Wade* decision of 1973. The unanimous decision of his court on July 24, 1974, to deny President Nixon's claim of executive privilege in the matter of the Watergate tapes, which were under subpoena by special prosecutor Leon Jaworski, led more or less directly to Nixon's resignation as president.

BURR, Aaron (1756–1836)

Aaron Burr was an American politician and statesman, and a native of New York, who ran for President of the United States in 1800. The election was thrown into the House of Representatives, and his opponent, Thomas Jefferson, was elected. Under the laws of the period, Burr then became vice president. As vice president, he presided over the Senate during Jefferson's unsuccessful attempt to impeach Supreme Court Associate Justice Samuel Chase on a charge of bias. Burr's handling of these highly politicized proceedings was commended for its fairness.

Burr's policies earned him the bitter enmity of Alexander Hamilton, who, in July 1804, goaded Burr into challenging him to a duel. Hamilton, as the challenged party, picked the weapons. Both parties fired, with Hamilton firing first. Hamilton's ball went over Burr's head, and Burr killed Hamilton. The seconds, rushing up to the dying Hamilton, recorded his last words as something like "I didn't intend to fire." People interpreted this to mean that Hamilton had no intention of harming Burr. But that belies the facts. Hamilton provoked the duel, and he did fire. He missed and Burr did not. Over a century later, while the dueling pistols that Hamilton had borrowed to use were being cleaned, an interesting fact was discovered. The pistols were fitted with a secret hair trigger. One with knowledge of the secret would have an almost insurmountable advantage in a duel. This puts a possible new light on Hamilton's last words. Perhaps he had not practiced enough with the hair trigger, which is why he fired too soon. He didn't intend to fire over Burr's head, he intended to put a ball into Burr's chest.

In 1805, when he finished his term as vice president, Burr was involved in a plot to invade and annex Mexico. The plot, as interpreted by his enemies, was an act of treason against the United States. In 1807, he was brought to trial for that offense in Virginia. Chief Justice of the Supreme Court JOHN MARSHALL conducted the trial, and Burr was acquitted.

Burr spent some time in Europe trying to raise money for a variety of schemes, most involving Mexico. It was said that he wanted to set himself up as king of a country carved out of Mexico and the American West, but nobody who actually spoke to him ever claimed such a thing. In 1812, he returned to New York, where he practiced law until his death in 1836.

BUTTON MAN

"Button man" was the term for the lowest ranking Mafia member, also called a "soldier" or a "wiseguy." The analogy with a soldier fails at several points. The button man is not normally paid a salary by his superiors, but must earn his own living. He may be given a piece of the loansharking action, or other illegal activity, or he may own part of one or more legitimate businesses that are under Mob control. For a good description of the life of a button man, read *The Valachi Papers* (1968) by Peter Maas or *Wiseguy* (1985) by Nicholas Pileggi.

C

CAMORRA

A secret society originating in Naples, Italy, the Camorra was coexistent with the Sicilian MAFIA. From the 1890s to the 1920s, the transplanted Camorristi and the Mafiosi elements in American cities feuded over the rights to extort money from their immigrant Italian compatriots, often using the device of the BLACK HAND in their operations. By the start of PROHIBITION, the American Mafia had won the feud and either eliminated or absorbed the American Camorra.

CAPITAL PUNISHMENT

Since the end of the nineteenth century, a trend among governments of the more enlightened countries around the world has been to eliminate execution as a form of judicial punishment. It was abolished in Russia in the eighteenth century for every crime but treason. It was abolished in Portugal in 1867, in Holland in 1870, in Switzerland in 1874, and in Italy in 1889. With occasional lapses, the trend has continued. Over the past two decades, it has been abolished in, among other countries, Australia, Cambodia, Denmark, France, Namibia, New Zealand, Portugal (again), and Rumania. The United States is one of the last Western democracies to maintain the death penalty.

At the time of this country's birth two centuries ago, capital punishment was inflicted for a large number of crimes. In the colony of Massachusetts in 1650, the list had been shortened until it only included idolatry, blasphemy, witchcraft, murder, manslaughter, poisoning, stealing, bearing false witness, cursing and smiting of parents, rebellious sons, Quakers and Jesuits returning after banishment, and treason. Later, horse stealing was considered a capital crime in many Western states. Gradually, the number of crimes for which the death penalty could be inflicted was reduced to include only first-degree murder and treason. Then, after the abduction of CHARLES LINDBERGH's baby in 1932, kidnapping was added to the number in several states. Now there is great political fervor to add the crime of being a "drug kingpin" to the list.

The use of the death penalty for political rather than judicial goals is a price that is paid in a participatory democracy. American politicians are extremely sensitive to polls; elected officials in the United States lead by seeing which way the mob is heading and then running to the front. Current polls have indicated that about three-quarters of the population are in favor of the death penalty. This polling figure is, however, misleading. When the question is rewritten to include life imprisonment without the possibility of parole as a possible punishment, the figure in favor of a death penalty goes down to 30 percent.

There is general agreement among professionals in criminology and penology that capital punishment is an ineffective deterrent. A century's worth of research shows that the death penalty has no appreciable positive effect on the commission of crime. Indeed, some studies suggest the opposite: William J. Bowers, a criminologist at Northeastern University, conducted a study of the murder rate in New York State from 1907 to 1963. He found that in the month following an execution the average murder rate was increased by two.

In 1967, the Supreme Court declared that the death penalty was cruel and/or inhuman, as it was then administered by the states. For the next nine years, there were no executions performed in the United States. During that time the rate of murders rose slightly. In 1976, there were 18,780 cases of murder and non-negligent manslaughter

METHODS OF EXECUTION BY STATE

State	*Method as of 1938*	*Method as of 1989*	*Number 1930–1989*	*Number 1977–1989*
		* Not authorized at this time		
Alabama	Electrocution	Electrocution	142	7
Alaska	*	*	0	0
Arizona	Lethal Gas	Lethal Gas	38	0
Arkansas	Electrocution	Lethal Injection/Electrocution	118	0
California	Hanging	Lethal Gas	292	0
Colorado	Lethal Gas	Lethal Injection	47	0
Connecticut	Electrocution	Electrocution	21	0
Delaware	Hanging	Lethal Injection	12	0
District of Columbia	Electrocution	*		0
Florida	Electrocution	Electrocution	191	21
Georgia	Electrocution	Electrocution	380	14
Hawaii	*	*	0	0
Idaho	Hanging	*	3	0
Illinois	Electrocution	Lethal Injection	90	0
Indiana	Electrocution	Lethal Injection	43	2
Iowa	Hanging	*	18	0
Kansas	Hanging	*	15	0
Kentucky	Electrocution	Electrocution	103	0
Louisiana	Hanging	Electrocution	151	18
Maine	*	*	0	0
Maryland	Hanging	Lethal Gas	68	0
Massachusetts	Electrocution	*	27	0
Michigan	*	*	0	0
Minnesota	*	*	0	0
Mississippi	Hanging	Lethal Injection/Lethal Gas	158	4
Missouri	Hanging	Lethal Injection/Lethal Gas	63	1
Montana	Hanging	Lethal Injection/Hanging	6	0
Nebraska	Electrocution	Electrocution	4	0
Nevada	Lethal Gas	Lethal Injection	33	4
New Hampshire	Hanging	Lethal Injection/Hanging	1	0
New Jersey	Electrocution	Lethal Injection	74	0
New Mexico	Electrocution	Lethal Injection	8	0
New York	Electrocution	*	329	0
North Carolina	Lethal Gas	Lethal Injection/Lethal Gas	266	3
North Dakota	*	*	0	0
Ohio	Electrocution	Electrocution	172	0
Oklahoma	Electrocution	Lethal Injection	60	0
Oregon	Hanging	Lethal Injection	19	0

METHODS OF EXECUTION BY STATE (*continued*)

State	Method as of 1938	Method as of 1989	Number 1930–1989	Number 1977–1989
			* Not authorized at this time	
Pennsylvania	Electrocution	Electrocution	152	0
Rhode Island	*	*	0	0
South Carolina	Electrocution	Electrocution	164	2
South Dakota	*	Lethal Injection	1	0
Tennessee	Electrocution	Electrocution	93	0
Texas	Electrocution	Lethal Injection	330	33
Utah	Hanging/Firing Squad	Lethal Injection/Firing Squad	16	3
Vermont	Electrocution	*	4	0
Virginia	Electrocution	Electrocution	100	8
Washington	Hanging	Lethal Injection/Hanging	47	0
West Virginia	Hanging	*	40	0
Wisconsin	*	*	0	0
Wyoming	Lethal Gas	Lethal Injection	7	0
Federal Government	Hanging		33	0
			TOTAL 3,979	TOTAL 120

known to the police. In 1977, the states, under public and political pressure, began revising their capital punishment statutes to fall under the Supreme Court guidelines, and executions began again in the United States. The murder rate continued its slow rise. In 1986, the number was 20,610.[1]

Of course, in one sense the death penalty is the ultimate deterrent: Once executed, the miscreant cannot kill again. The benefits of this are less than one might expect from the fulminations of its proponents. Hugo Adam Bedau of Tufts University cited a study of 2,646 murderers paroled or otherwise released in 12 states from 1900 through 1976. He reported that 16 of them, or slightly more than one-half of one percent, were convicted of murdering again. This is a recidivism rate much lower than that for any other violent crime.

But there is one thing that an execution does preclude: the pardon and release of those falsely convicted. False convictions, while not frequent, are common enough that they should give proponents of the death penalty pause. A report in the *Stanford Law Review* in 1987 details that at least 23 people were executed in the United States for crimes they did not commit in the years 1900–1985. According to an article by John Horgan in the July 1990 *Scientific American*, at least 27 people condemned to death over the past 18 years have later been found innocent by a higher court. Randall Dale Adams, convicted in Texas of murdering a police officer, spent 12 years on death row before his innocence was established. In 1894, in Mississippi, WILL PURVIS was actually hung, but he survived when the knot slipped and escaped before the attempt could be made again. A new governor commuted his sentence to life imprisonment and in 1898 he was pardoned. In 1917, another man confessed to the crime in sufficient detail to make it clear that he was the culprit. In 1920, Purvis was awarded $5,000 compensation by the Mississippi legislature.

[1] These numbers are from the 1990 *Sourcebook of Criminal Justice Statistics* published by the U.S. Department of Justice.

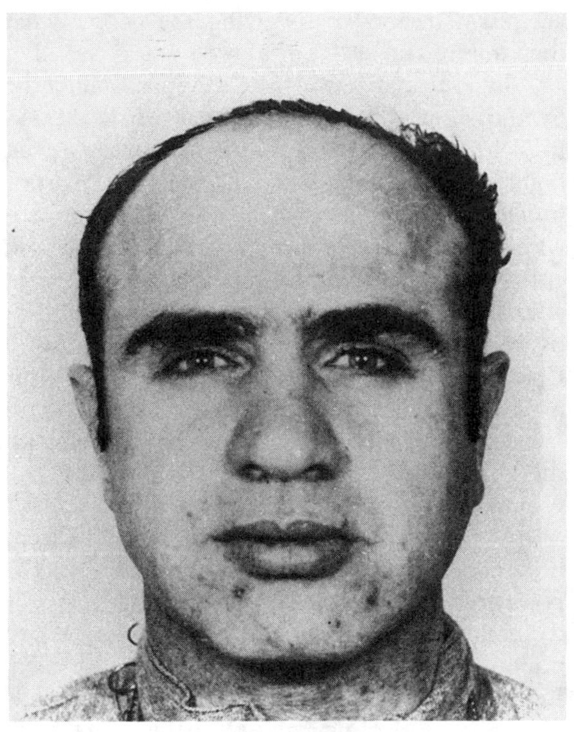

Alphonse "Al" Capone, the organizational genius who turned rumrunning into America's most profitable business. (Federal Bureau of Investigation.)

Also called "Scarface," Capone was responsible for the deaths of more than 500 men in Chicago before he was finally jailed on charges of income tax evasion. (Federal Bureau of Investigation.)

CAPONE, Al(phonse) "Scarface" (1899–1947)

HIS GENIUS FOR ORGANIZATION AND TALENT FOR KILLING MADE HIM CHICAGO'S GANGLORD

The most powerful and notorious of the gangster Capone brothers, Al Capone rose to head the Chicago crime syndicate by the time he was 28, but his criminal career was essentially over before he was 33. Born in Brooklyn, New York, he went to public school as far as the sixth grade and then dropped out in favor of hanging out with the FIVE POINTS GANG, a criminal association of street toughs headed by JOHN TORRIO. His friends and associates included such future luminaries as FRANKIE YALE, CHARLES "LUCKY" LUCIANO and MEYER LANSKY. While working as a bouncer in a combination bar and whorehouse owned by Torrio he received the scar on his cheek that would give him the nickname "Scarface." He was never fond of the nickname, which was not used in his presence, and liked to claim that he got the scar in combat in World War I.

Torrio was called to Chicago in 1909 to help his uncle, gang boss BIG JIM COLOSIMO, run his string of whorehouses, and when he needed help, he remembered his ambitious Brooklyn assistant. In 1919, Capone moved to Chicago to become Torrio's driver and bodyguard and soon his most trusted aide.

With the coming of PROHIBITION, Torrio wanted to get into the lucrative bootlegging business, but Colosimo, with a new young wife occupying his time and with his whores still pouring money into his account, was not interested. On May 11, 1920, with Torrio and Capone off the scene developing alibis, Big Jim Colosimo was murdered in his own restaurant. Colosimo had been told a large shipment of whiskey was coming in and was waiting for it by the front door when an unidentified assailant emerged from the hat check room and shot him to death. The probable assailant was gunman Frankie Yale, imported from Brooklyn to do the job. The technique was one Capone would remember years later when he planned the SAINT VALENTINE DAY'S MASSACRE.

The Torrio organization grew in all directions, taking over or eliminating other Chicago gangs that got in its way. When the North Side Gang, a mostly Irish group, proved intractible, Torrio had their leader DION O'BANION murdered, once again importing Frankie Yale to do the job. The North Siders, now led by HYMIE WEISS, refused to roll over, and waged a war against the Torrio Syndicate. In 1925, they shot Torrio from an ambush, and he barely survived. While in the hospital, he thought things over and decided that he had done well enough and had better get out of the rackets while he was still alive. "It's all yours, Al," he told Capone, and he took his estimated $30 million back to Brooklyn and retired.

The peculiar climate generated by Prohibition made bootleggers and gangsters heroes, and Capone found himself a popular figure. He tried to live up to the part, going to fashionable restaurants and speakeasies, hobnobbing with café society and giving quotes to any reporter who wanted to interview him. One of his pithiest quotes was "I am just a businessman, giving the people what they want."

In a sense that was true. Capone limited the Syndicate, as the Chicago branch of the MAFIA liked to call itself, to activities that were illegal, highly profitable, and had either public support or public tolerance, such as bootlegging, running whorehouses, and gambling. These were also crimes for which immunity could be bought in advance from venal public officials. Capone effectively took over the town of Cicero, Illinois, a Chicago suburb, keeping everyone from the mayor and police chief on his payroll.

Gradually Capone was winning his feud with the North Side Gang. Hymie Weiss tried to kill Capone in September 1926 by sending a convoy of cars by the Hawthorne Inn, Capone's Cicero headquarters, with machine guns blazing, but Capone emerged uninjured. A month later, Weiss died in an ambush as he crossed the street. When Capone discovered that three of his own men, John Scalise, Albert Anselmi and "Hop Toad" Giunta, were plotting against him, he invited them to a banquet then, over dessert, beat them to death with an Indian club.

On Saint Valentine's Day 1929, four men dressed as policemen entered a garage on Chicago's North Clark Street, lined seven members of GEORGE "BUGS" MORAN's gang up against the wall and machine gunned them to death. Moran, the real target, who was not there, said, "Only Capone kills like that." The savagery of the attack and the newspaper photographs of the dead bodies did much to turn the public's fondness for gangsters into revulsion.

The federal government went after Capone with both barrels. ELLIOT NESS and his Untouchables harassed Capone's mob and cut down their bootlegging profits, while an army of accountants studied Capone's establishable income and compared it with his income tax returns. After a year of careful research to garner convincing evidence, the government prosecuted Capone for income tax evasion. He was convicted and sentenced to 11 years in prison. While in prison, his mind and body, suffering for years from untreated syphilis in those years before penicillin, began to deteriorate at an alarming rate. By the time he was released from Alcatraz in 1939, he was no longer capable of continuous rational thought. He spent the last eight years of his life in seclusion at his home in Miami Beach.

CAPONE, Frank (1895–1924)

Older brother of AL CAPONE and RALPH CAPONE and younger brother of quondam lawman JAMES CAPONE, Frank Capone was regarded by his cohorts as the most vicious of all the Capone brothers. He believed in the direct approach when dealing with disputes and was quoted as explaining, "You never get no backtalk from a corpse." Like his brothers, he worked for Chicago mobster JOHNNY TORRIO in the early days of PROHIBITION. He was killed in a gun battle with police while trying to forcibly influence the outcome of city elections in Cicero, Illinois. *See also:* MAFIA

CAPONE, James (1887–1952)

Older brother of AL CAPONE, James Capone lived in Nebraska for years, and served as a lawman under the name of Richard James "Two-Gun" Hart. After traveling with a circus, he settled in Homer, Nebraska, where he became commander of the local American Legion post, the town marshal and eventually a state sheriff. He married a grocer's daughter named Kathleen Winch, and they had four sons.

James became a special officer in the Indian Service in 1922 but was often in trouble for cruelty toward the Indians he was supposed to be serving. He killed an Indian in a bar fight in Sioux City, Iowa, but was not charged. At some point, he lost an eye, probably in a bar fight, although he claimed he lost it in the war. When he was dismissed from his job in the Indian Service because of continued charges of brutality, he returned to Homer and resumed his position as town marshal. But he was soon relieved of that job as well. He was kicked out of the American Legion, when they found out he had never served in the armed forces. In the 1930s, jobless and destitute, he asked his brother Al for help, and lived off the largesse of his younger brother until his death.

CAPONE, Ralph "Bottles" (1894–1974)

Younger brother of mobster AL CAPONE, Ralph Capone served as an enforcer for his more famous brother during the Prohibition era. He earned his nickname "Bottles" because of his use of liquor bottles to convince speakeasy owners that they should use Al as their wholesaler. (A friendlier version is that he received the nickname because he owned a soft drink bottling plant in the 1920s and 1930s.) His only conviction was for income tax evasion, for which he served two years and four months in a federal prison. The IRS spent 35 years trying to collect back taxes that it claimed he owed from his activities during Prohibition. In 1963, federal marshals seized the assets of a business he owned, the Suburban Cigaret Service in Brookfield, a suburb of Chicago. They confiscated 262 vending machines, 100,000 packs of cigarettes and $7,500 in cash, using the proceeds as partial payment of the $223,294 Capone owed in taxes, interest and penalties. In his later years, Capone moved from Chicago to Mercer, Wisconsin, where he died.

CARUSO, Enrico (1873–1921)

Enrico Caruso was a famous Italian operatic tenor, who was an extortion victim of the BLACK HAND.

CASTELLAMMARESE WAR

In New York City in the 1920s, power within the immigrant Sicilian MAFIA was divided between the organization of GIUSEPPE "JOE THE BOSS" MASSERIA and a group of young dissidents concentrated in Brooklyn, headed by Salvatore Maranzano. Supporting Joe the Boss were such young and eager lieutenants as CHARLES "LUCKY" LUCIANO, VITO GENOVESE, FRANK COSTELLO, JOE ADONIS, and ALBERT ANASTASIA. On the Maranzano roster were Joe Bonanno, Joe Profaci, Tommy Lucchese (a defector from the Masseria camp) and others.

The struggle that broke out between the two groups was known as the Castellammarese War because so many of the younger Mafiosi had immigrated from the town of Castellammare del Golfo on the west coast of Sicily. To complicate the conflict, the young men on both sides felt that they had more in common with each other than with the MUSTACHE PETES who were their bosses. They even felt an affinity for their non-Sicilian compatriots, men like MEYER LANSKY and BENJAMIN "BUGSY" SIEGEL, who understood the advantages of working together instead of killing each other. While the two factions were fighting and killing each other, Luciano and his men were secretly talking to the other side, using Tommy Lucchese as their conduit. They mutually decided to eliminate their bosses and so end the war. Luciano went to lunch at a Coney Island restaurant with Joe the Boss, and they stayed to play cards and discuss policy. When the other patrons left the restaurant, Luciano excused himself to go to the bathroom. As he left, a hit squad made up of Joe Adonis, Albert Anastasia, Vito Genovese and Bugsy Siegel entered the front door and shot Masseria.

This allowed Luciano to make peace with Maranzano, a peace that lasted only a few months until Luciano could keep his word and have Maranzano, who now fancied himself as the "boss of bosses," killed. The end of the Castellammarese War marked the beginning of the consolidation of the New York Mafia, under Luciano, and the first stirrings of what would become the National Crime Syndicate.

CENTURION MINISTRIES, INC.

Centurion Ministries, Inc., is a Princeton, New Jersey, organization founded by JAMES MCCLOSKEY in the mid-1980s. Taking its name from the Roman soldier who looked up at Christ on the cross and said, "Surely this man is innocent," the organization tries to establish the innocence of imprisoned murderers and rapists who manage to convince McCloskey that they have been unjustly convicted.

CHAMBERS, Whittaker (1901–1961)

A principal figure in one of the two most notorious communist spy cases in the United States in the late 1940s, Whittaker Chambers sprang to national prominence when he appeared before the House Un-American Activities Committee on August 3, 1948, and named some of those with whom (he claimed) he had engaged in communist subversion against the United States in the 1930s. Among those he named was ALGER HISS, a former State Department official.

Chambers was born in Philadelphia, Pennsylvania, on April Fool's Day in 1901. When his father was notified of the birth, he thought it was a joke. Chambers attended Columbia University, supporting himself by working for the New York Public Library until he was fired for stealing books. In 1924, he joined the Communist party. He wrote for the *Daily Worker*, the Communist party newspaper, and soon became its editor. In 1932, he began working as a courier for the GRU (Soviet military intelligence). Five years later, he had an ideological conversion, stopped working for the GRU and quit the Communist party. For a while he worked as an editor for *Time* magazine.

Chambers approached the FBI and the State Department several times over the next few years, claiming that several high-ranking State Department officials were or had been members of the Communist party. The FBI investigated the charges but took no action.

In 1948, Chambers appeared before the House Committee on Un-American Activities and repeated his charges, giving some details of his life as a party member. He accused several government officials of being fellow members of "an underground organization of the United States Communist Party," including Alger Hiss, a former State Department official who had become head of the Carnegie Endowment for International Peace.

Hiss denied Chambers's story, challenging Chambers to repeat it out of the committee hearing room, where it was not a privileged statement. Chambers did, and Hiss sued for slander. Chambers produced some secret State Department documents he said Hiss had given him and five rolls of microfilm that had, according to Chambers, been hidden in a hollowed-out pumpkin.

Chambers and Hiss were called before a grand jury, which decided on the basis of Chambers's testimony that Hiss had committed perjury. He could not be tried for espionage because the statute of limitations had run out. Hiss's first trial resulted in a hung jury, but in January 1950, he was tried again and convicted. Hiss served three-and-a-half years in prison and continued to protest his innocence after he got out. In 1952, Chambers told his story in a book called *Witness*. In 1957, Hiss replied with his book *In the Court of Public Opinion*. Neither book resolved the question as to whether Hiss had been justly convicted or Chambers had been a consummate liar and rogue. Learned opinion has gone both ways over the years as new evidence has been uncovered.

On October 15, 1992, General Dmitri A. Volkogonov, chairman of the Russian military intelligence archives, completed a search of the Soviet intelligence records of the period. He concluded that Hiss was not, and had never been, an agent of the Soviet government. Chambers, it would appear, was indeed a liar and a rogue.

CHAPPLEAU, Joseph Ernst (1850–1911)

Convicted in 1889 of murdering a neighbor named Tabor, Joseph Chappleau, a New York farmer, was the first person ever sentenced to die in the electric chair in New York State. The dispute between Chappleau and Tabor, publicly about some poisoned cows, was rumored to actually have been about an affair between Tabor and Chappleau's wife. On Chappleau's appointed execution date, the electric chair was still under construction, so his sentence was commuted to life imprisonment. He was a model prisoner and was regarded by the prison staff and the other convicts as a victim of circumstance rather than a criminal. In 1905 at Clinton Prison, he saved the life of Lewis E. Lawes, a young prison guard who later became the warden of SING SING penitentiary. He died in prison.

CHICAGO

During the last half of the nineteenth century, the city of Chicago worked hard to earn its reputation as "the wickedest city in the United States." Home to some of the worst ROOKERIES in the 1860s, it and its suburbs became host to some of the most violent gangsters during the PROHIBITION era and is home to the Syndicate, as the Chicago MAFIA likes to call itself. *See also:* EVERLEIGH CLUB; LEOPOLD AND LOEB CASE

CHOWCHILLA KIDNAPPING

THE KIDNAPPING OF A SCHOOLBUS FULL OF CHILDREN THAT SHOCKED THE NATION

On July 15, 1976, the kidnapping with the greatest number of victims was accomplished on a road outside of Chowchilla, California. Three men wearing stocking masks blocked the road with a van and stopped a school bus carrying 7 boys and 19 girls home from summer school. The bus driver and his 26 charges, aged 6 to 14, were forced into the van and a second van, while one of the stocking-masked men drove the bus off the road and hid it in a creek bed.

The captives were driven to a rock quarry less

than 100 miles from the site of the abduction and placed in a large moving van that had been buried in a corner of the quarry. The van, 25 feet long and 8 feet wide, was furnished with bread, water, breakfast cereal and potato chips and contained several mattresses and a portable toilet. It was ventilated with two battery-operated fans blowing air through four-inch rubber tubing. It was, however, left unguarded.

The police immediately searched for the bus when it failed to deliver the children. It was found in the creek bed within a few hours, but no trace of the driver or children was evident.

Sixteen hours after the start of their ordeal, the bus driver and a few of the older children dug their way out of their makeshift cell. They freed all of the other children and then walked as a group until they found a quarry employee, who called the police.

Up to the time the children were freed, their parents had still not received a ransom demand. The bus driver was able to recall the license number of one of the vans under hypnosis, and the police traced it to an Oakland car dealer. The moving van had been purchased from a Palo Alto company. Employees of the two companies identified the purchaser from photographs as Frederick Newhall Woods, IV, the son of the owner of the quarry. His two cohorts were Richard Allen Schoenfeld and his brother James. It was to be a kidnapping for ransom, and they had worked on the details for over a year before attempting it. Richard Allen surrendered to police on July 23, and his brother was captured on July 29. Woods was located in Vancouver and arrested by the Royal Canadian Mounted Police on the same day.

The defendants chose their case to be heard by a judge rather than a jury, fearing that any jury would be implacably hostile to them. All three were convicted on 24 counts of kidnapping and 3 counts of kidnapping with bodily harm and received life sentences. It was stipulated that James Schoenfeld and Frederick Woods could never be paroled.

CHURCH, Benjamin (1734–c. 1777)

A Boston physician and minor poet, Benjamin Church was a member of the provincial congress of Massachusetts and was considered a Revolutionary War patriot. He was also a paid informer of General Thomas Gage, the British commander-in-chief and governor of Massachusetts. When General Gage, on the evening of April 18, 1775, sent British troops to capture the Rebels' store of munitions at Concord, thus provoking the "shot heard round the world," he was acting on information supplied by Church. Gage knew that the colonials had decided to fortify Bunker Hill more than a month before the event, thanks to Church.

Church went to Philadelphia to speak for Massachusetts Colony before the Continental Congress and impressed the congressmen with his fervor for the American cause. They appointed him director and chief physician of the first American army hospital in Cambridge, Massachusetts.

In August 1775, a letter in cipher from Church to someone in Boston fell into the hands of a suspicious patriot, who passed it on to General Washington. He had the courier, a young woman who apparently was Church's mistress, arrested and questioned at length. After some time, she confessed, and Church was arrested and his papers seized. But he seems to have been warned about his impending arrest, since no incriminating papers or documents were found. The cipher letter was read and was enough to convict him of treasonous communication with the enemy. As the Continental Army had no punishment for such an offense (its articles of war did not cover treason), the case was referred to the Continental Congress. The congress discovered that it, also, had not covered the offense and hastily passed a law providing the death penalty "or such other punishment as a general court martial shall think proper" for such cases in the future. It sentenced Church to "be close confined in some secure jail in the colony of Connecticut, without the use of pen, ink, and paper, and that no person be allowed to converse with him except in the presence and hearing of a magistrate of the town or the sheriff of the county where he shall be confined, and in the English language."

Church was kept in several different jails about the colonies until, sometime in 1777, he was permitted to leave the country. The schooner on which he sailed, probably for the West Indies, was never heard from again. Church's wife went to England, where she was granted a pension of 150 pounds a year in return for "certain services" her husband had performed.

The full extent of Church's treason was not known for over a century, when some of his early letters were found among General Gage's papers.

CLINE, Alfred L. (1888–1948)

Alfred Cline was a repetitive and methodical wife killer. At least eight times he married women, had them make out wills in his favor, and then took them on vacation. While in some resort hotel, he would give his wife a glass of buttermilk laced with a powerful sedative. He would then summon the hotel's doctor, claiming that his wife had just suffered "another heart attack." Then he would give his wife a further, heavier dose of the same sedative, which would kill her. The doctor would give a death certificate certifying heart failure, and Cline would have the body cremated.

In 1945, the authorities in California caught up with Cline. Because all of his deceased spouses had been cremated, a case for murder could not be made, but the state was able to prove that he had forged his wives' signature on various documents to get his hands on their money. Cline was sentenced to 126 years in prison and sent to Folsom Prison, where he died three years later.

CLIP JOINTS

Nightclubs that make a practice of fleecing their customers are called clip joints. Often unlicensed, they get their customers with "steerers," usually cab drivers or hotel bellmen. The forms of robbery practiced in such joints range from merely padding the bill to doping the customer's drinks, knocking him out, emptying his pockets, and dumping him in a convenient alley. Sometimes they provide women for lonely men. Instead of conferring the expected service, these women merely rob the mark in a different location.

COHEN, Mickey (1913–1976)

A Los Angeles bookmaker and general utility gangster, Mickey Cohen bucked the MAFIA family headed by Jack Dragna by siding with East Coast mobsters in an ongoing feud in the 1940s. Dragna then made a determined effort to kill him. Cohen was shot at with rifles, pistols and shotguns, and attacked with bombs that blew up his neighborhood in at least five different incidents, all of which left him totally unharmed. This gave Cohen an aura of invincibility, and gave Dragna's mob the nickname of "the Mickey-Mouse Mafia."

When BENJAMIN "BUGSY" SIEGEL settled in Los Angeles, reducing Dragna to an impotent second place in the organized crime structure, Siegel employed the man with the charmed life as his bodyguard. Unfortunately, Cohen was away the day two shots fired through a window ending Siegel's life. Cohen was not very communicative in his appearance before the KEFAUVER COMMITTEE investigation of organized crime in 1950. When asked by one of the senators, "Is it not a fact that you live . . . surrounded by violence?" Cohen indignantly replied, "What do you mean, 'surrounded by violence'? People are shooting at *me*!"

Cohen was convicted of tax evasion, serving 14 years in prison. When he was released in 1972, he retired from his criminal activities. In 1976, he died of natural causes.

COHEN, Morris (1910–) and Leona (1913–)

Members of the ATOMIC SPY RING in the United States after World War II, the Cohens fled the country before they could be arrested. Morris, a graduate of the University of Illinois, had been a schoolteacher in New York City.

Assuming the new identities of Peter and Helen Kroger, they moved to New Zealand, where they stayed for a few years before moving on to London in 1954. "Peter Kroger" opened a bookstore in the Strand specializing in Americana, from which he operated a letter drop. A shortwave transceiver was hidden in their Ruislip home with which they communicated with Moscow Center.

They were arrested by the Special Branch of Scotland Yard in 1961, in what became known as the "Portland Spy Case," and sentenced to 20 years in prison. In 1969, they were exchanged for a British professor named Gerald Brooke, who had been jailed by the Soviets for distributing subversive pamphlets, and disappeared behind the Iron Curtain.

COLOSIMO, Big Jim (1871–1920)

EARLY CHICAGO BROTHEL OWNER AND CRIME BOSS

Born in Italy, Big Jim Colosimo came to Chicago at the age of 24 and worked his way up from shoeshine boy to gang boss. He became a collector for "Bath-house John" Coughlin and Michael "Hinky Dink" Kenna, two aldermen who controlled much of the organized corruption in turn-of-the-century CHICAGO, including betting parlors and brothels.

In 1902, Colosimo married one of the madams he was collecting from, a stout middle-aged matron named Victoria Moresco. He settled down to manage her brothel, renaming it the Victoria. Under Colosimo's guidance, the whorehouse business flourished, and he soon opened a bevy of brothels around the city. As a sideline, he organized Chicago's street sweepers into a union—he had briefly been a street sweeper himself—and used it as a base for the various extortion rackets that have plagued those who deal with unions ever since. He settled into a nightclub on South Wabash Avenue called Colosimo's Café, which soon became a favorite late-night spot for Chicago's version of café society and an after-show hangout for entertainers working the Windy City.

In 1909, Colosimo was plagued by BLACK HAND extortion threats, so he brought his nephew, JOHNNY TORRIO, from Brooklyn into the business. Torrio, who had led the infamous FIVE POINTS GANG, was just the person to aid in enforcement and keep the Black Handers and other rival gangs at bay, so Big Jim could continue to enjoy the good life in his café. Torrio proved tough enough to eliminate the extortion demands and had several imaginative ideas for running a whorehouse (he had the girls dress as young virgins). Big Jim soon made Torrio his chief of staff and, in effect, turned over the business to him. Torrio had brought a young man named AL CAPONE, who had impressed him back in Brooklyn, to Chicago to work as his chauffeur, bodyguard and lieutenant. Colosimo concentrated his energy on his café and on a singer named Dale Winters who worked for him. In 1919, Colosimo left his wife and married Dale.

Torrio wanted to expand the criminal operations into the promising field of bootlegging, now that PROHIBITION was in effect, but Colosimo preferred the traditional rackets that he understood. On May 11, 1920, Big Jim was murdered by an unknown gunman in his own café. He had been asked by Torrio to be on hand to receive a large shipment of whiskey, but the whiskey never showed up. Both Torrio and Capone had excellent alibis. It is believed that they imported Brooklyn killer FRANKIE YALE to do the job. The method was similar to that used years later by Capone in the infamous SAINT VALENTINE DAY'S MASSACRE.

CONFIDENCE GAMES

A confidence game is an organized attempt by one or more swindlers (known as con men or con artists) to separate a victim from his money by guile and deceit rather than by violence or extortion. The two major divisions of confidence games are the big con (or BIG STORE), an elaborate operation which requires much preparation and usually involves between 3 and 20 people, and the SHORT CON, which is usually done on the spot and involves from one to three people, in addition to the victim. Confidence games are carefully constructed shows, designed to convince someone of facts contrary to truth and to keep him convinced long enough to separate him from his money. Some confidence games have been so successful at creating this aura of belief that the victim has come back two or three times to be further fleeced, and in some cases, the victims have refused to believe that they were swindled even while attending the trial of the swindlers.

Some of the more hardy confidence swindles are the SPANISH PRISONER con, which promises the mark great riches if he or she helps get the swindler out of jail; the GREEN GOODS GAME, which makes honest shopkeepers lust after nonexistent counterfeit money; the BADGER GAME, in which a man discovers that his new girlfriend has a husband, and the PIGEON DROP, in which the pigeon (victim) drops a lot of money. Some con men have transcended their grift to become institutions. CHARLES PONZI made a lot of money in the 1920s with a PETER TO PAUL SWINDLE, and OSCAR HARTZELL convinced a lot of people that they were heirs of Sir Francis Drake. Eighty years earlier, an enterprising band of con men had pulled a similar swindle convincing people named Baker that they could inherit a share of the BAKER ESTATE.

Following is a list of terms commonly used to describe confidence game swindles:

Ace—The fix; the assurance that local authorities are paid off and will look the other way.

Ace in the Hole—The simpler con that a worker can fall back on if the more complex or expensive con he is working *goes South*.

Against the Wall—In a confidence game, doing without a *big store* or other prepared location. Usually a *short con*, not a *big con*.

Bates—The person to be swindled; the *mark*.

Big Con—A major confidence game employing different locations, many workers, and usually a *big store*, all to fleece one *mark*. Big cons have been worked without creating a big store, by using an existing location such as an ocean liner, a bank, a hotel, or other massive prop.

Big Mitt—A big store operation revolving around a card game in a supposedly illicit casino.

Big Store—A venue made up to resemble an operating bank, bookmaking parlor, gambling casino, telegraph office, business office, or other location, employing shills to simulate employees, to impress the *mark*. [Note: the terms *big con* and *big store* are often used interchangeably, but there is a clear distinction: the *big con* is the operation, the *big store* is the location.]

The Blocks—The shell game (also, *the nuts*).

Blow-off—The last step in a confidence game, after the *mark* has been taken, designed to separate the con men from the mark, or to ensure his or her silence through embarrassment or fear of exposure.

Boiler Room—A room with a bank of telephones where pitchmen try to sell stories to *marks* over the phone.

Broad Tosser—The dealer at three-card monte.

The Broads—Three-card monte.

Bucket Shop—An operation where many con men gather together to sell large amounts of worthless paper, usually in the form of stock, to many *marks*. Usually involves use of a *boiler room*.

Build-up—The preparation of a *mark* for the *score*; all dealings with the mark that come before the act of collecting money from the mark.

Bunco—Any confidence game; the act of conning.

Cackle Bladder—A device worn under the shirt containing animal blood or simulated blood. If hit hard from the front it will burst, creating a very bloody shirt. It is used to simulate someone being shot. In a *blow-off*, it will convince the *mark* not to go to the police for fear of being implicated in a murder.

Capper—The person in a con game who the *mark* sees winning a lot of money, or who convinces the mark that there is something of value in the transaction under consideration.

Con—Confidence game.

Con Man—One who makes money through confidence games.

Convincer—The act that lures the *mark* into bringing his or her bankroll into play; it usually involves allowing the mark to win some money.

Dropping the Leather—The Pigeon Drop.

The Fix—An arrangement with the authorities assuring the con artist that he or she will not be arrested.

Flimflam—A confidence game.

Go South—When a con game in operation falls apart, it is said to go south.

Hype—A swindle in a minor business transaction, such as shortchanging a customer.

Inside Man—The person who takes the *mark* away from the *outside man* and tells the *tale*, getting the mark hooked on the idea of making some easy money. Also known as the *roper*.

Mark—The person to be swindled.

The Nuts—The shell game (also *the blocks*).

Outside Man—The con man who first makes contact with the *mark* and directs him or her to the *inside man*, often leaving him or her there. Also known as the steerer.

Paper—Counterfeit or genuine negotiable instruments; bad checks.

Paperhanger—Passer of bad checks.

Peter to Paul Scheme—*See* Ponzi Scheme.

Ponzi Scheme—Named after Charles Ponzi, who swindled tens of millions of dollars with it in 1920, it involves taking money from investors with the promise of paying indecently high interest through some clever manipulation of the laws of nature. In actuality, the interest is paid with the money taken in from new investors. Also known as a Peter to Paul Scheme.

Roper—*See* Inside Man.

The Score—The act of obtaining money from the mark; preceded by the build-up and followed by the blow-off. Also, and by extension, the money taken from the mark.

Short Con—A confidence game played without preparation for the amount of money that the *mark* has on him.

Spanish Prisoner—A classic confidence game that keeps reappearing in different variants. The *mark* is told that if he or she helps a prisoner get out of jail, by paying a large sum of money, then the prisoner will recover his or her fortune and share it with the mark.

Steerer—*See* Outside Man.

Three-Card Monte—A card game that is always a con.

CONSTITUTION OF THE UNITED STATES

See: FOURTH AMENDMENT; FIFTH AMENDMENT; BILL OF RIGHTS; MIRANDA RULE; SUPREME COURT

COONEY, Cecilia

On January 5, 1924, Cecilia Cooney and her husband Ed stole $688 from a Brooklyn, New York, store, beginning a crime spree that made Cecilia famous as the "Bobbed-Hair Bandit." The Cooneys were captured in Florida and spent the next six years in prison. Later that year, in reaction to the LEOPOLD-LOEB Case, Reverend Alva Vest King pronounced that "the only cure for youthful crime, boy brigands, and bobbed-hair bandits is the thorough training of the children in the principles of the Christian religion."

COOPER, D. B. (?)

HE HIJACKED AN AIRLINER AND DISAPPEARED WITH $200,000

On November 24, 1971, the day before Thanksgiving, a man giving the name of D. B. Cooper boarded a Northwest Orient Airlines flight from Portland, Oregon, to Seattle, Washington. When the Boeing 727 was airborne, Cooper called the stewardess over and told her that he had a bomb in his briefcase. In return for $200,000 in $20 bills and four parachutes, he would not set it off. Airplane hijacking was a new sport in the United States when Cooper made his demands, and there was no mechanism in place for dealing with it. Even though there was some doubt as to whether he really had a bomb or not, for the safety of the passengers and crew, it was decided to take him at his word. When the plane landed in Seattle, Cooper traded the 36 passengers and most of the crew for the money and parachutes. He then directed the three remaining crew members to take the plane and head for Reno. The crew was ordered to stay in the cockpit with the door closed. When the plane landed in Reno, Cooper, one parachute, and all the money were gone. The 727 Trijet was one of the few commercial airliners from which Cooper could have pulled this stunt safely, since it had a rear door facing directly backward with a built-in ramp.

Despite an intensive manhunt, Cooper and the money had disappeared. It was theorized that he jumped somewhere over southwest Washington, a heavily wooded region. As time passed and no trace of Cooper or the money was found, his deed became legend. The FBI believes that Cooper was never found because he was killed in the jump or shortly thereafter. Many people in the Pacific Northwest prefer to believe that he escaped. They celebrate D. B. Cooper Day on the anniversary of his crime. None of the money turned up until 1980, when some children near Vancouver, Washington, found a few thousand dollars of it buried in the mud along the north bank of the Columbia River. Whether Cooper buried it there, or whether it was washed downriver, is unknown.

The fact that, as far as is known, none of the money was ever spent would seem to indicate that D. B. Cooper was not alive to spend it. But there are many in the Pacific Northwest for whom D. B. Cooper will not be dead until his body is found, dangling from a parachute and clutching the money, somewhere amid the ancient redwoods.

COP

This slang expression for "policeman" coexists with its companion, "copper." There are many competing explanations of the origins of these two words, and which begat which. Some trace "cop" to the British C.O.P., Constable On Patrol, which bobbies signed to official documents. The only problem with this explanation is that bobbies did not sign C.O.P. or any variant of it. A competing apocryphal explanation is that it comes from the copper badges worn by the policemen.

The probable etymology of the word goes back to "to cop," meaning to steal or take, a still-prevalent slang usage that Partridge's *Dictionary of Slang and Unconventional English* traces back to c. 1700. A policeman was one who "copped" a miscreant, as is shown by the British "it's a fair cop," meaning it is a just arrest. Therefore he was a "copper," and soon a "cop." *See also:* POLICE

CORLL, Dean (1939–1973)

HE BUTCHERED TEENAGE BOYS—UNTIL ONE OF THEM FOUGHT BACK

A delicate child whose mother owned a candy company in Houston, Texas, Dean Corll was drafted into the army in 1964, but was out again with an honorable discharge in less than a year.

His mother had convinced the military that Dean was too sickly to be a soldier and that she needed him back home at the candy company. Dean started working out with weights to build up his strength, and his mother started seeing psychics to improve her sex life. She was estranged from her last husband, who now owned the candy company across the street. Her psychic sent her to a computer dating service, and she married a sailor with whom she was electronically compatible. Physically and emotionally, however, they turned out to be incompatible, and she soon moved first out of the house and then out of town.

Corll was forced to close the candy business and went to work for the Houston Lighting and Power Company. He befriended a 12-year-old boy named David Brooks, recently arrived from Louisiana, who moved in with him. Brooks's buddy Elmer Wayne Henley, Jr., joined the two, although he did not move in; he lived elsewhere with his mother and grandmother. Corll convinced Brooks and Henley to bring other children to the house, offering them large sums of money for each boy they delivered. The two lads would bring a companion to Corll's house and get him drunk or high on airplane glue. Then Corll would undress him, strap him to a plywood restraint and torture him to death. Sometimes the guest boys were not harmed on the first visit, or even the second, but continued partying at the Corll house meant eventual torture and death.

Corll never came up with as much money as he promised for Henley's and Brooks's assistance, but by now, the two were getting their own gratification out of the situation. Brooks satisfied himself with watching the proceedings, but Henley soon joined in. He did not find strangling as easy as he thought, and had to call in Corll to help him finish off several of his victims.

Corll moved more than 20 times in the next five years, always in the same general area of Houston. It seemed that the neighbors were constantly complaining about the noise. By 1973, when Corll moved into a house owned by his father in the Pasadena suburb of Houston, he and his cohorts had killed well over 20 youths. And, amazingly, none of them were missed. Occasionally, worried parents would notify the Houston police department, and a missing juvenile report would be filed, but the parents were always reassured that it was probably just "this hippie thing," and their son would come home when he was tired of living in sin in San Francisco or New York and doing drugs. Not only was there no systematic search to find these boys, there was no attempt made at all.

Corll's methods of torture varied from victim to victim as the mood struck him. Some were raped or sodomized; some were beaten to death; some were shot; some were strangled; some were cut up before they were killed. After he moved into his father's house, his need for victims became insatiable. Henley was afraid that Corll was losing control. He was right.

On August 7, 1973, Henley stayed overnight at Corll's house with two friends, a teen-age girl who was running away from home and her boyfriend. The next morning he awoke to find himself strapped to the torture table. It seems that Corll was aggravated that Henley would bring a girl into his home, and was going to kill the three of them. The floor was covered with plastic, the radio was turned up to cover the screams, and Corll had his knives out. He hit Henley in the face with the barrel of a pistol he was holding and told him what a mistake he had made bringing his friends there. Henley agreed and said that he would help Corll torture his two friends if Corll would release him. Corll released the straps and told Henley to cut the girl's clothes off and rape her, while he prepared the boy to be tortured.

As soon as Henley was free, he grabbed Corll's pistol. Corll laughed and told him he would never shoot and dived for the gun. Henley shot Corll six times and then called the police.

When the police arrived, Henley began telling them the whole story. They did not believe it. Henley took them into Corll's boat shed and pointed out the sacks of lime, the plastic bags full of male clothing and a bicycle belonging to a nine year-old boy who had disappeared from the neighborhood shortly after Corll moved in.

David Brooks at first denied knowing about the killings but then admitted to watching them. He put the number he had witnessed at somewhere between 25 and 30 and added that he had helped bury most of them. Most were teenagers, but the youngest was, Brooks estimated, three years old.

Elmer Wayne Henley was indicted for six of the murders. The trial was held in San Antonio, and on July 15, 1974, Henley was found guilty on all counts. His attorney appealed. Then David Brooks was tried and found guilty of one murder. He was sentenced to life in prison.

Henley's appeal was granted, and he was retried in June 1979. This time the trial was held in Corpus Christi, Texas. Once again, he was convicted on six counts of murder.

CORONA, Juan (1934–)

A migrant fruit picker who had worked his way up to being a labor contractor in California's Central Valley, Juan Corona was indicted on July 12, 1971, for murdering 25 of his fellow workers over the previous two years. The bodies of several migrants had been found in shallow graves, and with the bodies, the investigators found bank deposit slips with Corona's name on them. Police searched his house outside of Yuba City, and a bunkhouse on the nearby Sullivan ranch where he housed his transient workers, unearthing a total of 25 graves. The apparent motive for the killings was robbery. Corona was brought to trial, at which he pleaded innocent. The prosecutor introduced as evidence bloodstained knives, machetes and a pair of his bloodstained boots. The most damning evidence was a ledger Corona kept, dubbed his "death list" by the prosecutor, in which Corona enumerated his victims and their possessions.

The jury was out for 45 hours before returning with a verdict of guilty on 25 counts of murder. Corona was sentenced to 25 consecutive life terms. In 1973, Corona was attacked in Soledad prison, repeatedly stabbed and lost the use of one eye, which resulted in his separation and isolation from the general prison population for his own protection. In 1978, Corona was granted a new trial on the grounds that his defense was inadequate. The court felt that, although there was no doubt about his guilt, his attorney should have raised an insanity defense. He was found guilty again.

CORONERS

The office of coroner is the oldest existing position in English criminal law. The text *Jarvis on Coroners* (1829) refers to the *Article of Eyre* of 1194, at which time the office was already in existence. It was imported to North America as the colonies were established. The coroner, usually with, but in some jurisdictions without, a coroner's jury, held an inquest over a person's death when there was any reason to assume that the death was other than natural. The inquest was to determine the cause of death and, in cases of murder or manslaughter, whether there was probable cause to suspect anyone of the crime. If probable cause was found, an indictment could be handed down, and the suspect could be tried for the crime in a criminal court.

Coroner's inquests were commonly informal affairs. The coroner was often a political appointee and was not required to be either a lawyer or a doctor. Those questioned had no right to have an attorney present, although the coroner might allow one to be present if he chose. The procedures in the coroner's court were those that the coroner chose and were designed to establish the basic facts in a case, not to apportion guilt or innocence.

CORPUS DELICTI

Corpus delicti is a Latin phrase meaning "the body of the crime." The phrase is often misused in murder cases to mean the corpse of the victim, but it means the body of evidence that establishes that a crime has been committed. In a murder case, it is helpful to have the corpse, but murderers have been successfully prosecuted and convicted without finding the victim's body. In such cases, to establish the *corpus delicti*, it must be proved to a moral certainty that the victim is dead and that the victim died of unnatural causes.

Corpus delicti must be established in every crime. The two points necessary to prove *corpus delicti* are, as in a murder case, that an injury or loss has occurred and that a criminal act was the cause of that injury or loss.

COSA NOSTRA

An Italian phrase meaning "our thing," *Cosa Nostra* is what members of the MAFIA call their organization. The term was not generally known outside of the Mafia until 1962, when JOSEPH VALACHI used it during the KEFAUVER COMMITTEE's televised investigations into organized crime.

COSTELLO, Frank (1891–1973)

PEACEMAKER AND GRAND STRATEGIST OF THE MAFIA

The future "Prime Minister of the Underworld," Frank Costello was born Francesco Castiglia, son of Luigi Castiglia, in Cosenza, a little town in the toe of Italy, on January 26, 1891. In 1895, the family immigrated to the United States, settling in New York, where Luigi opened a grocery store.

When Francesco was 17, he was arrested for assaulting a woman and stealing her pocketbook, but his entire family swore that he was eating supper with them at the time, and the charges were dropped. When he was 21, he was arrested for assaulting a woman who was on her way to the bank and stealing $1,600, but again, he had an unassailable alibi, and the charges were dropped. Two years later, Francesco, who had by now Americanized his name to Frank Costello, was arrested for carrying a concealed weapon. This time he went to trial and was sentenced to a year in prison.

Costello took an extended course in the criminal arts while he was in prison, and when he got out he had graduated from assault and battery to more lucrative and safer forms of larceny. For a while, he ran a crap game. By 1919, when he was 28, Costello was a partner in the Horowitz Novelty Company, which was engaged in the ancient and honorable business of conducting a PUNCH-BOARD SCAM.

In 1920, the Horowitz Novelty Company went bankrupt, having made close to $100,000 for its partners in the year of its existence. In its bankruptcy filing, the company declared debts of a little more than $14,000 and substantial assets. But the creditors had small hope of collecting anything. As the court statement recorded: "The debts which are due the company cannot be collected by the bankrupts as they were all East Side gangsters."

After that, Costello went into the liquor importing business, which at the time was illegal in the United States, which was in the throes of PROHIBITION. With the backing of ARNOLD ROTHSTEIN, Costello would buy Scotch whiskey in Canada and arrange for its introduction into the United States. Costello was a respected and trusted businessman on the Canadian side, where his operation was legal. Those who did business with him reported that his word was his bond, and he never haggled about the price. And he paid in cash.

"He was a man of his word," one of his Canadian suppliers commented. "The guys liked him because he had money to spend and you could trust him. He had the kind of reputation where he could order 8,000 cases of Scotch for delivery in six months, and you'd be sure he'd show up and pay you off on the dot."

In 1928, Costello and an old-time associate named Dandy Phil Kastel formed a company (the

Tru-Mint Novelty Corporation) for the purpose of introducing mechanical gambling in New York City. They distributed over 5,000 nickel slot machines about the city. Other companies had slot machines, but what Frank and Dandy had was something more important—police protection. They paid off a TAMMANY HALL bag man by the name of Jimmy Hines, who made sure that slots with the sticker of the Tru-Mint Novelty Corporation did not get confiscated by the police.

In 1934, Fiorello La Guardia was elected mayor of New York City, and it was his declared intention to clean up vice, graft, corruption, and slot machines in the city. Costello and Kastel obtained an injunction against the city when La Guardia began breaking up their machines (there is a famous photograph of him, fire axe in hand, menacing a slot machine) and fought him all the way to the Supreme Court. They lost on a 5 to 4 split decision and quickly removed the machines that La Guardia did not get to first with his fire axe.

The Tru-Mint Novelty Corporation moved some of its machines down to Louisiana when Governor HUEY LONG decided to raise some revenue for his state by allowing—and taxing—certain games of chance. Unfortunately, Long was assassinated before the good citizens of Louisiana had a chance to weigh the salutary effects of legalized slots, and the new administration chased Costello and Kastel and their slot machines out of the state.

A complicated series of events beginning in 1934 moved Costello up in the Mob hierarchy. It started when THOMAS E. DEWEY was appointed special prosecutor in New York State by Governor Lehman, who had been shocked to discover that there was organized crime in his state. Dewey went after the crime bosses, and one of his first targets was DUTCH SCHULTZ, the New Jersey beer baron who had taken over the Harlem NUMBERS RACKET. Dutch, who had no sense of humor, took this personally. He decided that Dewey should be killed.

The cooler heads in the Mob, CHARLES "LUCKY" LUCIANO, LOUIS "LEPKE" BUCHALTER and others, decided that killing Dewey would not be wise. Dewey would be dead, but a horde of little Deweys would come to take his place. And they would be irascible. No, a better plan, according to Lepke, would be to see that the witnesses did not testify. What could not be done by threats and intimidation could surely be done by simple murder. But Schultz was adamant. He was determined to get Dewey, and his associates could see that he was serious.

On October 23, 1935, the Dutchman was having dinner in the Palace Chop House in Newark, New Jersey, when a gunman named CHARLIE "THE BUG" WORKMAN walked in with two assistants and three guns. When the Bug walked out, Dutch and three of his associates were dead or dying.

With the Dutchman gone, Dewey turned his attentions to Luciano. In 1936, Luciano was put on trial for compulsory prostitution. Which was not to say that he forced women to become prostitutes, but that once they had made that choice, he controlled the prices, working conditions and client lists of prostitutes, and his methods of enforcement were brutally direct. "First you got to sit on them, then you got to step on them," as he explained it.

When Luciano was convicted and sentenced to from 30 to 50 years in the penitentiary, control of his crime "family" went to VITO GENOVESE. But he proved unequal to the challenge and, after bungling an attempted murder and getting both the police and his compatriots mad at him, left for Italy in 1937 to give Mussolini the benefit of his experience in government.

This moved Costello up to the acting head of the Luciano crime family, although Luciano still put in an occasional word from the Dannemora State Penitentiary.

With the end of Prohibition in 1933, Costello diversified. He stayed in the now legal liquor business, first distributing and then buying a major interest in the Whiteley Distillery, the manufacturers of House of Lords and King's Ransom Scotch, then two of the best-selling labels in the country. The actual stock in the company was in the names of a variety of Costello's friends and relatives, since the federal and state governments frowned on racketeers having interests in the liquor industry.

Costello also had a major interest as a commission agent or "layoff man" in booking bets. This was a time before the pari-mutuel system came into the New York racetracks, and the betting was done at the track with a number of licensed bookmakers. Known felons could not get licenses, but they could lay off bets for those who had licenses.

In 1937, Costello and Dandy Phil Kastel, his partner in various slot-machine operations, were indicted for "violating Title 26, Sections 145 and 1639, United States Code by willfully attempting to evade and defeat a tax and the payment thereof." In other words, income-tax evasion.

The Treasury Department's theory was that many of the "partners" of the indicted pair in their various companies were partners in name only and reported and paid taxes on income that they then kicked back to Costello or Kastel. Costello's brother-in-law, for example, was shown to have reported an income of $150,000 a year, and yet was living in a $40-a-month apartment and buying furniture on the installment plan. The case was thrown out by the tax court, however, which felt that, although the facts were awfully suggestive, they didn't *prove* anything.

Costello had learned early that the best way to keep out of trouble was to own the people who could get you into trouble. He became so adept at buying politicians outright, or otherwise influencing the political process, that the rest of the Mob turned to him for help when they had political problems. This greatly enhanced his influence in and his value to the leadership of the Mob nationwide. In 1943, when the Bar Association of the State of New York brought disbarment proceedings against New York Magistrate Thomas A. Aurelio, who had just gotten the nomination to the New York State Supreme Court, because of his association with known gangsters, the extent of Frank Costello's influence on the public officials of the state became apparent. Perhaps as startling to the public was the size and extent of the criminal empire of interconnecting gangster "families" that made up the Mob—of which only a part was the Sicilian brotherhood called the MAFIA.

The exposure of the connection came when Manhattan District Attorney Frank Hogan, who had put a wiretap on Costello's telephone, overheard Aurelio thanking Costello for his help. Hogan was prepared to introduce this and other wiretap evidence to the grand jury when Costello testified in the Aurelio disbarment. Costello's attorney, George Wolf, advised him to tell the truth to the grand jury, pointing out that what Costello did was not illegal—using his influence to get a friend the nomination—but that lying to a grand jury was perjury, and Hogan had the wiretaps to prove it.

Costello did not volunteer any information to the grand jury, but Hogan knew the questions to ask. Costello, with Hogan's prompting, told the jury that he was a good friend of Michael Kennedy, who was then head of Tammany Hall, the Democratic political machine that ran the city in between reform mayors. He told them that he had asked Kennedy to see to Aurelio's Supreme Court nomination and that Kennedy had done that. Why would Kennedy do him a favor like that? Costello told the jury that he had spoken to the district leaders—all friends of his—about Kennedy's election as Tammany leader.

"What instructions did you give those leaders with respect to Kennedy?" Hogan asked.

Costello didn't quibble with the word *instructions*.

"I told [district leaders] Kelly, Sarubbi and Rosenthal that I would consider it a nice thing if they would go along."

Presumably no one wanted to find out what Costello would do if they did not go along with what he thought was "a nice thing." But to say that Costello controlled through fear alone would be unfair. Many of them were truly in his debt.

"I want to tell you something," Costello explained to the jury. "Here's the position I am in. I am born in New York. I am here all my life. I know everybody, and I am inclined to help mostly anybody if it is possible, with no interest, financial, physically or otherwise. When they are in trouble, sick or they need rent, and if I got it, I help them and I believe it's my reputation."

And so Costello owned Kennedy because he owned the people below Kennedy. And through Kennedy, he would have owned a Supreme Court justice if Aurelio was elected.

But who else did Costello know? Hogan brought that out for the jury.

> "Do you know Benjamin Siegel, also known as Bugsy Siegel?"
>
> "I've known him about 10 years."
>
> "Al Capone?"
>
> "20 years."
>
> "Frank Nitti . . . 'Trigger Mike' Coppola . . . Louis 'Lepke' Buchalter . . . Johnny Torrio . . . Lucky Luciano . . . Dutch Schultz . . . Dutch Goldberg . . . Owney Madden . . . 'Little Ziggy' . . . Vito Genovese?"
>
> "Yeah . . . yeah . . . yeah . . . him I don't know . . . sure . . . yeah . . . yeah . . . sure . . . yeah."

The person Costello claimed not to know was Johnny Torrio from Chicago—a gangster whom he surely did know. No one has ever been able to suggest a reason why Costello denied it. Perhaps he was just tired of saying yes.

As a result of this testimony, and the extensive coverage it got in the newspapers and news magazines around the country, Frank Costello suddenly found himself a household name. He spent the rest of his life trying to make those households forget his name, but never succeeded.

Thomas A. Aurelio was not disbarred, since, although they could prove that he knew Costello and that Costello had helped him, they could not prove that he knew Costello was a crook. He went on to be elected to the Supreme Court of New York (his name was already on both the Democratic and Republican ballots, and it was too late to take it off), and he served honorably and ably for 14 years, then moved up to the Court of Appeals.

In 1950, Costello was asked to speak before a subcommittee of the U.S. Senate's Commerce Committee on the subject of gambling. He appeared voluntarily before the committee and denied that he was, or had ever been, involved in bookmaking. "I have very little knowledge," he told them. "I don't feel I qualify."

What did he do?

"I am in the real estate business. I am interested in a nightclub in Louisiana, and I have some oil leases in Texas."

Was the Louisiana nightclub really a gambling casino?

"A little gambling," Costello explained, "The roulette wheel and dice."

Then why do the other witnesses keep referring to you as "the big shot"?

Costello explained that it was the result of bad press. "The newspapers have a great investment in me, just like Coca Cola . . . with them I'm number one."

They asked him if he thought the new law would prevent gambling. He shook his head. "If a man wants to gamble," he told them, "he'll find some trick to do it."

Senator Estes Kefauver observed all the attention that Costello had generated for the subcommittee, and there is nothing that a politician appreciates as much as attention. He wanted some of it for himself. On March 13, 1951, Frank Costello appeared in open—televised—hearings before the Kefauver Committee on Organized Crime. The hearings had begun in December 1950, and Costello's appearance was to be their climax.

Costello objected to being televised. He did not need the notoriety. So the cameras kept off his face. Instead they showed his hands as he testified. For a while, they were the most talked-about pair of hands in America. The committee was convinced that they would find Frank Costello to be the crime boss of the United States. They said so in public before Costello ever testified: "There is no doubt in the minds of the members of this committee that there do exist at least two major crime syndicates. There is one with an axis between New York and Miami headed by Frank Costello." They said so again while he was testifying. And Kefauver said so afterward. In his book *Crime in America*, he wrote:

> For sheer drama, for wholesale peeling back of layers of deceptive camouflage and perjury about the activities of criminals and certain politicians, the New York City open hearings were the climax. . . . Frank Costello, described in testimony before us as "the most influential underworld leader in America," [did] a remarkable job of demolishing, through his own testimony, his pose of present respectability and veracity. . . .
>
> Of all the witnesses from the crime world summoned before us in New York, Frank Costello was the focal point of interest. The remarkable thing about his appearance before us is that Costello, the vaunted "prime minister" of the underworld, made himself out—and needlessly so—to be unintelligent. This in itself is a paradox, for it is hard for anyone who has studied Costello's persistent criminal activities, his influence in criminal and political circles, and the skill with which he has covered up the tracks of some of his operations, to believe the man really is a fool.

The committee had Costello in a tight bind. If he answered their questions truthfully about some of his activities, he could go to jail for committing crimes. If he lied about it and was caught, he could go to jail for perjury. If he refused to answer—took his Fifth Amendment right against self-incrimination—he could be jailed for contempt of Congress.

Costello walked out twice during the proceedings. He said it was because of a sore throat from talking. Kefauver called it a cowardly attempt to evade answering questions. Costello's attorney, George Wolfe, revealed years later in a book about Costello that it was an attempt to save his friend William O'Dwyer, onetime mayor of New York City and then the Ambassador to Mexico, from being caught in perjury. The committee was curious about their friendship. O'Dwyer was coming back from Mexico to testify. Costello wanted O'Dwyer to talk about himself before Costello had to talk about O'Dwyer. The attempt worked, although O'Dwyer got into enough trouble with his own testimony.

After the hearings, Kefauver was determined to "get" Costello for contempt of Congress for walking out on him. Costello was charged with that and with refusing to answer certain questions concerning his net worth, which could have gotten him in trouble with the Internal Revenue Service. He was put on trial on January 7, 1952. The trial resulted in a hung jury—eleven for conviction and one for acquittal. Public sentiment was running so much against Costello that the one holdout juror was called before a grand jury to explain his vote.

Costello was retried. This time he hired an expensive Wall Street law firm but lost. He was sentenced to a year and a half in prison plus a $5,000 fine. In August 1952, for the second time in his life, 61-year-old Frank Costello went to prison. While he was in the federal penitentiary in Atlanta, the government made its next move against Frank Costello. He was accused, based on testimony given during the Kefauver hearings, of lying on his naturalization papers. The Department of Justice wanted to deport him to Italy, the country he had left when he was four years old.

In 1946, Vito Genovese, who had been reimported to this country to stand trial for murder, returned to his crime family and friends in New York. The witnesses against him at the murder trial had all mysteriously died. Over the next five years, Genovese had been getting more and more unhappy about the way Costello was running the New York rackets. His major complaint was that he wanted the job himself. While Frank was in prison, Vito consolidated his position. He murdered several of Costello's friends.

Costello was now spending as much time in prison as out. The government tried him for income tax evasion again, and this time got a conviction. The Supreme Court, in a decision that was considered "bad law" by many experts, upheld the conviction (it had been obtained on wholly hearsay evidence, usually not allowed).

On May 2, 1957, Frank Costello took a cab home from dinner at an East Side restaurant. He walked into his apartment house and was shot in the head by a fat man who was waiting there for him. The fat man fled into the night. By a miracle, the bullet had only grazed his scalp, and Costello lived. Vincent Gigante, a hoodlum working for Vito Genovese, was tried for the attempt and beat the rap. Later he became a good friend of Costello's, although he almost certainly was the gunman. But Costello was never the man to hold a grudge.

On October 25, 1957, Albert Anastasia was sitting in Chair #4 at the barbershop at the Park Sheraton Hotel when two gunmen ran into the shop, emptied their pistols into Anastasia's body and the chair and everything else around, and fled. Costello knew that his time was running out, that Genovese would surely try again.

On November 14, in what became known as the *APPALACHIAN CONFERENCE,* a congregation of Mafia leaders assembled at JOSEPH BARBARA's mansion in Apalachin, a small town in upstate New York. A state trooper named Sergeant Edgar Crosswell spotted the parade of long, black limousines going up the driveway of a known hoodlum, and wondered who was in them. He set up a roadblock outside the house to stop everyone leaving to identify them. The meeting, which had been set up by Vito Genovese to announce his takeover of the East Coast rackets, dissolved into a slapstick comedy of chaos as 58 of the top Mob bosses of the country were rounded up by a young state trooper, who did not even recognize most of them. Several other old, distinguished leaders of great crime families escaped by fleeing through the woods on foot.

Frank Costello, who had not been invited to the meeting, was a beneficiary of its fallout. As the last of his appeals was turned down, Costello returned to the Atlanta penitentiary to finish his term for tax evasion. Genovese, who had been arrested on drug charges, was sent to the same prison. The inmates, who thought Costello was a regular guy, decided to kill Genovese. But Costello would have none of it. Through George Wolfe, his attorney, he invited Genovese to a sit-down in the warden's office. The warden was glad to go along with the scheme as a way to prevent bloodshed and a potential riot. Genovese sat down, a picture was taken, and the prisoners decided to leave Vito alone. Vito sent a copy of the picture to his people in New York as a sign to leave Costello alone when he got out. Genovese had made peace. As he told Wolfe: "Frank is something. He is so smart I'm always wondering what's behind everything he says and then I find he's talking straight and I'm the jackass. He even warned me about holding that meeting in Apalachin and I didn't listen."

Frank Costello avoided deportation and lived the rest of his life, once out of prison, in Manhattan. He died in 1973, at the age of 82.

In November 1949, in an interview with journalist Bob Considine, Costello defined his life. "If you say I was or am a racketeer, I guess you'll be right, too. But for a long time I've been trying to figure just what a racketeer is. I never went to school past the third grade, but I've graduated from 10 universities of hard knocks. And I've decided that a racketeer is a fellow who tries to get power, prestige, or money at the expense of entrenched power, prestige, or money."

COUGHLIN, Blakely (1919–1920?)

Late Tuesday night, June 1, or early Wednesday morning, June 2, 1920, 13-month-old Blakely

Coughlin was stolen from his crib in the Coughlin house in Norristown, Pennsylvania. The family promptly notified the police, called in the Burns detective agency and offered a reward for the baby's safe return.

The Coughlins received several ransom notes, and a large volume of crank letters, which the family found at least as upsetting as the real ransom demands. By June 16, Mr. Coughlin had made contact with the kidnapper and paid a ransom of $12,000, but his son had not been returned. In August, the kidnapper, a man named August Pascal, attempted to collect another $10,000, and was arrested by the combined efforts of the state police, the U.S. Post Office investigators, and the Secret Service.

Pascal admitted to the kidnapping but steadfastly refused to tell where Baby Blakely was. After four months, he finally admitted that the child had smothered during the kidnapping and stated that he had weighted down the body and thrown it into the Schuylkill River. In October, the badly decomposed body of a male baby was found near the town from which the ransom letter had been mailed. The police believed that Blakely Coughlin had been found, but the parents refused to accept it and kept searching for their child.

Pascal pleaded guilty to second-degree murder and kidnapping for extortion. The prosecution accepted the plea, since first-degree murder could not be proven. The trial judge, in sentencing Pascal to life imprisonment, said: "I am sorry that I cannot impose the most extreme penalty known in law, the electric chair, because your crimes richly deserve such a penalty."

COUNTERFEITING

The Pilgrim fathers brought the notion and practice of counterfeiting with them from Europe, only to find the scheme already firmly established in the New World. While the less honest among them attempted to foist silver-coated lead coins on the Indians whose land they were appropriating, the Indians were passing counterfeit wampum to the Pilgrims. The Pilgrims had not brought much coinage with them from Europe, investing most of it in useful possessions before they left. Since there had to be some agreed-upon medium of exchange for goods and services, and the Pilgrim settlers were not equipped to produce their own coinage, the Indian wampum filled a definite need.

Wampum, circular beads made of seashells pierced in the center, circulated along with silver coinage in North America through the first quarter of the eighteenth century. It came in two varieties: white wampum, made from clam or whelk shells, and black wampum, made from quahog shells, which actually varied from pale violet to a rich purple in color. To the Iroquois and other tribes, wampum was more than an instrument of trade; the strung shells, arranged in different patterns, had great symbolic significance. To the Europeans, it was just another form of money, with one black wampum worth five white wampum. So the Indians passed their inferior wampum on to the settlers, and then started dyeing the white wampum purple with berries to make black wampum.

Counterfeiting continued to be a serious problem in colonial New England. One series of paper money bore the motto: "To Counterfeit Is Death," a warning designed to discourage would-be copiers. Benjamin Franklin purposely misspelled words on Pennsylvania money (e.g., "Pensylvania"), hoping that the counterfeiters would not notice—or so he claimed. But neither warning nor trick discouraged the brotherhood of the printing press. In 1768, a New York newspaper estimated that there were over 500 counterfeiters working in the colonies. Within the next 10 years, over 200,000 pounds in counterfeit money was put in circulation.

The counterfeiters were usually professional men or artisans: carpenters, weavers, teachers, doctors. The engravers were silversmiths or other skilled craftsmen. In *The American Way of Crime* (1980), Frank Browning and John Gerassi described one such counterfeiter:

Counterfeiting equipment and fake money seized by police in New York. The members of this counterfeiting ring passed more than $1,000,000 before they were caught. (Acme Photo Service)

The prince of colonial counterfeiters was the spry and agile Owen Sullivan, who first appeared in Boston in 1749 as a silversmith, pockets bulging with more money than his trade could have provided. He was indicted for passing false bills in 1750, the evidence drawn in part from his wife, who, on drunken binges, would pronounce him the "forty thousand pound money maker." For punishment he was taken to the pillory and given twenty lashes. Two years later he was convicted with several others in Providence of printing excellent though not quite perfect £16 Rhode Island bills. This time his ears were cropped and the letter C branded on his cheek. He escaped from his jailers a few days later, slipping through Connecticut to Dover in Dutchess County, New York. There he organized an infamous band of moneymakers who came to be called the Dover Money Club.

During the national confusion that was the Civil War, counterfeiters had a field day. In 1863,

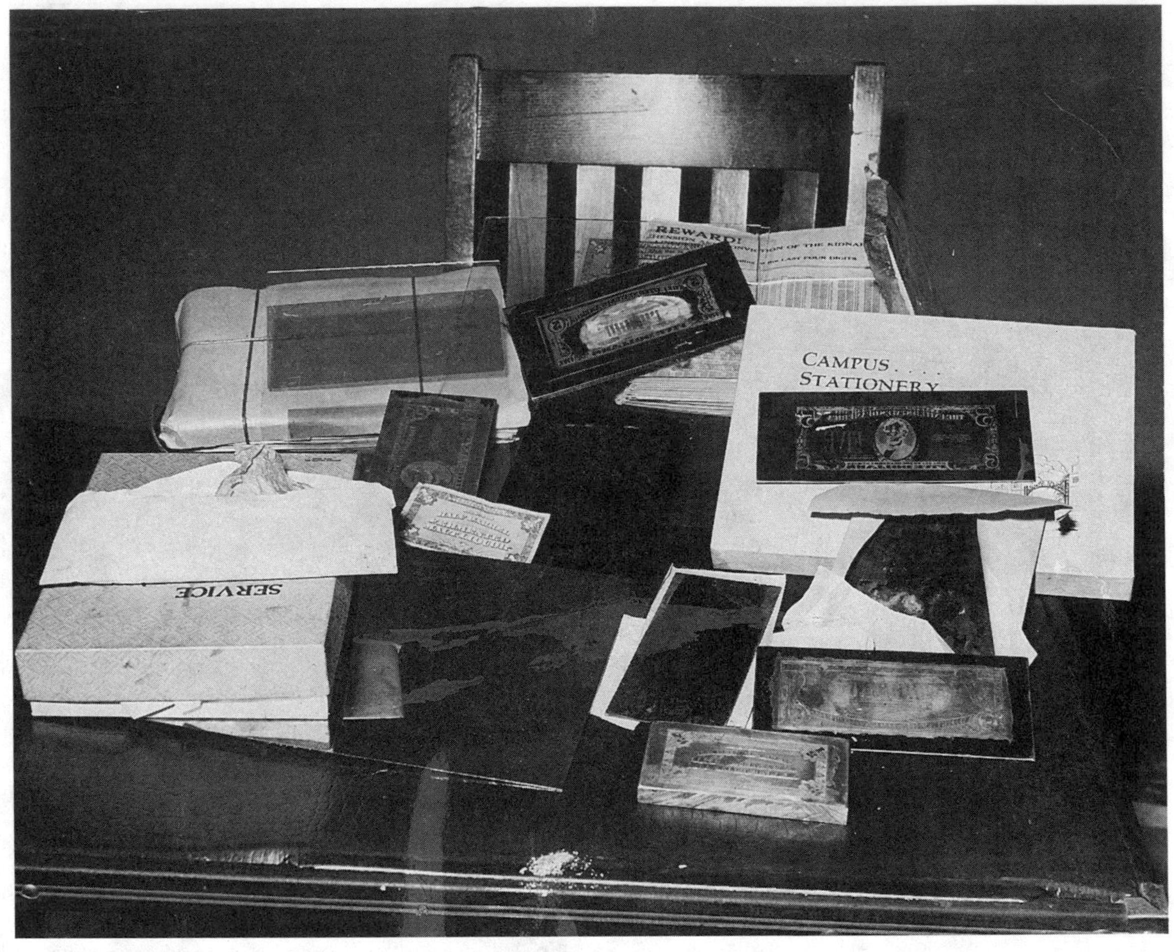

A complete outfit for printing counterfeit $5 bills, confiscated by the Secret Service in New York in 1934. (Acme Photo Service.)

the federal government issued the first national paper money to replace or at least supplement the private bank money then in use. By 1865, it was estimated that half of the paper money in circulation, both federal and bank currency, was counterfeit. WILLIAM P. WOOD, a man with a varied background in counterespionage, penology and law enforcement, was appointed the first chief of the newly formed United States SECRET SERVICE on July 5, 1865. The Solicitor of the Treasury Edward P. Jordan told Wood at his swearing-in that "the main object is to restore public confidence in the money of this country. Our policies and rules can take shape as your work progresses."

Wood and his 30-man Secret Service actively attacked the problem and the counterfeiters with such effect that within a year of his taking office over 200 counterfeiters had been arrested. Counterfeiting has never since then been a serious threat to the economy of this country. During World War II, the Nazi government set up an ambitious plan to counterfeit the money of Great Britain and the United States. They had some success with British money, enough to cause the British government to change the face of its currency as a precaution, but the war ended before any significant amount of American money was put in circulation.

With the development of the color photocopying machine, the Treasury Department's problems have multiplied. It used to require a skilled engraver or photolithographer to make a passable copy of United States currency, but no longer. With a little care, anyone can make money. The colors may not be right, but they are close enough. The Treasury is considering several options to counter this threat. A new 100-dollar bill, which incorporates several of these options, is already in circulation. A line of print so fine that a copying machine will pick it up as a solid line circles the president's picture, and a special plastic line runs down one side of the bill. Special watermarks are being considered, and in the future, we may see holographic images in our paper money. But however carefully our money is made, and whatever high-tech methods are used to protect it, someone will always attempt to counterfeit it.

See also: MISTER 880

CRATER, Joseph Force (1889–?)

THE JUDGE LEFT HIS HOUSE ONE DAY, AND JUST DISAPPEARED

A justice in the New York Supreme Court in the City of New York, Judge Joseph Force Crater created one of the country's long-standing mysteries on Wednesday, August 6, 1930, when he walked out of a restaurant on Manhattan's West 45th Street and hailed a cab. He climbed into the taxi, drove off and was never seen again.

His disappearance was kept quiet for a month, but when it was clear that he was not going to reappear, District Attorney Thomas C. T. Crain launched a search for him and a grand jury investigation into his disappearance.

Crater, a graduate of Lafayette College and Columbia Law School, had a successful New York City practice before his appointment to the bench in April 1930, some four months before his disappearance. His presidency of the Cayuga Democratic Club, an important adjunct to the city's TAMMANY HALL political machine, had certainly been a material consideration in New York State Governor Franklin D. Roosevelt's selection of Crater, but the choice was not purely political as shown by Crater's endorsement by the New York Bar Association.

Crater had cut short a vacation at his summer camp in Maine to return to the city and had spent part of Tuesday and Wednesday in his court chambers. His wife Stella, who had remained in Maine, could shed no light on the reason for Crater's return to New York, and she professed absolute bewilderment as to his disappearance. It was shown that he had withdrawn several thousand dollars from two bank accounts and sold $16,000 worth of stock shortly before he vanished. There was speculation that his disappearance was somehow connected to an investigation into corrupt city officials being conducted by State Attorney General Hamilton Ward, and the events spurred the broader Seabury investigation that followed, but no allegation of misconduct was ever brought against the absent judge.

After seeing many witnesses and taking hundreds of pages of testimony, the Crain grand jury disbanded on January 9, 1931, without discovering anything of value. Two weeks later, on the twentieth, Stella Crater announced that she had found in a desk drawer $6,690 in cash, a bundle of securities and a written list of debts owed to the absent judge. On the bottom of the list was penned a note: "Am very weary. Love, Joe."

Since the police had searched the apartment several times since the judge's disappearance, including the drawer that now held the newly discovered documents, this merely deepened the mystery. Sightings of Judge Crater were reported all over the country, and for a while, the police followed every lead. But they all came to naught. Seven years after he disappeared, he was declared legally dead, and Stella remarried, but she never gave up looking for her absent first husband.

In 1829, 101 years before Judge Crater disappeared, John Lansing, a justice of the Court of Chancery of the State of New York, left his hotel to mail a letter on the steamer for Albany. He was never seen again. It is probably no more than an interesting coincidence that Joseph Crater also served on the Court of Chancery.

CRIMINAL IDENTIFICATION

See: IDENTIFICATION OF INDIVIDUALS

CUMMINGS, Homer S. (1870–1956)

A PROSECUTING ATTORNEY WHO DID HIS JOB AS IT SHOULD BE DONE

President Franklin D. Roosevelt's first attorney general (1933–1934), Homer S. Cummings had been active in Democratic party politics for all of his professional life. He had been the keynote speaker at the 1920 Democratic National Convention in San Francisco, and chairman of the Democratic National Committee. In 1924, he was the prosecuting attorney for his home state of Connecticut and was expected to be the next governor.

In Bridgeport, Connecticut, on February 4, 1924, Father Hubert Dahme, the popular pastor of St. Joseph's Episcopal Church, was accosted on the street and killed. The city was outraged, and the police were under pressure to arrest someone for the heinous crime. They apprehended a 23-year-old drifter from Pennsylvania named Harold Israel, who was found in possession of a gun of the same caliber as the bullet that had killed Father Dahme. They took Israel into the back room of the police station and questioned him for some time, until he confessed. The gun was tested by a ballistics expert, who certified that it was the murder weapon. The police located some witnesses who had seen Israel do the killing.

This was the case that was handed to Cummings to prosecute, and no prosecutor has ever been handed a neater bundle. The public wanted a quick conviction, and the evidence was in his hand to secure one. Israel tried to retract his confession, claiming that the police had not let him sleep and that he had been exhausted, hungry and bewildered by the constant police pressure when he made it. But every defendant disowns every confession with some similar excuse. The defense attorney saw little hope for his client and planned to plead not guilty by reason of insanity.

But something about the case smelled. Cummings detected the odor of lying witnesses and became convinced that the confession had truly been coerced. To check the ballistics evidence, Cummings sent the gun and bullet out to six different ballistics experts without telling any one of them about the others. Every one of them came to the independent conclusion that the bullet that killed Father Dahme had not been fired from Israel's gun. There was also, they discovered, a mechanical flaw in the weapon.

At the trial, Cummings, in his opening statement, outlined the facts of the case as he knew them. He pointed out that because of lighting conditions, the witnesses could not have seen what they claimed to have seen; he demolished the police's ballistics expert with six experts of his own; and then he loaded Harold Israel's pistol, pointed it at the floor and pulled the trigger. The gun refused to fire. It had a defective firing pin and would not fire at the angle at which the murder weapon must have been held when Father Dahme was shot.

The judge directed that Israel be released, and Cummings personally took him to the train station. The townspeople, who wanted someone punished for Father Dahme's murder, somehow felt cheated that their prosecutor failed to prosecute, and Cummings never was elected governor. Unpopular though his actions might have been at the time, they are truly representative of the American ideal of justice.

While he was Roosevelt's attorney general, he intensified the federal efforts in the battle against JOHN DILLINGER, "PRETTY BOY" FLOYD, "MACHINE GUN" KELLY, and the other gangsters that were running wild through the country in the early 1930s, stating in a speech before the Daughters of the American Revolution, "We are now engaged in a war that threatens the safety of our country—a war with the organized forces of crime."

The story of Homer Cummings's search for the truth while a prosecuting attorney inspired the excellent 1947 film *Boomerang*, starring Dana Andrews and directed by Elia Kazan. No one was ever tried for the murder of Father Hubert Dahme.

CVETIC, Matt

Matt Cvetic, like HERBERT A. PHILBRICK, was an FBI informer within the American Communist party in the 1940s. He wrote a strident book about it called *The Big Decision* (fl. 1940s), and a movie called *I Was a Communist for the FBI* was made from his experiences.

CZOLGOSZ, Leon (1873–1901)

An unemployed worker and avowed anarchist, Leon Czolgosz stood on a receiving line at the Pan-American Exposition in Buffalo, New York, on September 6, 1901, to greet U.S. President William McKinley. When he reached the front of the line, he raised his bandage-wrapped right hand and fired two shots from the .32-caliber revolver concealed therein. One bullet bounced off a button on the president's jacket, but the other penetrated his abdomen. "I done my duty," Czolgosz yelled, as he was brought down by the guards.

McKinley clung to life for eight days, finally succumbing to gangrene of the pancreas. Bad medical treatment, even for the time, probably contributed as much to McKinley's death as had the assassin's bullet.

Except for professing his anarchist beliefs, Czolgosz stood mute at his trial. In a handwritten confession, he stated his belief that it was wrong that "one man should have so much service and another man should have none." He was electrocuted at Auburn Prison in New York on October 29. His last words were: "I killed the President because he was the enemy of the good people—the working people. I am not sorry for my crime." It is believed that his act was motivated partly by Gaetano Bresci's assassination of King Umberto of Italy near Milan a year earlier. It should be noted that even before the assassination, other anarchists regarded Czolgosz as a dangerous crank, or possibly an *agent provocateur*.

Czolgosz's act brought on a wave of anti-anarchist sentiment in this country and precipitated the arrests of noted anarchists Emma Goldman and Johann Must, among others.

D

DAHMER, Jeffrey (1960–)

HE INVITED YOUNG MEN TO HIS APARTMENT FOR BEER—AND THEN CUT OFF THEIR HEADS

At 11:25 P.M. on July 22, 1991, Tracy Edwards, a slender black man who looked younger than his 31 years, ran out onto a Milwaukee street, a pair of handcuffs dangling from his left wrist, and hysterically flagged down a passing police car. What he told the two policemen, Robert Rauth and Rolf Mueller, sounded like part of the plot of a particularly unbelievable horror novel.

Edwards had gone to the apartment of Jeffrey Dahmer, a man he had met in a bar with a bunch of his friends, believing that the friends were right behind him in another car. But the friends never showed up, and after a couple of beers, Dahmer had suddenly snapped a handcuff on Edwards's left wrist. Edwards had immediately started struggling, which prevented Dahmer from fastening his other wrist. Intent on his purpose, Dahmer's "face was completely changed," Edwards said. "I wouldn't have recognized him." Dahmer had pushed the tip of a large butcher knife against Edwards's chest and said, "You die if you don't do what I say."

After a couple of agonizing hours, during which Edwards was afraid for his life every second, he took a desperate chance and lashed out at Dahmer, knocking the wind out of him. Then he raced for the door and made it outside, where he stopped the police car.

When the two officers knocked at the door of apartment 213 of the Oxford Apartments, a calm and rational Dahmer answered. It was all a misunderstanding, he assured the officers. Merely a lovers' quarrel. The police ordered him to produce the handcuff key, and he balked. He was afraid to leave the door and let the police see inside. The officers insisted. Dahmer refused. He resisted the officers, who subdued him and put him in handcuffs. Then they looked around the apartment.

It was much worse than even Edwards had imagined. Photographs of naked men were on the walls. At a closer look, it was clear that some of them were dead. Some of the bodies had parts missing. A foul cloying stench permeated the apartment. One of the officers opened the refrigerator door, and a severed human head stared back at him from inside.

The subsequent investigation revealed a trail of murders going back to 1978, when Dahmer was 18. The apartment revealed the heads or skulls of 11 people. Body parts were found in the refrigerator, in a large barrel in the bedroom, in a kettle in the closet, and in a filing cabinet. A human heart was in the freezer.

A truly shocking story was uncovered when police found that two months before, a 14-year-old Laotian boy named Konerak Sinthasomphone had escaped from Dahmer's clutches and staggered bleeding into the street. But because he was drugged and acted incoherent and because he did not speak English very well, the policemen who investigated believed Dahmer when he told them it was just a lovers' quarrel. They did not want to get involved in a homosexual lovers' spat, and gave the boy back to Dahmer. Parts of his body were found in the apartment.

Dahmer was found guilty of 15 murders and sentenced to life imprisonment. In November 1992, the building Dahmer had lived in was razed to the ground so the neighbors could begin to forget the horrors that it held.

DALTON BROTHERS

THE LAST OF THE WESTERN OUTLAWS

Grattan "Grat" Dalton (1861–1892)
William Marion "Bill" Dalton (1863–1894)
Franklin "Frank" Dalton (1865?–1887)
Robert "Bob" Dalton (1870–1892)
Emmett Dalton (1871–1937)

Born a decade too late to be one of the famous bank robbing gangs of the Old West, such as the JAMES BROTHERS or the YOUNGER BROTHERS, the Daltons were nevertheless determined to make their mark. Legend has it that they were cousins to the Youngers, but although their mother's maiden name was indeed Younger, she was no relation to that notorious outlaw brood.

In 1884, Frank Dalton got a job as deputy marshal under the famous "Hanging Judge" ISAAC C. PARKER. Riding from Fort Smith, Arkansas, on the Oklahoma Territory border, the marshals earned their meager pay hunting the outlaws that rode into Indian Territory to evade justice elsewhere. There was a bonus of two dollars for every outlaw caught, but to balance that, the marshal had to pay to bury any man he killed trying to make an arrest. Frank was entitled to one assistant, called a "posseman," and he brought his brother Grat in to share the excitement.

In 1887, Frank was killed in a gun duel with a band of whiskey runners, who were illegally smuggling liquor to the Indians. Grat took over Frank's job as marshal and took brother Bob in as his posseman. Deciding that enforcing the law was overly dangerous and insufficiently profitable, they developed a system of extortion on the settlers making their way into Indian Territory. First, one of them would hide a bottle of whiskey in the wagon, then they would ride up, announce themselves as marshals, and search the wagon. When they found the booze, they would assess a fine for bringing illegal liquor into the territory, which the frightened settlers invariably paid.

In 1888, the Osage Indians, who were suffering from an influx of outlaws in their territory, asked the Federal District Court in Wichita, Kansas, to send them an experienced man to help them organize a police force and be its head. Bob Dalton applied for the job and was appointed. He made brother Emmett his assistant. After things got organized, he added his brother Grat to the ménage. For a while, the Daltons had an interesting triple play in operation: marshals under Judge Parker, chiefs of a tribal police force and heads of the largest horse-stealing ring in the territory. When that situation fell apart, the brothers headed for California, where Bill and Grat were caught robbing a train in 1891 and sentenced to 25 years in prison. Grat escaped and, with his remaining brothers, made it back to Oklahoma.

The Daltons now formed a gang and began robbing banks throughout the Midwest. For a while they did nothing noteworthy, but they were building up for the one great score that would make them rich and put their names in the bank robbers' hall of fame. What they conceived of became known as the Great Coffeyville Raid.

The town of Coffeyville, Kansas, had two banks, the First National Bank and the Condon & Company Bank, across the street from each other. Nobody had ever robbed two banks in the same town on the same day before.[1]

On October 5, 1892, Bob, Emmett and Grat Dalton, along with Dick Broadwell and Bill Powers, rode down Eight Street into downtown Coffeyville. The Daltons, who had grown up in the area, wore false beards so that they would not be recognized. But the beards were so patently false that people turned to watch them as they rode past. The hitching posts in front of the banks had

[1] This feat would not be tried again until March 27, 1915, when Henry Starr brought a band of five men into Stroud, Oklahoma. The Starr gang was caught by a posse on their way out of town.

The Dalton Brothers—Bill, Bob, Grat, and Emmett. (Collection of the author.)

been removed for street repairs, so the gang had to leave their horses in an alley about a block away. It would later be called Death Alley. Bob and Emmett took the First National Bank, while Grat, Dick and Bill entered the Condon & Company building. There was no attempt at finesse; instead, they did their best to intimidate the bank tellers and customers into obedience. The bank employees complied, but the town's citizens did not. As word spread that the banks were being robbed, the townspeople picked up weapons and headed toward the banks.

The robbers were still in the banks when the shooting started. Bob and Emmett made it out the back door of the First National and headed for the alley and their horses. They shot and killed several people on their way, but they made it. Grat, Powers and Broadwell were not so lucky. The cashier of the Condon & Company bank, who had known the Daltons as children and had little respect for Grat's intelligence, had told him the vault was locked by a time lock, and that the bank had no back door, which was not true. So when the shooting started, Grat and his compatriots had to race out the front door with only the $1,000 in cash that the tellers turned over. Bob and Emmett had to go back to try to help their brother.

When the smoke cleared, four townsmen, including Charlie Connelly, the town marshal, were dead, as were four of the five robbers. Only Emmett Dalton survived. He would have gotten away, but he went back to help his brother Bob when he was hit. Emmett was hit by a blast from a shotgun as he tried to put Bob on his horse, but he lived. He was tried and sentenced to life in the Kansas State Penitentiary.

In 1895 Bill Dalton was killed by lawmen in Oklahoma Territory.

In 1907 Emmett Dalton was released from prison and moved to California, where he became a movie scriptwriter, as well as appearing in bit parts in silent westerns.

DARROW, Clarence Seward (1857–1938)

THE MOST FAMOUS DEFENSE ATTORNEY OF OUR CENTURY

The most famous defense attorney in the first half of the twentieth century, Clarence Darrow earned his reputation not only for his ability to win his cases, but for his compassion for the underdog and his passionate belief in justice tempered by mercy. In 1894, when Darrow had been practicing for 16 years, he handled the appeal of Robert Prendergast, a convicted murderer. Darrow lost the appeal, and Prendergast was executed. As a result, Darrow developed a horror of capital punishment, and he vowed to never lose another client to the hangman. In representing over 50 clients accused of capital crimes, Darrow kept his vow.

Darrow began his career as a corporation lawyer, working for the big trusts. But his dislike of his clients grew to the point that he switched sides and took on the defense of socialist labor agitators when this was not a popular thing to do. In 1894, he took on the defense of socialist leader Eugene V. Debs during the Pullman strike. He won the case, and Debs went on to run for president five times as leader of the Social Democratic party. In 1907, Big Bill Haywood, leader of the International Workers of the World (IWW), was indicted for the murder of former Idaho Governor Frank Stenuenberg, in a guilt-by-association trial. Stenuenberg had been killed by a bomb planted on his porch, and Harry Orchard, the admitted murderer, an IWW thug, claimed that Haywood made him do it. Darrow took up Haywood's defense, and succeeded in having him acquitted.

Darrow always saw his cases in their larger context, and he tried to make juries share his view. Toward the end of his eleven-hour summation in the Haywood case, as taken from the court record, he told them:

> The eyes of the world are upon you—upon you twelve men of Idaho tonight. If you should decree Bill Haywood's death, in the railroad offices of our great cities men will applaud your names. If you decree his death, amongst the spiders of Wall Street will go up paeans of praise for these twelve good men and true. In every bank in the world, where men hate Haywood because he fights for the poor and against that accursed system upon which the favored live and grow rich and fat—from all those you will receive blessings and unstinted praise.

> But if your verdict should be "Not Guilty" in this case, there are still those who will reverently bow their heads and thank these twelve men for the life and reputation you have saved. Out on our broad prairies where men toil with their hands, out on the wide ocean where men are tossed and buffeted on the waves, through our mills and factories, and down deep under the earth, thousands of men, and of women and children will kneel tonight and ask their God to guide your hearts—these men and women and these little children, the poor, the weak, and the suffering of the world, are stretching out their helpless hands to this jury in mute appeal for Bill Haywood's life.

In a 1910 labor dispute, James and John McNamara were charged with murder after the bombing of the *Los Angeles Times* building. Darrow agreed to defend them and then found out that they were guilty and the prosecution could prove it. To save their lives, to him the overriding consideration, he pled them guilty. The union leaders, incensed that Darrow had not fought the case, refused to pay him his $50,000 fee. Darrow, who saw that they were more interested in a *cause célèbre*, even if the defendants were hanged, refused to ever take a labor case again. To compound his zeal over this case, *Times* owner Harrison Gray Otis, a rabid antiunionist, had Darrow indicted for jury tampering. Darrow beat the charge despite Otis's overpowering influence in the city. From then on he concentrated on criminal cases.

In 1924, when Darrow was 67 years old, he participated in his most famous capital trial, the LEOPOLD AND LOEB CASE. Nathan Leopold, 18, and Richard Loeb, 19, were accused of the thrill murder of Bobby Franks, 14. They had committed the crime, and the evidence against them was overwhelming. The case was already being called the "Crime of the Century" before it came to trial, and the Chicago press had sensationalized it into the crime of the millennium. There are times when 12 men constitute not a jury but a mob, and Darrow believed that this was one of them. He pled Leopold and Loeb guilty, to put the burden of sentencing them completely on the judge. He hoped to spare them the death penalty; he judged that he could do no more. He assumed that one man, in a profession that valued law, logic and rationality above all, might be more willing to go against public opinion than 12 members of that public. But, as quoted in Maureen McKernan's *The Amazing Crime and Trial of Leopold and Loeb*

Clarence Darrow, champion of the underdog and violent opponent of the death penalty, is still regarded as the greatest trial lawyer of this century. (Collection of the author.)

(1957), he was no less eloquent in addressing the one judge than he had been in the past in addressing a jury of 12:

> I have never yet tried a case where the State's Attorney did not say it was the most cold-blooded, inexcusable, premeditated case that ever occurred. If it was murder there never was such a murder. If it was robbery there never was such a robbery. If it was conspiracy it was the most terrible conspiracy that ever happened since the star chamber passed into oblivion. If it was larceny there never was such a larceny. . . .
>
> What about the matter of crime and punishment, anyway? I may know less than the rest, but I have at least tried to find out and I am fairly familiar with the best literature that has been written on that subject in the last hundred years. The more men study the more they doubt the effect of severe punishment on crime. And yet Mr. Savage [the State's Attorney] tells this court that if these boys are hanged there will be no more murder. Mr. Savage is an optimist. . . .
>
> I am not pleading so much for these boys as I am for infinite numbers of others who will follow, those who perhaps cannot be as well defended as they have been, those who may go down in the storm and the tempest without aid. It is of them I am thinking, and for them I am begging of this court not to turn backward toward the barbarous and cruel past. . . .
>
> I am pleading for the future. . . . Only pleading for a time when hatred and cruelty will not control the hearts of men.

Whether convinced by Darrow's eloquence or his logic, the judge sentenced the two teenage defendants to life in prison without possibility of parole. Darrow had once again cheated the hangman.

In 1925, John T. Scopes, a Dayton, Tennessee, schoolteacher, was accused of teaching Charles Darwin's theory of evolution, the propagation of which was illegal in Tennessee. It was, as H. L. Mencken put it, "a part of the world where you couldn't throw an egg out of a pullman car window without hitting a fundamentalist." The Tennessee Legislature had passed a bill making it unlawful "to teach any theory that denies the story of Divine creation of man as taught by the Bible, and to teach instead that man has descended from a lower order of animals." Scopes violated the law, and Scopes was brought to trial. The American Civil Liberties Union, feeling that it was not a religious but a First Amendment issue, brought in Clarence Darrow, among others, to defend Scopes. The World's Christian Fundamental Association felt that this was an assault upon Scripture and brought in William Jennings Bryan, three-time Democratic candidate for president of the United States and Woodrow Wilson's Secretary of State, to lead the prosecution. The trial became a verbal duel between Darrow and Bryan, who at one time agreed to take the stand to defend the Bible as the revealed Word of God. An excerpt of the duel from the published court record:

Darrow: Do you claim that everything in the Bible should be literally interpreted?

Bryan: I believe everything in the Bible should be accepted as it is given there; some of the Bible is given illustratively. For instance: "Ye are the salt of the earth." I would not insist that man was actually salt, or that he had flesh of salt, but it is used in the sense of salt as saving God's people.

Darrow: But when you read that Jonah swallowed the whale—or that the whale swallowed Jonah, excuse me, please—how do you literally interpret that?

Bryan: When I read that a big fish swallowed Jonah—it does not say whale.

Darrow: You don't know whether it was the ordinary mine-run of fish or made for that purpose?

Bryan: You may guess. You evolutionists guess.

Darrow: The Bible says Joshua commanded the

sun to stand still for the purpose of lengthening the day, doesn't it, and you believe it?

Bryan: I do.

Darrow: Have you any opinion as to whether whoever wrote the book, I believe it was Joshua—the Book of Joshua—thought the sun went around the earth or not?

Bryan: I believe that he was inspired.

They went on to discuss the Tower of Babel, the number of languages spoken on earth, the age of the glaciers and were interrupted by a prosecuting attorney, who asked the purpose of the questions.

Bryan: The purpose is to cast ridicule on everybody who believes in the Bible, and I am perfectly willing that the whole world shall know that these gentlemen have no other purpose than ridiculing every person who believes in the Bible.

Darrow: We have the purpose of preventing bigots and ignoramuses from controlling the education of the United States, and you know it, and that is all.

The questioning went on, Darrow asking and Bryan stating that he believed in Adam and Eve, that Eve was created from Adam's rib, that Eve was tempted by a serpent, that God kicked Adam and Eve out of Heaven, and punished women by making them give birth in pain.

Darrow and Bryan received more nationwide newspaper space during that trial than at any other time in their careers, the slant of the coverage depending on the geographic location and political leaning of the paper. In the end, Darrow made Bryan look foolish, but Scopes lost his case. He was fined $100, but the conviction was overturned by the Tennessee Court of Appeal.

Darrow was the author of, among other writings, *Crime: Its Cause and Treatment* (1922) and *The Story of My Life* (1932). He was a confirmed pessimist and agnostic, but a man of great bravery and compassion.

DEATH PENALTY

See: CAPITAL PUNISHMENT

DEFECATION

It has long been noted that a preculiarity of many burglars—particularly safecrackers, second-story men and those who burglarize fur vaults or other places of difficult access—often leave behind a memento in the form of a pile of defecation on the floor. Many policemen, in writing of this in their memoirs, cite it as an example of the burglar's disrespect for authority. Some psychiatrists have epoused the theory that the burglar is subconsciously offering a gift in return for what he is taking—an act that goes back to his relationship with his mother during early toilet training.

Irving Gold, a detective on the New York City Police Force, has offered an alternate explanation, pointing out that the burglar has to spend many hours, often all night, in opening the safe or drilling through the vault wall, and there are often no toilet facilities accessible to the burglar. He is not going to increase the risk in his already risky profession by going two floors down and to the other side of the building to use a bathroom.

DEGNAN, Suzanne

See: WILLIAM HEIRENS

DESALVO, Albert Henry (1931–1973)

"THE BOSTON STRANGLER," A MASS MURDERER WHO KEPT A CITY IN TERROR

Before he attained the peak of notoriety as the "Boston Strangler," Albert DeSalvo worked his way up a mountain of sex crimes, pausing at various plateaus long enough to interest the police before moving along a different path to his next set of crimes. Unfortunately for law enforcement, Albert was a true heterosexual polymorphous pervert; that is, while his aberrant and criminal sexuality focused on women, his pattern was constantly changing, making it difficult for the police to link all his crimes to the same man. It was not until Albert's eventual confession that the police realized that "the Measuring Man," "The Green Man," and "the Boston Strangler" were all the same person. Even then he had to work hard to convince them he was telling the truth.

Coming from that Republican ideal, a two-parent home, Albert DeSalvo had a violently abusive father who beat his young wife and six children regularly and severely with his fists and a studded leather belt. When Albert was sent to the Lyman School for Delinquent Boys at 13, he regarded his stay as a welcome respite from his home life. Albert grew up to become a tall and powerful young man, and he joined the army when he was 17. He was sent to Europe where he served in a tank outfit and boxed in the army's sports program, winning the middleweight boxing championship for Europe. When he was 20, he married a German woman named Irmgard and brought her back to the States with him. It was in 1955, while he was stationed at Fort Dix, New Jersey, that he was first reportedly involved in a sex crime. He reputedly touched a nine-year-old girl sexually while alone in a room with her. But her mother chose not to press charges, so the case was dropped.

DeSalvo was honorably discharged from the army in 1956, after which he moved back to the Boston area and took a variety of blue-collar jobs. He began a pattern of breaking into houses to steal what he found, usually small amounts of money. By 1959, he had a police record for numerous minor cases of B&E (breaking and entering). By now he and his wife had two children, a six-year-old girl who had been born with a bone disorder, and a one-year-old son.

In 1960, a new sort of sex criminal appeared in the Boston area. An innocent-looking, smooth-talking con man would knock on doors and tell the women who answered that he represented a modeling agency and that they had been recommended as models. "You can make as much as forty dollars an hour," he told them, and then when they acquiesced (or were merely too bewildered to respond), he would whip out a tape measure and take their measurements. By the time they realized that he was touching them intimately rather more than was necessary, he was finished and out the door. When DeSalvo talked about this later he said that the women who complained were only a small percentage of the women he accosted. Most let him take the measurements without complaint. Some removed their garments so that his measuring would be "more accurate." Some, he claimed, happily hopped into bed with him.

On March 17, 1961, the "Measuring Man" was arrested by the Boston police. DeSalvo was diagnosed as a sociopathic personality after a series of tests at the Westborough State Hospital, but the diagnosis fell short of legal insanity. He stood trial for assault and battery on some of the women he had measured and was sentenced to two years in the Middlesex County House of Correction. The authorities could not seem to decide whether his "Measuring Man" antics were merely a strange but comparatively harmless aberration, or whether they masked something more serious. But the something more serious they envisioned was burglary, not sex crimes. They feared that his posing as a modeling agent was merely an excuse to case apartments so he could come back later and burglarize them. Unfortunately their suspicions were misplaced. DeSalvo's sentence was reduced by the judge when he tearfully promised to reform, and the parole board was similarly lenient. By April 1962, DeSalvo was back on the streets again.

On Thursday, June 14, 1962, Juris Slesers went to pick up his 55-year-old mother Anna at her apartment on Gainsborough Street in Boston to take her to a memorial service at the Latvian Lutheran Church in Roxbury. When she did not answer the bell, he became alarmed and broke the door down. His mother was lying on the floor next to the bathroom, her blue housecoat spread apart below the shoulders rudely exposing her body, her legs spread grotesquely apart, the belt of the housecoat wrapped around her neck and tied with a peculiar knot. She had been strangled to death. The first policeman on the scene thought the death was a suicide, but he was soon disabused of this notion.

Two weeks later, on Saturday, June 30, Mrs. Marguerite Steadman, who lived with her attorney husband in a Boston suburb, was talking on the phone to her sister, 68-year-old Nina Nichols, when Nina interrupted the call. "There's my buzzer," she said. "I'll call you right back." Nina, who lived on Commonwealth Avenue in Boston, failed to call back. Marguerite's husband Charles called Nina's number, and received no answer. But Nina was supposed to be having dinner with them that evening. Perhaps she had merely forgotten to call and was even now on her way. By seven-thirty, when Nina had neither called nor arrived, Charles Steadman called Thomas Bruce, the building superintendent in Nina's building, and asked him to look outside and see if Nina's car was still in the parking lot. It was. Bruce went upstairs with his key to see if Mrs. Nichols perhaps needed help.

The body of Nina Nichols was lying on a hooked rug on the bedroom floor, naked from the waist down, her thin housecoat and slip pulled up to her shoulders. A pair of her nylon stockings had been twisted around her throat, pulled cruelly tight and knotted under her chin. There were signs that Mrs. Nichols had been criminally molested.

The apartment had been ransacked and belongings thrown all over, but nothing of importance seemed to have been taken. An expensive camera stood in plain sight and a drawer had been pulled open, exposing some valuable silver, which had not been touched. Boston detectives had a riddle on their hands, and every fact they unearthed just deepened the riddle. What had the killer been looking for in such a frenzy? Who had Nina Nichols admitted to her apartment while clad only in a flimsy pink housedress? Was it someone she knew?

On Monday, July 2, the body of 65-year-old Helen Blake was found in her apartment in Lynn, Massachusetts, a town close enough to Boston to be considered a suburb. With the exception that Helen was facedown on her bed, the pattern resembled that of the earlier killings. Her clothes had been pushed up around her shoulders, a nylon stocking had been tightened deeply around her neck and knotted. Her cotton brassiere was tied in a bow around her neck below the stocking. The apartment had been ransacked, all of her possessions pulled out and examined and nothing taken.

Boston Police Commissioner Edmund McNamara, a former FBI agent who had been on the job for about three months, was holding a conference on the first two murders when he was informed of the third. "Oh, God, we've got a madman loose!" was his heartfelt reaction.

The situation warranted his response. Forensic investigation showed that Helen Blake had been killed on the morning of Saturday, June 30, some hours before Nina Nichols. The killer, whoever he was, had murdered two women on the same day!

In the coming months, McNamara's feeling of frustration and Boston's anger and fear would only intensify. As Gerold Frank put it in his book, *The Boston Strangler* (1986):

> Boston could not know that these stranglings, each more bizarre than the one before, would give rise to the greatest manhunt in the history of modern crime, using every technique of detection, natural and supernatural: computers, clairvoyants, "sensitives," men and women claiming ESP powers, psychiatrists armed with hypnotic drugs, hallucinating agents and truth serums, specialists in anthropology, graphology, forensic law. Here was a city laid siege to by a killer whose insanity was equalled by his cunning, who apparently could materialize within locked apartments and not only kill but do fearful things to the women he killed—without leaving a clue.

Commissioner McNamara assigned every detective in his department to the homicide squad and asked the FBI to send a sex crimes expert to lecture 50 of his picked men. For two weeks, the detectives questioned neighbors of the victims, pulled in every known sex offender for questioning and followed every clue, however slight. A special phone number, DE 8-1212, was set up by the police to take phone calls from anyone who thought he or she could help. People were encouraged to call and did: women who were convinced that their boyfriends were the Strangler; women who had been followed home for years; women who saw men peeping in their windows; people who heard strange noises in the night; people who had neighbors with strange habits; people who had seen the Strangler in their dreams. And every call that made any sense at all was followed up.

On Tuesday, August 21, 75-year-old Ida Irga, a short, docile, patient woman, widowed for the past 30 years, was found murdered in her Grove Street apartment. She had been manually strangled and then a pillowcase had been wrapped around her neck. She had been sexually molested. Her corpse had been arranged, legs spread and propped on chairs, to expose her intimately to whoever came through the door.

On Thursday, August 30, 67-year-old Jane Sullivan, a nurse who worked the night shift at Longwood Hospital, was found murdered in her Dorchester apartment, across Boston from Ida Irga. She had been dead for about 10 days, which put her murder within a day or so of Ida Irga's death. After death, she had been taken into the bathroom and placed in the bathtub in an obscenely exposed position. Someone had methodically searched the apartment, but nothing had been taken.

For the next three months, there were no further killings that could be attributed to the Strangler, but the fear and hysteria in Boston, particularly among elderly women, remained.

Then, the Boston Strangler struck again. This time his victim was a 20-year-old black girl, a student at the Carnegie Institute of Medical Technology. Sophie Clark was alone in the apartment she shared with two other girls on Wednesday, December 5, 1962, when sometime between 2:30 P.M., as she was writing a letter, and 5:30 P.M., when one of her roommates found her body, a man entered and strangled her with her own stockings. She had been sexually assaulted, and there were signs that she had tried to fight the assailant off. Her body was rudely exposed as the others had been, and the apartment had been searched.

A downstairs neighbor reported that a man had rung her bell and told her that the landlord had sent him to paint the apartment. When the man suddenly started complimenting her on her figure, the woman got frightened. She put her finger to her lips and told him to be quiet or he would wake her husband. The man fled. It was not until some time later that she and the police realized that she had briefly entertained the Boston Strangler.

On December 31, 1962, 23-year-old secretary Patricia Bissette was found dead in her Back Bay apartment. She had been strangled with her own stockings and had recently had sexual intercourse, whether willingly or unwillingly the medical examiner could not say.

The Strangler had now picked victims from 20 to 75 years old, scattered all over Boston. They had all been alone in their apartments and had all apparently willingly let a stranger into their homes. It must have been someone that they trusted who turned on them. The fear in Boston ran deep as the city entered the new year.

Four months passed. Then on May 6, 1963, the lifeless body of 23-year-old Beverly Samans was found by her boyfriend in her apartment on University Road in Cambridge. She had been stabbed and strangled, the stab wounds forming a bizarre bull's-eye pattern centered on her left breast. As with the others, her body had been obscenely arranged to offend and horrify the eye of whoever entered the apartment. For a while detectives allowed themselves to be sidetracked by the possibility that her death was unrelated to the others, despite its apparent similarity. Samans had been doing research in the netherworld of sexual aberration, working on her master's thesis: "Factors Pertaining to the Etiology of Male Homosexuality." But the similarities to the other killings were overwhelming, and the police were forced to add Beverly Samans's name to the list of Strangler victims.

On September 8, Evelyn Corbin, a 58-year-old divorcee who looked much younger, was strangled to death in her Lafayette Street apartment. On November 23, the day after President John Kennedy was assassinated in Dallas, 23-year-old Joann Graff was murdered in her Essex Street apartment in Lawrence, Massachusetts.

On January 4, 1964, the Strangler killed his eleventh victim, in a horrible self-parody of the preceding ten. Nineteen-year-old Mary Sullivan was found in her Charles Street apartment by her two roommates. She had been strangled and propped up on her bed, her knees up, legs spread, her back against the headboard, her body from the breasts down exposed, and a broom handle had been inserted in her vagina. A stocking was wrapped around her neck, and two scarves were wrapped over that, one of them tied in a flowery bow. There were seminal stains on the blanket, and a viscous liquid dripped from her mouth. Resting against her left foot was a New Year's card, with the gaily colored words "Happy New Year" facing out.

Within two weeks Commonwealth Attorney General Edward W. Brooke, Jr. had personally taken over the Boston Strangler investigation. Squads of detectives examined all available evidence. A team of psychiatrists analyzed the apparent behavior of the killer and agonized over its decisions. The Strangler had started by killing only elderly women. Did he have a mother fixation? If so, why did he switch to young women? Were all the murders really the work of one man, or were there one or more copycat killers? Could he be captured by some clever trick? Could he be made to turn himself in by some clever appeal? Could he be stopped before he killed again?

Months passed and there were no more killings. But the police were no closer to catching the Strangler. Suspects were picked up, held, questioned, examined and released. Mystics and seers, including noted Dutch psychic Pieter Cornelis van der Hurk, better known as Peter Hurkos, volunteered their assistance, and the authorities were at the point where they would listen to anyone, no matter how firmly they had to thrust their tongues into their cheeks. The psychics contributed little beyond a certain amount of entertainment for the weary detectives and news copy for the reporters. Hurkos later claimed to have aided substantially in the solution, but Boston Detective Phil DeNatale, who worked with him, said categorically for a *Detroit Free Press* article that this was not so.

At 9:30 A.M. on October 27, 1964, 10 months after the last Strangler killing, Albert DeSalvo entered the apartment of a 20-year-old coed whose husband of a few months had just left for work. The young woman was still in bed. "Don't be afraid," DeSalvo told her, approaching the bed, "I'm a detective." He tied her to the bed, gagged her with her own underwear, and kissed and fondled her for some time. "Don't look at me," he told her, over and over again. But she could not help looking. Then he got up, untied her and left, telling her to be quiet for 10 minutes and adding "I'm sorry," just as he went out the door.

A police artist made a sketch based on her description, and Cambridge Detective Paul Cloran recognized it as the "Measuring Man." DeSalvo voluntarily came down to the Cambridge police station and insisted that he was innocent, even though the girl identified him. The police put his photograph on the teletype, which brought a cluster of Connecticut detectives. DeSalvo was identified as the man the Connecticut police were calling the "Green Man," for his habit of wearing green pants when he went in to burglarize houses and rape women. He was suspected of being responsible for hundreds of assaults in the Connecticut area, including four in four different towns on the same day. Despite the volume of complaints

Thomas E. Dewey was elected governor of New York and ran for president on the basis of his crime-busting successes. (Acme Photo Service.)

against the "Green Man," the police never suspected that he could also be the Strangler. After talking to his wife, DeSalvo broke down and confessed to the crimes, even telling them about some they had no record of. He had committed forcible rape in Massachusetts, Connecticut, New Hampshire, and Rhode Island. But, he insisted, he had never hurt anyone.

On February 4, 1965, after an extensive psychiatric evaluation, DeSalvo was committed to Bridgewater State Hospital "until further order of the court." While there, at the urging of his attorney, he confessed to the Boston Strangler crimes. At first, the authorities had a difficult time believing him; after all, many people had confessed over the past two years. But DeSalvo proved to have an almost eidetic memory, and as he recounted detail after detail that nobody but the killer and the police could know, he gradually convinced the Massachusetts Attorney General's office that he was, indeed, the Boston Strangler.

Confined in the Walpole State Prison, DeSalvo was stabbed to death by a fellow inmate in 1973.

DEWEY, Thomas E(dmund) (1902–1971)

NEW YORK'S FIGHTING DISTRICT ATTORNEY

On July 29, 1935, Herbert A. Lehman, Republican governor of New York State, at the urging of Fiorello La Guardia, reform mayor of New York City, appointed Wall Street lawyer Thomas E. Dewey as special prosecutor to combat the wave of ORGANIZED CRIME that was swamping the justice system in New York. Technically, Dewey was under the control of William Copeland Dodge, New York City's district attorney, but as Dodge was known to be controlled by TAMMANY HALL, Lehman and La Guardia made it clear that Dodge was to keep his hands off or find himself on the wrong side of the investigation.

Dewey devised the strategy of working his way up the hierarchy of racketeers, developing cases against the low-level hoodlums and then offering them plea bargains if they would testify against their bosses. By the time he was ready to tackle DUTCH SCHULTZ, beer baron and policy boss of the city, he had the organized crime bosses thoroughly alarmed. The Commission, the self-appointed bosses of organized crime, met in executive session to decide what to do about Dewey.

CHARLES "LUCKY" LUCIANO and MEYER LANSKY argued that they should close down some of their activities, maintain a low profile, concentrate on areas away from New York City and wait for Dewey's investigation to pass, as all things must. They had weathered investigations and investigators before, although none as adamant and unyielding as Dewey. It was bad policy, they felt, to kill lawmen, newspapermen or special investigators. Dutch Schultz disagreed, feeling that Dewey must be killed. And if nobody else would do it, the Dutchman would do it himself. When the Commission found out that Schultz had actually begun an operation against Dewey, they decided that Schultz must be hit first. On October 23, 1935, he and a couple of associates, including OTTO "ABBADABBA" BERMAN, were gunned down in the rear of a Newark, New Jersey, restaurant.

With Schultz out of the way, Dewey turned his legal gunsights on Lucky Luciano, who ironically had been one of the men who had saved his life. On May 11, 1936, he brought Luciano and a dozen of his associates to trial. He had wanted to get Luciano for industrial racketeering but had trouble finding businessmen who were brave enough to testify, so he had to be satisfied with going after Luciano for one of his other illegal enterprises. Fortunately, the victims of this undertaking were eager to testify, once they'd been granted immunity and a measure of physical safety.

"Frankly," Dewey told the jury, "my witnesses are prostitutes, madams, pimps, and ex-convicts. . . . I wish to call to your attention that these are the only witnesses we could possibly have brought here. We can't get bishops to testify in a case involving prostitution."

The trial was a circus: the first in a series of courtroom carnivals with Tom Dewey as ringmaster. The testimony was always colorful, frequently lurid and occasionally unprintable. The wood-paneled walls of Superior Courtroom Two rang with names like Jenny the Factory, Sadie the Chink, Frisco Jean, Nigger Ruth, Gashouse Lil, and Cokey Flo. New York City was enthralled, and Dewey's name became a household word. On June 7, 1935, the jury found Luciano guilty on 61 counts of compulsory prostitution (what used to be called WHITE SLAVERY).

Dewey ran for district attorney of New York City in 1937 and easily won. He then went after the remains of the Dutch Schultz organization and followed the trail leading from Schultz associates George Weinberg and mob lawyer Dixie Davis to Jimmie Hines. Known as "The Honest Blacksmith," Hines was a Tammany Hall functionary whom Dewey originally thought of as the Dutchman's bag man. As the case unfolded, it became clear that Hines was more like Schultz's partner, or maybe even his boss. Dewey tried him twice, the first time resulted in a mistrial, and finally secured a conviction. He then went on to run for governor of New York, winning that election during his second campaign. Dewey then ran for president twice, losing the first time to Franklin D. Roosevelt and the second time to Harry S. Truman. The contest against Truman was so close that several newspapers declared Dewey the winner before the final tally was in. It has been speculated that columnist Dorothy Kilgallen's comment that Dewey "looked like the little man on top of the wedding cake" may well have cost him the election.

DIAMOND, Jack "Legs" (1896–1931)

MOBSTER AND MURDERER WHO SUFFERED FROM THE DELUSION THAT HE WAS IMMORTAL

Born John T. Noland, Jack Diamond grew up in New York and started stealing when he was a teenager. A slender, handsome youth with cold eyes, he got his nickname from his ability to outrun anyone chasing him. In 1919, when he was released from the Disciplinary Barracks at Leavenworth, where he had been sent for deserting the army and stealing company funds, he began working for ARNOLD ROTHSTEIN as a muscle man. Two years later, with Rothstein's blessings and financing, Jack Diamond and his brother Eddie (who had also dropped the Noland last name, calling himself Eddie Diamond) organized a gang to prey on the unorganized rumrunners and bootleggers that were propagating like mayflies. During this period, Jack was arrested over a dozen times for various minor crimes, usually burglarizing stores, and released within a day or two for lack of evidence, or with the connivance of a judge in Rothstein's pocket. This began the legend that no jail could hold him.

On October 15, 1927, major New York racketeer Little Augie Orgen (Orgenstein) and Diamond, who was acting as his bodyguard, were ambushed in a New York City street by LOUIS "LEPKE" BUCHALTER, Jacob "Gurrah" Shapiro and Hyman "Little Hymie" Bernstein, in a dispute over territory. Little Augie died, but Diamond survived. This was the second time he had survived a determined attempt to kill him. Thus began the second half of the Legs Diamond legend: that he could not be killed.

When Diamond recovered, he made peace with Buchalter and the others, assuring them that he did not hold a grudge, and went on with his bootlegging operations. By this time, he controlled a substantial part of the Manhattan booze distribution. Diamond opened a nightclub, the "Hotsy Totsy Club," on Broadway and 54th Street, and it became a favorite watering hole for the gangster element, which made up a substantial part of New York's night life.

In 1929, Diamond became arrogantly overconfident. He and his henchman Charles Entratta shot a gangster named Red Cassidy to death right at the bar of the Hotsy Totsy Club, in full view of a cluster of witnesses. Diamond and Entratta went into hiding while, one by one, four of the witnesses, including the club's bartender, were eliminated. Another four disappeared, whereupon Diamond and Entratta resurfaced. The police, with no witnesses, were powerless to arrest Diamond, no matter how sure they were that he was responsible for the crimes.

In time, his control over the liquor distribution in Manhattan was disputed by beer baron DUTCH SCHULTZ who didn't like anyone having anything he didn't have. Schultz used Diamond's absence while avoiding the murder charge to move in on Diamond's operation. Diamond and his mob resisted, and a small-scale gang war broke out in Manhattan. Twice Schultz's hoodlums caught up with Diamond and filled him full of slugs. Both times he made remarkable recoveries, adding to the legend of his invincibility. But Schultz apparently was not superstitious. On December 18, 1931, Schultz's gunmen caught up with Diamond in an Albany, New York, rooming house and shot him three times in the head, disproving the legend that he could not be killed. On June 30, 1933, Diamond's widow, Alice, who had been threatening to talk (although nobody knew about what), was found dead in her Brooklyn apartment, shot through the head.

DILLINGER, John Herbert (1903–1934)

HE ROBBED BANKS AND BROKE OUT OF JAILS TO BECOME AN AMERICAN LEGEND

Son of an Indianapolis grocer who raised him with a combination of neglect and abuse, John Dillinger achieved the status of public enemy number one, before he was gunned down by the FBI while coming out of a Chicago movie house. It was during the last year of his life that what became known as the Dillinger mob, in which he was first among equals, caught the public imagination.

Many of the bank robbers of the Depression years attained a sort of Robin Hood status:

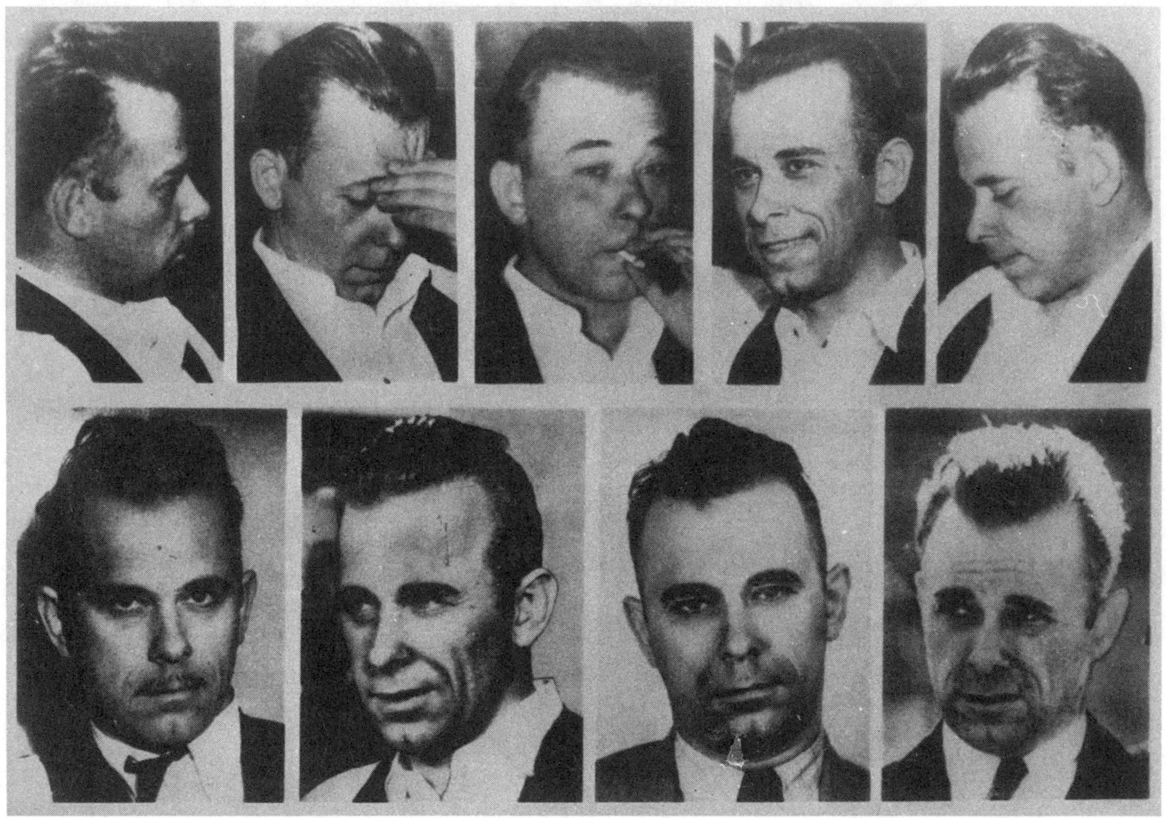

John Dillinger, who learned bank-robbing at the hands of a Prussian expert and whose exploits made him a popular hero. (Federal Bureau of Investigation.)

BONNIE AND CLYDE, "PRETTY BOY" FLOYD and WILLIE "THE ACTOR" SUTTON were among the heroes of the day. But John Dillinger, like Jesse James before him, captured the public's imagination, particularly in the poverty belt of the Midwest and West. Dillinger had class. He leapt over the rail of a bank like Douglas Fairbanks leaping over the rail of a pirate ship. He was chivalrous toward women. He thumbed his nose at the authorities. No police could catch him and no jail could hold him. Or so was the popular perception.

Dillinger committed his first crime of any importance when he was 21. He fell in with Ed Singleton, an older and wiser crook, and the pair attempted to rob a grocer as he walked home with the day's receipts. Dillinger's gun went off accidentally in a struggle with the grocer and, thinking that he had shot the man, Dillinger ran back to where Singleton was supposed to be waiting with the car. The older and wiser crook had fled, leaving Dillinger to escape as best he could.

Two days later, Dillinger was arrested at home and taken to the Martinsville, Indiana, jail. His father came and convinced him to confess, and he broke down and told the whole story to the prosecutor. His partner, who knew the system, drew a

LEAVE THIS SPACE BLANK

Name John Dillinger (Dead)
Alias
Class. O 32 W 1 R O / O 32 W 1 I M I
No. Color Sex Ref.

RIGHT HAND

1. Thumb	2. Index Finger	3. Middle Finger	4. Ring Finger	5. Little Finger

LEFT HAND

6. Thumb	7. Index Finger	8. Middle Finger	9. Ring Finger	10. Little Finger

Classified Assembled
Searched Verified
Index Card Answered
Note Amputations
Prisoner's Signature
Four Fingers Taken Simultaneously
Four Fingers Taken Simultaneously
Left Hand
L. Thumb R. Thumb
Right Hand

Deceased - Shot by Special Agents of the FBI, 7/22/34, while resisting arrest.

Dillinger's fingerprints, taken after his death. He unsuccessfully attempted to have his prints surgically altered. (Federal Bureau of Investigation.)

two-year sentence. Dillinger, who was assured by the prosecutor that the court would be lenient and he did not need an attorney, was sentenced to from 10 to 20 years in Pendleton Reformatory.

Despite his justifiable anger at the system, Dillinger behaved well in Pendleton, playing baseball and going to school. But when he came up for parole after five years, the chairman of the parole board told him: "Young man, you've served only a small part of your term and apparently you aren't amenable to prison life. Perhaps you'd better go back for a few years." By this time his erstwhile partner in crime had been loose on the street for three years.

Dillinger was transferred to the penitentiary at Michigan City at his own request, not realizing the seriousness of the move. Unlike the reform school, Michigan City was a prison for hard-core criminals. He thought they had a better baseball team. The rules were far stricter, and the punishments for infractions were harsh. A no-talking rule was enforced, prisoners marched in lockstep, and solitary confinement in "the hole" was given for extended periods of time. But there were some advantages for the crime novice who wanted to learn his craft. Here, there were men grown old in the practice of crime: con men, bank robbers, forgers, heistmen, and other professionals. Here was a postgraduate education in crime. Harry Pierpont and a couple of other men who had worked with the legendary "Baron" HERMAN K. LAMM befriended Dillinger and taught him the Baron's Prussian technique for robbing banks. When Dillinger finally got out he was ready for bigger things.

In return for his prison learning, he had agreed to help his tutors escape from prison. This required a plan and money. The plan was in place before Dillinger left the prison, and he immediately went about using his new skills to make the money. Gathering a small gang around him, he began robbing banks. After several small scores, Dillinger and his gang hit the State Bank on Massachusetts Avenue, Indianapolis, on September 6, 1933. The robbery happened to coincide with the preparation of a major payroll, and Dillinger made off with $24,800, an unbelievable amount of money in the middle of the Depression.

At the same time Dillinger was preparing the prison break, he was being hunted by Captain Matt Leach of the Indiana State Police, who had identified him as the leader of the new gang of bank robbers that was plaguing the state. When the plans for the prison break were complete, Dillinger went to visit a girlfriend named Mary Longnaker, sister of one of the prisoners. But the police were waiting for him and arrested him in her living room.

On September 26, 1933, while Dillinger was in jail in Lima, Ohio, Pierpont and nine of his companions escaped from the Michigan City prison. When Pierpont heard that Dillinger was in jail, he felt that he had an obligation to get him out. He and three companions raided the Lima jail and broke Dillinger out, killing Sheriff Jess Sarber by accident during the escape. Dillinger regretted the killing of Sarber, who had treated him well.

John Dillinger—"Public Enemy No. 1"—in a characteristic pose. (Federal Bureau of Investigation.)

Dillinger and Pierpont now turned their attention and talents to robbing banks. They made a good team; Pierpont had the experience at planning a good job, and Dillinger had those qualities of leadership that made the gang respect him and follow his lead. Over 30 bank robberies were attributed to them during the next few months. How many they actually were involved in is not known, since they were being blamed for every robbery in the Midwest, but the number they actually committed was probably about a dozen.

The gang went to Florida for a vacation over Christmas–New Year's, and then arrived in Tucson, Arizona, in late January. By a stroke of bad luck—someone recognized a member of the gang from a picture in the *Police Gazette*—the Tucson police arrested most of the gang. Dillinger was flown to Chicago, and then sent to a new "escape-proof" jail in Crown Point, Indiana.

Dillinger's lawyer for this case was Louis Piquett, who had worked as a city prosecutor for Chicago until his party went out of power, when he switched to the other side and started defending criminals. "They're the only ones who have money these days," he explained once, when a friend asked him about his choice of clients. Piquett looked over the situation and decided that there was only one way to save Dillinger. John Toland explained in *The Dillinger Days* (1963): "Sometime in the following week Piquett kept a rendezvous at the grounds of the Century of Progress. There he handed over an envelope containing several thousand dollars—to a prominent Indiana judge. The judge promised to smuggle a gun into the county jail."

With the gun, Dillinger made his way down-

The Biograph theater, where Dillinger saw his last movie. (Federal Bureau of Investigation.)

stairs, capturing one guard at a time, until he was in the receiving room. Fortuitously, there were two machine guns on the windowsill. Dillinger asked HERBERT YOUNGBLOOD, a large black man from Gary, Indiana, awaiting trial for murder, if he wanted out. Youngblood agreed and took one of the machine guns. With one hostage, they made their way to a Ford garage across from the jail and took a car. Dillinger was out of Indiana's "escape-proof" jail.

Two people who had observed the escape called the police and warned other people that Dillinger had escaped, but for some time, they were not believed. Dillinger and Youngblood separated after a couple of days, and Youngblood was killed in a gun battle a few weeks later.

It was this jailbreak that entered popular mythology with the story that Dillinger's gun was an imitation that had been carved out of a block of wood by Dillinger and dyed with shoe polish. The judge involved died before the truth was known, and the myth has proven to be stronger than truth.

Dillinger put another gang together, which included the short-tempered, violent GEORGE "BABY FACE" NELSON, who had the saving grace of being dependable in a robbery. Dillinger committed a couple of bank robberies to raise money for the defense of Pierpont and his companions, who were being tried for the murder of Sheriff Sarber. The money did no good, and Pierpont and one other man were sentenced to death. Dillinger was almost killed when the FBI caught up with him in St. Paul, but his girlfriend, Billie Frechette, drove off before the agents could do more than shoot him in the leg.

He and Billie were almost caught a month later at the Little Bohemia Lodge in Wisconsin, but they escaped before the FBI closed in. "Baby Face" Nelson shot it out with a couple of agents, and a couple of other agents shot three innocent

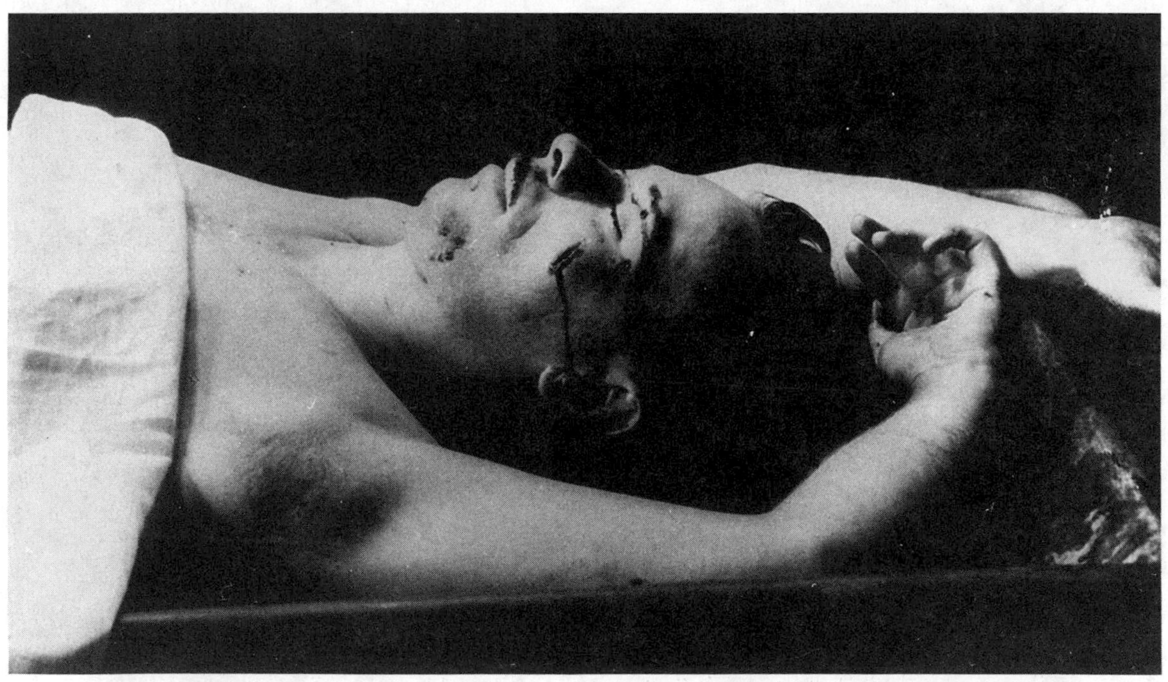

Dillinger, captured in death, at the Chicago morgue. (Federal Bureau of Investigation.)

bystanders who they mistook for gangsters, killing one of them. The incident caused widespread criticism and two Republican senators accused the FBI of bungling the business. A petition circulating in the area asked that FBI man MELVIN PURVIS be suspended and charged two other agents with "criminal stupidity." Toland relates that Will Rogers wrote: "Well, they had Dillinger surrounded and was all ready to shoot him when he come out, but another bunch of folks come out ahead, so they just shot them instead. Dillinger is going to accidentally get with some innocent bystanders some time, then he will get shot."

Early in 1933 Dillinger arranged to have plastic surgery to change his appearance, and even tried to have his fingerprints altered. The operation only managed to make his face look lopsided, and to scar his fingers, making him in fact more noticeable. Separated from Billie Frechette, he looked for other female companionship and met a waitress, Polly Hamilton, in a Chicago restaurant. Twenty-six years old and recently divorced from a Chicago policeman, she started going with the nice man who, the other waitresses kidded her, "looked like Dillinger."

Polly roomed with an older woman named Anna Sage, whose real name was Ana Cumpanas. Anna had operated a whorehouse in Gary, Indi-

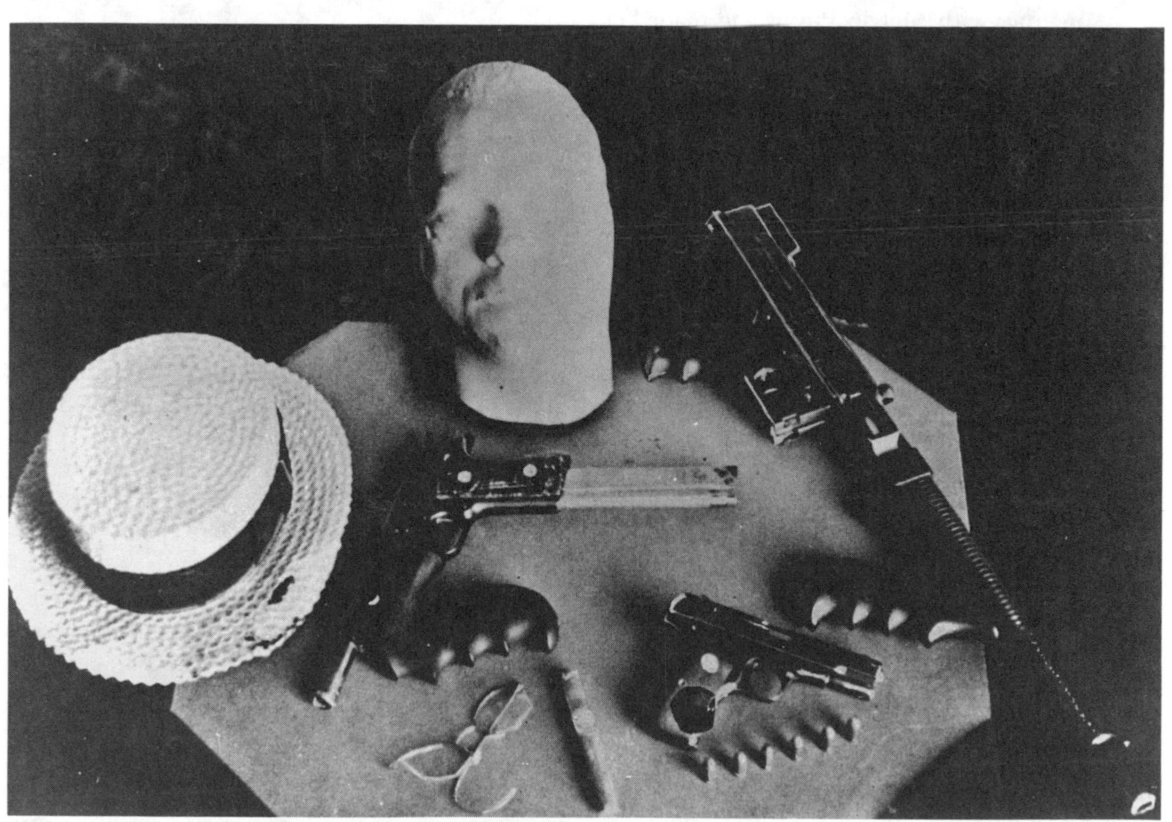

Death mask of Dillinger, exhibited with some of his personal effects at the Chicago FBI headquarters. (Federal Bureau of Investigation.)

ana, becoming locally famous as Katie from the Kostur Hotel. She had been convicted twice for operating a "disorderly house," and both times had been pardoned by then Governor Leslie. But now there was a new governor, and she was being threatened with deportation.

Anna soon figured out who her roommate's new boyfriend was, and she went to Sergeant Martin Zarkovich of the East Chicago, Indiana, Police Department, an old acquaintance. She knew where John Dillinger was, she told the sergeant, and if the deportation proceedings were dropped, she would set him up to be captured. The East Chicago police, after trying to make a deal with the Chicago police to kill Dillinger and being rebuffed, turned Anna over to the FBI.

Anna met with Melvin Purvis and made her offer: She would turn Dillinger over in return for having the deportation proceedings dropped and receiving a substantial piece of the reward. He promised to do what he could. Sage told Purvis that Dillinger would almost certainly take the two women to a movie the next day, either at the Marbro or the Biograph Theater. She would wear red, so as to be easily recognized.

The next day, Sunday, July 22, 1934, the temperature was over 101° F. in downtown Chicago. Purvis prepared to take Dillinger, telling his men to try to take him alive, but not to risk their own lives in the effort; the important thing was to get Dillinger, dead or alive. Without bothering to notify the Chicago police, the FBI staked out the two theaters.

Sometime after 8:00 P.M., Purvis, who was watching the Biograph, saw Anna Sage in her red dress pass by with two companions, a man and a woman. As planned, they allowed the trio to enter the theater. They would get Dillinger as he emerged.

The movie, *Manhattan Melodrama* with William Powell and Clark Gable, was over at 10:30. Dillinger and his two companions were among the first to leave. Purvis and another special agent closed in on Dillinger, while two other special

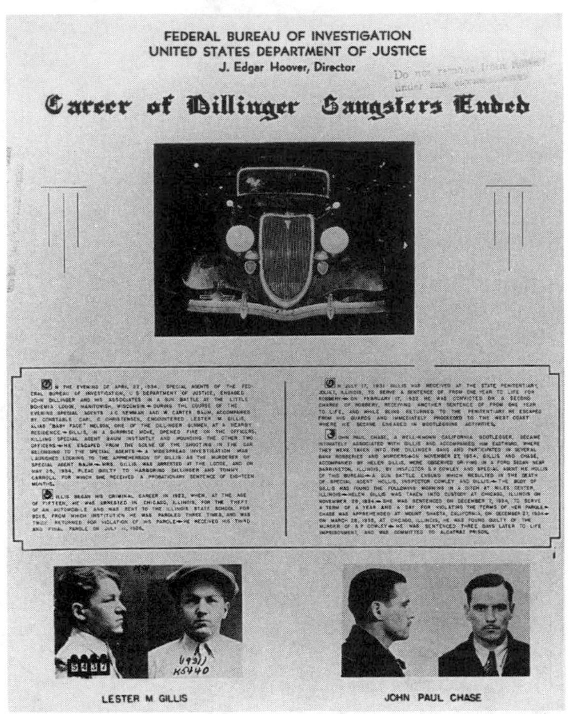

An FBI press release traces John Dillinger's career. (Federal Bureau of Investigation.)

agents casually walked in front. Dillinger suddenly drew a Colt automatic and, crouching down, ran toward the alley beside the theater. Purvis yelled, "Halt," and then the FBI special agents started shooting. One bullet went into Dillinger's left side. Another entered his bent-over back and exited his right eye.

J. EDGAR HOOVER refused to honor Purvis's commitment to Anna Sage, who entered American myth as the "Lady in Red," and she was deported to Rumania. Purvis, in disgust at this and other Hoover policies, resigned from the FBI.

DRAKE, Sir Francis, the heirs of

See: OSCAR HARTZELL

DRUCCI, Vincent "Schemer" (1895–1927)

The only Italian in CHARLES DION O'BANION's North Side Gang in Chicago, Vincent "Schemer" Drucci had a well-deserved reputation for crazy behavior, especially against his enemies. The Schemer received his nickname for the continuous flow of schemes that he developed to accomplish his aims. He tried to get the chef at AL CAPONE's favorite restaurant to poison Capone. When that did not work, he kidnapped the chef and murdered him, presumably just to annoy Capone. Capone referred to the Schemer as "the bedbug." Drucci effectively took over the North Side Gang after O'Banion and HYMIE WEISS died gangland deaths. In one gun battle against the Capone mob, Drucci was reputed to have roared with laughter as he skipped around the sidewalk to avoid rounds of gunfire.

In April 1927, Drucci was placed under arrest for election fraud. On the way to the station house, a police detective named Dan Healy suddenly pulled his gun and put four bullets into Drucci, who promptly died. It was alleged that Drucci had become violent, but the informed opinion was that Healy had murdered Drucci at Capone's instigation.

DRUGS

The personal use of certain chemical and pharmaceutical substances has been deemed against the interest of our society. The importation, growing, manufacturing, sale and use of these substances is either highly controlled or illegal. It should be recognized that the choice of which substances are banned is arbitrary, and more the result of cultural and religious patterns than in any innate property of the substance. Thus alcoholic beverages are strictly forbidden in Saudi Arabia and Iran; the Mormon religion discourages the drinking of coffee; and the United States government forbids the use of heroin, marijuana, cocaine, and a panoply of other narcotic or hallucinogenic drugs. The use of tobacco and alcohol, although discouraged, is legal.

Several thousand people a year die through the illegal use of banned or controlled substances in the United States, either through overdoses or the accidental introduction of poisonous impurities into the substance. Several thousand more die as a result of internecine battles over the sale and distribution of these substances. These facts are used as part of the argument for increasing the legal strictures over drug use, when some would argue that they are perhaps better arguments for decriminalizing them.

Over 25,000 people a year die as a direct result of the use of alcohol, mostly through automobile accidents. It is generally recognized that the answer to this problem is to make it more difficult and more socially undesirable to drive while intoxicated, rather than banning alcohol. In the government's effort to mobilize every weapon against narcotics offenders, including language, a person who uses one of the banned substances is said to be "abusing" it.

Some of the drugs more commonly abused in the United States are the following:

OPIUM and its chemical derivatives and analogues morphine, codeine, and heroin. Under the influence of these and other opiates, the user's mouth feels dry and the pupils of the eyes constrict. The skin becomes slightly flushed, moist and warm. The effect the user is paying for is a sensation of warmth and well-being; an extreme euphoria which has been described as a state "where all problems disappear and all things seem possible."

The opiate user develops a tolerance for the drug, which necessitates the use of larger and larger doses. But the intrinsic cost of producing and distributing the drug is so low that, were it legal, it could be given to addicts at a price that would alleviate any need for a life of crime to attain a drug supply. It is interesting to note that when heroin, an opium derivative, was first synthesized in Germany in 1898 it was recommended for use as an addiction-free substitute for other opiates. Contrary to popular belief, the use of opiates, while highly addictive, does not lead to the disintegration of character, insanity, nascent criminality or physical breakdown. An opiate addict, when supplied with his or her drug, can be a useful and productive member of society in every other way.

COCAINE has been used since 1844, when it was first isolated from the leaves of the coca plant and found to be a powerful mood raiser and an effective local anesthetic. It heightens the attention span, focuses the mind and produces a sense of well-being. In the form of crack cocaine, it produces what users describe as an irresistible euphoria. In the 1880s, Sigmund Freud used it to treat his own depression and wrote glowingly of its effects.

MARIJUANA, the dried leaves of the *Cannabis sativa* plant, is closely related to hashish, the dried tops of *Cannabis indica*, the Indian hemp plant. The 1938 *New American Encyclopedia* says of it that "narcotic officials named it 'The Assassin of Youth,' and state that it is as dangerous as a coiled rattlesnake. Its effects when smoked vary with different individuals. It may make of its victim a philosopher, a joyous reveler, a mad insensate, or a fiendish murderer."

LSD, PSILOCYBIN and other hallucinogenic drugs can profoundly influence the mental processes in doses that were once thought to be too small to have any physiological impact. The usual effect is an altering of the sensory processes of the brain, sometimes to the extent that complete tactile and visual hallucinations result.

Drug terms change constantly, sometimes cycling back upon themselves. These are some of the terms that have been in use in the last 25 years.

A—Amphetamines
Acapulco Gold—Marijuana
Ace—Marijuana
Acid—LSD
African Black—Marijuana
Alice B. Toklas—Marijuana
Angel Dust—Cocaine or LSD
Apple Jacks—Crack cocaine
Bazooka—Crack cocaine
Beam Me Up—Crack cocaine
Bennies or Bens—Amphetamine (Benzedrine)
Big C—Cocaine
Big H—Heroin
Black Beauties, Black Bombers or Blacks—Amphetamine pills
Blue Angels, Blue Birds—Barbiturates
Bomb—Amphetamines or heroin
Bones—Crack cocaine
Bong—Water pipe for smoking marijuana
Boo—Marijuana
Brick—Crack cocaine; hashish; opium
Cadillac—Cocaine
Canada Black—Marijuana
Charlie—Cocaine
China White—Heroin
Clocker—Street dealer in cocaine
Coke—Cocaine
Connection—Supplier
Cop—To obtain (a drug)
Crack—Cocaine chemically treated to be especially powerful and potentially lethal
Crystal—Powdered methamphetamine; powdered LSD
Cube—LSD in a sugar cube
Cut—To dilute a drug to the desired strength
Dex, Dexie—Dexedrine
Dice—Crack cocaine
Dolls—Amphetamines; barbiturates
Dope—Any substance that results in a chemically altered perception of reality
Down—Coming off a drug high, sometimes with concomitant uncomfortable side effects
Downers—Barbiturate pills
Drag—One puff on a marijuana cigarette
Dripper-dropper—Device for injecting heroin using a hypodermic needle fixed to the end of a glass dropper
Dust—Cocaine
501's—Crack cocaine
Flying Saucers—LSD
Freak—Addict who openly exhibits addictive behavior
Gangster—Marijuana
Gold Star—Marijuana
Goof Ball—Amphetamine and a barbiturate mixed

Grass—Marijuana
Gunja—Marijuana
Hamburger Helper—Crack cocaine
Hamster—Marijuana
Happy Dust—Cocaine
Head—Addict or constant user (A-head—Amphetamine addict)
Hemp—Hashish; marijuana
High—Under the effect of some drug (although some people claim to be high on life)
Hit—One puff on a marijuana cigarette
Horse—Heroin
Hot Shot—An injection of heroin sufficiently pure to cause the death of addict (normally heroin is cut to no more than 5% to 10% purity). Sometimes a mistake, often murder
Ice—Variously amphetamines, cocaine, and heroin (all white powders)
Idiot Pills—Barbiturates
Jive Stick—Marijuana cigarette
Joint—Marijuana cigarette
Junk—Heroin
Kansas Grass—Marijuana
Kee, Key—A kilo of marijuana
Keefer—Marijuana
Kibbles and Bits—Crack cocaine
Kif—Marijuana; hashish
Killer Weed—Marijuana; tobacco
M&Ms—Barbiturates
Magic Mushroom—Psilocybin
Mary Jane—Marijuana
Meth—Methamphetamine
Mexican Brown, Mexican Green—Marijuana
Mexican Horse—Heroin
Microdots—LSD
Muggles—Marijuana
Nark—Informer; narcotics agent
Nickel Bag—Specific amount of marijuana costing five dollars
Nose Candy, Nose Powder—Cocaine (because, in powdered form, it is sniffed)
Outfit—Set of equipment for shooting (injecting) heroin or other injectible drugs
Panama Red—Marijuana
PCP—Phencyclidine phosphate; a horse tranquilizer which has unpredictable mental and central nervous system effects on people, including possible hallucinations and great resistance to pain
Pep Pills—Amphetamines
Pot—Marijuana
Red Devils—Barbiturates
Red Flag—Ensuring injection of heroin into a vein by allowing some of the blood to be pulled up into the glass of the hypodermic syringe or dripper-dropper
Reds—Barbiturate capsules
Reefers—Marijuana cigarettes
Roach—The remains of a smoked marijuana cigarette
Santa Claus—Heroin
Sativa—Marijuana
Smack, Smeck—Heroin
Smith—LSD
Snow—Cocaine; heroin
Spaced [out]—Heavily under the influence of LSD, marijuana or an opiate
Speed—Amphetamines or (rarely) cocaine
Speedball—Cocaine and heroin combination
Speed Freak—Amphetamine addict
Spike—Hypodermic needle
Star Dust—Cocaine
Stuff—Heroin
Tabs—LSD
Tar—Hashish; opium
Tea—Marijuana
Tea Pad—Place where marijuana smokers gather (from 1960s)
Thing—Cocaine
Toke—One puff on a marijuana cigarette
Toot—Cocaine
Tripping—High on LSD or another hallucinogenic drug; also used for other drugs, but less frequently
Truck Driver—Amphetamines
Up—High on drugs
Uppers—Amphetamine pills
Wake Ups—Amphetamines

Weed—Marijuana
Whiffledust—Amphetamines
Yellow Jackets—Barbiturates

Drug terms, assembled by drug type, are listed below. Some entries are duplicated; the same term is used for more than one drug. These are in italics.

Amphetamines—A (or Ay), Bennies or Bens, Black Beauties, Black Bombs, Bombers or Blacks, Crystal (powdered methamphetamine), Dexies (Dexedrine pills), *Dolls*, *Ice*, Meth (methamphetamine), Pep Pills, Speed, Truck Driver, Uppers (pills), Wake Ups, Whiffledust

Barbiturates—Blue Angels, Blue Birds, *Dolls*, Downers (pills), Idiot Pills, M&Ms, Red Devils (pills), Reds, Yellow Jackets

Cocaine—*Angel Dust*, Big C, Cadillac, Charlie, Coke, Crack (when specially prepared), Dust, Happy Dust, *Ice*, Nose Candy, Nose Powder, *Snow*, Star Dust, Thing, Toot

Crack Cocaine—Apple Jacks, Bazooka, Beam Me Up, Bones, *Brick*, Dice, 501's, Hamburger Helper, Kibbles and Bits

Hashish—Bang, *Brick*, Hash, *Hemp*, *Kif*, *Tar*

Heroin—Big H, Black Gold, Black Tar, Blue Sky, *Bomb*, China White, H, Horse, *Ice*, Junk, Liquid Sky, Mexican Horse, Santa Claus, Smack, Smeck, *Snow*, Stuff, Tootsie Roll

LSD—Acid, *Angel Dust*, Cube, Flying Saucers, Microdots, Smith, Tabs

Marijuana—Acapulco Gold, Ace, African Black, Alice B. Toklas, Boo (spelled by the culturally elite "Bhu"), Canada Black, Dime Bag ($10 worth), Dope, Gangster, Gold Star, Grass, Gunja, Hamster, *Hemp*, Kansas Grass, Keefer, *Kif*, Killer Weed, Lid (a specific amount), Mary Jane, Mexican Brown, Mexican Green, Muggles (1930s), Nickel Bag ($5 worth), Panama Red, Pot, Sativa, Shit, Tea, Weed

Marijuana Cigarettes—Jive Sticks, Joints, Reefers, Roaches

Opium—*Brick*, *Tar*

EARP BROTHERS

HEROES OF THE OLD WEST, THEY WERE NO BETTER THAN THEY HAD TO BE

James C. Earp (1841–1926)
Virgil W. Earp (1843–1906)
Wyatt B. Earp (1848–1929)
Morgan Earp (1851–1882)
Warren B. Earp (1855–1900)

A family of lawmen, the Earps were neither more nor less honest than other lawmen of their period. James, the eldest, who was severely wounded in the Civil War and was not fit for the rigors of law enforcement, ran some of the Earps' shadier business interests. His wife was, for a while, madam of a bordello in Dodge City, Kansas.

Morgan Earp served as deputy sheriff in Dodge City, Kansas, and then moved to Butte, Montana, where he developed a reputation as a "town tamer."

Virgil Earp was the first one of the brothers to settle in Tombstone, Arizona, and he became the acting marshal in 1881 when the previous holder of that position was killed in a gunfight.

Wyatt Earp, who had been a stagecoach

driver, bartender, horse thief, buffalo hunter, and professional gambler, joined Virgil in Tombstone after serving a stint as deputy in Wichita and Dodge City, Kansas. His reputation as a fearless lawman was born in Dodge City, where he and BAT MASTERSON "cleaned up" the town. It was in Dodge City that his friendship with DOC HOLLIDAY developed.

The Earp clan settled in Tombstone and, with occasional help from Doc Holliday, who showed up shortly after the Earps arrived, kept the town clean and decent for the business interests. This was still by Eastern standards a wide-open town, since the principal business interests were those who ran the saloons, the gambling halls and the whorehouses. Often these three institutions were housed in the same building.

The opposing interests, mainly cattlemen who wanted control of the town taken out of the hands of the saloon owners, were supported by a group known as the Clanton gang, led by Ike and Billy Clanton. On October 26, 1881, after weeks of threats and counterthreats, the two opposing factions met at the O. K. Corral in the most famous gun battle of the century. On one side were Virgil, Wyatt and Morgan Earp and Doc Holliday, who had been deputized for the occasion. On the other side were Ike and Billy Clanton, Tom and Frank McLowery and Billy Claiborne. It was hardly a fair fight. The Earps were all noted gunfighters, and Doc Holliday had a reputation as a deadly shot and a cold-blooded killer. The Clanton gang, whatever else they might have been, had no such reputations. That the Earps provoked the fight is clearly shown by the fact that Sheriff John Behan, a friend of the Clantons, in an attempt to avoid bloodshed, offered to go ahead of the Earps and disarm the Clantons and get them out of town. His offer was refused.

The battle lasted less than half a minute and was effectively a one-sided slaughter. Frank McLowery had no chance to draw his gun before Wyatt Earp shot him in the stomach. Tom McLowery may not have had a gun, but he was shot anyway. Billy Claiborne fired a few shots at random and then scurried across the street to the shelter of Fly's Photographic Studio. A minute later the McLowery brothers and Billy Clanton were dead, Virgil Earp was shot in the leg, Morgan Earp in the shoulder, and Doc Holliday in the hip.

Public feeling ran against the Earps, and Wyatt Earp and Doc Holliday were charged with murder. But the charge was vacated at the preliminary hearing, and that ended the legal retribution.

Virgil Earp, already wounded in the gunfight, was bushwhacked a couple of months later by a man with a shotgun. He survived, but lost the use of his left arm. Morgan Earp was shot through the back by Clanton men on March 17, 1882, while playing pool in Bob Hatch's billiard parlor, and died about half an hour later.

Virgil and his family took a train to California, while Wyatt, Doc Holliday, and Warren Earp, who had arrived in Tombstone shortly after the O. K. Corral incident, went after the bushwhackers. They killed Frank Stillwell and Florentine Cruz, both of whom were involved in Morgan's murder and may have been responsible for the sudden decease of Curly Bill Brocius, the acting head of the Clanton gang. Then, with several murder charges hanging over their heads, the remaining Earps decided to move to California to join Virgil.

Warren Earp went back to Arizona in 1900 to take a job as a cattle detective. Shortly thereafter he was killed by a man named Johnny Boyett in a barroom brawl. Virgil Earp thought it was a bought killing, connected with the O. K. Corral fracas, and swore to get the man responsible. Virgil did not reveal who that man was, but it is generally understood that he kept his promise in 1905, the year before he died. He spent the last few years of his life in Prescott, Arizona.

Wyatt Earp was befriended by the movie community in Southern California in the 1920s, and the young screenwriters pumped him for material about the Old West. Many of the stories he told showed up in the two-reelers of the day, transformed by the camera into western melodramas.

EINSTEIN, Isadore

See: IZZIE AND MOE

ESPIONAGE

See: COLONEL RUDOLF IVANOVICH ABEL; ATOMIC SPY RING; WHITTAKER CHAMBERS; BENJAMIN CHURCH; MORRIS & LEONA COHEN; MATT CVETIC; FEDERAL BUREAU OF INVESTIGATION; HARRY GOLD; ALGER HISS; HERBERT A. PHILBRICK; ETHEL AND JULIUS ROSENBERG

EVANS, Charles (?–1875)

In April 1875, an 18-year-old boy named Seabolt was found dead in Indian Territory, part of what would later become the state of Oklahoma. His horse, boots and money were missing. A drifter named Charles (or sometimes Daniel) Evans was arrested for the murder when he was apprehended riding Seabolt's horse.

Evans claimed that he had bought the horse, and there was little other evidence against him, so he was found innocent. However, the presiding judge left the bench and the territory after the trial without signing Evans's release papers. So a pro-forma second trial was scheduled to officially release Evans.

The new judge, ISAAC C. PARKER, who would achieve notoriety as the Hanging Judge, was just starting his career at this time. The trial would have been over quickly, with Evans found not guilty, but the dead boy's father was in the audience. He noticed that Evans was wearing his son's missing boots. Evans was found guilty this time and hanged.

EVERLEIGH CLUB (1900–1911)

THE EVERLEIGH SISTERS GAVE CHICAGO A WHOREHOUSE TO BE PROUD OF, AND CHICAGO SHOWED ITS APPRECIATION

One of the grandest brothels ever to operate in the United States was the 50-room mansion run by the Everleigh sisters, located at 2131–33 South Dearborn Street, Chicago.

Ada and Minna Everleigh were born in a small village near Louisville, Kentucky, Ada in 1876 and Minna in 1879. The last name they were born with was probably Lester, as that is the name that Minna signed checks with, but that may have been the name of the brothers they married in Kentucky in 1879. The sisters left their husbands within a year, and never talked about them much, except to say that they were brutes who tried to strangle them. The story that has come down is that they named themselves Everleigh in honor of a grandmother, who used to sign her letters, "Everly Yours."

Ada and Minna joined a theatrical troupe, which toured the Midwest playing melodramas to small-town audiences. The sisters never rose above bit parts, and they decided to change professions when the troupe reached Omaha, Nebraska, just before the opening of the Trans-Mississippi Exposition in 1898. What Omaha needed, the girls decided, was a high-class, well-run bordello. They used a small inheritance to rent a place and furnish it in a parody of high fashion, brought in high-quality sporting girls, and charged the unheard-of prices of 10 dollars for a girl and 12 dollars for a bottle of wine. Despite their lack of experience in this enterprise, neither having been a prostitute or a madam before, the place prospered as long as the exposition ran.

When the exposition closed, and it became clear that the native Omahans were not big spenders, Ada and Minna looked around to see where the sporting life could support the sort of club that they liked to run. They chose Chicago and rented a mansion that had been built in 1890 by famous madam Lizzie Allen, who had called it the "House of Mirrors." When Lizzie retired in 1896, it had been leased to Madame Effie Hankins, but Effie was now anxious to ply her trade in New York and passed the place on to the Everleigh sisters.

The sisters bought the lease, fixtures and girls for $55,000, putting $20,000 down, with the balance due in six months. They immediately fired the girls and stripped the house down to its bare walls, hiring carpenters and decorators to come in and make it look like what they thought a high-priced bordello, catering only to gentlemen of quality, should look like. When they were done, the place was resplendent with thick, rich-looking carpets; mahogany tables topped with marble; curtains of golden silk; chairs and couches upholstered in silk damask; inlaid beds; gold-rimmed china and crystal glassware to go with the sterling silver dinner service, which was used on dining tables covered in Irish linen; paintings and tapestries and statues and hundreds of *objects d'art* in ornamental glass cases. It had a half-dozen pianos, one of them gilded, and gold spittoons and champagne buckets and a gilded bathtub especially for the guests. It was from this idea of gentility that the decorating style known as "Chicago Bordello" originated.

On February 1, 1900, the Everleigh Club opened for business, supplying fine wines and finer girls in a luxurious setting to those who could pay the tab. It was an instant success and stayed so for over a decade. The *Chicago Tribune* said of it: "No house of courtesans in the world was so richly furnished, so well advertised, and so continuously patronized by men of wealth and slight morals." Its pre-eminent position in the world of the *demimonde* was verified in 1902, when Prince Henry of Germany, brother of Kaiser Wilhelm II, visited Chicago and was entertained at the Everleigh Club. And the girls were the best that Ada and Minna could find. "I talk with each applicant myself," Ada said in a 1910 interview. "She must have worked somewhere else before coming here. We do not like amateurs. Inexperienced girls and young widows are too prone to accept offers of marriage and leave. To get in, a girl must have a good face and figure, must be in perfect health, must understand what it is to act like a lady. If she is addicted to drugs, or to drink, we do not want her." The girls were indeed at the top of their profession, and they were well treated and well paid for their efforts. Having worked at the Everleigh Club was a mark of distinction in the *demimonde*.

In his book, *Gem of the Prairie* (1940), Herbert Asbury describes what the club was like in its heyday:

> There were two entrances to the Everleigh Club, each leading into a spacious hallway fragrant with perfume and decorated with potted palms and other greenery, through which peeped statues of Greek Goddesses. From the hallways mahogany staircases wound gracefully upward to the love bowers of the courtesans, each of which was sumptuously furnished according to the taste of its occupant, with the exciting colors of red and gold dominating the decorative schemes. On the first floor were the music-room, the library, an art gallery which was said by connoisseurs of the period to contain a few really good paintings; the grand ballroom, lighted by chandeliers of cut glass, the hardwood floor inlaid with rare woods in mosaic patterns; the dining-room paneled in walnut and containing a mahogany table large enough for fifty diners; and the Pullman Buffet, a reproduction in mahogany of a section of a railroad dining-car. Also on this floor were some of the twelve parlors, each of which was virtually sound-proof and could be completely cut off from the remainder of the house by closing the heavy double doors. These parlors were called the Gold, Moorish, Silver, Copper, Red, Rose, Green, Blue, Oriental, Chinese, Egyptian, and Japanese Rooms, and were appropriately decorated and furnished. . . . And in every room

were the two objects that probably aroused more comment than any other feature of the brothel—the gold spittoon, and a fountain which at regular intervals squirted a jet of perfume into the incense-laden air.

To run the Everleigh Club, it cost from $50,000 to $75,000 a year, which included the rent and the salaries of the 20 or so cooks and maids; the three orchestras and one mandatory piano player; and the special entertainers for the occasional erotic "circuses" put on by the house. This did not include the girls, who were paid for performance on a piecework basis, receiving a full one-half of what the house charged for their services. This was much better than the competition, which ensured that the Everleigh Club always had its pick of the best talent available.

For the services of its girls, the club charged from $10 to $25 a client, depending on the service required and the length of time the client remained with the girl. In addition, a customer could order wine—at $12 a bottle in the parlor or $15 if delivered to one of the rooms—but neither beer nor hard liquor was available. Supper parties—a specialty of the house—cost a minimum of $50 a person, including wine but not any subsequent services of one of the girls. A customer was expected to spend at least $50 during the course of an evening. This was in a day when a good salary for a working man was $12 a week.

The club closed in 1911 when, on October 24, Chicago Mayor Carter Harrison, bowing to the influence of the reform groups, ordered the police to close it down. John McWeeny, the general superintendent of police, ignored the order until the next day, giving time for old friends and clients of the club to come back for one last evening. Then the girls disbursed to take one of the variety of offers that came by telegram and telephone from all over the country, the Everleigh sisters put all the furniture and fixtures in storage and left for Europe. Minna gave a last interview to the Chicago *American*: "You get everything in a life time. Of course, if the mayor says we must close, that settles it. What the mayor says goes, as far as I am concerned. I'm not going to be sore about it, either. I never was a knocker, and nothing the police of this town can do will change my disposition. . . . If the ship sinks we're going down with a cheer and a good drink under our belts, anyway."

When the sisters came back from Europe after six months, they moved to New York, where they lived out their days in respectable seclusion.

FEDERAL BUREAU OF INVESTIGATION

The Federal Bureau of Investigation (FBI), a branch of the United States Justice Department, is charged by statute with enforcing all federal criminal statutes not specifically assigned to another agency. It also investigates cases of espionage or subversion in the United States and its territories. It is, therefore, both the principal law enforcement agency and the principal counter-espionage organization of the federal government.

In 1870, the Attorney General was placed in charge of the newly formed United States Department of Justice. The department had a police force of sorts in the Federal Marshals, but it had no detective division and adopted the practice of hiring private detectives like ALLAN PINKERTON to conduct investigations. When Congress discouraged that in 1892, the Justice Department borrowed agents from the SECRET SERVICE. In 1907 the Secret Service was investigating land frauds in the Western states, and discovered that a number of congressmen were involved. Congress responded by restricting, in its appropriations act of 1908, Secret Service activities to the suppression of counterfeiting and other matters relating to the Treasury Department. This prompted President Theodore Roosevelt to request that the legislators appropriate money for a force of detectives for the Justice Department. His Attorney General, Charles J. Bonaparte, who was a grandnephew of French Emperor Napoleon I, took the plea to Congress himself.

Congress refused his request, fearing to allow the Federal Government any sort of "secret police." As Congressman Walter I. Smith of Iowa declared: "No general system of spying upon and espionage of the people, such as has prevailed in Russia, in France under the Empire, and at one time in Ireland, should be allowed to grow up."

Roosevelt decided that he could hire detectives for his Justice Department without a specific appropriation. When Congress adjourned he directed his Attorney General to create a new force of detectives. On July 1, 1908, eight of the finest Secret Service agents were transferred to the Justice Department. Congress was outraged, and both the Senate and the House started investigations. Bonaparte was called on the carpet. He blandly informed the investigating committee that it was all their own fault: since Congress forbade the Justice Department from borrowing detectives, they had to get their own. The furious investigators began hurling charges at the administration. Roosevelt fought back, declaring publicly that, in forbidding the Justice Department to borrow detectives, the congressmen were actively promoting crime. The public liked that simple explanation, and sided with the president. Congress hastily backed down, and the detective division thus survived the legislative attempt to drown it at birth.

In 1909, under President Taft, the group was given an official name: the Bureau of Investigation (BOI).

In 1916, at the beginning of the war in Europe that was to become World War I, the United States was still officially neutral, but was selling a lot of munitions and war supplies to Great Britain and France. Germany felt that America's neutrality was a little too one sided, and thought it was justified in mounting a campaign of espionage and sabotage within the United States.

DR. WALTER T. SCHEELE, a research chemist living in New Jersey who had been a German agent for over twenty years, designed and aided in the manufacture of "cigars": small, time-delay pipe bombs that could be placed in merchant ships to destroy much of the cargo, if not the ship itself, while on the high seas.

On July 30, 1916, the Black Tom arsenal in New York harbor blew up, detonating over two million pounds of dynamite in one of the largest chemical explosions of all time. The blast was heard over two hundred miles away. Windows in Manhattan, Brooklyn and Jersey City were broken, and heavy plate glass windows from storefronts littered the streets. Miraculously, since it was early morning, only three men and a child died in the explosion.

In January 1917, a shell assembly plant in Kingsland, New Jersey, blew up, scattering shells all around the plant area. Luckily the shells were not yet armed with their detonating fuzes, and few of them blew up. The damage was estimated at seventeen million dollars.

When the United States entered the war President Wilson requested and obtained from Congress a broad expansion of the Espionage Act, but not as broad as many in the administration and Congress desired. A patriotic fervor gripped the country, and a spy fever swept from coast to coast. Volunteer vigilante groups sprang up all around the country, spying on their neighbors and threatening dire consequences for those not deemed "loyal" enough.

The BOI was put in charge of rounding up

suspicious "enemy aliens," and had its staffing increased from three hundred to four hundred agents. Even the Secret Service had a few of its powers restored, and tracked German saboteurs. But with loyal Americans seeing spies and saboteurs under every bed, four hundred agents weren't nearly enough. A. M. Briggs, a Chicago advertising executive and the founder of one of the larger of the vigilante groups, the American Protective League (APL), convinced the Justice Department that a few thousand unofficial, unpaid volunteers would be of great assistance. With the approval of Attorney General Thomas W. Gregory, the APL investigated everyone it could get away with investigating, to the point of performing a "background check" on everyone the American Red Cross sent overseas.

With its quasi-official status, the APL rapidly grew in size, with over 250,000 members. For their one dollar dues, the members got little tin badges that said "Secret Service," and the right to snoop on their friends. When the Treasury Department pointed out that there was a real Secret Service, the APL changed the badge to read "Auxiliary to the U.S. Department of Justice."

In 1918 the BOI, with APL assistance, carried out a series of "slacker raids" in cities around the United States, meant to round up those young men who had failed to register for the draft. The raids succeeded in rounding up and throwing into jail thousands of young men, most of whom had registered for the draft but were not carrying their draft cards when they were caught up in the dragnet. Only one-half of one percent of those apprehended proved to be genuine draft dodgers. The ever-fickle public cried out in horror at what it now perceived as an excess of governmental zeal. Attorney General Gregory relented to the extent of no longer using anyone but bona fide full-time government employees on the raids.

In 1918 Congress passed the Alien Act, designed to "exclude and expel from the United States aliens who are members of the anarchistic classes." The postwar Attorney General, a Pennsylvania lawyer named A. MITCHELL PALMER, was moved to action by a series of anarchist bombings that occurred around the country in 1919, including one on the lawn of his own house in Washington, D.C. He appointed William J. Flynn, a former director of the Secret Service, to take over the bureau and actively fight radicals, anarchists, and subversives. To investigate these subversives, a new unit, the GENERAL INTELLIGENCE DIVISION (GID), was formed under the direction of Assistant Attorney General Francis P. Garvan. A young Department of Justice attorney named J(OHN) EDGAR HOOVER was appointed as his chief assistant.

The GID got off to a running start, soon compiling dossiers on more than two hundred thousand people. Palmer, with his eye on the White House, used the Alien Act to build a reputation with the American people, by now thoroughly alarmed over the continuing wave of anarchist bombings. Glorying in his new nickname of "The Fighting Quaker," he began a series of "Red Raids," using the Bureau to round up suspected anarchists. After a few small raids for practice, which mostly got a favorable press, although they resulted in many false arrests and only a few convictions or deportations, Palmer got down to business. On the night of January 2, 1920, the BOI raided locations in 33 cities and arrested approximately 10,000 people, many of them new immigrants who spoke no English and whose only crime was picking an unfortunate place in their neighborhoods to stop for a cup of coffee or a bowl of soup. Some of the "aliens" Palmer tried to deport were actually American citizens, who were too confused and frightened by the proceedings to speak up. The jails were not prepared for the sudden influx of "traitors," and in many localities had little interest in treating them humanely anyway. According to Frederick Lewis Allen in *Only Yesterday* (1931): "In Detroit, over a hundred men were herded into a bull-pen measuring twenty-four by thirty feet and kept there for a week under conditions which the mayor of the city called intolerable. In Hartford, while the suspects

A. Bruce Bielaski, Chief of the Bureau of Investigation from 1912 to 1919. (Federal Bureau of Investigation.)

were in jail the authorities took the further precaution of arresting and incarcerating all visitors who came to see them, a friendly call being regarded as *prima facie* evidence of affiliation with the Communist party." Most of the detainees, even the few guilty ones, had been arrested without warrants, and were subsequently released by the courts.

The country was divided in its feelings about the raids. Many felt that Palmer was defending the American way, and was a hero; but as word of the way the raids were conducted and the country's laws were being flouted by its own police, public opinion once again swung around to denounce what now became known as the "Palmer Raids."

Under the administration of President Warren G. Harding, the reputation of the bureau fell to a new low. William J. Flynn was replaced as director by "famous international sleuth" William J. Burns, who had also once been the director of the Secret Service. After his retirement from the Secret Service in 1909, Burns had founded the William J. Burns National Detective Agency, which became known for its impressive client list and its lack of ethical standards.

Burns brought his lack of ethics to his new job, and the BOI now routinely engaged in illegal wiretaps, committed burglaries to examine documents, beat up prisoners to get confessions, and engaged in vendettas against those who criticized

William J. Burns, former director of the Secret Service, who took over the Bureau of Investigation during the Harding Administration. (Federal Bureau of Investigation.)

Chiefs of police from all over attending the FBI's national police academy during the 1940s. (Dept. of Special Collections, University Research Library, UCLA.)

the administration, the Department of Justice or the Bureau itself, including senators and congressmen. It also continued its preoccupation with the radical elements of the country, or, as Attorney General Dougherty put it, "Red Agents of the Soviet Government," who, he believed, were getting their instructions directly from Moscow and had, he was sure, caused the railroad strike that tied up much of the country's transportation.

By the time Harding died and Calvin Coolidge became president, the Bureau of Investigation was thoroughly discredited and ineffectual. Coolidge fired Attorney General Dougherty, and appointed Harlan Fiske Stone, the former dean of the Columbia University Law School, to take his place. Stone, in turn, fired Burns and looked around for a replacement. On May 10, 1924, he offered the job to J. Edgar Hoover.

"I'll take the job," Hoover is reported to have said, "on certain conditions. First, the Bureau must be divorced from politics and not be a catch-all for political hacks. Appointments must be based on merit. Second, promotions will be made on proved ability, and, third, the Bureau will be responsible only to the Attorney General."

Those were the conditions that Stone, himself, had in mind, and Hoover got the job.

Within a few days, Stone made a public statement outlining the new policies of the BOI. It, he declared,

> is not concerned with political or other opinions of individuals. It is concerned only with their conduct and then only with such conduct as is forbidden by the laws of the United States. When a police system passes beyond these limits, it is dangerous to the proper administration of justice and to human liberty, which should be our first concern to cherish. Within them it should rightly be a terror to the wrongdoer.

Under Hoover's stewardship, and after a vigorous housecleaning, the bureau grew and prospered. After temporary name changes to the Division of Investigation, and the United States Bureau of Investigation, it received, in 1935, its present designation of the Federal Bureau of Investigation. As such it was (and is) within the Department of Justice, but entirely separate from it at all levels below that of the attorney general, who is the FBI Director's boss.

In a comparatively short time Hoover changed the bureau's image to one of squeaky-clean honesty, incorruptibility and efficiency in law enforcement. He recruited college graduates as special agents (all field operators were and are "special agents"), preferring those with law or accounting degrees. Hoover took everything on himself, and everything that was done in the Bureau was done in his name. This developed a cult of personality within the Bureau, but also clearly placed responsibility. The buck really did stop at Hoover's desk.

In 1924 Congress appropriated funds to expand and centralize the country's existing criminal identification records. The fingerprint files of the International Association of Police Chiefs and the convict fingerprint records kept at the federal penitentiary at Leavenworth, Kansas, were brought to the Bureau's Identification Division and added to the existing fingerprint records and the old BERTILLON measurement files. This gave the Identification Division a base of 810,188 fingerprint records to build on. In 1930 Congress authorized the formation of the National Division of Identification and Information within the Bureau, and it soon became a major resource for police forces around the country.

In 1932 the Bureau, now the United States Bureau of Investigation, established a crime laboratory patterned after that at Northwestern University, which serviced the Chicago Police Department. They rapidly developed an expertise on forged documents and typewriter type identification, as well as the analysis and identification of bloodstains, hair, paint, ink, tire treads, and the myriad of other bits of physical evidence that might be found at a crime scene. They made the crime lab available to local police chiefs, and even sent their experts to testify in local criminal prosecutions when requested.

Hoover's goal was to become indispensable to the nation's police forces, and he worked to minimize the inevitable friction that would develop when two such organizations tried to work together. To a large extent he succeeded, although there was occasional grumbling when the Bureau or Hoover himself took the credit for an arrest that a local police force felt it could have accomplished without their aid.

It wasn't until June 18, 1934, that Congress gave the Bureau's special agents the power of arrest and the authority to carry firearms. Until then a special agent had to either make a citizen's arrest or call in a U.S. Marshal or a member of the local police. On July 1, 1935, the Bureau officially became the Federal Bureau of Investigation, under the Department of Justice Appropriations bill, Public Law 22, signed by President Franklin D. Roosevelt on March 22, 1935.

For many years, up until the APALACHIN CONFERENCE in 1957 and the revelations of the MCCLELLAN COMMITTEE in the 1960s, Hoover, and thus the FBI, refused to address the problem of large-scale ORGANIZED CRIME, or admit the existence of an American MAFIA. In his book *The Bureau* (1979), William Sullivan, who for years was Hoover's right-hand man, quotes Hoover as explaining, "They're just a bunch of hoodlums." The only organized conspiracy that interested Hoover was what he still perceived as the threat of International Communism.

A secondary effect of the Depression, which began with the stock market collapse of 1929, was a wave of hooliganism, mostly bank robbery and kidnapping, that alternately thrilled and frightened the American public. From the early 1930s the Bureau took vigorous action against the hooligans. In 1932 the Bureau joined in the investigation of the LINDBERGH KIDNAPPING under the special direction of President Hoover, since it had no jurisdiction. As a result of that case, the Federal Kidnapping Statute, popularly known as the "Lindbergh Kidnap Law," was enacted, giving the FBI authority to investigate a kidnapping, but only after it was established that the kidnap victim had been taken across a state line.

On September 26, 1933, kidnapper and bank robber GEORGE "MACHINE GUN" KELLY was captured in Memphis, Tennessee. He supposedly yelled, "Don't shoot, G-Men, don't shoot!" when the special agents arrested him, thus creating a term (G-MEN) for federal agents that has gone into the language. On April 22, 1934 GEORGE "BABY FACE" NELSON killed a special agent, W. Carter Baum, in a shootout in rural Wisconsin.

In one of the most famous episodes of the period, bank robber JOHN HERBERT DILLINGER was killed as he was leaving the Biograph Theater in Chicago on July 22, 1934, by special agents MELVIN PURVIS and Samuel P. Cowley. Cowley and another agent, Herman F. Hollis, caught up with "Baby Face" Nelson on November 27, 1934, on a highway near Barrington, Illinois. Nelson was killed in the ensuing gun battle, and the two agents were both mortally wounded.

The wave of bank robberies crested in 1935,

and subsided rapidly thereafter, partly because of the FBI's vigilance, and partly because the worst of the Depression was over, and people could find other occupations besides robbing banks. But some of the Bureau's most spectacular arrests came as the wave reached its peak. On January 8, 1935, the Bureau broke up the BARKER-KARPIS GANG with the Chicago arrest of Arthur "Dock" Barker and the killing of Russel Gibson, who tried shooting it out with the special agents who came to arrest him. "MA" BARKER and her son Fred were killed in a gun battle with agents at Lake Weir, Florida. Alvin "Creepy" Karpis was arrested by Hoover personally in New Orleans on April 30, 1936.

On August 24, 1939, LOUIS "LEPKE" BUCHALTER, head of MURDER, INCORPORATED, arranged through columnist Walter Winchell to surrender directly to Hoover.

As World War II approached, Hoover and his Bureau were among the first American institutions to publicly realize the evils of Fascism, and to come out against Nazi infiltration of the United States. Hoover sought a wide role for the FBI in the coming battle against the forces of darkness, and was deeply disappointed when the Office of Strategic Services (OSS) was formed, and the Bureau was restricted to counterintelligence duties in the Western Hemisphere (the Bureau had authority over North, Central, and South America, with the exception of Canada, a trusted ally which had the RCMP, and the Panama Canal Zone, which was protected by the United States Army).

In 1941 Dusko Popov, a British double agent code-named "Tricycle," came to the United States with a list of questions from the Abwehr (German military intelligence), who believed he was working for them. Hoover refused even to look at the Abwehr-supplied questionnaire. Had he, the overwhelming number of questions concerning the defenses of the Hawaiian Islands might have given him an idea of what was about to happen, and possibly changed the course of the war. But Popov was a Yugoslav, and a "playboy," and Hoover (and thus the FBI) didn't trust him.

With the outbreak of war, the FBI infiltrated neo-Nazi groups, wiretapped suspected German and Japanese agents, and worked closely with the Office of Censorship to keep tabs on suspected enemy agents, potential enemy agents, and anyone else of interest. It arrested enemy saboteurs who were being periodically landed from U-boats (many of whom turned themselves in, a fact seldom mentioned in Hoover's press releases). It is to Hoover's credit that he strongly recommended against the internment of Japanese-Americans, feeling that such a move was totally unnecessary to safeguard the nation's security.

One of the Bureau's success stories was the double agent William G. Sebold, who was used to round up one of the principal Nazi spy rings working in the United States. Simon Emil Koedel, a German sleeper agent, managed to elude the Bureau for years, sending over 600 messages of varying importance back to the Abwehr until he and his daughter were finally apprehended in October 1944. The last two Nazi agents to arrive in the United States, William Colepaugh and Erich Gimpel, were landed by U-boat off the coast of Maine on November 28, 1943. The FBI had them both apprehended before New Year's Day, 1944.

Habits, once acquired, are hard to break, and the habit the Bureau had nurtured over the war years of searching for subversives found a welcome continuation after the war with the nationwide Communist paranoia that developed in the late 1940s and early 1950s. There were, of course, actual Soviet spies, and many of them were or had been avowed Communists. But many of the cases developed by the Bureau were not so clear. There was the case of Philip Jaffe, editor of *Amerasia*, a magazine which focused on the Far East. The magazine published information from classified government documents, and Jaffe was put under surveillance by the Bureau. He was seen visiting the home of Earl Browder, head of the American Communist Party, as well as the Soviet consulate in New York. Several government officials were seen associating with him.

But when the case was brought to a grand jury it became evident that the Bureau had no evidence that any information had been passed to the Soviets; and further, that what evidence they did have had been developed with the aid of illegal wiretaps and "bag jobs" (the Bureau's term for warrantless breaking and entering for the purpose of securing information).

The revelations of internal subversion that Hoover and the House Un-American Activities Committee (HUAC) had suspected all along were made tangible with the confession *ad nauseam* before HUAC of Elizabeth Terril Bentley, who had decided to tell all upon the death of her lover and spymaster, Jacob N. Golos. In acting as a courier for Golos, Miss Bentley had become aware of the extent of the Soviet spy ring that he was operating out of his New York travel agency.

Miss Bentley was merely the first of a gaggle of ex–Communist spies who were now determined to tell all to their fellow countrymen, who were by now awaiting breathlessly the next installment of the continuing saga of perfidy and collusion. WHITTAKER CHAMBERS, a journalist and one-time editor of *Time* magazine, revealed the names of many government officials who he claimed had been secret Communists, and traitors to their country, culminating on August 3, 1948, with his accusations against ALGER HISS, an erstwhile high official in the American State Department who was, at the time of Chambers's accusation, president of the Carnegie Endowment for International Peace. Many books and articles have been written on the Hiss case since his conviction (for perjury) in January 1950. The facts regarding his guilt or innocence have never been satisfactorily resolved, and even today a convincing case could be made supporting either conclusion. In 1992 a Russian intelligence officer revealed that a search of relevant Soviet documents shows Hiss to be innocent.

In March of 1949 the FBI arrested Judith Coplon, an employee of the Justice Department, while she was walking down a New York street with Valentin A. Gubitchev, an attaché to the Soviet delegation to the United Nations, who was also arrested. Coplon had in her possession a sheaf of documents that would have been incriminating if she had actually passed them over to Gubitchev, but she was apprehended before she had a chance to do so. During her trial her attorney tried to picture her as a victim of her own passion for Gubitchev, which must have seriously annoyed his wife.

The two were convicted of espionage and sentenced to fifteen years in prison. Gubitchev never served his sentence, being deported to the Soviet Union instead. He might have made the wrong choice, as a later defector reported that he had been sent to Siberia, presumably as a punishment for getting caught. Coplon's two convictions were overturned when the appellate court learned that the FBI had illegally wiretapped her home phone and that of her parents, as well as her office phone and the phone that she used to talk to her lawyer during her first trial. The Bureau had then destroyed some of the relevant records, and stood mute as the federal prosecutors had denied during the trials that any taps had been used.

In contrast to the Coplon case, the case built up against ETHEL AND JULIUS ROSENBERG was flawless and free of error. In this the Bureau was helped by the trial judge, Irving R. Kaufman. Although public feeling was high at the time of the trial and subsequently that the Rosenbergs had been railroaded (counterbalanced by equally strong feeling from another segment of the public that electrocution was too good for the dirty traitors), it wasn't until many years later that FBI records released under the FREEDOM OF INFORMATION ACT showed that the Bureau may have indeed been too zealous. In retrospect it seems clear that the Rosenbergs were indeed guilty, but perhaps not quite as guilty as Hoover would have the world think.

In the 1960s the attention of the Federal Government focused on the institutionalized segregation that existed throughout the South, and a determined attempt began to integrate schools, public transportation, and businesses. The segregationists fought back, resurrecting that traditional foe of Negroes, Jews, Catholics, and all things Northern, the KU KLUX KLAN. Hoover had some experience of fighting the Klan in the 1920s, when the Governor of Louisiana asked the help of the Federal Government in cleansing his state of a pervasive Klan influence that reached even into the Governor's office and controlled most of the state's organs, including the State Police. As Fred J. Cook describes in *The FBI Nobody Knows* (1964):

> With Hoover playing the leading role, arrangements were made to send Bureau of Investigation agents into Louisiana. It was, for the Klan, the beginning of the end. The cooperation of the Bureau's agents with untainted local authorities led to the prosecution and, more important, to public exposure of the viciousness of the Klan. In New Orleans, the Bureau's agents caught up with Imperial Kleagle Clarke, who was subsequently indicted in Houston, Texas, on a white slavery charge. He pleaded guilty in March, 1924, and was fined $5,000. The Klan, at the time, was at the height of its power, but with the prosecution of Kleagle Clarke and others, the end was in sight.

Now, four decades later, the Klan had returned. By the mid-1960s, the FBI estimated membership in the resurgent Klan at close to 15,000, and suspected it of many acts of lawless violence, including cross burnings, assaults, bombings, kidnappings and murders. The Bureau infiltrated the Klan, using paid informants, and did its best to disrupt the various Klan organizations from within. The techniques, which it had developed in years of infiltrating the American Communist Party, were effective, and held Klan influence and violence to a minimum. A Bureau informant, Gary Thomas Rowe, was riding in the car in Alabama when Michigan civil rights worker Viola Liuzzo was murdered. He was unable to prevent the murder, but his testimony convicted the murderers.

Regarding the use of informants, William Sullivan, who retired from the FBI as Assistant Director in 1971, says in *The Bureau*:

> Although we certainly wouldn't have broken the Klan without them, informants could cause tremendous problems for the bureau. After they've been working for us for a while, informants get to know the kind of information we want and many of them tailor their stories to suit the occasion. It's very easy to embellish a little at first—a small exaggeration here and there will convince the bureau that it's getting its money's worth. If our informant starts to run out of facts altogether, however, little exaggerations can turn into great big lies.
>
> That's why we always try to have more than one informant in the same group. Three in a group of thirty would be ideal. Each would be unknown to the others, of course, so that we could compare three separate reports of the group's activities. That way it's easy to spot major discrepancies in the reports, run it out ourselves, and see who is mistaken or lying.

During the Vietnam era of the late 1960s the Bureau's counter intelligence programs, called COINTELPRO within the Bureau, completed a slide toward disruptive tactics that had been going on for ten years. The perceived dangers of the American Communist Party, the Socialist Workers Party, the Black Panthers, the Jewish Defense League, and other organizations that Hoover thought to be subversive made such tactics seem desirable, even though all involved realized that they were illegal. They went from police procedures, which permit the gathering of information even by clandestine means for the purpose of prosecuting wrongdoers, to tactics designed to harass and confuse the target, and make them lose credibility in the eyes of the public. A 1974 Justice Department report, as cited by Sanford J. Unbar in his book *FBI* (1975), says:

The most popular technique was to send anonymous or false materials to organizations or their members in the hope of stirring up dissension over policies and plans and then disrupting those plans. Agents sought out "friendly media representatives" and leaked derogatory public record information—arrests, controversial background—to stimulate bad publicity about the "target." Sometimes the same was done with secret information from the Bureau's files "for the purpose of exposing the nature, aims and membership of the various groups." The Bureau also called any civil or criminal violation by groups or their members, however large or small, to the attention of other local, state, or federal authorities, on the theory that if they could be immobilized with legal problems they would be less active. In some instances, especially with the Old Left, informants were sent into organizations with specific instructions to stir up dissension and exploit internal differences to render the group less effective and coherent. The Bureau also surreptitiously notified "credit bureaus, creditors, employers and prospective employers" about individuals' "illegal, immoral, radical and Communist Party activities in order to affect adversely their credit standing or employment status."

All COINTELPRO actions were stopped by Hoover in 1971, with no apologies. Similar activities, although on a less formalized basis, continued until Hoover's death. His successors halted their casual use, and took measures to see that any such actions in the future would have to be first approved at the highest levels.

Since Hoover's demise in 1972, under the stewardship of Clarence M. Kelley (1973–1978), William H. Webster (1978–1987), and William S. Sessions (1987–) the FBI has become both more sensitive and more effective when it comes to handling counterintelligence and "internal security" cases. It is recruiting men and women of different races and ethnic backgrounds, both as a measure of affirmative action and because they make useful special agents in such a heterogeneous country. Several recent complaints from minority groups within the Bureau show that perhaps the assimilation process has not gone as far as it might, but at least it is under way.

HEADS OF THE FBI AND PREDECESSOR AGENCIES

July 26, 1908—Stanley W. Finch appointed head of the Special Agent Force.

March 16, 1909—The Special Agent Force is replaced by the Bureau of Investigation [BOI]. Stanley W. Finch is Chief of the BOI.

April 30, 1912—A(lexander) Bruce Bielaski appointed head of BOI.

February 10, 1919—William E. Allen appointed acting head of BOI.

July 1, 1919—William J. Flynn appointed head of BOI.

August 22, 1921—William J. Burns appointed head of BOI.

May 10, 1924—J. Edgar Hoover designated Acting Director of BOI.

December 10, 1924—J. Edgar Hoover appointed Director of BOI.

July 1, 1932—The BOI becomes the United States Bureau of Investigation. Hoover continues as Director.

August 10, 1933—The Division of Investigation, which includes the BOI, is formed. Hoover continues as Director.

July 1, 1935—The Federal Bureau of Investigation comes into existence, with J. Edgar Hoover as Director.

May 3, 1972—L. Patrick Gray becomes Acting Director of the FBI.

April 27, 1973—William D. Ruckelshaus becomes Acting Director of the FBI.

July 9, 1973—Clarence M. Kelley is appointed Director of the FBI.

February 23, 1978—William H. Webster is appointed Director of the FBI.

May 26, 1987—John Otto becomes Acting Director of the FBI.

November 2, 1987—William Steele Sessions is appointed Director of the FBI.

FIFTH AMENDMENT

> No person shall be held to answer for a capital, or otherwise infamous crime, unless on a presentment or indictment of a Grand Jury, except in cases arising in the land or naval forces, or in the Militia, when in actual service in time of War or public danger; nor shall any person be subject for the same offence to be twice put in jeopardy of life or limb; nor shall be compelled in any criminal case to be a witness against himself, nor be deprived of life, liberty, or property, without due process of law; nor shall private property be taken for public use, without just compensation.

The BILL OF RIGHTS, in codifying the personal liberties of U.S. citizens, has provided a vast and continuing amount of work for lawyers and jurists. Among the most fecund of the 10 articles is the Fifth Amendment, which provides for GRAND JURY indictments for major crimes and prevents double jeopardy and self-incrimination. The first person to use the Fifth Amendment for protection during a trial was NICKY ARNSTEIN, on trial in a federal court for bond theft in the 1920s. His attorney, William Fallon, had him refuse to answer certain questions on the grounds that the answers might incriminate him. The judge, who had never heard of such a thing, cited him for contempt. The case went to the Supreme Court, and the justices ruled for Arnstein and the Fifth Amendment. Since then the phrase, "I refuse to answer on the grounds that it may tend to incriminate me," has become a courtroom litany of gangsters and investment bankers.

FIND THE LADY

See: THREE-CARD MONTE

FINGERPRINT IDENTIFICATION

The identification value of the whorls, arches and loops in the skin at the ends of fingers has been recognized for many centuries. In the Babylonia of Hammurabi, 4,000 years ago, contracts were written on clay tablets and sealed with the thumbprints of the parties involved. In one tablet of the period, preserved by the British Museum, a Babylonian official records that he was ordered to confiscate some property, make arrests and secure the fingerprints of the defendants.

The Chinese historian Kia Kung-yen, writing during the Tang period (c. A.D. 650), commented that in earlier times "wooden tablets were inscribed with the terms of the contract, and notches were cut in the sides at identical places so that the tablets could later be matched, thus proving them genuine. The significance of the notches was the same as that of the fingerprint (*hua chi*) of the present time." In the twelfth century, Shi-naingan, a Chinese detective story writer, speaks of recording criminals' fingerprints as though the practice were common in the era.

In seventeenth-century Europe, several medical researchers commented on the ridge patterns of fingers and one, Professor Marcello Maloighi of the University of Bologna, peered through the newly invented microscope to describe the "diverse figures on palmar surfaces, and loops and spirals." In 1823, Anatomy Professor John Evangelist Purkinje of the University of Breslau wrote a thesis on fingerprints, in which he remarked that he had identified nine "principal varieties of curvature according to which tactile furrows . . . are disposed upon the inner surface of the last phalanx of the fingers."

In 1858, Sir William John Herschel, chief administrative officer for the Old East India Company of the Hooghly district, Bengal, India, began using handprints on contracts to impress his native contractors with the solemnity of the occasion. He later modified his technique to record just the last finger joint. In 1877, Herschel began using finger-

The fact that fingerprints are unique to every individual became useful in the identification of criminals when scientists had broken the prints down to their basic types and developed a system for characterizing them. (Federal Bureau of Investigation.)

print records as a means of identifying prisoners. He recommended extending its use to other districts, but his recommendation was not put into effect.

A British doctor, Henry Faulds, who was working at the Tsukiji Hospital in Tokyo in the 1870s, became interested in fingerprints when he noticed the imprint of the fingers of ancient potters left accidentally in the markings of their pots. This inspired him to make an exhaustive study of fingerprints, and in 1880 he published an article in the magazine *Nature* in which he discussed the possibility of identifying criminals by the latent fingerprints they left behind. He had already proven the practicality of his methods by developing fingerprint evidence in two minor criminal cases, proving the guilt of one person and establishing the innocence of the other.

It was by now generally recognized that a person could be identified by fingerprints, but what was still needed was a practical method of classifying them so that one set of fingerprints could be found out of the thousands that would be on record in criminal identification bureaus. In 1892, Sir Francis Galton, a famed British anthropologist and cousin of Charles Darwin, published *Fingerprints*, the study of which he had been pursuing for 12 years. The book covered the anatomy of fingerprints, along with practical methods for recording them and several suggestions as to ways to best classify them. He also verified that an individual's fingerprints are unique to the individual and established that an individual's fingerprints remain essentially unchanged and recognizable throughout his or her lifetime. In 1894, Galton's system of fingerprinting was adopted by Scotland Yard, which continued to use it along with ALPHONSE BERTILLON's anthropometry until the latter was dropped in the 1920s.

One of the first Americans to recognize the value of fingerprints was Mark Twain, who tells of a murderer being identified by his thumbprint in his 1883 book *Life on the Mississippi*. In *Pudd'nhead Wilson* (1893), a part of the convoluted plot involves sorting out a pair of young men, mixed-up as babies, by fingerprint identification. The earliest known official use of fingerprints in the United States was in 1882, when Gilbert Thompson of the U.S. Geological Survey put his fingerprint on his own official orders to prevent their being counterfeited.

The first systematic fingerprint files were kept by Argentinean police official Juan Vucetich, who based his work on the Galton system. Vucetich became the first criminologist to solve a murder by identifying fingerprints left at the scene of the crime in 1892 in La Plata, Argentina. The system developed by Vucetich became the basis for the systems used in many South and Central American countries.

In 1900, Sir Edward Richard Henry, commissioner of the London Metropolitan Police, published *Classification and Uses of Finger Prints*, which codified and extended the discoveries of Galton. The Henry system is today in use in practically all parts of the world that do not use the Vucetich system. A fingerprint is analyzed in terms of its arches, loops and whorls; thus, the Galton-Henry system is commonly known as the A-L-W method. In Germany in 1909, the Klatt system was in use, but it was found to be inadequate and elements of the Henry system were added.

Dr. Henry P. DeForest induced the New York Civil Service Commission to use fingerprinting to identify applicants for civil service testing in 1902. On June 5, 1903, SING SING prison in New York officially adopted the fingerprint system of identification. The St. Louis Police Department began a fingerprint bureau in 1904 with the help of a serendipitously visiting sergeant from Scotland Yard. That same year the federal penitentiary at Leavenworth, Kansas, started its own fingerprint bureau. Leavenworth offered a fingerprint exchange service to interested police departments around the country. In 1905, the United States Army began fingerprinting for identification, followed by the Navy in 1907, and the Marine Corps in 1908.

The International Association of Chiefs of Police set up the National Bureau of Criminal Identification (NBCI) and encouraged local police departments to send copies of their fingerprints to this central registry. In 1924, the Identification Division was established within the BOI, precursor to the FBI, by an act of Congress. Fingerprint records from Leavenworth Penitentiary and the NBCI were combined in the new division, which thus started with a nucleus of 810,188 fingerprint records and has been growing ever since.

An international exchange of fingerprint data was organized in 1932. In 1933, the BOI set up a civil identification section, and a single fingerprint section for the technical examination of latent prints.

It is not actually impossible for two people to have the same fingerprints, but it is highly unlikely. The estimates of exactly how personal fingerprints are vary tremendously, but one of the lower figures quoted by fingerprint experts is that there is no more than one chance in 64 billion that the print of any one finger on one person could be duplicated exactly on another person. Since the total number of people who have ever lived is less than one-fifth of that, the reliability of fingerprint identification is statistically secure.

Several criminals have attempted in various ways to "beat" the fingerprint system. JOHN DILLINGER had a doctor burn his fingertips with acid to remove the prints. But within a few weeks the ridges in his fingers grew back in the same pattern that had been destroyed, and when he was killed in a gun battle his body was positively identified by his fingerprints.

Although fingerprints present a positive method of individual identification, the comparison must be made by people trained in the taking of prints and their examination. Under the Henry system and its various modifications, prints are filed by a classification based on all 10 fingers. If the classification is done incorrectly, then the prints will be forever lost in the file room. Over the years, the basic Henry system of classification has been expanded, extended, modified and adapted to local conditions in various countries.

Until recently there was no practical way to identify a single fingerprint unless the investigator had a fairly good idea of who might have left it. Several methods of classifying single prints were developed, such as the Battley single-fingerprint system, which uses a special magnifying glass, or the FBI's Five-Finger System, but they demand meticulous classifying and even more meticulous searching for a match. And, as was in most cases, if the suspect print was not codified in one of these systems, direct comparisons would have to be made with the suspect prints until a match was found; a tedious task at best, and practically impossible if there were a large number of possibilities. Today there are computer matching systems, but it is still a time-consuming process.

The presentation of fingerprint evidence in courtrooms is also a specialized skill, as it is necessary to be able to show the comparison between the fingerprint lifted at the crime scene and the print of the suspect in a way that will make their relationship clear to an untrained jury. Using greatly enlarged photographs with lines drawn pointing to at least 14 points of similarity is an accepted method.

The techniques of lifting latent fingerprints has advanced continuously, and it is now possible to lift prints from surfaces that were once thought to be all but impossible, like paper, leather and fabric. Chemical fumes that react with body amino acids will develop a fingerprint in situations where nothing else will even show that one is present. Some work has even been done in trying to tell something about a person's profession or physical condition from his or her fingerprint. So far this has been successful only in unusual cases.

FINK, Isador (1895?–1929)

A LOCKED-ROOM MYSTERY THAT HAS NEVER BEEN SOLVED

A classic form of the detective story is the Locked Room Mystery, where a person is found murdered in a room which is locked from the inside, with no apparent means of egress for the murderer. One of the few occasions when it happened in real life was on March 9, 1929, in the killing of laundryman Isador Fink in his laundry on East 132nd Street in New York City.

Patrolman Albert Kattenborn arrived in response to a call to the police from a next-door neighbor, who heard three shots, close together, and the sound of something falling. The front door of Fink's tiny laundry was locked and bolted. Kattenborn boosted a boy up to the transom, but that was also locked, and he had to smash the glass to get in. The boy unbolted and unlocked the door for Patrolman Kattenborn, who entered and found Fink's dead body on the floor. He had three bullet wounds in him: two in the chest and one in the wrist.

The investigating detectives looked the place over carefully. The doors and windows were all bolted from the inside—Fink had a fear of robbery—and there were no secret panels, hidden doors or trap doors in the floor or ceiling. The detectives were inclined to call it a suicide except for two things: the wound in the wrist, which indicated that he was defending himself from his assailant, and the absence of a gun. Perhaps it was suicide, and Fink had lived long enough to hide the gun. They searched the store thoroughly, looking through all the bins and cupboards, and through the washed clothing and the clothing to be washed. They tore up the floorboards, they sounded the walls and ceiling—no gun.

A special squad of men was sent from police headquarters to search the store. They literally tore the place apart, and they found nothing.

The case was never solved.

FISH, Albert (1870–1936)

A serial killer whose grotesque and macabre crimes shocked and horrified the nation when he was finally caught, Albert Fish was a mild-looking housepainter with a wife—until she ran off with a half-wit—and six children. His personal habits were bizarre, including a predilection for sticking needles into himself and having himself beaten with a paddle studded with nails, but the various psychiatrists who looked at him always found him sane, if a bit odd. Of course, they were unaware of some of his more socially unacceptable pastimes. He killed his first man in Wilmington, Delaware, in 1910. He then apparently molested hundreds of children, preferring children for their innocence and because, as he wrote in his confession, "they don't tell."

Over the years, he killed at least 15 children, usually cooking and eating parts of their bodies before disposing of the bones. In New York City in 1928 he killed and made a stew of his last known victim, 12-year-old Grace Budd. The police were baffled by the girl's disappearance. In 1934, Fish wrote the girl's parents a letter detailing what had happened to Grace. The police traced the letter to Fish and took him into custody, after which he confessed to a wide variety of crimes in over 20 states.

When Fish was sentenced to die in the electric chair at Sing Sing he commented, "It will be the supreme thrill; the only one I haven't tried." He got his chance on January 16, 1936, and was described by press observers as positively delighted as he was strapped into the chair. It took two jolts of electricity to kill him. *See also:* MASS MURDERERS

FISHER, Amy Elizabeth (1974–)

SHE WANTED HER BOYFRIEND JOEY BUTTAFUOCO TO LOVE HER—SO SHE SHOT HIS WIFE

Shortly after 11:30 A.M. on May 19, 1992, six weeks before she was due to graduate from John F. Kennedy High School in Bellmore, Long Island, 17-year-old Amy Fisher knocked on the door of a house in Massapequa, Long Island. When 37-year-old Mary Jo Buttafuoco came to the door, the two had a brief conversation, and then Amy shot Mary Jo through the head with a .25 caliber pistol. Amy ran to the car she had come in, and was driven off by a friend. Neighbors who had heard the shot called 911, and Mary Jo was rushed by police helicopter to Nassau County Medical Center in East Meadow, a few miles away. Joey Buttafuoco, Mary Jo's husband, was called at Complete Auto Body and Repair in Baldwin, Long Island, where he worked (his father and brother owned the business), and he rushed home in time to see his wife being airlifted away. Also 37, he and Mary Jo had been high school sweethearts.

Mary Jo was in surgery for over seven hours, and the doctors were not hopeful when they released her to the recovery room. They had not been able to remove the bullet, which was lodged at the base of her skull, and she had suffered a small stroke while on the operating table. But by next morning Mary Jo was awake and answering questions by painstakingly printing notes—she couldn't speak because of the tube down her throat. When she wrote that she had been shot by "a nineteen-year-old girl," Joey tearfully told the detectives that he knew who it must be.

When the Nassau County detectives went to pick up Amy Fisher, with whom Joey told them he'd been having an affair for the past year (he has since denied ever saying that), they thought they had a pretty good understanding of the case. As they described it to the press when Amy was in custody, it was a simple matter of the lover spurned. Amy still wanted Joey, who had cast her aside. So in an act of spite, or vengeance, or a misguided attempt to win him back, she had tried to eliminate her rival, Joey's wife.

But the case had layers that they had not yet begun to unravel. Amy was sexually promiscuous, although Joey was her true love. An insecure girl with limited feelings of self-worth, she needed the approval of the older man, and she earned it in bed. She worked on call at the ABBA escort service, where she worked as what amounted to a high-priced prostitute with a select client list of men who liked young girls. She claims Joey got her the job, but he denies it. All this while attending high school, dating, and living at home with her parents, who didn't suspect anything about her double life. There had been a moment when she was diagnosed with genital herpes that she told her parents that Joey Buttafuoco had given it to her. Her father, furious at the auto mechanic, threatened to have him prosecuted for statutory rape. But Joey came to the house and insisted that, although Amy was infatuated with him, he had never touched her. Amy, perhaps realizing the trouble she could get Joey into, renounced her story and said she had made it up. Her parents allowed themselves to be mollified.

After the shooting of Mary Jo, Amy was held on two million dollars bail. Her attorney, Eric Naiburg, tried to get it reduced, but the prosecutor, Fred Klein, fought any attempt to lower it. He told the judge that Amy "could slide into that sleazy world and no one would be able to find her, and she'd be able to support herself very well." This posits the interesting theory that prostitutes are invisible. Considering the media coverage given to Amy it is doubtful that she could have gone anywhere without at least two camera crews tagging along. Klein clinched his argument by telling the judge that Amy "is as dangerous as John Gotti." The judge refused to reduce her bail. It took Amy's parents over two months to come up with the bail bond.

The police found the gun, a Titan .25 automatic, in the sewer near Amy's house. They traced it to Peter Guagenti, who sold it to Amy and who drove her to the Buttafuoco's house when she shot Mary Jo. He claimed that, although Amy had said she was going to shoot Mrs. Buttafuoco, he didn't really think she'd go through with it. Which is probably true. It is possible that Amy herself didn't think she'd go through with it.

Within two weeks after the shooting, the whole affair had become an incredible media circus. Naiburg decided to sell Amy's story to the highest bidder in order to raise the money to bail Amy out of jail. Television shows like "A Current Affair," "Inside Edition," and "Hard Copy" and lesser news feature shows on all three television networks presented "fatal attraction" stories night after night, interviewing anyone even faintly concerned with the events or the people involved. Both the Fisher and Buttafuoco families found television cameramen camped on their doorsteps twenty-four hours a day.

On September 23, 1992, a plea bargain was reached between the defense and prosecution lawyers, which resulted in Amy being sentenced to from five to fifteen years in prison. Three days later she overdosed on tranquilizers and was rushed to the hospital to have her stomach pumped. She remained in the hospital psychiatric unit for a month. On December 1, she began serving her sentence.

The fascination with the case continued unabated. On December 28 the made-for-television movie *Amy Fisher—My Story* was aired on NBC. A week later *The Amy Fisher Story* was aired on ABC on the same night that CBS showed *Casualties of Love: The "Long Island Lolita" Story*. All three earned high ratings.

On April 15, 1993, Joey Buttafuoco was charged with statutory rape and sodomy. The case against him was supported by Amy's testimony, as well as that of people who worked in his garage. There were also motel registration records. Joey claimed they were forged. His wife said she believes him. As this book goes to press, this case is still unresolved.

FIVE POINTS

See: ROOKERY; FIVE POINTS GANG

FIVE POINTS GANG

Coming from a tradition begun in the ROOKERIES of New York City, the Five Points Gang flourished for the first two decades of the twentieth century. At its height, its chief, Paul Kelly (born Paolo Antonini Vaccarelli), controlled a group of over 1,000 hoodlums for hire, mostly of Italian origin. They were used to bust up rival saloons or other businesses, as strikebreakers and for other jobs demanding muscle and small respect for the law. They committed mayhem for a price, on a graduated scale from arm-breaking to murder. On their own, they practiced extortion, hijacking, saloon keeping and pimping. *See also:* AL(PHONSE) "SCARFACE" CAPONE; JOHN TORRIO

FLEGENHEIMER, Arthur

See: DUTCH SCHULTZ

FLOYD, Charles Arthur "Pretty Boy" (1901–1934)

PUBLIC ENEMY # 1 AND POPULAR HERO, FLOYD HAD AN UNCANNY ABILITY TO AVOID POLICE TRAPS—UNTIL THE LAST ONE

Born and raised in Oklahoma, Charles Floyd turned to crime in his early twenties as a convenient way to support his young wife and child. Released from prison after serving half of a

CHARLES ARTHUR FLOYD

ALIAS "PRETTY BOY FLOYD"

- HIGHWAY ROBBER, BANK ROBBER AND KILLER.
- PARTICIPATED IN KANSAS CITY MASSACRE, JUNE 17, 1933.
- HE WAS KILLED ON OCTOBER 22, 1934, BY FBI AGENTS AND LOCAL POLICE OFFICERS NEAR EAST LIVERPOOL, OHIO, WHILE RESISTING ARREST.

FBI information sheet on "Pretty Boy" Floyd, "highway robber, bank robber and killer." (Federal Bureau of Investigation.)

three-year sentence for a payroll robbery, he concentrated on robbing banks for the next few years. On March 11, 1930, he and his associates Jack Atkins and Tom Bradley robbed the Sylvania, Ohio, bank, making off with about $2,000. It was the Depression, and even the banks were poor. The robbers were pursued by motorcycle policemen and, in a running gun battle, one of the policemen, Harlan F. Manes, was shot and the gang's getaway car crashed into a telephone pole, resulting in their capture. Bradley received the death penalty for killing Manes, Atkins was sentenced to life imprisonment, and Floyd received a 10- to 25-year sentence. While on the train taking him to prison, Floyd kicked out a window and jumped to freedom just shy of the prison walls. This would be the last time he was in the hands of the authorities until his death four years later.

Floyd worked his way to Toledo, Ohio, where he joined Bill "the Killer" Miller. They started robbing filling stations and then proceeded to banks, hitting a dozen or so by the time they reached Kansas City. There, they stayed at Mother Ash's Kansas City Whorehouse, a well-known establishment that was known to have police protection. Legend has it that Floyd was given his nickname there, when Mother Ash told him, "I want you all to myself, pretty boy." But another legend, just as plausible, holds that he got the nickname in childhood from his habit of constantly slicking down his hair with a comb.

At Mother Ash's, the two bank robbers found romance. Floyd favored Mother Ash's daughter-in-law Rose, and Miller decided he liked Rose's sister Beulah Bird. Mother Ash's two sons, William and Wallace Ash, resented the pair's attention to the sisters, who happened to be their wives, and decided to turn Floyd and Miller in to the police. Floyd and Miller murdered the Ash brothers on March 25, 1931, and left town with the girls. Floyd returned a few months later long enough to kill PROHIBITION agent Curtis C. Burks, who accidentally came across his Kansas City hideout.

Later that year, Miller was killed in a shootout with the Bowling Green, Ohio, police, which also claimed the life of Police Chief Carl Galliher. The two girls were wounded in the incident, and Floyd fled. Returning to Oklahoma, Floyd teamed up with preacher-turned–bank robber George Birdwell, and they went on a bank robbing spree, freely killing guards and bystanders, but making no more than a couple of hundred dollars from each bank. Floyd and Birdwell made it a practice of tearing up any mortgage deeds they could find in the bank while they were taking its money, and they often scattered money out of the car window while leaving town. This made them popular with those citizens of Oklahoma that didn't own bank stock, and put them at one with the other legendary bank robbers of the period like JOHN DILLINGER and "BABY FACE" NELSON.

Floyd's seeming invincibility made his Robin Hood legend grow, despite his propensity for wanton killing. The authorities decided to concentrate on capturing him and the two or three other popular hero bank robbers. On February 11, 1932, Floyd barely escaped a police trap in Tulsa, Oklahoma. On April 7, he killed Erv A. Kelley, a special investigator for the State of Oklahoma, while escaping from another trap near Bixby, Oklahoma. On November 1, 1932, Floyd and Birdwell, along with Aussie Elliot, went after the Sallisaw Bank in Sallisaw, Oklahoma, Floyd's home town. Several of the town's citizens recognized him as he strode down the street toward the bank with a machine gun under his arm.

"Howdy, Chock," one of them called, using Floyd's old nickname. "Where you headed?"

"Howdy, Newt," Floyd replied. "Going to rob the bank."

"Give 'em hell, Chock!" another farmer yelled.

This was the attitude that the government desperately wanted to discourage.

A week later the trio picked up a good score at Henryetta, Oklahoma, leaving the town's bank with $11,352.20. Shortly after that George Birdwell was killed by the police while engaging in a solo bank robbery.

Floyd and his partner Adam Richetti were suspected of being involved in the KANSAS CITY MASSACRE of June 18, 1933, where several federal officers and local policemen were killed, but the evidence of his involvement was thin. In October 1934, Floyd was spotted in a wooded area outside of Wellsville, Ohio, and FBI head gangster hunter MELVIN PURVIS went down to apprehend him. Floyd was shot down in a cornfield outside East Liverpool, Ohio, on October 22, and the bank robber went down with eight bullets in him. As he lay dying, Purvis asked him if he was involved in the Kansas City Massacre, but Floyd had other things on his mind and gave an evasive answer. His last words were, "I won't tell you nothing."

With John Dillinger dead several months before, and "Baby Face" Nelson with barely a month to live, the age of the Robin Hood bank robbers was just about over.

FOSTER, Mathan (1753–1819)

In Masonville, New York, 66-year-old Mathan Foster bought some arsenic from the local druggist, remarking in a jocular fashion that he was "looking about for a new wife." The druggist remembered the remark when Mathan's wife Eleanor died a few days later, and he informed the authorities. Arsenic was detected in Eleanor's body, and Mathan was tried by Martin Van Buren (who was attorney general of New York before he was elected president), found guilty, and hanged.

FOURTH AMENDMENT

The right to be secure from unreasonable searches and seizures, as established by the Fourth Amendment to the Constitution of the United States, is the constitutional guarantee that makes advocates of "law and order" the most unhappy. The amendment reads:

> The right of the people to be secure in their persons, houses, papers and effects, against unreasonable searches and seizures, shall not be violated, and no Warrants shall issue, but upon probable cause, supported by Oath or affirmation, and particularly describing the place to be searched, and the persons or things to be secured.

It must be admitted that the necessity of getting a warrant and showing probable cause has prevented numerous police searches that would have turned up evidence of serious crimes. And that the failure to get a proper warrant has resulted in the exclusion of evidence necessary for the conviction of criminals who were certainly guilty of serious crimes.

On the other hand, allowing police authorities to stop whomever they please or search wherever they please would be putting excessive power in the hands of the guardians of the law—Lord Acton's comment that power tends to corrupt has been confirmed time after time in country after country. The framers of the Bill of Rights wisely chose to temper the power of the police with the authority of the courts.

Several Supreme Court decisions have helped draw the line as to what constitutes unreasonable searches and seizures. In the 1952 case *Rochin v. California*, Los Angeles County deputy sheriffs forced a tube down Mr. Rochin's throat and had his stomach pumped because they believed that he swallowed the evidence, in this case two capsules containing morphine. The capsules were recovered and used in evidence against him, over the defendant's objection. He was convicted and sentenced to 60 days in jail. The Supreme Court overturned the conviction, saying in part,

> the proceedings by which this conviction was obtained do more than offend some fastidious squeamishness or private sentimentalism about combatting crime too energetically. This is conduct that shocks the conscience, illegally breaking into the privacy of the petitioner, the struggle to open his mouth and remove what was there, the forcible extraction of his stomach's contents—this course of proceeding by agents of government to obtain evidence is bound to offend even hardened sensibilities. They are methods too close to the rack and the screw to permit of constitutional differentiation.

See also: MIRANDA RULE

FRANKS, Bobby (1910–1924); THE FRANKS CASE

Fourteen-year-old Bobby Franks was the victim of Nathan Leopold and Richard Loeb in what is known as either the Franks Case or the LEOPOLD AND LOEB CASE.

FREEDOM OF INFORMATION ACT

Passed in 1966 and revised in 1974, the Freedom of Information Act (FOIA) permits private citizens access to government records except when it is against the national interest to do so. This act has been used by the media and those with special interests to uncover cases of fraud and abuse of power within the government and to make available government information on business practices.

The FBI's use of COINTELPRO, their Counter Intelligence Program, to disrupt and "neutralize" groups that J. EDGAR HOOVER considered subversive was first brought to light in documents released through a FOIA lawsuit brought by Carl Stern, an NBC reporter. The children of ETHEL AND JULIUS ROSENBERG used the FOIA to force the FBI to release the extensive records of its investigation against their parents. The files revealed that, while the FBI was undeniably overzealous, the Rosenbergs were certainly guilty as charged.

The FOIA has also been used for such diverse purposes as establishing the severe environmental problems developing around federal nuclear weapons plants and documenting the hazards of the gas tank design in the Ford Pinto.

G

G-MEN

"G-Men" is a slang expression for government agents popularized through the "dime novels" that made up a large part of the reading of America's youth in the half-century after the Civil War. Applied at first to SECRET SERVICE agents and then to special agents of the FBI, the term came into the language firmly enough so that when GEORGE "MACHINE GUN" KELLY was captured in a Memphis boarding house in 1933, he was reported as screaming, "Don't shoot, G-men—don't shoot!" The story is apocryphal, since Kelly was actually captured by Memphis detectives and is probably the product of J. EDGAR HOOVER's public relations efforts.

GACY, John Wayne (1942–   )

THE "KILLER CLOWN" WHO LOVED YOUNG BOYS TO DEATH, GACY HOLDS THE OFFICIAL AMERICAN MASS MURDER RECORD

The nicest guy on the block, John Wayne Gacy, a successful building contractor, was always the life of the party in his Knollwood Park Township neighborhood; always the neighbor who was glad to help out; everybody's uncle; the man who loved to put on a clown costume and entertain the kids at block parties. Nobody in Knollwood Park, a Chicago suburb, had any idea of the perverted secret sexual life that Gacy was acting out.

Gacy was his parent's middle child, with an older and younger sister. He grew up in a suburban area of Chicago. His father, John Stanley Gacy, a skilled machinist, was also an abusive drunk who beat his wife and children. When displeased with his son, which was often, he called him "dumb and stupid," a redundant phrase which stuck in Gacy's mind ever after, and had a special belt to beat him with. The father had a particular dislike for "sissies" and homosexuals. John Wayne Gacy suffered from seizures and fainting spells in his youth, which his father regarded as either a sissy symptom, or a deliberate attempt at malingering to get out of going to school. When he was eight years old Gacy's mother took him to a doctor and he was put on barbiturates for five years, until

A jovial John Wayne Gacy poses as "Pogo the Clown." (Collection of the author)

a new doctor recognized his symptoms as a form of psychomotor epilepsy.

A dumpy, unattractive youth in high school, Gacy had a notable lack of success with girls. When one girl did go so far as to neck with him in a car, he passed out as it began getting serious.

When Gacy was 19 he moved away from his parents and got a job at the Palm Mortuary in Las Vegas. There he developed a certain fondness for dead bodies, as evidenced by the fact that the owner began finding that some of his clients' bodies had been undressed, with the clothes neatly folded alongside the corpse. Gacy quit before the owner or the police could determine just what unnatural acts the youth was performing on the bodies, and the matter was dropped. He moved back to Chicago and enrolled in business college. When he graduated in 1963 he moved to Springfield, Illinois, to live with an aunt and uncle, and went to work as a shoe salesman in a local Robinson's department store.

He joined the Junior Chamber of Commerce and achieved instant popularity, taking on all the jobs that the group needed done and doing them well.

In Springfield he met and married Marlynn Myers, who worked in the same department store, and shortly thereafter took a job his new father-in-law offered him managing three Kentucky Fried Chicken franchises in Waterloo, Iowa. He attended Kentucky Fried Chicken University to prepare himself, and then the couple settled down to a happy life in Waterloo, had two children, and became a part of the community. Gacy joined the Waterloo Jaycees and took an interest in the Waterloo Merchant Patrol, a volunteer protection force that served as a sort of police auxiliary. He installed a red light in his car and took to carrying a gun. It was during this period that Gacy began giving in to his strange sexual fantasies, and succeeded in pulling the facade of his life down in shreds around him.

The disintegration began with 15-year-old Donald Voorhees and 16-year-old Edward Lynch. Gacy took Voorhees, the attractive blond son of a fellow jaycee member, to his house when his wife was absent and showed him some stag movies, and then coaxed the boy into having mutual oral sex with him. The boy apparently came back several times, exchanging sex for money. In March, 1968, when Donald's father found out about his son's activities with Gacy, he called the police. At the grand jury hearing Lynch, who worked in Gacy's KFC franchise, came forward with a story more frightening than a sex-for-money transaction. He told the jury that he had been at Gacy's house in August, 1967, and Gacy had insisted on a sexual encounter. When Lynch refused, Gacy pulled a knife and ordered him into the bedroom. The two struggled over the knife, and Lynch received several minor cuts before Gacy dropped the knife. Then Gacy suddenly stopped fighting and apologized, offering to show Lynch a stag movie to make up for it. A short time later Gacy picked up a length of chain and tried to bind Lynch with it. They fought again, and Gacy choked the boy into unconsciousness. When Lynch came to a few moments later, Gacy was once again contrite, and took the boy home.

Gacy claimed that the story was made up, and offered to take a lie detector examination. He was given the test twice, at his own suggestion, and both times his examiner, Police Lieutenant Kenneth Vanous, found his reactions were "indicative of deception." A private firm reexamined him a month later, again at his own request. And again the finding was that his answers were less than truthful. Then, before the case came to trial, Gacy had the bright idea of hiring 18-year-old Russell Schroeder to beat up Voorhees and convince him not to testify. Schroeder did as requested, and Voorhees promptly reported this to the police. The prosecution brought additional charges against Gacy.

By the time the case was tried the prosecutors had flushed a covey of additional witnesses out of the teen-age population of Waterloo. An impressive roster of young men, mostly boys who had worked at the Gacy-managed Kentucky Fried Chicken, came forward and described their sexual encounters with Gacy. One told how Gacy's wife had seduced him, and then Gacy had demanded sexual favors in return. Another reported that Gacy had told several boys that he was conducting sexual experiments for the Governor of Iowa, paying them five dollars each for participating. He was a member of a sexual "commission," he told them, and showed them a certificate attesting to this. Gacy was sentenced to ten years in the Iowa State Reformatory for Men at Anamosa. His wife divorced him while he was incarcerated and moved away with the children. He proved to be a model prisoner, and walked out of Anamosa on parole after 18 months.

Gacy then moved back to Chicago and lived with his mother—his father had died while he was in prison. He went into the maintenance business with 20-year-old Mickel Reid, with whom he had a homosexual relationship, but Ried moved out when Gacy hit him with a hammer. Shortly after that Gacy remarried. His new bride was Cathy Hull, a girl who had gone to high school with his sister. Their marriage quickly disintegrated into an armed truce, when it became clear that Gacy preferred boys. By 1975 their sex life was over, and Cathy had a pretty good idea that he preferred boys.

Cathy gradually became aware of a peculiar smell coming up from the crawl space under the house. Gacy told her it must be the sewers, and spread lime down there to kill the odor. But it kept getting worse.

Gacy was now a successful contractor, but in the dark of the night and the privacy of his own home he acted as though he were in the grip of an irresistible impulse, sexually molesting and then murdering young men. To the public Gacy was well liked, helpful to neighbors, the host of many pleasant parties. Dressed up as "Pogo the Clown," he entertained the local children at birthday parties.

From 1972 until he was apprehended in 1978, with ever-increasing frequency, Gacy lured boys and young men to his home. Usually he promised them jobs with his construction company. Sometimes he would just drive around and see if he could pick up some young homeless boy off the street. Often he claimed to be "Detective Jack Hanley" when he picked up the young runaways. Once at home with the boy he would show him the "handcuff game," putting on a pair of trick handcuffs and magically snapping them off. But when the boy tried it, the cuffs wouldn't open. Then Gacy would play the "rope game," twisting a rope around the boy's neck and tightening it until the boy was only semi-conscious. He would keep the boy in this state, sometimes for hours, while he sodomized him. Then he would pull the rope tight one last time and kill the boy, burying him in a mass grave under the house.

When 15-year-old Robert Piest disappeared in 1978, he was traced to Gacy's house. Gacy admitted to police that the youth had been there, but said that he had left and Gacy didn't know where he had gone. After all, a lot of boys run away from home every year.

The police, unsatisfied with Gacy's story, investigated further. They came back with a search warrant a few days later and found many suggestive items, such as pornography, a high-school ring with the initials J.A.S.—clearly not Gacy's—an 18-inch dildo, a collection of police badges in the attic, and a three-foot board with holes drilled at each end that looked like some strange sort of homemade bondage device. But nothing substantial enough to arrest Gacy. One item, a photo developing receipt from a drugstore, would eventually be tied in to the missing boy, but they didn't know that then. They instituted a close surveillance of Gacy, both to wear him down and to prevent him from killing any other boys. On Thursday, December 21, they arrested him on a drug charge—he had passed a packet of marijuana to a garage attendant—and got a second search warrant. This time they dug into the crawlspace beneath the house. What they found there and in his garage was more horrifying than anything they had imagined. The stench was horrible once the top layer of lime was disturbed. Pieces of flesh, skin and bones filled the buckets that they were using to drain away the water. Bodies filled the crawlspace, in some places three and four deep. Some of them still had the cords around their necks that Gacy had strangled them with. By the end of December they had recovered 29 bodies. The final count, including some that Gacy had thrown in the river, was 35.

Gacy began confessing shortly after he was taken into custody, admitting killing somewhere between 25 and 30 young men—he was unsure of the total. But, he insisted, they had all deserved it. He also insisted that he had never used force, and that he was not a homosexual.

He was actually charged with 33 deaths, which makes him the largest official mass murderer in American history. He was tried in March, 1980, and sentenced to death. The sentence was later commuted to life imprisonment.

GAFF

A gaff is a secretly prepared device that provides an advantage to its owner, most often in the context of cheating at gambling. Although secret, it is not always hidden; frequently, a gaff is disguised as a normal object. The word *gaff* can also be used as a verb, meaning to prepare such a device.

GAMBLING AND GAMBLERS

The history of gambling in the United States is as old as the history of America, and for most of that time and over most of the country, it has been prevalent and illegal. Card games have been the overwhelming favorite of the gambling fraternity, with craps a close second because of the ease of transportation of the required apparatus, but, where available, the gambling games have included chuck-a-luck, backgammon, chess, roulette, punch boards, keno, lotto, policy, bolita, penny-pitching, and a legion of SHORT CON games known as bar bets. Over the past two centuries, Americans have also bet on wild animal contests, bullfights, dogfights, cockfights, human fights (boxing, wrestling, mud wrestling, kick-boxing, quarterstaff fighting, arm wrestling and thumb wrestling), footraces, dog races, horse races (trotter, bareback, and saddle; thoroughbred, quarterhorse), dog sled races, automobile races, boat races, airplane races, frog jumping contests, worm races, rat races, baseball, football, basketball, soccer, tennis, swimming and jai alai.

Illicit gambling has been a major source of income for ORGANIZED CRIME, as major crime figures in the cities control the NUMBERS RACKET, or policy houses, the bookmakers that take bets on sporting events, and the illegal casinos. In the 1930s and 1940s, gambling ships stood off the coast of California, beyond the three-mile limit, and serviced their customers by speedboat throughout the day and night. Slot machines were in every candy store, barbershop, and corner drugstore in New York City until Mayor Fiorello La Guardia cracked down in the late 1930s. Even pinball machines were used for gambling, storekeepers paying off on the free games won. Las Vegas, the gambling capital of the world, was created by the Mob, when gangster BUGSY SIEGEL saw its potential in the 1940s and built the Flamingo Casino-Hotel, the first large casino on the strip, named after his girlfriend, VIRGINIA HILL.

Gambling can be a valid form of entertainment, if kept under control. An evening at the blackjack table might cost no more than an evening at the theater and can provide at least an equal amount of excitement. But if done to excess, it is sometimes considered a disease and should be treated as such.

Police detectives destroying gaming equipment during a raid on an illegal gambling casino in Los Angeles. (Dept. of Special Collections, University Research Library, UCLA.)

In 1894, *Koschitz's Manual of Useful Information*, a pamphlet-sized book on card manipulation and how to avoid it, was published. Although especially aimed at draw poker, its assertions are worth reading by all card players. Age has not staled the usefulness of the advice found therein. Among the comments in its General Remarks section are the following:

Every transaction at the card table should be spot cash.

Excessive talking of a merry, abusive, or of a boisterous nature, having a tendency to intoxicate the mind, ought, like excessive drinking, not to be tolerated.

Innocence or over simplicity of action on an opponent's part merits distrust.

The movements of opponents whose eyes one too frequently encounters demand notice.

One who insists in holding the deck otherwise than level is not fitted to be a participant.

A dealer who in shuffling screens the pack is well worthy of reprimand.

One who, in handling checks [chips], cigar, etc., habitually crosses his arms over the hand holding the deck, or quota, is a dangerous associate.

The wearing of hand bandages need be viewed with distrust.

No more participants should be admitted than the table can comfortably accommodate, for no room should be given for an excuse to withdraw the hands from the top thereof.

The pack should be so riffled as to displace all cards from their former position, and no one should be privileged with the knowledge of even the bottom card.

An unbanded, seamless, and untorn covering forms so important a feature as to call for the avoidance of all tables otherwise arranged.

Preposterous as the suggestion may sound, it may nevertheless stand one in hand to notice the backs of the cards shown down, to see whether they are of the same pack.

The value of an alleged best hand should be well examined before throwing one's own hand away, for anyone is apt to make mistakes.

An opponent, when called, should be compelled to spread his own hand out plainly; this to prevent confederates from aiding its value by adding a card thereto.

Practical education being of more value than theoretical, the inexperienced should check his anxiety for a bout with a known cheater, unless indifferent as to the price which such an experience may cost him.

The sudden darkening of the room while a deal is being made or a "pot" is being contested for is to be taken as an indication that something is about to occur which, if overlooked, may have to be dearly paid for.

As the fingering of the "pot" is not apt to increase the volume of the stakes therein, that habit should be rigidly prohibited.

Following are some gambling terms commonly used today:

Bottom Dealing—Taking the card from the bottom of the deck while allowing the viewer to think it came from the top

Broad Tosser—Dealer of three-card monte; also Spieler

Cold Deck—A deck that has been stacked in a useful manner that is ready to be unobtrusively exchanged for the deck in play

Fakir—(Carny, 1890–1910) A grifter traveling with a circus or carnival to toss the broads or work the nuts, or run another grift

False Cut—A manner of cutting cards so that they end up in the same relative order as they started

Grift—A confidence game or the act of running one; to be "on the grift" is to be knowledgeable about and actively engaged in confidence games

Hold Out—A device for keeping one or more cards on one's person and ready to reinsert into play

Marked Cards—Playing cards in which the backs have been altered in a subtle fashion with ink or another substance, or with scratches or pinholes, so that a knowledgeable player can read their value without seeing their faces

Mechanic—An expert at cheating with a deck of cards

Number Two Man—A dealer in a card game who can deal the second card from the top, retaining the top card, if it is to his advantage; a mechanic

Privilege—The right to do something illegal, like run a three-card monte game; purchased from the police or as a concession on a carnival or circus lot

Shill—Player in a gambling game who covertly works for the house. Sometimes merely to make the table look busy, the shill is allowed to win to create interest in the game

Spieler—Dealer of three-card monte; also broad tosser

Stacked Deck—A deck of cards arranged in a manner useful to the dealer, especially when used with a false cut

Tipping—Inadvertently showing a card to another player

Tossing the Broads—Dealing three-card monte

Vigorish—The house cut in a gambling house

See also: PUNCH BOARD SCAM; NUMBERS RACKET; THREE-CARD MONTE

GARCIA, Manuel Philip (?–1821)

On March 20, 1820, Manuel Garcia, a burglar and head of a band of highwaymen, took Peter Lagoardette and Jose Castillano, both members of his band, to an empty house outside of Norfolk, Virginia. There Garcia accused Lagoardette of consorting with Garcia's woman and attacked him with a cutlass. Castillano may or may not have aided in the murder, but he certainly helped Garcia hack Lagoardette's body into pieces and stuff them in the fireplace, which was then set afire: a job that was so bloody and messy that the men changed shirts before leaving.

The smell of the smoldering body attracted the neighbors, who called the local constables. One of them recalled how police in England had recently caught a murderer by tracing the laundry marks on abandoned clothing and determined to try the same thing with the bloody shirts found at the scene. As a result of this attempt at scientific police work, the two murderers were soon apprehended. This was the first known case where laundry marks figured in a police investigation in the United States. Garcia and Castillano were tried, found guilty and hanged in Norfolk on June 1, 1821.

GARFIELD, James A(bram) (1831–1881)

Twentieth president of the United States, James A. Garfield was assassinated on July 2, 1881, in a Washington railroad station by disappointed office seeker CHARLES JULIUS GUITEAU. Garfield, who had just taken office on March 4, was widely regarded as a good, decent man who would make a fine president. The royal courts of Europe declared a day of mourning for Garfield, the first ever declared for a citizen of a republic.

GEIN, Edward (1906–1984)

THE WISCONSIN FARMER WHO TOOK GHOULISHNESS TO NEW HEIGHTS

Ed Gein (rhymes with mean) and his brother Henry grew up on the family farm outside of Plainfield, Wisconsin. His mother, a strict disciplinarian with a particular distaste for sex (which may have been intensified by the fact that her husband, Gein's father, was an abusive alcoholic) warned her children often about the dangers of premarital sex. Gein's father died in 1940, and his brother was killed fighting a fire in 1944. The following year his mother died of a stroke, leaving Gein alone on a primitive farm, with no electricity, in a desolate area far from town. After his beloved mother died he boarded up her bedroom and sitting room, leaving them as they had been in her lifetime as a sort of shrine.

In 1952 Gein read of the sex change operation, one of the first such procedures, performed on Christine Jorgensen and was fascinated. He studied textbooks on anatomy and visited the local graveyard and dug up female corpses to dissect. He reasoned that he could turn himself into a female by covering himself with female parts. He made a belt of nipples and a vest of a human torso, complete with breasts. Skulls were used as decoration or fashioned into bowls. By this time he was, by any standard, completely mad. He would leave his house at night and dance naked under the moon, festooned with female body parts. The house slowly filled up with debris and garbage and the macabre mementos of his ghoulish experiments.

Sometime during this period he began killing local women and taking the bodies home. On November 16, 1957, he found 58-year-old Bernice Worden alone in her Plainfield hardware store and killed her. He took her body and the store's cash register with him when he left. The investigators found a half-written receipt for antifreeze on the counter, and Mrs. Worden's son remembered that Gein had mentioned needing antifreeze the day before.

When officers went to Gein's house to investigate they were confronted with a scene that has seldom been equalled for grotesque horror. The house was festooned with skulls and shrunken heads. Some of the skulls had been fashioned into drinking cups. There were pieces of furniture upholstered in human skin, and articles of clothing and bracelets created from human skin. A human heart was resting in a skillet on the stove. In a shed to the side of the house they found the missing

Mrs. Worden. As Judge Robert H. Gollmar described in *Edward Gein: America's Most Bizarre Murderer* (1981):

> . . . Mrs. Worden had been completely dressed out like a deer with her head cut off at the shoulders. Gein had slit the skin on the back of her ankles and inserted a wooden rod, 3½ feet long, and about 4 inches in diameter, and sharpened to a point at both ends, through the cut tendons on the back of her ankles. Both hands were tied to her side with binder twine. The center of the rod was attached to a pulley on a block and tackle. The body was pulled up so that the feet were near the ceiling.

One of the heads found in the house was identified as Mary Hogan, who had disappeared from the tavern she managed in Pine Grove, Wisconsin, on December 8, 1954. Some remains were not identified, or were thought to have come from deceased individuals when Gein acquired them. The body parts indicated that at least 15 people, living or dead, had been dismembered, disemboweled, and otherwise disfigured at the hands of Ed Gein. He confessed to killing Mary Hogan and Bernice Worden, and to stealing bodies from the cemetery. The authorities suspected him of at least three other murders, but couldn't prove them, and it is not known how many victims there might have been. The two they could prove were enough to get Gein committed to the Central State Hospital at Waupun, Wisconsin, where he spent the rest of his life, dying there in 1984.

Gein was the inspiration for the ghoulish villains in the 1959 novel *Psycho* by Robert Bloch, made into a movie by Alfred Hitchcock, and the 1990 novel *Silence of the Lambs* by Thomas Harris, adapted for the screen by Ted Tally and directed by Jonathan Demme.

GENERAL INTELLIGENCE DIVISION

In 1919, A. MITCHELL PALMER, attorney general under President Woodrow Wilson, established the General Intelligence Division (GID) of the U.S. Department of Justice. There was general concern at the time over the rise of violent anarchy around the country, accompanied by a rash of bombings. The mission of the GID was to investigate and compile dossiers on anarchists and other subversives throughout the country. Francis P. Garvan, an assistant attorney general, was put in charge, and appointed as his direct assistant was a young Justice Department lawyer named J. EDGAR HOOVER. The GID was involved in the infamous "Palmer Raids," in which thousands of people, including many native-born Americans, suspected of being "alien radicals" were arrested, held without warrants, due process or probable cause and barely escaped being deported. In 1925, the GID was made a part of the Justice Department's Bureau of Investigation, which eventually became the FEDERAL BUREAU OF INVESTIGATION (FBI).

GENOVESE, Catherine "Kitty" (1935–1964)

THIRTY-EIGHT PEOPLE WATCHED AS SHE WAS STABBED TO DEATH

In the early morning hours of March 13, 1964, Kitty Genovese, an attractive 28-year-old brunette, was returning to her apartment in Kew Gardens, Queens, New York, when she was brutally attacked by a man who had followed her from the subway. According to newspaper accounts, she screamed, "Oh my God, he stabbed me! Please help me! Please help me!"

Several lights went on in the surrounding apartments, and one man opened his window and yelled "Let that girl alone!", at which, the attacker moved away. But nobody came downstairs to assist the wounded girl. A minute later, when the window had closed and the lights were turned off, the attacker returned and stabbed her again. "I'm dying, I'm dying!" she screamed. Still no one came to her assistance or even called the police.

An overview of the neighborhood in which Kitty Genovese was killed showing (1) where she parked her car, (2) and (3) where she was attacked and (4) where her body was found. (Collection of the author.)

Her assailant left her and went back to his car, a white sedan parked down the street. Kitty crawled to a back door of her apartment house and collapsed in the doorway. Perhaps fearing that she was not dead, her attacker left his car and found her once again, stabbing her repeatedly before he finally left the scene and drove away. The time from the first attack to the last was 35 minutes. When the police were finally called, a patrol car was at the scene within two minutes. They found Kitty Genovese dead in the doorway.

Six days later, Winston Mosely, a 29-year-old factory worker, was arrested for the murder. He confessed to the crime and two other murders and was sentenced to life imprisonment.

Thirty-eight people watched or listened to Kitty Genovese being slowly murdered for half an hour, and not one of them came to her assistance or even called the police until it was too late. When questioned about this, the standard answer was, "I didn't want to get involved."

GENOVESE, Vito (1897–1969)

THE MAFIA CRIME BOSS WHOSE PARANOIA MADE JOE VALACHI SING

A member of CHARLES "LUCKY" LUCIANO's crime family, Vito Genovese worked his way up in the crime hierarchy by performing murder for hire. He was also not above murdering for his own benefit. He is reputed to have murdered Gerardo Vernotico in 1932 so he could marry Gerardo's wife Anna. In 1934, he murdered Ferdinand "Shadow" Boccia, when Boccia demanded his share of the profits from a money machine swindle. In 1937, learning that the New York authorities were gathering evidence about this earlier murder, he fled to Italy and became a lieutenant in another crime family, that of Benito Mussolini, that ruled Italy at the time. The story is that he supplied drugs to Mussolini's son-in-law Count Ciano.

As the Allied forces made their way up the Italian peninsula, Genovese switched allegiance and went to work as an interpreter for the U.S. Army. He helped the army close down several black market gangs in southern Italy, but his own black market operation prospered.

After the war, Genovese was extradited to New York to stand trial on the old murder charges, but the witnesses against him had mysteriously disappeared over the years. Genovese tried to wrest control of the Luciano crime family from

FRANK COSTELLO, its caretaker boss since Luciano had been deported to Italy. On May 2, 1957, a lone gunman put one shot into Costello's head as he entered his apartment building. Costello survived. Then somebody murdered ALBERT ANASTASIA, a dangerous friend of Costello.

Genovese tried to arrange a meeting to smooth things over, and a sit-down of crime bosses from around the country was scheduled at gangster JOSEPH BARBARA's Apalachin, New York, estate. The meeting was thwarted, either accidentally or as part of a clever plot, and Genovese was thus prevented from having his takeover of the Luciano operation okayed by the national board.

In 1958, Anna Genovese, Vito's wife by murder, sued him for divorce. In her demands for a property settlement, she gave the court details of what she knew of Vito's finances. By her calculations, Genovese's income was in excess of $40,000 a week. The IRS estimated that Vito Genovese had made over $30 million, on which he had not paid any income taxes.

At about the same time, Genovese's crime career began to deteriorate. A small-time Puerto Rican drug pusher named Nelson Cantellops, who was spending five years in SING SING, talked to the federal narcotics people. He told them how he had worked directly for Don Vito Genovese in a variety of illegal errands. It seemed too good to be true, so the agents gave him a battery of lie detector tests and spent hours recording his story down to the most minute details. But he passed the tests, and his story checked out. In July 1958, Genovese and 23 of his lieutenants and soldiers were indicted for conspiracy to traffic in drugs. Genovese was convicted and sentenced to 15 years in prison.

Genovese became increasingly paranoid in prison and started blaming everyone around him for his troubles. And those he blamed, he ordered killed. When Mafia button man and fellow prisoner JOSEPH M. VALACHI found out that Genovese had put out a contract on him, Valachi killed a prisoner whom he mistakenly thought was the hit man and then asked for federal protection in return for information. Valachi spent the next few years telling the authorities much about the activities of the Mafia. Not since the revelations of ABE "KID TWIST" RELES had the authorities had such an inside view of the workings of ORGANIZED CRIME.

Genovese died in prison in 1969. *See also:* APALACHIN CONFERENCE

GID

See: GENERAL INTELLIGENCE DIVISION

GILLARS, Mildred (1901–1988)

American-born Mildred Gillars broadcast music and Nazi propaganda under the name of "Axis Sally" to American troops from a German radio station during World War II. After the war, she spent 12 years in prison and then moved to Columbus, Ohio, where she taught German and music in a convent school.

GILLIS, Lester

See: GEORGE "BABY FACE" NELSON

GILMORE, Gary Mark (1940–1977)

In July 1976, Gary Gilmore was convicted by a Utah court of the murders of a gas station attendant and a motel room clerk and sentenced to execution by the firing squad. A decision of the U.S. Supreme Court in 1967 had put all of the states' capital punishment statutes in question and had caused a *de facto* moratorium on executions within the United States. The execution of Gary Gilmore, under a new capital punishment law designed to meet the Supreme Court's objections, would be the first in the United States in 10 years.

Despite the fact that Gilmore had refused to allow an appeal and had tried to commit suicide twice in his cell, a movement was started to stay his execution. The Supreme Court granted one stay at the request of Gilmore's mother, suggesting that the State of Utah prove that Gilmore had been of sound mind when he refused to appeal his death sentence. Then, in a five-to-four decision, the Court ruled that the state's death penalty law was constitutional. On January 17, 1977, a five-man firing squad put Gilmore to death.

GOLD, Harry (1912–1972)

A KEY CONSPIRATOR IN THE ATOM SPY RING, HE HELPED MAKE THE CASE AGAINST THE ROSENBERGS

Harry Gold, the member of the Atom bomb spy ring whose revelations led the FBI to the Rosenbergs. (Federal Bureau of Investigation.)

A member of the ATOMIC SPY RING rounded up by the FBI, Harry Gold was born in Berne, Switzerland (as Heinrich Golodnitsky), and immigrated to the United States with his parents in 1914, when he was two years old. He grew up in Philadelphia, Pennsylvania, and attended the University of Pennsylvania, but was unable to finish his studies because of lack of money. He went to work for the Pennsylvania Sugar Company as a laboratory assistant but was laid off in December 1932, in the midst of the Depression. A friend named Tom Black got him a job in Jersey City and tried to enlist him in the American Communist party. Capitalism, Black told Gold, "was doomed here in the United States. . . . The only country to which the working man owed allegiance was the Soviet Union, and that the only reasonable way of life was Communism."

Gold went with Black to party meetings but was not impressed with what he saw. When he got a chance to return to work for the Pennsylvania Sugar Company, he took it.

Despite his lack of enthusiasm for the Communist party, Gold shared Black's belief that helping the Soviet Union was helping the working man. Black showed up in Philadelphia in 1935 and told Gold that he now worked for AMTORG, the Soviet trade organization, in an unofficial but highly important capacity. He was supplying the Soviets with confidential industrial recipes, formulas and other proprietary information, passed on by other true believers. This saved the workers' paradise from having to pay royalties or do the research themselves.

Gold agreed to help and soon passed on to a man known as Paul Smith—the first real Soviet agent that Gold met—his company's formula for converting waste bone black and sulfuric acid into phosphoric acid.

When the Pennsylvania Sugar Company ran out of useful secrets, Gold did not need much convincing to take the job of courier and go-between to gather information from other Communist supporters and pass them on to his Soviet controller, who was Semon Markovich Semenov. "Sam" impressed Gold with his impeccable, although slightly accented, English, his good manners and his knowledge of chemical engineering and English literature.

In 1943, Gold's assignments became more interesting, when he became the go-between for "a group of American scientists in New York." In 1944 "Sam" left, turning Gold over to "John," who was actually Anatoli Yakovlev, a vice consul at the Soviet consulate in New York City.

Gold, who had a dull home life, fell naturally into the life of a spy. It gave him a secret existence, a chance to feel important in a way that his job and his family could not provide. He was able to compartmentalize his spying from his regular life, a trait shared by other agents. As he put it:

> When on a mission, I just completely subordinated myself to the task at hand, whether it was delivering data I had myself obtained, or a report I had written or whether it concerned getting information from a person such as Klaus Fuchs or Al Slack or Abe Rothman. Once I had started out on a trip, I totally forgot home and family and work and friends and just became a single-minded automaton, set to do a job. . . . And when the task was completed and I returned home, the same process again took place, but this time in reverse. I would return to work and . . . cast away and bury all thought and all memory of everything that had happened on the trip.

But Gold took the process of mental separation a step further and added one additional compartment: a wholly imaginary one. To have something to talk about with his new contacts, Gold invented a family: a wife named Sarah and twin children named David and Eppie. Soon the invention took on a life of its own. He related to his contacts how Sarah was having troubles with an old boyfriend, an underworld character named "Nigger Nate," and how one of the twins had come down with polio. He reported quarrels with Sarah, and once she almost left him. The stories were so realistic that no one he shared them with suspected that Sarah, David and Eppie existed only in Gold's imagination.

In 1943, Yakovlev sent Gold to Santa Fe, New Mexico. It was one of several meetings with Klaus Fuchs, the expatriate German physicist, who passed valuable information concerning the construction of the plutonium bomb, the gaseous diffusion process and other atomic secrets to the Soviets over a period of years until shortly before his arrest in 1950.

Gold came under FBI scrutiny first in 1947, as a result of the serial confessions of Elizabeth Bentley, the "Red Spy Queen," who had related the story of her life with Soviet Case Officer Jacob Golos to a horrified federal grand jury. The part of her story that involved Gold's sometime boss Abe Brothman and peripherally Gold, had not been enough for the grand jury to indict either man, but their names were now in the FBI index.

When Klaus Fuchs was arrested for espionage in Great Britain in 1950, he described his American contact, whom he had met several times in New York City, and who had come to see him at Los Alamos; a man he knew only as "Raymond." The description fit Harry Gold, and the FBI went to work immediately to make the identification positive. On May 22, 1950, Fuchs positively identified Gold from motion picture film and some still photographs. On the same day, FBI agents searching Gold's apartment (with his permission) found a map of Santa Fe in his closet. Gold, who until that moment had sworn he had never been west of the Mississippi, promptly confessed to a decade of espionage. He described his career as "Raymond" the courier in detail, but at first, not wanting to be a "squealer," he refused to reveal the identities of his fellow spies.

The FBI worked on him relentlessly to break him down. They cross-checked everything he said and pressed him for more and more detail. This quest for detail paid off with a bit of information that was the first step in the tortuous path that would lead to the trial and execution of ETHEL AND JULIUS ROSENBERG. In several of his meetings with Klaus Fuchs in Santa Fe, Gold related that he "traveled . . . via train to Chicago then by train to Albuquerque, and finally by bus to Santa Fe."

It was not necessary to go to Santa Fe by way of Albuquerque. Why had Gold done so? The FBI kept asking him this, and finally he told them. He had met a soldier and traded him $500 for information on the layout of Los Alamos, and "some bit of structural equipment of a machine." Gold could not remember the man's name, but he described him as about 25, five feet seven inches tall, sturdily built, with curly black or dark brown hair. He had visited the man's apartment, and remembered meeting his wife, whose name might have been Ruth.

Within days, the FBI determined that this soldier must have been David Greenglass, a relative of the Rosenbergs. They showed Gold photographs of Greenglass, but Gold was unable to make the identification. They showed him films of the house in Albuquerque, but it had changed so much he did not recognize it. Finally they located some old photographs of Greenglass, taken in 1945. Gold was immediately able to recognize the man in the pictures as the man he had met in Albuquerque. Although the FBI still had no hard evidence, they pulled in David Greenglass for questioning. He confessed during this first interview.

On July 20, 1950, Harry Gold pled guilty to a charge of espionage in a federal courtroom in Philadelphia. The U.S. attorney asked for a sentence of 25 years in prison for Gold's crimes. The judge, at Gold's sentencing in December 1950, increased it to 30.

Gold testified at a number of espionage trials over the next few years, the most important of which was the trial of Julius and Ethel Rosenberg for passing "atomic secrets" to the Soviets. The Rosenbergs were found guilty and given the death sentence. In 1953, they were executed. In *Invitation to an Inquest* (1983), Walter and Miriam Schneir attempted to defend the Rosenbergs in retrospect and made the claim that Gold had offered perjured testimony at their trial. Gold, who was still in Lewisburg Penitentiary, wrote an 84-page refutation of the Schneirs' claims. It included circumstantial detail that he would not have known had he not been where he had claimed. The facts were checked, and they corroborated his story.

GOLD BRICK GAME

See: SHORT CONS

GOTTI, John Joseph, Jr. "Johnny Boy" (1940–)

CRIMINAL CHARGES JUST DIDN'T STICK TO THE "TEFLON DON"—UNTIL ONE LAST TRIAL PUT HIM AWAY.

John Gotti, Jr., mobster son of immigrant Neapolitan laborer John Gotti, Sr., and his wife Fannie, grew up as one of 13 children in the Gotti apartment in New York City's South Bronx. When he was ten the family moved to a house on East 13th Street in Sheepshead Bay, a far corner of Brooklyn near the ocean. Two years later the house was sold, and the Gotti clan was forced to move to the Brownsville-East New York section of Brooklyn, an immigrant ghetto and breeding ground for many Italian and Jewish mobsters, home in the 1930s of the notorious MURDER, INCORPORATED. (It should not be necessary to point out that many attorneys, judges, doctors, teachers, and a few writers and artists also come from Brownsville).

In the late 1950s Gotti dropped out of high school and joined the Rockaway Boys, one of the numerous Brooklyn teen-age gangs of the period. Neighborhood groups with a tendency toward racial or ethnic uniformity, the gangs were constantly rumbling (fighting) amongst themselves. The Rockaway Boys and other local gangs such as the Mau Mau Chaplins, the Brownsville Stompers and the Ozone Park Saints formed a pool of violent street punks from which the adult mobsters in the neighborhood could recruit new talent as needed.

When Gotti was 17 he was caught stealing copper tubing from a construction site. He pleaded guilty and was sentenced to two years' probation as a juvenile. When he was 19 he was picked up in a raid on a gambling house—gambling was already and would remain a passion with him—and he received a 60-day suspended sentence. The ease with which he walked away from the consequences of his crimes evoked within him a deep disdain for the legal process that grew as time passed. His subsequent brushes with the law over the years did nothing to change his opinion.

When he was in his early 20s, Gotti married Victoria L. DiGiorgio. Their daughter, Angela, first of five children, was born in April, 1961. By 1966 Gotti was hijacking trucks by night and spending his days at the Bergin Hunt and Fish Club in Queens, a mob hangout which would become one of his headquarters in later years. Caught in a hijacking operation in 1968, Gotti spent three years in the Federal Penitentiary at Lewisberg, Pennsylvania. When he got out he returned to the Bergin to enjoy the increased status of one who has graduated from a federal prison. By this time he had become an underboss in the Gambino crime family by attrition.

In May, 1972, Emanuel Gambino, the nephew of family boss Carlo Gambino, had been kidnapped, snatched right off a New York City street. The family had paid a $100,000 ransom, but Emanuel had not been returned. His body was found on January 26, 1973, buried in a shallow grave on the grounds of a federal ammunition depot in New Jersey. The Gambinos believed, rightly or wrongly, that the Westies, a Manhattan gang of mostly Irish extraction, had carried out the kidnapping. They determined that James McBratney was the head of the gang, and was responsible for the kidnapping. In this they may well have been wrong, but Carlo Gambino did not insist on courtroom standards of evidence.

The MAFIA professes to believe that a member cannot fully be trusted until he has killed a man for the family. The process is called "making your bones." John Gotti was given the chance to make his bones with James McBratney. At about eleven in the evening on Tuesday, May 22, 1973, Gotti entered Snoope's Bar & Grill on Staten Island. With him were Gambino button men Angelo Ruggiero and Ralph Galione. They walked over to McBratney, who was drinking a creme de menthe on the rocks at the bar, and, claiming to be policemen, pulled guns on McBratney. When one of the other bar patrons asked to see a badge, Galione responded by firing a shot into the ceiling. The three Gambino men tried dragging McBratney out of the bar while the other customers scattered, but he resisted. While Gotti and Ruggiero held McBratney, Galione put three bullets into the Irish gang chieftain, killing him. The trio raced out of the bar.

Ruggiero and Galione were identified shortly after the hit and arrested. Galione was murdered before he could come to trial. Ruggiero's trial ended in a hung jury. Gotti was heard bragging about the hit by an FBI informer known as Source Wahoo, and the Bureau passed the information on to the New York City police. Gotti's picture was then picked out of a photo spread by witnesses, and he was apprehended and charged. Gotti and Ruggiero were then scheduled to be tried together. Their lawyer was Roy M. Cohn, former associate of Senator Joseph McCarthy. A powerful attorney with many connections and an impressive client list that included politicians, hoodlums and the Roman Catholic Diocese of New York, Cohn had an uncanny way of bending the legal system to his clients' needs.

On June 2, 1975, Gotti and Ruggiero pled guilty to a very reduced charge of attempted manslaughter, and the Staten Island District Attorney's office, possibly leery of getting a conviction because of the hung jury in Ruggiero's first trial, accepted the plea. For committing what most of us would consider first degree murder in front of a bar full of witnesses, Gotti was sentenced to four years in prison. With normal time off, he would be out in two.

Gotti went through the ceremony of formal initiation into the Gambino crime family shortly after getting out of prison in 1977. Although his position of authority within the gang was such that he could have been "made" much earlier, Don Carlo Gambino had closed the book on new initiations some time before. But Carlo had died while Gotti was in prison, and the new boss of the family, Paul Castellano, had opened the book again.

On Tuesday, March 18, 1980, John Favara, a neighbor of John Gotti in the Howard Beach area of Queens, ran into a 12-year-old boy on a minibike while he was driving home from work. He was heading west, into the setting sun, when the boy darted out from behind a dumpster. The boy, Frank Gotti, John Gotti's younger son, was killed. After an investigation the police ruled it a tragic accident. Favara found a death threat in his mailbox a few days later, and someone called the local police precinct to warn them that Favara would be killed, but he refused to believe it. After all, his son Scott and Gotti's oldest son, John, were good friends. But the threats kept coming.

On Friday, July 25, John Gotti took his wife to Florida for a week. The following Monday John Favara was kidnapped by several men as he was leaving work. He was never seen again. An informant told the FBI that Gotti had promised his wife revenge, and added that John Favara's body would never be found. It never has been.

Over the next decade, as Gotti rose in power and influence in the ranks of ORGANIZED CRIME, he managed to remain comparatively unknown to the general public. But the FBI had taken note of him, and had received authorization to place wiretaps in several locations that Gotti and his henchmen frequented, such as the Bergin Hunt and Fish Club in Queens and the Ravenite Social Club in Manhattan's Little Italy. This was done under the authority of RICO, The Racketeer-Influenced and Corrupt Organization Act, passed by Congress in 1970. The taps produced a wealth of information about the organization of the mob and captured vividly the mobsters' conversational proclivity for almost continuous profanity, scatology, and obscenity. The tapes also provided evidence of a pattern of crime including extortion, hijacking, narcotics trafficking, and murder. The Gambino family had long had a ban against trafficking in narcotics, not for moral reasons but because the penalties against it were so strict that a family member prosecuted on such a charge might be tempted to "turn" and become an informer for the authorities. But the narcotics business was so lucrative that the ban was constantly being broken, even thought the penalty was death if the trafficker was caught. Eventually the information on the tapes laid the groundwork for a series of prosecutions against important gang figures, including Gotti.

On September 11, 1984, a chain of events began that would thrust Gotti into the public eye. Romual Piecyk, a 35-year-old refrigeration repairman, found his car blocked by a car double parked outside the Cozy Corner Bar in Maspeth, Queens. He honked. When nothing happened, he honked again. And again. Eventually Frank Colletta, a Gotti henchman, came out of the bar. Coming over to the driver's side window, he reached into the car and slapped Piecyk across the face. For good measure he took a roll of money out of Piecyk's shirt pocked and walked off. Piecyk, who had just cashed his weekly paycheck and had $325 in the roll, didn't think this was funny. A tough, husky man, who could take care of himself in a brawl, he got out of his car and grabbed for Colletta. By this time Gotti had emerged from the bar, and joined in the tussle, and the two of them roughed Piecyk up. When the police arrived Gotti and Colletta had returned to the bar, and Piecyk was standing on the street, his face puffy and his right arm cut and bloody. Piecyk identified Gotti and Colletta, who were handcuffed by the police and led away. Gotti was annoyed.

By the time the case came to trial Piecyk had been informed, both by the newspapers and by a series of anonymous phone calls, just who John Gotti was. When he took the stand he refused to identify his assailants. "I don't remember who slapped me," he testified. "I have no recollection of what the two men looked like or how they were dressed." The *New York Post* reported the event under the memorable headline: I FORGOTTI! In a later interview Piecyk explained: "Any human being would lie to save his life."

All this time the U.S. Attorney's office was constructing a RICO case against Gotti and others in New York's crime families, with the help of wiretaps and several secret informants within the Gambino organization. While they were building their case, Gotti was continuing his rise in the Gambino family. He was among a select group of family members, including Angelo Ruggiero and Gotti's brother Gene, who defied Paul Castellano's ban on dealing drugs by importing and distributing heroin. They had worked out a lucrative deal with the Inzerillo clan, an important Sicilian crime family. In 1985 Gotti and his confederates became concerned that Castellano would discover their drug dealing when it was revealed that Ruggiero's house had been wired for sound. Castellano was trying to get his hands on tapes of the recorded conversations, and Gotti, unsure of what the tapes would reveal and fearing Castellano's wrath, felt that he had to act first.

On December 16, 1985, Castellano and the man he had just anointed as the new Gambino family underboss, Tommy Bilotti, drove up to Sparks Steak House on East 46th Street in Manhattan. They were gunned down in the street as they emerged from their Lincoln town car. In a matter of weeks John Gotti was appointed Paul Castellano's successor as head of the Gambino crime family, which is, as Ralph Blumenthal points out in his foreword to *The Gotti Tapes* (1992), ". . . long considered to be the richest, most powerful Mafia clan in America, with some 300 made members, 2,000 associates, and uncounted hundreds of millions of dollars of assets and illicit revenues."

In 1986 Federal prosecutor Diane F. Giacalone of the Brooklyn office of the U.S. Attorney filed RICO charges against Gotti, a case that she had been building since 1984. In the process, despite strong protests by the FBI, she indicted Wilfred "Willie Boy" Johnson, a member of the Gambino family and confidant of Gotti. The indictment revealed that he was, and had for some time been, an informer (the FBI's "Source Wahoo"). She saw this as a way to bring pressure on Johnson to testify, since if he turned state's evidence he would be put into the Federal witness protection program. If not he would surely be killed by his disillusioned comrades. The FBI pointed out that Johnson had many times assured them that he would never testify, and that he was much more valuable as a mole within the Gambino organization than as a man on the run in fear for his life.

Johnson, as he had said, refused to testify. He denied under oath that he had been an informer. The prosecution had him held in "protective custody" as a flight risk for a year and a half. He was released, still refusing to testify. In 1988 he was murdered. Giacalone also revealed another FBI source, code named "BQ," by naming him as an unindicted coconspirator in her case. He warned his FBI contacts that, if named, he would disappear. In January, 1986, 53-year-old bookmaker William Battista, known to the FBI as source BQ, disappeared.

Gotti's first RICO trial commenced in August, 1986. Ninety hoodlums testified, many of them in prison and hoping to get some time off their sentences in return for cooperation. Gotti's attorney, Bruce Cutler, took full advantage of this perceived ulterior motive, blasting the witnesses in his cross-examination. When the trial ended in March, 1987, Gotti was found not guilty. It was then that the newspapers began referring to Gotti as "the Teflon don." Cutler's skills as a defense attorney may have been aided by an unseen hand; the prosecution later filed charges that one of the jurors had been subverted by members of the Gambino family.

In 1989 the government tried again. This time Gotti was charged in State court with ordering the 1986 shooting of John O'Connor, a leader of the Carpenter's Union. The evidence was based on a tape recording from a bug planted in the Bergin clubhouse, on which Gotti is heard to give the order to "bust him up." Gotti was acquitted once again, and once again it subsequently seemed that one or more members of the jury had been reached.

In 1992 the Federal prosecutors tried one more time, but this time they had an edge. After hearing himself on tape from FBI bugs, Salvatore "Sammy the Bull" Gravano, a Gotti henchman, agreed to turn state's evidence. His testimony was deadly. For example:

Q: How many murders were you charged with?
A: Three.
Q: When you decided to cooperate, you told the government about sixteen others, correct?
A: Yes.
. . .
Q: Can you describe the different roles you had?
A: Sometimes I was a shooter. Sometimes I was a backup guy. Sometimes I set the guy up. Sometimes I just talked about it.
. . .
Q: Now the top ten names on the list span the period from December 16, 1985, Paul Castellano and Thomas Bilotti, to October of 1990, Correct?
A: Yes.
Q: Of these, how many involved John Gotti?
A: All of them.

The jury deliberated for a day and a half. On April 2, 1992, Gotti was found guilty of 14 counts, including murder, tax evasion, and racketeering. He received a life sentence which he is currently serving at the Federal Penitentiary in Marlow, Illinois.

GOUZENKO, Igor (1919–)

On September 2, 1945, Lieutenant Igor Gouzenko, a code clerk at the Soviet Embassy in Ottawa, Canada, took his wife Anna and their small child with him and defected to the West. He also took a bundle of papers documenting the existence of a large Soviet espionage *apparat*.

At first, the Canadian authorities did not want to listen to him, for fear of starting an international incident. And then they did not want to believe him. Prime Minister Mackenzie King's first reaction was to have the authorities tell Gouzenko to take his papers back to the embassy. When the Canadians finally decided to listen to him and examined the papers, they became aware for the first time of the existence of a series of interlocking Soviet espionage rings working in North America and Great Britain under the direction of NKVD Colonel Nikolai Zabotin. This was the so-called ATOMIC SPY RING, including Allan Nunn May, HARRY GOLD and ETHEL AND JULIUS ROSENBERG.

When the Canadians realized the importance of this information, Prime Minister King secretly consulted with Prime Minister Clement Attlee in London and President Harry S Truman in Washington, D.C.

Gouzenko gave Western intelligence agencies their first glimpse into the organization and inner workings of the Soviet intelligence *apparat*. He also provided the West with the first hints that Soviet Intelligence had penetrated the top levels of Western Intelligence services, and that there were one or more moles in the higher levels of British Intelligence.

Gouzenko testified at the trials of various

members of the *apparat* who were apprehended by the Canadian police, after which he and his family settled in Canada under the protective eye of the Royal Canadian Mounted Police.

GRAHAM, Jack Gilbert (1932–1957)

On November 1, 1955, United Airlines Flight 629, a DC-6B, blew apart in the air 11 minutes after taking off from Denver's Stapleton Airport, killing 44 people. Investigators found traces of a bomb in the plane's luggage compartment, and the case was turned over to the FBI. Their attention soon focused on Jack Graham, the son of passenger Daisy Walker King, who died in the crash. Witnesses testified to his erratic behavior at the airport: He was seen nervously buying several life insurance policies from airport vending machines totaling $37,000, and getting his mother to sign them. When his home was searched, material for the manufacture of bombs was found in his basement. After intensive questioning by the police, Graham confessed to planting a time bomb containing 25 sticks of dynamite in his mother's luggage.

Graham, who was found to be sane, recanted his confession at the trial, but he was convicted on the evidence. He never showed any remorse over the death of his mother or the deaths of the 43 innocent travelers on the plane with her. Refusing to appeal his death sentence, he died in the gas chamber of the Colorado State Penitentiary on January 11, 1957.

GRAND JURY

In most states, before a person can be tried for a felony, an indictment must be handed down by a grand jury. A grand jury is usually made up of 23 people picked from the regular jury rolls. Its job is not to decide on the guilt or innocence of the accused but to certify that there is enough evidence to conclude that a crime has been committed and that the accused is possibly responsible. This is an ancient procedure in English common law and has evolved from the assize at which the knights assembled to hear criminal matters in the county. In federal courts, all felonies must be heard by a grand jury before an indictment, called a "true bill," can be issued. This protection is guaranteed by the Fifth Amendment to the Constitution, but the Supreme Court has ruled that states do not have to offer this protection. As noted, most states use grand juries, but in some jurisdictions, a grand jury is not necessary on all cases; instead, the prosecutor, upon a finding of probable cause, can return an information, which is a legal document sufficient to bind the accused over for trial.

The most ancient archive of the Court of General Sessions in New York records, on its first page, the empaneling of a grand jury:

> PROVENCE OF NEW YORK. Att the General Quarter Sessions of our Lord the King held att the Citty Hall in the Citty of New-York for Our Sayd Lord the King, and the body of the sayd Citty and County of New-York, that is to say on Tuesday the 8th day of February, in the Six and thirtieth year of the Reigne of our Sovereigne Lord Charles the Second of England, Scottland, France and Ireland, King, Defender of the faith, & before Cornelis Steenyck, Esqr, May^{r} of the sayd Citty, and James Graham, Recorder, Nicholas Bayard, John Inians, Wm Pinho . . . Guyl. Ver Plank, Jn^{r} Robinson and William Cox, Esq^{rs}, Aldermen and Justices of the Peace of the sayd Citty and County, Commisionated by Authority und^{r} his Royal Highness James Duke of York and Albany Lord Propriet^{r} of the Province afores^{d}. . . ."
>
> The Grand Jury . . . was called and sworne According to An Oath Agreed On by the Court, and was as followeth," viz^{tt}.:
>
> "You shall diligently Enquire and true Presentm^{t} make of all Such things and matt^{rs} as shall be giuen you in Charge Or shall Come to your knowledge this Present Servise. The Kings, His Royal Highness Lord Propriet^{r} and this City Councell Yo^{r} fallows and you^{r} owne you shall well and

> Truely keep secreet. You shall present nothing for Malace or Euill will that you Bare to Any Person, Neither shall you Leaue anything unpresented for Loue, favour, affecttion Reward Or Any hopes thereof, but in all things that shall Concerne this Present Servise you Shall Present the truth the whole truth and nothing but the truth, According to yo[r] best skill and knowledge—Soe help you God.
>
> M[r] Francis Rumbout was apoynted foreman.

This first case was against Henry Thomassen, who was charged with burglary. The grand jury brought a true bill against him and was then informed by the "Sherriff" that Mr. Thomassen had "Broak Prison." The "Sherriff" was ordered to "Persue him." He caught him, and the felon was tried at the next session.

GRAVANO, Salvatore "Sammy the Bull"

See: JOHN GOTTI

GRAY, Henry Judd (1894–1928)

Henry Judd Gray was a corset salesman who helped his lover RUTH BROWN SNYDER murder her husband in 1927.

GREAT COFFEYVILLE RAID

See: DALTON BROTHERS

GREEN GOODS GAME

One of the oldest CONFIDENCE GAMES still being practiced, and an exemplar of the con man's favorite saying, "You can't cheat an honest man," the Green Goods Game first appeared shortly after the Civil War. In it, the mark (victim), usually a shopkeeper or banker in a small town, was sounded out in some fashion as to his innate honesty. If he passed the test, he was induced to buy what he believed was a supply of counterfeit money. He was given bills to examine to show him how good their quality was.

If the con men misjudged their mark, and he took the sample "green goods" to the police, he would discover that they were genuine bills. And, until states enacted BUNCO statutes, there was no law against offering to sell someone real money under the claim that it was counterfeit. If he fell for the con and purchased a supply, when he opened the package he would find the money had been switched for carefully cut stacks of newspaper. At that point, it was very difficult for the mark to complain to the police. Few tradesmen and fewer bankers would care to admit to the authorities that they had been swindled while trying to buy counterfeit money. For that reason, it is hard to tell how prevalent the con is today, but a few people are known to fall for it every year.

GUITEAU, Charles Julius (1844–1882)

On July 2, 1881, as President JAMES A. GARFIELD walked into the Baltimore & Potomac railroad station in Washington, D.C., on his way to Williams College, Charles Julius Guiteau came up behind the president and fired twice, the second shot hitting the president in the back. Garfield died on September 19, 1881.

Guiteau, an insane religious fanatic, who was displeased that Garfield had not appointed him ambassador to France, had followed Garfield for some time before finding a convenient location to shoot. He acted as his own attorney at his trial, alternating moments of civility with moments of rabid insanity, during which he called everyone in sight every name he could think of. He called the prosecutor a "low-livered whelp." The jury, which he called "low, consummate jackasses," convicted him. Taken to the gallows on June 3, 1882, he recited a song he had composed in prison, which opened with the words, "I am going to the Lordy," immediately before he was hung.

GUNFIGHT AT THE O. K. CORRAL

A famous battle in Tombstone, Arizona, on October 26, 1881, between Wyatt Earp and his supporters and the Clanton gang. *See also:* EARP BROTHERS; JOHN HENRY "DOC" HOLLIDAY

GUNNESS, Belle (1859–?)

SHE ENTICED MEN TO HER FARM WITH PROMISES OF MARRIAGE—BUT DELIVERED SOMETHING ELSE

There is a consensus among people who write about such things that mass murder is a recent phenomenon and that mass murderers are invariably male. Brynhilde Poulsatter Sorenson Gunness, "Belle" to her friends, contradicts this theory.

Born in Selbe, Norway, in 1859, Belle came to the United States in 1868 and settled in Illinois. She married Mads Sorenson in 1883, and he died in 1900, leaving her with two children and $13,000 from life insurance and the sale of their home. In 1901, she bought a 40-acre farm about a mile out of La Porte, Indiana, put a six-foot wire fence around the house and yard and settled down.

Belle was five foot seven and about 200 pounds but could not be described as fat. "Hefty" and "rugged" were the terms most often used. A photograph of her from those days shows a stocky woman whose looks could charitably be called plain. But a good, solid wife who could heft a sack of grain was an asset to a farmer in those days, and Belle was a first-class farmer. She raised calves and hogs and did her own butchering, selling the meat in La Porte.

In April 1902, Belle married again, wedding Peter Gunness, a decent, friendly Norwegian, who was much liked by the neighbors. In December, Gunness was killed when a sausage-grinder unaccountably fell off a shelf, hitting him on the head. At least that is what Belle told the La Porte coroner. One of her children later told a friend that "Mama brained Papa with an axe. Don't tell a soul." She kept his name and $4,000 from a life insurance policy.

Belle put ads in the matrimonial journals, a form of periodical that was popular around the turn of the century. She was looking for a kind, honest man of Scandinavian birth, preferably Norwegian, who had a little ready cash to help her pay off the mortgage. "Triflers need not apply."

In 1906, a 50-year-old Norwegian gentleman named John Moo came to Belle's farm from Elbow Lake, Minnesota, in response to one of her ads. To show his earnestness he brought with him $1,000 in cash for the mortgage. To neighbors who saw him about the house he was introduced as "Cousin John." After about a week, neighbors stopped seeing him about the house. He was never seen by anyone again.

Shortly thereafter, George Anderson, another Norwegian, came to La Porte from Tarkio, Missouri. He was initially charmed by Belle and, after a couple of days on the farm, was seriously thinking of going home to get his money—for the mortgage—and proposing marriage. But he awoke one night from a deep dream of peace to find Belle, a lighted candle in her hand, bending over him and peering intently into his face. There was, as he said later, a very odd look in her eyes. He screamed. She screamed and ran out of the room. He quickly gathered his clothing and ran out of the house and straight to the La Porte railroad station, whence he took the next train back to Tarkio.

Shortly after Anderson departed, Belle hired a slow-witted young French-Canadian named Ray L'Amphere (who soon Anglicized his name to Lamphere) to work around the farm. About this time, a 16-year-old girl named Jenny Olson, who had been staying with Belle, disappeared. Belle said she had left to go to school in California. She never returned.

It might have been the strength of her epistolary style that lured suitors across the prairie. Never underestimate the power of the simple declarative sentence. One surviving letter reads:

> To the Dearest Friend in the World: No woman in the world is happier than I am. I know

> that you are now to come to me and be my own. I can tell from your letters that you are the man I want. It does not take one long to tell when to like a person, and you I like better than anyone in the world, I know.
>
> Think how we will enjoy each other's company. You, the sweetest man in the whole world. We will be all alone with each other. Can you conceive of anything nicer? I think of you constantly. When I hear your name mentioned, and this is when one of the dear children speaks of you or I hear myself humming it with the words of an old love song, it is beautiful music to my ears.
>
> My heart beats in wild rapture for you. My Andrew, I love you. Come prepared to stay for ever.

Perhaps she took the main ideas of the letter from one of the love-letter writing manuals that were sold in those innocent days. But the last sentence of that letter is surely her own addition. It reverberates with horror.

To the Gunness farm over the next few years came a steady stream of men, most of whom were never seen again. Some of them we know about. In April 1907, Ole Budsberg brought $2,000 in cash. In January 1908, Andrew K. Helgelien, a wheat grower of Aberdeen, South Dakota, brought $3,000. It was he to whom the above epistle was sent.

A month or so after Helgelien had responded to Belle's tender entreaties, his brother Asle Helgelien wrote demanding news of Andrew. Belle responded that Andrew had left, perhaps to return to Norway.

Now Belle, who had had several public disputes with her handyman, Lamphere, had her will drawn up, telling the attorney that she was in fear of her life from Lamphere. The next morning the Gunness farmhouse burned to the ground. Lying on a mattress in the cellar of the burned house were the bodies of Belle's three children, and the headless corpse of an older woman. It was wearing Belle's dress and some of Belle's jewelry, but somehow it did not look like Belle.

The doctors who examined the remains of the headless corpse affirmed that it was that of a woman five feet three inches tall and about 150 pounds in weight. Four inches too short and 50 pounds too light to have been Belle Gunness.

Asle Helgelien showed up in town the day after the fire, looking for his brother Andrew. He went out with the sheriff to view the house and grounds, and Asle pointed out several suspicious-looking depressions in the ground. The sheriff's deputies dug one of them up and, under a layer of rubbish, found a gunnysack. In it was a chopped-up body. Asle examined it. "That's Andy," he told the sheriff.

Thus encouraged, the deputies dug at the other sites, and before the day was over had unearthed four more bodies, two of them of small children. They went back a second day and found four more bodies. On the third day, they uncovered only one body. They also uncovered hundreds of unconnected bones that indicated that more corpses, perhaps many more, had been scattered about the Gunness farm. They looked with alarm at the cellar, which had been fitted out as an efficient abattoir—for slaughtering pigs, the neighbors had always thought.

The debris from the fire was sluiced by an expert miner who lived in the area, and he came up with a set of false teeth that the dentist identified as Belle's. Even though the anchor tooth was included, this failed to convince the local population that Belle had burned. Lamphere, who had been seen near the burning building, was arrested for arson. When questioned, he denied setting the fire and suggested that Belle had done it herself. He had firsthand knowledge of some of Belle's strange courtship customs, and related in his statement:

> Mrs. Gunness made me a proposal of marriage, and after we had become lovers she said that before the ceremony was performed I must insure my life. This I did, making a will in her favor. But

> somehow, once she got the will, she kept postponing the marriage. Then one day I found a strange man in the house. It was Andrew Helgelien. They thought themselves alone, but I heard my mistress say she was tired of having Lamphere around and intended to get rid of him. Late one afternoon she sent me to the station to meet her cousin, a Mr. Moo. She told me that if he did not arrive I was to stay in town overnight. I met the train at Michigan City, but there was no Mr. Moo on it. I knew then that Mrs. Gunness had concocted the story to get me out of the way. I at once returned to La Porte, and when it was getting near to midnight I stole out to the farm. In the yellow light from a stable lamp I saw Mrs. Gunness bending over a hole in the ground. I walked up to a wire fence around the yard and saw she was sprinkling lime on a dead body. Suddenly she seemed to feel that someone was watching her, and turning she gasped, "My God! I thought you were a ghost." I did nothing but stepped through the gate. Helgelien's head lay staring up at me from the grave. The body was in a gunny sack and the arms and legs had been tossed in upon it. I helped Mrs. Gunness to fill up the hole. From that night on I had her in my power.

How relieved Lamphere must have been to discover that his mistress was not cheating on him, but merely murdering her latest suitor. He was tried and convicted of arson but acquitted of murder.

Lamphere died in prison in 1909. Before he died, he gave more details of his version of his relationship with Belle and that final day to a fellow prisoner, who passed it on to the authorities after Lamphere died. He claimed that Belle had entertained 42 suitors at her farm, and only one had left alive—presumably Mr. Anderson. She drugged their coffee and then clubbed them to death before they woke. Then she cut up the bodies on the butchering table in her cellar and distributed the body parts around the farm. The children whose bodies had been found had been left to board with Belle.

The day of the fire, she had lured a woman out to the farm with the promise of a job, then killed her, removed her head and buried it in a quicklime-filled hole in the swamp. Then she had killed her own children, because they knew too much, dressed the headless woman in her clothes, put all the bodies on a mattress in the cellar, and fired the house. Lamphere admitted to helping dispose of a few of the bodies, but claimed that he had never killed anyone. Undoubtedly his account of his own actions was sanitized, but the story of Belle's actions rings true.

Sightings of Belle were reported as late as 1936, when she would have been 77. But she was never caught. In the years after her disappearance, as she entered the realm of folklore, a ballad was written to be sung to the tune of "Love, O Careless Love." It goes like this:

> Belle Gunness lived in In-di-an,
> She always, always had a man,
> Ten at least went to her door,
> And were never, never seen no more.
>
> Now, all these men were Norska folk
> Who came to Belle from Minn-e-sote.
> They liked their coffee and their gin.
> They got it—plus a mickey finn.
>
> And now with cleaver poised so sure
> Belle neatly cut their jug-u-lar;
> She put them in a bath of lime,
> And left them for quite some time.
>
> There's red upon the Hoosier moon
> For Belle was strong and full of doom;
> And think of all them Norska men
> Who'll never see St. Paul again.

GUZIK, Jake "Greasy Thumb" (1887–1956)

One of the many Jews to rise to high positions in what is usually thought of as the all-Sicilian

MAFIA, Jake Guzik was accountant and treasurer for the Chicago North Side mob while AL CAPONE headed it and for a long while thereafter. It is reputed that one evening in May 1924, a gangster named Joe Howard beat up the short, dumpy Guzik in a bar. When Capone heard about it, he accosted Howard in Heinie Jacobs's saloon on South Wabash Avenue and asked him why he had hit his friend. Howard supposedly replied, with a momentary lapse of good judgment, "Go back to your girls, you dago pimp." Capone pulled his gun and put six bullets into Howard. Guzik remained Capone's faithful friend from then on, seeing that she was taken care of while he was in prison, and supporting him during his declining years in Florida, when he was dying of paresis and incapable of supporting himself.

Guzik was the top-level bag man for the Syndicate, paying off a generation of Chicago mayors and police chiefs and other officials. His one stretch in prison was, like Capone's, on tax charges, and when he got out he went right back to his old job. For 30 years, some of the toughest mobsters in the world trusted him to handle their money and, as far as is known, they never had any cause for complaint. His testimony before the KEFAUVER COMMITTEE was one long recital of his FIFTH AMENDMENT rights. He died of a heart attack while eating dinner at a restaurant on February 21, 1956.

HALL-MILLS CASE

DID THE REVEREND LOVE THE CHOIR SINGER? AND WHO KILLED THEM BOTH?

The Reverend Mister Edward Wheeler Hall, rector of the Episcopal Church of St. John the Evangelist, in New Brunswick, New Jersey, and Mrs. Eleanor R. Mills, a singer in the church choir and wife of the church sexton, were found together in death on the morning of Saturday, September 16, 1922. Their bodies lay arranged in close communion in a crab apple orchard, by a lonely dirt road named De Russey's Lane, a block away from Easton Avenue, on the outskirts of New Brunswick.

Reverend Hall, 41, had a bullet in his head. Mrs. Mills, 34, had three bullets in her body and her throat had been savagely ripped open. Love letters from Mrs. Mills to Reverend Hall were scattered about the bodies, and one of Reverend Hall's calling cards was sticking up in the grass a few inches from his foot. One expended shell from a .32 pistol was found in the grass, as well as a three-foot-long iron bar, two handkerchiefs with the letter "H" embroidered into one corner and a bunch of keys. The keys were determined to belong to Reverend Hall. A later investigation turned up two more expended .32 caliber shells.

The border between Somerset County and Middlesex County, unfortunately for the ensuing investigation, ran between De Russey's Lane and the homes of the victims. The Somerset County police, who had authority over the location where the bodies were found, decided that they had been moved and tried to pass the responsibility for the investigation over to Middlesex County. The Middlesex County police did their best to decline the honor. This impasse continued throughout the investigation, which as a result was bungled, muddled and mishandled. Standard procedure in murder cases is to perform an autopsy, no matter how obvious the cause of death may seem to be, but no

Sidney Carpenter, Willie Stevens, and Henry Carpenter in court, accused of aiding the wife of Rev. Hall in the murder of her husband and his lover. (International Newsreel Photo.)

autopsy was performed on either body at the time. Such physical evidence as existed was grossly mishandled.

After having dinner with his wife, her brother Willie Stevens and a young niece, Reverend Hall left his home at 23 Nichol Avenue at about 7:30 Thursday evening, saying that he had some church business to take care of and that he was going to speak with Mrs. Mills about a doctor's bill. When he failed to come home all night, Mrs. Hall called the New Brunswick police on Friday morning to see if an accident of some sort had been reported. There was no such report. When it was known that a private watchman had seen a woman entering the Hall house at about 3:00 Friday morning, Mrs. Hall amplified her statement. Unable to sleep and worried over her husband's absence, she awakened her brother William at about 2:30, and the two of them went to the church to look for Reverend Hall. Not finding him there, they continued on to the Mills's house, thinking someone might be sick. But since no lights were on in the house, she and William went home. The next morning she asked Mills, who vouchsafed that he knew nothing of Reverend Hall's absence and added that his own wife had not come home.

The double murder of the respected minister and the beautiful choir singer made the front page in newspapers all over the country and stayed there for weeks. The discovery of the love affair between Mrs. Mills and the reverend was of at least as much journalistic interest as the murders. Letters were found from Reverend Hall to his paramour to complement the ones penciled by Mrs. Mills that had been recovered around the bodies. The theory espoused by the newspapers, with which the county prosecutors also agreed, was that Mrs. Hall, discovering her husband's extra-clerical activities with his choir singer, had followed them to their trysting site and murdered them both. Feeling that she could not have acted alone, the authorities questioned Willie, who was regarded as slightly feebleminded, and another brother, Henry, who lived about 50 miles away from his sister, and was known as a crack shotgun marksman. Henry claimed that he was surf fishing for bluefish on Thursday night. Willie, after initially refusing to talk, changed his mind and garrulously confirmed his sister's version of events. Willie was found to have a .32 caliber revolver, but its firing pin had been filed down and it would not shoot. Judging by the ejected shells, it was probably an automatic that was used in the murders.

Suddenly and unexpectedly an amazing witness turned up. Her name was Mrs. Jane Gibson, she was about 50 years old, and she worked a 60-acre farm near the murder scene with her son. Most of her income was derived from fattening up pigs for sale, and she immediately became known

Somerville County Courthouse, opening day of Hall-Mills trial. (International Newsreel Photo.)

as "the Pig Woman." Her story was that, on the night of the murders, she chased a thief who had been raiding her corn patch; she on her mule Jenny, and he driving a wagon. When she reached the unnamed lane and the crab apple orchard, she saw and heard three men and two women engaged in a furious argument. The scene was illuminated in the headlights of a parked car and the beam of a flashlight one of the men was carrying. She dismounted from her mule and approached the scene cautiously. Suddenly she heard a shot and ran back to her mule. Before she could mount and exit, she heard three more shots, and a woman screamed, "Oh my! Oh my! Oh my!" And then another woman screamed, "Oh Henry!"

The prosecutors decided that they had better have autopsy evidence after all, and both bodies were exhumed and examined. It was then that they established that Mrs. Mills had been shot three times—they had thought only once, and that Reverend Hall had been shot only once—they had thought twice. Mrs. Mills also had deep lacerations on the backs of her hands and wrists.

On November 27, 1922, the grand jury, after hearing all pertinent evidence, deliberated for 18 hours and refused to hand down an indictment. Mrs. Hall went to Italy to recover from the excitement and stayed away a year. When she came back, she put her life in order and tried to put the past behind her.

Three years later, four years after the murder, the past rose up to haunt her. It began when Arthur Riehl, a piano salesman, sued his wife, the former Louise Geist, for an annulment of their marriage. It was necessary at that time to give substantial cause for such an action. Miss Geist had been a parlor maid in the household of the Rev. Hall when she met Riehl and had married him shortly after the murders. Riehl accused his wife of having had illicit sex with the deceased Rev. Hall and further of having accepted a $5,000 bribe from Mrs. Hall not to tell what she knew of the murders.

In addition, the *New York Daily Mirror*, under the editorship of Philip Payne, was looking for something to boost circulation. Anything would do, but a sensational murder would do better than most. The paper resurrected the old story with such headlines as "Unsolved Mystery of the Slain Minister and His Beautiful Choir Singer." It strongly suggested that Mrs. Hall and her wealthy family had bought off the investigation, and justice had been thwarted. Other newspapers took up the theme, and the new governor of New Jersey, Harry A. Moore, felt the hot breath of the press on his political neck. He appointed Alexander Simpson, a respected attorney then serving as a state senator, as special deputy attorney general to the Hall-Mills case.

Simpson lost no time. He looked over the situation in amazement and berated his predecessors. In *They Escaped the Hangman* (1953), Francis X. Busch described the case:

> [Simpson] began by charging that the former prosecutors and police had made a mess of the earlier investigations. After the discovery of the bodies the police had taken no pains to safeguard the scene of the crime for expert investigation for clues. No examination had been made of the clothing of the victims for outsiders' fingerprints. There had been no coroner's inquest. Material witnesses who had presented themselves to the police and prosecutors had been spurned. In some of the police investigations, witnesses had been bullied and induced to change their stories. Officers who had shown too keen a disposition to track down the murderers had been taken off the case. Such clues as existed had not been followed up. The autopsies conducted after exhumation of the bodies were slipshod and inadequate. The evidence submitted to the 1922 grand jury had not been carefully prepared or convincingly presented. Now, he said, important papers—original statements and affidavits of witnesses and the original grand-jury minutes—were missing, and vital exhibits still in the possession of the State showed evidence of having been tampered with.

Despite these difficulties, Simpson determined to proceed. He arrested Mrs. Hall and her brothers Willie and Henry Stevens and a cousin named Henry de la Bruyere Carpender. His detectives contacted witnesses corroborating the Pig Woman's story and poking holes in the alibis of Mrs. Hall and her male relations.

On November 3, 1926, the case went to court. According to New Jersey law at that time, two judges had to sit on capital crimes, and so Supreme Court Justice Charles W. Parker and Judge of the Court of Common Pleas Frank L. Cleary jointly presided. A flock of defense attorneys, headed by Robert H. McCarter, a former attorney general of New Jersey, faced a plethora of prosecuting attorneys, headed by Simpson. The jury was made up of a blacksmith, a mason, a teamster, a factory superintendent, two clerks and six farmers.

The prosecutor told the jury that the crime they were trying, the murder of Eleanor Mills, was the cruelest and most fiendish murder in the criminal history of the state of New Jersey; a fairly standard opening statement for a murder trial. He spoke of an intimacy between the two victims "that was not spiritual." He gave the jurors to understand that Mrs. Hall, somehow hearing of her husband's infidelity (he guessed an overheard telephone conversation), had gathered together her brothers and her cousin and gone in search of the amorous couple. On finding them, a quarrel broke out, and a double murder resulted. He called 84 witnesses to establish his case.

The high point of the trial was the reading of the love letters. Stylistically they are not models of amorous prose, but they do serve to indicate a certain level of passion.

The Reverend Hall wrote:

> Dear, Dear, Tender Wonderheart of Mine . . . I have so longed to talk, talk, talk with you while holding you in my arms. I am not wild or fierce today or possessive, but calm, strong, exalted. . . . Dearie, dear heart, I want to hold you close, commune with you, hold you tight with my left arm and drag your dear firm face and body with my right arm and look deep down into those wonder eyes, hazel eyes. Dearest, you are like crystal to me. I will call you "crystal eyes." I seem to see and feel all of the awe and wonder of the universe in them, and I am full of awe and wonder today.

Eleanor Mills wrote:

> Dear Darling Boy: I love you more when you love me as you did today—not so much physically but prayerfully, exalted, and you see, darling, the physical fits in and doesn't dominate—it was there just the same and not to be denied, never. Dearest, believe me, won't you? Never will I say you want my body rather than me—what I really am. I know that if you love me you will long and ache for my body . . . As you said today, our hearts are as true as steel. I am not pretty. I know there are girls with shapely bodies but I am not caring what they have. I have the greatest of all blessings—a noble man's deep, true, eternal love—and my heart is his. My life is his. All I have is his. I am his forever. Honey, I am awful lonesome for you tonight.

Prosecutor Simpson established beyond any doubt whatsoever that Reverend Hall and Mrs. Mills were having an affair. What he could not prove, except by innuendo, gossip and supposition, was that Mrs. Hall had any idea of her husband's intrigues. He produced witnesses, Mr. and Mrs. John Dixon, who remembered a man coming to their house, near the site of the murders, at 8:30 on the evening of the murders, and asking directions. The man was wearing a derby hat, a bow tie, a gold watch with a gold chain, and had a hesitant stutter. When asked if he could identify the man, Mr. Dixon walked across the courtroom and grabbed Willie Stevens's hand. The jury was much impressed until the defense established that Willie never owned a derby hat, never had a silver watch and chain and had never stuttered.

Dying of cancer, the Pig Woman was brought in on a stretcher and transferred to a hospital bed to give her testimony. She was attended by a doctor and nurse in the courtroom, and her testimony was frequently interrupted for them to minister to her needs. Her story had expanded in the four years since the murders. She now related a lot more conversation, including a fair amount of cursing and had clearly heard a woman say, "Explain those letters!" What she could not explain was why she hadn't remembered this dialogue the first time she told the story.

The trial lasted for a month. The jury was out for five hours. It returned a verdict of not guilty for all defendants on all charges.

No one was ever convicted for the murders of Rev. Hall and Mrs. Mills. Two possible alternate solutions to the crime have been offered. One is that the KU KLUX KLAN, which was very active in New Jersey at that time, and was known to punish what it regarded as immorality, might have found out about the illicit love affair and corrected things its own way. Another is the possibility that simple robbery was the motive. The Rev. Hall carried a heavy gold watch and chain, wore solid gold cuff links, and always had a wallet filled with money. None of these items was found on Hall's body. But, if the lovers were not killed in a jealous rage, why were the love letters scattered over the bodies? And just what did the Pig Woman really see?

HARDING, Warren Gamaliel (1865–1923)

Twenty-ninth president of the United States, Warren G. Harding's administration was plagued by scandal, much of which came to light after his untimely death.

See also: GASTON BULLOCK MEANS; OHIO GANG

HARRIS, Carlyle (1869–1893)

WHEN THE MEDICAL STUDENT'S SECRET WIFE DIED MYSTERIOUSLY, THE JURY SAID MURDER—BUT FOR JUST WHAT SIN WERE THEY PUNISHING HIM?

At eleven o'clock in the morning of Sunday, February 1, 1891, 19-year-old Mary Helen Neilson Potts died. At the time Miss Potts was a student and boarder at the Comstock Select Boarding School for Young Ladies at 32 West 40th Street, New York City. She had suddenly taken ill at about nine o'clock the previous evening, when her roommates had awakened her after returning from the theater. An hour later the school physician, Dr. Edward Fowler, who lived a few doors down the street, was called in, and he spent the night ministering to the girl. But his efforts were in vain, and she expired. Believing that the illness might have been caused by something the girl had ingested, Dr. Fowler and Miss Lydia Day, the headmistress of the Comstock School, searched her room for some clue of what the substance could be. They found an empty pill box labeled "C.W.H. Student."

Miss Day recollected that one of Helen Potts's friends was a young medical student named Carlyle Harris, and the young man was sent for to see what light he could shed on the mysterious empty box. Harris, a tall, handsome young man, arrived at about seven in the morning. He appeared shocked at Helen's condition, and confirmed that he had written a prescription for insomnia at Helen's request, which he had filled at the Ewen McIntyre & Sons Pharmacy on Sixth Avenue. It seems that in those ancient and halcyon days medical students regularly wrote prescriptions (though they technically weren't supposed to). No one thought it was strange, although it was a bit irregular. Carlyle Harris's prescription read:

℞

1-20-91

Quin. Sulph. gr. xxv
Morph. Sulph. gr. i
In capsules vi
Sig. One before retiring
(Signed) C.W.H. Student

Which translated to 25 grains of quinine and one grain of morphine, a form of opium, to be divided between six capsules. This gave one-sixth of a grain of morphine for each capsule, hardly enough to endanger a normally healthy baby mouse. As a further precaution Harris had only given Miss Potts four of the six pills, withholding two for future need. Or so he told the doctor. He had given Helen the capsules on January 21, just before leaving on a trip to Old Point Comfort, Virginia. He had received a letter from Helen while he was in Virginia in which she had written that she had taken one of the capsules and it had not helped her, and that "she would change doctors if he could not do better." Perhaps, Harris suggested, she had taken the other three capsules at the same time.

When Helen's mother, Mrs. Cynthia Potts, arrived from their home in New Jersey, she informed them that Helen had a history of heart trouble since she was a little girl. Perhaps even a small amount of morphine could prove dangerous to a diseased heart.

Coroner Louis Schultze and his deputy, Dr. Albert Weston, arrived shortly after the girl died.

After examining the deceased girl and the physical evidence, and hearing Helen Potts's history from those present, they concurred in agreeing that Helen's death was probably caused by "action of the opium in conjunction with her heart trouble." But there were other possibilities. The compounding pharmacist might have made a mistake, for example, or Helen might have taken the three pills all at once.

Harris happened to have one of the remaining pills with him—the other, he said, had been mislaid. Coroner Schultze took the pill to have it analyzed. "The inquest will be held as soon as possible," he said in a statement to the press. "It will depend upon the results of the analysis of the pill. It is very dangerous for anyone, even the most experienced physician, to prescribe morphine for a patient suffering from heart trouble . . . I am not prepared now to say what can be done in the case of the medical student who gave the prescription. Many students do give prescriptions, and it seems never to have attracted any particular attention until now."

The *New York World* explored for its readers the various possibilities in the death of Helen Potts. Perhaps the pills were improperly compounded by the pharmacist, or perhaps Helen had refilled the prescription and taken all the pills at once. The *World* also looked into the background of Carlyle Harris, and found that he had been arrested in August, 1890, for running a "blind pig," an after-hours drinking establishment. Further, that he had been indicted under the false name of C. W. Harkis at the time. The case had not yet come to trial.

When Harris was interviewed, he freely admitted the charge, but said it was all a mistake. He was the secretary-treasurer of the Neptune Club, a restaurant in Asbury Park, New Jersey, and he had leased part of the club to other organizations. One of these must have been using the premisses as a blind pig without his knowledge. As to the false name, he had given his right name when he was arrested, the officer must have written it down incorrectly. His candidness and sincerity impressed the reporters.

Mary Helen Neilson Potts was not buried until February 7, six days after her death, because her father convinced himself that he saw signs of life in the corpse. After a watch kept around the bier for four days failed to confirm the father's observation, he allowed his daughter to be interred. The *World* noted the suspicious fact that Carlyle Harris was not present at either the funeral or the belated burial, but accepted the explanation that it was his grief and fear of breaking down that kept him away. But public interest in the case was strong, and the *World* kept digging.

On Saturday, March 21, the newspaper struck paydirt. The District Attorney of New York County, DeLancey Nicoll, had two affidavits; one sworn to by Mrs. Potts, the dead girl's mother, and the other by one Dr. Charles Treverton, Helen's uncle, who practiced medicine in Scranton, Pennsylvania.

According to Mrs. Potts, Carlyle Harris and Helen Potts had been secretly married on February 8, 1890, using the names Charles Harris and Helen Neilson. Mrs. Potts had learned of the marriage when Dr. Treverton called her to Scranton. Helen was at Dr. Treverton's home to be treated for a condition which, as Mrs. Potts put it, "the doctor assured me was the effect of sin."

Dr. Treverton in his turn had sworn that Helen came to him in July needing an abortion to save her life as a result of three previous attempts at abortion, the girl had told him, two by Harris and one by another doctor in New York. The suspicion was articulated by Mrs. Potts that her daughter's death was the result of foul play. The verdict of the coroner's jury added to this view: "We the jury find that Helen Potts met her death from opium poisoning. We also find that the amount of morphine known to have been in her possession was not sufficient to cause death." The analysis of the one remaining capsule had revealed it to be properly compounded.

Upon hearing this, Carlyle Harris immediately went to District Attorney Nicoll and offered to give himself up, but Nicoll determined that there was not yet sufficient cause to arrest him. Harris admitted the secret marriage, but specifically denied each of the other allegations against him. He had, he declared, never performed an abortion on his wife, the operation performed by the uncle was without his consent, and he had in no way fooled with the capsules he had given Helen. The marriage had been kept secret, he maintained, for two reasons; the first because of Helen's father's known objection to the union, and the second because of the harm it might do to Harris's position as a medical student and, indeed, to Helen Potts's status as a student at the Comstock School. Had Headmistress Day known that Miss Potts was actually Mrs. Harris, she would have been out of the school, bag and baggage, as fast as she could pack. And as for Harris, even before the story broke he had been suspended from medical school "in consequence of charges of a serious nature involving his moral character."

Now Mrs. Potts revealed one bit of information that drew the net of suspicion firmly around Harris. Her daughter Helen, she avowed, had not suffered from heart disease. She had told that story to prevent an autopsy, for fear it would show that Helen had had an abortion which would disgrace her and her family.

On Wednesday, March 25, the body of Helen Potts Harris was exhumed and an autopsy performed. Five days later, on Monday, March 30, Carlyle Harris was indicted for murder by the grand jury.

The trial did not begin for eight months, both sides having an interest in delaying it. The prosecution was busy gathering all the incriminating information about Carlyle Harris it could find, while Harris's attorneys were happy to wait for the intense ill feeling against their client to die down. At the time of the indictment one clergyman, the Reverend Frank C. Colby of Asbury Park's First Baptist Church, declared to his congregation that Harris "was the vilest wretch ever vomited out of hell—and he should be thrown back there again!"

Harris's defense team was made up of Charles Davison, who had been his lawyer before his troubles, John A. Taylor, an extremely competent advocate who had been Corporate Counsel of Brooklyn, and William Travers Jerome, who would years later become one of New York City's most famous and successful district attorneys. In 1906 he would prosecute millionaire HARRY THAW for the murder of architect Stanford White.

Heading the prosecution was Assistant District Attorney Francis Wellman, a brilliant trial lawyer who would later write *The Art of Cross-Examination*, and *My Day In Court*, two highly regarded books on the craft of the barrister.

In his opening address Wellman described for the jury the chain of events which, he hoped to prove, led up to the murder of Helen Potts. He told of the secret marriage; Helen's trip to Scranton, with her mother following shortly after; Mrs. Potts's finding out about the marriage and insisting that Harris make it public and the couple remarried before a minister; the compounding of the pills, and Helen's death. He also described various peccadilloes and infidelities that various witnesses would accuse Carlyle Harris of committing. But all this was background for the big question, which could only be answered by circumstantial evidence and the jury's reading of the character and intent of Carlyle Harris: did he refill one of the capsules with morphine, deliberately causing Helen's death?

As reported in Charles Boswell and Lewis Thompson's book *Surrender to Love* (1955), Wellman met the question head on:

> "In a case of death by willful poisoning a jury must expect to find as defendant a cunning, shrewd, clever, calculating man, one who weighs circumstances and prepares for them. He lays his plans carefully and discounts in advance possible failures in his calculations. Such a one is Carlyle Harris. He was a medical student. It is fair to presume that if he

gave this morphine in the manner described, he knew just what the effects would be and he knew the difficulty of detection in a post-mortem examination. All the medical authorities agree that morphine is so quickly absorbed into the system that only traces can be found in the stomach after death. Had not Helen's roommates gone to the concert that night, had they gone to bed as ordinarily with her, had they not come in late and awakened her, the first sleep produced by the drug would have been the sleep of death. Had his plan succeeded there would have been no talk of investigation. It would have been said that she died from natural causes, and Harris would have gone to his wife's funeral an object of sympathy to all her friends and relatives. But the plans of the shedder of human blood always fail. So this one has failed. Murder will out because God wills it so!"

The defense team was not impressed by this preliminary oration, certain that the case was going to prove to be a battle of the experts. If it could be shown that Helen Potts died of an overdose of morphine, then Carlyle Harris's life was in jeopardy. If the jury could be made to believe that the girl had a predisposition to be sensitive to small doses of morphine, or that she had died of some other cause entirely, then Carlyle Harris would walk from the courtroom a free man. It was an open question in a day when pathology was still more of an art than a science.

The prosecution built its case carefully and methodically. First Wellman called on Headmistress Day and then on Frances Carson, one of Helen's roommates, to establish the facts prior to the girl's death. Then Doctor Fowler testified as to the girl's condition when he treated her: "I found her in a state of coma, with a pale and blue surface of skin, and very labored respiration, about two per minute. The breathing was stertorous. I found the pupils of both eyes contracted to a point almost beyond being perceptible. The pupils were symmetrically contracted in both eyes." The prosecution brought out that Fowler recognized in these symptoms a case of opiate poisoning, and that he was familiar with the symptoms, having treated at least seventy-five cases of opium poisoning in his thirty-five years in practice. Fowler told about finding the pill box and sending for Carlyle Harris.

The next morning the dead girl's mother, Mrs. Potts, took the stand. She told of the secret marriage and Harris's reluctance to acknowledge it. Then Dr. Charles Treverton of Scranton was sworn. He told of performing an abortion on Helen necessitated by a botched abortion that had been attempted by Harris earlier. He claimed that Harris, who had come up to Scranton to be with Helen, admitted performing the earlier procedure, and said that he had done it several times before, always with success, and couldn't understand what went wrong this time. He also testified that he had given a fair amount of morphine to Helen at the time to kill her pain, thus disposing of one defense argument; that the girl had an abnormal sensitivity to the drug.

On cross examination the defense brought out a letter that Dr. Treverton had written to Harris to get him up to Scranton. It contained this passage: "Things must be attended to at once, or you must know the result—disgrace for us all—and above all I shall need medical aid and money. Will you stand the bill? If you will, things can be made all right again, and no one the wiser. If not, we will take other steps . . . I shall handle this thing to your sorrow if you fail to appear." The scent of greed and blackmail in the letter undercut the doctor's testimony.

As Jerome had suspected, the case finally came down to a battle of experts. The prosecution put a parade of witnesses on the stand who blackened Harris's character. Charles Oliver, a cousin to the Potts, told of Harris bragging of his successes with women, and his dealing with the occasional issue of those successes by either performing an abortion or suggesting a "lying-in hospital" and subsequent adoption. The Lathams, husband and wife, testified that even while Helen was recovering from her painful and dangerous operation Harris was consorting with a young lady with the felicitous name of Queenie Drew.

Harris, interviewed in his jail cell by reporters, impressed them all as being calm and earnest. And he refuted the testimony with passion and logic. "Do you believe," he asked the reporters, "that if I were guilty of the things Treverton, Latham and Oliver suggested, that I would have confided in them, all of whom were virtual strangers to me?"

The trial evidence now moved into the realm of medical forensics. The prosecution, after a brief intercourse with the druggist, who explained how carefully he compounded medications, brought to the stand a succession of distinguished physicians. Dr. Allan McLane Hamilton testified that he had performed an autopsy on the exhumed body of Helen Potts. He had, he said, found no sign of disease of the heart, but great congestion of the brain, a symptom of narcotic poisoning. Dr. George D. Smith, who had assisted at the autopsy, agreed. Dr. Rudolph Witthaus of New York University Medical School testified as to the laboratory analysis of certain specimens taken from Helen Potts's body. The specimens, he explained, were the stomach, the whole intestine, the left kidney, the spleen, the heart and the brain. He declared that he had performed extensive tests on these body parts and found no quinine, but minute traces of opium.

On cross-examination Jerome got Dr. Witthaus to admit that atropine, one of the medicines which Dr. Fowler had administered to the dying girl, could have turned into opium in the body by losing two atoms of hydrogen. He also suggested the quinine in the pills as a possible source for breakdown products which would test as opium, and even brought up the possibility of pepperin, a constituent of pepper, as a source.

After a few more doctors appeared for the prosecution, the defense got to present its expert witnesses. First Harris's aunt testified as to what a nice boy Carlyle was. Then Dr. Horatio C. Wood of Philadelphia, a leading medical expert of the day, testified that in his learned opinion opium poisoning could not be reliably detected in a post mortem on an embalmed body. He could not reliably state what Helen Potts had died of, and he didn't think anyone else could either. On cross-examination, however, Wellman brought out that Dr. Wood hadn't treated more than one overdose of morphine case in the past fifteen years. Based on this he managed to effectively destroy Wood's value as a defense witness.

The next person on the stand, Dr. Herman M. Biggs, Professor of Pathology at Bellevue Medical School, would be a powerful witness for the defense, but his testimony was interrupted by the physical collapse of defense attorney Jerome, who was suffering from exhaustion and extreme lack of sleep due to the immense amount of preparation he had done in the weeks before the start of the trial. The judge adjourned the proceedings for the weekend to allow Jerome time to recover.

Over the weekend the authorities of Asbury Park, New Jersey, grabbed a couple of headlines by announcing that if, by any chance, Harris were found innocent of the charges against him in New York City, they had every intention of proceeding against him for the violations of the Neptune Club, where they claimed to have discovered, "orgies were of nightly occurrence."

Jerome, much recovered on Monday, resumed his examination of Dr. Biggs. Harris was likewise in good spirits. "I cannot feel myself in danger," he had told reporters over the weekend. "I have tried to force myself into the belief that my life is in jeopardy, but I cannot. I have gone over the testimony of each witness and . . . I cannot see how an intelligent jury can send me to the chair on the strength of it."

Dr. Briggs testified that he could not see how any determination of the cause of death could have been made from an analysis of the internal organs of the victim. They were "absolutely worthless for the purpose of pathological examination." On cross examination Wellman tried to weaken the testimony, but did not succeed.

Jerome called several other expert witnesses, ending with Dr. Dana, Professor of Nervous Diseases at Dartmouth Medical School and President of the American Pathological Society. Dr. Dana confirmed that no proper pathological examination could have confirmed that Helen Potts died of morphine poisoning. He further stated that, "The entire autopsy was worthless. No embalming fluid will preserve the organs without changing them."

Wellman tried to discredit Dr. Dana as he had Dr. Wood of Philadelphia, but had worse luck. "Have you examined many kidneys?" he asked the doctor.

> "Yes."
>
> "How many?"
>
> "Oh, I should say three or four hundred."
>
> Wellman pushed on. "Have you made microscopic examinations of any kidneys?"
>
> "Yes.—I should think ten or fifteen thousand."
>
> Wellman gave up, and the defense rested.

It was the consensus of court watchers, including the reporters, the judge, and both sets of attorneys, that the jury would be out for a long time. They were mistaken. Twenty-two minutes after the judge gave the case to the jury the twelve jurors filed back into the courtroom. In that time they found the defendant guilty of murder in the first degree.

On Monday, February 8, 1892, the judge, who made it clear that he agreed with the jury's verdict, sentenced Harris to die in what New York State was then calling its "electrical chair." A last-ditch fight to save Harris was waged by the notorious legal firm of Howe and Hummel, who were known to cross the bounds of propriety and legality to aid their clients, and who would eventually both be disbarred. William Howe, the senior partner, managed to find several witnesses who would swear that Helen Potts had been a secret morphine addict. He also interviewed one of the original jurors who told him that he would not have voted for conviction had he known, or so Mr. Howe claimed. By these techniques he managed to delay the execution for over a year, but he was unable to change the final outcome. On Monday, May 8, 1893, Carlyle Harris was executed in the electrical chair at Sing Sing prison. His mother had a brass plate fastened to the top of his coffin, with the following inscription engraved on it:

Carlyle W. Harris
Murdered May 8th, 1893
Aged 23 yrs., 7 mos., 15 days
"We would not if we had known."
—THE JURY

HART, Richard James "Two-Gun"

See: JAMES CAPONE

HARTFORD CIRCUS FIRE

On July 6, 1944, while the Ringling Bros., Barnum & Bailey Circus was playing Hartford, Connecticut, a fire started in the main tent. Within minutes, the big top was engulfed in flames, and before it was put out 168 people died in the conflagration. Connecticut authorities conducted a six-month investigation and concluded that a cigarette, carelessly tossed from the stands onto dry hay below, caused the tragedy.

On June 28, 1950, 20-year-old Robert Dale Segee, while under investigation for arson near Columbus, Ohio, confessed to the Ohio State Police that he had set the fire in Hartford six years before. At the time of the fire, he was a husky 14-year-old who had joined the circus a week before and was working as a roustabout. He admitted to the Ohio troopers that he had set between 25 and 30 major fires near his home in Portland, Maine, when he was growing up. He also admitted to setting two small fires prior to the big one at the circus during the week he worked there.

Segee confessed because of bad dreams that

he had, starting right after the fire, about all the people who had died. In his dreams, their faces appeared and accused him of killing them. He did not remember actually setting the fire, but admitted that he must have, because he usually blacked out when he set a fire, and a frightening "red man" with fiery red chest hair and fangs and claws and flame coming out of the top of his head would appear in a dream. Which was what happened in this case.

The Ohio authorities sent the file on Segee, including his 33-page, single-spaced signed confession, to the Connecticut State Police. But since their investigation had already concluded that the fire was an accident, they did not pursue it.

In 1991, 47 years after the fire, Hartford Fire Lieutenant Rick Davey concluded a nine-year re-investigation of the case and determined that the fire had indeed been deliberately set. Davey reviewed the records in light of new scientific techniques that were not available to the original investigators. For example, a study conducted in California in the 1970s showed that a smoldering cigarette would not ignite dry hay if the relative humidity was over 23 percent. At 2:00 P.M. on the day of the Hartford fire, the humidity was 42 percent.

Segee was convicted of arson in Ohio and sentenced to the Ohio State Reformatory in Mansfield. While there, he was questioned about his confession and repudiated it, claiming it was the result of his bad dreams and vivid imagination. Segee, now in his sixties, is living in Ohio, and will not talk about the fire. Even if his culpability for the Hartford fire were to be established at this late date, it is not clear what, if anything, he could be charged with. There was no law specifically for arson murder in Connecticut in 1944, so the police would have to establish that he intended to kill someone in the fire to bring murder charges against him. The statute of limitations has long since run out on anything else with which he could be charged.

HARTZELL, Oscar Merril

A MASTER SWINDLER

An Iowa farm boy who became a consummate master at swindling his neighbors, Oscar Hartzell began by falling for the swindle that he would adopt, adapt and make his own. In Des Moines, Iowa, in 1919, Hartzell and his mother were among an elite group of Iowa citizens who were solicited to give money to a widow known as Mrs. Sudie B. Whitaker to purchase shares in the estate of Sir Francis Drake. Mrs. Hartzell invested $6,000 in the proposition. After thinking it over, Hartzell saw the light and took the train to Sioux City to visit Mrs. Whitaker and her partner Milo F. Lewis. When Hartzell took them to task for swindling his mother, they admitted the con. To their surprise, he told them they were pikers, and he could show them how to make real money.

It seems that Sir Francis Drake had fathered an illegitimate son. The son had been jailed to prevent scandal and had never claimed his share in his father's estate. According to Hartzell's scheme, a Missouri man named Ernest Drake, the only legitimate heir to Sir Francis Drake's illegitimate son, was now preparing to claim that share, which had grown in value in the past 300 years to some 22 billion dollars. Since pushing the claim through British courts would require money, lucky midwesterners named Drake, or a suitable facsimile, would be invited to invest in the claim. When the eventual victory came, the investors, known as "donators," would be repaid at the rate of 500 to 1.

Hartzell and his new partners opened an office as the Sir Francis Drake Association. Then they traveled through Iowa, Missouri and Illinois looking for people named Drake. They had an irresistible proposition for the Drakes of the Midwest, and soon they broadened it to include people who had once been named Drake, people who thought they might have been named Drake, people who liked the name of Drake and anybody else who liked a good story.

Choosing not to conduct his business through the mails, probably because of federal statutes dealing with using the mails to defraud, Hartzell set up a network of agents in Iowa and the nearby states to deal with the thousands of donators. The agents would meet in secret conclave with their donators to read telegrams from Hartzell, who had moved to London to be closer to the action. The donators were pledged to "silence, secrecy and nondisturbance," and they kept their pledge with a fanatical devotion. Soon the necessity for a Drake connection on the part of the donators was dropped, and midwesterners of all surnames were permitted to pass money to Oscar Hartzell.

Hartzell's telegrams relating the successes and failures of the Drake heir made the donators participants in an exciting adventure story with international repercussions. The Depression, they understood, was being caused by Britain's fear of having to pay this vast sum. Every fluctuation in the British pound caused heart-pounding excitement among the faithful. Meanwhile, Hartzell, who was receiving $2,500 a week from his agents, was living in high style in London.

Finally, in 1932, when some of his agents had been careless enough to accept donations through the mails, the Post Office inspectors stepped in. Several of the agents were indicted for postal fraud, and the inspectors were going after Hartzell. The donators were not fazed. They understood what was going on: the United States was trying to embarrass the heir and his supporters on behalf of the British government.

In January 1933, Hartzell was deported back to New York as an undesirable alien. New York forwarded him to Iowa, where he was thrown in jail. Hartzell got word to his agents that this was good news! It showed that both governments were frightened. He requested and received more than $150,000 from the faithful for posting his bail, as well as legal fees and other expenses. This amount was exorbitant at a time when a full dinner at an expensive restaurant cost fifty cents, with tip.

As part of its case, the government sent an investigator to look up Sir Francis Drake's will in the Historical Documents Room of Somerset House, London. Drake left everything to his wife and his brother, Tom. There was no mention of a child, legitimate or otherwise. An English expert on the statutes of limitations was imported for the trial. He explained that, even were there a direct descendant of an illegitimate son of Sir Francis Drake, and even were another will or other document found acknowledging the paternity, the descendant would not be heir to anything, as the limitations to such a claim had run out centuries ago. Hartzell was convicted of "causing to have sent mail to defraud" and sentenced to 10 years in prison.

It is an interesting attribute of the human mind that, once it believes something, it is hard to make it disbelieve. Contrary evidence is either ignored or mentally twisted to make it conform. This is the principle of faith that organized religions and con men depend upon. Hartzell's conviction and imprisonment served to convince the faithful that the U.S. government was conniving with the king of England to swindle the heir out of his rightful inheritance.

The swindle persisted with Hartzell in prison. His agents continued to solicit and receive money from the donators. But not through the mail. Unfortunately for the agents, some of them did answer letters through the mail. Eight of the agents were brought to trial. Some of the donators were subpoenaed to appear as witnesses. When the receipts for their investments were passed around the court, they were visibly agitated. "Careful of those, please," they pled. "They are very valuable."

Despite the continuing faith of the donators, the agents were convicted.

HARVARD UNIVERSITY

In one of the most celebrated crimes in American academia, Dr. George Parkman, Harvard professor of anatomy, was murdered by DR. JOHN WHITE WEBSTER, Harvard professor of chemistry and mineralogy, in 1849.

HARVEY, Julian (1916–1961)

The ketch *Bluebelle* sailed from Fort Lauderdale, Florida, on November 8, 1961, with its captain, retired Air Force Lieutenant Colonel Julian Harvey, his wife Mary, Arthur Dupperrault and his wife, and the Dupperrault children: 14-year-old son Brian and two daughters, 11-year-old Terry Jo and 7-year-old Renee.

Five days later the Coast Guard picked up a dinghy holding Captain Harvey and the drowned body of young Renee Dupperrault. Harvey told them that the ketch had caught fire, and he was barely able to escape with his life. His passengers were below, and he could not get to any of them before the boat sank. He had found the body of Renee floating in the water.

Three days later, while he was telling this story to the Coast Guard board of inquiry, Terry Jo Dupperrault was rescued from a cork raft she had been floating in since the tragedy. Harvey was at the Coast Guard board of inquiry when word came that the girl had been found. He promptly went back to his motel room and slit his wrists with a razor blade.

Terry Jo told her rescuers a far different story of the incident from that offered by Harvey. Her mother, father and brother, and Harvey's wife, had all been murdered by Harvey. She had seen their bodies all covered with blood. Then Harvey had opened the boat's sea cocks and left in his dinghy. Terry Jo did not know why he had left her alive; she had barely been able to release the raft and climb aboard before the boat sank.

It was later discovered that Harvey's first wife and her mother had died in a violent accident in 1949, while Harvey was on active duty with the Air Force. His car had gone off a bridge into the Florida bayou with the three on board, and somehow he had survived.

Harvey was, as his suicide note requested, buried at sea.

HAUPTMANN, Bruno Richard (1899–1936)

The accused kidnapper of the infant son of Charles Lindbergh, Bruno Hauptmann was convicted and executed for the crime. In past years, however, there has been considerable doubt cast on his guilt.
See also: LINDBERGH KIDNAPPING

HEARST, Patricia Campbell (1955–)

FROM KIDNAPPED HEIRESS TO BANK ROBBER AND FUGITIVE

On February 5, 1974, Patricia Campbell Hearst, 19-year-old daughter of newspaper magnate Randolph Hearst, was kidnapped from the Berkeley, California, apartment she shared with her boyfriend Steven Weed. The kidnappers, two black men and a white woman, claimed to be members of a new terrorist group they called the Symbionese Liberation Army. The kidnapping of Patty Hearst was not their first venture into the realm of terrorism; several months before, they had murdered Oakland School Superintendent Marcus Foster with cyanide-tipped bullets and sent a letter to the *San Francisco Chronicle* explaining their actions. The letter expressed the tone of the group: "This attack is also to serve notice on the fascist Board of Education and its fascist supporters that The Court of the People have issued a death Warrant on All Members and Supporters of the Internal Warfare Identification Computer System. This shoot-on-sight order will stay in effect until such time as all political police are removed from our schools and all photos and other forms of identification are dropped." The letter ended: "Death to the fascist insect that preys upon the life of the people."

Apparently, the SLA had murdered a respected black school superintendent because he was trying to institute a program of student photo identification to keep the drug dealers out of the grammar schools. The police suspected that this group was involved in Hearst's kidnapping because cyanide stains appeared on the walls of her apartment where shots had been fired. But they knew nothing about the group. The only thing to do was to wait for a ransom demand.

The ransom demand came in the form of a tape to Berkeley radio station KPFA, along with an eight-page letter. The demand was extreme: "General Field Marshal Cinque" demanded that Randolph Hearst arrange for the distribution of free food to anyone with welfare cards, social security cards, food stamp cards, disabled veteran cards, medical cards, parole or probation papers, and jail or bail-release slips. If Hearst had attempted to comply with the demand it would have cost approximately $400 million, and although he would have given anything to get his daughter back, his personal fortune was less than one percent of that. Patty's voice was on the tape, and she spoke slowly and seemed unconcerned for her parents' feelings. This started the myth that she was involved in her own kidnapping. A much higher probability is that she had been drugged, frightened beyond emotion and was reading from a prepared script.

In a second tape recording from Patty, she told the startled world that she had taken the name of "Tanya," and would fight with the SLA for "the freedom of the oppressed people." On April 15th, she participated in an SLA bank robbery, holding a gun. The news media used this as proof that "Tanya" had been brainwashed and was now working for the SLA. The SLA used this press reaction to convince Patty that her family had given up on her, that the police were against her and that her only salvation lay in staying with the SLA. Patty, who had been holding an unloaded gun during the robbery, and had been forced to participate, no longer knew whom to trust.

Meanwhile, the police and FBI were identifying and locating the members of the SLA. On May 17, authorities caught up with six of them in a house on 54th Street in Los Angeles. In the six-hour shoot-out that followed, the house was burned to the ground and all six SLA members died. They were: Donald David DeFreeze, who called himself "Field Marshal Cinque"; Nancy Ling Perry; Patricia "Mizmoon" Soltysik; Camilla Hall; Angela Atwood; and Willie Wolfe. For a while, it was feared that Patty Hearst's body would be found in the burned-out house, but that proved groundless.

In September 1975, the remaining members of the SLA were taken into custody. William and Emily Harris, two of the gang that originally kidnapped Patty, were captured hours before Patty was picked up in a house in San Francisco with Wendy Yoshimura.

Patty was tried for bank robbery in February 1976. The defense of fear and brainwashing was rejected by the jury, and she was convicted. Sentenced to seven years' imprisonment, she served 28 months. William and Emily Harris were sentenced to 10 years to life for the kidnapping.

Patty Hearst's conviction and incarceration seemed like the last act of a bad tragic opera. The prosecution refused to believe that a 19-year-old girl could be brainwashed by being kept locked in a closet, taken out only to be raped by one or another of her male abductors. Dr. Joel Fort, a witness for the prosecution, cited her previous sexual experience as proof that she must have been willing. In retrospect, it seems that the State was too anxious for a conviction. The natural order of things had been turned upside-down: a rich girl had robbed a bank and somebody had to be punished.

WANTED BY THE FBI

NATIONAL FIREARMS ACT; MATERIAL WITNESS

William Taylor Harris

FBI No. 308,668 L5 Date photographs taken unknown
Aliases: Richard Frank Dennis, William Kinder, Jonathan Maris, Jonathan Mark Salamone
Age: 29, born January 22, 1945, Fort Sill, Oklahoma (not supported by birth records)
Height: 5'7" **Eyes:** Hazel
Weight: 145 pounds **Complexion:** Medium
Build: Medium **Race:** White
Hair: Brown, short **Nationality:** American
Occupation: Postal clerk
Remarks: Reportedly wears Fu Manchu type mustache, may wear glasses, upper right center tooth may be chipped, reportedly jogs, swims and rides bicycle for exercise, was last seen wearing army type boots and dark jacket
Social Security Numbers Used: 315-46-2467; 553-27-8400; 359-48-5467
Fingerprint Classification: 20 L 1 At 12 / S 1 Ut

Emily Montague Harris

FBI No. 325,804 L2 Date photographs taken unknown
Aliases: Mrs. William Taylor Harris, Anna Lindenberg, Cynthia Sue Mankins, Emily Montague Schwartz
Age: 27, born February 11, 1947, Baltimore, Maryland (not supported by birth records)
Height: 5'3" **Eyes:** Blue
Weight: 115 pounds **Complexion:** Fair
Build: Small **Race:** White
Hair: Blonde **Nationality:** American
Occupations: Secretary, teacher
Remarks: Hair may be worn one inch below ear level, may wear glasses or contact lenses; reportedly has partial upper plate, pierced ears, is a natural food fadist, exercises by jogging, swimming and bicycle riding, usually wears slacks or street length dresses, was last seen wearing jeans and waist length shiny black leather coat
Social Security Numbers Used: 327-42-2356; 429-42-8003

Patricia Campbell Hearst

FBI No. 325,805 L10 Date photograph taken unknown
Alias: Tania
Age: 20, born February 20, 1954, San Francisco, California
Height: 5'3" **Eyes:** Brown
Weight: 110 pounds **Complexion:** Fair
Build: Small **Race:** White
Hair: Light brown **Nationality:** American
Scars and Marks: Mole on lower right corner of mouth, scar near right ankle
Remarks: Hair naturally light brown, straight and worn about three inches below shoulders in length, however, may wear wigs, including Afro style, dark brown of medium length; was last seen wearing black sweater, plaid slacks, brown hiking boots and carrying a knife in her belt

CAUTION

THE ABOVE INDIVIDUALS ARE SELF-PROCLAIMED MEMBERS OF THE SYMBIONESE LIBERATION ARMY AND REPORTEDLY HAVE BEEN IN POSSESSION OF NUMEROUS FIREARMS INCLUDING AUTOMATIC WEAPONS. WILLIAM HARRIS AND PATRICIA HEARST ALLEGEDLY HAVE RECENTLY USED GUNS TO AVOID ARREST. ALL THREE SHOULD BE CONSIDERED ARMED AND VERY DANGEROUS

Federal warrants were issued on May 20, 1974, at Los Angeles, California, charging the Harris' and Hearst with violation of the National Firearms Act. Hearst was also charged in a Federal complaint on April 15, 1974, at San Francisco, California, as a material witness to a bank robbery which occurred April 15, 1974.

IF YOU HAVE ANY INFORMATION CONCERNING THESE PERSONS, PLEASE NOTIFY ME OR CONTACT YOUR LOCAL FBI OFFICE. TELEPHONE NUMBERS AND ADDRESSES OF ALL FBI OFFICES LISTED ON BACK.

CM Kelley
DIRECTOR
FEDERAL BUREAU OF INVESTIGATION
UNITED STATES DEPARTMENT OF JUSTICE
WASHINGTON, D. C. 20535
TELEPHONE, NATIONAL 8-7117

Entered NCIC
Wanted Flyer 475
May 20, 1974

HEIRENS, William (1929–)

THE MULTIPLE KILLER WHO CRIED OUT TO BE CAUGHT

A psychopathic killer, and the author of one of the most famous quotes in homicide history, William Heirens, who grew up in Chicago, began demonstrating abnormal behavior before he was 10, committing burglaries to steal women's undergarments, which he would admire, and sometimes wear, in the privacy of his room. He was arrested at 13 for walking the streets with a loaded pistol and sent to a correction facility. But for all of his troubles, he managed to keep a good grade average in school. When he was 16 he enrolled in the University of Chicago.

On the night of January 7, 1946, Heirens broke into the bedroom of six-year-old Suzanne Degnan and abducted her, leaving the window wide open and an oily piece of paper crumpled on the floor.

The first detective on the scene was Otto Kreuzer, who in later years became chief of Chicago's detective force. He discovered the piece of paper, which looked like a discarded facial tissue. On spreading it open he discovered that it was a crudely written ransom note reading: "Get $20,000. Waite for word. Get $5 bills. Do not notify police or FBI for safty of child."

There was something about the scene that made Kreuzer fear for the girl's life. Unfortunately, he was right. Heirens had killed the girl and dismembered the body into six pieces, distributing the body parts in the sewer system, not too distant from the Degnan house. One peculiarity of the killing that interested the crime psychologists was that, despite the ghastly treatment of the girl's body, each segment had been carefully washed and wiped clean before disposal.

A late-night walker reported seeing a man with a shopping bag a block away from the Degnan house at one o'clock the previous morning. In a basement one block east of the Degnans' house, the detectives located a laundry tub that had distinct traces of blood around the rim. When they opened the drain, they found pieces of human flesh and strands of blonde hair.

The FBI Crime Laboratory in Washington, D.C., examined the ransom note at the request of the Chicago police. On it they found some clear fingerprints as well as the print of a left palm.

Six months later, on June 26, Heirens was arrested for burglary. There was also reason to believe that he might have been involved in a series of earlier burglaries, mostly on the North Side of Chicago, in which the burglar seemed as interested in taking women's clothes as he was in taking valuables. His fingerprints were taken and routinely checked against the fingerprints from the ransom note. They matched. This led the police to question him about a number of unsolved crimes, including two other murders.

Feeling sure that they had the right man, the state's attorney's office decided to question Heirens under sodium pentothal, which was then highly touted as a truth serum. The shots were administered by Dr. Roy R. Grinker, director of the Psychiatric Institute of Michael Reese Hospital. Dr. Grinker warned Assistant State's Attorney Wilbert F. Crowley that the drug was not dependable, and that any revelations that Heirens came up with under the drug's influence would not be admissible as evidence; but they went ahead with the procedure.

Under the drug's influence, Heirens told of a companion named George Merman who had actually committed the burglaries and the murders. "I used to take him to church on Sunday but he never paid attention to the services," he told them. Unfortunately Heirens's friend turned out to be a figment of Heirens's imagination. The American Civil Liberties Union protested this use of sodium pentothal as a probable violation of Heirens' civil rights. Years later, Heirens admitted that he had been taking sodium pentothal for almost a year—he thought it would stimulate his mind—and so the drug had little effect on him.

On his attorney's advice, Heirens agreed to confess—a move that they hoped might save him from a death sentence. But when the time came and Heirens walked into the room to talk to the Cook County state's attorney, he found 30 other people gathered around staring at him. He balked and refused to continue. His attorneys arranged with the prosecuting attorney to try again, with the understanding that the crowd would be drastically reduced. This time the state's attorney had pared the crowd down to a mere dozen or so. Heirens managed a partial confession, admitting his guilt but withholding the more grisly details. As Fred E. Inbau put it in *Lie Detection and Criminal Interrogation* (second edition, 1948): "It is indeed a sad commentary upon current police interrogation practices when a seventeen year old boy has to impart an elementary lesson to top-ranking law enforcement officials to the effect that it is psychologically unsound to ask a person to confess a crime in the presence of thirty spectators."

Heirens also confessed to two earlier murders. The first was the June 1945 knifing of 43-year-old Josephine Ross, described in the newspapers as "an attractive widow," as she lay asleep in her bed. The second, which had been dubbed by the press "the Lipstick Murder Case," was the shooting and knifing death of 30-year-old Frances Brown in her hotel room in December 1945, less than a month before the Degnan murder. Both women had been found nude, with their bodies carefully washed. In each case, as with Suzanne Degnan, there was no sign of sexual molestation. On Frances Brown's living room wall, Heirens had written, using her lipstick as a crayon:

> For heaven's
> sake catch me
> before I kill more.
> I cannot control myself.

Heirens's psychiatric examination established several abnormalities. It seemed that Heirens's sexual urges were satisfied by the burglaries, and he often experienced orgasm during the act of entering a household. The murders were incidental, although he felt a strong urge to wash and clean the bodies of his victims. It was also established that he had a very high pain threshold, showing little or no reaction when a sharp needle was pressed into the skin under his fingernails.

The judge accepted Heirens's plea of guilty to three murders and 26 burglaries and sentenced him to serve three consecutive life terms at Stateville Penitentiary (Joliet) for the murders and one to 20 years on the burglaries. He added the recommendation that Heirens never be paroled.

Heirens was transferred to the state prison for the criminally insane at Chester (Menard) after a month, but later went back to Stateville. In 1954, he unsuccessfully tried to get the Illinois Supreme Court to review his case.

HEIRS OF SIR FRANCIS DRAKE

See: OSCAR MERRIL HARTZELL

HELTER SKELTER

See: CHARLES MANSON

HENLEY, Elmer Wayne, Jr. (1956–)

Elmer Henley, Jr., was the teenage assistant-in-crime and eventual murderer of DEAN CORLL.

HILL, Virginia (1918–1966)

Lover and mistress to a pride of Mafiosi, including ANTHONY ACCARDO, FRANK NITTI, JOE ADONIS, FRANK COSTELLO, and finally BUGSY SIEGEL, Virginia Hill was a beautiful, intelligent, capable woman who served the MAFIA in a variety of areas outside of the bedroom. She was a layoff woman for major horse-racing books, going to the track to place pari-mutuel bets to cover long-odds bets. Later she was a world-traveling bag lady for major ORGANIZED CRIME figures. It is believed that she carried tens of millions of dollars to and from bank accounts in Europe and the Caribbean for her paramours and others, a sign of how well trusted she was by a group of highly suspicious men. For her various skills, she was well paid, and she lived well.

Bugsy Siegel, the man who created Las Vegas, named the first major casino on the strip "The Flamingo" after Hill, who had picked up that nickname at 16, when she was a dancer at the 1934 Chicago World's Fair. It was in her Los Angeles house that he was murdered in 1947, while she was on a trip to Europe.

Hill was one of the more flamboyant witnesses at the 1950 KEFAUVER COMMITTEE hearings. When a senator asked her where she got her money, she told him "men like to give me money." When asked why so many mob figures were so fond of her, her slightly expurgated reply was, "I'm the best goddamned lay in the world."

In March 1966, in Salzburg, Austria, Virginia Hill died after taking an overdose of sleeping pills.

HINES, Jimmie J. (1877–1957)

See: THOMAS E(DMUND) DEWEY; DUTCH SCHULTZ; TAMMANY HALL

HINCKLEY, John W., Jr. (1955–)

A psychopathic drifter who decided to make his mark in the world by assassinating a U.S. president, 25-year-old John Hinckley, Jr., emptied his .22-caliber revolver aiming at President Ronald Reagan on March 30, 1981, as Reagan was leaving Washington's Hilton Hotel after giving a speech. Bullets hit Reagan in the chest under his left arm and James Brady, Reagan's press secretary; Timothy J. McCarthy, a Secret Service agent; and Thomas Delahanty, a District of Columbia police officer. Reagan was pushed into a limousine by a Secret Service agent and rushed to the hospital. He survived, as did the other three men wounded in the attack.

The son of an oil executive, Hinckley grew up in Dallas, Texas, moving to Colorado in 1974 with his family. He attended Texas Tech, but never graduated, and joined the American Nazi Party, but was dropped from membership because of his "violent nature." A letter found in his hotel room revealed that he had a fixation on Jodie Foster, a young movie actress who was then a student at Yale. He had written her several letters, which she had not answered. He shot Reagan hoping to thereby win Miss Foster's affection.

Hinckley was judged insane by a jury and committed to a mental facility. The pistol that he used was purchased at a Dallas pawnshop a few days before the attack. Since the attack, the Brady Bill, named in honor of James Brady, who was the most seriously injured in the incident, has been proposed in Congress. The Brady Bill does not prohibit the ownership of handguns but merely puts into effect a three-day waiting period for buying such weapons so that the authorities can check the criminal record of the purchaser. To date the bill has been successfully blocked by the gun lobby.

HISS, Alger (1904–)

Accused by WHITTAKER CHAMBERS of being a Soviet agent and convicted of perjury for denying it under oath, Alger Hiss was a brilliant lawyer who graduated at the top of his Harvard Law School class in 1929. He served as law clerk for Supreme Court Justice Oliver Wendell Holmes for two years before going into private practice in Boston and New York City. In 1933, he entered government service, and by 1947, he was director of the office in charge of United Nations affairs. He attended the Yalta Conference and was secretary-general at the San Francisco Conference at which the Charter of the United Nations was drafted. At the time of Chambers's accusations,

Hiss was president of the Carnegie Endowment for International Peace.

Chambers claimed to the House Committee on Un-American Activities that Hiss was part of his secret Communist cell and that Hiss passed him secret documents to photograph and pass on to the Soviets. Hiss denied this vehemently under oath:

> I am not and never have been a member of the Communist Party. I do not and never have adhered to the tenets of the Communist Party. I am not and never have been a member of any Communist-front organization. I have never followed the Communist Party line, directly or indirectly. To the best of my knowledge, none of my friends is a Communist.

Chambers produced documents that he claimed Hiss had given him and microfilm that had been hidden in a hollowed-out pumpkin. Pictures of the pumpkin appeared in all the papers, with Chambers on one side of it and committee member Richard Nixon on the other. Hiss was indicted by a grand jury and, after two trials, convicted of perjury. He served three and a half years in prison. During that time, and after he was released, he continued to work to prove his innocence and establish that it was Chambers who had perjured himself. He wrote a long, analytical book about his experience, *In the Court of Public Opinion*, published in 1957, in which he did his best to logically and methodically refute the charges.

On October 15, 1992, General Dmitri A. Volkogonov, chairman of the Russian military intelligence archives, completed a search of the Soviet intelligence records of the period. He concluded that Hiss was not, and had never been, an agent of the Soviet government. Hiss, now 87, said, "For 44 years I have been trying to set the record straight about the false charges against me." He said he had no bitterness against Chambers, who he had always felt "was not of sound mind." He felt that Nixon had been misled by Chambers, but that "Nixon wanted to be fooled. He didn't try very hard to find out the true facts."

HOCH, Johann Otto (1862–1906)

WIDOWER, quiet and home loving, with comfortable income and well-furnished house wishes acquaintances of congenial widow without children. Object, matrimony. Write Box B-103

Mrs. Marie Walcker, a 46-year-old widow, answered the above ad in a Chicago German-language newspaper in late 1904. On December 4, 1904, she and Johann Hoch were married. Almost immediately she sickened and died, leaving her new husband all her worldly belongings. Hoch immediately proposed to Marie's sister Amelia and married her a week after Marie's death. Amelia gave him $750 of her money to handle, after which he promptly disappeared. Amelia went to the police.

Inspector George Shippy of the Chicago police, who had been on the trail of what he believed was a name-changing wife-murderer for some time, promptly had Marie Walcker-Hoch's body exhumed. An impressively large dose of arsenic was found. Shippy checked with the mortician and established that arsenic had not been used in the embalming fluids and put out an all-points bulletin on the missing Hoch.

Hoch was arrested in New York, turned over to the police by the landlady of the rooming house he moved into, who recognized his picture as the man who, under the name of Henry Bartels, had proposed marriage to her the same day he moved into her house. The New York police searched his room and found several wedding rings with the inscriptions filed off, a dozen suits with the labels ripped out, a revolver, 58 grains of arsenic hidden in a fountain pen, and $625 cash. He was extradited to Chicago to stand trial.

Inspector Shippy slowly put together Hoch's history. He had been born in Horweiler, Germany, with the name John Schmidt. He married

Christine Ramb, had three children, left Christine and the children in 1887 to come to the United States and embarked on a career of bigamy, embezzlement and murder. He was identified by the Reverend Hermann C. A. Haas of Wheeling, West Virginia, as the man who, as Jacob Huff, had married and then poisoned Caroline Hoch in 1895. He then took all her money, collected her life insurance, sold her house and disappeared. The poisoning could not be proved because when the authorities disinterred the remains of Mrs. Huff they discovered a sight that shocked even the hardened physicians at the scene: The entire midsection of the dead woman had been removed.

Huff then apparently roamed the Midwest, marrying and murdering wealthy widows. Bodies of his former wives were examined in New York, St. Louis, Philadelphia, Minneapolis, and as far west as San Francisco. All had more than the expected amount of arsenic in them. Unfortunately, because some arsenic had been used in the embalming process, murder could not be proved, except in the case of Mrs. Walcker-Hoch's body, which was embalmed by a new process.

Hoch kept protesting his innocence through the trial, but when it was over and he was convicted of his latest wife's murder, he was heard to murmur as he was led away, "It serves me right." On February 23, 1906, he was hanged.

HOFFA, James R. (1913–1975?)

THE UNION LEADER WENT FOR A RIDE, AND NEVER CAME BACK

On July 30, 1975, James Hoffa, erstwhile boss of the Teamsters Union (1957–1967) and convict (1967–1971), walked out of the Manchus Red Fox restaurant in Detroit and was never seen again. He thus, like the missing JUDGE JOSEPH CRATER, left the world of the mundane and entered American myth.

Hoffa fought his way to the top of the Teamsters Union in the 1930s, organizing Detroit locals in an atmosphere that approached physical war between union and management. His brother was shot. Their cars were bombed, their offices wrecked, strikebreakers and police would assault them on the street. It was a time when the distinction between the unions, the management and ORGANIZED CRIME were blurred. MAFIA figures worked for both sides, and the Teamsters proved more adept than most at using violence as an organizational tool.

When Hoffa took over from Dave Beck as Teamster president in 1957, the intertwining of the union and organized crime was an established fact. The union leadership needed the gangsters to supply muscle in strike situations and to keep the faithful in line during local elections. Hoffa, with the Mob's help, used the power of the union as a whip to extort money from companies employing teamsters. He used the union's pension funds as his own private bank and used the money to buy political favors. As William Balsamo and George Carpozi explained in *Under the Clock* (1988):

> "Everybody has his price" was the credo by which Jimmy Hoffa managed the union. That policy resulted in payoffs for some and promises of political support or special favors for others. He kept no bank accounts, drew no checks, and when he travelled he carried an attache case that contained up to $500,000 in cash. . . .
>
> Each month of every one of the ten years he steered the Teamster steamroller through the nation's Upper and Lower Houses, some of Hoffa's most trusted intimates would enter the offices of the representatives and senators who were on the union's "friendship rolls" and plunk down a large manila envelope on each of those lawmakers' desks.
>
> "Here's your copy of the magazine," Hoffa's emissaries said. Indeed, that month's issue of *International Teamster* was in the envelope—but so were

$500 to $1000 in crisp legal tender of $50- or $100-bill denominations.

When Robert Kennedy became chief counsel to the Senate Select Committee on Improper Activities in the Labor or Management Field—more generally known as the MCCLELLAN COMMITTEE—he targeted Hoffa for special attention, describing the Teamsters' leadership as a "conspiracy of evil." Kennedy continued the attention when his brother JOHN F. KENNEDY was elected president and appointed Robert as his attorney general. In 1962, Hoffa went on trial for extortion and managed to get a hung jury. How he accomplished this was demonstrated when he subsequently was put on trial for jury tampering. This time he was convicted and drew an eight-year sentence. In 1964, he was put on trial again and convicted of defrauding the union pension fund of close to two million dollars. In 1967, when his lawyers ran out of appeals, he began serving his sentence in the federal penitentiary at Lewisburg, Pennsylvania. Hoffa tried to keep his hold on the union from Lewisburg and had his protégé Frank Fitzsimmons appointed president in his place.

Fitzsimmons, however, showed an unexpected stubbornness and refused to take orders from the imprisoned Hoffa. A very annoyed Hoffa vowed that when he got out of prison he would regain the union leadership.

In 1971, President Richard Nixon agreed to commute Hoffa's term to time served—but with the proviso that Hoffa agree to renounce the Teamsters' presidency and stay out of union politics, including any seat on the ruling councils, for 10 years. Four years later, at 2:00 P.M. on July 30, 1975, Hoffa went to the Manchus Red Fox restaurant in Detroit to meet three men. Half an hour later he called his wife to say the men had not arrived yet. Shortly after that he was seen entering a car in the restaurant parking lot with a couple of other men. Who the other men were is not known. Whether Hoffa ever got out of that car alive is not known. The FBI later found traces of hair and blood in the car, but no trace of Hoffa has ever been found.

HOLE IN THE WALL GANG

The Hole in the Wall was an outlaw refuge in Wyoming, about one day's ride from Casper. Many western badmen rode out of Hole in the Wall, including many gangs. The one that is usually referred to as the Hole in the Wall Gang is the group led by Butch Cassidy, which is also known as the Wild Bunch. After they left, the title shifted to a group led by BLACK JACK KETCHUM, and then to the Laughing Sam Carey Gang. Laughing Sam is regarded by some historians as being the most inept outlaw to ever attempt to rob a bank or hold up a train. Most of those who rode with him did not live to regret it. Once he and his gang tried to hold up the Spearfish Bank in South Dakota. They were all killed but Laughing Sam, and he had three bullets in him. But for some reason, he never lacked for recruits. Perhaps it was as Butch Cassidy is supposed to have said to the Sundance Kid, "Kid, there's a lot of dummies at Hole in the Wall."

HOLLIDAY, John Henry "Doc" (1852–1887)

An Atlanta, Georgia, dentist who went west for his health in 1873 after contracting tuberculosis, Doc Holliday soon became a heavy drinker, a professional gambler, and a psychopathic killer. He fell in with the EARP BROTHERS in Dodge City and once saved Wyatt Earp's life when Earp was town marshal of Dodge. Doc left Dodge City in 1879 and moved around through Texas and New Mexico Territory. He ran a saloon in Las Vegas, where he supposedly murdered a man named Mike Gordon who tried to leave town with one of the saloon's working girls.

Holliday came to Tombstone, Arizona, when Wyatt Earp was appointed town marshal and worked as the house gambler at the Oriental Saloon. At the time, he was suspected of being involved in a number of illegal activities, including stagecoach robberies, but nothing was ever proved. As a friend of the Earps he had many enemies. Holliday was involved in the infamous gunfight at the O. K. Corral and helped Wyatt Earp avenge his brothers who were bushwhacked afterward by followers of the Clanton gang. Doc Holliday died of tuberculosis in a sanatorium in Glenwood Springs, Colorado, on November 8, 1887.

HOLMES, H. H.

See: HERMAN WEBSTER MUDGETT

HOLMES, Oliver Wendell, Jr. (1841–1935)

Born in Boston, Massachusetts, Oliver Wendell Holmes served as an associate justice of the Supreme Court from 1902 to 1932. He was a lonely liberal in a conservative court. He became known as the "Great Dissenter" because of his forcefully written minority opinions supporting social legislation, which he believed should be regarded as constitutional unless it specifically violated the Constitution.

HOOD

See: HOODLUM

HOODLUM

Hoodlum is a term meaning a tough; an uncouth troublemaker; especially a member of a gang of toughs. This American expression dates back to the 1870s and probably originated in San Francisco. Eric Partridge, in his *Dictionary of Slang and Unconventional English*, points out that *noodlum* is back-slang for *Muldoon*, the leader of a gang of San Francisco street arabs. It is possible that a printer copied "hoodlum" for "noodlum," and thus created a new expression. Another possibility, that it comes from a gang cry: "Huddle 'em," is regarded as unlikely.

HOOVER, J(ohn) Edgar (1895–1972)

THE FIRST DIRECTOR OF THE FBI MOLDED IT INTO HIS OWN IMAGE

Appointed head of the FEDERAL BUREAU OF INVESTIGATION in 1924, J. Edgar Hoover, the man who would become known as "the nation's top cop," kept his office for 48 years, until his death in 1972. Hoover served under eight presidents and 16 attorney generals, many of whom disliked him intensely. To his credit, he brought the FBI from a minor federal investigative group without the authority to make arrests or even to carry guns to the premier crime-fighting organization in the United States. But his flaws were many, and they prevented the FBI, which he ran with autocratic zeal, from ever truly becoming the agency that his public relations campaign convinced the public that it already was.

With a Master of Laws degree earned attending night school at George Washington University, Hoover joined the Department of Justice in 1917. Soon he was working under John Lord O'Brian, the special assistant to the attorney general for war work. O'Brian was so impressed with Hoover's work (he was registering enemy aliens) that he promoted the young man several times.

In 1919, Hoover was put in charge of the new GENERAL INTELLIGENCE DIVISION (GID), with the rank of special assistant to Attorney General A. Mitchell Palmer. There had been a series of bombings in the country, presumably the work of Communist radicals. The GID was set up to collect information on "subversives," and the hunt for subversives was to become a theme in Hoover's life. The subversives in question were anarchists, Communists, Wobblies (members of the International Workers of the World [IWW], a Communist-oriented trade union), men with long hair, women with short hair, and other radical elements.

J. Edgar Hoover, the official photograph. (Federal Bureau of Investigation.)

In 1921, Harry M. Daugherty was made President Warren G. Harding's new attorney general, and he promptly appointed Hoover as assistant director of the Justice Department's Bureau of Investigation. An inefficient, unprofessional and corrupt organization, burdened by political patronage, rocked by scandal, the popular abhorrence for the Red-baiting Attorney General's raids of 1919, and the Wall Street bombing by anarchists in 1920, the Bureau did not seem a particularly advantageous place for an ambitious young attorney to hang his hat. The next three years of the Harding administration, shaken by the Teapot Dome Scandal among others, did nothing to improve its stature.

In 1924, Calvin Coolidge was the new president, and his attorney general, Harlan Fiske Stone, abolished the GID and appointed Hoover as head of the Bureau of Investigation. Hoover was to concentrate on investigating federal crimes, leaving the subversive-hunting to others. His first job was to clean up the bureau, eliminating the corrupt ward heelers, con men and crooks who had crept in during the Harding administration, and establish high professional standards for his agents—standards that would win the respect, if not the love, of the public and the Congress and the eight presidents who would become his bosses over the next 48 years. He promptly swept the bureau clean, firing many of its 358 agents, setting up an inspection procedure over field operations and overhauling record-keeping and oversight procedures. As Harlan Stone, by then an associate justice of the Supreme Court, wrote to Felix Frankfurter in 1933:

> [Hoover] removed from the Bureau every man as to whose character there was any ground for suspicion. He refused to yield to any kind of political pressure; he appointed to the Bureau men of intelligence and education, and strove to build up a morale such as should control such an organization. He withdrew it wholly from its extra-legal activities, and made it an efficient organization for the investigation of criminal offenses against the United States.

In 1935, President Franklin D. Roosevelt renamed the Bureau the Federal Bureau of Investigation. This was the era of the gangster, when figures like JOHN DILLINGER, BABY FACE NELSON, and AL CAPONE had achieved the status of public heroes. Hoover decided that part of his job was to demystify these hoodlums and transfer the public's affection to the FBI and other law enforcement agencies. "If there is going to be publicity," he said, "let it be on the side of law and order." As it worked out, law and order meant the

FBI and Hoover. Hoover, through the FBI, did his best over the years to control everything that appeared in print, in movies and on radio or television concerning himself and the FBI. In the late thirties, he carefully stage-managed a "personal" capture of the wanted gangster Pretty Boy Floyd, which put Hoover on the folk-hero list, along with the gangsters he was chasing. Radio and television shows such as "This is Your FBI" and "The FBI in Peace and War" constantly presented a favorable image of the FBI and its activities to the public. Movie after movie made the taciturn, fearless special agents of the FBI into heroes and role models for small (male) children. And Hoover *was* the FBI. As a CIA officer was heard to gripe in the late sixties: "When we screw up, we appear before Congress; when the FBI screws up, Hoover just has Hollywood make another movie."

Despite Hoover's tendency to put himself and the FBI in the limelight, his sympathy for the ordinary police officer was real. As he wrote in an article in the November 1968 *Reader's Digest*:

> Obviously an adequate police force is the prime line of defence against crime. And many cities have been able to deter crime dramatically by sharply increasing the number of patrolmen in high-crime areas. But, again, the public must support the police fully. We must reject the current fashion of condemning the police and fawning on the felon. The man who daily places his life on the line for us against murderers, robbers, and unpredictable young thugs should not have to moonlight as a cab driver. He deserves fair compensation, which he does not get for the hazardous duty performed—the average policeman's salary is about $500 a month. Give him better tools with which to protect you. And these must be backed by proper research into the causes of crime and the improvements necessary to prevent it.

In 1937, President Roosevelt added to the FBI's tasks a job for which Hoover had been lobbying: counterespionage within the United States. With the start of World War II, Hoover attempted to expand the functions of the FBI to include intelligence gathering and counterintelligence all over the world. The job was instead given to William Donovan and his Office of Strategic Services (OSS), but Hoover and the FBI were allowed to keep Central and South America as their sphere of influence.

Hoover worked hard to professionalize the FBI, and it was soon recognized worldwide as among the finest criminal investigation agencies in existence. His "special agents"—all of his field officers were "special agents"—were recruited largely from people with legal or accounting backgrounds. He established a forensic science laboratory that not only stayed state of the art, but created many of the techniques that are now in general use in police departments throughout the world. The FBI's National Academy has trained its own agents as well as the top law enforcement officers from around the country since 1935.

At first suspicious of wiretapping as a tool of law enforcement, feeling that its use discouraged "ethical, scientific and sound investigative technique," Hoover allowed the FBI to use it in cases of national security. The Supreme Court, which in a 1928 decision allowed wiretapping evidence in court, changed its mind in 1939, but by then Hoover had come to depend on the fruits of wiretap. He was assured by the Justice Department that what was now forbidden was not wiretapping, but merely the disclosure of wiretap evidence. President Roosevelt authorized the continued use of wiretap in cases of suspected subversion, but directed that it should be limited as far as possible to aliens.

Hoover won ungrudging respect for his honesty, his integrity, his patriotism and his essential lack of bias. The FBI upheld the law, but it did not take sides. Hoover was strongly against the government's policy in 1942 of interning citizens of Japanese ancestry, for example. But as the years passed, Hoover changed, becoming more and more withdrawn, stubborn, rigid and paranoid, and his views became those of the FBI. He focused the attentions of the FBI on internal subversion, carrying on the hunt for domestic Communists to the exclusion of suppressing crime. In the 1950s, the FBI had no information on ORGANIZED CRIME and took the stand that the MAFIA simply did not exist. Hoover felt, as he testified before a 1951 Senate committee, that the principal responsibility for controlling organized crime lay with state and local law enforcement.

To Hoover in his last years, any dissent was suspect. Any criticism of himself or the FBI was anti-American. He went after Communists, hippies and civil rights workers with the same fervor. He put more resources into investigating Dr. Martin Luther King and Joan Baez than he did into investigating the five "families" controlling the American Mafia.

In 1961, Hoover reached retirement age, but he didn't want to retire. So he continued in office until he died in his sleep on the night of May 1, 1972. During his long years in office, Hoover built up a collection of personal files on important individuals, in and out of government, that, it was widely rumored, protected him from being ousted by any incoming administration. These files were burned by his secretary after his death.

Recently there have been allegations that Hoover was a closet homosexual, and that organized crime figures' knowledge of this was what kept Hoover and the FBI from investigating organized crime for so many years.

I

IDENTIFICATION OF INDIVIDUALS

The early attempts by the police to identify specific individuals and to communicate this identification to distant authorities, thus enabling them to recognize and apprehend wanted felons, were inconsistent and ineffective. A man arrested in one jurisdiction would frequently not be identified as the man wanted for a serious crime two counties away. Handbills and wanted posters were distributed, but the pictures were muddy and the physical descriptions were vague and inaccurate.

ALPHONSE BERTILLON, a French criminologist, was one of the first to attempt to remedy this. In the 1880s, he devised the system he called anthropometry, to classify prisoners according to body measurements, and the *PORTRAIT PARLÉ* (spoken picture) to codify descriptions of them. He also developed the technique of metric photography, by which the camera lens and the subject's distance from the camera are regularized so that the actual dimensions of the subject's head can be determined directly from the photograph.

By the 1920s, anthropometry gave way to FINGERPRINT IDENTIFICATION, and the *portrait parlé*, cumbersome and difficult to use, gave way to a generally standardized descriptive form.

One early version of this identification form, as given in Söderman and O'Connell's *Modern Criminal Investigation* (1935), looks like this:

NAME—
SEX—
COLOR—
NATIONALITY—
OCCUPATION—
AGE—
HEIGHT—
WEIGHT—
BUILD—Large; stout or very stout; medium; slim; stooped or square-shouldered; stocky

COMPLEXION—Florid; sallow; pale; fair; dark
HAIR—Color; thick or thin; bald or partly bald; curly; kinky; wavy; how cut or parted; style of hairdress
EYES—Color of the iris; eyes bulgy or small; any peculiarities
EYEBROWS—Slanting, up or down; bushy or meeting; arched, wavy, horizontal; as to texture, strong; thin; short or long-haired; penciled
NOSE—Small or large; pug, hooked, straight, flat
WHISKERS—Color; vandyke; straight; rounded; chin whiskers; goatee; side whiskers
MUSTACHE—Color; short; stubby; long; pointed ends; turned-up ends; Kaiser style
CHIN—Small, large; square; dimpled; double; flat; arched
FACE—Long; round; square; peg-top; fat; thin
NECK—Long; short; thick; thin; folds in back of neck; puffed neck; prominent Adam's apple
LIPS—Thick; thin; puffy; drooping lower; upturned upper
MOUTH—Large; small; drooping or upturned at corners; open; crooked; distorted during speech or laughter; contorted
HEAD—Posture of—bent forward; turned sideways; to left or right; inclined backwards or to left or right
EARS—Small; large; close to or projecting out from head; pierced
FOREHEAD—High; low; sloping; bulging; straight; receding
DISTINCTIVE MARKS—Scars; moles; missing fingers or teeth; gold teeth; tattoo marks; lameness; bow legs; pigeon toes; knock-knees; cauliflower ears; pockmarked; flat feet; nicotine fingers; freckles; birthmarks
PECULIARITIES—Twitching of features; rapid or slow gait; long or short steps; wearing of eyeglasses; carrying a cane; stuttering; gruff or effeminate voice
CLOTHES—Hat and shoes—color and style; suit—color; cut; maker's name; shirt and collar—style and color; tie—style and color; dressed neatly or carelessly
JEWELRY—Kind of; where worn
WHERE LIKELY TO BE FOUND—Residence; former residences; places frequented or hangouts; where employed; residences of relatives, etc.
PERSONAL ASSOCIATES—Friends who would be most likely to know of the movements or whereabouts of the person wanted, or with whom he would be most likely to communicate
HABITS—Heavy drinker or smoker; drug addiction; gambler; frequenter of pool parlors; dance halls; cabarets; baseball games; resorts, etc.
HOW HE LEFT THE SCENE OF THE CRIME—Running; walking; by vehicle; direction taken

Although descriptions are still considered useful, the photograph and the fingerprint are now the preferred methods of identification. Special cameras are used, and the placement of the subject is very important. Front and side views (or, in officialese, anterior and profile) are taken, and retouching the photographs is discouraged. The right side is preferred, and the angle of the subject's head in relation to the background is controlled. In the past some cameras used a mirror arrangement to take both views simultaneously, but that practice has fallen out of favor. It has been found that initial identification is easier with the front view, but that the side view shows more detail and is more positive.

Many police forces now take three views; front, right side, and left quarter view.

ISRAEL, Harold (1901–)

Harold Israel was a suspect in the 1924 murder of Father Hubert Dahme, an Episcopal priest, in Bridgeport, Connecticut. His innocence was established by HOMER S. CUMMINGS, the prosecuting attorney.

IZZY AND MOE

THEY BROUGHT HUMOR TO THE JOB OF ENFORCING PROHIBITION

On January 16, 1920, PROHIBITION became the law of the land, and Americans stopped drinking alcoholic beverages. Within six months, there were more speakeasies operating than there had been saloons when drinking was legal. It became clear that the 1,500 Prohibition enforcement agents, whose job it was to see that 125 million Americans stayed dry, were going to have quite a job on their hands. Most of these "revenuers" were a dull, dour, humorless lot. Bad pay, an unpopular and impossible job and miserable working conditions were nothing to chortle about. In Chicago, ELIOT NESS and his "Untouchables," in their war against the booze empire of AL CAPONE, were honest, brave, loyal, efficient and capable, but they were not very amusing.

New York City produced another breed of Prohibition agent, personified by Isadore Einstein and Moe Smith, whom the newspapers took to their hearts as "Izzie and Moe," because their exploits could be written about with the tongue planted firmly in the cheek, to amuse a public who found it impossible to take Prohibition very seriously.

Before he joined the Federal Prohibition Bureau, Isadore Einstein was a clerk for the Post Office in New York City. He lived in a $14-a-month apartment on Manhattan's Lower East Side with his wife and four children. He was attracted to the bureau, he cheerfully admitted, by the $2,000-a-year salary paid to an enforcement officer.

According to "the Merry Antics of Izzy and Moe," a *New Yorker* article by Hurbert Asbury, James Shevlin, chief enforcement agent for the Southern District of New York, pondered Izzy's application. "I must say Mr. Einstein," he is quoted as saying to the short, fat, cheerful man in his forties standing before him, "you don't look much like a detective." But Einstein had possibly useful abilities. Aside from English, he was fluent in Yiddish, German, Polish and Hungarian, and spoke passable French, Italian and Russian. Also, Shevlin decided, considering the problems some of his men were having just getting through the door of a speakeasy, it might be an advantage not to look much like a detective. It was necessary to get an agent inside a speakeasy to buy a drink so that the illegality could be established before the proprietor could be given a summons. In those early days of Prohibition, the Bureau just gave summonses; raiding speakeasies and breaking up the furniture came later.

For Izzy's first job he was sent to a suspected Brooklyn speakeasy that seemed to have an unerring eye for keeping out law officers. Izzy did not waste time trying to figure out a subtle approach; he walked up to the door and knocked. An eye appeared at a peephole and stared wonderingly at Izzy.

Izzy stared back. "I'm Izzy Einstein," he said. "I want a drink."

"Who sent you?" the eye inquired.

"My boss sent me. I'm a Prohibition agent. I just got appointed."

The doorkeeper thought that was hilarious and ushered Izzy in. The bartender, going along with the gag, asked Izzy to show him his badge. Izzy produced the badge, and the bartender examined it. "Looks just like the real thing," he said, pouring Izzy a drink.

Izzy downed the drink. "It is real," he told the bartender.

Moe Smith, an old Lower East Side buddy of Izzy's, went to work for the bureau a few weeks after Izzy. A little taller and a little lighter than Izzy, he also did not look like a detective. They made a great team and were especially adept at getting into places that other revenuers could not enter. They used rudimentary disguises, more to adapt their appearance to local demands than to conceal their features. Izzy's big secret was always to carry something. If the speakeasy was a musicians' hangout, he would carry a trombone, if it was a neighborhood joint, he'd carry the groceries. One day he went on half-a-dozen raids lugging a big pail of dill pickles. As he said: "Who'd ever think a fat man with pickles was an agent?"

The reporters loved Izzy and Moe and started following them around on their raids. Speakeasies put their pictures up as a warning, but somehow could not believe that the fat, friendly, slightly goofy men outside wanting in were really Izzy and Moe. Once Izzy went into a place that had his picture above the bar and asked for a drink. The bartender asked for identification.

"That's me," Izzy said, pointing to his picture. "Izzy Epstein, the famous Prohibition detective."

"That bum's name is Einstein," the bartender corrected.

"I should know my own name," Izzy said, betting the bartender a drink.

The bartender called someone else over to settle the bet. Izzy lost and bought the drinks—and then arrested the bartender for serving them. Newspaper readers all over the country chuckled at the antics of Izzy and Moe. And then, on November 13, 1925, they were both retired "for the good of the service." Izzy said it was because the bureau wanted to transfer them to Chicago, and they did not want to go. But some cynical newsmen were of the opinion that it was because the chubby duo were getting more newspaper attention than the high dry brass in Washington, and the brass was jealous. Einstein and Smith went into the insurance business, where they did very well.

J

JAMES BROTHERS

A MATCHED PAIR OF LEGENDARY WESTERN OUTLAWS

Frank James (1843–1915)
Jesse Woodson James (1847–1882)

Born in Clay County, Missouri, the James brothers, sons of the Reverend Robert James, were natural-born outlaws. In their time they were heroes, and after Jesse's death, they became legends. Neither of these results was deserved. Frank joined Quantrill's Raiders during the Civil War. Masquerading as guerrilla soldiers, these men were actually ruthless and murderous highwaymen. Jesse fought with Bloody Bill Anderson's group of Confederate guerrillas, where he was seriously wounded. When he recovered, the war was over. The James boys decided they liked what they had been doing, war or no war, so they teamed up with the YOUNGER BROTHERS and turned to bank robbery.

Their first known bank robbery was on February 13, 1866, in Liberty, Missouri, where they scored $17,000. It was also their first known civilian killing, when they shot a bystander. In 1873, they robbed their first train, derailing a Chicago and Rock Island express near Adair, Iowa. The unpopularity of railroads in the Midwest, due to their seizure of land for right-of-way for scandalously low payments, greatly increased the popularity of the James boys. Almost unnoticed was the murder of the engineer during the derailment. The James brothers killed people in many of their robberies; a fact that somehow got lost as their Robin Hood legend grew.

The railroads were using the PINKERTON organization to hunt down the robbers, and in January 1875, the "Pinks" thought they had the James brothers cornered in their mother's house. The detectives tossed in what they later insisted was a flare and the house blew up. The James's mother lost her right arm, and their little half-brother Archie was killed. The Pinks were already unpopular, and this incident did nothing to improve their status.

In 1876, a large gang including the James brothers and the Younger brothers tried to rob the First National Bank of Northfield, Minnesota. The whole town, or a substantial part of it, came out shooting to defend their bank. Everyone but Frank and Jesse was either killed or captured. The brothers decided to lay low for a few years. In 1879, they reconstituted a gang with new people, including the brothers Bob and Charles Ford. But the Fords decided there was an easier way to make money than robbing banks. There was a reward on both Jameses, and they determined to collect it. They made a deal with Missouri Governor Thomas Crittenden to collect a $10,000 reward for Jesse James, dead or alive.

On the evening of April 3, 1882, the Fords were visiting Jesse at his house, where he was living under the name Howard. Jesse got up on a chair to straighten out a picture, and Bob Ford pulled out his gun and shot Jesse in the back.

Six months later, Frank James walked into Governor Crittenden's office and surrendered. He was tried in several states for several murders, but the James legend stood him well, and he was found innocent each time. Eventually he took up farming.

JOHNSON, Ray (1926–)

A one-time armed robber who spent about 25 of his first 50 years in prison, Ray Johnson reformed and wrote *Too Dangerous To Be at Large* (1975), about his experiences as a criminal and a convict. A very readable book, it gives interesting insights into criminal behavior and the realities of the California penal system.

JUDD, Winnie Ruth (1909–)

SHE TOOK HER TWO CLOSEST FRIENDS FOR A RIDE ON A TRAIN, AFTER STUFFING THEM IN A TRUNK

Soon to be known to the press as "The Trunk Murderess" and "The Tiger Woman," Winnie Ruth Judd, the young wife of Dr. William C. Judd, went to visit two of her closest friends, Agnes LeRoi and Hedvig "Sammy" Samuelson, at their apartment in Phoenix, Arizona, on October 16, 1931. Two days later Judd took a train from Phoenix to her home in Los Angeles, California, bringing with her two trunks. A station attendant in Los Angeles who was helping her move the trunks noticed a red liquid dripping from one of them. He insisted that she open the trunk, suspecting that she was transporting illicit deer meat.

Winnie told the attendant that the keys were in her car but drove off hurriedly instead of returning. The authorities opened the trunks to find Winnie's two closest friends. Agnes and part of Hedvig were in the large trunk, and the rest of Hedvig in the smaller trunk. An arrest notice was issued for "Winnie Ruth Judd, American, 26, fair complexion, grey-blue eyes, light brown hair. She weighs 125 pounds, is five feet seven inches and was wearing a black and white dress and a black hat."

As days passed and no sign of Winnie was

found, Dr. Judd was afraid that his wife had cast herself into the ocean. In case she had not, he made a plea through the Los Angeles newspapers for her to surrender and retained a trio of prominent attorneys to defend her. She called Dr. Judd and arranged to surrender, meeting him and the police at an undertaking parlor at Court and Olive Streets in Los Angeles. The macabre location for the meeting was apparently one of convenience with no special significance. Winnie issued the following statement to explain the events leading to the killings:

> I had gone to the girls' home to remonstrate with Miss Samuelson for some nasty things she had said about Mrs. LeRoi. Miss Samuelson got hold of a gun and shot me in the left hand. I struggled with her and the gun fell. Mrs. LeRoi grabbed an ironing board and started to strike me over the head with it. In the struggle, I got hold of the gun and Sammy got shot. Mrs. LeRoi was still coming at me with the ironing board, and I had to shoot her. Then I ran from the place—

She was taken to the Georgia Street Receiving Hospital to have her hand looked at, and part of her story was strengthened when the doctor removed a .25-caliber bullet from the base of her middle finger. Before she was arrested in Los Angeles, she wrote a long, rambling letter to her husband and then changed her mind and attempted to flush it down the toilet in the Broadway department store, where she had spent one night hiding in the drapery department. A plumber fixing the drains found a scrap of paper with the name Judd on it and fished around for more. He came up with ten water-soaked telegraph blanks with Winnie's handwriting on them. The letter went into her past sexual history and indicated that she was not a stable personality. Its account of the murder differed in details from the account she gave police but still indicated that her actions constituted self-defense.

Judd was extradited to Arizona to stand trial, and a jury found her guilty of both murders. She was sentenced to hang. A week before the scheduled execution, the warden of the prison sent out the invitations, 50 black-bordered cards reading, "You are invited to be present at the state prison, Florence, April 21, to witness the execution of Winnie Ruth Judd."

On April 18, Winnie Ruth was granted a sanity hearing before a judge and jury. The jury was admonished to consider only Winnie's sanity, not the specter of the rope that loomed over her. Preparations for the hanging continued. But, despite the prosecutor's insistence that she was just trying to cheat the hangman, the hearing found her insane and her sentence was commuted to life imprisonment in a state mental asylum.

Once in the mental home, Winnie escaped seven times over the next 30 years, once staying free for six years. During all this time, she harmed no one and was a useful member of society. In 1969, she was recaptured in California, and Governor Ronald Reagan allowed her extradition to Arizona. There she was adjudged sane and put in a regular prison. In 1971, 40 years after her crimes were committed, she was paroled. At this writing, she is still living, under an assumed name.

JUICE RACKET; JUICE OPERATORS

See: LOAN SHARKS

JURY TRIALS

The Sixth Amendment to the Constitution of the United States guarantees to all criminal defendants the right of trial by jury. The Supreme Court has decided that this protection must be extended to all offenders whose crime is punishable by more than six-months imprisonment. In all federal and most state criminal courts, guilt must be decided beyond a reasonable doubt by the unanimous vote of a jury of 12 of the defendant's peers. Federal courts must adhere to this, but state courts are free, if the state wishes, to convict on a nonunanimous verdict of as low as nine to three. Juries of as few as six members are also permissible in some jurisdictions, but then the verdict must be unanimous. The states that make use of these possibilities tend to reserve them for misdemeanor trials or other cases in which the penalty is not too severe.

Why 12 came to be the number appropriate to a jury panel is lost in antiquity, and probably has a biblical basis. Duncomb's *Trials*, an early British law treatise, has this explanation:

> And first as to their number twelve: and this number is no less esteemed by our law than by Holy Writ. If the twelve apostles on their twelve thrones must try us in our eternal state, good reason has the law to appoint the number of twelve to try our temporal. The tribes of Israel were twelve, the patriarchs were twelve, and Solomon's officers were twelve. Therefore not only matters of fact were tried by twelve, but of ancient times twelve judges were to try matters in law, in the Exchequer Chamber, and there are twelve counsellors of state for matters of state; and he that wageth his law must have eleven others with him who believe he says true. And the law is so precise in this number of twelve that if the trial be by more or less, it is a mistrial.

Although the judge decides the applicable law in a criminal trial, the jury is the only judge of fact, and nobody can overrule or alter a jury's decision if the jury finds the defendant innocent. A judge, however, may find, as a point of law, that a defendant cannot be convicted on the evidence presented even if the jury feels otherwise. The phrase "a jury of his peers" is taken seriously, and the trend seems to be to take it more seriously every year. If blacks or women are systematically excluded from a jury, that is reason to nullify a trial. In *Witherspoon v. the State of Illinois*, the Supreme Court ruled that a state law allowing the prosecution to exclude jurors who had qualms against the death sentence unfairly biased the jury against the defendant. In its decision, it said in part:

> A man who opposes the death penalty, no less than one who favors it, can make the discretionary judgment entrusted to him by the State and can thus obey the oath he takes as a juror. But a jury from which all such men have been excluded cannot perform the task demanded of it. Guided by neither rule nor standard . . . A jury that must choose between life imprisonment and capital punishment can do little more—and must do nothing less—than express the conscience of the community on the ultimate question of life or death. Yet, in a nation less than half of whose people believe in the death penalty, a jury composed exclusively of such people cannot speak for the community. . . .
>
> Whatever else might be said of capital punishment, it is at least clear that its imposition by a hanging jury cannot be squared with the Constitution. The State of Illinois has stacked the deck against the petitioner. To execute this death sentence would deprive him of his life without due process of law.

The jury system is the great protector of our civil liberties. Those who choose not to serve on juries, and use various excuses to get out of service, should reflect that if they are ever accused of a crime, they will also be tried by only those people who could not get out of jury service.

KABER, Eva Catherine (1882–1931)

SHE HAD HER RICH HUSBAND KILLED SO SHE COULD MOVE TO NEW YORK

On the night of July 18, 1919, Daniel D. Kaber, an affluent, well-respected publisher, was lying in bed in his mansion in Lakewood, an exclusive suburb of Cleveland, Ohio, as he had been for the last six weeks, partially paralyzed after suffering a stroke. His male nurse F. W. Utterbach was in an upstairs bedroom taking a nap, and his stepdaughter, Marian McArdle, an 18-year-old undergraduate at Smith College, was downstairs with a friend, Anna Baehr. His wife Eva was not home, she was visiting her sister in Cedar Point, Ohio, but her mother, Mrs. Mary Brickel, was rocking peacefully on the front porch.

At exactly 10:20 P.M. Utterbach awoke to the sounds of screaming coming from Kaber's bedroom. He raced to the bedroom and found his patient lying on the floor, covered with blood. Utterbach, seeing that Kaber was suffering from multiple stab wounds, called an ambulance and the police and then did his best for his bleeding patient. In a cursory search of the room, he found a razor and a sharpened nail file, both covered with blood, and a single blood-soaked glove. In addition to these weapons, the police found that the house had been robbed in a perfunctory manner. One drawer in the dining room sideboard had been pried open, and much of the family's silver was missing. Some of the missing silver was subsequently found on the front lawn.

The ambulance took Kaber to Lakewood Hospital, where doctors labored over him, doing their best to patch up his 23 stab wounds. But he had lost too much blood. He died a few hours later, saying with his dying breath: "The man in the cap did it. The man in the cap. That woman had me killed."

Moses Kaber, Daniel's 75-year-old father, believed that "that woman" was Daniel's wife Eva. The local prosecutor, Samuel Doerfler, agreed. At the coroner's inquest, he accused the weeping widow of her husband's murder. "Are you crazy?" she responded. He was at least a bit premature, as there was then no evidence to connect Eva with her husband's death. The coroner's jury brought in a verdict of death "by person or persons unknown," and Eva collected her husband's life insurance. She promptly moved with her daughter to New York City, where she opened a millinery shop, and Marian became a Broadway chorus girl. Moses took legal action to prevent Eva from inheriting his son's estate and hired PINKERTON detectives to investigate the crime and his daughter-in-law. He also posted a $2,000 reward.

The reward offer had an unexpected result. Two Cleveland ladies resolved to solve the crime: Mrs. Ethel Berman moved to New York to befriend Eva Kaber, and Mrs. M. A. Deering worked on her mother, Mrs. Brickel. Within a couple of months, Mrs. Berman had a job in Mrs. Kaber's millinery shop and was on intimate terms with the widow, and Mrs. Deering was a confidant of Mrs. Brickel. The pair of amateur detectives drew from the two women details of Eva's relationship with her husband that did nothing to discourage the belief that she was implicated in his death.

The union with Daniel Kaber was Eva's third marriage, she having divorced her first two husbands at a time when divorce was still a scandalous activity. She married him for his money and social position, and once she had them she ceased any attempt at being a good, or even a cordial, wife. When Daniel had his stroke, Eva started going to fortune tellers, trying to find out how long she would have to put up with a sick husband. Then Eva overheard Daniel telling his father that he intended to cut his ungrateful wife out of his will. She determined to get him first. She offered an acquaintance's chauffeur, named Frank Di Carpo, $5,000 to run her husband over—$200 in advance and the rest on completion. The shocked chauffeur refused. She consulted several mediums, asking if they could arrange her husband's demise through the spirit world, perhaps by sticking pins in a wax likeness of Daniel. "I use my powers only for good, not evil," one of them, Mrs. Mary Wade, told her indignantly.

Then Eva went to Sandusky, Ohio, to consult with Erminia Colavito, a midwife and psychic. "Big Emma," as she was known, gave Eva a powder to dust over her husband's food. It would make him more agreeable, she said with a wink. It did not work. If the spirits would not cooperate, Big Emma was prepared to resort to more direct means. She produced two burly-looking men, "Sam"—Salvatore Cala—and "Tony"—Vittorio Pisselli, who were experienced at making men more agreeable—in this world or the next.

Two years after the killing, a persistent Moses Kaber put the information his private detectives had collected in the hands of the authorities. On Friday, June 2, 1921, the district attorney of Cuyahoga County, Ohio, wired the New York City Police Department to find and arrest Mrs. Eva Kaber and her daughter Marian McArdle for murder and complicity in murder. The New York detectives questioned the two women separately for many hours. Marian admitted to breaking the sideboard drawer open with an ice pick and removing some of the silver, at her mother's request. Eva spent much time explaining to the detectives how mean her husband had been to her before admitting to having two men "play ghosts" and give her husband "a rough shaking to scare him." Why they carried a sharpened file and a razor into his room and stabbed him repeatedly, she did not know.

In the meantime, two men in Lakewood were negotiating with the police to give important information. Salvatore Cala and Vittorio Pisselli had never been paid by Mrs. Kaber and wanted to collect the reward for turning her in.

The mother and daughter were extradited back to Ohio, where they and Big Emma stood trial. One of the prosecution's principal witnesses was Mrs. Mary Brickel, who was indicted as an accomplice and turned state's evidence against her daughter. She told of setting fire to the Lakewood mansion a year before the murder because her daughter was "tired of home life and wanted to go to a hotel." Big Emma told of a rehearsal on the Wednesday before the murder, where the two killers were led through the house and shown what to do, while Daniel lay in bed upstairs and Marian sat at the piano downstairs playing loudly to drown out any noise the plotters might make.

Eva Kaber, Erminia "Big Emma" Colavito and Salvatore Cala were all convicted and sentenced to life imprisonment. Mrs. Brickel and Marian McArdle were released. Vittorio Pisselli was apprehended in Italy, where he had fled, and put in an Italian prison. Eva, a troublesome prisoner given to escape attempts and temper tantrums, died in the Prison for Women at Marysville, Ohio, in 1931.

KAMPILES, William P.

William P. Kampiles joined the Central Intelligence Agency (CIA) in March 1977 with dreams of becoming an officer in the top-secret Clandestine Service. He was not deemed suitable for this assignment and was put to work as a watch officer in the Operations Center. This was not what he had in mind, and he resigned in November.

Kampiles traveled to Athens, Greece, bringing with him a copy of the agency's KH-11 Reconnaissance Satellite operations manual, which he had removed from the Operations Center. He contacted the Soviet Embassy in Athens and sold them the manual for $3,000.

Kampiles was apprehended by American counterespionage and explained his actions in terms of his fantasy. He had, he explained, been trying to win the confidence of Soviet intelligence, and was planning to become a double agent. The court was not impressed with his story, and he was sentenced to 40 years in prison for espionage.

The harm he did to American reconnaissance efforts was great, as the KH-11 was the country's most sophisticated satellite system.

KANSAS CITY MASSACRE

GANGLORD RESCUE GONE SOUR OR POLITICAL ASSASSINATION?

On June 16, 1933, agents of the U.S. Bureau of Investigation (USBI; to be renamed the FEDERAL BUREAU OF INVESTIGATION within a year) and Octo Reed, police chief of McAlester, Oklahoma, arrested bank robber Frank "Jelly" Nash in the White Front Pool Hall in Hot Springs, Arkansas. They took him by car to Kansas City, where they planned to put him on a train for the federal penitentiary at Leavenworth. Along the way, the authorities picked up a few local lawmen as escorts. They did not ask for help from the Hot Springs police, as Hot Springs was generally recognized as a town controlled by the criminals who used it as a hideaway. Someone did in fact phone ahead to Kansas City and arrange a welcome for the group.

As they emerged from their car at Kansas City's Union Station, Nash and his captors were attacked by four men with machine guns. One of the attackers yelled, "Up! Up! Get 'em up!" When one of the lawmen went for his gun, four machine guns poured a murderous cross fire into the vehicle. Nash, screaming, "For God's sake, don't shoot me," was one of the first killed. Also killed were Police Chief Reed, USBI agent Raymond Caffrey and Kansas City detectives W. J. "Red" Grooms and Frank Hermanson. USBI agents F. L. Lackey and R. E. Vetterli were wounded, as was one of the attackers. USBI agent Frank Smith was unharmed. All four of the gunmen escaped.

Whether the incident was a rescue attempt gone sour or whether it was a plot to murder Nash, and the lawmen were killed just because they were there, has never been cleared up. One theory was that the rescuers failed to recognize the bald Nash because he was wearing a red wig. But if they did not recognize him, why would they attack at all?

The USBI named CHARLES ARTHUR "PRETTY BOY" FLOYD and his partner Adam Richetti as two of the assailants, but Floyd denied this to his dying day, going so far as to write a letter to the newspapers protesting his innocence. Since he never bothered to do this for any of the other crimes he was accused of, many just as serious, he may have been telling the truth.

In 1954, underworld character James Henry "Blackie" Audett told crime author J. Robert Nash that the perpetrators had been Verne Miller, William "Solly" Weissman and brothers Maurice and Homer Denning. He also claimed that it was a political assassination arranged by Kansas City's Pendergast political machine for reasons of their own. To bolster this view, six months later the nude body of Verne Miller was found in a ditch outside of Detroit, and two weeks after that, the body of Solly Weissman was found in similar circumstances.

KARPIS, Alvin "Creepy" (1907–1979)

See: BARKER-KARPIS GANG

KEET, Lloyd (1916–1917)

On May 30, 1917, Lloyd Keet, the infant son of a Springfield, Missouri, banker, was abducted from his home. A note demanding a $6,000 ransom was mailed to the parents. The father attempted

In the aftermath of the Kansas City Massacre, local citizens inspect the scene of the crime. (Federal Bureau of Investigation.)

to deliver the money, but the kidnappers failed to show up, possibly because of a bad storm. A few days later six people were arrested, who admitted to planning several abductions, but they declared that the Keet child was not one of them, and they had not taken him. When word got out about the arrest, a mob started to form, and the sheriff put the suspects in a car to take them to the state prison in Jefferson City for their own protection.

The next day, the body of Baby Keet was found thrown down the well of an abandoned farm. Now the mob formed in earnest and set out after the sheriff and his prisoners. They caught up to them about 45 miles outside of Springfield and hung one of the prisoners—a man named Piersol. They let him down just before he choked to death and told him the treatment would continue until he confessed. This he refused to do, and they pulled him up again. When he was let down, he once again protested the innocence of himself and his companions. This went on a few more times, until he was finally allowed to live, although the mob was still not convinced of his innocence. Enough evidence was eventually gathered to convict Piersol of kidnapping, but not of the murder, and he was sentenced to 35 years in prison.

KEFAUVER COMMITTEE

From May 1950, to March 1951, the Senate Special Committee to Investigate Crime in Interstate Commerce, chaired by Democratic Senator Estes Kefauver of Tennessee, launched a nationwide investigation of ORGANIZED CRIME. The other members of the committee were Democrats Herbert O'Conor of Maryland and Lester C. Hunt of Wyoming and Republicans Charles W. Tobey of New Hampshire and Alexander Wiley of Wisconsin. The chief counsel was Rudolph Halley. Beginning in Miami, Florida, the committee traveled to 13 cities to take testimony. The hearings, which were televised, were generally adjudged to be the finest dramatic program to show on television that year.

A Chattanooga lawyer, whose father was a dairy farmer, Kefauver entered politics as a reform candidate and part of a Southern progressive

Testimony at the Kefauver hearings led to new federal legislation against organized crime. (Dept. of Special Collections, University Research Library, UCLA.)

The Kefauver Committee hearings proved that while you could swear crime bosses in you couldn't make them talk, as dozens of witnesses took the Fifth Amendment. (Dept. of Special Collections, University Research Library, UCLA.)

Senator Estes Kefauver, whose televised Senate crime hearings made the public acutely aware of the pervasiveness of organized crime. (Dept. of Special Collections, University Research Library, UCLA.)

movement to support the New Deal policies of Franklin Roosevelt. After five terms in the House, he ran for the Senate and won. An independent-minded senator, he was not part of the Senate's power elite when the hearings brought him to national prominence.

Kefauver and the committee got little help from the FBI in their investigations. J. EDGAR HOOVER had always maintained that the MAFIA was an illusion and that the gangsters were "just a bunch of hoodlums" rather than an organized syndicate. At first Halley agreed with Hoover, but as the evidence was presented to the committee, he became a believer. The committee listened as witnesses drew a picture of an organized crime community throughout the United States that was taking tens of millions of dollars from the public.

Major organized crime figures were subpoenaed to testify, but they contributed little directly. JAKE "GREASY THUMB" GUZIK of Chicago refused to answer because his words might "discriminate against me," and the FIFTH AMENDMENT became a favorite refuge of the wicked. New Jersey crime boss Willie Moretti provided the comic relief at the hearings, but his fellow mobsters thought he was talking too much, and he was subsequently shot to death. VIRGINIA HILL, mob bag lady and the girlfriend of several gangsters including GEORGE "BUGSY" SIEGEL, was asked where she got the large sums of cash she was known to have. "Men like to give me money," she testified. FRANK COSTELLO, a star witness saved for the last days of the hearings, refused to testify at all if the television cameras were aimed at him. The committee reached a compromise with him in which they agreed that the cameras would not show his face, and the picture of Costello's hands nervously fidgeting as he tried to avoid answering the committee's questions appeared on television sets all over the country. He walked out when faced by questions that especially annoyed him, earning him a sentence of 18 months for contempt of Congress.

The Kefauver hearings opened the eyes of the public to the extent to which organized crime impinged upon their lives, caused the FBI to admit the existence of a Mafia and made possible the serious crackdowns that were to follow. Kefauver's appearance on television sets all over the country brought him to national prominence and made him a vice-presidential candidate in the next election.

KELLEY, John (1873–1963)

"Honest" John Kelley was a lawyer for the Ringling Brothers–Barnum and Bailey Combined Shows when the income tax became law in the United States in 1918. In 1932, the IRS took him to court, deciding that, for the last 14 years, Kelley had been overly zealous in shielding the profits of the Greatest Show on Earth from the tax collectors. He declared depreciation on thousands of items that the circus never possessed, he wrote off the props for shows in the 1920s that had actually been done in the 1890s and he declared payments to suppliers far in excess of what they were actually paid. After a circus rhinoceros died, he "abandoned" it at a purchase price of $35,000, which was 10 times what the animal had actually cost. He liked the trick so much that he "abandoned" the same rhinoceros for the next three years. There was also, according to Kelley, an epidemic among the polar bears, and many fictitious bears died to pad the Ringling Brothers' expenses. In 1927, he declared the "abandonment" of 46 elephants in Bridgeport, Connecticut. A circuit court judge who happened to be from Bridgeport sat on the appeal and asked Kelley to explain just where he had left the elephants. His response was vague.

John Ringling, the last survivor of the four Ringling brothers, turned over all the company's books to the authorities. He claimed to be astounded at what the books showed, and he may well have been. The only problem the IRS agents had in dealing with him was his hours. He refused to conduct business before midnight, and preferred 3:00 A.M. Kelley claimed to have been acting under the orders of the late Charles Ringling, but he could not prove it. The brothers apparently signed whatever Kelley put in front of them. Ringling died before the case went to trial.

On April 26, 1938, Kelley was convicted of "aiding and assisting the counseling, procuring, and advising the filing of false and fraudulent returns" for the Ringlings. He was fined $10,000 and sentenced to jail for two years. The circus was assessed $3,600,000, and the government, faced with the prospect of running a circus if they seized it for back taxes, settled for $800,000.

The reputation of bank robber and kidnapper George "Machine Gun" Kelly exceeded his abilities. (Federal Bureau of Investigation.)

KELLY, George R. "Machine Gun" (1895–1954)

A bank robber and kidnapper of great reputation in the Midwest, Kelly was actually a mediocre bandit who never amounted to much until he met Kathryn Thorne. Thorne was the widow of bootlegger Charlie Thorne, who had been found dead with a note reading, "I can't live with her or without her, hence I am departing this life." Although friends were sure that Charlie had never said or written "hence" in his life, and a gas station attendant had heard Kathryn state, "I'm bound for Coleman, Texas, to kill that goddamned Charlie Thorne," the coroner's jury ruled it suicide.

Kathryn began calling Kelly "Machine Gun" and encouraged him to have higher goals. After a three-year hiatus, which Kelly spent in Leavenworth for smuggling liquor onto an Indian reservation, Kathryn married him. She nursed him through several small bank robberies, which went smoothly, and then set their sights on the kidnapping of a wealthy businessman. "Machine Gun" and an associate named Albert Bates broke into the Oklahoma City home of millionaire oilman Charley Urschel and took him away, demanding a

$200,000 ransom. Kathryn wanted to kill Urschel after they collected the ransom, but Kelly insisted they let him go, which they did.

The FBI, now eligible to hunt kidnappers because of federal legislation passed after the LINDBERGH KIDNAPPING, went after the Urschel kidnappers. Bates, arrested in Denver on another charge, was found to have some of the ransom money on him. The Kellys were captured in Memphis, Tennessee, by detectives of the Memphis police. J. EDGAR HOOVER took credit for the arrest, spreading the apocryphal story that Kelly, when cornered, had yelled, "Don't shoot, G-men, don't shoot." But there were no G-MEN present when Mr. and Mrs. Kelly were captured.

The Kellys were sentenced to life imprisonment for the kidnapping. George died in Leavenworth in 1954, and Kathryn was released from prison in 1958.

KENNEDY, John Fitzgerald (1917–1963)

Thirty-fifth president of the United States, John F. Kennedy was assassinated in Dallas on November 22, 1963, after two years and 10 months in office, by LEE HARVEY OSWALD. The Warren Commission, chaired by Chief Justice Earl Warren, which officially investigated the assassination, concluded that Oswald worked alone and was not part of a conspiracy, although there are several conflicting theories which present Oswald as a member of a complex network, or even an innocent patsy who was set up to take the blame for the acts of others.

KETCHUM, Black Jack (1862–1901)

Born Thomas Ketchum, Black Jack and his brother Sam were notorious outlaws and train robbers in the American Southwest at the end of the nineteenth century. They and a group of outlaws from the infamous HOLE IN THE WALL GANG held up Train Number 1 near Twin Mountains, New Mexico Territory, in 1898. The robbery was so successful that they held up the same train at the same place again. And again. By the fourth time, the authorities had figured out the pattern, and were ready for them. A posse cornered the gang at Turkey Canyon, near Cimarron. Several lawmen were killed in the ensuing gunfight. Most of the gang were captured, but Ketchum, although wounded in the shoulder, escaped and hid out for a few days until he was caught. He was brought to trial in Santa Fe for attempted train robbery, a capital offense.

On April 26, 1901, Black Jack Ketchum was brought to the gallows. "I'll be in hell before you start breakfast, boys!" he yelled to the assembled onlookers. When the black hood was placed on his head, he yelled, "Let 'er rip!"

The trap was sprung and Black Jack dropped. Because of a badly adjusted rope, his head was torn from his body at the end of the drop.

Earlier, Sam Ketchum had tried to carry on his brother's tradition, holding up Train Number 1 for a fifth time on August 16, 1899. He and most of his gang were killed in the attempt.

KETCHUM, Sam (1860–1899)

See: BLACK JACK KETCHUM

KIDD, Captain William (1645?–1701)

THE LEGENDARY PIRATE CAPTAIN

One of the most famous pirates in the mythology of piracy, Captain Kidd was in actuality a minor buccaneer, guilty of no more than two or three piratical acts, and there is even some doubt about them.

Owner of several small ships and a working captain, Kidd lived with his wife and children in New York. He fought several successful maneuvers against French privateers in the Atlantic around 1690. In April 1691, the Provincial Council of New York passed a resolution to reward

Kidd for his "many good services done to this Province."

In 1695, Kidd sailed a trading sloop to England, anchoring in the Thames. In London he was approached by a private syndicate that was trying to outfit a privateer to sail against pirates attacking British shipping and to capture whatever French shipping it might run across. King William III had authorized it, and five Whig noblemen headed by the Earl of Bellomont agreed to put up four-fifths of the money if Kidd could raise the other fifth, to a total of 6,000 pounds. Kidd was to head the venture and captain the ship. By November 1695, the sponsors had raised their 4,800 pounds, and a ship had been acquired: the *Adventure Galley*, of 287 tons burden, carrying 34 guns, and a crew of 70. The crew size would be more than doubled when the ship next sailed; privateering was a very crew-heavy pursuit.

By January 1696, Kidd received his Letter of Mark and Reprisal from the High Court of Admiralty of England, authorizing him to prey upon "the Ships Vessels and Goods belonging to the French King or his Subjects or inhabitants within the Dominions of the said French King; and such other Ships Vessels and Goods as are or shall be liable for confiscation; according to the said Commission granted unto us for that Purpose." He also received a specific warrant from King William III authorizing him to apprehend and seize "Captain Thomas Too, John Ireland, Captain Thomas Wake, Captain William Maze or Mace, And other of our Subjects, Natives or Inhabitants of New England, New York, and elsewhere in our Plantations in America," as well as "such Pirates, Freebooters, and Sea-Rovers, being either our own Subjects or of other Nations associated with them, which you shall meet upon the said Coasts or Seas of America, or in any other Seas or Parts, with their Ships and Vessels; And also such Merchandizes, Money, Goods, and Wares, as shall be found on board."

Captain Kidd was thus required to raid the French and to apprehend those who had raided the English. Also under the terms of his agreement with his sponsors, neither he nor the crew were to receive any salary, but only shares of the profit from what they might capture. On February 27, 1696, having gathered a suitable crew and completed all the paperwork, Captain Kidd and the *Adventure Galley* set sail from Deptford into a sea of misfortune. It began when his ship was stopped by British men of war on the way to sea, and a large number of his crew were pressed for service in the navy, leaving him with 80 men. Although there is no record of this, it is certain that the Royal Navy took the best men, leaving Kidd with the inexperienced landsmen and the troublesome sailors. The practice of pressing, or forcing men to serve, the time-honored way for the Royal Navy to keep its manpower requirements met, would be directly responsible for the War of 1812 a century later. It was also responsible for Kidd's eventual plunge into piracy.

Kidd crossed the Atlantic to New York, picking up a small French prize on the way, and used the money from that to buy additional supplies for his ship and to raise the ship's complement to 155. Unlike the English crew, carefully picked for their dependability and loyalty, these colonial sailors were the dregs of the docks, and for some of them, piracy was probably an occupation they were already familiar with.

When his outfitting was complete, Kidd raised sail for the East Indies, where the *Adventure Galley* roamed about for six months without finding any prizes worth taking. Then, in February 1697, he had to beach the ship on Mohéli, one of the Comoro Islands near Madagascar, for repairs, as it was taking on too much water. Within a week of the beaching, 50 members of his crew had sickened and died of what was probably cholera. It was here that Captain Kidd's troubles climaxed. The crew, sick, frightened, angry and penniless, came to some sort of deal with their captain. Just what it was will never be known but can be judged by the subsequent adventures of the *Adventure Galley*.

In July 1697, Kidd met and boarded a Moorish ketch with an English captain named Parker. He appropriated bales of paper and of coffee and some myrrh, but could not find any money on board. He had several of the crew strung up and beaten with cutlasses, but they failed to disclose the location of any hidden money, if such existed. He sent the Moorish ship away and sailed off with Captain Parker and a Portuguese ship's officer as captives. The next time they made port, two of his crew deserted, claiming to the authorities that they had done so because Kidd "was going upon an ill design of piracy."

When the *Adventure Galley* again put to sea, it was attacked by a Portuguese frigate, which it drove away after a long fight. Then they came upon a Dutch ship, the *Loyal Captain*. Taking the ship would have been obvious piracy, as opposed to their own commission, and Kidd refused to allow his crew to make the attempt. Perhaps he was trying to reform before things got too far out of hand, or perhaps he just thought that the *Loyal Captain* was too strong to take, but the crew disagreed strongly. Two weeks later, Kidd had words with William Moore, the gunner, over the decision not to go after the Dutch ship. In a fit of anger, Kidd hit Moore on the head with an iron bound bucket. Moore died less than a day later. Captain Kidd was now guilty of murder.

For the next four months, Kidd and his crew stopped and looted Dutch, Moorish and Portuguese ships, culminating with his taking of the *Quedagh Merchant*, an Armenian ship of over 400 tons burden, with an English captain named Wright and a rich cargo, including gold and other treasure. Kidd put Captain Wright and his crew into longboats and claimed the *Quedagh Merchant* as a prize. When they arrived at Madagascar, they anchored, transferred all belongings and prize cargo to the *Quedagh Merchant* and scuttled the *Adventure Galley*, which was leaking too badly to be reliable. They also sank a smaller prize, the *Maiden*, which they had taken sometime earlier. While in Madagascar, they fraternized with several known pirate captains and their crews without trying to apprehend and seize them, a fact that was duly noted at Captain Kidd's trial.

By November 1698, Kidd was being hunted as a pirate. In 1699, he returned to Boston, landing first at Gardiners Island, where he left off several chests and other cargo. He was arrested, although he protested his innocence of the charges against him, and was taken in irons to London for trial. There were four separate trials on the charges, and he was found guilty at each proceeding. On May 21, 1701, he was hanged at Execution Dock, the traditional termination point for pirates. His last words while standing on the dock were reported to be, "This is a very fickle and faithless generation." The first time he dropped the rope broke, throwing him to the ground still conscious. A new rope was hastily put in place and he was hanged again.

The *Quedagh Merchant* has never been found, nor has the treasure it was supposed to be laden with. One report said that the ship was burned and the treasure sold up and down the West Indies. But another said that Captain Kidd had hidden the ship and its treasure, planning to go back for them when he was cleared of the piracy charges. This has resulted in many treasure hunts in the West Indies and along the New England coast.

KIDNAPPING

> ***"He hath brought many captives home to Rome whose ransoms did the general coffers fill."***
>
> ***—Shakespeare, Julius Caesar, III.ii***

Kidnapping is an ancient, if not honorable, occupation among the various tribes of humanity. Abduction has been used as a form of marriage, as a means of procuring slaves, as a system for manning armies and ships of war, as a way of neutralizing an enemy, as a precursor to sexual subjugation and as a method of transferring wealth. The term *kidnap* originated in seventeenth-century Britain to describe the abduction of people, usually children, to be sent to the American colonies as bondservants.

In the United States, the two most frequently encountered forms of kidnapping are child stealing by a divorced parent and kidnapping for ransom. But there are others. At various times and places, allegations of kidnapping young girls into WHITE SLAVERY (forced prostitution) have surfaced, but they have usually proved to be exaggerated. Kidnappings sometimes occur as a part of other crimes, such as during a botched robbery attempt, when the criminals take hostages in order to have a bargaining position with the encircling police. In his book *Ransom Kidnapping in America* (1978), *1874–1974*, Ernest Kahlar Alix lists 15 subdivisions of the crime.

But the majority of kidnappings that are not part of, or the result of, other crimes involve the forcible removal of a person from one place and his or her concealment in another place for the purpose of collecting a ransom. Around the beginning of the twentieth century, some BLACK HAND gangs extorted money from Italian immigrants in large cities by threatening to kidnap, and occasionally carried out their threat to maintain their credibility. For a while it was a major problem. On August 30, 1911, an article in the *New York Times* pointed out that New York's Little Italy was "almost in a state of panic. Fathers and mothers, never able to tell where the 'Black Hander's' lightning will strike next, live in dread that at any hour their child may be snatched up and carried off." The article quoted a resident of the neighborhood, uncle to a kidnap victim, as saying, "You put [Black Handers] in prison for ten or fifteen years, but that doesn't do any good. They ought to be put on the shelf for life. Then the others would be frightened and go out of the business. You don't hear anything in the old country about kidnapping children. They hold up and rob men, but they are afraid to kidnap children."

The first important American kidnapping was the 1874 abduction of CHARLES BREWSTER ROSS, a four-year-old child, from his home in Philadelphia. The suspected kidnappers were shot while attempting a burglary a few months later, but although one of them lived long enough to confess the crime, little Charlie Ross was never found, living or dead.

Kidnapping continued as a minor occupation among the criminal classes over the next couple of decades. A rich bachelor was kidnapped in March 1891, in Detroit. The ransom note demanded $15,000, but the man's banker refused to permit the withdrawal of such a sum from his account. The man was released, unharmed, the next evening. In March 1892, Ward Waterbury, the eight-year-old son of a New York farmer, was taken and a ransom of $6,000 demanded. But in this case, too, the boy was returned unharmed without the ransom having been paid.

The first successful kidnapping for ransom was the abduction, on December 18, 1900, of 15-year-old Eddie Cudahy, son of Omaha meatpacker millionaire E. A. Cudahy. The father called the police, hired the PINKERTONS and sent 50 of his employees to scout around the city for Eddie, but to no avail. The next day, after receiving a letter threatening to blind his son with acid, Cudahy paid a $25,000 ransom, and the boy was returned. Cudahy then offered a $25,000 reward for the apprehension of the kidnappers, but there was some question as to what could be done with them if they were caught. There was no Nebraska law against kidnapping, as long as the victim was not removed from the state.

The 1917 LLOYD KEET kidnapping, in which the child was killed, followed by the 1920 abduction of 13-month-old BLAKELY COUGHLIN, also killed, raised the public consciousness regarding kidnappings and created a climate in which more severe sentences for kidnappers were being demanded by the public. The 1921 kidnapping and murder of five-year-old Giuseppi Verotta by a Black Hand gang, and the subsequent arrest and conviction of 40 of those involved, ended the Black Hand's open season on Italian immigrants.

In 1924, one of the two most notorious kidnappings of the century occurred in Chicago: 14-year-old Bobby Franks was kidnapped and murdered by two college students, Nathan Leopold and Richard Loeb, both from wealthy families, who committed the crime for warped psychological reasons of their own. The LEOPOLD AND LOEB CASE was called the crime of the century for eight years, until, in 1932, the LINDBERGH KIDNAPPING deprived a true American hero of his young son. The result of all this was a federal antikidnapping law, which was christened the Lindbergh Law, and several state laws.

Under the combined influence of the Depression and the repeal of PROHIBITION, gangs of desperadoes appeared in various places around the country. Bank robbery and kidnapping were two of their favorite sports. On February 12, 1933, Charles Boettcher, II, a Denver, Colorado, millionaire, was taken from his own driveway by two gunmen. They demanded a ransom of $60,000 and got it, whereupon Boettcher was returned unharmed. When he revealed that he had been taken across the state line, the federal authorities formally sprang into action. Under the terms of the Lindbergh Law, they had to either wait seven days or know that a state line had been crossed. J. EDGAR HOOVER's agents usually got into the act much earlier, but it was unofficial until one of the two criteria had been met.

The group responsible for the kidnapping was known as the Sankey-Alcorn gang, headed by Verne Sankey and Gordon Alcorn. Four of them were arrested on March 6, although the two leaders escaped. Sankey was later captured, and the group was the first to be tried under the new federal statutes.

During 1933, there was a rash of kidnappings. Twenty-five-year-old Mary McElroy, daughter of the city manager of Kansas City, Missouri, was kidnapped in May. The girl's abductors asked for a $60,000 ransom, but accepted $30,000 and released her unharmed. They were later captured and sentenced to death under Missouri's antikidnapping law. In June, William Hamm, Jr., a wealthy St. Paul, Minnesota, brewer, was kidnapped by the BARKER-KARPIS GANG. He was released unharmed on payment of a $100,000 ransom. John King Ottley, a rich banker, was kidnapped in Atlanta, and a $40,000 ransom was paid. The next day, John J. O'Connell, Jr., of Albany, New York, 24-year-old son of an important Democratic politician, was taken and a $250,000 ransom was demanded. Illinois banker August Luer was kidnapped and held for five days, but then released without any ransom being paid. On July 22, Charles F. Urschel of Oklahoma City was taken by Albert Bates and GEORGE "MACHINE GUN" KELLY. He was released after a $200,000 ransom was paid. In addition, gangsters were also kidnapping each other for ransom. Several Chicago gangsters are known to have been abducted and held for large sums of money.

With the intervention of the federal authorities, and the increasingly severe penalties for kidnapping, the wave of abductions subsided, but did not entirely die out, by the late 1930s. In 1946, WILLIAM HEIRENS was arrested for the kidnapping and murder of little Suzanne Degnan on fingerprint evidence developed by the FBI. On September 28, 1953, Robert Greenlease, the six-year-old son of a Kansas City businessman, was abducted by Carl Austin Hall and Bonnie B. Heady; Bonnie Heady picked up the child at school by pretending to have been sent by the boy's mother. They demanded a $600,000 ransom, which was paid. But the child was already dead, having been killed and buried the day of the kidnapping. Hall and Heady have the twin distinctions of collecting the largest ransom paid for a victim up to that time and being put to death in the shortest time after their crime: 81 days. Heady was also the first woman executed under the federal Lindbergh Law.

On July 4, 1956, Peter Weinberger, the one-month-old son of a Westbury, New York, businessman, was taken from his carriage outside the family home. A $2,000 ransom note was left, in which the kidnapper apologized for asking for the money but threatened to kill the baby if he did not get it. The money was placed where the kidnapper specified, and he drove up to get it with the victim in the car, but he was frightened away by crowds of sightseers gathered around the victim's home. He deserted the baby in a thicket, where it died of exposure. On August 23, the kidnapper, Angelo John LaMarca, was apprehended by the FBI. He was tried under New York law, convicted and executed. The Greenlease and Weinberger cases convinced Congress to amend the Lindbergh Law to allow the FBI to investigate a kidnapping case after 24 hours, instead of waiting seven days.

In December 1963, the 19-year-old son of singer Frank Sinatra, Frank Sinatra, Jr., was abducted at gunpoint from a motel in Stateline, California. He was taken to a house in Los Angeles and held until his father paid a $240,000 ransom, whereupon he was released unharmed. Three men, John W. Irwin, Barry W. Keenan, and Joseph C. Amsler, were apprehended and tried for the crime under federal law. The case was complicated by the kidnappers' claim that the whole thing had been a publicity stunt and that Frank Jr. had been a willing victim. They were convicted, but an appeals court later reversed two of the convictions and the third had his sentence greatly reduced.

In December 1968, Barbara Mackle was kidnapped and put in an underground capsule for more than 3 days until a $500,000 ransom was paid. Twenty-three-year-old GARY STEVEN KRIST and 26-year-old Ruth Eisemann Schier were arrested and convicted for the crime.

On February 5, 1974, PATRICIA HEARST was kidnapped by a group with pseudo-political motives, calling itself the Symbionese Liberation Army, which seemed to unleash a wave of kidnappings. Twenty-seven kidnappings were reported for the year—the most since the 1933 outbreak.

On July 15, 1976, in a plot unequaled for number of victims or bizarre and cruel technique, 26 schoolchildren were kidnapped on a school bus in CHOWCHILLA, California. Three men, Frederick Newhall Woods, IV, and brothers James and Richard Allen Schoenfeld, were convicted of the crime and sentenced to life imprisonment. *See also:* ARTHUR D. SEALE

KNAPP COMMISSION

In 1970, in response to suggestive articles in the city's newspapers, New York City Mayor John V. Lindsay appointed the Knapp Commission to investigate charges of corruption in the Police Department. After two-and-a-half years of taking testimony and listening to tapes secretly recorded by a policeman who agreed, under pressure, to tape his dealings with the Police Department's less moral officers, the commission concluded that corruption was rampant within the department. Although the majority of officers were not corrupt, those who had not succumbed to the temptations of easy money had become cynical about the system.

Two honest cops, Detective Frank Serpico and Sergeant David Durk, had done a lot of undercover work and supplied a lot of information. They were not well thought of by some of their fellow officers, even the uncorrupted ones, who had been brainwashed into the mindset that male bonding was more important than honesty, integrity and doing the job that one has sworn to do.

The commission found that the pervasive sources of corruption were ORGANIZED CRIME and the construction industry, which in New York City were often one and the same. They found that double-parked cars along certain streets would not get ticketed if they had matchbooks or menus from certain bars along the street on their dashboard. The most frightening thing the commission discovered was that graft from drug peddlers, which used to be considered dirty money, had become acceptable, and that one of the more common corrupt acts was the taking of drugs or drug money when making a drug-related arrest.

The commission found evidence, which it did not follow up because its scope of investigation was only the Police Department, that corruption involving drugs was also engulfing the court system, including prosecutors, attorneys and even judges. While this did not excuse the actions of the corrupt officers in the Police Department, it did help put their activities into perspective.

Police Commissioner Patrick V. Murphy and the district attorneys of the various New York jurisdictions moved strongly against the corruption, based upon evidence collected by the Knapp Commission and their own independent investigations.

KRIST, Gary Steven (1945–)

On December 17, 1968, in a crime that attracted a great deal of attention because of the bizarre and heartless behavior of the kidnappers, Barbara Jane Mackle, a 20-year-old college student, was taken from a motel room she was sharing with her mother. The mother was bound and gagged and left behind. Barbara was buried underground in a capsule which contained a life-support system that would keep her alive for a limited number of hours. When the kidnappers collected a $500,000 ransom, they told the authorities the location of the capsule, and Barbara was rescued after spending more than 80 hours buried underground. By the time rescuers reached the girl, her battery-powered light was dead, and she was about out of food and water.

Twenty-three-year-old Gary Steven Krist and 26-year-old Ruth Eisemann Schier were suspected of the crime based on information discovered by the FBI from a 1966 Volvo found near the scene of the ransom pickup. The two were put on the FBI's TEN MOST WANTED list; Ruth Eisemann Schier had the distinction of being the first woman on the list. Krist was arrested in Florida and Eisemann Schier was picked up in Oklahoma. They were tried and convicted, Krist being sentenced to life imprisonment and Eisemann Schier, who was believed to be under Krist's influence, getting a seven-year sentence.

In May 1979, Krist was granted a parole, under the condition that he go to and remain in Alaska, where his family lives. He publicly apologized to Barbara Mackle, his victim, and thanked her for "having the Christian charity" not to oppose his parole.

KROGER, Peter and Helen

See: MORRIS AND LEONA COHEN

KU KLUX KLAN

WHAT BEGAN AS A JOKE GREW INTO AN EVIL EMPIRE

The Ku Klux Klan was started as a social organization by six young ex–Confederate Army officers in Pulaski, Tennessee, in May 1866. The name was a joke: They were going to call it "the Circle," and one of them suggested they use the Greek word for circle—*kuklos*. So, they called their little circle Kuklux and, in a moment of inspiration, added "Klan." It was a fraternal organization with a sense of fun, using secret passwords and initiation rites. They met in the cellar of a ruined home outside of Pulaski and sent mysterious notes to the local newspapers to attract new members.

Then, in March 1867, after the Fourteenth Amendment, which gave the right to vote to black men, had been rejected by 10 southern states, Congress passed the first of the Reconstruction acts. The former Confederacy was divided into five military districts under federal control; former Confederate soldiers were forbidden to vote; federal troops registered over 700,000 blacks and over 6,000 formerly nonvoting whites. The South was flooded with "carpetbaggers," northerners who came south to help the blacks or merely to do well for themselves, and with "scalawags," south-

New recruits to the Ku Klux Klan taking the oath and kneeling before the Klan alter in 1948. (Acme Telephoto.)

erners who were willing to abide by the decision to allow blacks to vote.

As the New York *World* put it in one of a series of articles published in 1921:

> Almost at once the Ku Klux Klan became transformed from burlesquers into a band of regulators. The best authority on the change is a little history of the Ku Klux Klan written years afterward by Capt. John C. Lester, one of the six original members [in which he stated] that the transformation was effected first by the impressions it made upon those who joined it; second by the impressions it made upon the public; and third, by the anomalous and peculiar conditions then prevailing.
>
> The impression made on those who joined was that behind the amusement features, and unexpressed in its ritualistic work, was a deep purpose—a solemn mission to be undertaken later. What it was none knew, but the feeling spread that the mission existed just the same.
>
> The impression made upon the public showed that the organization possessed a certain power nobody had imagined it would possess. This power was largely one of fright and intimidation and was shown in the case of the ignorant Negro more than in the white people. Negroes would see the ghostly,

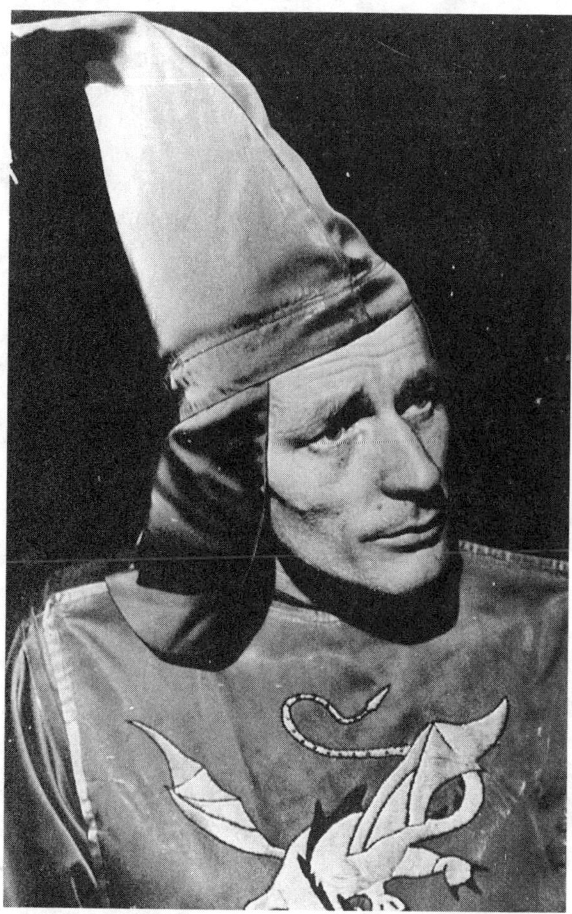

National Grand Wizard of the Ku Klux Klan, Bobby Shelton, at a Klan rally in Montgomery, Alabama, in November 1960. (Acme Telephoto.)

nocturnal Ku Kluxes and imagine they were spirits of deceased Confederate soldiers, and the Klansmen were quick to use the idea to the utmost advantage.

A figure in white would ride up to a Negro's house and ask for a drink of water. The frightened Negro would hand him a gourd, which the rider would pour into a rubber bag concealed under his robe; then demand a bucketful of water and dispose of it in the same way, remarking it was the first drink he had tasted since he was "killed at Shiloh."

The Klan in its new guise was the postwar inheritor of such prewar terrorist organizations as the Knights of the Golden Circle, the Minute Men, the Knights of the Columbian Order and The Precipitation, all dedicated to preserving "southern rights," in opposition to the abolitionists and other spreaders of northern notions in the 1840s and 1850s. The Klan spread rapidly through the South. Then, in April 1867, the disparate elements organized. Representatives of the various chapters met at the Maxwell House in Nashville, Tennessee, and drew up their governing regulations, which they called a prescript. The weak, innocent, defenseless and oppressed were to be defended; the Constitution of the United States and all constitutional laws were to be upheld. The Invisible Empire was divided into realms, dominions, provinces and dens headed by Grand Dragons, Titans, Giants and Cyclopses. The individual members were titled Ghouls. Confederate General Nathan Bedford Forrest was elected the first Grand Wizard.

The Klan was strongest in the rural areas of the nine southern states: Florida, Georgia, Mississippi, North and South Carolina, Mississippi, Arkansas, Tennessee and Texas. Despite their jocular beginnings, the Ghouls rapidly turned serious. As David M. Chalmers says in his book *Hooded Americanism* (1965):

> The method of the Klan was violence. It threatened, exiled, flogged, mutilated, shot, stabbed, and hanged. It disposed of Negroes who were not respectful, or committed crimes, or belonged to military or political organizations such as the Loyal and Union Leagues. It drove out Northern schoolteachers and Yankee storekeepers and politicians, and "took care of" Negroes who gained land and prospered, or made inflammatory speeches or talked about equal rights. It assaulted carpetbag judges, intimidated juries, and spirited away pris-

oners. It attacked officials who registered Negroes, who did not give whites priority, or who foreclosed property.

The reign of the original Klan was short. By 1869, it was outwardly successful and internally out of control. A secret, masked society proved impossible for even its leaders to rule, and an anarchic element was rapidly taking over as the southern aristocracy dropped out. And besides, in many areas its political objective was being achieved and the rule of the southern white was again ensured. Negroes were no longer slaves in name, but the system had once again enslaved them in fact. In January 1869, Imperial Wizard Forrest ordered the disbanding of the Klan and the destruction of all its records.

The order to disband was generally followed, although pockets of Klan activity remained and similar unrelated organizations, such as the Knights of the White Camellia (which was sworn "to observe a marked distinction between the races"), continued their enlightened policies. By 1877, when President Rutherford B. Hayes removed the last of the occupying federal troops from the South, and local government control was firmly back in the hands of the white aristocracy, the last remnants of the Ku Klux Klan dissolved and disappeared.

Then, in 1902, Thomas Dixon, Jr., published *The Leopard's Spots*, which was followed in 1905 by *The Clansman, An Historic Romance of the Ku Klux Klan*. Colorful, highly romanticized, one-sided stories of the war and Reconstruction, they painted the United States Senate as the villain, with the southern Negro as its henchman. The heroes were Abraham Lincoln and the Knights of the Ku Klux Klan. D. W. Griffith, the brilliant young film director, bought the rights to *The Clansman* and turned it into one of the longest, most powerful, most innovative and controversial films ever made. It was released in 1915. He moved the beginning of the story back to colonial days and concluded it with the end of Reconstruction. Griffith, originally from Kentucky, originally called it *The Clansman* but, at Thomas Dixon's suggestion, changed the title to *The Birth of a Nation*. Its view of southern womanhood suffering bravely through the rapine and pillage of the Negro and the white carpetbagger shone as revealed truth. The film was immensely popular in the South and provoked riots and packed houses in the North. Adjusting for inflation, it is still one of the biggest grossing pictures of all time.

The release of *The Birth of a Nation* stirred William Joseph Simmons, a failed preacher and one-time seller of ladies' undergarments, to reestablish the Ku Klux Klan. A week before the movie opened in Atlanta, Georgia, he gathered a group of like-minded citizens at the Piedmont Hotel and ferried them to Stone Mountain, some 16 miles away. There he fired a kerosene-soaked cross and, by a stone altar holding the American Flag, an open Bible, a naked sword and a canteen of "holy" river water, declared that "under a blazing, fiery torch the Invisible Empire was called from its slumber of half a century to take up a new task and fulfill a new mission for humanity's good and to call back to mortal habitation the good angel of practical fraternity among men." Simmons then declared himself the new Grand Wizard, administered an oath of allegiance and they all went back to the hotel.

Simmons proved to be a great man with ritual but an untalented organizer and money-maker. After five years, the rejuvenated Klan had no more than 2,000 members. World War I intervened, and for two years, the Klan hunted down enemy aliens, homegrown traitors, spies, slackers, idlers, strike leaders and immoral women and marched patriotically in parades. But still, after the war the Klan had not progressed nearly as far as Simmons had hoped.

Simmons found assistance in the Southern Publicity Association and its proprietors Edward Young Clarke and Mrs. Elizabeth Tyler. The association raised funds for the Salvation Army, the Young Men's Christian Association, the Anti-

Saloon League, the Theodore Roosevelt Memorial Fund, and Near East Relief, taking a substantial tithe for their troubles. They saw great potential in the Klan as a money-making proposition and, in June 1920, struck a deal with Simmons. Clarke and Tyler were to get 8 dollars out of every 10-dollar membership fee they brought in and two dollars from every membership fee brought in by existing Klan branches. In return, they would publicize the Klan.

Clarke and Tyler underestimated the depth of bigotry in the country. What they expected to be a nice cash cow, situated mainly in the South, turned out to be a money cascade, bringing in members from all over the United States. By 1921, the Klan membership had reached 100,000 and, by 1924, close to 4,000,000. The Klan of the 1920s broadened its scope of hatred to include blacks, Jews, Roman Catholics, Japanese, Chinese and all other non-"Aryan" peoples. It also pledged to fight bootlegging, dope, graft, nightclubs and roadhouses, breaking the Sabbath, unfair business dealings, sexual perversions, infidelity and violations of the Ten Commandments.

Simmons named or renamed every Klan activity and title to conform to a pattern. The individual associations, once Dens, were now Klaverns. They gathered at Konklaves and Klanvocations. The Klan court was a Kloncilium. The members, under the Exalted Cyclops, were either Klaliffs, Klokards, Kligrapps, Klabees, Kladds, Klageros, Klexters or Klokanns. The official Klan Bible (or perhaps Book of Kommon Prayer) was the Kloran, and the preacher was a Kludd. At meetings, they sang Klodes and spoke in their private Klanguage.

Clarke, who was now the Imperial Kleagle of the Klan, revised the fee structure. The country was divided into domains, which were essentially sales districts, each headed by a Grand Goblin. Each state was under the jurisdiction of a King Kleagle, under whom worked the regular Kleagles, who did the recruiting. The $10 Klectoken (initiation fee) was broken up as follows: $4.00 to the recruiting Kleagle; $1.00 to the King Kleagle; $0.50 to the Grand Goblin; $2.50 to the Imperial Kleagle; and $2.00 to the Grand Wizard.

The Klan in its internal structure was like a juvenile version of the Masons; indeed, some of the Imperial Kleagle's best recruiting was done from within the Masons and other highly ritualistic fraternal orders. The Klan in its outward behavior was a mob of self-righteous, bigoted vigilantes, who delighted in taking the law into their own hands and keeping "the Jews and Niggers" in their place. Klansmen were asked to reply in the affirmative to the following catechism:

1. Is the motive prompting your ambition to be a Klansman serious and unselfish?

2. Are you a native born, white, Gentile American citizen?

3. Are you absolutely opposed to and free of any allegiance of any nature to any cause, government, people, sect or ruler that is foreign to the United States of America?

4. Do you believe in the tenets of the Christian religion?

5. Do you esteem the United States of America and its institutions above any other government, civil, political, or ecclesiastical in the whole world?

6. Will you, without mental reservation, take a solemn oath to defend, preserve, and enforce same?

7. Do you believe in clanishness, and will you faithfully practice same towards Klansmen?

8. Do you believe in and will you faithfully strive for the eternal maintenance of white supremacy?

9. Will you faithfully obey our constitution and laws, and conform willingly to all our usages, requirements, and regulations?

10. Can you always be depended on?

In 1921, the New York *World* began running a series of exposés of Klan activities, which failed to frighten the Klan—they did not have a very big hold on New York. But then Congress threatened to take action. A Massachusetts congressman introduced a resolution claiming that the Klan had been guilty of violating the First, Fourth, Fifth, Sixth and Thirteenth Amendments. It had, the resolution claimed, outraged religious freedom and violated the prohibitions against illegal seizure, trial, punishment and involuntary servitude. It also had not been paying its income taxes. The Rules Committee of the U.S. House of Representatives held hearings in October.

The hearings lasted a week and came to nothing. It culminated with Simmons admitting that incidents had occurred, but they were probably committed by people hiding behind white sheets and pretending to be Klansmen. "If this organization is unworthy," he declared, "then let me know and I will destroy it, but if it is not, then let it stand." He then called "upon the Father to forgive those who have persecuted the Klan" and collapsed unconscious on the floor. The result of the newspaper exposés and the congressional investigation was a tremendous increase in Klan membership. "Congress made us," Simmons would say many years later.

In 1922, a group of dissident Klansmen led by Imperial Kligrapp (national secretary) Hiram Wesley Evans, a Texas dentist, wrested control of the Klan away from Simmons, who was promoted to the figurehead post of Emperor of the Klan, and ousted Clarke and Tyler (who had been caught in a sexual tryst in a hotel room and therefore were anathema to the righteous moralists of the Klan). For a while in the 1920s, the Klan was a country within a country, and in some states, the Klan was the law. In Texas, it elected a senator and almost elected a governor. In Oklahoma, the governor tried to stop it and was driven from office. In Arkansas, Klan primaries decided who would win in the regular party primaries. In Oregon, the Klan elected the governor and enough members of the legislature to pass bills outlawing parochial schools. In Colorado, the Klan elected both of the state's senators. In southern California, the Klan burned and whipped and raged and controlled many local police forces. In Indiana, the Klan elected a governor, a senator and much of the legislature.

The Klan punished whites for violating its primitive Protestant sense of morality and blacks for being black. Tarring and feathering, along with branding, were popular pastimes for the vigilante Klansmen. In many areas in the South and Midwest, the police authorities were either members of the Klan, Klan sympathizers or afraid to get involved, and so the Klan ran the show. The Klan also practiced economic clannishness; shop windows bore signs reading TWK (Trade With Klan), and "undesirable" shopkeepers were boycotted and run out of business, if not out of town.

In Texas during 1922, to use one state as a representative example, the Klan took out and beat a divorced man in Dallas, a lawyer from Houston who annoyed girls, a Timpson man who left his wife and a Brenham man who spoke German. A woman in Tenha was suspected of having married for a second time without the formality of divorcing her first husband. She was taken from the hotel she worked in, stripped, beaten with a wet rope and then tarred and feathered. In Dallas, the Klan had a special whipping meadow along the Trinity River bottom, where it flogged 68 people during the spring of 1922.

The Klan did not stop with beatings or tar and featherings. It also practiced murder. In Texarkana, Arkansas, on July 28, 1922, John West, a black road worker, was lynched for asking a foreman if he could drink out of a cup that had been used by whites. On December 19, 1925, in Clarksdale, Mississippi, a black man named Lindsay Coleman was found innocent of a murder charge. He was nonetheless grabbed as he left the courthouse and lynched by the Klan. These incidents are picked at random from a long and horrible list.

It should be understood that, even in the southern states, the Klan was never a majority, merely a strident and dangerous minority. The

Klan was all the more dangerous because Klansmen operated under the cover of anonymity, drawing a white sheet over their identities. In 1924, the Klan effectively controlled the Democratic National Convention. They succeeded in preventing the nomination of Alfred E. Smith as the Democratic presidential candidate because he was a Catholic. They succeeded, by a narrow margin, in defeating a plank in the party platform that would have condemned the Klan by name. Imperial Wizard Evans was elated, and the Klan hierarchy was convinced that in four years they would be electing a president. But, although nobody knew it at the time, the Klan was already at its apex.

By 1924, the tide had turned and the state officials started taking measures to regain control of their own states. In Louisiana, the legislature passed three bills that effectively removed the mystical power of the Klan. The first required the annual filing of membership lists by all fraternal organizations. Anyone attending a meeting of a society not filing its membership list was committing a crime punishable by imprisonment. The second prohibited the wearing of masks in public except for Halloween, school fairs, minstrel shows and Mardi Gras. The third made any offense or breach of the peace, including simply threatening someone, a felony if committed by a person wearing a mask.

The Klan went down kicking and screaming and was a long time in the dying. In 1925, it held a parade down Pennsylvania Avenue in Washington, D.C., with over 40,000 marchers. But public opinion had shifted against the Klan, in part because of a nationwide radio broadcast by Imperial Wizard Evans that spouted the Klan's usual anti-black, anti-Catholic, anti-Jewish rhetoric. It was not unusual for a Klan meeting, but it was a first for nationwide radio. For the first time, people all over the country heard Evans's contention that "only the White Anglo-Saxon Protestants of the Klan can truly claim one hundred percent Americanism."

Evans had gone too far. The Klan's disclaimer was no longer believed. It was clear that the atrocities were not random acts, but were being committed with the full knowledge and authority of the Imperial Wizard. Catholic and Jewish leaders organized against the Klan. President Calvin Coolidge publicly condemned the Klan and promised to use the authority of the Executive Office to help quash it. The American Federation of Labor and the United Mineworkers Union told their membership that anyone who belonged to the Klan would immediately lose union membership and all benefits. The American Legion offered a standing award of $3,000 for the arrest and conviction of Klan criminals.

The final blow to the Klan's image came when DAVID C. STEPHENSON, Grand Wizard of the Indiana Klan, was tried and convicted of murdering a young lady upon whom he had forced his unwelcome attentions. Membership in the Klan dropped over the next decade, and it lost much of its political clout.

In 1939, Imperial Wizard Evans was deposed, and the Grand Dragon of the Realm of Ohio, former veterinarian Dr. James A. Colescott, took the reins. The Klan had a brief love affair with the Fascist German American Bund, a Nazi front organization, but then withheld its affections with the beginning of World War II. The end of this incarnation of the Ku Klux Klan came in 1944, when the IRS decided that the Klan owed more than $685,000 in back taxes on income from the 1920s. Colescott resigned and went back to veterinary practice, explaining, "The Revenuers knocked on my door and said they had come to collect three-quarters of a million dollars that the government just figured out the Klan owed as taxes. . . . We had to sell our assets and hand over the proceeds to the Government and go out of business. Maybe the Government can make something out of the Klan—I never could."

After World War II, with the first stirrings of civil rights, the Klan was again reborn. Its new patriarch was a 55-year-old Atlanta obstetrician named Dr. Samuel Green, who had been in the earlier Klan since the 1920s. In 1946, a ceremony of rebirth was held on Stone Mountain, and the Klan began again its insidious growth. It professed its intolerance for blacks, Jews, Catholics and labor organizers, but this time, the federal and state governments were determined to limit the damage. President Truman ordered the FBI to investigate civil rights abuses, and the authorities in California, Indiana, Kentucky, Michigan, New Jersey, New York and Pennsylvania took steps to have the Klan investigated and controlled. As a result, the Klan languished.

It sprouted again to oppose the civil rights movements of the 1950s, beginning with the May 17, 1954, Supreme Court decision that banned segregated public schools. Eldon Edwards, a paint sprayer at the General Motors plant in Atlanta, received a state charter for the "U.S. Klans, Knights of the Ku Klux Klan," and took over what was left of Green's organization. It was then that the Klan added bombings to their repertory of floggings, rapings, castrations and lynchings. By now there were many competing Klan organizations that all claimed descent from the one true Klan; the Original Ku Klux Klan competed for membership with the U.S. Klans, the United Klans, the Association of Arkansas Klans, the Southern Knights of the Ku Klux Klan, the Invisible Empire Knights of the Ku Klux Klan and the Independent Knights of the Ku Klux Klan. They fought each other, as well as their traditional enemies, and their bigotry, now with a sharp focus, prospered.

But their support was not as wide or deep as they supposed. Most people despised them, but many were afraid to take action. Opposing the Klan was still a good way to be tarred and feathered—or murdered.

The North Carolina Klan received a surprise when they decided to harass the Lumbee Indians. They burned three crosses outside the Lumbee reservation and then announced that they were coming back for a fourth time. When the 75 Klansmen torched the cross, they suddenly became aware that 350 shotgun-toting Lumbees were advancing from across the road. The Indians shot out the tires of the Klansmen's cars, they shot out lights and speaker systems and they disbursed the brave Klansmen.

In the past decade, as integration has become an established fact, the Klan has become a marginal entity. In what may be the final irony, a federal jury in Mobile, Alabama, gave a $7 million award in a damage suit brought by Beulah Mae Donald, the mother of Michael Donald, a 19-year-old black man who was savagely assaulted and hanged by Klansmen in March 1981. They were avenging the murder of a white policeman by an unknown black malefactor. The United Klans of America had to sign over all their assets, including the headquarters building in Tuscaloosa, to Mrs. Donald. *See also:* LYNCHING

L

LAMM, Herman K. "Baron" (1890?–1930)

THE MASTER BANK ROBBER WHO TAUGHT DILLINGER THE TRICKS OF THE TRADE

A former Prussian Army officer, whose conduct was not deemed worthy of that high profession, Herman Lamm immigrated to the United States when he was caught cheating at cards. Upon arrival, he turned to robbing banks, which he did with military planning and precision. He spent a short time in prison in Utah in 1917, when his method apparently was not yet perfected. After that, he and his gang committed numerous bank robberies for 12 years before they were finally stopped.

The technique he developed, which became known as the Baron Lamm System, was essentially an adaptation of Prussian military planning to the problem of robbing banks. It involved working from an accurate floor plan of the bank, finding out which bank workers were responsible for opening the safe, noting where the alarms were located and of what sort they were and determining what the best escape route was. Lamm then assigned each of his associates a specific job and drilled them until they understood just what they were to do, sometimes creating a mock-up of the bank to rehearse in. The escape route was gone over by the driver until he was familiar with it, and several alternates were plotted in case of need.

The baron's greatest innovation was precise timing. Every element of the robbery was timed, and the gang stuck to the schedule, even to the point of leaving money behind if it was time to go.

The system worked fine until December 13, 1930, when the baron and his gang held up the Citizen's State Bank of Clinton, Indiana. The robbery went fine, but the getaway driver panicked when he saw a man approaching with a shotgun, and he blew a tire in executing a quick U-turn. The gang immediately stole another car, but this one had a governor installed by the owner to prevent his elderly father from speeding. The fugitives went through a couple of other vehicles before they were cornered by over 200 lawmen. Baron Lamm and the driver were killed in the gun battle; Dad Landy, a 70-year-old ex-con, shot himself rather than go back to prison and the two other gang members, Walter Dietrich and Oklahoma Jack Clark, were convicted and sent to prison. Fellow inmate JOHN DILLINGER agreed to help them escape in a massive breakout, provided they would teach him the fundamentals of the Baron Lamm system. They did so, and he applied what he learned, becoming one of the most successful bank robbers in an era of bank robbers.

LANSKY, Meyer (1902–1983)

THE CHAIRMAN OF THE BOARD OF ORGANIZED CRIME

The man who is believed to have run the National Crime Syndicate for over two decades was born Maier Suchowljansky in Grodno, Russia. When he was nine years old, his family moved to New York City, where in 1917, he graduated from the eighth grade of P.S. 34. By the time he was 20, he and his young companion BENJAMIN "BUGSY" SIEGEL had moved from petty theft to running their own gang. Known as the Bugs and Meyer Gang, it

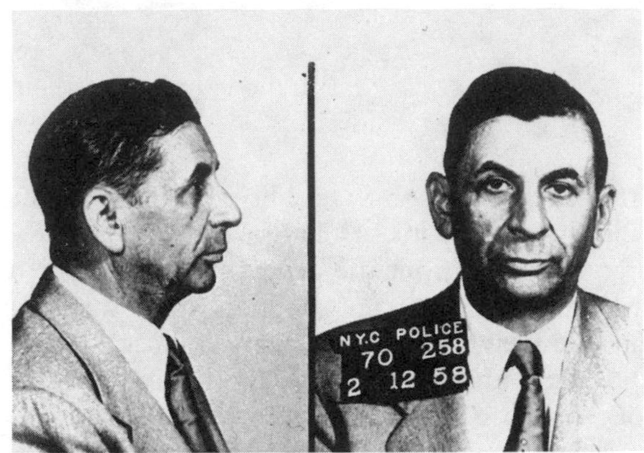

New York City police mug shot of Meyer Lansky. (Federal Bureau of Investigation.)

practiced theft, extortion, general mayhem and murder for a fee. Siegel, who was considered so crazy that it was dangerous to cross him, was the enforcer, while Lansky was the brains.

Over the next two decades, Lansky gradually moved from being the brains of the Bugs and Meyer Gang to being the brains behind the National Crime Syndicate. It is probable that were it not for Meyer Lansky's manipulative intelligence, the National Crime Syndicate, called by its associates the Syndicate, the Outfit or the Combination, never would have developed. It started with the realization by Lansky and CHARLEY "LUCKY" LUCIANO, who was a lieutenant in the organization of GIUSEPPE "JOE THE BOSS" MASSERIA, that they had a commonality of interests. Joe the Boss was one of the old-fashioned MUSTACHE PETES who believed that anyone not from the same hometown in Sicily was a natural enemy. With the help of Lansky, Luciano and his Young Turks eliminated Masseria and the other Mustache Petes to bring the CASTELLAMMARESE WAR to an abrupt end and started a new reign of criminal cooperation to maximize profits during the wonderful opportunity presented by PROHIBITION.

As the wealth and power of the organized crime cartel grew, Lansky allowed Luciano, DUTCH SCHULTZ and others to get all the publicity, while he remained the gray eminence behind the throne. Lansky introduced the Outfit to new ways of making money, and he handled, banked or invested the surplus money—a sign of the respect, fear and trust in which he was held. He brought the Outfit to Cuba, making a deal with dictator Fulgencio Batista to allow Mob-run luxury casinos in Havana to operate with little interference. The Mob gave the military junta headed by Batista a large weekly payoff, but the colonels and generals had to come to the casinos to collect the cash; by the time they left, they had dropped the money at the craps tables or the roulette wheels.

In 1970, when the U.S. government made a determined effort to put him away for tax evasion and to have him deported as an undesirable alien, Lansky moved to Israel. Under the Israeli Law of Return, anyone born Jewish (which meant having a Jewish mother) could not be denied citizenship in Israel. But somehow the Israeli government, under pressure from the U.S. government, made Lansky an exception. In 1972, he was forced to leave Israel, and he moved to Miami, Florida.

In 1973, while Lansky was recuperating from open heart surgery, the government moved against him. Income tax charges were brought, and Lansky stood trial in Miami. The government, possibly suffering from an excess of hubris because of past successes, failed to make its case. Lansky was found innocent and spent the rest of his life in semiretirement, free of significant harassment from the federal government.

LEBRON, Lolita (1920–)

On March 1, 1954, Lolita Lebron, a Puerto Rican nationalist and mother of two, along with three male companions, made a valiant if criminal attempt to "free Puerto Rico" (their battle cry). The four of them attended a session of the U.S. House of Representatives and, from the visitors gallery, fired pistols at the congressmen assembled below.

Five representatives were wounded, none seriously, and the four Puerto Ricans were sentenced to life imprisonment. They served 25 years, until their sentences were commuted to time served by President Jimmy Carter on September 6, 1979. Four years earlier, GRISELIO TORRESOLA and a companion made an attempt on the life of President Harry S Truman for similar reasons—and with similar results.

LEGAL DEFINITIONS

See: GLOSSARY OF LEGAL DEFINITIONS

LEOPOLD AND LOEB CASE

TWO TEEN-AGE BOYS COMMITTED THE "CRIME OF THE CENTURY" BY KIDNAPPING AND MURDERING 14-YEAR-OLD BOBBY FRANKS

> These boys, neither one of them, could possibly have committed this act excepting by coming together. It was not the act of one; it was the act of two. It was the act of their planning, their conniving, their believing in each other; their thinking themselves supermen. Without it they could not have done it. It would not have happened. Their parents happened to meet, these boys happened to meet; some sort of chemical alchemy operated so that they cared for each other, and poor Bobby Franks' dead body was found in the culvert as a result. Neither of them could have done it alone.
>
> —Clarence Darrow, counsel for the defense

Born into wealthy Jewish families, Nathan Leopold, Richard Loeb and their victim, Bobby Franks,[1] all lived in the exclusive Kenwood district of Chicago within blocks of each other. Leopold, 19 years old, and Loeb, 18, were precocious, brilliant youths; Leopold graduated Phi Beta Kappa from the University of Chicago at the age of 18, while Loeb at 17 had been the youngest graduate of the University of Michigan.

[1] Although born Jewish, Franks's parents were professed Christian Scientists at the time of the murder.

Richard Loeb had what today would be called a sociopathic personality. When he was four years old, he was put in the care of a governess named Miss Struthers, who was overprotective and overly strict. In response to Miss Struthers's curiosity about his every action, he became an accomplished and inveterate liar. From the age of eight or nine, he began stealing from friends and relatives, for the thrill it gave him and to reinforce the feeling of superiority he felt over others. When caught, he displayed neither guilt nor remorse, but merely chagrin. The items he stole were usually of no use to him, and quite often, he threw them away.

Nathan Leopold, Jr., was brilliant and precocious from infancy. According to family legend, he spoke his first words when he was only four months old. He suffered from a variety of congenital illnesses and deficiencies: an atrophying pineal gland, a diseased and overactive thyroid and what was described as a disorder of the nervous control of the blood vessels. He was also an incipient diabetic. The youngest of the Leopold children, the small, sickly youth bore the family nickname of "Babe." He became interested in birds when he was quite young and was a noted amateur ornithologist by the time he was in his early teens. Unable to make friends easily, he was an outsider and loner in school, possibly through choice, but more probably because his behavior caused him to be shunned by his classmates.

The two boys met when Leopold was 14 and Loeb was 13 and immediately became fast friends. Loeb entered the University of Chicago at 14, and Leopold at 16. They transferred together to the University of Michigan, where Loeb joined the Zeta Beta Tau fraternity. The fraternity boys liked the gregarious Loeb, but disliked his strange young friend. They supposedly told Loeb that they would put him up for membership if he dropped Leopold, which he promptly did. Leopold transferred back to the University of Chicago, from which he graduated Phi Beta Kappa in 1923. The following fall he entered the University of Chicago's law school. Loeb had graduated from Michigan the same year and was taking some history courses at Chicago, with the idea of entering the law school the next quarter. Although Leopold was hurt by Loeb's behavior, he quickly forgave him.

The relationship between Leopold and Loeb was the meshing of two different but complementary fantasies. Leopold's self-image was enhanced by associating with the popular and socially competent Loeb. Loeb's feeling of superiority was enhanced by his closeness to the brilliant Leopold, whose IQ tested at 210 to Loeb's 160 (both scores are in the genius range). Since IQ is a measure of what one knows compared to the norm for one's age group, the fact that both boys had received years of extra tutoring from governesses may well have inflated the scores.

Loeb's life was predicated on his imagined superiority to other people; a superiority that was expressed not in accomplishments, but in successful lies and petty thefts. He fantasized about being a master criminal. He often imagined himself as the "mastermind" of a gang of expert crooks.

Leopold, from the age of five, had master-slave fantasies, in which he was sometimes the master but much more often—nine times out of ten—the slave. He dreamed of saving the life of his king and then refusing to accept his king's offer of freedom. He read Friedrich Nietzsche's theories of the *übermensch*, the superman, and saw himself and Dickie Loeb in that role: supermen, far above other mortals. He knew that Loeb constantly lied about everything, even to him, but in his mind that somehow increased Dickie's superiority. In his scale of the perfect man, he gave Loeb a score of 90 and himself a score of 63. Everyone else ranged from 30 to 40. As supermen, Babe felt, there was no room for emotions, only intellect. For *übermenschen*, no sin is possible except an intellectual error. Dickie and Babe showed their intellectual superiority by cheating at cards when playing with their friends and worked out an elaborate system of hand signals to accomplish this.

It was the combination of Loeb's fantasy criminal mastermind and Leopold's fantasy super-slave, and the fear that each had of losing face in the eyes of the other, that killed Bobby Franks that afternoon in May 1924.

The pair began their active criminal career with malicious phone calls and soon progressed to turning in false fire alarms. When these thrills wore thin, they set fire to an empty shack and joined the gathering crowd to watch it burn, enjoying the feeling of superiority over the crowd and their ignorant guesses as to what had started the fire.

Their first venture into serious crime was burglarizing a pair of fraternity houses at the University of Michigan: the Zeta Beta Tau house, where Loeb had lived for two years, and a random one of Leopold's choice. They made off with a variety of items of varying utility from Zeta Beta Tau, including an Underwood portable typewriter that Leopold took home with him. At the second house they were frightened off and only came away with a camera.

After this robbery, their relationship took a strange turn. As the Hubert and Bowman Report, prepared by the two psychiatrists before the trial, explained:

> Each one was disgusted with the other's work in the robberies. They raised other personal questions, about which they were disharmonious, and their friendship threatened to collapse. . . . However, both gained by this friendship in several ways and therefore they came to an agreement . . . that [Loeb] should have complete domination over [Leopold] so that he might call upon him whenever he wished for implicit obedience. In order, however, that [Leopold] should not accede to [Loeb] in every minor request and under all conditions, it was understood that [Leopold] should use his own discretion about accepting [Loeb's] suggestions or

> commands except when [Loeb] should say "for Robert's sake." Whenever [Loeb] used this phrase in a request it meant that it was a part of this contract, and that [Leopold] should do as [Loeb] suggested.

On Wednesday, May 7, 1924, Loeb and Leopold began actively preparing for an adventure that they had begun discussing after the fraternity house robbery, and that they had been planning for the last six months. It was to be the masterstroke that would establish them as the supermen that they knew they were: kidnapping for ransom and murdering the victim. They had spent some time trying to decide who the victim should be. Leopold suggested kidnapping and raping a girl, but Loeb vetoed that: girls were too closely watched. Loeb suggested his own younger brother but realized that getting away to collect the ransom would be difficult (he later stated that he liked his brother and had suggested him only as a joke). Several mutual acquaintances were suggested and vetoed for a variety of reasons. They finally decided to leave the choice of the victim to chance, the only caveat being that it had to be someone younger and smaller than themselves so he would not be too difficult to subdue.

On that Wednesday, they rented a hotel room and opened a bank account in the name of Morton D. Ballard. On Friday, May 9, Leopold went to the Rent-A-Car Company to rent a car in the Ballard name. Loeb waited at a nearby phone booth to be "Louis Mason," one of "Ballard's" references, in case the rental company chose to call. The company did call, and "Mason" gave "Ballard" a glowing reference. Leopold drove the car around for a short while and then returned it, telling the man that he might be back soon to take it out again.

On Tuesday, May 20, Loeb went into a hardware store and bought a chisel and 35 feet of rope. The next day Leopold typed the ransom notes on the portable Underwood in his study. The wording had been planned for some time. The stationery was plain, cheap paper purchased a few days before at a store near the university. The notes were not addressed, as the victim had not yet been picked.

On Wednesday, May 21, Leopold, as "Ballard," again rented the Willys-Knight touring car that he had taken out two weeks before. He and Loeb had lunch and then, around 1:00 P.M., dropped Leopold's own car off at his house and left together in the rental car.

They drove to Jackson Park where one of them wrapped the blade of the chisel with adhesive tape from Leopold's bathroom medicine chest (in their confessions each of them claimed the other had done it). Then, they drove around the neighborhood inspecting groups of schoolchildren for a likely prospect. Leopold briefly returned home to pick up a pair of field glasses, and they continued their search for a candidate. After considering and rejecting several for various reasons, they saw 14-year-old Robert Franks, a boy whom Loeb knew casually, coming toward them. He was on his way home from the Harvard School for Boys; a private day school a few blocks away that he attended (Leopold had graduated from the Harvard School, and Loeb's younger brother was a current student). They passed him and turned the car around, driving slowly to allow Franks time to get clear of a pedestrian on the same side of the street.

The events of the next few minutes are in dispute. The driver of the car pulled over to the sidewalk and Loeb invited Franks into the car. The boy did not want to get in, but Loeb said he wanted to talk to him about a new tennis racket, and Franks was a tennis fanatic, so he entered the car. The driver of the car went up to the corner and made a left turn, whereupon the other person hit Bobby Franks with the handle of the chisel several times, rendering him unconscious.

The dispute is over who was driving and who actually hit and killed the Franks child. Each of them claims that he was driving and that the other committed the actual murder. The point is moot, since the culpability of each is complete no matter whose hand wielded the chisel, but at least one of them thought it was important. On balance, it would seem that Leopold was driving and Loeb lured Franks into the car, since Leopold had rented the car, and since Loeb was a habitual liar even about unimportant things. But we can never be sure.

The murderer threw the groaning, bleeding, semiconscious child onto the floor of the back seat and thrust a gag into his mouth. The boy made no further noises and died shortly thereafter.

They drove around in the car waiting for it to get dark enough to dispose of the body. Sometime in the afternoon, they stopped at the Dew Drop Inn, a hot dog stand on Fifteenth Street and Calumet Avenue, where Leopold purchased hot dogs and root beers to go while Loeb waited. They ate in the car, with Bobby Franks's body in the back seat.

Shortly after dark, they drove to Avenue F and 108th Street and followed a dirt road into the marsh near Wolf Lake. They had originally planned to kill Franks at this point, debating whether to use ether or strangle him with the rope they had bought. They had decided on the rope because each could take an end and jointly share the ultimate responsibility. But the boy was already dead.

They took Franks's clothing off and poured hydrochloric acid over the face and body to make it more difficult to identify. Using a lap robe to remove the body from the car, they stuffed it as far into a culvert as they could manage, Leopold donning a pair of rubber boots to wade through the wet marsh and push the body well in. They assumed that the body would never be found and, if by chance it was, it would be too far decomposed to be identified. Wrapping all of Franks's clothing in the robe, they tossed the bundle into the back of the car. One of Bobby's stockings fell out of the bundle, and a pair of eyeglasses fell unnoticed from the pocket of Leopold's jacket.

They stopped on the way home so that Leopold could call his father and say he would be late getting home. Then they stopped again and looked up the address and phone number of Jacob Franks, Bobby's father, in the phone book. They addressed the prewritten ransom note and mailed it.

They burned Franks's clothes in the furnace in the basement of Loeb's house—all but the robe, which was too big and would cause a stench. They hid the robe behind the greenhouse and spent some time washing the bloodstains out of the Willys-Knight. Then they went over to Leopold's house.

By early evening, Jacob and Flora Franks were becoming concerned about the absence of their son Robert and a bit angry about his staying out so late without telling them. Jacob, a wealthy 67-year-old man, walked around the neighborhood asking if anyone had seen Bobby, and Flora called the parents of Bobby's friends. Nobody had seen him since school. The older Franks children, Jack and Josephine, had no suggestions. By 9:00 P.M., with no hint of Bobby's whereabouts, the anger had been replaced by worry. Fearing—or perhaps hoping—that he had been inadvertently locked in at the Harvard School, Jacob and a family friend, former state senator Samuel Ettelson, arranged to enter and search the building, with no result.

Sometime after nine o'clock, the phone rang at the Franks house, and Flora Franks answered. A strange man (Leopold) asked for her husband, and she said he was out.

"Your son has been kidnapped," the voice told her. "He is all right. There will be further news in the morning." She asked the voice who he was, and the voice said, "Johnson." She asked what he wanted, and the voice hung up.

Bobby Franks's mother fell to the floor in a faint.

Jacob and Sam returned home to find Flora lying on the floor, unconscious. They revived her, and crying hysterically, she told them about the phone call. They talked it over, trying to decide what to do. At two in the morning, when the kidnappers had still not called back, Jacob decided to inform the police. They drove to the police station and told the duty officer, Lieutenant Welling, what they knew. After a discussion, it was decided to do nothing until morning, for fear of endangering the child's life.

The next morning, the ransom letter was delivered, and Jacob Franks opened it. Its two typewritten sheets read as follows:

> Dear Sir
>
> As you no doubt know by this time, your son has been kidnapped. Allow us to assure you that he is at present well and safe. You need fear no physical harm for him, provided you live up carefully to the following instructions, and such others as you will receive by future communications. Should you, however, disobey any of our instructions, even slightly, his death will be the penalty.
>
> **1.** For obvious reasons make absolutely no attempt to communicate with either police authorities or any private agency. Should you already have communicated with the police, allow them to continue their investigations, but do not mention this letter.
>
> **2.** Secure before noon today $10,000. This money must be composed entirely of old bills of the following denominations:
>
> $2000 in $20 bills.
> $8000 in $50 bills.
>
> The money must be old. Any attempt to include new or marked bills will render the entire venture futile.
>
> **3.** The money should be placed in a large cigar box, or if this is impossible, in a heavy cardboard box, securely closed and wrapped in white paper. The wrapping paper should be sealed at all openings with sealing wax.
>
> **4.** Have the money with you, prepared as directed above, and remain at home after one o'clock P.M. See that the telephone is not in use.
>
> You will receive a further communication instructing you as to your final course.
>
> As a final word of warning, this is a strictly commercial proposition, and we are prepared to put our threat into execution should we have reasonable grounds to believe that you have committed an infraction of the above instructions. However, should you carefully follow out our instructions to the letter, we can assure you that your son will be safely returned to you within six hours of our receipt of the money.
>
> Yours truly,
> George Johnson

At about the same time as Jacob Franks was reading the ransom note, a Polish immigrant named Tony Mankowski, who was crossing the marsh near Wolf Lake, thought he saw something in a culvert under the Pennsylvania Railroad track. He looked closer and then excitedly flagged down a pair of motorized handcars that were approaching on the track. The four signalmen on the cars stopped to look. Two small bare feet were sticking out of the culvert.

The five of them pulled the naked body of Bobby Franks out of the culvert, wrapped it in a tarpaulin and placed it on one of the handcars. Thinking that he might have drowned in an ill-advised attempt to swim, they looked around for his clothing. They found nothing but a pair of horn-rim eyeglasses, which one of the signalmen put in his pocket. They took the body on the handcar to the nearest telephone and called the police. The policeman, when hearing about the glasses, assumed that they had belonged to the corpse and placed them on the body.

Jacob Franks went to his bank and withdrew the ransom money, in old bills as the note demanded. Then he went home to await word from the kidnapper.

The Chicago *Daily News* had received a tip about the kidnapping, which they confirmed with Sam Ettelson, who requested them not to publish until further notice. They also learned that the body of a young boy had been found in a culvert and wondered if there might be a connection.

A *Daily News* reporter described for the Franks family the corpse, which had been taken to a funeral home. Jacob Franks was sure it was not Bobby. He was older and lighter and, most important, did not wear glasses. But just to be sure, Franks's brother-in-law went to look at the body.

Finally, in late afternoon, the kidnapper called, instructing Mr. Franks to take the taxicab that would appear at his front door to a certain drugstore and await instructions. Franks hung up and then realized in a panic that he had forgotten the address of the drugstore. They checked with the cab driver, but he had just been instructed by phone to pick up someone at the Franks' house. But it did not matter. Before Franks could leave the house there was a second phone call. It was his brother-in-law. The body was that of Bobby.

Leopold and Loeb had realized that the two greatest difficulties in a kidnapping were the possibility of identification by the victim, and the possibility of being caught in collecting the ransom money. They eliminated the first possibility by killing the victim. For the second, they evolved an elaborate scheme. After obtaining the money, the subject would receive telephoned instructions to go directly to a specific "Help Keep Our City Clean" box, where he would find a typewritten note directing him to a drugstore to await a phone call. This call would have him rush to the I.C. Railroad station and board the next train, where he would find the next note in a telegraph box in the rear car. This note would instruct him to toss the cigar box full of money out of the train just as it passed a specific spot: a factory with a black water tower. The two master criminals would be waiting below for the package.

The morning after the murder, after various errands such as cleaning the rest of the blood out of the rental car and breaking the Underwood portable up and depositing its pieces in various ponds in Jackson Park, the two killers went to a public phone and Leopold made the call to the Franks house. They had abbreviated their master plan and instructed Jacob Franks to go directly to the drugstore. To save time, Leopold had already called a yellow cab. After the call, they saw a headline on the latest edition of a newspaper at a newsstand: "Unidentified Boy Found in Swamp." Loeb was convinced the game was over. Leopold thought it was at least worth the phone call to the drugstore. He tried twice, but no one answered. They returned the rental car and went home.

From the beginning, it was understood that this was no ordinary crime. At a time when gangland killings had become commonplace, in a city with a murder rate of more than one a day, the callous killing of a 14-year-old boy from a wealthy family struck a responsive chord, and the citizens vibrated with fear and anger. If Bobby Franks was not safe within three blocks of his own home, then nobody was safe anywhere. State's Attorney Robert E. Crowe and Chief of Police Morgan A. Collins headed the hunt for the murderers, establishing a special headquarters in the Drake Hotel for the various authorities involved. Jacob Franks offered a $5,000 reward for information leading to the capture of the killers, the major Chicago newspapers each offered similar amounts for exclusive information, and Police Chief Collins put up $1,000.

The major clues in the hands of the police were the ransom note and the eyeglasses, which they now knew did not belong to Bobby Franks. An expert from the Royal Typewriter Company examined the note and decided that it had been typed on an Underwood portable. And probably, judging by the uneven pressure, by someone who was not a touch typist.

Loeb took a strong interest in this murder investigation. After all, Loeb's brother went to the Harvard School, and little Bobby Franks had played tennis on the Loeb family court. Loeb actually suggested to some reporters that they try to find the drugstore to which the kidnappers had directed Mr. Franks. They piled into a car and drove around, asking at various drugstores whether there had been a phone call for a Mr. Franks. Loeb was very proud of himself when they actually found the right drugstore. Later, driving to the inquest, one of the reporters asked Loeb what he had thought of the murdered boy. Loeb smiled. "If I were going to murder anybody, I would murder just such a cocky little son of a bitch as Bobby Franks," he replied.

At 11:00 A.M. on Sunday, May 25, four days after the killing, routine police procedure turned up the name of Nathan Leopold, and he was brought in for questioning. He was on a list of people who went birding in the area where the Franks boy was found. He admitted to having been there the Sunday before the killing, said he occasionally wore glasses, was not asked to produce them and went home.

During the weeks after the murder, many false clues were uncovered, false leads were followed and false testimony was taken; and several innocent people were arrested. Two bootleggers staying at the Sheraton Plaza Hotel were held on general principles. John Shackleford, a railway switchman, reported watching three men and a woman take a bundle from a sedan stopped near Wolf Lake and disappear into the woods with it. When they returned, Shackleford helped tow their car out of the mud. This, according to Crowe, was "an important clue."

The police were most serious about holding Walter Wilson and Mott Kirk Mitchell, two teachers from the Harvard School. Wilson, the mathematics teacher, had taken Bobby and his brother to an amusement park the year before and they had returned home late. Mitchell, English teacher and assistant headmaster, showed signs of being homosexual. Under the intense police pressure—Wilson later charged that he had been beaten with a rubber hose—Mitchell eventually confessed to having committed "numerous acts of perversion," but adamantly maintained that he had nothing to do with Bobby Franks's murder.

Charles Heath, a Chicago druggist, attempted to commit suicide. The police thought that very suspicious, as they had received a letter purporting to come from the kidnapper, saying that he was going to take his own life. They put Heath under guard at Mercy Hospital, but he escaped and went to Louisville, Kentucky, where he was discovered after taking an overdose of drugs in a hotel room and rushed to a hospital. He had a pocket full of clippings about the Franks kidnapping. "This certainly looks good," Collins said, sending two detectives down to question Heath. Unfortunately Heath died without regaining consciousness.

The kidnappers, according to a telegram sent to the Chicago police by Eugenic Dennis, a psychic from Kansas, were two men and a woman with red hair. "One of the men is in custody now, and the other one, the light-complexioned one . . . is hiding."

Jacob Franks could not help brooding about his son's death. And his brooding was more apt than a lot of the police work and expert theorizing. "I have been racking my brains trying to think who [the kidnappers] could be," he said. "Robert knew the murderers. That is why they choked him to death. And since Robert knew them, I must know them."

The break in the case came a week and a day after the killing. On Thursday, May 29, 1924, authorities succeeded in tracing the eyeglasses that had been found with the body. Almer Coe & Company identified the glasses as theirs because of an almost-invisible diamond mark that they put on all their lenses. They checked through over 50,000 records for the police. The prescription was common, as were the frames. The hinges on the frames, however, by pure chance, were rare. Only three pairs of horn-rim glasses with those hinges had been sold: one to an attorney who was then in Europe, one to a woman who was wearing them when she was interviewed and the third, in November 1923, to Nathan Leopold, Jr., for $11.50.

Leopold was taken in for questioning for the second time. He searched his house for his glasses and could not find them. He suggested that he had lost them while birding in the area. He fell down several times to show how they might have fallen from his breast pocket. They refused to oblige, staying firmly in the pocket. The district attorney found this a telling point, but his reasoning is obscure: Whether Leopold was birding or murdering, the glasses did fall out of his pocket.

Leopold had prearranged an alibi with Loeb when the glasses were discovered, on the off chance that they might lead back to him. The two had agreed on a time limit of seven days after the crime for the use of the alibi. Leopold had been picked up several hours before he thought the alibi ran out, so he used it. Loeb was picked up some hours later, and he chose to reckon from the start of the crime, so he did not use the alibi.

After several hours of saying he could not remember where he was on that Wednesday evening, Leopold slowly and artfully revealed the prepared alibi under intense questioning. He and his pal Dickie Loeb, he told the investigators, had eaten dinner together at the Coconut Grove Restaurant and then cruised around in his car with a hip flask of gin, looking for a couple of girls to pick up. They found a pair: Edna and Mae, and parked with them in Jackson Park for a couple of hours. But the girls "wouldn't come across, so we asked them to leave. And then we went home."

Loeb, who was being questioned separately by Assistant State's Attorney Bert Cronson, held out for longer than Leopold in revealing their common alibi, but he finally and grudgingly told the tale of Edna and Mae. His interrogators thought he was more sensitive than Leopold, more unwilling to hurt his parents with details of his girl-chasing evening; but the truth was that he felt that the time period for using that alibi had expired, and he was angry at Leopold for using it.

The investigators had almost become convinced of the boys' innocence, when their whole alibi fell apart. Sven Englund, the Leopolds' chauffeur, was asked if he remembered the events of May 21. He did, he told them, because that was the day his little girl got sick and had to go to the doctor. That day he had oiled the brakes on Nathan's car.

What time, they asked him, did Nathan Leopold take his car out that evening.

"I worked on that car all day," Englund told them. "They used some other car."

That was it. Bert Cronson checked on the date of the prescription written for Englund's little girl, and then went in to his boss's office and told him the story. "God damn, I think we've got them!" said State's Attorney Crowe.

Collaterally, at the same time, a couple of reporters were establishing that Leopold had possessed an Underwood portable typewriter.

Loeb was the first to confess. When confronted with the chauffeur's testimony, he said, "Shit!" and asked for a cigarette. Then he spent over an hour telling the story of the crime to State's Attorney Crowe and to E. M. Allen, a court reporter.

It was 4:00 A.M. before Crowe got back to Leopold, who refused at first to believe that Loeb had confessed. But when Crowe started telling him intimate details of the crime and added that Loeb had said that Leopold had wielded the chisel, Leopold then spent the next hour telling his version of the events. At about 6:00, Crowe announced to the press that the Bobby Franks case had been solved, and Richard Loeb and Nathan Leopold, Jr., had been charged with kidnapping and murder.

The district attorney prepared his case with meticulous care. Every item in the pair of confessions that could be confirmed was confirmed. The broken pieces of Underwood portable typewriter were dredged out of the various ponds and assembled, and their provenance traced back to the Zeta Beta Tau robbery a half-year before. The actions of the two defendants were checked and verified, as much as humanly possible, every step of the way. Crowe took them on a re-enactment of the day of the crime. They drove here and there and pointed out to him where they had first seen Bobby Franks, where they had hit him with the chisel, where they had stopped to eat and where they had taken the body. Once they started confessing, they could not seem to stop.

The only possible defense seemed to be a plea of insanity, and Crowe was determined to fight that tooth and nail. He wanted a conviction, and he wanted the death penalty. He brought in his own alienists, as psychiatrists were called then, who examined the two boys and pronounced them sane.

The families of Leopold and Loeb hired Benjamin Bachrach, a noted criminal lawyer, to conduct the defense. Bachrach urged that they also hire CLARENCE DARROW.

Sixty-seven years old when Jacob Loeb, Richard's father, went up to his hotel room to see him, Darrow was an author, a philosopher, a humanist and the leading criminal attorney of his day. He defended the poor, the oppressed, the defenseless and the unpopular, and by all reports, he was a marvel to watch in the courtroom. He had defended over 100 capital cases and not one of his clients had gotten the death penalty. He was an avid opponent of capital punishment. He did not want to take the two boys as clients; he was tired and in constant pain from various ills concomitant with his age. But he feared that if he did not take the case, the boys would die. "For God's sake," Jacob Loeb reportedly said, falling to his knees by the side of Darrow's bed, "don't let them hang!"

Darrow's first move was to hire his own alienists, attracting some of the finest psychiatric minds in the country by offering them a chance to examine these two boys. Two of the defense alienists, Dr. Carl M. Bowman of Boston, Massachusetts, and Dr. Harold S. Hubert, of Oak Park, Illinois, saw the defendants over a period of weeks and interviewed various of their friends and relatives. The resulting document, the Hubert and Bowman Report, was one of the most extensive psychiatric studies of the minds of murderers ever done. It treated with each of the defendants separately and covered them from infancy to the present. The boys were, as far as can be checked, amazingly honest with their questioners. Loeb found it boring, although he cooperated, but Leopold found the process fascinating and went out of his way to help out as much as he could.

The case against Nathan Leopold, Jr., and Richard Loeb for kidnapping and murder was brought to trial at 10:00 A.M. on Monday, July 21, 1924. It began with a bombshell: Darrow and Bachrach changed their clients' plea to guilty on both counts. Darrow and Bachrach reasoned that the finding of guilty was inevitable. In the climate created by the crime's publicity, no jury would have gone for an insanity plea. But, by pleading the boys guilty, they eliminated the jury. The penalty phase of the trial, technically a hearing to hear evidence in "mitigation and aggravation" of the crime, would be heard only by the judge, 63-year-old John R. Caverly, who had spent the last 14 years on the bench.

The hearing went on for 32 days, far longer than most murder trials in which the verdict is in doubt. Crowe was determined that none of his preparation to prove the defendants guilty would be wasted merely because they had already pled guilty. The public wanted to hear it all. And Crowe, with one eye on his political career, wanted the public to wallow in every word. He wanted these two teenage boys to hang, and he would pull the trap himself if they would let him.

While Crowe tried the two boys, Darrow tried the death penalty. In his two-day summation, he went over the state's case, pointed out that no boys so young had ever been executed in Illinois, that few defendants that pled guilty had ever been sentenced to death, that the prosecution's thirst for blood was no more wholesome than the defendants'; he quoted poetry, and he spoke of the progress of humanity. He said:

> I knew, your honor, that ninety unfortunate human beings had been hanged by the neck until

dead in the city of Chicago in our history. We would not have civilization except for those ninety that were hanged, and if we cannot make it ninety-two we shall have to shut up shop.

. . . It might shock the fine sensibilities of the state's counsel that [Bobby Franks] was put into a culvert and left after he was dead, but, your honor, I can think of a scene that makes this pale into insignificance. I can think . . . of taking two boys, one eighteen and the other nineteen, irresponsible, weak, diseased, penning them up in a cell, checking off the days and the hours and the minutes, until they will be taken out and hanged. Wouldn't it be a glorious triumph for the State's Attorney? Wouldn't it be a glorious illustration for Christianity and kindness and charity? I can picture them, wakened in the gray light of morning, furnished a suit of clothes by the state, led to the scaffold, their feet tied, black caps drawn over their heads, stood on a trap-door, the hangman pressing a spring, so that it gives way under them; I can see them fall through space—and—stopped by the rope around their necks.

Judge Caverly listened to Darrow's summation, a short comment by Bachrach and then to State's Attorney Crowe's summation for the state. Crowe seemed preoccupied with his belief that the defendants were "perverts" and was more concerned with the possibility that they had sexually molested Bobby Franks than the fact that they killed him. He had brought forth no evidence of this possibility during the hearing, and it seems extremely improbable. Crowe was also concerned that, if the court listened to the pernicious doctrine of Clarence Darrow that it was wrong to hang people, "a greater blow has been struck to our institutions than by a hundred, yes, a thousand murders."

On Wednesday, September 10, 1924, after deliberating for a week, Judge Caverly handed down his sentence:

"For the crime of murder, confinement at the penitentiary at Joliet for the term of their natural lives.

"For the crime of kidnapping for ransom, similar confinement for the term of ninety-nine years."

He further recommended that if either of the defendants ever became eligible for parole, it be denied.

Examining the crime with the lack of passion made possible by the passing of most of a century, it is clear that the "Crime of the Century" was the badly planned, badly botched exercise of diseased juvenile minds. Committing a motiveless crime is a sign of insanity, and it is clear that the $10,000 ransom was not the motive for the crime. Were Leopold's glasses not dropped at the site, there were still many clues by which the two boys would have been caught. The murder left large amounts of blood in the rented car, which was hastily and badly cleaned up. One of the many people who saw the two boys in the rental car might have come forward. It was pure chance that no one looking out a window saw Franks getting into the murder car. And, as they all lived in that neighborhood, the odds were good that, had they been seen, they would have been recognized.

The chisel that was used to kill Franks was thrown away on the street and found by a passerby, who thought that there were bloodstains on the handle and turned it over to the police. Investigators would have traced it to the store that sold it and had a description of the purchaser.

The ransom note, which State's Attorney Crowe used as an example of the high intelligence of the perpetrators, was a bad parody of the sort of ransom note found in stories in most every issue of *Dime Detective Story Magazine,* which Loeb read regularly.

Loeb died in prison in 1936, murdered by James Day, a fellow inmate. Day, who had used a straight razor to cut Loeb's throat and inflict 57 other wounds on the body, was acquitted when he claimed that Loeb had made homosexual advances toward him.

Leopold was paroled in 1958, after serving 33 years in prison. While in prison, he wrote the book *Life Plus 99 Years* (1958), which is a fascinating record of his 30 years in a state penitentiary. He moved to Puerto Rico, got married and eventually taught at the University of Puerto Rico. He died in 1971.

LEPKE, Louis
See: LOUIS "LEPKE" BUCHALTER

LICATA, Nick (1897–)
An important MAFIA don in Southern California, Nick Licata came to the United States from Camporeale, Trapani, Italy, in 1913. He took control of Mafia interests in the Southwest after the death of Frank DeSimone in 1968. Licata was cited for contempt in 1959, when he told a California state assembly subcommittee that he knew nothing of the Mafia, but the charges were dropped.

LINCOLN, Abraham (1809–1865)
The sixteenth president of the United States, Abraham Lincoln was assassinated by JOHN WILKES BOOTH in Ford's Theater, in Washington, D.C. Before he went into politics, Lincoln was an able defense attorney. He once won a murder case by discrediting an eyewitness who had claimed to have seen the events, which he described in detail, in the light of the full moon. Lincoln pulled out a farmer's almanac and showed that the moon had been at the quarter and would have provided little light.

LINDBERGH, Charles Augustus
See: LINDBERGH KIDNAPPING

LINDBERGH KIDNAPPING

THE CRIME THAT SHOCKED A NATION, FOR WHICH AN INNOCENT MAN MAY HAVE BEEN EXECUTED

On March 1, 1932, Charles Augustus Lindbergh, Jr., the 20-month-old son of famed flyer Colonel Charles Augustus Lindbergh and his wife Anne Morrow Lindbergh, was kidnapped from his crib in his upstairs bedroom in the Lindbergh home in the Sourland Hills of Hunterdon County, New Jersey, outside of Hopewell and northwest of Princeton.

Charles "Lucky Lindy" Lindbergh had been a national hero since he became the first person to fly solo across the Atlantic Ocean, taking off from Mineola, New York, in the *Spirit of St. Louis* on May 20, 1927, and landing in Paris, France, the next day. This earned him the sobriquet of "the Lone Eagle," and a level of public adoration that was not seen again until the Beatles came to New York. His marriage two years later to Anne Spencer Morrow, a poet and the daughter of Dwight W. Morrow, then ambassador to Mexico, and reputed to be one of the richest men in America, was the closest thing to a royal wedding this country had ever seen. When their child was born, common people rejoiced.

On the evening of the kidnapping, Charles, Jr., called "Little It" by his parents, was put to bed by Anne Lindbergh and the child's nurse, Betty Gow, at about eight o'clock, and the nurse stayed with him until he fell asleep. When Anne came to look in on her baby at nine o'clock, he was peacefully sleeping. When Betty Gow checked fifty minutes later, the baby was gone. The two women's first thought was that it was a practical joke; Lucky Lindy was fond of practical jokes and had actually hidden his son and heir in a closet only a couple of months before. But this time it was no joke. Lindbergh told the butler to call the police and then

Charles Lindbergh during a break at the trial. His efforts may have hindered the kidnapping investigation as much as they helped. (Associated Press.)

grabbed a loaded rifle and searched the grounds. The only clue he found was a wooden ladder lying on the ground outside the nursery window.

A ransom note in an envelope was left on the windowsill. Lindbergh would not let anyone open the envelope until the police arrived and it could be dusted for fingerprints. Chief Harry Wolf of the Hopewell police was the first person of authority to arrive, but before he could do anything constructive, the New Jersey State Police arrived in force and took over the investigation. As Henry Morton Robinson described the scene in *Science Versus Crime*:

> Bend your glance backward to the opening chapter of the Lindbergh case. Do you remember—could anyone ever forget—the foaming and senseless cataract of gorgeously uniformed state troopers that descended on the Lindbergh home in motorcycles, roared up and down the road trampling every available clue into the March mud, systematically covering with impenetrable layers of stupidity every fingerprint, footprint, dust trace on the estate?

Sometime after midnight, a fingerprint expert arrived and dusted the ransom envelope for prints. Nothing useful was found. He opened the envelope and examined the letter within. It had no prints. It read:

> Have fifty thousand dollars ready, 25,000 in twenty-dollar bills 15,000 in ten-dollar bills, and 10,000 in five-dollar bills. In 4–5 days we will inform you where to deliver the money. We warn you for making anyding public or for notify the police. The child is in gute care Indication for all letters are signature and three holes.

Unfortunately the police were already there, and as for making anything public, there had not been anything so public since P. T. Barnum added

Nurse Betty Gow takes the Lindbergh baby out for a walk six months before the kidnapping. (Associated Press.)

After the kidnapping, nurse Gow was one of the insiders initially suspected of being involved in the crime. (International News Photo.)

the third ring to the American circus. Newscasters had already spread the word of the kidnapping all over the world. The assembled experts decided on the basis of spelling and grammar that the letter was probably the work of a semiliterate German.

The ladder and a chisel found on the ground nearby were examined. It was assumed that the chisel had been used to pry open the nursery window. The ladder was a three-sectioned, noncommercial product that had been made by a less than skilled carpenter. Impressions in the earth outside the nursery window showed where it had been leaned against the house. One of the rungs near the top was broken, presumably having given way during the kidnapping. When placed against the side of the house, the top rung of the ladder fell some 30 inches below the bottom of the window. It would have been difficult, although not impossible, for one man to transit from the window ledge to the ladder while carrying a 30-pound baby, and close the window behind him. Police reported finding two sets of footprints at the foot of the ladder, but nobody could be sure who had walked there since the kidnapping was discovered. The nursery was dusted all over for fingerprints—walls, furniture, crib, windowsill, doors and doorknobs—but no prints were found. It was as though someone had wiped the entire room clean. This fact led to the recurring theme that the kidnapping was an inside job, although it is as possible that the housekeeping staff was very efficient, and the kidnapper wore gloves.

In the night, a quartet of colonels assembled to decide what to do next. Of the four, only one had any police background—Colonel H. Norman Schwarzkopf, a West Point graduate who was now the superintendent of the New Jersey State Police. The other three were Colonel William Joseph "Wild Bill" Donovan, a World War I hero who was preparing to run for governor of New York (he would lose that, but go on to head the OSS during World War II); Colonel Henry Breckinridge, a very social Wall Street lawyer; and Colonel Lindbergh.

From the beginning, the investigation of the case was fragmented and mishandled, and it suffered from the triple liabilities of Lindbergh's fame, ego, and tendency to manage everything. Everyone that dealt with him was conscious that it was Colonel Lindbergh they were talking to and deferred to his opinions. Lindbergh, too, had a very high opinion of himself. He tended to give orders when it would have been more profitable to listen to advice.

The four colonels decided that the "snatch" was probably a gangland job. They decided to ask the aid of Mickey Rosner, a Broadway character who was believed to have underworld connections. He put them in touch with Salvatore "Salvy" Spitale and Irving Bitz, a pair of New Yorkers who ran speakeasies. Lindbergh, at Rosner's suggestion, appointed them the official intermediaries in dealing with the kidnappers. Spitale and Bitz, it later turned out, had been foisted on Rosner, and thus on Lindbergh, by the New York *Daily News*, who hoped to use them as conduits into the Lindbergh home to keep on top of what was happening. Spitale's contribution was to call a press conference in his New York apartment and announce to the assembled reporters: "I been in touch all around, and I come to the conclusion that this one was pulled by an independent."

President Herbert Hoover was notified of the crime the morning after the kidnapping by U.S. Attorney General James Mitchell, who discussed with him what action the federal government should take. Legally, the government could take no action, since there was no federal kidnapping law, but there was no room for legal niceties where the Lone Eagle was concerned. The attorney general announced that "although there is no development to suggest that the case is one within Federal jurisdiction," the full law enforcement machinery of the government was being mobilized. This would include the cooperation of the Justice Department's Bureau of Investigation (not yet called the FBI), headed by young J. EDGAR HOOVER; the services of the U.S. Post Office Department's investigators; and the assistance as required of the Coast Guard, the Customs and Immigration Services, the Washington, D.C., police force and as many of the 563 Prohibition Bureau agents as required.

The first of a series of follow-up ransom letters arrived for Lindbergh, identified as genuine by a pair of red and blue circles punctuated by three holes, which were the same as the note left on the windowsill. The police wanted to examine it, but Lindbergh gave it to Rosner, who rushed it to New York to show to his gangster connections. What they were supposed to do with it is not known. What somebody did do with it was make a photograph and peddle copies of it all over town at five dollars a copy. When the second note arrived, the police observed that it had been mailed from the same area of Brooklyn as the first note. Perhaps the kidnappers were not aware that one could tell the mailing location by the postmark. New York City Police Commissioner Ed Mulrooney came up with the idea of staking out the mailboxes in that area. A special device would be installed in each box to isolate the letters as they were put in, and the mailer of any letter to Lindbergh or anyone connected to him would be tailed.

Lindbergh forbade the scheme, feeling that any such attempt might endanger the life of his son. Mulrooney argued for his idea, assuring Lindbergh that his men were professional, that the subject would never know he was being tailed and that rather than risk being found out, they would drop the tail. He also pointed out that if they knew where the boy was being held, they could attempt to rescue him.

Lindbergh put his foot down. He assured Mulrooney that if the chief went ahead with the scheme, he would use all his influence to see that Mulrooney was broken. Mulrooney had no choice but to acquiesce. The next day, a third ransom note was dropped into one of the boxes that would have been watched.

At this point, a strange character came into the act. Dr. John F. Condon, a 72-year-old schoolteacher, who was principal of a public school in the

John F. "Jafsie" Condon, the self-appointed intermediary between the family and the alleged kidnappers. (Associated Press.)

Bronx and had some eccentric extra-curricular activities. He wrote letters to the newspapers, usually the Bronx *Home News*, on some topic of current interest. The letters, which took the form of articles, poems, essays and calls-to-arms, were not signed with his name. He took his model from an earlier time and signed his pieces P. A. Triot, L. O. Nestar, L. O. Nehand or J. U. Stice.

Condon had the *Home News* print a story saying that he was offering his services as an intermediary. He offered a reward of $1,000 for information leading to the safe return of the "Little Eaglet," as the newspapers were calling the missing baby. This was certainly an impressive gesture, probably representing a larger percentage of his net worth than the Lindberghs' $50,000 reward represented of theirs. With the State of New Jersey's offer of a $25,000 reward, the total reward offered was $76,000; a fairly hefty amount for 1932.

Condon's article in the *Home News* actually brought a response. A letter with the red and blue rings and the three punched holes came to his mailbox, stating that the kidnappers would accept him as intermediary, if indeed it was the kidnappers who sent the letter. He rushed to the Lindbergh estate. Lindbergh, noting the circles and holes, promptly accepted the letter as genuine. Neither Lindbergh nor Condon knew that copies of the first letter were being retailed throughout the country at five dollars a print. In explaining his qualifications to Anne Morrow Lindbergh, Condon informed her that he had once won a $20 prize by submitting the following New Year's resolution to the *Home News*: "That I shall, to the best of my ability, and at all times, help anyone in distress."

Condon replied as the letter instructed: three words in the agony column of the *New York American*, with his new signature, formed from the pronunciation of the three initials of his name:

Money is ready. Jafsie

While this was going on, a professional lawman and consummate swindler named GASTON BULLOCK MEANS became involved. A one-time Bureau of Investigation agent and Burns detective, and an all-time rogue and confidence man, Means was called upon by Evalyn Walsh McLean, a Washington socialite, to help her solve the Lindbergh kidnapping. Where she got the idea that Means could help her is unknown, but Means told her that he, indeed, could get in touch with the kidnappers. His extensive underworld connections, he explained, would make it a snap. He went away and came back, and told her that the kidnappers had talked to him and had agreed to use him as the middleman. For proof, he offered the fact, held back from the press, that the sleeping suit that the Little Eaglet had been wearing had no flap in the back, whereas most suits of that brand had such a flap.

Mrs. McLean called a friend, Rear Admiral Emory Land, who happened to be a relative of Lindbergh. Land passed on Means's description to Lindbergh. "He's absolutely right," Lindbergh said.

Means told Mrs. McLean that the kidnappers would accept her as an intermediary. The only problem was that they had raised the price to $100,000, and they wanted it now.

This, strangely enough, tied in with what the letter writer was now saying: Since Lindbergh had called in the cops, it would now cost him double the price to get his baby back. But nobody could explain why two different groups were trying to collect the ransom. Nonetheless, Lindbergh told Land/McLean/Means to go ahead.

Mrs. McLean raised the money. Means told her that the kidnappers would turn the baby over only to a Catholic priest. She called Father Francis J. Hurney. Two messengers brought $100,000 in assorted currency to her house. Father Hurney said a prayer over Means and the money, and Means took the money away. The next morning Means added a personal request for an extra $4,000 for himself for expenses, and directed Mrs. McLean, Father Hurney and Admiral Land to go to a house Mrs. McLean owned in the Maryland countryside. The kidnappers, he assured them, would contact her there. They went, bringing a butler and maid to ensure their comfort while they waited.

At the same time as Means was delivering Mrs. McLean's money to his set of kidnappers, Jafsie was in the Woodlawn Cemetery in the Bronx having a conversation with one of his set of kidnappers. This was in response to a phone call by the man he met in the cemetery. The kidnapper told Jafsie that his name was John, that he was a Scandinavian sailor and that there were five other members of the gang: three men and two women. The Little Eaglet, John claimed, was being held on a boat.

Jafsie tried for verification. Where, he asked, had the original note been left. "In crib," John told him.

Jafsie waved two safety pins that he had taken from the baby's blanket. "What are these?"

"Safety pins."

"Where are they from?"

"The crib."

Jafsie decided that only the kidnapper could know that. Furthermore the kidnapper promised to supply the baby's sleeping suit, the one without the flap in back.

At Lindbergh's insistence, Commissioner Mulrooney was not told of this meeting. Therefore "John" was not shadowed when he left the cemetery.

Now came yet another twist in the ransom saga. Commodore John Hughes Curtis of Norfolk, Virginia, claimed to have been approached by a man named "Sam" while leaving a club in Norfolk. Sam said that he was one of the gang that had kidnapped the Lindbergh baby, and he had selected Curtis as the go-between. He was, he claimed, having a feud with the other kidnappers. He was willing to deliver the baby for only $25,000. Curtis brought in Dean H. Dobson Peacock, an Episcopal clergyman, and Rear Admiral G. H. Burrage, who had been in command of the ship that brought Lindbergh back from France. Admiral Burrage informed Lindbergh of these events.

When Jafsie heard of this new development, he grew quite perturbed. "They're frauds!" he snarled. A few days later, he received a package in the mail containing a baby's sleeping suit that Lindbergh identified as his son's. On what basis he made this identification is not known, since the garment contained no laundrymark or other means of distinguishing it from the thousands of others identical to it sold in the stores. It is hard to believe, especially considering that the baby had a mother and a nurse, that Colonel Lindbergh had an intimate knowledge of his son's sleeping garments.

Jafsie by now was growing bored with his anonymity. What was the fun in being the go-between if nobody knew about it? He put an ad in the *Home News*:

> Money is ready. No cops. No secret service. I come alone, like last time.
>
> Jafsie

He took to going around in fancy costume, one time dressing as a woman, with his pants legs rolled up and his mustache hidden behind a drawn-up collar. He tried hard to be recognized, but the newspapermen, who had spotted the Jafsie ads and were wondering who he was, somehow did not recognize him. The New York police also wanted to know who "Jafsie" was, but Lindbergh would not tell them.

In the meantime, Gaston Means had appeared at Mrs. McLean's country house—which was experiencing a burst of poltergeist phenomena—and told them that the baby was held on a boat. So they adjourned to another McLean house in Aiken, South Carolina, to await developments. After spending a week having the furniture thrown at them by invisible entities, they were delighted to leave. A man Means called "the Fox" came and examined the new house without saying a word. Means said he was one of the kidnappers. He wore gloves and wiped every doorknob that he touched with a handkerchief. But the baby did not appear, and Means moved the entourage to El Paso, Texas. The baby, Means now claimed, had been moved to Juarez, across the Mexican border.

On Friday, April 1, a portent nobody wanted to think about, Jafsie got a letter telling him to prepare to pay the ransom. The agreed-upon amount was now $70,000. The baby had now been missing for one month to the day. The ransom was packaged with $50,000 in a wooden box, carefully constructed out of several different woods for later identification, and the remaining $20,000 wrapped in brown paper. The serial numbers of all the bills had been noted, and $20,000 of it was in gold notes—gold-backed currency that was just then going out of circulation and therefore would be that much more noticeable.

The next night, a man in the Bronx hailed a taxi. He gave the driver a letter to deliver to Jafsie. It was the final ransom note, telling Jafsie to proceed immediately to a flower shop and look under a stone in front of the door. By chance, Lindbergh was with Jafsie when the taxi driver delivered the letter, and he drove the histrionic schoolteacher to the flower shop. They found the note under the stone. It directed Jafsie to nearby St. Raymond's Cemetery. There Jafsie met a man whom he thought was the same John he had met before. The man asked for the $70,000. Jafsie told him they could not raise that much; they had only $50,000. The man agreed to settle for the smaller amount. Jafsie went back to Lindbergh's car to get the box, smugly satisfied with himself at having saved Lindbergh $20,000. He gave John the money, and John gave him a note and faded away over the tombstones. Again the police had not been notified, and the man was not followed.

The note said the baby was being held on a boat called the Nelly, which was off Martha's Vineyard, a resort town on an island off Cape Cod, Massachusetts. Lindbergh flew to Martha's Vineyard and spent two days buzzing every boat in the area before he was willing to admit that they had been hoaxed.

Gaston Means, in the meantime, had been able to string Mrs. McLean only so far, but he had no way to get rid of the lady and keep the money. Mrs. McLean wanted either the Lindbergh baby or her money back. She was very firm about it. Means could produce neither. She called the cops, and Means and a co-conspirator named Norman Whittaker, an erstwhile lawyer who had assumed the role of "the Fox," went to prison.

Now, Commodore John Hughes Curtis was in the hot seat. He could not produce even one of the six kidnappers he said he had been in touch with. The New Jersey State Police felt frustrated at this, and responded the way police so often do when they are frustrated. A police captain named John J. Lamb took Commodore Curtis down to the cellar of the Lindbergh house and beat the tar out of him, demanding that Curtis produce at least one kidnapper.

The result was not expected. As Alan Hynd told it in *Murder, Mayhem and Mystery* (1958):

> After he recovered from his beating, Commodore Curtis signed a confession that Sam and the five other members of the kidnap gang were merely characters in a fiction story he had dreamed up. His purpose in becoming an author had been to sell his story to the *New York Herald-Tribune* and use the proceeds to pay off hot-breathed creditors. Somewhere along the way, however, the confession was forgotten. The commodore was taken into court and charged with obstructing justice. Specifically, he was supposed to have dealt with six persons who had stolen the Lindbergh baby and, by not letting the state police in on what he was doing, prevented the apprehension of the kidnappers. The commodore was fined one thousand dollars and sentenced to a year in jail, though the jail sentence was suspended.

Seventy-two days after the Little Eaglet vanished, William Allen, a truck driver, parked his truck on a road near the Lindbergh house and trotted into the woods to relieve himself. Before he had a chance to do so, he found the unclothed corpse of a small child lying in the underbrush. He notified the police, and the body was taken to the morgue in Trenton, about 12 miles away. Lindbergh and Betty Gow, the nurse, came to the morgue to identify the body. After examining it for less than three minutes, they agreed that it was the missing baby.

There is strong presumptive evidence that the identification was wrong and that the body was not that of the Lindbergh baby. The corpse was badly decomposed, to such a state that it was impossible to tell even the sex of the child by looking at it. The left leg was missing from the knee down, and the right foot was missing, so Lindbergh couldn't have depended on a slight physical deformity of the baby's toes for identification. Dr. Philip Van Ingen, a New York physician who was the baby's doctor, examined the corpse carefully. He had examined Charles, Jr., only a couple of weeks before the kidnapping. "If someone were to come in here and offer me ten million dollars," he told the coroner, "I simply wouldn't be able to identify these remains." Nonetheless, the body was promptly cremated at Lindbergh's request.

One of the most famous detectives of the day, a shrewd, self-taught catcher of murderers named Ellis Parker, lived in nearby Burlington County, New Jersey. In his 30 years as a detective, he had a hand in the conviction of over 100 murderers, a cumulative feat that had earned him the nickname of "the Old Fox" (not to be confused with "the Fox" who was Gaston Means' confederate). He was learned in the way of the criminal and practiced in the sort of inductive reasoning that solves crimes. Parker frequently guest lectured in criminology and psychology classes at Columbia University and the University of Pennsylvania.

Parker thought that the finding of the body was very odd. He knew that the area had been gone over before by the state police, and it was unlikely that they would have missed a body just lying there on the ground. He looked at pictures of the corpse and realized that it was overly decomposed for the length of time it was supposed to have been there. He checked the mean temperatures over the months in question and found it had indeed been too cool for the decomposition to have reached such an advanced state.

Parker compared the physical records. The missing baby had been 29 inches tall. The dead child, allowing for the missing foot, had been 33½ inches long. Parker concluded that it was not the Lindbergh baby. After some thought, he developed the theory that bootleggers, who had been seriously inconvenienced by all the police interest in stopping and examining cars and searching remote areas for the baby, had provided the authorities with the corpse they were looking for. Perhaps they had known of the deformed toes, and that is why the corpse's feet were missing.

Neither Lindbergh nor the police were interested in Parker's theories. The police went back to harassing the Lindberghs' household staff. The maid at the New Jersey house, a British woman named Violet Sharp, had originally lied about where she had been the night of the kidnapping. Apparently this was because she was out with a young man who was not her regular boyfriend. The police decided to probe deeper into this and questioned Violet severely, letting her know in the strongest possible terms that they did not believe her story. These were the same police that had beat up a suspect in the Lindbergh basement only a few weeks before, and Violet must have known about that. Violet, a neurotic, sensitive girl, committed suicide.

Congress, which had before it a bill to make kidnapping a federal offense, had been holding off passing it so as not to endanger the Little Eaglet. Now that the baby had been found dead, Congress passed what immediately became known as the Lindbergh law. This legitimized allowing J. Edgar Hoover's Bureau of Investigation to join the New Jersey State Police and the New York City Police in tramping around the Lindberghs' estate, searching for clues.

As time passed and nothing more was discovered, the police concentrated on the ransom money. Copies of the list of numbers on the bills were sent to every bank and many businesses. One bill—a $20 gold certificate—turned up in New Castle, Pennsylvania, two months after the ransom drop. Nobody saw who spent it. For a year, there were no further developments. Then, a year after the kidnapping, the United States went off the gold standard. People were required to turn in their gold-backed money by a certain date or it would no longer be honored.

Shortly before the May 1 deadline, a man entered the Federal Reserve Bank in Manhattan and plumped down $2,990 of the ransom money goldbacks for exchange. Unfortunately, the bank was so busy that nobody remembered what the man looked like. The deposit slip he filled out gave his name as J. J. Faulkner of 537 West 159th Street. Experts could not decide whether it was or was not the same as the handwriting on the ransom notes. There was no Faulkner living at 537 West 159th, and had not been in the memory of the postman, who had been delivering mail to that apartment house for 18 years.

But the Treasury Department investigators were thorough. They went through old city directories and telephone books until they came up with a Jane Faulkner who had lived at that address in 1913.

In 1921, Miss Faulkner had married a German named Gerhardt. They traced the Gerhardts and interviewed them; both denied any knowledge of the crime or the money. Gerhardt had a son and daughter by a previous marriage. The son worked in a flower shop. He had recently moved from an apartment on Decatur Avenue, one block from Jafsie's house. The daughter was married to a German landscape gardener. Handwriting samples of the various Gerhardts produced nothing but disagreement. The theory that handwriting can be definitely associated with the writer has resulted in the conviction of many suspects. Nonetheless, it is merely a theory and has never been proven.

Jafsie came at the invitation of the police to look at and listen to the three male members of the Gerhardt family. He said that the daughter's husband—the German landscape gardener—sounded a lot like Cemetery John. Then he said he was not sure. Then, he said the man did not sound anything at all like John. The harassment of the Gerhardts by the police continued until the son-in-law committed suicide. Then the police lost interest.

During the following months, as nothing more was discovered, Jafsie began suffering from rejection syndrome. He took to visiting police stations and announcing, "I am Jafsie. Let me look at your prisoners. Cemetery John may be among them." One day while he was riding a city bus he suddenly yelled, "Stop this bus! I am Jafsie. I see the Lindbergh kidnapper—there across the street!" By the time Jafsie had run across the street, the suspect had disappeared.

The FBI compiled Jafsie's various contradictory descriptions of Cemetery John, and found that they were looking for a five-foot-eight inch tall man who was six feet tall; small-framed and barrel-chested; with a square chin that came to a point; with large brown, small blue eyes; above a small-large nose.

A small number of the ransom bills began turning up in circulation in the Bronx, but they were always identified too late to trace back to their source. A five-dollar bill was used to buy a ticket to a movie at the Loew's Sheridan Square Theater in Greenwich Village (*Broadway Through a Keyhole*, a gangster film written by Walter Winchell), in November 1933. The ticket seller, Mrs. Cecilia Barr, thought the purchaser looked "furtive." She examined the bill after he left her window, thinking it might be a counterfeit, and found that it was a Lindbergh bill. By the time the police arrived, the man was nowhere to be found.

Bruno Richard Hauptmann, the alleged kidnapper, entering the courtroom. Although he was executed for the crime, the question of his guilt remains an open one. (Associated Press.)

Ten months later, two-and-a-half years after the kidnapping, a gas station attendant in the Bronx received a ransom bill from a man who bought gas at his station. He had taken the license number of the man's car because of what he described as the man's "furtive behavior."

The next day a German carpenter named Bruno Hauptmann was placed under arrest at his home in the Bronx. A search of his garage turned up almost $15,000 in ransom bills. Hauptmann, who was married and had a son who had been born around the time of the kidnapping, asserted that he had no knowledge of the crime. According to Hauptmann, the money had been turned over to him by a friend named Isadore Fisch, who asked him to hold it while he went back to Germany. He had spent some of it because Fisch owed him money. The police determined that there was an Isadore Fisch, but he had died in Germany and was thus unavailable to confirm Hauptmann's story.

Mrs. Barr, the cashier at the Loew's Sheridan Square Theater, identified Hauptmann as the man who had passed her the ransom bill a year before. The cab driver who had taken a ransom note to Jafsie's house picked Hauptmann out of a lineup, consisting of Hauptmann and two uniformed officers. Jafsie was brought in to look at Hauptmann.

"That is not the man," he told the investigators, "Cemetery John was much heavier."

The New Jersey State Police were determined to try and convict someone for the Lindbergh baby snatch. They now came up with two witnesses who placed Hauptmann near the scene of the crime at the time of the crime: Millard Whited and Amandus Hockmuth. Both had previously been questioned and denied seeing anyone. Now they suddenly changed their stories. It was never brought out at the trial—at which they both testified—that Whited had been in trouble with the police and might be buying his way out with his testimony and that Hockmuth suffered from cataracts and was legally blind.

The police had Hauptmann write a series of letters to compare them with the ransom notes. Hauptmann was later to maintain that they had dictated the letters—including misspellings—to him, and he had put down what they told him. Several handwriting experts were called to make the comparison. They split about down the middle, some convinced that he had written the notes, and some convinced that he had not. The police thanked the experts who said he had not written the notes and sent them home, keeping the ones who said he had.

Hauptmann was put on trial for kidnapping and murder in the courthouse in Flemington, New Jersey. The trial was destined to be a carnival, and Flemington made the most of it. Every bed in town and most of the pool tables were rented for the duration. The tabloid New York *Daily Mirror* supplied Hauptmann with an attorney: a flamboyant, incompetent drunk named Edward J. Reilly. Called "The Old Lion" in public, and "Death House Reilly" behind his back, Reilly had a prodigious reputation for creating a large and newsworthy fuss as his clients in capital cases were convicted and executed. He had two local lawyers as co-counsels, but he was in charge.

A wood expert employed by the New Jersey State Police testified that one of the pieces of wood in the kidnap ladder was sawed from a plank that was part of the floor in Hauptmann's attic. Nobody could suggest why Hauptmann should have done such a thing, but there it was. Jafsie's phone number was found written in pencil on a closet door in Hauptmann's house. When the state cautiously introduced evidence about the corpse in the woods, Reilly stood up, weaving slightly, and announced, "We concede that the corpse that was found was that of the Lindbergh baby." Both his co-counsels and the state's attorneys were astounded at this give-away, but there it was.

Jafsie positively identified Hauptmann as Cemetery John, despite his earlier statement that Hauptmann could not have been Cemetery John. Several other people identified Hauptmann as someone they had seen either at the cemetery or around Jafsie. The identifications were highly questionable, but Reilly did not question them. The legally blind Hockmuth testified to seeing Hauptmann around the Lindbergh house, and Reilly did not question him.

Hauptmann was convicted and sentenced to death. On April 3, 1936, four years, one month and two days after the kidnapping, Bruno Richard Hauptmann was electrocuted in the prison in Trenton, New Jersey. He went to his death protesting his innocence. It was later revealed that the penciled phone number in his closet, one of the strong points against him, had been made after his arrest by a reporter who was trying to strengthen the story he was writing.

The only thing we can be sure Hauptmann was guilty of was possession of some of the ransom money. The rest, incidentally, has never turned up. To an unbiased observer, it was never established that Hauptmann was Cemetery John; it was never established that Cemetery John was connected to the kidnapping, and not just an extortionist; and it was never established that the body in the woods was that of the Lindbergh baby.

Three months before Hauptmann's execution, the Lindberghs secretly moved to England. They had another son now, born between the kidnapping and the discovery of the body.

As for Lindbergh, who contributed so much to the failure to resolve the kidnapping, he could be considered a prisoner of his own fame. Harold Nicolson, an English writer who rented his home to the Lindberghs when they fled the United States, had this to say:

> It was almost with ferocity that he struggled to remain himself. And in the process of that arduous struggle his simplicity became muscle-bound; his virility-ideal became not merely inflexible, but actually rigid; his self-control thickened into arrogance, and his convictions hardened into granite. He became impervious to anything outside his own legend—the legend of the young lad from Minnesota whose head could not be turned.

LITTLE GREEN HOUSE

"The Little Green House" was the name given to the house in Washington, D.C., out of which operated the OHIO GANG during the Harding administration.

LOAN SHARKS

One of the linchpins of ORGANIZED CRIME, the loan sharking industry, also called the juice racket, creates as much grief and disruption as any of the more violent crimes; takes in far more money; and provides the organized crime syndicate with a handle to use in grasping for legitimate businesses.

Loan sharks advance money to customers at an interest rate usually quoted as "six for five," which amounts to 20 percent—a week. At the lowest level, the borrowers are blue- or white-collar workers who need a few dollars to make it until the next payday. At a higher level, the borrowers are businessmen who have to pay bills and are having trouble with their accounts receivable. At the highest level, top executives of large but troubled corporations borrow money for their companies in hopes that a reorganization or a new product will save them from bankruptcy.

Loan sharks have no offices and do not advertise for customers. They work out of bars or restaurants and use bartenders or others who might hear of someone's financial troubles as steerers. For larger loans, they might be referred by an insurance agent, or a bank loan officer might explain that while the bank cannot make the loan, he or she knows someone who might oblige.

The terms of interest and the surety demanded are infinitely flexible, depending on the amount involved and what the ultimate goals of the shark are in the transaction. For small amounts of money, for instance, under $10,000 or $20,000, there is usually no surety demanded. The customer's word is enough. If the customer fails to pay, an "enforcer" will be sent out. The sharks have found that the threat of physical mayhem will convince the most recalcitrant. If an occasional leg is broken, that is even more convincing. If an occasional customer is beaten to death, those remaining will be especially eager to pay.

At the higher levels, a more insidious method is used to accomplish a more devious goal. For example, a small businessman borrows $10,000 from a loan shark at a weekly rate of 10 percent. He has to repay $1,000 a week just to stay even. One week he cannot make the payment. "Okay," the shark tells him, "but I'm going to add the $1,000 to the principal of the loan, and I'm upping the interest to 12 percent." The businessman's only option is to pay off the loan, and if he could do that he would not have borrowed it. After three or four months, he has paid twice what he borrowed, and still owes twice what he borrowed. After six months, the shark owns the company.

The Illinois Crime Investigating Commission, in a report titled *Juice Racketeers: Report on Criminal Usury in the Chicago Area* (June 1970), quoted a witness as saying: "Juice customers are squeezed of their money, blood, morals, and soul. Unbearable burdens of meeting exorbitant interest rates, suffering inexorable physical reprisals when payments cannot be met, put unfortunate victims in a vise that squeezes them unmercifully. Sometimes the only escape is suicide."

LOOSE, Carl (?–1909)

A New Yorker who immigrated from Bremen, Germany, Carl Loose, a God-fearing, Bible-quoting baker, had obviously been overly impressed by the story of Lot, for he made a habit of lying with his own daughters. When his daughter Maria became pregnant, Carl convinced her boyfriend, Billy Rooney, that the child was his, and Rooney did the honorable thing. But when the birth date of the baby indicated that it was conceived before Rooney had even met Maria, he ran off.

At this point, Maria told the police about her father's habits, and Carl was brought before a judge who suggested that he be deported. Before the deportation hearings, Carl jumped up from the breakfast table one morning and, waving a pistol and screaming *"Verflucht sei jeder mann hier!"*, he began shooting his family. His daughter Meta was killed and his son Frederick wounded before the police arrived, whereupon he surrendered without protest.

Loose was sentenced to death, the judge declaring: "The gruesome annals of awful crime contain nothing more shocking than this crime of which you stand convicted." He was executed at Sing Sing.

LOTTERY SCAM

The lottery scam is the latest form of the PIGEON DROP, a classic CONFIDENCE GAME.

LOVEJOY, Elijah Parish (1802–1837)

Editor of the *Alton Observer*, an antislavery newspaper, in Alton, Illinois, Elijah Lovejoy had the temerity to say in an editorial that slavery was a sin. A mob of proslavery citizens protested this usage and affirmed the morality of their position by breaking into the newspaper office, destroying the press and murdering Lovejoy.

LUCIANO, Charles "Lucky" (1897–1962)

THE LEGENDARY HEAD OF THE NEW YORK MAFIA WHO HELPED THE U.S. WIN WORLD WAR II FROM BEHIND PRISON BARS

At the age of nine, Salvatore Lucania came to New York from Lercara Friddi, near Palermo in Sicily. The family settled in Manhattan's Lower East Side, a short walk from the Brooklyn Bridge. At the age of ten, Salvatore was arrested for shoplifting. At 16, he was caught delivering a packet of heroin for a drug dealer and was put in jail for six months. By the time he was 20, Charley "Lucky" Luciano was a rising star in the FIVE POINTS GANG, breaking ground for many of the 1930s' more important gangsters. Luciano was an equal opportunity gangster. Unlike the old-time MUSTACHE PETES who were his bosses, he saw no reason to be clannishly Sicilian in the new world. With the start of PROHIBITION, Luciano made lasting ties with the Bugs and Meyer Gang, headed by MEYER LANSKY and BUGSY SIEGEL, and their financier, ARNOLD ROTHSTEIN. Luciano and Lansky formed a friendship that lasted a lifetime and was responsible for much of what followed. It was Lansky's incisive brain and the fact that Luciano and other crime leaders trusted him that shaped the future of ORGANIZED CRIME for the next half century.

Luciano's chief, GIUSEPPE "JOE THE BOSS" MASSERIA, one of the Mustache Petes and head of one of the two most important MAFIA families in New York, did not believe in cross-ethnic associations. He did not even like to deal with gangsters with roots in other towns in Sicily. In 1928, the feud between Masseria and rival chieftain Salvatore Maranzano broke out into the CASTELLAMMARESE WAR, setting Sicilians from one town against Sicilians from another. Luciano and a few other lieutenants on both sides of the war held clandestine meetings and agreed that the feud was ridiculous and that they would all be better off if a new generation took control of the gangs. A secret arrangement was made to kill both of the current bosses and make peace.

By 1931, everything was in place for the transition. Luciano took his chief, Joe the Boss, to a restaurant in Coney Island. After the meal, they began playing a friendly game of cards. Luciano excused himself to go to the restroom, and three men walked through the front door and shot down Joe the Boss. He died with the ace of diamonds firmly clutched in his hand. For a brief moment, Maranzano thought that meant that he had won. He divided the New York area into five Mafia families and prepared to declare himself the *capo di tutti capi*, the "boss of all bosses," but this was not to be his destiny. Within a few months, the pact was honored and Maranzano was killed.

There is a Mafia legend that this marked the "Night of the Sicilian Vespers," when the younger generation of hoods all over the country knocked off the Mustache Petes. But in fact this never happened. Most of them died off or were murdered at other times for other reasons. But this did mark the ascension to power of the new generation, headed by such men as Luciano and FRANK COSTELLO in New York and AL CAPONE in Chicago. After consolidating their own positions, these Mafia leaders developed associations with Mafia and other mob bosses all over the country. A nationwide syndicate evolved, largely ethnically Jewish and Italian, headed by Lucky Luciano, Meyer Lansky, Frank Costello, DUTCH SCHULTZ, Al Capone, LOUIS "LEPKE" BUCHALTER and others. The "boss of all bosses" was replaced by a national "board of directors."

Luciano showed great organizational skills and consolidated the bootlegging in New York. The organized mobs also divided up loan sharking, prostitution, bookmaking, narcotics, labor racketeering, and even ran auto theft rings and major theft rings on the docks of New York and New Jersey. As William Balsamo and George Garpozi, Jr., describe in *Under the Clock* (1988):

> By 1935, Luciano was the most dominant Mob leader the United States had ever known. He had made Al Capone's rule over Chicago gangland look like a kindergarten. He directed his vast empire like a potentate of a legendary kingdom. His base of power was seated in New York's world-famous Waldorf Astoria Hotel, where he was registered as a year-round resident in a sumptuous suite under the name of Charles Rose.
>
> No gambling enterprise, no dock racket—whether it was protection, pilfering, or loansharking—and no Garment District extortion operation could be conducted without his sanction, not unless an ironclad agreement had been reached beforehand for his very substantial cut of the action.

Luciano's authority and power rested on three legs: (1) the continuing national combination of local gangs, orchestrated by Meyer Lansky; (2) a vast system of payoffs and accommodations with the sachems of TAMMANY HALL and other political power structures in New York, aided by Frank Costello; and (3) the naked fear and power engendered by the 1,000 Mafia soldiers at his command. And his final argument, and that of the other National Board members, was the surgical striking force known as MURDER, INCORPORATED, which did their bidding.

But political reform was in the air. New York's Governor Herbert H. Lehman appointed a special prosecutor named THOMAS A. DEWEY to clean up organized crime. With the applause and assistance of the city's mayor, a feisty Italian named Fiorello La Guardia, Dewey went after the mobs. He began showing extreme interest in the activities of Dutch Schultz, who decided to eliminate Dewey. This violated one of the prime directives of the National Board: never kill cops or reporters; it created too much heat. But Schultz insisted that he was going to take out a contract and have Dewey "hit." So Luciano and the other members of the board felt that they had no choice. On October 23, 1935, Schultz and three of his employees were gunned down in a restaurant in Newark, New Jersey.

With Dutch Schultz removed, Dewey, in an ironic twist, resolved to go after Luciano. One of Luciano's enterprises, minor but profitable to the tune of about $10,000,000 a year, was organized prostitution. Luciano's mob controlled over 200 madams and their associated brothels; most concentrated in the Harlem area. Dewey wanted to get Luciano on charges of labor racketeering, but he was unable to get the frightened businessmen to testify. So he went after Luciano for compulsory prostitution. Luciano had small respect for his stable of girls, and when they got out of line he would have them beaten into compliance. "Whores is whores," he explained to an associate. "They can always be handled. They ain't got no guts." But the ladies of the night proved to have more guts than the businessmen. Girls with monikers like Cokey Flo Brown, Sadie the Chink, Nigger Ruth and Jennie the Factory testified against him. "We can't get bishops to testify in a case involving prostitution," Dewey reminded the jury.

On June 7, 1936, Charley "Lucky" Luciano was found guilty on 62 counts of WHITE SLAVERY, and sentenced to 30 to 65 years in prison. He went to the state penitentiary in Dannemora, New York.

Luciano's control of his mob was so complete that he continued as the boss from prison. And his influence in other fields remained strong. In 1946, Dewey, now governor of New York, pardoned Luciano. The story was that it was for "wartime services to the country." Luciano supposedly saw to it that the security on the New York and New Jersey docks was kept tight. A strong possibility was that Luciano caused the conditions—theft and sabotage—that required the tightened security. Another story was that Luciano somehow aided the Allied invasion of Sicily, supposedly by telling the Sicilian Mafia to cooperate. This is doubtful.

After his release, Luciano was deported to Italy. He subsequently spent some time in Cuba, to be closer to his business interests, but returned to Italy when U.S. government agents put pressure on the Batista government. The reins of Luciano's New York empire were transferred to the incapable hands of VITO GENOVESE. Toward the end of his life, Luciano became loquacious, talking to American journalists who came to visit him in Italy. He told the story of his life to Martin Gosch, an American screenwriter, over a ten-month period before his death. Published after his death as *The Last Testament of Lucky Luciano* (1974), by Martin A. Gosch and Richard Hammer, it is a fascinating if one-sided account of the life of America's premier gangster. On the evening of January 25, 1962, Luciano died of a heart attack in the airport at Naples where he had gone to pick up Gosch.

LYNCHING

The derivation of the term *lynching* is uncertain, but authorities are sure that it is of American origin. It is said to have begun with James Lynch, a Virginia farmer who acted as an informal justice in the eighteenth century; with Charles Lynch, a Virginia justice of the peace; and with Lynche's Creek, South Carolina, where a vigilante group called the Regulators met in the 1780s to practice their form of justice. The term first appeared in print in 1817, although it was probably in use at least 20 years before this.

A southern practice, that form of mob activity known as lynch law was a powerful form of intimidation for keeping blacks in their place for almost 100 years after the end of the Civil War. Spontaneous lynchings occurred in all the southern states when black men were accused of crimes involving white women. Whether the accused was guilty was not relevant; many victims were lynched after having been found innocent in a jury trial. The KU KLUX KLAN planned many lynchings, often picking completely innocent victims, just to symbolize their power. They lynched blacks, those who sympathized with blacks and those who opposed Klan power. From 1884 to 1900, there were over 2,500 lynchings in the southern states.

On July 16, 1921, the *Washington Eagle* described the lynching of a black man named John Henry Williams in Moultrie, Georgia:

> There are many things about the Williams burning more disgraceful than have been published. A sick woman and her child, who had nothing to do with the matter, were beaten into insensibility and left to die because of hoodlumism of the mob. Colored churches were burned, colored farmers chased from their homes.
>
> Williams was brought from Moultrie on Friday night by sheriffs from fifty counties. Saturday court was called. Not a single colored person was allowed nearer than a block of the courthouse. The trial took half an hour. Then Williams, surrounded by fifty sheriffs armed with machine guns, started out of the courthouse door toward the jail.
>
> Immediately a cracker by the name of Ken Murphy gave the Confederate yell: "Whoo-whoolet's get the nigger!" Simultaneously 500 poor pecks rushed the armed sheriffs, who made no resistance whatsoever. They tore the negro's clothing off before he was placed in a waiting automobile. This was done in broad daylight. The negro was unsexed, as usual, and made to eat a portion of his anatomy which had been cut away. Another portion was sent by parcel post to Governor Dorsey, whom the people of this section hate bitterly.
>
> The negro was taken to a grove, where each one of more than 500 people, in Ku Klux ceremonial, had placed a pine knot around a stump, making a pyramid to the height of ten feet. The negro was chained to the stump and asked if he had anything to say. Castrated and in indescribable torture, the negro asked for a cigarette, lit it and blew the smoke in the face of his tormenters. The pyre was lit and a hundred men and women, old and young, grandmothers among them, joined hands and danced around the negro while he burned, and began to sing "Nearer My God to Thee."

Blacks were not the only subjects of lynchings. In 1915, in Atlanta, Georgia, a Jewish factory manager named Leo Frank was taken from prison and lynched for the rape and murder of a young girl, a crime of which he was innocent. In 1933, in San Jose, California, John Maurice Holmes and Thomas Harold Thurmond, confessed kidnappers and murderers, were broken out of jail and lynched by a mob of over 2,000 citizens. The governor of California, James "Sunny Jim" Rolfe, with a fine disrespect for law and order, sided with the kidnappers, saying: "I would like to parole all kidnappers in San Quentin and Folsom to the fine patriotic citizens of San Jose."

In the last half of the twentieth century, lynching has become uncommon, although there is still an occasional outbreak.

LYNDS, Elam (1784–1855)

The first warden of New York's SING SING prison, Lynds had a well-deserved reputation as the wickedest warden in America. Beginning his career in penology as keeper of the Auburn, New York, prison, and taking over as warden of that institution in 1821 when the old warden died, Lynds began a regime of unrelenting cruelty. He set up 80 solitary confinement cells, where prisoners were to be kept for their entire sentences. They were to keep complete silence, a rule that was enforced by the rawhide whips carried by the guards. After two years all but two of the prisoners so incarcerated had either died or become incurably insane. The prisoners not in solitary confinement were allowed to work at hard labor during the day, and at dusk, they were sent back to their individual cells. On Sundays, they did not have to work but were kept confined all the day in their cells. They moved from place to place in lockstep, their heads down, in complete silence.

When the state legislature authorized the construction of a new prison at Sing Sing, along the Hudson River, Lynds offered to build it for them free of cost with prison labor. The legislature gratefully accepted the offer.

Lynds arrived at the Sing Sing site with 100 prisoners from Auburn, dressed in a striped uniform he had devised to make them better targets if any tried to escape. He had the prison built in three years, without one escape. He also had extra stone quarried by the prisoners, which he sold to builders along the river, pocketing the profit.

Lynds used to creep along the corridors of the prison at night, hoping to catch some poor convict whispering. If he did, he would throw the cell door open and begin lashing the miscreant with his whip. Many times, a man who was talking in his sleep would be rudely awakened by the sting of Lynds's lash.

Lynds was removed from his post in 1845 when it was proven that he was taking kickbacks from the prison's victuallers and allowing them to supply food much inferior in quality to that which the state thought it was buying. It also was discovered that Lynds's record of no escapes was false; several men had escaped, but were still carried on the books so as not to spoil the record.

McCLELLAN COMMITTEE

There exists in America today what appears to be a close-knit, clandestine, criminal syndicate. This group has made fortunes in the illegal liquor traffic during prohibition, and later in narcotics, vice and gambling. These illicit profits present the syndicate with a financial problem, which they solve through investment in legitimate business. These legitimate businesses also provide convenient cover for their continued illegal activities.

—Senator John L. McClellan

The Senate Select Committee on Improper Activities in the Labor or Management Field, usually known as the McClellan Committee after its chairman, Arkansas Senator John L. McClellan, began an intensive investigation into Mob activities in the marketplace in 1957. The committee's chief counsel was Robert Kennedy, and McClellan and Kennedy declared war on gangsters. As Stephen Fox saw it in *Blood and Power* (1989):

> Confronting witnesses, seated elbow to elbow in close quarters, McClellan and Kennedy made a peculiar team. The older man, twenty-nine years Kennedy's senior, resembled a large mastiff, slow and deliberate, measured and dignified. In rough going he often took over the interrogation. A scowl line between his eyes deepened, his face darkened into an expression of incredulous exasperation, as he leaned forward and tapped the table in cadence with his deep, rumbling drawl. Beside him, the younger and smaller Kennedy, sarcastic and needling, an excitable terrier occasionally brought to heels by his boss, yapped at the witnesses in his flat, nasal Boston Irish voice. As the investigations unfolded it became essentially a joint undertaking of these two oddly matched allies.

The McClellan Committee was concerned with the penetration of unions by ORGANIZED CRIME. It investigated former Teamsters President Dave Beck and explored his illegal expropriation of union funds. It looked into the current Teamsters president, JIMMY HOFFA, and his relations with the MAFIA. It investigated other unions infiltrated by gangsters, such as the Hotel and Restaurant Employees, the Longshoremen and the Operating Engineers, but it concentrated on the Teamsters. The hearings became a parade of union officials and gang bosses taking refuge under the FIFTH AMENDMENT.

McClellan, a Southern WASP conservative, seemed particularly bothered that so many of the gangsters were not WASPs. "We should rid the country of characters who come here from other lands and take advantage of the great freedom and opportunity our country affords, who come here to exploit these advantages with criminal activities," he said. "They do not belong to our land, and they ought to be sent somewhere else. In my book, they are human parasites on society, and they violate every law of decency and humanity."

The committee looked into the recent APALACHIN CONFERENCE of gang bosses, when over 60 of the top mobsters in the country gathered at the home of Joseph Barbara at Apalachin, New York. They concluded that there probably was such a thing as organized crime. Martin F. Pera, a U.S. Bureau of Narcotics special agent, told the committee about the drug connection:

> The smuggling of heroin into the United States has taken place through different routes during different years, but generally, predominantly, most of the heroin smuggled, let's say, within the last 10 years, has taken place in the following manner:
>
> The opium was produced . . . in the Near East, in Turkey and Iran, and perhaps in Yugoslavia, and is processed into morphine base. . . .
>
> From Beirut, Lebanon, or perhaps Aleppo, Syria, this morphine base is shipped to clandestine laboratories in France for conversion into heroin . . . They are operated by Corsican traffickers, and we might point out there that the Corsican underworld element are cousins to the Sicilians. They call each other cousins. They speak Italian. Many of them immigrated originally to Corsica from the Italian islands. . . .
>
> The laboratories in France are operated by Corsican violators who, in turn, arrange for the smuggling of these drugs, of heroin, into the United States, via French seamen smugglers, couriers, as it were, or else in some instances the heroin is sent back to the traffickers in Sicily or in Italy, and it is brought over here by means of concealment in trunks or the personal effects of immigrants.

Pera emphasized the close family ties between the different elements in the drug trafficking and the nationwide import of their activities. An extremely ethnocentric presentation, it had a strong influence on the committee. Since then, it has become clear that one does not have to be Sicilian or Corsican to deal dope.

For Kennedy, these hearings were the start of what seemed to some a vindictive campaign to get Hoffa, an attack that continued when he became attorney general under his brother President John F. Kennedy. But it must have been easy to feel strongly about Hoffa, when one saw how he was illegally helping himself to the retirement funds of thousands of Teamsters.

In closing the committee's hearings, McClellan declared:

> The testimony we have heard can leave no doubt that there has been a concerted effort by members of the American criminal syndicate to achieve legitimacy through association and control of labor unions and business firms. The extent of this infiltration poses a serious threat to the very economy of our country.
>
> The criminal syndicate which we have identified here as the Mafia has revealed an arrogant challenge to the Government and to the decent people of this country. The contempt with which the leaders of the underworld, as they have displayed it here in the witness stand, regard both their Government and the citizens of this country has been demonstrated repeatedly during this past week by their refusal to cooperate, even in the slightest degree, with this committee, which has a mandate to carry out an important function of this Government.

McCLOSKEY, James (1943–)

The founder of Centurion Ministries, Inc., James McCloskey works to save prisoners who are able to convince him that they have been falsely convicted of murder or rape. In 1979, dissatisfied with his life as a Philadelphia businessman, McCloskey entered the Princeton Theological Seminary. In his second year, he worked as a student chaplain at Trenton State Prison, where he became convinced that one of the inmates might be innocent. The man, a drug addict named George "Chiefie" De Los Santos, had been convicted of murdering a used car salesman in Newark, New Jersey. After reading the trial transcript, McCloskey worked for two-and-a-half years to establish that the chief witness against De Los Santos had perjured himself. The experience convinced him that his calling lay in this work, and he founded the nonprofit Centurion Ministries.

Financed by donations (which average under $150,000 a year), and taking cases only when they are convinced of the innocence of the petitioner, McCloskey and his two full-time assistants have had an impressive rate of success. Aided by two other licensed investigators, who are called in on a case-by-case basis, their post-trial researches have succeeded in having over a dozen people released from prison or saved from execution. Clarence Brandley, a black man accused and convicted of raping and murdering a 16-year-old girl in the Conroe, Texas, high school where he worked as a janitor, was saved scant days before his scheduled execution when McCloskey talked to another janitor who confessed, with tears in his eyes, that he had watched silently as two white janitors kidnapped the girl, and then had been afraid to come forward.

The Ministries took on the case of Clarence Chance and Benny Powell, convicted of the 1973 murder of a Los Angeles County deputy sheriff, 17 years after the pair went to prison. McCloskey and his associates located three women who had testified that Powell and Chance had bragged to them of the killing. All three recanted, claiming that the police detectives had pressured them into the statements. Although the detectives denied wrongdoing, this was enough for the district attorney's office to reopen the investigation. They found that the testimony of one of the major witnesses, a jailhouse informant named Larry Wilson, was so corrupt that it should have been excluded. On March 25, 1992, Judge Florence-Marie Cooper of the Los Angeles County Superior Court, calling the conduct of the police officers "reprehensible," ordered Powell and Chance released. She told them: "On behalf of the people of the State of California and the criminal justice system in particular, I offer to each of you gentlemen sincere apologies for the gross injustices perpetrated in these cases."

McCloskey has not won every challenge that he has taken on. Jimmy Wingo was sentenced to death in Louisiana in 1982, after a one-day murder trial. McCloskey secured the videotaped statement of a woman who had been a key witness at the trial, in which she claimed that she had lied on the stand because a deputy sheriff threatened to take away her children if she did not. He handed the tape to one of the governor's aides, who promised to look at it and take it up with the governor. But the aide never called McCloskey back and Wingo was executed.

McCloskey also failed in the Virginia case of Roger Coleman, who was convicted of raping and murdering his sister-in-law. The case received national attention, but despite strong doubts as to his guilt and new evidence developed by McCloskey, it ended with Coleman's execution in May 1992.

McCloskey's experiences have colored his view of American justice. As an article by Trip Gabriel in the *New York Times* magazine put it: "After a decade of probing the excesses of the criminal-justice system, McCloskey has a dark opinion of justice in America. He has learned that the police can and do coerce witnesses to commit perjury. That prosecutors can and do suborn the self-serving lies of jailhouse informants. And that defendants on the margins of society may receive sloppy and uncaring defense lawyering. McCloskey estimates that 10 percent of all defendants brought to trial for violent crimes—rape, murder, assault—are wrongfully convicted."

Even if McCloskey's estimate is off by half, it should give pause to rabid advocates of the death penalty.

McKINLEY, William (1843–1901)

Twenty-fifth president of the United States, William McKinley was assassinated by self-described anarchist LEON CZOLGOSZ on September 6, 1901, at the Pan-American Exposition in Buffalo, New York.

McPHERSON, Aimee Semple (1890–1944)

THE CHARISMATIC EVANGELICAL PREACHER WHO WAS ALL TOO HUMAN

Aimee Semple MacPherson, "the world's most pulchritudinist evangelist," whose 1926 disappearance made national headlines. (International News Photo.)

"The World's Most Pulchritudinous Evangelist," as she called herself, Sister Aimee Semple McPherson grew up on a farm near Ingersoll, Ontario, Canada. When she was 17, she married a Pentecostal boilermaker named Robert Semple, who then decided that his true calling was to be a missionary, so he took his young wife to China, where she had a little girl and he died. She and her daughter returned to the United States, where she married a New England grocer named Harold McPherson with whom she had a son. While Harold kept up the grocery business, Aimee took up evangelism and began tent preaching in various cities around the country. It soon became evident that an evangelical calling and marriage to a grocer did not mix very well. Harold filed a divorce action against Aimee for desertion. "I do not wish to come in contact with her in any way shape or form," he said in 1926. Aimee went into preaching full time.

After following the preaching circuit for a while, Aimee decided to settle in Los Angeles and build a congregation. Los Angeles at the time was a city "where the conditions of climate and the mental sea-level of the majority of inhabitants have combined to create a veritable Canaan for the religio-commercial *entrepreneur*," as David Warren Ryder wrote in *The Nation*.

Aimee prospered over the next decade. She founded the International Institute of Four-Square Evangelism and, by 1926, had built for it the $1.5 million Angelus Temple which could, and often did, hold 5,000 fervent believers. According to a description in *The New Republic*, "Every Sunday morning, in a city where each family, rich or poor, has at least one automobile, the streets around the Temple present a problem to the police like a Yale-Harvard football game. Thousands of cars packed like dominoes in a box. Tens of thousands of eager, would-be communicants, only a fraction of whom will ever squeeze their way in to see the far-away, tiny figure in white beside the altar and the microphone, buoyant, eager, on tiptoe, shouting her message, the message which is so exactly, to a hair's breadth, what you would expect."

Sister Aimee opened a radio station at the temple, so that the increasing masses of faithful could at least hear her preach, but the experience was not the same. To see the small, sensual figure bathed in colored lights as she moved about the stage in her long, white silk gowns, her long blond hair adorned with flowers, while listening to her exhort you to come to the Lord, was enough to induce a religious frenzy in the massed congregation. Hundreds of people swooned at every service. Because she found the sounds of coins dropping into the collection boxes embarrassing, she rigged up clotheslines in the temple. The faithful would pin their offering onto the clothesline, and Sister Aimee would reel in the money.

In May 1926, Sister Aimee went to a beach near Venice, California, with her secretary, Miss Shafer. She went for a swim, while Miss Shafer went into a nearby hotel to use the telephone. When Miss Shafer returned to the water, the evangelist had disappeared. She was not in the water, she was not on the beach and no one had seen her leave. Sister Aimee was known to be a good swimmer, and the water was calm, so the mystery was complete. A fainting spell, or a sudden case of cramps, was the best that the beach police could come up with, and it seemed hardly adequate.

By late that night, with no word of her, the temple staff were giving up hope. Aimee's mother, Mrs. Kennedy, announced, "We know she is with Jesus. Pray for her." A $25,000 reward was posted, but no one had any hope that it would be claimed. As Carey McWilliams described in "Sunlight On My Soul," a chapter in the book *The Aspirin Age* (1949):

> During the succeeding thirty-two days armies of the faithful kept a night and day vigil at the Temple and at the beach, where they built bonfires, wept, prayed, moaned, and sang hymns. Patrols were sent up and down the beach; airplanes swept low over the waters; and deep-sea divers prowled the ocean floor, looking for the body of a marathon swimmer in a green bathing suit. A girl committed suicide. One of the deep-sea prowlers died of exposure. On May 20 an ecstatic follower, glimpsing an image of Aimee on the bright, shimmering waters of the Pacific, was forcefully restrained from plunging into the waves. On May 23 one Robert Browning, twenty-six, leaped into the sea crying, "I'm going after her," and was drowned.

And then, on June 23, a frightened and exhausted Mrs. McPherson appeared on the outskirts of Douglas, Arizona, with quite a story to tell. She had, she claimed, been abducted, held against her will and tortured by three kidnappers, two men and a woman, named "Jake," "Steve" and "Rose." But, never abandoning her faith in the Lord, she had managed to break free and struggle across the desert to freedom. After a brief stay in a hospital in Douglas, she returned to Los Angeles to a heroine's reception. A hundred thousand people gathered in the streets to welcome her back.

It soon became clear that her story was untenable. She could not have crossed the desert in the heat of the day without suffering some effects of dehydration. It was noted that Kenneth G. Ormiston, the man who operated the temple radio station, had disappeared at about the same time as Sister Aimee. Reporters followed the lead and traced the couple to the Andrews Hotel in San Luis Obispo, as "Mr. and Mrs. Frank Gibson," on May 29. Although the faithful continued to believe, Aimee rapidly became a laughingstock around the rest of the country. Newspaper columnists wrote funny stories; radio comedians told funny jokes.

It would have died down soon, after all there was no proof, she had committed no crime and if

McPherson burying one of her flock. (International News Photo.)

one wanted to believe that Sister Aimee had been kidnapped, one were perfectly free to do so. But Aimee insisted that the authorities find and punish the kidnappers. So a grand jury looked into her story. They found that Mrs. McPherson and Mr. Ormiston had stayed as man and wife in a cottage in Carmel. They had registered as Mr. and Mrs. McIntyre, but four witnesses positively identified Aimee as being the woman. On September 17 a criminal complaint was filed, charging Aimee and others with conspiring to obstruct justice.

During this time, Ormiston stayed hidden, whether to shield Aimee or merely to protect himself is not known. As the trial progressed, more and more damning evidence was brought out. Although Aimee, claiming "I am like a lamb led to the slaughter" and still sticking to her "kidnapping" story, managed a few bombshells of her own: for example, she had overheard her kidnappers plotting to abduct Mary Pickford. On December 17, Ormiston was found in Harrisburg, Pennsylvania, and the results seemed certain. And then, on January 4, 1927, District Attorney Asa Keyes moved to dismiss the case. The rumor went around that he had been offered a $30,000 payoff to drop the case, but there was no proof. Some credence was added to the story a few years later when he was convicted of corruption in office.

The temple did not fold, although it seemed for a while that it might, and Aimee continued to preach, although the fire was not as hot as it once was. Throughout the Depression, the temple fed the homeless, and those who heard Aimee preach said it was still quite a stirring experience. On September 26, 1944, Sister Aimee gave a sermon to a crowd of 10,000 in the municipal auditorium in Oakland, California. It was to be the start of a new crusade. The next morning she was found unconscious on the floor of her room at the Hotel Leamington, and she died that day. Carey McWilliams said of her:

> A woman who could arouse such love and devotion and blind loyalty in the hearts of thousands of little people possessed qualities that perhaps justified certification to God's Hall of Fame. She believed, with all her heart, in goodness and kindness, and before this fact all else was meaningless. . . . It is not surprising, therefore, that Los Angeles has already begun to miss Sister Aimee and to wish that she were back at the Temple, chasing the Devil around with a pitchfork, calling the lonely to love in her unforgettable voice.

MAD BOMBER

See: GEORGE METESKY

MAFIA

The name Mafia comes from a Sicilian secret brotherhood that took root in the United States, mainly in East Coast cities, in the 1890s. For the first quarter of the twentieth century, it was often known as *L'Unione Siciliano*. Gradually, it has become a loose confederation of "crime families," the members of which are largely, but not exclusively, Sicilian in origin, and which substantially control the major criminal activities and many noncriminal activities which they have criminalized, in many different areas of the country. To the classic pursuits of protection; LOAN SHARKING; GAMBLING; prostitution; extortion; KIDNAPPING; bootlegging; murder; auto theft; and simple burglary, robbery, and assault, these career criminals have also added control of labor unions, produce vendors, contractors, breweries, distilleries, movie studios, as well as politicians, judges and whole police forces.

For a long time, law enforcement authorities and academics in the field of social science refused to publicly admit the existence of a Mafia in the United States. Although the Federal Bureau of Narcotics, under the direction of Harry Anslinger, insisted that their investigations into the drug trade had shown the existence of such an organization, J. EDGAR HOOVER publicly stated that there was no such thing as a Mafia, and his FEDERAL BUREAU OF INVESTIGATION, preoccupied by its witch hunt for Communists, did not investigate ORGANIZED CRIME until prodded by Attorney General Robert Kennedy in the early 1960s.

In 1959, Daniel Bell wrote in *The End of Ideology* that "the legend of the Mafia has been fostered in recent years largely by the peephole writing team of Jack Lait and Lee Mortimer. In their *Chicago Confidential*, they rattled off a series of names and titles that made the organization sound like a rival to an Amos and Andy Kingfish society. Few serious reporters, however, give it much credence. Burton Turkus, the Brooklyn prosecutor who broke up the 'Murder, Inc.' ring denies the existence of the Mafia. Nor could Senator Kefauver even make out much of a case for his picture of a national crime syndicate."

As late as 1976, Professor Dwight C. Smith, Jr., of the State University of New York at Albany wrote an article for the *Annals of the American Academy of Political and Social Sciences* called "Mafia: The Prototypical Alien Conspiracy," in which he stated his belief that the United States needs a new conspiracy to believe in every few years, and that the Mafia was a creation of the Federal Bureau of Narcotics, which required a boogie man to scare increasingly larger appropriations out of Congress for its war on DRUGS.

The United States is indeed conspiracy crazy and has been for much of this century, but nonetheless, there is a Mafia. Since World War II, it has been pushed more into the open, its membership and its practices have become subjects for public discussion, but it still thrives. The name "Mafia" has become synonymous with "criminal organization," so that one sees references to, for example, a "Black Mafia," a "Chinese Mafia," a "Jewish Mafia," a "RUSSIAN MAFIA" or a "Mexican Mafia," which describe indigenous groups that have nothing to do with the quondam Sicilian organization.

The Mafia in the United States has been called a number of things at various times and in different areas. Aside from *L'Unione Siciliano*, it has also been known as the Arm, the Clique, the Combination, the Combine, the Organization, the Outfit, the Syndicate, the Tradition and among formalists, the Honored Society. At the turn of the twentieth century, it was known as the BLACK HAND, but that was always just a cover name for extortion, blackmail and murder. In 1963, while appearing before the MCCLELLAN COMMITTEE, convicted gangster JOSEPH VALACHI revealed that Mafia members referred in private to their organization as *la Cosa Nostra* (Italian for "this thing of ours"). This name is now used in the press and elsewhere as frequently as Mafia.

HISTORY

Sicily

Sometime after the fifteenth century, an organization known as the Mafia was born in Sicily. Its chroniclers disagree as to when or how it came into being, and even as to what the name means and where it came from, but there is general agreement as to why. Legend has it that originally, and for most of its existence, the Mafia was a secret organization of "men of honor," formed by the local peasants and small landholders to combat the organized terrorism imposed upon them by their absent masters. The Sicilian peasants suffered through several thousand years of absentee landlords, who were interested in Sicily only for what its land could produce through the labor of its serfs.

One story suggests that the Mafia came into existence to resist the powers of the Holy Office of the Inquisition, whose predominately Spanish officers were using the authority of the Church to condemn anyone whose property, or whose wife or daughter, they coveted. As Sicily was an occupied land, its natives had no influence in the courts of the Church or the nobles. There was no protection, no evasion and no appeal from the predations of the inquisitors.

Another story suggests that it was the Bourbon princes who provoked the response. *Mafia*, in this version, stands for *Morte alla Francia Italia anela* (Death to France is Italy's cry). This is certainly apocryphal, if for no other reason than that no Sicilian would have referred thus to Italy. The word *Mafia* is much more likely a Sicilian derivation by way of the Arabic (the Moors also held Sicily for a while) that means "courage, strength and endurance." In his article "Mafia," in *Encyclopedia of the Social Sciences* (1952), Gaetano Mosca defines it thus:

> Mafia describes the attitude which assumes that recourse to legal authority in cases of persecution by private enemies is a symptom of weakness, almost of cowardice. It is an exaggeration of the sentiment, more or less common in Latin countries, that appeal to law against offenses involving personal insult, for instance, adultery, is unmanly and that the duel is the proper means of recovering lost honor. Sicilian circles affected by mafist psychology held that many offenses must be avenged by personal action or by that of relatives and friends. Common theft, for example, was considered a sign of lack of respect indicating that the thief did not fear vengeance.

In any case the "Men of Honor" and the vendetta were the only protection the Sicilian peasants had from their masters. But the protectors soon turned into the oppressors. The Mafia, spread all over western Sicily, divided into small groups called *cosche* (singular *cosca*; Sicilian dialect for "tuft"). Their principal occupations were cattle rustling, extortion and kidnapping for ransom. Eventually, as their presence evoked fear (which they called "respect"), they no longer had to commit the crimes very often; the local small farmers and peasants just paid them in various ways not to extort, rustle or kidnap. In America, this time-honored Mafia device would become known as the protection racket.

Gay Talese put a happy face on this relationship in *Honor Thy Father* (1971):

> They believed that there was no equality under the law; the law was written by the conquerors. In the tumultuous history of Sicily, going back more than two thousand years, the island had been governed by Greek law, Roman law, Arab law, the laws of Goths, Normans, Angevins, Aragonese—each new fleet of conquerors brought new laws to the land, and no matter whose law it was, it seemed that it favored the rich over the poor, the powerful over the weak. . . .
>
> Under such an unenlightened leadership, feudalism was permitted to exist until the nineteenth century, and illiteracy prevailed in much of Sicily through the midtwentieth century, particularly in the barren mountain villages of the western region. Here in an atmosphere of neglect and isolation, families became more insular, more suspicious of strangers, held to old habits. The official government was often the enemy, the outlaw often a hero, and family clans such as the Bonannos, the Magaddinos, and numbers of other large families in neighboring seaside villages or interior towns were held in awe by their townsmen. Though certain of these leaders were vengeful and corrupt, they identified with the plight of the poor and often shared what they had stolen from the rich. Their word was nearly always good, and they did not betray a trust. Usually they went about their business quietly, walked arm in arm with the village priest through the square, or sat in the shade of cafés while lesser men stopped to greet them and perhaps seek a favor. While they bore the humble manner of other men in the town, there was nevertheless an easy confidence about them, a certain strength of character. They were more ambitious, shrewder, bolder, perhaps more cynical about life than their resigned *paesani*, who relied largely upon God. They were often spoken of in hushed tones by other men but were never called mafiosi. They were usually referred to as the *amici*, friends, or *uomini rispettati*, men of respect.

The United States

Italians began coming to America in meaningful numbers in the 1880s, settling largely in the major cities. They brought with them, like the other immigrant groups, the poverty, ignorance, fears, customs and criminals of their homeland. The rich and well educated seldom emigrated. The criminal classes found the new land rich in exploitive opportunities. They began by exploiting their fellow immigrants. Black Hand extortion gangs preyed on the Italian shopkeepers, pushcart peddlers and craftsmen.

The old-time Sicilian Mafia bosses—called "MUSTACHE PETES" by their "young Turk" lieutenants—were xenophobic and set in their ways. They did not want to deal with anyone who was not from their own home town back in Sicily, and they did not want to experiment with any of the cornucopia of new crimes possible in this new world.

While building a case for counterfeiting against some New York City Mafiosi in 1909, the SECRET SERVICE discovered a notebook belonging to Giuseppe Palermo which contained, in Italian, the following rules, as translated and condensed in Walter S. Bowen and Harry Edward Neal's book *The United States Secret Service* (1960):

> **1.** Whoever reveals to a non-member any operations of his companions, or offends or quarrels with a fellow-member, or refuses to comply with

an order, or who leaves town for more than one day without notice, shall be fined $20 and cannot "come to his place." But the companions who judge him must be all of one accord, pro or con. . . .

2. He who swears falsely . . . who draws a weapon without his companion draws another of the same dimension, always with the point uncovered, if it is a knife, or who fights a duel with a companion of the Society without the permission of the Society, shall be undressed (summarily deprived of his rights).

3. The companion who knows of the fault of another and does not inform the Society at large is liable to the same penalty.

4. He that does not attend at the precise hour of the meeting of the blackmailers of the day, to do his duty without any orders, shall be punished. If he explains his lateness in a manner satisfactory to the Society he will be pardoned and may take his place. Otherwise he may not participate at the next division.

5. A recruit who produces gain to the Society is entitled to one-fifth of it as his own share.

6. The Society cannot act without the consent of all the companions. Even the opposition of one mouth is enough to overrule the opinions of all the others, always provided the person objecting gives a reasonable explanation of his views.

7. No companion who becomes a member of the Society may in any way alter its rules.

8. Every meeting of the Society must be announced to those on duty on the day of the meeting at least 24 hours before it takes place, except in case of emergency.

9. The date and place of meetings is absolutely in the hands of the head of the Society, and none may oppose him.

If these were, indeed, the rules of the Mafia at that time, then it was a much more democratic organization than it was to become.

In New York in 1928, a feud that became known as the CASTELLAMMARESE WAR broke out between the gangs of two Mustache Petes: "JOE THE BOSS" MASSERIA and Salvatore Maranzano. Young Turks, men like CHARLES "LUCKY" LUCIANO, FRANK COSTELLO and VITO GENOVESE, thought the war was stupid; there was enough loot for everyone, and it was smarter to work together. The old bosses could not be convinced, so they were eliminated. First, Masseria was killed and then Maranzano. Luciano, the "first among equals," formed a coalition with the Bugs and Meyer mob of BUGSY SIEGEL and MEYER LANSKY, as well as reaching out to AL CAPONE in Chicago and to other mob bosses around the country. A national crime syndicate was formed, and a board of directors appointed, including Lansky, Luciano, Capone, DUTCH SCHULTZ and others. The size of the board is usually given as nine.

With the start of PROHIBITION and the sudden existence of a product that everybody wanted but that could only be obtained illegally, the mobs consolidated. This action gave the Mafia the money and power to move into legitimate businesses and to corrupt policemen, judges and other public officials sufficiently to ensure, not only their safety, but their virtual control of the processes of government in some cities. Everyone in the mobs who did not get killed or go to prison got rich. Even many of those who went to prison got rich first.

By the end of Prohibition, the Mafia was into every sort of crime that could be organized, and many that could not. They controlled gambling, prostitution, loan sharking, labor racketeering and were heavily into legitimate businesses in the construction industry, hauling, produce, show business and the restaurant business.

For a long time, law enforcement authorities, including J. Edgar Hoover, refused to admit the existence of the Mafia or of any national crime organization, calling it an urban myth. But with the revelations of ABE "KID TWIST" RELES and Joe Valachi, among others, the doubters have been silenced.

In *The Valachi Papers* (1968) by Peter Maas, Joe Valachi, the man who confirmed the existence of the Mafia in the United States for the McClellan Committee, described his initiation into that organization in 1930, at the start of what became known as the Castellammarese War:

> I'd say about forty guys were sitting at the table, and everybody got up when I came in. . . .
>
> I was led to the other end of the table past them, and the other guy with me said, "Joe, meet Don Salvatore Maranzano. He is going to be the boss for all of us throughout the whole trouble we are having."
>
> Now Mr. Maranzano said to everybody around the table, "This is Joe Cago," which I must explain to you is what most of the guys know me by. Then he tells me to sit down in an empty chair on his right. When I sit down, so does the whole table. Someone put a gun and a knife on the table in front of me. I remember the gun was a .38, and the knife was what you would call a dagger. After that, Maranzano motions us up again, and we all hold hands and he says some words in Italian. Then we sit down, and he turns to me, still in Italian, and talks about the gun and the knife. "This represents that you live by the gun and the knife," he says, "and you die by the gun and the knife." Next he asks me, "Which finger do you shoot with?"
>
> I said, "This one," and I hold up my right forefinger.
>
> I was still wondering what he meant by this when he told me to make a cup out of my hands. Then he put a piece of paper in them and lit it with a match and told me to say after him, as I was moving the paper back and forth, "This is the way I will burn if I betray the secret of this Cosa Nostra." All of this was in Italian. In English Cosa Nostra would mean "this thing of ours." It comes before everything—our blood family, our religion, our country.
>
> After that Mr. Maranzano says, "This being a time of war, I am going to make it short. Here are the two most important things you have to remember. Drill them into your head. The first is that to betray the secret of Cosa Nostra means death without trial. Second, to violate any member's wife means death without trial. . . ."
>
> Mr. Maranzano then says, "Everybody up. Throw a finger from zero to five." So all the guys around the table threw out their right hand at the same time. [They add up the fingers and count around the table to that number. It comes out to Joe Bananas.] When Mr. Maranzano saw where the number fell, he started to laugh and said to me, "Well Joe, that's your *gombah*"—meaning he was kind of my godfather and was responsible for me.
>
> So Joe Bananas laughs too, and comes to me and says, "Give me that finger you shoot with." I hand him the finger, and he pricks the end of it with a pin and squeezes until the blood comes out.
>
> When that happens, Mr. Maranzano says, "This blood means that we are now one Family."

The FBI's current list of Cosa Nostra families in the United States includes:

In New York:
The Bonanno family
The Columbo family
The Gambino family
The Genovese family
The Luchese family
and in Newark the DeCavalcante family
Also there are alleged to be Mafia families or organizations in:
New England (Boston, Massachusetts / Providence Rhode Island)
Rochester, New York
Buffalo, New York
Philadelphia, Pennsylvania
Pittston, Pennsylvania
Pittsburgh, Pennsylvania
Cleveland, Ohio
Detroit, Michigan
Milwaukee, Wisconsin
Chicago, Illinois
St. Louis, Missouri
Kansas City, Missouri

Tampa, Florida
New Orleans, Louisiana
San Jose, California
San Francisco, California

MOB MONAKER LIST

Many practitioners of organized crime and their associates were known by MONAKERS, which artfully disguised their legal names. Some of the more well known and interesting are listed below:

MONAKER	*REAL NAME*
Abbadabba	Otto Berman
Little Angy	Angelo Tuminaro
Little Augie	Jacob Orgen
The Baker	Joe Liberito
Joe the Baker	Joseph Catania
Joe Bananas	Joseph Bonanno
Joe Bandy	Joseph Biondo
The Bathhouse	John Coughlin
Joe Batters	Tony Accardo
Joe Beck	Joseph Dipalermo
Tony Bender	Anthony Strollo
Jimmy Blue Eyes	Vincent Alo
Bottles	Ralph Capone
The Bug	Charlie Workman
The Camel	Murray Humphries
Don Cheech	Frank Scalice
Cherry Nose	Charles Gioe
The Chin	Vincent Gigante
The Dasher	Frank Abbandando
Dimples	Moey Wolinsky
Johnny Dio	John Dioguardi
Bobby Doyle	Girolamo Santucci
Tony Ducks	Antonio Corallo
Dynamite	Joe Brooks
Big Ed	Edward (Eddie) Vogel
The Enforcer	Frank Nitti
Gameboy	Samuel Miller
The Goat	Thomas Duffy
Golf Bag	Sam Hunt
Greasy Thumb	Jake Guzik
Big Greeny	Harry Greenberg
Jake Gurrah	Jacob Shapiro
The Gyp	Angelo DeCarlo
Hop Toad	Joseph Giunta
Kid Twist	Abe Reles
Legs	Jack Diamond
Lepke	Louis Buchalter
Little Big Man	Carlos Marcello
Little New York	Louis Campagna
Charlie Lucky	Charles Luciano
Mad Dog	Vincent Coll
Trigger Mike	Michael Coppola
Mitters	John Foley
Tony Mops	Anthony Volpe
Mossy	Maurice Enright
Mr. Neil	Aniello Dellacroce
Peppy	Joseph Genero
Pittsburgh Phil	Harry Strauss
Mike the Pike	Michael Heitler
Little Augie Pisano	Anthony Carfano
Puggy	Irving Feinstein
Izzy the Rat	Isadore Buchalsky
Johnny Roberts	John Robilotto
Tommy Ryan	Thomas Eboli
Dom the Sailor	Dominick DeQuatro
Scarface	Alphonse Capone
The Schemer	Vincent Drucci
Dutch Schultz	Arthur Flegenheimer
Screwy	Claude Maddox
The Scourge	Orassio Tropio
The Shadow	Ferdinand Boccia
The Snake	Carmine Persico
Socks	Joseph Lanza
Joe Stretch	Joseph Straci
The Thief	Nick Capuzzi
Three-Finger Brown	Thomas Lucchese
Three-Fingered Jack	William White
Tough Tony	Anthony Capezio
Two-Gun	Louis Alterie
The Waiter	Paul Ricca
The Wolf	Joseph Lupo
Frank Yale	Frank Uale
Zarumba	Louis Rothkopf

Following are a few terms that are heard frequently in discussions about the Mafia:

Button Men—Low-ranking members of a crime family; soldiers
Caporegima—A middle-ranking member of a Mafia crime family; a lieutenant over Mafia soldiers
The Commission—The national council created to prevent the Mafia families from fighting each other
Connected—Not a member of a Mafia family, but having a business or friendship relationship with one
Consigliere—Italian word for "counselor"; the advisor to the boss of a crime family
Cosa Nostra—Literally "our thing"; the Mafia's own term for itself revealed by Joseph Valachi to the McClellan Committee in 1963
A Friend of Our Friends—*see* Connected
Made his bones—*see* A Made Man
A Made Man—Someone who had completed the necessary requirements for being accepted as a full-fledged member of a Mafia family. Usually involves committing at least one murder
Mattresses—A Mafia family is said to go "to the mattresses" when it becomes involved in a war with another family. This is from the mattresses that are laid on the floor of rooms in safe houses so that the participants can have a safe place to sleep
Mustache Petes—The first-generation Sicilians who brought the Mafia over with them when they emigrated; the original American Mafia
Omerta—The fabled "code of silence" that prevents Mafia members from talking about the organization
The Organization—The New York Mafia's name for itself
The Outfit—The Chicago Mafia's name for itself (*see also* the Syndicate)
Soldiers—Rank-and-file members of a Mafia crime family
The Syndicate—The Chicago Mafia's name for itself (*see also* the Outfit)

Although there still is a Mafia in the traditional sense, made up of crime families of largely Sicilian origin, organized crime today is a multiethnic, multi-racial phenomenon. There are black gangs, Puerto Rican gangs, Mexican gangs, Chinese gangs, Korean gangs and gangs affiliated by a common interest in something—like motorcycles. Between them all they bleed tens of billion dollars out of the American economy every year. It is a vast hidden tax that we all pay in higher prices, higher insurance rates, higher taxes to pay for police protection and a pervasive fear of our own streets.

MAGADDINO, Stefano (1891–)

With his brother Antonino, Stefano Magaddino, who was born in Castellammare, Sicily, was head of the Buffalo, New York, Mafia crime family in the 1960s. He was one of those present at the unfortunate meeting of top crime family bosses at Apalachin, New York, in 1957. *See also:* APALACHIN CONFERENCE

MANN ACT

Properly named the White Slave Traffic Act, this law sponsored in 1910 by Congressman James Robert Mann of Illinois was intended to put a halt to what was known as the white slave traffic. Under the Constitutional clause giving the federal government the authority to regulate interstate commerce, it forbade the transport of women across state lines for immoral purposes. Farm girls, it was widely believed, were being lured into the cities, where they were ravished by professional ravishers and then "turned out" as prostitutes and sold to houses of prostitution. There is no doubt that this did happen, but many more of the "working girls" chose life in a brothel willingly over life on the farm.

Charles Manson being interviewed by talk-show host Geraldo Rivera at San Quentin in April 1988. (Paul Stojanovich.)

The purpose of the act was quickly subverted, as it was used as a defender of Puritan morality. Unmarried couples traveling for a vacation or a weekend of innocent pleasure who happened to cross a state line were subject to interception and arrest (for the male) by federal authorities. They did not have to be caught *in flagrante delicto*, the intent to fornicate was assumed. As D. H. Lawrence once said, "To the Puritan all things are impure."

MANSON, Charles (1934–)

THE GURU OF EVIL WHO MADE OTHERS KILL IN HIS NAME

Before he was 18, Charles Manson, the illegitimate son of an Ohio prostitute, spent time in various state institutions in the Midwest for a variety of crimes including burglary and robbery. At 18, just before he was to be released from a boys' school, he raped another boy at knife point and spent the next two years in a federal youth facility. When he

Members of Charles Manson's "family." Though Manson never wielded a weapon, he was the inspiration behind the gang's killing spree. (Federal Bureau of Investigation.)

was released, he got married, stole a car, and drove his pregnant wife to Los Angeles. Upon arrival, he was promptly sent to another prison. He spent the next 10 years of his life in and out of several prisons for a variety of charges, including credit card theft and pimping.

In 1967, Manson emerged from prison and went to Berkeley, California. He was now a complete paranoid and had the magnetic personality that some paranoids unfortunately develop. Convinced that he was going to become a great guitarist and song writer, he had become familiar with pop psychology, Scientology, hypnotism, mysticism, the occult and black magic. He had also read Robert Heinlein's college cult science fiction book, *Stranger in a Strange Land*, and picked up a warped version of its idea of group living.

Manson's magnetic personality and his guru appearance turned him into an instant cult figure. He gradually picked up a harem of worshipful young girls, such as librarian Mary Brunner, Lynette "Squeeky" Fromme, Susan Atkins, Linda Kasabian, and Bible-reading Patricia Krenwinkel. Abused by their parents, ignored by the world, unloved by a society that did not understand them, the runaways, the homeless and the hopeless turned to Charles Manson and found a god.

He picked up a few men, too, such as Bruce Davis, Charles "Tex" Watson and Bobby Beausoleil, holding them with his hodge-podge philosophy and the sexual favors of his harem. Manson's philosophy was slowly evolving, and by 1969, it included the concept of an inevitable war between the races. They hid supplies of food and munitions in the desert to prepare for the coming war. He and his troupe had moved back to Los Angeles by then, living in the houses of people they could interest in the "movement," or in the sexual favors of one of Charlie's girls.

Manson sent the girls out to burglarize houses. Then, overcome with his own power, he sent his followers out to kill. They probably began with an occasional casual murder, killing runaways and castoffs who would not be missed. They certainly killed Gary Hinman, a music teacher who Bobby Beausoleil had been living with when he met Manson.

It was late July when Bobby Beausoleil went to his old roommate, along with Susan Atkins and Mary Brunner. They tied Hinman to a chair and tortured him to reveal where he had his money hidden. Why they thought he had money hidden is not known. Hinman told them he had no money. They called Manson, who came over to try his hand at torturing. Hinman still insisted that he had no money hidden anywhere in the house, so Manson forced Hinman to sign over the title to his two cars, a Volkswagen bus and a Fiat, and told his group to kill Hinman after he left. They stabbed him over and over, Atkins wrote "political piggy" on the wall in Hinman's blood, they wiped away their fingerprints and they left.

The Los Angeles Sheriff detectives who investigated Hinman's murder, Paul Whitely and Charles Guenther, found a fingerprint that the murderous trio missed when they cleaned up. It would prove to be from the finger of Bobby Beausoleil. The next day a highway patrolman stopped to assist Beausoleil, whose van had broken down on the highway. The patrolman ran the plate number and arrested Beausoleil when it turned out to be Hinman's van.

Manson decided that now was the time to start the class war that he was convinced was coming. He had read it in the stars. He had confirmed it by a secret message that he found in a Beatles album. It would be called "Helter Skelter," and it would bring the millennium. On August 9, 1969, Manson sent his followers to Terry Melcher's house on Cielo Drive. Manson thought that Melcher, a producer, had not done enough to further Manson's musical career. He ordered his followers to kill everyone in the house. What he did not know was that since he had been there last Melcher had moved out, renting the house to film director Roman Polanski and his wife, actress Sharon Tate. But it would not have made a difference: Helter Skelter demanded human life, and it did not much matter whose.

Tex Watson parked his car outside the estate and cut the wires to the electric fence. Then he and his three companions, Patricia Krenwinkel, Leslie Van Houten, and Susan Atkins, climbed the fence. As they went in, a car was leaving. They stopped the car and killed the driver, 18-year-old Steve Parent who had the misfortune to be visiting the house. Then they went into the main house and murdered everyone there. Roman Polanski was in Europe, but his wife and three friends were there. Voytek Frykowski, a Polish writer and producer, and his girlfriend coffee heiress Abigail Folger were keeping Sharon Tate, who was eight months pregnant, company while Polanski was away. They found Frykowski asleep on the living room couch and tied him up. They dragged Abigail Folger from her bedroom. They found Sharon Tate and an old friend, hair stylist Jay Sebring, in another room and dragged them downstairs. The four victims in the house were shot and stabbed over 100 times. Atkins smeared the word *pig* over the door in somebody's blood.

Two days later, Manson drove around with the clan for a couple of hours and stopped at a random house. Manson entered through a window and tied up the owners, Leno and Rosemary LaBianca. Then he left the house while Tex Watson, Leslie Van Houten and Patricia Krenwinkel carved up the LaBiancas. Watson carved the word *war* onto Leno's stomach and "DEATH TO PIGS" and "RISE" were written in blood on the walls. Krenwinkel wrote "HEALTER SKEALTER" on the refrigerator, misspelling the words. They then took a shower, ate a meal and left.

The police did not officially connect the Tate-Frykowski-Folger-Sebring-Parent murders with the LaBianca killings for some time. They suspected a dope connection in the Tate killings. Eventually all the pieces fell into place, and the various members of the Manson family were arrested and assembled for trial. Deputy District Attorneys Vincent Bugliosi and Aaron Stovitz were assigned to prosecute the case. Their biggest problem was to present the evidence so that what they knew to be true—that Charles Manson had masterminded and ordered the murders, although he was not present—would be evident to the jury.

Their case was made when Linda Kasabian surrendered to the police and volunteered to confess everything she knew. She was the only one involved who had not directly participated in any of the murders. Manson, Atkins, Krenwinkel and Van Houten had separate lawyers. Charles Watson was in Texas fighting extradition, and they decided not to wait but to try him separately later.

The Manson family continued to take in converts, even while Manson and his major disciples were on trial for multiple murder. An entourage of them stood vigil outside the courtroom, handing out leaflets protesting the "second crucifixion of Christ." Linda Kasabian was on the witness stand for a week, and during that time, Manson glared at her from his seat with a glare of overpowering evil.

But she refused to be overpowered, and there were close to 50 pieces of circumstantial evidence to support her story of the two murder nights.

After a trial that went on for nine-and-a-half months, the jury found the four suspects guilty on all counts. At the separate penalty hearing, for which the three girls had shaved their heads, the jury voted for execution. But their lives were spared by the Supreme Court's decision on CAPITAL PUNISHMENT later that year, which automatically spared all those currently awaiting execution, and commuted their sentences to life imprisonment.

In September 1976, Lynette "Squeeky" Fromme, who had not been convicted of anything, went to Sacramento and pointed an automatic pistol at President Gerald Ford from point-blank range, and pulled the trigger. She had, however, neglected to put a bullet in the chamber of the gun, although the clip was loaded, it did not fire. Her plan was to call Manson as a witness, so that he could preach to the world from the witness stand, but the judge failed to see the relevance of his testimony and it was not permitted. She was sentenced to life imprisonment.

Neither Manson nor any of his murderous disciples has ever shown the slightest sign of remorse or regret over what they did. They have been eligible for parole since 1978, but none have been released. In 1984, another prisoner doused Manson with a flammable liquid and set him on fire, causing severe burns to his face and chest. When it was shown that Manson had been threatening to kill several of the other inmates, the prison authorities decided it was self-defense and charges were dropped.

MARSHALL, John (1755–1835)

John Marshall was chief justice of the SUPREME COURT from 1801–1835. A Revolutionary War officer, Marshall saw action at Monmouth and Stony Point and spent the winter of 1777 at George Washington's encampment at Valley Forge. He served as a congressman and secretary of state before accepting President John Adams's nomination as Chief Justice of the Supreme Court. In the 1803 *Marbury v. Madison* decision, his court affirmed the authority of the Court itself to determine constitutionality and asserted that in disputes over jurisdiction, the nation necessarily took precedence over a state or a section. Marshall presided over the treason trial of AARON BURR in 1807.

MASS MURDERERS

There is a common delusion today that the mass murderer is a recent phenomenon. Actually, there have been examples of such antisocial individuals throughout history. The biggest killers, of course, have been dictators and religious leaders who have been able to mobilize armies of the convinced or the conscripted to do their killing for them. Those with an overwhelming lust for power, and those possessed of a sure knowledge of "the truth," whatever that truth might be, seem most willing to kill other people for the good of the state or the salvation of their souls.

There is also an impression that mass murder is a masculine trait. As BELLE GUNNESS and JANE TOPPAN so amply demonstrate, females can exhibit such grisly behavior as well.

The ease of murder, even for the individual killer, has increased with the rise of civilization and the increasing sophistication of modern technology. It is possible today to kill 500 people by placing one small explosive device in the cargo hold of a large passenger aircraft. It is possible to travel in a car and kill people in 10 different states in as many days, thanks to the high-speed interstate highway system. It is possible, with a high-powered, rapid-fire rifle and a good location, to kill or wound scores of people before the police intervene.

A distinction in behavior and psychology must be made between the group mass murderer, who kills many people at one time, or in one extended incident, and the serial killer, who kills sequentially, usually one at a time. The typical group murderer is a person with a grudge; the typical serial killer is a person with a compulsion. There are those who combine these traits, such as CHARLES MANSON in California or New York's Mad Bomber, GEORGE METESKY, who planted bombs all over the city for a decade and only by the wildest of chances failed to kill anyone, although he permanently crippled several people. *See also:* JOE BALL; TED BUNDY; JEFFREY DAHMER; ALBERT HENRY DESALVO; JOHN WAYNE GACY; ED GEIN; HERMAN MUDGETT; RICHARD SPECK

MASSERIA, Giuseppe "Joe the Boss" (c. 1880–1931)

An Italian immigrant, Giuseppe Masseria became the leader of the major MAFIA family in New York City in the early 1920s. One of the most important of the MUSTACHE PETES, he initiated what came to be known as the CASTELLAMMARESE WAR and was killed by his lieutenants, at the instigation of CHARLEY "LUCKY" LUCIANO, who wanted to get on with business instead of carrying on a pointless feud.

MASSIE, Lieutenant Thomas H.

A COMPLEX STORY OF MURDER AND RACE ON AN ISLAND PARADISE

On the night of September 12, 1931, U.S. Navy Lt. Tommy Massie and his wife Thalia Massie were at a party at the Ala Wai Inn in Honolulu, Hawaii. Thalia, oppressed by the heat and cigarette smoke, and having had a minor quarrel with her husband, left the party to walk in the night air and clear her head.

She had not gone far when a car pulled up alongside her and four men leaped out and grabbed her, throwing her into the back seat of the car. They drove to a deserted location and raped her repeatedly, one of them hitting her hard enough to break her jaw to subdue her. When they were done they drove away, leaving her lying on the ground contused, lacerated and hysterical. She made her way to the road and flagged down a passing car, which took her home.

She called her husband, who was still at the party, and he rushed home and called the police. They took her to the hospital and questioned her about the rape. Mrs. Massie was able to describe the men who assaulted her, and even had spotted and memorized the license number of the car.

Mrs. Massie was not the first woman who reported being raped by men driving that car. A Hawaiian woman married to a Caucasian man named Peebles had reported a similar tale, including the license number. She had identified her assailants as two Hawaiians, two Japanese and a Chinese, but the quintet had been released for lack of corroborating evidence. One of the Hawaiians, Joe Kahahawi, was famed on the island as a talented boxer.

The five suspects were picked up and brought in for Mrs. Massie to look at from her hospital bed. She unhesitatingly identified them. "I'd know those savages anywhere," she said. She identified Joe Kahahawi as the man who had broken her jaw.

As the trial date for the five approached, the sentiment in the islands split along racial and ethnic lines. The Territory of Hawaii was a United States protectorate at the time, and the population was a mixture of native Hawaiians, Japanese, Chinese, Portuguese, with an overlay of American administrators and military personnel. None of the ethnic groups were particularly fond of any of the others. The American whites in particular looked down on those they were administering as social and intellectual inferiors.

In this case, the whites, as represented by the navy and the local government, felt that a white woman had been violated and that the natives should pay for it. The natives felt that something had happened to Mrs. Massie—it was not clear what—and the accused were scapegoats to white vengeance. On the Massies' side was the evidence of Mrs. Peebles, and the fact that two of the accused had been previously convicted of sex crimes. On the accused's side was the fact that the hospital doctors certified that Mrs. Massie had been attacked but would not state that she had been raped. No trace of sperm had been found either inside or outside her body.

Thalia Massie's mother, the socially prominent Mrs. Grace Glanville-Fortescue, flew to her daughter's side from her home on Long Island, New York. Tempers were short on both sides of the ethnic gulf as the case readied for trial. The commander of the U.S. Navy base on the island, Admiral Yates Stirling, in a masterful example of self-control, tried to cool things down by advising that they must be patient and allow the authorities to carry out the law, although, "our first inclination is to seize these brutes and string them up on trees."

Trial was held on November 19. After listening to 15 days of testimony, the jury of five whites and seven nonwhites was unable to reach a verdict. The five defendants were released on bond while a new trial was readied.

Tensions rose even higher. The native and oriental races set up a defense fund for the five martyrs. White women bought handguns for self-defense in record numbers. Admiral Stirling wrote in his memoirs: "The criminal assault of a white woman by the five dark-skinned citizens had gone unpunished by the Courts. Sympathies have been aroused in favor of the accused men. Conviction was thus impossible." He did not think it necessary to include the fact that reputable witnesses had testified to the men's presence on other parts of the island at the time of the alleged rape. This might or might not have been true, but it was certainly enough to hang a jury.

On Saturday, December 13, a party of naval officers seized one of the defendants, took him to a deserted spot and beat him, leaving him to find his own way home.

This dash of adolescent poetic justice was not enough for Massie and Mrs. Fortescue. On January 8, at 8:30 A.M., Tommy and Mrs. Fortescue, with the aid of two enlisted men, kidnapped Joe Kahahawi from the street in front of the courthouse and took him in a rented Buick back to the bungalow Mrs. Fortescue had rented for her stay on the island. There Tommy brandished a loaded .32 at the frightened boxer and extorted a confession from him. A second later the gun went off, and Joe Kahahawi fell to the floor with a bullet in his chest.

When the police, who had been told of the abduction by bystanders, arrived a short while later they found Kahahawi's body in the back seat of the rented Buick wrapped in canvas.

Lieutenant Massie, Mrs. Fortescue, and the two sailors were arrested and charged with second-degree murder. Sentiment on the mainland remained with them; sentiment on the islands was mixed. Trial was set for April 5, 1932, and 75-year-old CLARENCE DARROW, who had saved LEOPOLD AND LOEB from hanging eight years before, was brought out of retirement to appear for the defense. He wanted no part of the case, but he was offered a $25,000 fee, and he needed the money.

Darrow quickly decided that no jury would accept Massie's claim that the gun had gone off accidentally. His defense was based on "mental illness brought on by extreme provocation," a version of the old "unwritten law" theory of justice.

Even Darrow's eloquence was unable to influence the jury sufficiently. Mrs. Fortescue, Lieutenant Massie and the two seamen were found guilty of manslaughter, a compromise verdict, and sentenced to 10 years imprisonment.

After the verdict, Darrow and the prosecuting attorney had a meeting. Intense pressure was already being brought on the prosecution from the mainland to quash the verdict. President Herbert Hoover had called. The navy had begun an unofficial boycott of island businesses. Members of Congress were pushing for a presidential pardon. An agreement was reached between Darrow and the prosecutor that the sentence would be changed to one hour's detention in the courtroom, provided that the accused left the islands immediately afterward.

Darrow agreed, but added a condition of his own: The second trial against the accused rapists should be dropped. "Set them free," he said, "and let's bury this whole shabby business."

Rumors persisted that the true events of that night were not at all as Thalia Massie had asserted, but no authoritative version of the story ever came forward. Two years later the Massies were divorced. Thomas Massie eventually remarried. Thalia Massie attempted suicide several times over the years until finally, in 1963, she succeeded.

MASTERSON, William B. "Bat" (1853–1921)

THE LEGENDARY LAWMAN, GUNFIGHTER, AND SPORTS REPORTER

The middle (in age) of a trio of gunfighting lawmen, Bat Masterson achieved more fame than his equally competent brothers Edward (1852–1878) and James (1855–1895). This was due in equal parts to his style, his ability and his longevity.

Bat worked as assistant city marshal of Dodge City, Kansas, with his brother Edward until Edward died in a gunfight with two drunken cowboys at the Lady Gay Dance Hall. Bat and his brother managed to kill both of the drunks even as Edward was killed.

A renowned gunfighter with pistol and rifle, Bat once picked an escaping murderer named Spike Kennedy off his horse with a rifle shot at what onlookers described as an amazing distance. In a duel with a gunman named Mel King in a dance hall, Bat was wounded when King fired first and probably would have been killed had not a dance hall girl named Molly Brennan stepped in front of him to take the next bullet. Masterson killed King, but Molly died of her wound.

Masterson helped Wyatt Earp in the process of civilizing Dodge City before the city fathers kicked him out for being too uncivilized himself. It should be understood that the job of lawmen in Dodge City, as in most Western towns of the era, was to make the town safe for saloons, gambling dens and whorehouses—a job that Masterson and his compatriots, many of whom had an interest in the various businesses, did very well.

In later years, Masterson spent time as a gambler in Colorado and then moved on to New York City, where he became sports editor of the *New York Morning Telegraph*. It was there that one of the most famous Western legends began, that of gunfighters putting a notch in the butt of their gun after every kill. The story is that a dime-novel writer, who wrote Western stories (although he had never been west of Hoboken) and collected Western memorabilia, begged Masterson to give him his "six-shooter," offering him the tremendous sum of $100 for it. Masterson, who considered guns as tools, had not kept his original weapon, since it was too big to easily conceal under eastern-style clothing. So he went to a pawn shop and purchased an appropriate weapon, without noticing that there were five notches filed into the handle. When he handed it over, the collector noticed and asked Masterson the story behind the notches—and a myth was born. After this, Masterson is reputed to have made a small business out of selling notched six-shooters to collectors.

In 1915, Masterson went to Havana, Cuba, and sent back some memorable coverage of the heavyweight title fight between Jess Willard and Jack Johnson (Willard won). His writing style is exemplified by his much quoted observation: "There are many in this old world who hold that things break about even for us. I have observed, for example, that we all get about the same amount of ice. The rich get it in the summer-time and the poor get it in the winter." *See also:* EARP BROTHERS

MEANS, Gaston Bullock (1880–1938)

LAWMAN, CON MAN, THIEF AND MURDERER—MEANS DID IT ALL

Born in North Carolina, Gaston Means went through a variety of careers: cotton broker, school superintendent, private detective, attorney and special agent of the U.S. Bureau of Investigation (precursor to the FBI). All of these were secondary to his true calling of consummate swindler and confidence man.

In 1910, Gaston went to work for the Burns Detective Agency and was declared by his boss, William J. Burns, to be "the greatest natural detective ever known." It took Burns five years to figure out that Means was using his badge as a means of depriving the gullible of their wealth. What successes he had as a detective were due to a closer association with the criminal element than even private eyes were supposed to sustain.

In 1915, Means arranged to meet millionaire heiress Maud R. King. He accomplished this by rescuing the attractive young widow from a pair of thugs he had hired to accost and rob her on a Chicago street. Means parlayed this meeting into a position handling Mrs. King's financial affairs. In two years, he managed to transfer over $150,000 from the widow's purse to his own. When, in mid-1917, she became curious about his disposition of her fortune, Means took Mrs. King on a hunting trip in North Carolina. While out in the woods, Mrs. King somehow contrived to shoot herself behind the right ear. It sounds unbelievable, but Means had seen the whole thing, and he so testified. A jury of his peers brought in a verdict of suicide.

During World War I, Means managed to hire himself out to both the British and the Germans, and also took a job with U.S. Army Intelligence. He confused the Germans for the British, the British for the Germans and the U.S. Army for his own enjoyment. He claimed to have recovered two large trunks full of "defense secrets," but before he could deliver them a platoon of enemy agents jumped him and took them back.

In 1920, Means flimflammed a Chicago lawyer named Roy D. Keehn by collecting a $57,000 settlement on the East Coast for Keehn, and mailing it through the Southeastern Express Company. When Keehn opened the package, he found a block of wood in place of the currency. Keehn sued Means, and Means sued the express company, claiming someone there had substituted wood for his stack of currency. Somehow the case was never tried.

In 1921, William Burns, Means's former boss, told Means that he expected the incoming President Warren G. Harding to appoint Burns head of the Bureau of Investigation if he could get a few letters of recommendation from influential people. Means supplied the letters, and when Burns got the job, he appointed Means as a special investigator. This incensed the young J. EDGAR HOOVER, who was then assistant director of the bureau. Means served as a conduit between the OHIO GANG, a group of corrupt cronies of President Harding, and the people getting special favors from the government.

Means then decided to blackmail the president, who had been carrying on a long-term affair with a young lady named Nan Britton. Before he could collect, the president died of a blood clot on the brain while on a trip to the West Coast. Means cast about for a way to salvage his research and decided to collaborate with Miss Britton on a book called *The President's Daughter*, in which they alleged that Harding had sired an illegitimate baby. Means followed that up with a solo effort called *The Strange Death of President Harding*, which intimated that the President's wife had poisoned him. This became a best-seller.

During the 1920s, Means became an intrepid fighter of international communism. He took thousands of dollars from Mrs. Finley Shepherd of Tarrytown, New York, who had formed a committee to fight communism, by convincing her that "agents from Moscow" had been sent to kill her and her family. He soon broadened his scope, taking money from anti-Communists all over the country.

Means's final stunt involved bilking Evalyn Walsh McLean, a copper mine heiress and wife of a member of the Ohio Gang. In March 1932, after the LINDBERGH KIDNAPPING, Mrs. McLean decided to help rescue the child. The kidnapping promised to dominate the news for a long time to come, and Mrs. McLean was fond of publicity. Means convinced her that he was in touch with the kidnappers and took $100,000 ransom money from her, plus $4,000 for expenses. After moving Mrs. McLean and her associates around the country for a month, he claimed that the deal had fallen through. Mrs. McLean demanded return of her $100,000, and Means was unable to produce it. He was convicted of fraud and sent to Leavenworth for 15 years.

Means did not survive his sentence, dying of a heart attack in 1938. The $100,000 ransom money, which Means had presumably hidden somewhere, was never found. *See also:* CONFIDENCE GAMES

METESKY, George Peter (1903–)

THE "MAD BOMBER" WHO KEPT NEW YORKERS NERVOUS FOR A DECADE, METESKY WAS TRULY A MAN WITH A GRUDGE

During 10 years of planting bombs around New York City, George Metesky managed to scare the city to death but miraculously failed to kill anybody. Known by the press as the "Mad Bomber," Metesky conducted two periods of bombings. From 1940 to 1941, he planted a number of bombs, most of which failed to go off. Then he spent nine years brooding and perfecting his craft and, in 1950, began an eight-year reign of terror, planting bombs in Grand Central Station, Pennsylvania Station, Radio City Music Hall and various other landmarks, theaters and public places.

Interspersed between the bombings were a series of letters he sent to the newspapers complaining about the abuses of Consolidated Edison (Con Ed), the city's electric power company, signing himself "Fair Play." The police took the hint and checked disgruntled employees and former employees of Con Ed, but they did not go back far enough. Finally, in 1958, one of his letters accused the company of giving him tuberculosis, which provided a needed clue. Con Ed records showed that Metesky had been an employee years before. He had been injured on the job in 1931 and had claimed that he had developed tuberculosis through his work.

The police arrested him at his home in Waterbury, Connecticut, and he was found criminally insane and sent to a state mental hospital. In 1973, when Metesky was 70, he was released and went to live with his sister. During the course of his bombings he had injured 15 people, several seriously, killed no one and kept millions of people in a state of anxiety for eight years. It is estimated that the cost to the New York City theater district was millions of dollars in lost business.

MILLER, Richard W. (1937–)

A special agent of the FEDERAL BUREAU OF INVESTIGATION (FBI), Richard Miller has the distinction of being the first agent charged with espionage against his country. This was the result of a version of the classic intelligence ploy of sexual entrapment known as the "honey trap."

Miller began a sexual liaison with Svetlana Ogorodnikov, an attractive young Soviet emigré, in May 1984. Shortly after the affair began, she informed him that she was a major in the KGB (Soviet intelligence service) and asked him to pass on classified FBI documents. Her husband, Nikolai, concurred in this request. Miller agreed to do so and passed several documents to her. He later claimed that this was an effort to entrap and eventually "turn" Svetlana Ogorodnikov, but he neglected to inform his superiors of any such plan.

In October 1984, Miller and the Ogorodnikovs were arrested by the FBI. They were tried separately. The Ogorodnikovs pled guilty. Nikolai received an eight-year sentence. Svetlana got 18 years. After a mistrial, Miller was found guilty in his second trial of six counts of espionage and one count of bribery and was sentenced to two concurrent life sentences and an additional concurrent 50 years.

MINEO, Sal(vatore) (1939–1976)

Son of an immigrant coffin maker, Salvatore Mineo, Jr., was a streetwise tough kid from the Bronx who faced a bleak future until he turned his life around by attending the New York City High School for the Performing Arts. He became a talented actor, opening in the Broadway production of *The Rose Tattoo* and going on to play the crown prince in *The King and I*, with Yul Brynner playing the king. When he was 16, he played Plato, a delicate, sensitive, mixed-up adolescent, in the film *Rebel Without a Cause*. This role resulted in the first of two Academy Award nominations. In 1960, he played Dov Landau in *Exodus* and received his second Oscar nomination. Unfortunately, his career stalled at this point, and at the age of 21, he began the slow slide toward anonymity.

In 1976, after a series of small parts, he was preparing to make a second assault on stardom. As part of this campaign, he was rehearsing for the Los Angeles production of the play *P.S. Your Cat Is Dead*, which he and his agent hoped would refocus attention on his great acting ability. On the evening of February 12, 1976, he was parking his car—an aged Chevette—in the carpark of his modest apartment building, when he was attacked and stabbed by a random robber. Neighbors heard him scream for help and rushed to the car park in time to see a man fleeing the scene. Mineo was dead before the ambulance reached the scene.

The statements of the witnesses, who had seen a white man fleeing in a small yellow car, proved of no help to the police. Time passed, and no one was arrested for the crime. All of the unfortunate rumors that accompany a celebrity death were ground from the mill: Mineo was killed in a drug deal gone bad; Mineo was killed by his homosexual lover.

Fifteen months after the crime, a black girl named Theresa Williams told the police a story. Her husband, 19-year-old (at the time) Lionel Ray Williams, who had been working as a pizza delivery man, killed Mineo, she claimed. He had bragged to her about having "just killed this dude in Hollywood."

Although Williams had a history of violence, arrested four times before he was 18, the police did not believe Theresa. First, Williams was black, and the witnesses had said the fleeing man was white. Second, Williams had claimed knowledge of the crime a few days after the killing, when he was picked up on a robbery charge and offered to trade the information for leniency. But he had said it was a drug killing, and the police thought he was lying.

Later, it was confirmed that he was lying. There were no drugs involved; it was a botched robbery attempt. A prison informer—Williams was in a Michigan prison on a forgery rap—claimed that Williams not only bragged to his fellow prisoners about having killed Mineo, but demonstrated how he had handled the knife. His shadow-stabbing matched the pathologist's opinion of how Mineo had been stabbed. Also he was a very light-skinned black man and had been driving a borrowed yellow Dodge Colt on the night of the murder.

In January 1979, nearly three years after the murder, Lionel Ray Williams was tried for Sal Mineo's death, with 11 additional felony counts for robberies in Beverly Hills, West Hollywood and the Wilshire district. He was convicted of second-degree murder and 10 robbery counts and sentenced to 51 years in prison.

MIRANDA RULE

On June 13, 1966, the Supreme Court ruled (5–4) in the case of *Miranda v. Arizona* that a criminal suspect must be informed of his or her rights before being questioned. Basing its decision on the FIFTH AMENDMENT guarantee against self-incrimination, the decision stated that the prosecution "may not use statements, whether exculpatory or inculpatory, stemming from custodial interrogation of the defendant unless it demonstrates the use of procedural safeguards effective to secure the privilege against self-incrimination. By custodial interrogation, we mean questioning initiated by law enforcement officers after a person has been taken into custody or otherwise deprived of his freedom of action in any significant way."

In this expansion of the 1936 *BROWN V. MISSISSIPPI* decision, the Court ruled that psychological as well as physical interrogation can be a violation of a suspect's rights. By the use of the word *demonstrates*, the Supreme Court put the burden upon the prosecution to prove that its guidelines had been followed. As to the necessary safeguards, it specified that unless other "fully effective" measures could be developed, the arresting authority had the following responsibility:

> Prior to any questioning, the person must be warned that he has a right to remain silent, that any statement he does make may be used as evidence against him, and that he has a right to the presence of an attorney, either retained or appointed. The defendant may waive effectuation of these rights, provided the waiver is made voluntarily, knowingly, and intelligently. If, however, he indicates in any manner and at any stage of the process that he wishes to consult with an attorney before speaking there can be no questioning. Likewise, if the individual is alone and indicates in any manner that he does not wish to be interrogated, the police may not question him. The mere fact that he may have answered some questions or volunteered some statements on his own does not deprive him of the right to refrain from answering any further inquiries until he has consulted with an attorney and thereafter consents to be questioned.

The ruling came from a 1963 Arizona case in which a 22-year-old drifter named Ernesto Miranda was arrested for theft. While being held on this charge he was picked out of a line-up by a young girl as the man who had kidnapped and raped her. After two hours of police interrogation, Miranda was induced to give a written confession to the crime. The confession was used in court, and Miranda was convicted of kidnapping and rape and sentenced to 20 to 30 years imprisonment for each offense. On appeal, the Supreme Court of Arizona ruled that the conviction should stand, noting that Miranda did not ask for an attorney.

In the U.S. Supreme Court reversal of the Arizona court decision, it noted that:

> Again we stress that the modern practice of in-custody interrogation is psychologically rather than physically oriented.
>
> Interrogation still takes place in privacy. Privacy results in secrecy and this in turn results in a gap in our knowledge as to what in fact goes on in the interrogation rooms. A valuable source of information about present police practices, however, may be found in various police manuals and texts which document procedures employed with success in the past, and which recommend various other effective tactics. These texts are used by law enforcement agencies themselves as guides. It should be noted that these texts professedly present the most enlightened and effective means presently used to obtain statements through custodial interrogation. . . .
>
> To highlight the isolation and unfamiliar surroundings, the manuals instruct the police to display an air of confidence in the suspect's guilt and from outward appearance to maintain only an interest in confirming certain details. The guilt of the subject is to be posited as a fact. The interrogator

> should direct his comments toward the reasons why the subject committed the act, rather than court failure by asking the subject whether he did it. . . . The officers are instructed to minimize the moral seriousness of the offense, to cast blame on the victim or on society. These tactics are designed to put the subject in a psychological state where his story is but an elaboration of what the police purport to know already—that he is guilty. Explanations to the contrary are dismissed and discouraged.

The Miranda rule caused a shock wave throughout the law enforcement community, complete with dire predictions that it would now be impossible to convict criminals. This has proved to be an exaggeration. When Ernesto Miranda was retried on the rape charge, with the confession inadmissible, he was again convicted.

The word *Miranda* has now come into the police lexicon. To Mirandize someone is to read him his rights, which are read off of a Miranda Card. The usual formulation reads something like this:

> You have the right to remain silent. If you give up the right to remain silent, what you say may be taken down and used in evidence against you. You have the right to have an attorney present during questioning. If you cannot afford an attorney one will be provided for you. Do you understand these rights?

MISTER 880

HE COUNTERFEITED DOLLAR BILLS—AND DROVE THE SECRET SERVICE CRAZY

Edward Mueller (1875–   ), who became known as "Mr. 880," was a counterfeiter of U.S. currency who managed to manufacture and pass his bogus bills for almost 10 years, an elusiveness which seriously annoyed the Treasury Department. He succeeded in this because of his unassuming manner, his naïveté, his lack of ambition and his desire not to hurt anyone—a combination of character traits not usually associated with success in the criminal world.

Mueller worked as a superintendent for apartment buildings in New York City's Upper East Side until his wife died in 1937, when he was 62. He had several close brushes with success as an inventor in his early years. In 1905, he sent blueprints for a new camera design to Eastman Kodak, which replied with a letter complimenting him on his "extraordinary ingeniousness," although they declined the idea as not commercially practicable. A few years later he designed an improved mechanism for a Venetian blind, which a manufacturer to whom he showed it declared was "simple and clever," but which he deemed would be too expensive to manufacture. Mueller seems to never have followed through with these ideas by improving them or even showing them to other companies after their initial rejection. He contented himself with pulling out the letter from Eastman Kodak and showing it to visitors at the slightest excuse.

In 1938, having retired from the building superintendent trade, Mueller moved into an apartment on West 96th Street, off Broadway, bought an old pushcart and set himself up in the junk business. He would push the cart for miles through the city, picking up anything salvageable from vacant lots or along the waterfront, and sell his finds to wholesale junk dealers.

At about this time, he set up a small, hand-cranked printing press in his kitchen and, using an old plate camera, took pictures of the front and back of a dollar bill. He photoengraved the pictures onto a pair of zinc plates, producing muddy images that lacked any semblance of the clarity of the money manufactured by the U.S. Bureau of Engraving and Printing. After passing a few samples of his product, he realized just how poor they were and touched up the plates as best as he could, trying to make the picture of Washington on the front more recognizable, and cleaning up the president's name below his portrait, which had come out particularly muddy.

When the bills began appearing in late 1938, the U.S. Secret Service, charged with suppressing counterfeiting and apprehending counterfeiters, opened file number 880 on the new series of counterfeit money. The opening memorandum read in part:

> New York reports the appearance November 19th of new counterfeit $1 Silver Certificate, 1935 Series; check letter "K"; face plate No. 1371; back plate No. 601; serial No. K70025356A; W.A. Julian, Treasurer of the United States; Henry Morgenthau, Jr., Secretary of the Treasury; portrait of Washington.
>
> This counterfeit is printed on one sheet of cheap quality bond paper from crude photo-etched plates. The portrait is poorly executed against a black background which fails to show any line work. The left eye is represented by a black spot. A heavy line forms the lower lid of the right eye, which is almond shaped.

Mueller's attempt to remedy the worst defects in his bills produced an error that the Treasury agents found particularly annoying. In re-engraving the president's name under his portrait, Mueller transposed two of the letters, so that it read "Wahsington." Despite this flaw, merchants all over New York City continued to take the "880" bills without noticing who gave them to them.

The bills were being passed at the rate of about two a day; an amount that would not seriously damage the economy but that would not make "880" easy to catch either. The amounts involved were so small that a theory developed in the Secret Service that the counterfeiter was a crank with a grudge against the Treasury Department.

As the years passed, "880" became "Mr. 880," and eventually "Old Mr. 880." A large map of the city was posted to the wall of the Secret Service branch office in New York, and a red thumb tack was placed at every location where Mr. 880 was known to have passed a bill. Soon a mosaic of red dots covered the map, with a concentration on Manhattan's Upper West Side. Some of the bills were being found by banks in other East Coast cities, and one even made it to a bank in Seattle. But the Treasury agents were sure that Mr. 880 never left New York City. The bills were being included in bank-to-bank shipments.

Mueller went on passing his poor-quality dollar bills. His needs were simple, and he seldom bought anything he did not need. He also was concerned that no shopkeeper be out more than a dollar, so he never returned to the same place. His frugality and his concern for merchants made it exceedingly difficult to apprehend him.

In January 1948, Mueller's apartment house caught fire. The firemen, in an excess of zeal, threw a lot of the "junk" in Mueller's apartment, including the zinc engraving plates and a bundle of "WAHSINGTON" dollar bills, out the window into a vacant lot next door. Mueller went to stay with his married daughter while the building was repaired. A couple of days later some teenage boys playing in the lot came across the zinc plates and the bundle of money. The bills that had fooled merchants, and even bank tellers, for a decade did not fool the teenagers for an instant. They decided it was stage money and divided it up to play with. One of them took the zinc plates to experiment with. He inked the plate and tried making an image on toilet paper, but the results were unsatisfactory and he abandoned the attempt.

The father of one of the boys thought the bills might be something more serious, and brought one of them into the West 100th Street Police Station to show to the desk sergeant. The sergeant passed it on to detectives North and Behrens, who called the Secret Service. When the Secret Service agent heard that the name under the president's picture was spelled "WAHSINGTON," he told the detectives to wait where they were, someone would be right over.

Simple legwork took the Secret Service men to the fire-damaged apartment building, where they interviewed Alexander Flynn, the superintendent. He told them about the wonderful, friendly old man who lived on the top floor, whose junk the firemen had tossed out the window. His name was Edward Mueller, and he had just returned after staying with his daughter. They went upstairs, where Mueller met them at his door. They looked around the apartment, and found the small press in the kitchen and a bundle of WAHSINGTON dollar bills in a kitchen drawer.

Mueller freely admitted his hobby. He seemed to believe that, since he manufactured only dollar bills and had never passed more than one in any one place, that he had not hurt anybody.

On September 3, 1948, Mueller came before Judge John W. Clancy in the U.S. District Court of the Southern District of New York. He pled guilty on two of the three counts against him: possessing counterfeit plates and passing counterfeit bills. But on the third count, manufacturing counterfeit money, he stubbornly refused to plead guilty. He insisted that "a man named Henry" had done the actual manufacturing. There was no trace of "Henry," and no one in Mueller's building had ever seen him coming or going. Despite evidence to the contrary, he held out on this one point.

The prosecutor dropped the third charge and recommended a suspended sentence, "despite the heinousness of the crime," due to the defendant's advanced age and lack of a prior criminal record. The judge believed that the crime had to be punished, and sentenced Mr. 880 to nine months in prison. The prosecutor reminded the judge that, due to a peculiarity of the law, a nine-month sentence would have to be served to the day, while a sentence of a year and a day would make the prisoner eligible for parole in four months. So, taking pity on the prisoner, the judge raised the sentence. Mueller was also fined one dollar.

A few years later a film, *Mister 880*, was made of his story, which Mueller went to see. He enjoyed it very much.

MONAKERS, also MONIKERS

A monaker refers to the name or nickname by which a criminal is known to his or her associates. The monaker is often based upon a physical or mental peculiarity or habit of the subject and is sometimes a cruel comment. Nobody ever dared call AL CAPONE "Scarface" to his scarred face. Likewise, "BUGSY" SIEGEL and "Crazy Joey" Gallo were never confronted with their appellations. Many times the monaker replaces the subject's name in the perception of everyone except, perhaps, the subject's parents. Sometimes the monaker is based upon a professional characteristic or accidental circumstance. In New York City's Greenwich Village, in the 1960s, two of the more popular drug pushers were "Hypo Herb," who had once owned a pharmacy, and "Duncan Yo-yo," who received his monaker because he wore a leather jacket, purchased at a used clothing store, which said on the back, "Duncan Yo-Yo Champion, Brooklyn, 1952." One must be careful in attempting to fix the derivation of monakers. "Yellow Kid" Weil, the famous turn-of-the-century con artist, for example, received his monaker because of his love for wearing yellow gloves, not for any imagined cowardice.

It should be noted that monakers tend to be reused, although some, such as "Tin Lizzie Jones," become too dated to recur. Some monakers from the past include:

Ace High
Adopted
Airbrake Smith
Alibi Good Kid
Ant Eater
Apple Jaw
Ax Handle
Bad Weather
Battle Axe Williams

Bird Legs
Bow and Arrow Kid
Butterfly Mary
Calamity Zim
Careful Kelly
Chicago May
Cokey Flo
The Dis and Dat Kid
Dried Apple Joe
Easy Walking James
Eight Mile Blackie
Fifty Dollar Joe
Free Lunch
Jenny the Factory
Lill the Legend
Mile Away Bill
Paddle Foot
Peaceable Jones
Peaceful Henry
Pint and a Half
The Preacher
Rooster Face
Sad Sam
Safety Pin
Sally Two-and-a-Half
Saturday Night Johnnie
Slow Death
Snow Peters
Suit Case Simpson
Willie Round Legs
Wooden Ears
The Yob (Cockney back slang: "boy")

MOODY, Walter Leroy, Jr. (1933–)

In 1972, Walter Moody was convicted for possessing a pipe bomb, a conviction that was upheld by the U.S. 11th Circuit Court of Appeals. He evidently thought the verdict was unfair and developed a belief that blacks received preferential treatment in the courts. In December 1989, he mailed pipe bombs to the Alabama home of Robert S. Vance, a judge of the 11th Circuit Court, and to the Savannah, Georgia, office of Robert E. Robinson, an attorney, both of whom were killed when the devices went off. He also mailed bombs to the Jackson, Florida, office of the National Association for the Advancement of Colored People and to the federal court building in Atlanta, Georgia.

Moody was apprehended because the pipe bombs used in the murders were identical with the ones he was jailed for making. Because of the pretrial publicity, the trial was moved to St. Paul, Minnesota. On August 20, 1991, Moody was convicted of both murders and attempted murder and sentenced to seven life terms plus 400 years in prison with no possibility of parole.

MORAN, George "Bugs" (1893–1957)

Born in Minnesota with an Irish father and a Polish mother, George Moran grew up on Chicago's North Side and naturally gravitated into DION O'BANION's North Side Gang, where he soon became a trusted aide of O'Banion. The North Side Gang was in an ongoing territorial dispute with JOHNNY TORRIO's mob, a Chicago branch of the American MAFIA, which liked to call itself the Syndicate. It was the middle of PROHIBITION, and there were enough bootlegging profits for all, but intermural jealousies and racial rivalries kept the combat alive. Moran was known for his direct and violent solution to such disputes, his favorite tool of diplomacy being the machine gun.

When O'Banion was murdered by the Torrio mob in 1924, the mantle of leadership fell upon HYMIE WEISS, who was in turn murdered in 1926, and then to VINCENT "SCHEMER" DRUCCI, who was killed in a dispute with a police detective in 1927. Thus, Bugs Moran was elevated to the leadership of the gang. In the meantime, Torrio, who narrowly missed being murdered by Moran, had turned the leadership of his mob over to AL CAPONE and retired to Italy.

Moran moved the gang's headquarters to a garage at 2122 North Clark Street and continued his battles with Capone's syndicate over booze and territory. They tried for many an armistice but each would soon be violated, usually by hoods from one side who were unable to resist hijacking one or more beer trucks of the other side.

On February 14, 1929, four men, two in police uniforms, parked their Cadillac across the street and entered the garage. Moran, who was just coming up the street to be on hand for an expected shipment of booze supposedly hijacked in Detroit, decided to wait across the street during what he believed was a police roust. When he heard the blatting of machine guns from inside the garage, he knew that the visitors were not cops. The gunmen ran back to their Cadillac and drove away, leaving six men dead and one dying on the floor of the garage. This event became known as the infamous SAINT VALENTINE'S DAY MASSACRE.

When Moran was asked what he thought had happened, he had a ready answer. "Only Capone kills like that," he said.

Moran, along with JOSEPH AIELLO and several other gang leaders, made a determined effort to get Capone by bribing some of Capone's own soldiers. But their loyalty to Capone—or their fear of him—was greater than any inducement Moran could offer, so the plot came to nothing. By 1935, Capone and the Syndicate effectively controlled Chicago crime, and Moran eventually moved to Ohio. In July 1946, he was arrested for bank robbery and sent to prison. He died in Leavenworth Prison in 1957.

MORELLI BROTHERS

Five Sicilian lads from Brooklyn who moved up to Providence, Rhode Island, around the beginning of the twentieth century, the Morelli brothers, led by Joe and Butsey, founded the New England branch of the MAFIA. Joe had been a suspect in the murder of Herman Rosenthal in New York in 1912, a fact of which he was inordinately proud. It is probable that the Morellis committed the 1920 payroll robbery of the Slater and Morrill Shoe Company in South Braintree, Massachusetts, for which anarchists Nicola Sacco and Bartolomeo Vanzetti were convicted and eventually executed. Years later, Butsey Morelli told VINNE TERESA, "We whacked them out, we killed those guys in the robbery. These two greaseballs took it on the chin for us. That shows you how much justice there really is."

See also: SACCO AND VANZETTI

MOSSMAN, Captain Burton C. (1867–1956)

A cowman and lawman, Mossman was the first captain of the ARIZONA RANGERS. Originally from Aurora, Illinois, he moved west to work cattle, and by the age of 30, he was managing the sizable Hash Knife Ranch in Arizona Territory. His ability to keep the area clear of badmen brought him to the attention of Arizona Governor Nathan O. Murphy, who in 1901 asked him to head his newly formed law organization. Mossman personally went into Mexico to lure Augustine Chacon, a notorious Mexican bandit who was believed to have killed over 30 people, into Arizona Territory where he could be arrested. Mossman headed the rangers for two years before returning to ranching. A successful rancher in the West that he had helped to tame, he died in Roswell, New Mexico, in 1956.

MUDGETT, Herman Webster (1860–1896)

THE MADMAN WHO BUILT HIS OWN CASTLE OF MURDER WHERE MORE THAN A HUNDRED PEOPLE DIED

Possibly the greatest mass murderer in American history, Herman Mudgett created a "murder castle" in Chicago in the early 1890s. The estimates of the number of people he killed, mostly but not exclusively young women, range from 50 to more than 200.

Mudgett grew up in Gilmanton, New Hampshire. While a student at the University of Michigan Medical School at Ann Arbor, he began in a small way those practices that would eventually get him hanged. He took out an insurance policy on himself, using another name, making himself, under his real name, the beneficiary. Then he took a body from the medical school morgue, dosed the face with acid, and placed it where it would be found. Then he went to identify the body at the city morgue and collected the insurance. Since the scheme worked so well, he did it again and again, taking the precaution of changing insurance companies with each cadaver. The only time he came close to getting caught was when someone stopped him while removing a female corpse from the medical school morgue. But the theft was treated as a schoolboy prank, and he was merely given a lecture.

Bored with his medical studies, Mudgett moved to Chicago and married a fairly well-to-do woman named Murta Belknap, changing his name to Herman Howard Holmes, since he had left a wife behind in Michigan. When Murta figured out that he was spending her money, and her uncle's, and kicked him out, he promptly found a new scam. He rented a wagonload of furniture from a rental company and took it across town and sold it. He continued this activity until he ran out of furniture rental companies. Then Mudgett took a job at a drugstore until he could think of another gimmick. Soon he was running the drugstore for Mrs. Holton, who was a widow. Within a year, the drugstore was in his name, and Mrs. Holton had disappeared.

Mudgett had some big plans, but first he decided he needed some working capital. With a sometime partner named Ben Pietzel, he swiped a body from a Chicago medical school to work the insurance scam one last time. They stuffed the body into a trunk, and Mudgett took it on a train to upper Michigan, where it was to be discovered. But the body was already decomposing and the baggage car guard complained about the smell of Mudgett's luggage. So Mudgett took the trunk off the train and loaded it up with ice before taking the next train. Then that train was wrecked. Mudgett dragged the trunk away from the wreck and managed to get it to a hotel in a nearby town. The next morning, he dressed the corpse in his clothes, with a lot of his identification, and placed it under a tree on the edge of town. This project netted him about $20,000.

Mudgett bought the empty lot across the street from the drugstore and began construction of a very peculiar building. He installed the furnace for the Warner Glass Bending Company in the cellar with the investment of his partner in the project, Mr. Warner. Then he put Mr. Warner in the furnace to see how well it worked. Warner was reduced to ashes. He built an apartment house above the furnace and rented out the rooms. He advertised in the papers that he had jobs for young girls and in the marriage journals that he was seeking a wife. When applicants came for either of these positions, he would invite them to dinner, make sure that nobody knew where they had gone and then imprison them in one of the several rooms he kept for that purpose. Promising to marry the girls, he would send them home sometimes to get all their money before locking them up and torturing them to death.

Some of the upstairs rooms were air tight, so that he could slowly suffocate his victims. One was fitted out with a poison gas inlet. One had asbestos walls and a flamethrower device to burn its victims to death. Some of the rooms were fitted out as torture chambers, with torture tables and racks and walls lined with various implements designed to cause pain.

Chicago was host to the 1893 World's Fair, and the town was crammed with people who had come to find work at the fair. Many of them disappeared forever into Mudgett's building. He had expected to make a profit from this enterprise, but many of his victims had no money, and he kept killing his tenants before they could pay their rent, so he decided to conduct his insurance swindle one more time. He sent Ben Pietzel to Philadelphia to establish his identity and insure his life. Then, according to the plan, he would go to Philadelphia with a corpse to substitute for Ben, and Mrs. Pietzel would collect the insurance. At the last minute, he decided it would be less work to merely kill Ben, so he got him drunk in the hotel room and set him on fire, making it look like an accident.

A lawyer supplied by Mudgett put in a claim, and the Fidelity Mutual Life Assurance Company paid Mrs. Pietzel double indemnity, $10,000, for the accidental death. She, in all innocence, turned it over to Mudgett. But now Fidelity Mutual found out that Mudgett had been asking around for a crooked lawyer for an insurance scam. They notified Philadelphia police detective Frank Geyer, who investigated. He interviewed Mudgett in Philadelphia and found him evasive, so he followed Mudgett. By now Mrs. Pietzel and her children had also disappeared. Geyer found the skeleton of Pietzel's son in a stove in a Toronto apartment and the two other children buried in the basement.

Geyer went on to Chicago and broke into Mudgett's rooms in the apartment house. He discovered a secret passage that wound around, giving access to most of the rooms and revealing several hidden rooms. In the cellar he found a fully equipped torture chamber, with a neatly stacked pile of human skeletons in one corner. (Mudgett used to sell the articulated skeletons to medical supply houses.)

Geyer called in the Chicago police, and a work crew came and unearthed the remains of well over 100 corpses. Mudgett was tried in Philadelphia for the murder of Ben Pietzel, which was sufficient. While in prison awaiting execution, Mudgett wrote a paper detailing 27 of his murders, but then recanted and claimed that he had made it all up and had never murdered anybody. He professed astonishment over the bodies found in his castle and wondered how they could have gotten there. On May 7, 1896, he was hanged. The murder castle was thoroughly searched for body parts and then razed to the ground.

MUGGING

A form of robbery in which the victim is grabbed from behind, an arm is placed around the victim's throat so that the elbow protrudes forward, and then is squeezed. At the same time a knee goes into the small of the victim's back. This combination renders the victim off-balance, bewildered and helpless. A confederate then goes through the victim's pockets or purse. This used to be called "strongarming."

MURDER

The root of the word *murder* is thought to be the Old English *morth*, meaning secret. Thus, a murder was originally a killing done in secret, "where of it cannot be known by whom it was done" (*Britton*, c. 1290). The meaning gradually altered, as public homicide became a less popular pastime, to mean a felonious killing "with malice aforethought." Then it became further subdivided, until by the time British common law was passed on to the American colonies, its definitions were fixed.

The killing of one human being by another is divided, in most states, into six categories: murder in the first degree, murder in the second degree, manslaughter in the first degree, manslaughter in the second degree, justifiable homicide and accidental death.

Murder in the first degree is the willful, deliberate and premeditated killing of another. That is, the killer is aware of what he or she is doing, does it with conscious purpose and has planned to do it. The planning does not have to be over any extended period of time to establish premeditation. The act of going into another room to get a gun before returning to use it is, in most instances, premeditation enough. A death resulting from a felony is also, in most jurisdictions, first-degree murder. If Andy robs a liquor store and the owner reaches for a gun, and Andy shoots him, this is first-degree murder even though Andy did not enter the store intending to kill the owner.

If Andy and Bob rob a liquor store and Andy shoots the owner, both Andy and Bob can be tried for first-degree murder, since Bob was an accessory in the crime that caused the murder. Interestingly, if Andy and Bob rob a liquor store and the owner reaches for a gun and shoots and kills Bob, Andy can be held for first-degree murder. Since the owner acted in self-defense, it has been held that it was Andy's initial act of robbery that resulted in Bob's death.

Murder in the second degree is a killing in which the malice aforethought is present, but the premeditation is absent. Killing one person while attempting to kill another is one example. Killing someone at random while firing into a crowd would be another.

Manslaughter in the first degree, or voluntary manslaughter, is the intentional killing of another without malice aforethought. A killing in the heat of extreme anger or jealousy or other passion, when the passion has been caused by the victim, is one example. Unreasonable or grossly negligent conduct, such as waving a loaded gun around, which results in a death, is also voluntary manslaughter.

Manslaughter in the second degree, or involuntary manslaughter, is "criminally negligent homicide." The classic example is a homicide resulting from reckless driving.

When we speak of murder, we are usually considering what in law would be murder in the first degree—usually with premeditation and certainly with malice aforethought. The motives for murder can be simplified to a basic six: murder for gain, murder for revenge, murder to eliminate an obstacle, murder to escape discovery of another crime, murder from political or religious conviction and domestic violence.

In the category of murder for gain we can put all MAFIA and other gangland killings. The BLACK HAND extortions and murders at the turn of the century are another example. BELLE GUNNESS, who liked to get married, LOUISE PEETE, who liked to tell stories, and DR. JOHN WHITE WEBSTER of Harvard, who liked to live well, also fit the definition.

Murder for revenge, called by the Italians *vendetta*, is an ancient human habit. The murder laws came into being partly to stop the blood feuds that erupted between families that could decimate towns and disturb the order of the state. The practice has until recently, in some places, still been carried to extremes. In the hills of western Sicily, on the island of Corsica and in the Ozark Mountains, whole families have been wiped out in a seesaw of murders, sometimes carried over generations. The EARP BROTHERS were on such a seesaw for a while. Many of those who seek revenge to the point of death are mentally unbalanced, and their grievance is either imaginary or not of a quality that would drive a normal person to such an act. CLARA PHILLIPS, the "Tiger Woman," DANIEL SICKLES and HARRY KENDALL THAW were three such people.

Murder to eliminate an obstacle, such as RUTH SNYDER's husband, or JACK GILBERT GRAHAM's mother, is the crime of a sociopath, as are many murders in general. A sociopath is a person who regards all other people as objects to be manipulated or disposed of at will. When combined with another pathology, such as extreme paranoia, the result is a CHARLES MANSON or a HERMAN MUDGETT. Unfortunately, there is usually no way to readily detect this pathology before it results in a serious crime.

Murder to escape discovery of another crime is usually a spur-of-the-moment act of desperation, but in some cases of KIDNAPPING, it can be premeditated. Most ASSASSINATIONS are murders from political or religious conviction, although some assassins merely want to ensure their own immortality by killing someone famous enough to put their own name in the history books.

The category of domestic violence is actually the most prevalent form of homicide, although this is rarely murder in the first degree. We exempt from this category, of course, the premeditated killing of a spouse or close relative for gain or to be relieved of a burden. The husband who kills in a drunken rage; the wife who kills in fear of her husband's drunken rage; the spouse who kills from jealousy or anger or another overwhelming passion make up the bulk of the murders in any year.

The weapon that statistically is to be most feared is not the handgun in the hands of a felonious stranger but the handgun kept in a bureau drawer at home. According to recent federal statistics, of the murderers in state prisons, 23.7 percent of their victims were either relatives or intimates, and another 33.5 percent were friends or acquaintances. Over half of the homicide victims were killed by people they knew, and almost half of those were killed by relatives or intimates. *See also:* MASS MURDERERS

MURDER, INCORPORATED

BROOKYN'S CONTRACT KILLERS WHO DID THE BIDDING OF THE COSA NOSTRA

PROHIBITION and the 1920s created a new set of rules for everyone to live by, for example, gangsters and hoodlums became bootleggers and were invited to the best parties. During this time, the various mobs around the country discovered the advantages of working together, but this was something at which they had no practice. By 1930, the rules of cooperative behavior had been laid down, the various territories and permissible activities had been mapped and divided up and a National Board of Directors was put in place over the local mobs. The board is usually said to have been made up of such MAFIA kingpins as "LUCKY" LUCIANO, FRANK COSTELLO and JOHNNY TORRIO, and such non-Mafia luminaries as MEYER LANSKY and DUTCH SCHULTZ.

As it became clear that the days of Prohibition were numbered, the board divided up ORGANIZED CRIME's other lucrative businesses, such as protection, loan sharking, gambling, labor racketeering, prostitution and NARCOTICS. But since the local mobs being organized were not as amenable to control as ordinary citizens, the board needed some means of enforcing its edicts.

A small Jewish-Italian mob in Brooklyn headed by ALBERT ANASTASIA and LOUIS "LEPKE" BUCHALTER was used as the board's enforcement arm. It committed contract murders for different crime "families" all over the country—murders that had to be approved by the board before they were permitted. When an organized crime boss wanted to "hit" (murder) another organized crime figure, he had to get the permission of the board, and then often, he would send word to Midnight Rose's candy store, in Brownsville, Brooklyn, and Anastasia's boys would take it from there. This served to strongly discourage the internecine warfare that was giving organized crime such a bad image. The murder of ordinary citizens was discouraged, and the killing of journalists or law enforcement officials was prohibited; the heat that such killings brought was not worth any possible gain. As Burton B. Turkis and Sid Feder put it in their book *Murder Inc.*, (1951). "The Brooklyn experts were not for hire. Their outside work was solely on contract service for other Syndicate gangs—the same as a garbage disposal company contracts to haul off the refuse from a suburban block every day; not just one garbage can from one house that summons it on one particular day."

Anastasia's troops performed their job so well that they had an effective monopoly on contract killings within organized crime. Such killers as ABE "KID TWIST" RELES, FRANK "THE DASHER" ABBANDANDO, Buggsy Goldstein, PITTSBURGH PHIL Strauss and Vito "Chicken Head" Gurino brought a quality of professionalism to the task of murder. During the 1930s, the Brownsville mob is known to have been responsible for killings all over the United States, with over 300 in the New York area alone.

Law enforcement found out about Murder,

Columnist Inez Robb interviews Brooklyn District Attorney William O'Dwyer in the midst of investigations that revealed the existence of Murder, Inc. (International News Photo.)

Incorporated, in 1940, when Abe Reles, feeling that he was about to be implicated in several murders, decided to turn state's evidence before anyone else had a chance to. Brooklyn District Attorney William O'Dwyer, who would become mayor of New York on the basis of the prosecutions developed from Reles's testimony, was astounded by what he heard. The existence of a major national crime syndicate, as well as a Brownsville gang responsible for over 1,000 murders, was revealed by Reles as he appeared as a witness in a series of prosecutions. The name "Murder Incorporated" was coined by *New York World Telegram* police reporter Harry Feeney, and it immediately went into the language.

Reles's testimony broke up the gang and, eventually, sent many of his compatriots to the electric chair, including Frank Abbandando, Happy Maione, Mendy Weiss, Pittsburgh Phil and finally "Lepke" Buchalter. Reles either committed suicide or was pushed out of the window of the Brooklyn hotel where he was being held.

MURDEROUS MARY (c. 1885–1916)

Probably the strangest lynching in the history of the American South took place on September 13, 1916, when Mary, an elephant with the Sparks–World Famous Shows, was hanged from a railroad derrick in Erwin, Tennessee, at the insistence of the local townspeople.

Mary had attacked and killed her trainer, Walter "Red" Eldridge, shortly after a matinee in Kingsport, Tennessee. Stories varied as to why she attacked her trainer. One possibility was that he denied her a piece of watermelon she wanted; another was that she went mad with suffering from a painfully abscessed tooth. A more unlikely possibility was that Eldridge treated her cruelly; if true, this would have been known around the circus.

In a macabre episode in American justice, "Murderous Mary" is hung by the neck until dead. (Collection of the author)

Although the Sparks circus had toured Mary for 15 years, and she had never hurt anyone in that time, the rumor spread around the area that "Murderous Mary" was a known killer, who had done away with between three and eighteen people over the years. The public demanded that she be killed, and the circus, for whatever reason, acquiesced. Mary's hanging took place in the yards of the CC&O Railroad, where a chain was wrapped around her neck, and she was hoisted into the air. The first seven-eighths-inch chain broke, and Mary fell down in a stupor. Before she could awaken, a second chain was put in place, and she was again raised into the air. This time she died.

MURPHY GAME

A SHORT CON of unfailing popularity that has been around since before the Civil War, the Murphy game preys on tourists, businessmen, sailors or other male visitors to the big city in search of female companionship. A typical "Murphy" scenario might go as follows:

An out-of-town visitor walks into a bar or coffee shop in New York's Greenwich Village, New Orleans's Storyville, San Francisco's North Beach or some other area known for its free and easy lifestyle. He tentatively approaches a couple of women who are waiting for their boyfriends and is rebuffed. Thus he establishes that he is a potential mark (victim).

"Murphy" walks over to the mark and commiserates with him on the difficulty of finding accessible women. "I happen to know a very attractive young lady who is not averse to having some kind gentleman help her with her rent in return for an evening of sexual delights," he says. "Shall I call her?"

The mark agrees. Murphy makes the call and comes back to the table. "She is home. I told her what an attractive man you are, and she is looking forward to meeting you." The mark salivates.

They walk over to the girl's apartment together. Downstairs Murphy is struck by a sudden thought. "Say," he says, "you're not a cop, are you?"

The mark assures him that he is certainly not a policeman.

"Just to be sure," Murphy says. "You'd better give me the young lady's—ah—fee before you go upstairs. That way you can't arrest the girl for being a prostitute, which would break her mother's heart."

The mark, flattered at being thought macho enough to possibly be an undercover policeman, gives Murphy the money and then goes upstairs to the apartment Murphy indicated. There is no girl there. When the mark comes back downstairs, Murphy and his money are long gone.

MUSTACHE PETES

"Mustache Petes" was the name given to the first generation of MAFIA bosses in the United States. It referred to their traditional Sicilian handlebar mustaches and was not a term of respect. The Sicilian Mafiosi transplants continued the old ways and primarily preyed on the Sicilians and Italians that had come over with them. In the teens and twenties such old-time dons as Lupo the Wolf, Salvatore Maranzano and "JOE THE BOSS" MASSERIA built their own organizations, but their ideas were rooted in the last century, and they were not open to change. They had no interest in considering the new opportunities in crime that PROHIBITION and the other peculiarities of the new world made possible. They also were actively opposed to allegiances with anyone they had not known since childhood. They provoked constant wars for dominance within the Mafia circle, which drained lives and energy, and took time away from more profitable enterprises.

The new generation of mobsters, such as ALBERT ANASTASIA, VITO GENOVESE, FRANK COSTELLO and LUCKY LUCIANO, felt the need for change, for expansion, for making a lot more money and having a lot more power. With what became known as the CASTELLAMMARESE WAR in New York, and a series of actions around the rest of the country, most of the Mustache Petes were killed, and the rest were forced into retirement. There is a legend, even within the Mafia, that these bosses were all killed off on the "Night of the Sicilian Vespers," which supposedly was September 10, 1931. This was the day that Salvatore Maranzano was assassinated, but there is no record of the 40 or so other Mustache Petes supposedly murdered on that day.

N

NARCOTICS

A class of drugs used to produce sleep or unconsciousness. Although this defines a wide variety of substances, including chloral hydrate, belladonna and alcohol, the criminal law meaning is usually restricted to opiates, such as heroin, morphine and codeine.

See also: DRUGS

NATIONAL ACADEMY

The FBI National Academy, now located in Quantico, Virginia, was founded by J. EDGAR HOOVER in 1935 to train selected state and local law enforcement officers. It was first called the FBI Police Training School and then the FBI National Police Academy. In 1945, it assumed its present name. The FBI describes it as "the West Point of law enforcement," and there are few in law enforcement who would disagree. When the first class of 23 police officers from all over the country went through its 12-week course, there was little training in police science available in the United States beyond the basic training given to rookie policemen in some of the larger city forces and the more advanced state police.

Over the years, the academy has taken the best officers of local forces, 200 at a time, and trained them in criminal law, modern techniques of forensic science and such elementary skills as marksmanship and interrogation. The schooling was free, and even transportation was paid by the government, thus putting no strain on the budgets of overburdened police forces. In recent years, the school has been enlarged to handle larger classes. Candidates are chosen on the basis of a geographical quota system, and in larger cities, competition for a spot in each class is keen.

The idea of a national police force has been proposed several times as a way of combating the increasing mobility of criminals and has been forcefully rejected. The two main objections for a national police force are a basic antipathy for giving the government more police powers than it has now, and the desire of state and local governments to maintain as much control over their own affairs as possible. J. Edgar Hoover used the National Academy as a substitute, accomplishing several of the desired results of a national police force without actually establishing one. With a body of similarly trained men in high positions in local police forces—and many academy graduates quickly rose to the top of their own forces—a degree of desired uniformity was achieved. Because training is provided by the FBI, graduates tend to look toward the bureau when in need of help, which encourages good relations between local police forces and the FBI.

NELSON, George "Baby Face" (1908–1934)

LAST OF THE MYTHICAL "ROBIN HOOD" BANK ROBBERS, IN REALITY A COLD-BLOODED KILLER

Brought up in the Chicago packing house district, Lester Gillis started his career of crime when barely a teenager by stealing cars, for which he was sent to the St. Charles School for Boys. When he emerged in April 1924, he had discarded what remained of his childhood and his name, choosing instead to be George Nelson, which for some reason he thought was more manly. He was called "Baby Face" by those who knew him, but never to his face, for he had a quick temper and a tendency to kill people who annoyed him.

In 1931, Nelson was caught robbing a bank and was sentenced to one year to life in Joliet Penitentiary in Illinois. A year later, while going back to prison after a court appearance, he escaped and fled to Los Angeles, California, where he tried his hand at bootlegging. Bootlegging was not exciting enough for him, so he went back to Chicago and robbing banks. He brought John Paul Chase, a California gangster, back to Chicago with him, and the two worked together for the rest of Nelson's life. Nelson joined with JOHN DILLINGER, a partnership of utility rather than affection; Nelson resented Dillinger's pre-eminence in the bank-robbing field, and Dillinger thought Nelson was a dangerous madman. During a robbery, Nelson could be depended on to kill or wound at least one innocent bystander, which Dillinger realized was bad for public relations. At the famous gun battle at the Little Bohemia Lodge in Wisconsin, where the Dillinger gang shot it out with MELVIN PURVIS and the FBI, Nelson killed Special Agent H. Carter Baum and escaped in one of the bureau's cars.

By 1934, the increased local and federal

George "Baby Face" Nelson. Behind an innocent face, he had the instincts of a killer. (Federal Bureau of Investigation.)

enforcement efforts were making bank robbery a risky profession. The FBI killed Dillinger outside a Chicago theater, giving Baby Face Nelson his fondest wish: he was now Public Enemy Number One. His triumph was brief. On the evening of November 27, 1934, Nelson, his wife Helen and Chase were driving a Ford near Barrington, Illinois, when they were spotted by William Ryan and Thomas McDade, two FBI special agents from the Chicago office. In the resulting running gun battle, Nelson lost the two agents but a bullet shot through the car's radiator. A little later his car stalled, enabling a second FBI car to catch up. Inspector Sam Cowley and Special Agent Herman Hollis jumped out and a gun battle began. Nelson's wife ran out into the field, while Nelson and Chase fired from behind their car. John Toland, in *The Dillinger Days* (1963), describes the battle:

Nelson impatiently grabbed a machine gun and said, "I'm going down there and get those sons of bitches."

A group of men planting trees several hundred feet away were horrified to see Baby Face walk toward the FBI car, upright, his gun blazing from the hip—like a movie gangster.

Cowley fired from the ditch as Nelson shot at him. One of Cowley's bullets hit Nelson in the side. But he didn't fall; he kept sweeping the ditch with bullets until Cowley dropped, fatally wounded.

Hollis was firing his shotgun. Half a dozen slugs tore into Nelson's legs but he plodded forward. Hollis dropped the empty shotgun, pulled out a pistol, and ran for the protection of a telephone pole. Before he reached it a bullet from Nelson's machine gun hit him in the head, killing him.

Nelson, his wife and Chase drove off in the FBI car. The next morning Nelson's nude body was found by the side of the road. The corpse had 17 bullet wounds in it. Two days later Helen Nelson surrendered. Chase was caught a few weeks later in California and spent the rest of his life in prison.

NESS, Eliot (1902–1957)

The king of the PROHIBITION agents, Ness and his 10 "Untouchables" did their best to disrupt the flow of booze from AL CAPONE's spigots to the drinkers of Chicago.

Ness was 26 years old and a Chicago University graduate, when he was told to create a special unit within the Prohibition enforcement department for the particular purpose of harassing Al Capone. Ness looked through the files of agents and picked nine associates whom he felt, based on their records, would be "untouchable," that is, completely honest and not susceptible to bribery.

Ness and his Untouchables succeeded mainly in distracting Capone, but never succeeded in disrupting his operation to any meaningful extent. However, they may have made it possible for the federal agents to infiltrate Capone's organization and gather the information that eventually ended in his conviction on income tax evasion charges.

Ness became head of the Prohibition investigators in the Chicago area and, with the end of Prohibition, took a job as Public Safety Director for Cleveland, Ohio. Cleveland was, at the time, mired in corruption, which extended to its police department. Ness, despite threats, bribes and an attempted frame-up, cleaned up Cleveland. By the end of his six-year term, Cleveland had been changed from a lawless battleground to one of the safest cities in America.

During World War II, Ness served as federal director of the Division of Social Protection for the Office of Defense. At the end of the war, he retired from public service and became a private citizen.

NEU, Kenneth (?–1935)

On September 2, 1933, in New York City, Lawrence Shead, a wealthy businessman, picked up Kenneth Neu and took him to his hotel room. Neu, a youthful, unemployed singer, murdered Shead and took his money and his best suit. He headed south where he killed Sheffield Clark, Sr., who owned a hardware store in New Orleans. On his way back north in Clark's car, Neu was arrested. With little urging he confessed to both murders and was tried and convicted. He was hanged on February 1, 1935. On his way to the scaffold he sang a song, which he wrote especially for the occasion: "I'm Fit as a Fiddle and Ready to Hang." He died wearing Shead's best suit.

NEW ORLEANS AXEMAN

AN EARLY SERIAL KILLER WHO KEPT NEW ORLEANS IN TERROR

On August 6, 1918, the people of New Orleans were given something more immediate to worry about than the war news from Europe. The New Orleans *Times-Picayune* headline that morning asked, IS AN AXEMAN AT LARGE IN NEW ORLEANS?

Seven years before, in 1911, three Italian grocers named Rosetti, Crui and Schiambra had been axed to death. Rosetti and Schiambra's wives had been killed along with them. No one had been prosecuted for the crimes, and it was generally thought to have been the work of the BLACK HAND.

For seven years the axeman remained dormant, or perhaps went elsewhere, but on May 24, 1918, he was back. He chiseled through a panel of the back door to the apartment of Joseph Maggio, an Italian grocer, and attacked Maggio and his wife as they slept. Maggio's two brothers, Jake and Andrew, lived across the hall. Jake heard what he described as "groaning noises" at about five in the morning and woke up Andrew. They ran across to Joseph's apartment and found Joseph half out of bed and his wife sprawled on the floor. They had each been hit once with an axe and then their throats had been slit with a straight razor. The razor lay on the floor; the axe—Maggio's own axe—was on the rear steps. Neither Mrs. Maggio's jewelry on the dresser nor the $100 in cash under the pillow had been taken. The wall safe was open and empty, but the brothers thought there had been nothing in it. The brothers immediately called the police.

The police arrived, looked the scene over and immediately arrested the two brothers. A neighbor had seen Andrew coming home between one and two in the morning. What that had to do with Joseph Maggio and his wife being axed to death three hours later is not recorded.

On the sidewalk about a block away someone had chalked: "Mrs. Maggio is going to sit up tonight just like Mrs. Toney." Somebody remembered that one of the 1911 axe victims had been named Tony Schiambra. Was his wife, who had also been killed, the "Mrs. Toney"? Was this another Black Hand killing?

On the morning of June 28, a Polish grocer named Louis Besumer and a woman thought to be Mrs. Besumer were attacked in his apartment behind the grocery store. It was the arrival of John Zanca, a baker, who was making his morning bread deliveries, that probably saved their lives. The store was closed, so Zanca went around to the back. He noticed that a panel had been chiseled out of the rear door, though it was still locked. He pounded on the door. A bloody Besumer opened the door, moaning "My God! My God!" Through the door, Zanca could see the woman on the bed, her head in a pool of blood. She was rushed to Charity Hospital, where she remained unconscious for several days.

The police found a bloody axe—belonging to Besumer—in the bathroom. They found letters written in Russian, German and Yiddish in a trunk. They learned that Besumer was new to New Orleans, arriving from South America, by way of Jacksonville, Florida, a scant three months before. The whole country was in the middle of a great, albeit unwarranted, spy scare, so the newspapers jumped to the obvious conclusion. The next morning the *Times-Picayune* headlined: "Spy Nest Suspected!"

Besumer's story was published the next day. He was not a German spy, he explained, he was not even a German. He was a Pole. The injured woman was not his wife, but Mrs. Harriet Lowe, who had come from Jacksonville with him. His wife was ill and was staying with relatives in Cincinnati. He had been hit while asleep and did not know who hit him or why. When he came to, he had found Mrs. Lowe lying on the floor and carried her to the bed. He was about to go for help when Zanca arrived.

But government agents had decided to look into the suspicious case of this Pole who had been hit by an axe while in possession of letters written in foreign languages. When Besumer went to the hospital to see Mrs. Lowe the next day, they refused to let him in. A bathrobe he had brought for her was taken and ripped apart to see what lay concealed within. The next day Besumer's grocery and apartment were searched. Nothing incriminating was found. But on July 5, Louis Besumer was arrested. It was told to the press that Mrs. Lowe had awakened, and the first thing she said was, "I have long suspected that Mr. Besumer was a German spy."

When she was interviewed the next day, Mrs. Lowe, in a vain effort to protect her reputation, said she was, indeed, married to Besumer. "I did not say Mr. Besumer was a German spy," she added. "That is perfectly ridiculous." Besumer was released.

Mrs. Lowe said that she had been knocked unconscious by someone she did not see. When she awoke, a tall, heavy-set man with an axe was standing over her. She screamed and "the next thing I remember is lying out on the gallery with my face in a pool of blood."

Mrs. Lowe changed the details of her story several times, which the police found suspicious. On August 5th she died, murmuring something like, "Besumer hit me with the axe," with her last breath. Or that is what it sounded like to the policeman writing it down. The police arrested Besumer again.

That night Edward Schneider, a young man who had been working late at the office, came home to find his pregnant wife laying in a pool of blood on the floor. He rushed her to Charity Hospital in time to save her life. She remembered only that she had awakened to see a man with a raised axe standing over her and that she had screamed as he brought it down. For a change the axe was not found at the scene. She recovered and had a healthy baby a week later.

The next morning the *Times-Picayune* headlined its rhetorical question.

On August 7, 1918, the mystery axeman was attacking Joseph Romano, when Romano's nieces, 18-year-old Pauline and 13-year-old Mary, heard the noise and burst into their uncle's bedroom. Pauline saw a "dark, tall, heavy-set [man] wearing a dark suit and a black slouch hat" standing by her uncle's bed and hitting him with an axe. When they came in, the dark man disappeared with frightening suddenness. They rushed their uncle to the hospital, where he died two days later. In a break with tradition, the police didn't arrest the two girls.

Axeman hysteria swept New Orleans after this incident. The police were inundated with calls from people who saw mysterious strangers chiseling panels from doors, leaping over back fences or creeping through the streets with axes in their hands. The growing paranoia was understandable. As the New Orleans *States* reported:

> Armed men are keeping watch over their sleeping families while the police are seeking to solve the mysteries of the axe attacks. Five victims have fallen under the dreadful blows of this weapon within the last few months. Extra police are being put to work daily.

But the axeman had stopped swinging his axe. Gradually the paranoia died down, and people forgot. World War I ended, the Eighteenth Amendment was ratified and people prepared to give up alcoholic beverages.

Then, on March 10, 1919, nine months after the last attack, the axeman struck again. In the town of Gretna, just across the river south of New Orleans, Charles Cortimiglia and his wife Rosie and infant daughter Mary were attacked in their home with the Cortimiglias' own axe. Iorlando Jordano, 69 years old, and his 18-year-old son Frank, who lived across the street, heard screaming and rushed over to help. They bandaged up the Cortimiglias and called the ambulance, but it was too late for little Mary, who was dead in her mother's arms.

Now a strange twist was added to the story. Rosie Cortimiglia, who had told of waking to find a tall, dark man over her, changed her story. It was the Jordanos, she now insisted, who had attacked her and her husband and killed her baby. The motive, she said, was jealousy because the Cortimiglia grocery store and the Jordano grocery store were across the street from each other. Her husband refuted her story, expressing bewilderment that she should claim such a thing, but she stuck to her guns.

The police experimented and discovered that the hefty Frank Jordano could not have wedged himself through the hole in the door where the panel had been removed. They also admitted that the *modus operandi* was exactly that of the axe killer. But, nonetheless, they arrested the Jordanos and scheduled a trial for May.

A few days later the *Times-Picayune* received a letter:

Hell, March 13, 1919

Editor of the *Times-Picayune*
New Orleans, Louisiana

Esteemed Mortal:

They have never caught me and they never will. They have never seen me, for I am invisible, even as the ether that surrounds your earth. I am not a human being, but a spirit and a fell demon from the hottest hell. I am what you Orleanians and your foolish police call the Axeman.

When I see fit, I shall come again and claim other victims. I alone know who they shall be. I shall leave no clue except my bloody axe, besmeared with the blood and brains of him whom I have sent below to keep me company.

If you wish you may tell the police not to rile me. Of course I am a reasonable spirit. I take no offense at the way they have conducted their investigations in the past. In fact, they have been so utterly stupid as to amuse not only me, but His Satanic Majesty, Francis Josef, etc. But tell them to beware. Let them not try to discover what I am, for it were better that they were never born than to incur the wrath of the Axeman. I don't think there is any need of such a warning, for I feel sure the police will always dodge me, as they have in the past. They are wise and know how to keep away from all harm.

Undoubtedly, you Orleanians think of me as a most horrible murderer, which I am, but I could be very much worse if I wanted to. If I wished, I could pay a visit to your city every night. At will I could slay thousands of your best citizens, for I am in close relationship to the Angel of Death.

Now, to be exact, at 12.15 (earthly time) on next Tuesday night, I am going to visit New Orleans again. In my infinite mercy, I am going to make a proposition to you people. Here it is:

I am very fond of jazz music, and I swear by all the devils in the nether regions that every person shall be spared in whose home a jazz band is in full swing at the time I have mentioned. If everyone has a jazz band going, well, then, so much the better for you people. One thing is certain and that is that some of the people who do not jazz it on Tuesday night (if there be any) will get the axe.

Well, as I am cold and crave the warmth of my native Tartarus, and as it is about time that I leave your earthly home, I will cease my discourse. Hoping that thou wilt publish this, that it may go well with thee, I have been, am and will be the worst spirit that ever existed either in fact or realm of fancy.

THE AXEMAN

The letter could, of course, have been a fraud. But there was something about it that commanded respect. On Tuesday, March 19, St. Joseph's Night, sounds of jazz permeated the city. One of the most popular piano pieces that night was the recently published "The Mysterious Axeman's Jazz." The axeman stayed home.

On April 30, the long-delayed trial of Louis Besumer began. With the war hysteria over, and nobody seriously believing that Besumer had been a German spy, the weakness of the prosecution's case was evident. The jury stayed out for only 10 minutes before returning with a verdict of not guilty.

On May 21, Iorlando Jordano and his son Frank were put on trial. Rosie and Charles Cortimiglia sat apart and did not speak or look at each other; they had separated after her accusation of the Jordanos. Each of them took to the stand, Rosie testifying against and Charles for the Jordanos. The defense called a parade of character witnesses, along with a reporter for the New Orleans *States*, Andrew Ojeda, who had interviewed Rosie shortly after she regained consciousness in the hospital. He testified that she had said, "I don't know who killed Mary. I believe my husband did it!" At this revelation the courtroom went wild, and it took the judge some time to regain order.

After three more days of competing witnesses, the case went to the jury. They were out for less than an hour, and when they returned they found the Jordanos, father and son, guilty.

The judge sentenced Frank Jordano to be hanged; his father to spend the rest of his life in prison.

On the morning of August 10, Frank Genusa answered a knocking at his door, and his friend Steve Boca fell into his arms. Boca, a grocer who lived down the alley, was covered with blood; a deep axe blow had split his head open. Genusa called an ambulance, and Boca was taken to Charity Hospital, where he recovered. But he remembered nothing useful; a dark man had stood over him with an axe, he had seen the blow coming and then nothing.

The police, over Boca's protests, arrested Genusa. They eventually let him go.

William Carson, a druggist, was up late reading on September 2, when he heard noises at his back door. He asked who was there and, when he got no reply, fired several shots from his revolver through the door. The next morning the police found chisel marks on one of the panels of the door.

The next day, neighbors of 19-year-old Sarah Laumann broke into her house when she failed to answer the bell. They found her in bed with minor head wounds and a concussion. A bloody axe was found outside one of her windows. The axeman had not entered through a door panel for a change. It is possible that he was frightened off by the ringing bell before he had time to complete his bloody task. The girl recovered but remembered nothing at all.

On October 27, a grocer named Mike Pepitone was attacked in bed and killed. His wife, who was sleeping in the next room, was awakened by the noise and opened the door to her husband's room just in time to see a black figure fleeing out the other door. When questioned she stated that she did not recognize him, that it was too dark and her glimpse was too fleeting.

Mike Pepitone was, as far as is known, the axeman's last victim. But the story has several sequels. On December 2, 1920, a woman dressed in black and heavily veiled stepped from a doorway in Los Angeles and shot and killed Joseph Mumfre. She was taken into custody, and told the police only that her name was Mrs. Esther Albano. Why she stood mute is unknown. Several days later she told all. Esther Albano was really Mrs. Mike Pepitone, wife of the New Orleans Axeman's last victim. She claimed that Mumfre was the axeman and that she had seen him running from her husband's room. "I believe that he killed all those people," she said.

Although both the Los Angeles and the New Orleans police forces were dubious at first, her story checked out to the extent that it could be checked. Mumfre had been released from prison in 1911, just in time to have killed the first five victims. Then he had gone back to prison for an unrelated offense and was released again less than a month before the attack on the Maggios. Between August 1918 and March 1919, when the axeman was strangely inactive, Mumfre had been in prison for burglary. The facts fit perfectly, but it was all coincidental with no proof but Mrs. Pepitone's word.

On December 7, 1920, Rosie Cortimiglia went to the city room of the *Times-Picayune* and asked to speak to a reporter. When several appeared, she fell to her knees and burst out crying. "I lied! I lied!" she shrieked. "God forgive me, I lied! It was not the Jordanos who killed my baby. I did not know the man who attacked us."

Rosie, thin, pale and ill-looking, was led to a chair. "Look at me," she told the reporters. "I have had smallpox. I have suffered for my lie. I hated the Jordanos, but they did not kill Mary. St. Joseph told me I must tell the truth no matter what it cost me. You mustn't let them hang Frank!"

She was taken to the Gretna jail, where she threw herself to the floor. "Forgive me! Forgive me!" she screamed at him. "You are innocent. God has punished me more than you. Look at my face! I have lost everything—my baby is dead, my husband has left me, I have had smallpox. God has punished me until I have suffered more than you!" The Jordanos were released.

In April 1921, Mrs. Pepitone stood trial. Her attorney tried for justifiable homicide, but although the court was sympathetic, he was not successful. She was sentenced to 10 years. She was out in three and disappeared from history.

Whether Joseph Mumfre was the man with an axe and a grudge against, mostly, Italian grocers, or whether it was the Black Hand after all, or some third party, will never be known. But the axe attacks did stop with Mumfre's death. The final toll was eleven dead, six wounded, and a city scared out of its wits for almost two years.

NEW YORK CITY

New York City has been infested with gangs since the Revolution, when the Mechanics lurked on street corners to patriotically rob any British sympathizers they happened upon. If British sympathizers were scarce, they would change sides and rob Patriots.

In the days before the Civil War, the city was divided into gang turfs; for example, the FIVE POINTS GANG operated in Five Points, an area around what is now Centre Street. By the 1850s, the area had become one of the worst ROOKERIES, a thieves' warren, which respectable people avoided.

As the various groups of immigrants moved into the city, they brought their own gangsters, until by the 1920s, there were Irish gangs, Jewish gangs, Italian gangs, and a few nonethnic gangs. At the start of PROHIBITION in 1920, the gangs grew larger and stronger. Internecine rivalry gave way to amalgamation and agreements dividing turf between the rival parties. Gang leaders like LUCKY LUCIANO and MEYER LANSKY, forged alliances that resulted in the formation of a national board of directors, with enforcement power vested in Brooklyn's MURDER, INCORPORATED.

When JOSEPH VALACHI and subsequent informers exposed the degree of MAFIA control of unions and legitimate businesses, the federal authorities and local police stepped up their campaign to eliminate the power of ORGANIZED CRIME in the city. But their success, to date, has been marginal at best.

NICKNAMES (criminal)

See: MONAKERS

NIGHT OF THE SICILIAN VESPERS

See: MUSTACHE PETES

NITTI, Frank (1884–1943)

Chicago gangster Frank Nitti broke into the underworld as a barber with a large hoodlum clientele. With the start of PROHIBITION, he became a small-time bootlegger and ended up fronting for the Syndicate. After AL CAPONE went to prison, the newspapers were looking for a candidate to be the head of ORGANIZED CRIME in Chicago. Since the real leaders had become increasingly publicity shy, Nitti was thrust forward to take the glare. In 1932, newly elected Mayor Anton J. Cermak, believing what he read in the papers, determined to replace Nitti with his own gangsters. Two policemen burst into Nitti's office and shot him while "resisting arrest," an experience he barely lived through.

Nitti began to believe his own publicity and acted as though he really were in charge of the Syndicate. When he was disabused of this notion and told that he was not only a front man but a fall guy, and would be expected to go to prison "taking the fall" for the more important gangsters, he could not bear it. On March 19, 1943, he committed suicide.

NOLAND, John T.

See: JACK "LEGS" DIAMOND

NORTH WEST POLICE AGENCY

See: ALLAN PINKERTON

NUMBERS RACKET

TEN CENTS PAY SIXTY DOLLARS—IF YOU WIN

Dating back in the United States to at least the 1870s, numbers games—also called at various times "policy," "Italian lottery," or "bolito"—have remained popular, particularly in the poorer areas of large cities, despite the best efforts of law enforcement to quash them. And often, due to the protection money that the large profits of the numbers racket makes possible, the police use something less than their best efforts to stop these games.

The basic pattern of numbers, a form of lottery, has remained constant over the years. The gambler picks a three-digit number, from 000 to 999, and places a bet with a local numbers runner. If the number comes up, the gambler wins at odds of (typically) 600 for one. That is, $6.00 for every penny bet. The figure used to produce the winning number is usually one that is regarded as unfixable by the people involved. It is the last three digits on some ever-changing large number, like the amount of money that the Federal Reserve publishes as in circulation that day, the total stock sales on the New York Exchange for the day or some other number regularly printed on the financial page of the newspaper. In the 1930s, the established number was based on the pari-mutuel handle of the third, fifth and seventh races at a given track for the day—the total amount of money bet on each of these races at the track.

A variant that was added to the game in the 1940s was "single action." After the better placed the main bet, a separate wager on any of the three separate numbers could be added. That is, if the bet were for the number 375, the better could then bet on the 3 in the first position, the 7 in the second position, or the 5 in the third position separately. These bets paid 8 to 1.

In some areas, two different games are run, in which case the one described above is the numbers game. The second, called a policy wheel, works as follows: A policy ticket has 24 numbers on it between 1 and 78. The winning numbers are drawn from a wheel supposedly containing all the numbers. The better tries to pick the numbers that will be drawn. Betting on two numbers is a "daddle"; three is a "gig."

The greatest advance in numbers popularity came in the second decade of the twentieth century, when the price of a ticket was lowered from a quarter to a nickel, or even a penny. This made it the poor man's game, and the profits increased as the price came down. "Dream books," pamphlets that would reduce a dream to a three-digit number, became big sellers in poor neighborhoods.

For a long time, numbers games were purely local in scope. A policy shop would service its own block, or a small policy bank would operate a group of policy shops. In the early 1930s there were an estimated 100 policy shops in Harlem and a total of 300 around New York City, with a gross handle of $300,000 a day. This profitability attracted DUTCH SCHULTZ, a Prohibition beer baron and racketeer, to the numbers racket. He quickly centralized it, offering the smaller banks the services of his one large bank. He offered protection from being wiped out by one heavily played number being hit and protection from the police and other gangs. For those who did not wish to go along, he offered assorted forms of mayhem from broken legs to sudden death. Soon, he controlled the numbers racket throughout New York City.

What made the game attractive to the numbers players was the large payoff: For a nickel one could win $32. What made the game attractive to the policy shops was the large spread between the payoff, at 600 for 1, and the true odds of 1,000 to 1. This meant that, on the average, for every $1,000 bet only $600 would be paid back as winnings.

Dutch Schultz wanted to improve the odds.

He used OTTO "ABBADABBA" BERMAN, a lightning calculator, to make last-second bets at the track to pull the pari-mutuel total away from heavily played numbers. The value of this service can be judged by Abbadabba's salary of $10,000 a week.

In the Chicago black community, policy wheels were first organized between 1895 and 1905 by "Policy Sam" Young. In the 1940s, the Jones Brothers, who then ran the racket, were sharing accommodations at the Terre Haute, Indiana, Jail with Mob boss Sam Giancana. They made the mistake of telling Sam that the yearly handle from numbers in the Chicago area was in excess of $30,000,000. Sam was released in 1946, and after a two-year turf battle, the Chicago Syndicate had taken over the numbers game. The Syndicate then discovered that black players disliked giving their money to Italian or Jewish numbers runners, and the games dried up. So the Mob gave the numbers play back to the black banks but took a hefty "insurance" premium off the top. Policy is believed to be the money base for the black, Chicano and Puerto Rican mobs in Chicago, as in other big cities.

Even with the proliferation of state lotteries and legalized off-track betting in some states, the numbers racket continues to flourish in big cities under the firm control of ORGANIZED CRIME.

O

O'BANION, Charles Dion (1892–1924)

Born in the "Little Hell" section of Chicago's North Side, Dion O'Banion progressed through the school of street crime to leader of the powerful North Side Gang, boss of such future luminaries as GEORGE "BUGS" MORAN, Dapper Dan McCarthy, HYMIE WEISS, and VINCENT "SCHEMER" DRUCCI. The gang, already organized and in place, was in a good position to take advantage of the opportunities presented when PROHIBITION became the law of the land. From his North State Street flower shop, Dion O'Banion and his men controlled over half of Chicago's illegal booze-running rackets.

The North Side Gang and JOHNNY TORRIO's syndicate, which represented the organized MAFIA in Chicago, came into constant conflict over the distribution of booze. Both sides recognized that there was enough profit for all, but they could not resist stealing from each other, and they had no hesitation about murdering each other. O'Banion tried to supply his North Side speakeasies by hijacking Torrio's beer trucks. Torrio and his lieutenant AL CAPONE responded by killing O'Banion's foot soldiers.

It seemed as if peace would finally be achieved when O'Banion announced that he wanted to get out of the booze racket and offered to sell Torrio his main illicit brewery for half a million dollars. Torrio eagerly took the offer and was properly amazed when, a few days later, federal Prohibition agents raided the brewery, shutting it down and arresting Torrio. O'Banion, who had advance information that the raid was coming, was very pleased with the results of his ploy and refused to even consider giving the money back to Torrio. He had cheated him fair and square, and if Torrio and Capone did not like it, then, as O'Banion said to Weiss, "To hell with them Sicilians."

The Sicilians had other ideas. On November 10, 1924, three men walked into O'Banion's flower shop. O'Banion thought they had come to pick up a floral order for the funeral of politician Mike Merlo, who had died two days before. One of the three took O'Banion by the hand and held tight, so that O'Banion could not draw his gun, while the other two men pulled their pistols and pumped bullet after bullet into the Irish gang leader. It is believed that the principal gunman was FRANKIE YALE, imported from Brooklyn for the occasion.

O'Banion had one of the finest funerals in Chicago's history.

OCUISH, Hannah (1864–1876)

In New London, Connecticut, in 1876, 12-year-old Hannah Ocuish was tried for the murder of 6-year-old Eunice Bolles during an argument over some strawberries. Hannah, an abandoned child with Indian blood, who was believed to be feeble-minded, was found guilty and, on December 20, hanged. "She said very little and appeared greatly afraid and seemed to want somebody to help her," according to a witness at the execution.

OFF THE WALL

See: SHORT CONS

OHIO GANG

A CROOKED POLITICIAN CAN STEAL MORE WITH A SMILE AND A PEN THAN ANY HOODLUM WITH A GUN

Warren Gamaliel Harding of Ohio took office as president of the United States in 1921. He rose through the political ranks, not because of any innate intelligence or ability, but because, as one of his aides said, "He looked like a President ought to look." And he gave good speeches.

He brought to Washington with him an assortment of his old Ohio cronies, such as Harry Daugherty, Charley Forbes, Ned McLean, Jesse Smith, his personal physician "Doc" Sawyer and old pal bootlegger "Mort" Mortimer. He appointed some good men to the Cabinet, but he paid little attention to their advice. He spent much of his time playing poker with his old buddies. As Alice Roosevelt Longworth described in *Crowded Hours* (1933):

> No rumor could have exceeded the reality; the study was filled with cronies . . . the air heavy with tobacco smoke, trays with bottles containing every imaginable brand of whiskey stood about, cards and poker chips ready at hand—a general atmosphere of waistcoat unbuttoned, feet on desk, and spittoons alongside.

While the members of the Cabinet tried to run the government with no help from the president, the president's buddies, who became known as the "Ohio Gang," set up officekeeping in a small green house at 1625 K Street, which became promptly and logically known as "The Little Green House." There, as Samuel Hopkins Adams described in "The Timely Death of President Harding," (from *The Aspirin Age* [1949], edited by Isabel Leighton) "they dealt in liquor withdrawal permits, appointments to office, illegal concessions, immunity from prosecution, pardons and paroles for criminals, and various minor grafts. It was in its way a *maison de joie* as well as a commercial center. Senators, Congressmen, Cabinet members, and other officeholders—and the place was patronized by all these classes—could find drinks at any hour and be accommodated with feminine companions from a choice list of ladies-at-call."

The Ohio Gang made the Little Green House pay well. When Daugherty became Harding's attorney general, his net worth was minus $18,000. Two years later, on a salary of $12,000 a year, he had managed to save well over $100,000. Jesse Smith was the administration's bag man. He worked out of the Department of Justice, dispensing the government's largess and collecting large sums of (preferably) cash. He traveled on a departmental pass, used the department's letterhead, and put his mail through the department's mail room.

He was not an employee of the Justice Department, but nobody seemed to notice.

Bureau of Investigation agent GASTON BULLOCK MEANS was a Little Green House habitué. He may not have been from Ohio, but he was one of the most consummate con men who ever wore a badge, and he had a lot to teach his Ohio Gang confreres. In the fullness of time, he would go to prison for bilking Ned McLean's wife out of $100,000.

The graft ring quickly spread beyond Harding's Ohio cronies. Albert B. Fall, a former Senator from New Mexico, was appointed Secretary of the Interior and had responsibility for the oil reserves at Teapot Dome, Wyoming, and Elk Hills Fields, California, taken from the Department of the Navy and given to the Interior Department. Then he proceeded to lease them, without competitive bidding, to his buddies Edward L. Doheny of the Pan-American Petroleum Company and Harry B. Sinclair of Sinclair Oil. For this slight favor, worth over $100 million to the two oilmen, Fall collected over $300,000, of which $100,000 was delivered in cash in a little black bag.

Harding made the mistake of trusting his friends, for he apparently knew nothing of what was going on. When he found out, he was upset. A White House visitor, who opened the wrong door, saw the president trying to strangle Charley Forbes, screaming, "You yellow rat! You double-crossing bastard!" As the skein of deceit started to unravel, Charles F. Cramer, Charley Forbes's right-hand man, committed suicide. Harding called in Jesse Smith for a long, heart-to-heart talk. Jesse apparently told all and then went back to his hotel and blew his brains out.

Harding died of a blood clot on the brain in August 1923, before the scandals broke on an astonished country. After Harding died, the incredible story of graft and corruption unfolded in a series of criminal trials. Charley Forbes and Albert B. Fall went to prison. Harry F. Sinclair went to jail for jury-tampering and contempt of court. Alien property custodian Thomas W. Miller went to prison. Navy Secretary Edwin Denby, who had turned the oil property over to Fall, resigned when it became clear that, although innocent of any criminal involvement, he was too ignorant to hold his job.

ORGANIZED CRIME

THE RICHEST CORPORATION IN THE WORLD

Organized crime is a special and delicate sprout of the weed of crime, which requires a long period of nurturing and encouragement. It needs a peculiar interrelationship between the criminal, the politician, the police, and the public. If these conditions are met, it will become major industry, as it has today in the United States, with a larger gross revenue than Mexico or France.

One of the problems in discussing this subject is the definition of "organized crime." The term is in common use by law enforcement and the media, but as with Humpty Dumpty in *Alice in Wonderland*, it means whatever its user wants it to mean. While many observers used the term *organized crime* as a euphemism for the MAFIA, many others refused to admit the existence of a Mafia. For years, the FEDERAL BUREAU OF INVESTIGATION denied the existence of any criminal organizations larger than a local gang. Part of this was political, allowing the FBI to focus on J. EDGAR HOOVER's major interest: domestic subversion. But part of it was the fact that organized criminals have very strong reasons for not discussing the doings, or even the existence, of their organization.

In *The American Way of Crime* (1980), Frank Browning and John Gerassi noted that

> Gangsters are not noted for opening their books to investigative reporters, so most writers on organized crime have had to depend upon raw police files. There is, therefore, a shadowy quality to all the

accounts, not unlike Plato's allegory of the cave, in which we can only surmise what the actors are doing because we are only permitted to face the wall watching the movement of their shadows. Are the two figures whose shadows briefly merge merely passing one another from an oblique angle, or have they met to discuss an agreement? As bosses rise and fall before each other's knives and bullets, as family organizations prosper and wither in their struggle for new territories, as unions and insurance funds and gambling combines and hotel chains conspire and collapse, there remain always the questions of who is in control, for how long, and why American society has been uniquely supportive of such large-scale racketeering.

The professional criminal is a sociopath; a person who sees other human beings as two-dimensional cutouts to be manipulated, who cannot empathize with them, and sees no reason not to deprive them of property or even life if it is to his or her benefit. An organization of professional criminals is, then, a precarious creation, since each member is just as liable to prey on fellow members as on the public. This is true even when the base of the organization is the family. What keeps them together is a social organization sanctified by usage, a boss able to inspire fear in the rank and file and a public that is easier to prey on than their fellow criminals. There must also be an object to this criminal association—something that is more easily gained in concert than separately. This "something" is political protection. A criminal organization subverts the police, local judges, and local politicians and, in that subversion, is its strength and its reason for existing. Occasionally, a city which harbors organized crime will have a clean-up campaign, and a reform mayor will come into office, but the organized criminals can weather such periods, for their structure is already in place.

Crime was organized in America, in one sense or another, since before the Revolution. It has drawn its membership from every ethnic group in the succeeding waves of immigration that so enriched our cultural heritage. The English, Irish, Chinese, Germans, Jews, Italians, Latinos and Japanese have produced gangsters, as well as judges, teachers and doctors. The first successful large-scale organized criminals in North America were the PIRATES who plied the coastal waters and struck as far afield as the Mediterranean and the Pacific Ocean from bases in the Carolinas, Maryland and Long Island. The Reconstruction period after the Civil War brought the KU KLUX KLAN. In the years before World War I, there were the Mechanics, the Molly McGuires and the Tongs of New York and San Francisco, among others, but the real beginning of what we now think of as organized crime in America was PROHIBITION, established in 1920, and the attempts to enforce it.

The organization criminal is a man who purveys a product that the public wants. It is the product that produces the organization. The desire for the product by the public makes the subversion of authority possible. A policeman or judge who would not countenance burglary might wink at bootlegging and take a bribe for the wink. By the time the official finds himself winking at murder, it is far too late for him to back out.

If there is a market for bootleg Scotch, then that market will be filled. But to buy Scotch in Scotland, ship it to Canada, run it across the border into the United States, and then distribute it to speakeasies from San Francisco to New Orleans, without being stopped by the law, takes a large and well-run organization. Ships have to be unloaded. Trucks have to be at the right place at the right time. Warehouses have to be rented. Local police captains and commissioners have to be bought. Federal agents have to be avoided.

Following the example of bootlegging, small gangs or individual entrepreneurs dealing in gambling, prostitution, or other social "necessities" found it to their advantage to combine and work together. But they were not used to working together, and problems of authority and leadership cropped up. A guiding hand was needed to establish overall control.

The question as to whose hand would do the guiding led to some of the more colorful disputes of the 1920s, one of the better known culminating in the ST. VALENTINE'S DAY MASSACRE in a Chicago garage, which made AL CAPONE the undisputed boss of midwestern hootch-purveying.

The bloody warfare was unproductive and dangerous, so the leaders of the various organizations met together and produced an uneasy alliance, which reduced the intramural shootings to an acceptable minimum.

With the repeal of Prohibition in 1933, the bootleggers were suddenly out of business. Used to the free flow of money that can only come with illegal enterprise, they turned to various other forms of crime. After a brief fling with kidnapping, which proved unsatisfactory for all concerned, they settled on gambling, loan sharking, narcotics, prostitution, smuggling (cigarettes and liquor from no-tax states to high-tax states), and infiltrating unions and legitimate businesses. They had been involved in all of these enterprises before Prohibition, but now they were tightly organized and much more effective.

By this time, the gangs had staked out territories, with the Commission firmly in place to handle any questions of overlap or new opportunities. Increasingly, the legitimate enterprises were of greater importance, albeit run with the same illegitimate methods of coercive force, graft, extortion, larceny and murder. Occasionally, as with the APALACHIN CONFERENCE of 1957, large groups of mobsters would gather to handle all the petty problems that crop up in any major business. Of the 75 or so mobsters at Apalachin, 9 were in the coin-operated machine industry, 16 were in the garment industry, 10 owned grocery stores, 17 owned bars or restaurants, 11 were in the olive oil and cheese business, and 9 were in the construction business. Others were involved with automobile agencies, coal companies, entertainment, funeral homes, linen and laundry enterprises, trucking, waterfront activities, and bakeries. Some owned race horses, and a few owned pieces of race tracks.

As newer waves of immigration entered the country, the traditional Italian, Jewish, Irish, black, and nondenominational gangsters were joined by, and threatened by, Puerto Rican, Cuban, Chinese, Japanese and other ethnic groups which quickly learned the American ethos of free enterprise. Colombian gangsters have come north with their coca leaves to bring indiscriminate murder to American cities.

Today, organized crime is flourishing as never before, with the sale of cocaine bolstering the takeover of legitimate businesses and unions, which are then gutted and left. Government enforcement has been strengthened with laws that enable it to take away the profits if it can prove the crime, or even a pattern of criminal intent. But criminal intent is often in the eye of the beholder, and some enforcement officers see criminal intent behind every bush. The use of overly coercive laws with too broad of a focus, which occasionally inflict unjust penalties on innocent bystanders, may prove increasingly unpopular as the public comes to understand their effect. When someone's house or car is taken away without due process because he or she unwittingly let a drug dealer use it, or when someone goes to jail for unwittingly selling an aircraft to a drug transporter, this creates an ever-enlarging pool of people with lessened respect for the law. This method of fighting organized crime may simply help create the climate in which organized crime can prosper.

See also: RICO

OSWALD, Lee Harvey (1939–1963)

THE MAN WHO ASSASSINATED PRESIDENT JOHN F. KENNEDY AND CREATED A FLOURISHING INDUSTRY FOR CONSPIRACY THEORIES

Although Lee Harvey Oswald is known as the man who assassinated John F. Kennedy, thirty-fifth president of the United States, there are several versions of the events surrounding the president's death. The official one, put forth by the Warren Commission which investigated on behalf of the government immediately afterward, is that Oswald was a lone gunman with a grudge. On the morning of November 22, 1963, Oswald went to a sixth-floor window of the Texas School Book Depository, where he worked as a stock handler, and waited for the Kennedy motorcade to pass. A few weeks earlier, he had purchased a mail-order rifle, a bolt action 6.5mm Mannlicher-Carcano, made in the early 1940s for the Italian Army. He brought the rifle to work that morning, wrapped up with some curtain rods.

At 12:31 P.M., Oswald rested the rifle on the windowsill and fired three shots at the Kennedy limousine as it went down Elm Street past the book depository, hitting Kennedy and Texas Governor John B. Connally. Kennedy, fatally wounded, was dead before the limousine reached the hospital. Connally, with chest and shoulder wounds, survived.

Oswald left the rifle behind, concealing it in some crates, and casually exited the book depository. He went home to pick up a pistol and left again. Where he was heading is not known. He was stopped on the street by Dallas policeman J. D. Tippit, and he shot the officer four times, killing him, to get away. He fled to a movie house, where other Dallas policemen cornered him and placed him under arrest.

Oswald refused to admit killing Kennedy, but he also refused to admit killing Tippit, and there were several witnesses to that murder. Oswald's palm print was found on the Mannlicher-Carcano left behind in the book depository. Oswald's past history did not mark him as a killer, but it did show a mixed-up man with uncertain goals, who might decide to do something drastic to achieve the recognition he desired. He quit the Marines in 1959 with a hardship discharge to help his mother recover from an injury. But after a few days at home, he left for Soviet Russia, where he renounced his American citizenship and married Marina Pruskova, the niece of a KGB officer. In 1962, he tired of life in the Soviet Union and moved back to the United States with his wife and small child. In 1963, he moved to New Orleans, where he became associated with pro-Castro and anti-Castro Cubans.

Two days after the assassination, while Dallas police were moving Oswald from the city lock-up to the county jail for greater security, Oswald was shot to death by Jack Ruby, a Dallas nightclub owner with ORGANIZED CRIME connections. Oswald was surrounded by 70 Dallas policemen and blanketed by media when the murder occurred; the shooting was shown over live television. Ruby, who was a police buff, managed to get into position to shoot at Oswald because all the policemen knew him and considered him harmless. He insisted that he had acted alone and out of extreme emotion. He was convicted of the murder and died in prison shortly thereafter of cancer.

A motion picture of the Kennedy assassination was taken by amateur photographer Abraham Zapruder with a new 8mm Bell and Howell camera that he was testing. He was fortuitously photographing the Kennedy motorcade at the moment of the assassination, and his film shows the event in graphic detail. The film has been used both to bolster the Warren Commission conclusions and to refute them.

Because of continued doubts over the results of the Warren Commission report, the House Select Committee on Assassinations conducted an investigation of its own in 1978. A new bit of evidence was introduced: a tape recording of the police radio channel that might have caught the sounds of the shots. An acoustical analysis was conducted of the tape, which existed because the send button on a motorcycle policeman's radio was stuck in the "on" position. The analyst concluded that there were four shots, not three, and that the third shot was fired from a "grassy knoll" in front of the motorcade, not from Oswald's window behind the motorcade. Other analysts refuted this, claiming that all the noises on the tape were backfires or other neutral sounds.

The conspiracy theorists, who believe that Oswald did not act alone, are divided on what happened. Some believe that the assassination was a KGB plot, with Oswald as a Soviet agent. Some hold that Castro set up the killing; others believe that anti-Castro Cubans did it. Some blame the Mafia, and others suspect extreme right-wing Americans, possibly ex–CIA agents. Also blamed are the FBI, the CIA and Odessa, the secret Nazi underground organization.

The strongest presumption against any conspiracy theory, which includes the Warren Commission covering up evidence, is that Robert Kennedy was attorney general during the investigation, and it is hard to believe that he would have any motive in covering up information that might lead to his brother's killers.

OUTFIT, THE

See: MAFIA

PALMER, A. Mitchell

Attorney general of the United States under President Woodrow Wilson, A. Mitchell Palmer instituted the Palmer Raids of the 1920s to rid the country of "Bolsheviks." *See also:* FEDERAL BUREAU OF INVESTIGATION; J. Edgar Hoover

PANEL THIEF

A panel thief works with a prostitute to rob a man while his attention is otherwise engaged. The thief is stationed behind a sliding panel placed near the spot where the john (as prostitutes call their customers) will probably put his clothes. While the john is busy with the prostitute, the panel thief slides the panel and removes the john's wallet and other valuables. The prostitute has several ways of cooling the john down when he discovers his loss: the easiest way is to refuse to believe him and demand her payment until he leaves in disgust. The term, and the game it describes, dates back at least 150 years and is still being practiced.

A panel house is a brothel, hotel or motel that has rooms provided with the necessary sliding panels.

PARKER, Bonnie

See: BONNIE AND CLYDE

PARKER, Isaac C. (1838–1896)

THE FAMOUS "HANGING JUDGE" WHO WEPT AS HE SENTENCED MEN TO DIE

"Hanging Judge" Isaac Parker was named to the federal bench in 1875 by President Ulysses S. Grant. He rode the Arkansas circuit, which covered what was then known as Indian Territory, and sentenced more men to death than any judge before or since. He would bow his head when passing sentence and declaim, with a tear in his eye, "I do not desire to hang you men. It is the law." Over the next 21 years, 172 defendants that appeared before him received the death sentence. Of these, 88 were executed. Appeals court decisions and presidential pardons deprived him of the rest.

Parker's reputation grew as those he had sentenced died. It became clear by the sheer volume of his death sentences, and because he seldom passed any other sentence if capital punishment was available, that he liked killing people.

When, in 1889, appeals were allowed for the first time from the Indian Territory, 30 out of 46 of those Parker had sentenced to death were found to have had unfair trials. The Supreme Court felt moved to tell Parker that the rules of evidence were the same in all parts of the country. In 1895, just before he died, Congress removed the Indian Territory from Parker's jurisdiction.

As Parker was about to pronounce sentence on a bandit named Henry Starr in 1895, Starr interrupted, shouting:

> Don't try to stare me down, old Nero. I've looked many a better man than you in the eye. Cut out the rot and save your wind for your next victim. If I am a monster, you are a fiend, for I have put only one man to death, while almost as many men have been slaughtered by your jawbone as Samson slew with the jawbone of that other historic ass.

Parker managed to swallow his astonishment long enough to pass the death sentence, which was later reversed by the Supreme Court.

PARKMAN, Dr. George (?–1849)

See: DR. JOHN WHITE WEBSTER

Louise Peete, the gentle-seeming lady whom nobody could believe was a murderess, including the people she killed. (Collection of the author)

PEETE, Louise (c. 1887–1947)

A MEEK-LOOKING SOCIOPATH, COMPULSIVE LIAR, AND COLD-BLOODED KILLER

The second woman to be executed for murder in San Quentin's gas chamber (the first was Ethel

Leta Juanita Spinelli), Louise Peete was guilty of at least two murders, and strangely, at least three people committed suicide after becoming intimate with her.

Peete did not look like a killer. She looked, according to Warden Clinton Duffy of San Quentin, like a clubwoman. "If you had met her without knowing who she was, you would have thought her a leader of civic activities in some suburban town," he said. She clearly thought of herself as cultured and well mannered, and except for those few moments when she was murdering her friends and lovers, perhaps she was.

Peete was born in Shreveport, Louisiana, in 1883, the daughter, according to her, of a schoolteacher. Her name seems to have been Lofie Louise Preslar, but she soon, and understandably, dropped the "Lofie."

In 1903, she married a traveling salesman named Henry Bosley. Within a year he divorced her. He died in 1906. She then, it is reported, turned to prostitution. She went to Boston but soon was kicked out of town for stealing knickknacks from her customers' houses as she left. In 1914, she was in Dallas, where she may or may not have married a hotel clerk named Harry Faurote. He was shortly found dead with a bullet in his head and a diamond ring missing. Louise was questioned and released. As we will see, she was an inveterate and inventive liar.

In 1915, she married a salesman named Richard Peete in Denver, Colorado. A year later, they had a baby daughter. In 1920, Louise left her husband and child and moved to Los Angeles. She rented a room on South Catalina Street from Jacob C. Denton, a wealthy widower who lived in the house. Whether their relationship was more than landlord and tenant, as has been alleged, is not truly relevant.

Denton was not seen alive after May 30, 1920, and Louise began throwing parties in his house. She ordered clothing on his charge accounts and signed his name to checks. When she ran low on money, she sold his belongings. When Denton's daughter and nephew began to question what had happened to their relative, she explained, in some detail, that Denton was "in hiding." He had, it seemed, lost an arm when a "Spanish-looking woman" who was visiting him got in an argument with him and pulled a knife. This was why Louise had to sign checks for him. When her stories were not believed, she shrugged and went back to Denver.

In September 1920, Denton's body was found in his cellar. He had been shot through the back of the head. Peete was asked to explain, and she and her husband voluntarily came to Los Angeles to shed what light they could on the mystery. Every time she told her story, she improved it a little, patching up the weak spots. She was arrested and held for trial. In *Murderers Sane and Mad* (1965), Miriam Allen deFord quotes Louise before the trial:

> I am able to preserve an attitude of calm because I am innocent. I have no visions of a murdered man to shake my nerves; no torments of remorse to disturb my sleep. There are other women in this jail who are charged with the murder of men. Some cannot sleep. Perhaps their minds mirror death agonies. I have seen them pace the floor and wring their hands. I have felt tremendous sympathy for them. My heart has been wrung with the wish that I could help them. At the same time I have thanked God that I am not tormented as they are.

In January 1921, Louise Peete was tried for the murder of Jacob Denton. She was convicted and sentenced to life imprisonment. Her husband stood by her through the trial and then returned to Denver. He wrote her letters saying he wished he could change places with her. In 1924, in Tucson, Arizona, he committed suicide. The daughter went to his relatives in the East.

In 1927, Louise gave a newspaper interview from her cell in the San Quentin women's department. "We need stepping-stones and people send us roll-skates," she said. "We don't ask for the advantages of a country club or a university, but we seek curative treatment so that when we are liberated we shall be prepared against any recurrence of the so-called mental illness that brought us here."

Peete expressed a belief in class distinctions among murderesses: "There should be some way, too, of segregating the better educated more refined women from those who have been brought up in close touch with life's slime and filth. They should be protected against being sullied by it."

When asked what her desire was, she replied: "I wish I could see a sunrise or a sunset. It has been so many years since I have watched the glories of either." Ironically, San Quentin, situated on a promontory in San Francisco Bay, has a wonderful view of the rising and setting sun.

In November 1933, the California Institution for Women at Tehachapi was opened, and Peete joined the rest of the San Quentin women prisoners in occupying the new facility.

In April 1939, after 18 years in prison, Peete was paroled. Because of the notoriety of her case, the parole office allowed her to use the name "Anna B. Lee" when she went out into the world.

During World War II, Anna operated a canteen for servicemen in Los Angeles. A woman who lived in the building disappeared, and Anna was questioned. She explained that the woman had hurt her hip and then died. The authorities pursued the case no further, having more important things on their minds.

While Louise was in prison, she had been befriended by Margaret Logan, a social worker from Los Angeles, and her husband Arthur. When Margaret visited Tehachapi she would make a point of seeing Louise. She found it hard to believe that this sweet, plump lady could be guilty of any serious crime. When Louise's parole officer, Mrs. Latham, died of, as far as we know, natural causes in 1943, Louise, who had been living with Mrs. Latham, moved in with the Logans and Margaret Logan assumed the role of parole officer. Louise took with her Mrs. Latham's .32 caliber revolver.

Once established with the Logans, the old pattern reasserted itself. The first problem was to get rid of Arthur Logan, an elderly man who was rapidly going senile. She convinced Margaret Logan to send him to the Los Angeles General Hospital for psychiatric observation, but they kept him for only 19 days. So Louise tried a different tactic. On May 30, 1944—24 years to the day since the disappearance of Jacob Denton—Margaret Logan disappeared. Her husband, who was not too senile to notice that his wife was absent, wondered aloud where she was. Louise explained that she was in the hospital. Arthur wanted to visit her. Louise had Arthur committed to the State Hospital for the Insane in Patton. He died in December, and she had the body turned over to the Loma Linda Medical College.

While this was going on, "Anna Lee" had married a bank messenger from Glendale, California, named Lee Judson. She now moved him into the Logan house. She followed her old pattern of forging checks and selling off choice articles belonging to the Logans, which nobody noticed. But the parole board did notice a change in Margaret Logan's monthly reports. As Louise's parole officer, Logan's reports had been favorable. But the reports that came in now were positively ardent. The parole board was suspicious, and in December, they sent someone to investigate.

They found Margaret Logan buried in her own back yard. She had been shot through the back of the neck, but that had not killed her, so her skull had been pounded in with the butt of the gun. They questioned Louise. She admitted to burying Margaret but insisted that Arthur Logan had killed his wife in a fit of insanity. Louise had not wanted to get involved, afraid that someone would suspect her because of her previous record, so she buried the body.

Her new husband was taken along for questioning. By January 12, 1945, the authorities were convinced that he was an unwitting dupe, so they

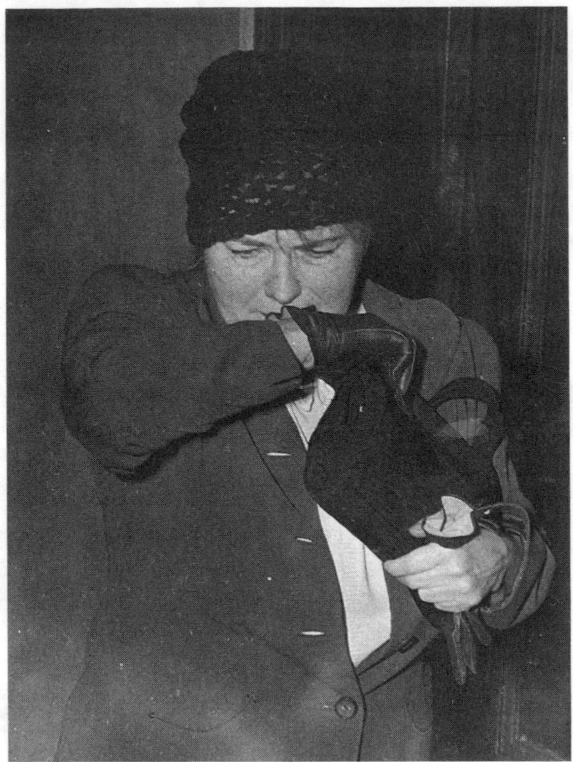

Mrs. Peete is taken into custody to be questioned about the disappearance of her employer, Margaret Logan. A few hours after this picture was taken on December 12, 1944, Mrs. Logan's body was discovered buried in the backyard. (Acme Photo Service.)

released him. The next day he jumped out of a window on the thirteenth floor of an office building.

It did not take the jury of eleven women and one man long to convict Louise of first-degree murder. She was sentenced to die in the gas chamber. It took two years for the appeals process to wind down, and then she was driven from Tehachapi to San Quentin and strapped into the green metal chair in the gas chamber. She met her death like a lady.

PETER TO PAUL SWINDLE

From the expression "robbing Peter to pay Paul," the Peter to Paul swindle is a close relative of the PYRAMID SCHEME and is the sort of CONFIDENCE GAME best exemplified by the operations of CHARLES PONZI in Boston in the 1920s.

PHILBRICK, Herbert A. (1914–)

The man who "led three lives," Herbert A. Philbrick was a member of the Communist party of the United States from 1940 to 1949, while secretly working as an unpaid informer for the FBI. After his cover was blown when he testified for the government in the 1949 subversion trial of eleven leaders of the Communist party, he gladly returned to his "third life" of private citizen and advertising executive. In 1952, he wrote *I Led Three Lives*, an autobiography of those 10 years and a classic exposé of Communist methods, tactics and goals within the United States. In 1953, the book was made into a television series of the same name starring Richard Carlson.

PHILLIPS, Clara (1899–)

THE "TIGER WOMAN" WHO KILLED HER HUSBAND'S MISTRESS WITH A HAMMER

A former vaudeville chorus girl, Clara Phillips retired from the stage to become the wife of oil-stock salesman Armour Phillips. Armour had little money, but he had a briefcase, a winning personality, a good line of patter and big prospects. With oil strikes common in 1920s Los Angeles, he believed in living on his expectations. Clara and Armour lived in a large house replete with a wide lawn, expensive furnishings, servants and three sets of silver.

Armour tried to keep from Clara the facts that

would upset her: his lack of success in selling oil stocks, the creditors pressing at their door and the affair he was having with a beautiful 21-year-old widow named Alberta Meadows. But Clara had a natural curiosity as to her husband's affairs and began to listen to his late-night telephone conversations on the upstairs extension. By June 1922, the conversations had become so interesting that Clara followed Armour around in taxicabs when he went out at night.

On July 5, 1922, Clara bought a claw hammer from a dime store and hid it in her purse. The next day she met a fellow former chorine, Mrs. Peggy Caffee, and poured out her troubles over glasses of gin in a Long Beach speakeasy. At half past four that afternoon, the two ladies found themselves in the parking lot of the Los Angeles bank where Mrs. Meadows worked.

When Alberta Meadows came out to get her car, she was accosted by the two tipsy women. They wanted, they told her, a ride to Clara's sister's house in Montecito Heights. Alberta presumably realized that more than transportation was in Clara's mind, but thought that now was as good a time as any to have it out with her rival, and she took the two ladies in her Ford. On the way to Montecito, Clara was drunkenly sweet, complimenting Alberta on her car, her dress and her new gold wristwatch. "My husband bought you that, didn't he?" she asked, suddenly turning nasty. Alberta denied it.

She stopped the car and the three women got out to talk. Clara quickly went into a frenzy, pulling the hammer out of her purse and chasing the now thoroughly frightened Alberta down the street. Peggy tried to interpose herself between the two struggling women, but Clara shoved her aside. When Peggy saw Clara knock Alberta down with the hammer and continue to strike savagely at Alberta's head and face, she fainted. As she came to moments later, Clara was standing over her rival's body, continuing to rain blows down on the prostrate and shattered form. Peggy vomited and fainted again when she saw her friend disemboweling the body with the claw end of the hammer.

Clara pulled Peggy into the Ford and drove off, leaving the bloody, mutilated body by the side of the road. She dropped Peggy off at home and then drove to her own home, parking the Ford in her driveway. Armour looked out the living room window and saw his wife emerging from his mistress's Ford. When she entered the living room he saw that her hands and arms were covered with blood. She crossed the room without saying anything and poured herself a drink. Then she turned calmly to him and said, "I guess it's murder."

"What's murder?" her husband asked.

"I killed your lover, Alberta."

We can only guess at Armour Phillips's emotions. But his actions were to tell Clara to drive the Ford up into the hills and abandon it. He would follow in his car to bring her home. An abandoned car in Los Angeles, even as early as 1922, was not strange enough to be noteworthy. With luck it would be stolen by someone and disappear forever. Phillips then put his wife on a train for Mexico.

By now the police had found Alberta Meadows's body in Montecito Heights. "It looked like she'd been attacked by a tiger," one policeman told the reporters. The newspapers put the brutal murder and mutilation of a beautiful young woman—as yet unidentified—all over their front pages. What sort of fiend was loose in Los Angeles?

Once over the initial shock of what had happened and the need to act, Armour paused to reflect. It occurred to him that he should see his lawyer. His attorney, John Haas, was stern and unsympathetic. He seemed to think that Armour, in his haste, had acted in a manner less than wise. Clara should give herself up. And Armour should certainly not aide and abet his wife in killing his mistress. The police would never understand. Haas called the sheriff's office and asked Undersheriff Gene Biscailuz, an old friend, to come over. Armour told Biscailuz what he knew of the crime.

A warrant was issued for Clara Phillips, and she was apprehended in Tucson, Arizona, and taken off the train. During the two days it took to get her back to Los Angeles, the newspapers had a heyday. They created "the Tiger Woman" before any of them had seen Clara. But the real woman, if anything, surpassed their hopes. Young, photogenic, willing to pose and answer questions, and stoutly denying that she knew anything about the murder, she managed to keep the front pages full during an otherwise dull summer.

Public interest continued through the trial. Seats were unobtainable, and the curious stood three-deep outside the courthouse each day for a glimpse of the Tiger Woman as she was brought in or out. Peggy Caffee told her story and pointed to Clara as the killer. Clara reversed the story. She claimed that she had, indeed, met with Alberta. In the heat of passion, she had called Alberta a dirty dog. Alberta had then slapped her, whereupon they struggled. And then Peggy, who happened to have a hammer in *her* purse, came to Clara's defense and struck down Alberta.

The jury was not convinced. They found her guilty of murder in the first degree. On November 16, 1922, the judge gave her 10 years to life in San Quentin. On December 5, while she was still in the Los Angeles County Jail awaiting an appeal, Clara Phillips escaped. An old boyfriend named Jesse Carson slipped her a hacksaw blade, and she sawed off one of the bars in her cell window. Then she wriggled through the 10 by 13-inch hole, inched around the corner of the building on a narrow ledge, slid 50 feet down a vent pipe, went down a rope another 50 feet to the ground, ran down an alley and climbed a metal fence to where Carson's car waited.

The pair hid under a house in Pomona while the hunt for Clara continued, and then moved to an apartment in Redlands owned by a woman who could not read newspapers. In early January, they crossed the country to New Orleans. From there, Clara took a boat to Mexico, where shortly she was joined by Carson and her younger sister Etta Mae Jackson.

A Los Angeles *Examiner* reporter, named Morris Levine, reasoned that if you cannot trace the woman, trace the money. Through some banking friends of Alberta Meadows, he found that Armour Phillips was sending money, in a roundabout way, to an address in Mexico. He passed his information on to the police, who telegraphed Mexico City police. But the Tiger Woman skipped to Guatemala before they could pick her up. She stayed one step ahead of the law, moving to Honduras before the Guatemalan police could arrest her. But in Tegucigalpa, Honduras, her luck ran out. Carson was arrested for gun smuggling, and Clara was arrested and held for extradition. Sheriff Eugene Biscailuz came down to get her, and Morris Levine came along to get the story. Clara lived up to his expectations as the saga of the Tiger Woman continued.

The diplomatic pouch with the extradition papers arrived, but when it was opened, it was empty. Supporters of Clara, who felt that she was just upholding her womanhood, and that the *Yanqui* despoiler of families had gotten no more than she deserved, had removed the papers. It would take at least another week to get another pouch. In the meantime, Clara might be released—she had, after all, committed no crime in Tegucigalpa—and once again disappear. Biscailuz and the American ambassador, Franklin Morales, went to see President Gutierrez of Honduras and an agreement was reached to take Clara to Puerto Cortez, a town two days away on the north coast, and hold her until the new papers arrived. Biscailuz and Levine took Clara out of town by car, then transferred to a dugout canoe for the trip across Lake Yojoa, and then rode the narrow-gauge railroad to San Pedro, where the local military commander skillfully hinted that he needed a bribe before allowing them to continue to Puerto Cortez. In Puerto Cortez, they received word that the extradition papers had arrived, but they were worded incorrectly and were thus invalid. The Honduran supreme court was about to meet and order Clara Phillips freed.

Levine, who had been listening to Clara explain her innocence during the two-day trip, now invited her to prove it. After all, an appeal had been filed. If she were truly innocent, she would get aboard the American ship in the harbor and go back to New Orleans with them. If she were guilty, she had better flee like hell. Clara thought it over and boarded the *S.S. Copan* with them. From New Orleans, they phoned ahead to Los Angeles and then took the train.

In a final twist to the story, Clara was never granted her appeal. Under California law, an appeal must be filed within five days. Her lawyer, for some reason, had waited nine. And nobody could ask him why because he had died of a heart attack the day of her escape.

In 1933, the women's prison at Tehachapi was opened, and Clara Phillips, along with all the other women prisoners, was transferred from San Quentin. On June 21, 1935, the Tiger Woman was paroled. In 1961, she petitioned the parole board to be allowed to move to Texas and practice dentistry. They said yes, and she did.

PICKPOCKETS

As with any specialized profession, pickpockets have developed their own argot to describe themselves and what they do. A professional pickpocket used to be called a "gun," but with the inevitable expansion of language, he has now become a "cannon." A female pickpocket has been a "gun moll" for the past 50 years. There are pickpockets who work alone, but most prefer to work in groups of three or four, called "mobs."

The two jobs in a pickpocket mob are the "tool," or "mechanic," and the "stall," who may either "front" the "mark" (victim), or serve as a "backstop." The action is fast and positive. After spotting a mark, the stall moves ahead of the mark and gets into position to front. This is the act of distracting and confusing the mark for a second, possibly by stopping abruptly if they are moving in a line or in a crowd. If there is a second stall, he will backstop by moving into position in the rear to shield the actions of the tool, who actually goes into the mark's pocket for the poke (wallet). Contrary to popular myth, a tool can take a wallet out of any pocket, although some are better at one pocket than another.

Women who work as stalls are very successful at fronting male marks. When an attractive woman pushes her rear into a man's groin, however seemingly accidentally, his thoughts are probably not on his wallet for the next few seconds. As David W. Maurer says in *Whiz Mob* (1955), his study of the argot and behavior pattern of pickpockets: "The girls used as stalls of this sort are sharp, attractive girls, very well dressed and in no way resembling prostitutes. Their effect on upper middle-class men is immediate and disastrous."

When the tool has scored the poke—obtained the wallet—he hands it off to one of the stalls, who will hold it until they have a chance to divide up the profits. The handoff is done so that, if by chance the mark feels something, when he turns around to grab the tool, the poke is already gone, and the tool can be searched, all the while loudly protesting his innocence. Since pickpocketing is hard to prove unless the tool is caught with his hands in a pocket, the police have created a crime called "jostling," which enables them to arrest suspicious people in crowds.

Pickpockets tend to go where the crowds are, and they dress to blend in with the crowd. If you are attending the opening night of the opera, the three distinguished-looking gentlemen in expensively cut tuxedos standing next to you might be a tool and his two stalls.

The pickpocket's jargon is very specialized. Here are some of the terms:

Breech—Side pants pocket
Bridge—Left or right front pocket

Cannon—Pickpocket
Chump—Victim
Dip—Police term for pickpocket
Framing—Positioning the mark with the stalls
Gun—Pickpocket
Gun Moll—Lady pickpocket
Leather—Wallet
Lush Worker—One who steals from drunks
Mark—Victim
Mechanic—*See* Tool
Moll whiz—Lady pickpocket
Office—Oral or visual cue that the leather has been lifted
Pit—Inside jacket pocket
Prat—Rear pants pocket
Prat worker—A tool who specializes in rear pants pockets
Shade—To conceal the actions of the tool from the mark
Single O—A pickpocket working alone
Single O tool—A pickpocket who prefers to work alone
Slum—Jewelry
Stall—One who frames the mark
Tip—A crowd
Tool—The pickpocket who actually removes the wallet from the mark's pocket
Whiz Mob—Gang of pickpockets
Wire—*See* Tool

PIGEON DROP

Possibly the oldest, most elegant CONFIDENCE GAME, the pigeon drop preys on the cupidity of humans and in the willingness to believe in miracles. Since it preys equally on rich and poor, it has caused a spectrum of grief over the years. A good practitioner of the ancient art can clean a mark (victim) out of his or her life savings within four hours.

In its classic form, the pigeon drop uses three people: the "steerer," the "roper" and the "authority." The following is a sample scenario:

The steerer befriends the mark, perhaps in a restaurant. Together they leave and, after walking a block or two, see a wallet, purse or briefcase on the sidewalk. As they pick it up, a third person (the roper) reaches for it at the same time. There is then some discussion as to what to do with it, each of them kept honest (apparently) by the presence of the other two. They look in the rescued article and find something that might be valuable—perhaps a rare postage stamp. As luck would have it, one of them knows a rare stamp dealer around the corner. They go around the corner and intercept the dealer just as he is leaving his shop. The authority verifies that it is, indeed, quite valuable. He offers to buy it from them for $50,000.

As they are congratulating themselves on their good fortune, he asks them where they got the stamp. They tell him they found it. That changes things. The dealer cannot buy the stamp for a period of time—say, two weeks. He has to make sure it is not reported stolen.

But who will hold the stamp? They decide that the mark can hold the stamp, but first he has to show financial responsibility. Perhaps all three have to show financial responsibility. This consists of taking as much money as they think the mark is good for out of the bank and showing it to the others. He can even keep it, along with the stamp, for the two weeks. They just want to see it.

The mark goes to the bank and withdraws some substantial portion of his life savings. He brings it to the meeting place and shows it to the others. Perhaps the others show him similar sums of money. The money and the stamp are sealed into a package and given to the mark. He is to take it home and return with it to the meeting place in two weeks—still sealed. When he returns, his former companions fail to show up. After waiting as long as he can stand, he opens the package. He then discovers that he has been tricked, the package has somehow been switched and all he has is a bunch of carefully trimmed newspaper. He slowly comes to realize what has taken place.

The lottery scam is the latest twist on the pigeon drop, with perhaps an overtone of the SPANISH PRISONER. The mark is approached by an old sick man with a lottery ticket. Perhaps the man claims to be an illegal immigrant. He has the winning lottery ticket, worth millions of dollars! But he is afraid to cash it in because he is too sick, or illegal, and they will merely deport him instead of paying him. If his new friend would take the lottery ticket for him and collect the money, he would gladly split it with him. But, of course, his new friend should put up some good faith money first—say, his life savings.

Needless to say the ticket is counterfeit, and the sick old illegal is long gone by the time the mark finds this out.

PINKERTON, Allan (1819–1884)

POLICEMAN, DETECTIVE, AND SECRET SERVICE AGENT WHO FOUNDED THE AGENCY THAT STILL BEARS HIS NAME

Allan Pinkerton ran the Union Army's Secret Service during the Civil War and founded the first nationwide private detective service. He was born in Glasgow, Scotland, on August 25, 1819. When he was still a child, his father, a city policeman, was invalided out of the force due to wounds received in a street riot. Allan was apprenticed to a cooper at the age of 10, and he spent his teen years learning the trade and becoming increasingly appalled by the working conditions endured by the common laborer in Great Britain. He became a Chartist, a political persuasion dedicated to helping workers achieve some rights. This point of view was not favored by the government, and Pinkerton hurriedly left for the United States in 1842.

He started a cooperage in Dundee, a small town 40 miles from Chicago, inhabited mainly by expatriate Scots. It was here that, by default, he became interested in police work. Gangs of counterfeiters infested the countryside, making life difficult for small merchants. Pinkerton discovered one such gang and directed the local police to them. This made him an expert on COUNTERFEITING and counterfeiters in the eyes of neighboring merchants, and they implored him to help the sheriff stop the problem. He acquiesced, and the sheriff deputized him to watch for counterfeiters while he ran his cooperage, which by now included eight apprentices.

Among the subjects that Pinkerton had explicit views on was slavery, and his views soon made him a conductor on the "underground railroad" that smuggled escaped slaves into Canada. At the time, the abolitionist view was not popular in northeastern Illinois. In 1848, Pinkerton ran as a candidate for the Illinois state constitutional convention on the Liberty ticket, and came in last in a field of nine. He was also induced to resign his membership in the local Baptist church. Shortly thereafter, he moved to Chicago, which held more liberal views concerning abolition.

At the time, most federal government agencies did not have their own investigators but contracted for their services when required. Pinkerton worked for the Treasury Department to suppress counterfeiting in Illinois and was also employed by the Post Office to stop pilfering from the outside and inside. His success—he caught several employees stealing large amounts of money from the mails—brought him a certain amount of popularity among the citizens of Chicago.

The railroads, expanding throughout the country, had unique law enforcement problems. A given railroad line might stretch through dozens, if not hundreds, of police jurisdictions, with hundreds of miles of unprotected area, and railway predators could attack it anywhere along its length. On February 1, 1855, Allan Pinkerton was given a chance to address this problem.

Representatives of six railroads gave Pinkerton $10,000 to found the North West Police Agency, the first such private service, which would become the paradigm for all those to follow it. His job was not merely to protect the trains from outside marauders, but to defend the railroads' earnings from parasitic employees. The worst offenders were conductors, who collected fares from those who boarded the train between stations and those who arrived at the station too late to buy a ticket at the ticket window. The amount they collected was substantial, and there were few controls beyond their intrinsic loyalty and honesty to prevent them from pocketing a large part of this.

North West Police Agency agents began spying on railroad employees, which the employees understandably resented bitterly. When Oscar Calswell, a conductor of the Chicago Burlington Railroad, was arrested for pocketing ticket fares, railroad employees rallied around and hired the best lawyers in Chicago to defend him. He was nonetheless found guilty and sentenced to one year in jail, which enraged the workers. They petitioned the governor to declare a mistrial, but he refused.

In 1850, Allan Pinkerton founded Pinkerton's National Detective Agency, supplying guards and solving crimes for railroads, jewelry stores, banks and local and federal governments. In 1861, hearing of a plot to assassinate the newly elected President ABRAHAM LINCOLN before he could arrive in Washington, D.C., to take the oath of office, Pinkerton and his men managed to spirit the president-elect from Baltimore into Washington without incident. At that time, Lincoln and Pinkerton developed a high respect and regard for each other. With the outbreak of the Civil War, Pinkerton proposed an espionage and counterespionage service for the president with the following letter, sent by the hand of Timothy Webster, one of Pinkerton's best agents:

To His Excellency
A. Lincoln
Prest. of the U.S.
Dear sir:

When I saw you last I said that if the time should ever come that I could be of service to you I was ready. If that time has come I am on hand.

I have in my Force from Sixteen to Eighteen persons on whose courage, Skill and Devotion to their country I can rely. If they with myself at the head can be of service in the way of obtaining information of the movements of the Traitors, or Safely conveying your letters or dispatches, on that class of Secret Service which is the most dangerous, I am at your command.

In the present disturbed state of affairs I dare not trust this to the mail, so send by one of My Force who was with me at Baltimore. You may safely trust him with any Message for me—written or verbal. I fully guarantee his fidelity. He will act as you direct and return here with your answer.

Secrecy is the great lever I propose to operate with. Hence the necessity of this movement (if you contemplate it) being kept *Strictly Private*, and that should you desire another interview with the Bearer that you should so arrange it as that he will not be noticed.

The bearer will hand you a copy of a Telegraph Cipher which you may use if you desire to telegraph me.

My force comprises both sexes—all of good character and well skilled in their business.

Respectfully yours,
Allan Pinkerton

Lincoln arranged for a meeting with Pinkerton, who was put in charge of a SECRET SERVICE operation under General George B. McClellan, commander of the Army of the Potomac. Pinkerton and Webster served on both sides of the lines. Webster was eventually caught and hanged as a spy by Confederate forces in Richmond, Virginia. When Lincoln was assassinated at the end of the war, Pinkerton was asked to aid in capturing the plotters.

After the war, Pinkerton's engaged in all sorts of commercial police and detective work, helping towns and cities where the police force was too small or too corrupt to handle the local criminals, guarding the railroads and going after the JAMES BROTHERS, the YOUNGER BROTHERS and other train robbers of the era. Allan Pinkerton died in

1884, passing control of the agency to his sons, William and Robert.

Pinkerton's prized its reputation for honesty and integrity with its clients, but in the 1880s, when the agency was used for strikebreaking and union busting, its reputation with the common people began to suffer. In 1937, when Congress made labor spying illegal, Pinkerton's gave up that activity. But that had been only a small part of Pinkerton's operations. It worked with law enforcement agencies at breaking up the BLACK HAND gangs around the turn of the century. It provided guards for the Barnum and Bailey Circus on tour: When local policemen would sneak in to watch the show, the Pinks would stay on guard. It provided agents who worked for defense attorneys to gather evidence in criminal trials. Pinkerton's had such a great success in catching bank robbers that the thieves started staying away from Pinkerton-protected banks. When the FBI was started, its founders modeled its structure on that set up by Allan Pinkerton in 1850.

THE PINKERTON DETECTIVE AGENCY

See: ALLAN PINKERTON

PIRATES

In an honest Service there is thin Commons, low Wages and hard Labour; in this Plenty and Satiety, Pleasure and Ease, Liberty and Power. And who would not ballance Creditor on this Side when all the Hazard that is run for it, at worst, is only a forelock or two at choaking.

—*Bartholomew Roberts, pirate captain*

An old established custom, imported from the old world to the new with the earliest voyagers and explorers, piracy flourished from the sixteenth to the mid-nineteenth century off the coasts of North and South America and especially in and around the islands of the Caribbean Sea. The term *buccaneers* comes from the pirates who made Hispaniola (now Haiti) their home base. It was their custom to carry with them long strips of smoke-dried, salted meat called "boucans," in preference to the barrels of salt pork that was the staple food of most European mariners.

The pirate ship was run as a practical democracy. Since each man was risking his life for shares, each man had a vote as to how the ship was run, who was to captain it and where it would sail. But when the ship entered combat, the captain became sole commander, and anyone disobeying his orders could be punished or killed.

The self-imposed regulations that pirates sailed under varied from ship to ship and year to year, but a typical set are listed below, drawn up by the crew of the *Revenge* under Captain John Phillips, to which each member of the crew affixed his mark, in 1723:

1. Every man shall obey civil Command; the Captain shall have one full Share and a half in all prizes; the Master, Carpenter, Boatswain, and Gunner shall have one Share and a quarter.

2. If any Man shall offer to run away, or keep any Secret from the Company, he shall be marroon'd with one Bottle of Powder, one Bottle of Water, one small Arm, and Shot.

3. If any Man shall steal any Thing in the Company, or game, to the Value of a Piece of Eight, he shall be marroon'd or shot.

4. If at any Time we shall meet another Marrooner (that is Pyrate) that Man shall sign his Articles without the Consent of our Company, shall suffer such Punishment as the Captain and Company shall think fit.

5. That Man that shall strike another whilst these Articles are in force, shall receive Moses' Law (that is 40 stripes lacking one) on the bare Back.

6. That Man that shall snap his Arms or smoak Tobacco in the Hold, without a Cap to his Pipe, or carry a Candle lighted without a Lanthorn, shall suffer the same Punishment as in the former Article.

7. That Man that shall not keep his Arms

clean, fit for an Engagement, or Neglect his Business, shall be cut off from his Share, and suffer such other Punishment as the Captain and the Company shall think fit.

8. If any Man shall lose a joint in time of an Engagement, shall have 400 Pieces of Eight; if a limb 800.

9. If at any time you meet with a prudent Woman, that Man that offers to meddle with her, without her Consent, shall suffer present Death.

Until the beginning of the nineteenth century, it was not always easy to tell whether someone was or was not a pirate, even when most of his actions were not in dispute. England, France, Spain and the other maritime nations habitually issued what were termed "letters of marque," or "letters of marque and reprisal," which were in effect licenses to attack the shipping of countries with which the issuing country was at war. Those sailing under such authority were called privateers. The Constitution of the United States reserved the right to employ privateers to the federal government: "No state shall . . . grant letters of marque and reprisal." (Article I, Section 10) It was an inexpensive and effective way of harassing an enemy, particularly for England during its extended hostility with Spain. Spain was a great and wealthy kingdom, largely as a result of its two centuries of organized looting in its American colonies. Privateers sailing under letters of marque from English governors in North America bled off a noticeable part of that wealth as it was brought across the ocean. But the line between privateering and piracy was a thin one. CAPTAIN WILLIAM KIDD sailed as a privateer in 1696 and was hanged as a pirate in 1701.

When the wars paused from time to time, the pirates saw little reason to stop their profitable enterprises. Joined by deserters, runaway slaves, escaped criminals and gentlemen seeking fortune and adventure, they boarded and plundered any ship they caught at sea and, when they felt strong enough, went ashore to pillage seaside towns. The line between privateers and pirates was crossed often enough for the European countries to turn against the practice of privateering, and the use of letters of marque was outlawed by the Congress of Paris in 1856.

The last outbreak of piracy in North America took place in the Caribbean and the Gulf of Mexico in the first quarter of the nineteenth century. After the War of 1812, when pirate chief Jean Lafitte and his men were pardoned from their previous crimes in return for their aid before and during the Battle of New Orleans, the number and quality of pirates declined rapidly. With the U.S. Navy active in suppressing pirates in the years after the War of 1812, piracy all but disappeared off the U.S. coast by 1830.

In the past decade, a new sort of piracy has emerged: drug smugglers seizing private yachts and powerboats, killing those aboard and using the boats to run shipments of drugs. The crafts are then abandoned or sunk. Fortunately, as drug smugglers find more efficient ways to move their product into this country, the expedient of piracy is becoming rare. *See also:* EDWARD TEACH

PITTSBURGH PHIL (1908–1941)

Harry Strauss, known to his friends as Pittsburgh Phil, was one of the most accomplished hit men of MURDER, INCORPORATED during the 1930s. A tall, slender man known as a sharp dresser, Phil had a reputation for vicious behavior, even among his fellow killers. A consummate contract killer, Phil enjoyed his job and frequently volunteered for the more interesting out-of-town "contracts." When ABE "KID TWIST" RELES told authorities about the Murder, Incorporated operation, Pittsburgh Phil and his associate, Buggsy Goldstein, were indicted for one of his estimated 100 murders, the death of Puggy Feinstein. As he had no other possible defense, Phil decided to feign insanity during and after the trial. He refused to shave or change clothes, chewed on his attorney's briefcase strap, glared at everyone in the courtroom and did his best to foam at the mouth. The jury found him guilty anyway. At 11:06 P.M. on June 12, 1941, Pittsburgh Phil Strauss followed Buggsy Goldstein to the electric chair.

POLICE

THE THIN BLUE LINE BETWEEN ORDER AND ANARCHY

The United States is a patchwork of overlapping police authorities, both in function and in area or population served. Most of what we usually regard as police business—intervening in crimes in progress, investigating felonies and misdemeanors and making arrests, ensuring public morality and enforcing the traffic laws is performed at the local level by city or county police forces. Above them in the hierarchical structure, although not necessarily in authority, is the state police, in some states known as the Highway Patrol, and, in Texas, as the TEXAS RANGERS. Many states have their own detective division, such as California's Criminal Investigations Division or the Illinois Bureau of Investigation.

At the federal level, police powers are vested in the FEDERAL BUREAU OF INVESTIGATION, the Marshals Service, the Postal Inspection Service, the SECRET SERVICE, the Drug Enforcement Administration, the Coast Guard and several others. Each of the military services has its own police force, but its powers are normally restricted to offenses against the Uniform Code of Military Justice that are not covered by civil statutes, committed by military personnel or crimes committed on a military installation.

The states came into being without police authority of their own; all law enforcement existed at the federal level or the county and city level. The governors were the chief executives of their states but had no enforcement power short of calling out the militia. Around the turn of the century, however, state police forces came into existence. As Governor Samuel Whitaker Pennypacker of Pennsylvania explained:

> In the year 1903, when I assumed the office of chief executive of the state, I found myself thereby invested with supreme executive authority. I found that no power existed to interfere with me in my duty to enforce the laws of the state, and that by the same token, no conditions could release me from my duty to do so. I then looked about me to see what instruments I possessed wherewith to accomplish this bounden obligation—what instruments on whose loyalty and obedience I could truly rely. I perceived three such instruments—my private secretary, a very small man; my woman stenographer; and the janitor . . . So I made the state police.

The English colonies in North America adopted the police practices with which they were most familiar and which were most suitable to their surroundings. In the North, New England and New York, the towns established night watches, usually made up of a rotation of all able-bodied men over the age of 16. During the daylight hours, the townspeople were the police, as in England, responding to the "hue and cry" when a crime was committed. As the towns grew larger, it seemed more sensible to employ full-time constables, and the day watches were established. These constables had small salaries, and made most of their money as retrievers of stolen goods, either charging fees or collecting offered rewards. It was soon discovered that this system encouraged collusion between the constables and the thieves they were supposed to apprehend, so better methods were sought.

Along with the influx of European immigrants to the American cities beginning in the 1820s came exponential growth of population and a concomitant growth in crime. This was partly because the European peasants who came over took a while to adjust to the necessities of city life, and partly because, along with the huddled masses yearning for freedom, many criminals arrived yearning to escape prosecution for their previous escapades. The cities soon realized that the night-watch system aided by an occasional constable no longer worked.

In 1833, Philadelphia created a police force of 144 men, under the command of a captain appointed by the mayor. Twenty-four men were to patrol during the day and 120 during the night. The creation of the police force was made possible by Philadelphian Stephen Girard, who died in 1831, leaving a part of his large fortune to establish a "competent police." Perhaps because of the wording of his will, promotion within the force was entirely on the merit system, a practice that other cities took many years to adopt. Boston, in 1838, organized a day watch, which by 1844 employed 30 constables. It did not coordinate with the obligatory night watch, which continued to exist separately. In 1854, the city switched to a regular police force.

In 1844, The New York State Legislature established a unified day and night watch of 800 men for NEW YORK CITY, under a chief of police. In each city that established a police force, there was resistance to the wearing of uniforms, which, to the citizens was suspiciously like establishing a standing army. But gradually these fears faded. San Francisco had a chief of police and a seven-man force by 1850. By 1878, the force had grown to 400 men. New Orleans and Cincinnati established police forces in 1852, CHICAGO in 1855 and Baltimore followed in 1857.

In the South, where most of the settlers were farmers on small farms, which gradually grew into large plantations, another English custom was adopted—the county sheriff.[1] This became the norm in rural America as the country grew. Usually an elected officer of the county, the sheriff is still an important component of American justice.

The evolution of the big city police department has been a gradual and continuous one, changing as it learned to cope with the needs of the city. New York revised its police force in 1857, enlarging its jurisdiction and putting it under control of a seven-man police commission, including the mayors of New York City and Brooklyn. This was called the Metropolitan Police District and included the cities of New York and Brooklyn and the counties of New York, Kings, Richmond, Westchester and part of Queens (all of these, except Westchester, are today part of New York City). In 1870, a new charter passed control of the police department from the state legislature to the respective cities. The New York City Police was put under the supervision of four commissioners appointed by the mayor with the consent of the Board of Aldermen. Its composition was a superintendent, 4 inspectors, 32 captains, 128 sergeants, 64 roundsmen and 2,085 patrolmen, detectives, doorkeepers and other rankers. It was the inspectors' job to listen to and act on complaints made by citizens against the police force. The city was divided into 32 precincts, with a police station in each precinct.

The 2,085 patrolmen were kept busy. In 1869, there were 72,984 arrests made in New York. They can be broken down into these major categories:

	MALES	*FEMALES*
Assault and Battery	5,638	1,161
Disorderly Conduct	9,376	5,559
Intoxication	15,918	8,105
Intoxication and Disorderly Conduct	5,232	3,466
Petty Larceny	3,700	1,209
Grand Larceny	1,623	499
Malicious Mischief	1,081	32
Vagrancy	1,065	701

The recruitment regulations for the force set up by the Board of Municipal Police in 1870 and used until well into the next century reads as follows:

[1] The etymology of the word *sheriff* is noteworthy. In Anglo-Saxon England, the bailiff or other officer appointed by the king was called the "reeve." The head of a county—called a "shire"—was a "shire-reeve."

No person will be appointed a Patrolman of the Metropolitan Police Force unless he
First, is able to read and write the English language understandingly.
Second, is a citizen of the United States.
Third, has been a resident of this State for a term of one year next prior to his application for the office.
Fourth, has never been convicted of a crime.
Fifth, is at least five feet eight inches in height.
Sixth, is less than thirty-five years of age.
Seventh, is in good health, and of sound body and mind.
Eighth, is of good moral character and habits.
Applicants for the office must present to the Board of Commissioners a petition signed by not less than five citizens of good character and habits, and verified by the affidavit of one of them.

In the 1872 book *Lights and Shadows of New York Life* by James D. McCabe, Jr., the duties of a policeman are described as follows:

> The general misdemeanors of which the police are bound to take notice are: Attempts to pick a pocket, especially where the thief is a known pickpocket; cruel usage of animals in public places; interfering with the telegraph wires; selling or carrying a slungshot; aiding in any way in a prize fight, dog fight, or cock fight; destroying fences, trees, or lamps, or defacing property; aiding in theatrical entertainments on Sunday; disorderly conduct; participating in or inciting to riots; assaults; drunkenness on the streets; gambling; discharging firearms on the streets; and other stated offenses. The officer must be careful to arrest the true offender, and not to interfere with any innocent person, and is forbidden to use violence unless the resistance of his prisoner is such as to render violence absolutely necessary, and even then he is held responsible for the particular degree of force exerted. If he is himself unable to make the arrest, or if he has good reason to fear an attempt at a rescue of the prisoner, it is his duty to call upon the bystanders for assistance; and any person who refuses him when so called on, is guilty of a misdemeanor, for which he may be arrested and punished.

A patrolman was paid a little under $20 a week, which even in 1870 was not overly generous. If a policeman became permanently disabled "whilst in the actual performance of his duty," the Board of Municipal Police could authorize the Municipal Police Life Insurance Fund to award him a benefit of not more than $150 a year. If he was killed in the line of duty, then his widow received the $150. "But nothing herein contained shall render any payment of said annuity obligatory upon said Board, or the said trustees, or chargeable as a matter of right. The Board of Municipal Police, in its discretion, may at any time order such annuity to cease."

In his book *Memoirs of a Murder Man* (1930), about his years in the New York City Police Department, Arthur A. Carey describes the duties of a beat patrolman at the end of the last century:

> After a month of probation duty I was assigned to a regular post on April 3, 1889. It was in the lower section of the city, not far from the old Chambers Street station house . . . I took care of the multiplicity of duties that befall a uniformed policeman in a big city. There were, in addition to the watch kept for crimes and their perpetrators, the duties of guardianship. Women and children had to be helped across streets, guided to their destinations; lost youngsters to be found and returned to their parents. Watch had to be kept for fires, cracked water mains, street lamps that were out; for suspicious characters and unseemly happenings. Traffic had not yet become a problem.

Another view is presented by Police Captain Cornelius Willemse in his 1931 book *Behind the Green Lights*:

> The individual policeman was respected and feared in the '90's much more than he is today.

> There weren't many policemen on the Bowery, but the toughest gangsters took to their heels whenever one of them appeared. They were powerful, fearless men, mostly of Irish birth, and they dispensed the law with the night-stick, seldom bothering to make arrests. The toughs of that day dreaded the club far more than they did a jail, and with good reason. If you ran afoul of the law it was a hundred-to-one chance that you'd wind up in a hospital.

Police terms vary from department to department, but some are more or less standard. The following is a representative listing of jargon and slang taken from New York City Police Department, Philadelphia Police Department and Los Angeles Police Department usages:

ACU—Anti-Crime Unit; working from the precinct to combat street crime
Brownie—Traffic officer (after the color of their uniforms)
Bug—A completely sociopathic criminal
Chicken Hawk—A sex criminal who prefers children
CO—Commanding officer
Collar—An arrest; a good collar: an arrest with enough evidence to make the charge stick and with no MIRANDA or other legal problems
CP—Command post; a control point set up for a specific operation
CSU—Crime Scene Unit; the group of specially trained officers who gather forensic evidence at a crime scene
Desk Officer/Desk Sergeant—The officer at the precinct station house who is responsible for bookings and whatever else happens at the station, under the watch commander
Drop Gun/Drop Knife—An untraceable weapon carried by a police officer to drop at the scene of a suspect shooting, in case the suspect did not have one of his own
First Officer—The first uniformed officer to arrive at the scene of a major crime, usually a homicide
Green Book—The book kept in each detective jurisdiction to record homicides
IAD—Internal Affairs Division; the New York Police division that investigates crimes allegedly committed by serving police officers
M.E.—Medical examiner
Perp—Perpetrator; one suspected of committing a specific crime
Shoe Fly—An officer assigned to the Internal Affairs Division
Street Crime Unit—Precinct detectives assigned to concentrate on street crimes such as assaults, muggings and pickpockets
Ten Code—The verbal code used on police radios, for brevity, uniformity and ease of understanding
10–4—I hear and will comply
10–5—Please repeat
10–7—Leaving car for lunch
10–13—Officer needs assistance
10–20—My location is ________

See also: KNAPP COMMISSION

POLICE STRIKE

See: BOSTON POLICE STRIKE

POLICY

See: NUMBERS RACKET

POLLARD, Jonathan Jay (1954–   )

HE ALWAYS WANTED TO BE AN ISRAELI SPY—AND ISRAELI INTELLIGENCE MADE HIS DREAM COME TRUE

A civilian intelligence analyst for the United States Navy, Jonathan Pollard was arrested on November 21, 1985, for spying for Israeli Intelligence.

Pollard grew up in South Bend, Indiana, and was a graduate of Stanford University. Somehow, possibly because his parents were Jewish, he became an avowed Zionist. During his Stanford days, he claimed (falsely) to friends that he was a captain, or sometimes a colonel, in the Israeli Army and an agent of the Mossad, Israel's intelligence service.

In 1984, when Pollard was introduced to an Israeli Air Force officer, he made his claim true. He told the officer, a colonel named Aviem Sella, that he worked in U.S. Naval Intelligence and that he knew that the United States was not sharing all the information it should be with the Israelis under existing agreements. He offered to help redress the situation.

Sella passed the information about this possible intelligence turncoat up the chain of command until it reached someone in the top-secret Lakam agency. Lakam, an acronym for the Hebrew phrase meaning Science Liaison Bureau, had been established to safeguard Israel's nuclear secrets, but had gradually expanded its mandate to include the collection of technical information of military value. Israeli intelligence agencies had an agreement with U.S. intelligence agencies to share information of value to both countries, principally that regarding Arab countries or international terrorism. But the Israelis knew that not all information was being shared. And here, it seemed, was a man who was in a position to tell them what they were missing.

Mossad had a policy of never using members of the Jewish population of a country to spy on that country. It also regarded spying on the United States in the United States as a serious breach of professional etiquette, since its information exchanges with the Central Intelligence Agency were of great value. But Lakam was under no such strictures and was further motivated by a desire to compete with Mossad at its own game.

Pollard was taken up on his offer, and he started supplying information of great interest to the Israelis. There were bundles of documents on arms purchases by various Arab states, on Syria's progress toward developing chemical weapons, on Iraq's quest toward a nuclear bomb. Pollard, the walk-in spy, was obviously going to be of value.

At first, Lakam used Colonel Sella as Pollard's case officer, but then transferred him over to Yossi Yagur, science consul at the Israeli consulate in New York and the local Lakam station chief. In November 1984, the Israelis brought Pollard and his fiancée, Anne Henderson, to Paris to introduce them to Pollard's new handler. They bought him a diamond and sapphire ring to give to Anne as an engagement ring. In a classic intelligence ploy, they gave Pollard $10,000 cash and informed him that he was being put on a salary of $1,500 a month, the money to be held for him in a Swiss bank account for 10 years until he could claim it. Such action is done to build up an agent's sense of self worth and to put the agent under a sense of obligation to his or her handlers. If the agent is getting paid, he or she may be willing to take more risks or to work harder to earn the money.

Pollard brought stacks of documents to his Lakam handlers every two weeks. Using a courier card he had been issued, he was able to collect files from many agencies besides his own. Lakam later began giving him lists of documents they would like to see, a fact that later made the FBI wonder if the Israelis had another agent within the U.S. intelligence community feeding the names of documents to them. That question has not yet been resolved, at least publicly.

It was Pollard's supervisor, Navy Commander Jerry Agee, who started watching Pollard because of erratic behavior and soon figured out that the civilian analyst was probably a spy. He noticed that Pollard was assembling large amounts of data for which he had no evident use, and that much of it dealt with the Middle East. He informed the FBI, which was too busy at that moment to take action, and naval counterintelligence, which put him under surveillance.

On November 18, 1985, Pollard was detained for questioning. The Navy investigators allowed him to call his wife, and during the conversation, he used a pre-arranged code phrase that told her to gather any incriminating documents and get them out of the house. Unfortunately, while they had thought to arrange a code phrase, they had not discussed what to do afterward. Anne put all the classified documents in the house in a large suitcase and took it over to a friend's apartment. The friend was alarmed by Anne's manner and saw that there were top secret naval documents in the suitcase. As the daughter of a Navy officer, she could not condone espionage, even from a friend, and she called the Naval Investigative Service.

When Pollard arrived at home he called Yagur, his handler, at the Israeli consulate. He requested asylum for himself and his wife at the Israeli embassy and transportation to Israel. Yagur told him that if he could shake his surveillance he could come to the embassy, and they would try to help.

On November 21, 1985, Pollard and his wife drove up to the Israeli embassy in Washington, D.C., with the FBI one step behind. It was an intolerable situation for the embassy. Legally, they could have offered the Pollards sanctuary, but with the FBI sitting at the gate demanding the Pollards' return "for questioning," it would have created a major incident. Israel valued its good relations with the United States. The embassy turned the Pollards away, and they were arrested by the FBI.

Considering the amount of evidence that piled up against them, much of it contained in the suitcase that Anne Pollard had tried to conceal, the Pollards' lawyers concentrated on trying to cut the best deal they could for their clients on a plea bargain. At the same time, the Israelis began constructing a cover-up in which they attempted to minimize the damage to Israeli-American relations without admitting anything or accepting any of the consequences. It was a policy that could not work, given the amount of information that was bound to come out.

Despite his pleading guilty with the understanding that the prosecution would try to get him a lesser sentence, Pollard was sentenced to life imprisonment by the trial judge. His wife, Anne, who was charged only with handling classified documents, was sentenced to five years. The severity of the sentences was due partly to Pollard's boasting about the value of his work to the Israelis, and partly to the letter that Defense Secretary Caspar Weinberger wrote to the judge, in which he said, "It is difficult for me to conceive of a greater harm to national security than that caused by the defendant."

In spite of a pledge to help the American investigators uncover the truth about what they described as a "rogue operation," the Israelis did their best to obfuscate all details of the operation: who was handling Pollard, for whom he was being handled, what information was being sought and, most importantly, who authorized the operation. Lakam paid the penalty for its amateurish handling of Pollard and was officially disbanded. Pollard's first handler, Colonel Sella, by now a brigadier general, was put in charge of Israel's largest military air base, Tel Nof. When the Americans protested, pointing out that Sella had been charged with criminal offenses in the United States and made it clear that no American official would visit Tel Nof while Sella was in charge, the Israelis bowed to pressure and Sella resigned his command.

It is clear that relations between Israeli and United States intelligence agencies have been hurt by the Pollard affair. What is not clear is why it was undertaken in the first place when any risk-benefit analysis would have shown that the risk was too great for the perceived benefit. The best guess is that the decision to run Pollard was simply a case of Lakam trying to outdo Mossad.

PONVENIR MASSACRE

See: TEXAS RANGERS

PONZI, Charles (1889–1949)

HIS METHOD OF MAKING MONEY WAS SO SUCCESSFUL THAT HIS NAME HAS BECOME SYNONYMOUS WITH A MASTER SWINDLER

"Of all the get-rich-quick magnates who have operated, he was the king. He was ignorant of business, knew little or nothing of banking, his knowledge of foreign exchange was ludicrous, his statements to newspapers and businessmen's clubs were grotesque in their absurdity—and yet the faith in him was not shaken."

—*Boston Post*

In 1920, in the midst of what would become the greatest era of self-indulgent capitalism until the 1980s, a small-time swindler named Charles Ponzi, or sometimes Charles Ponsi, or occasionally Charles Bianchi, stumbled across a scheme so elegantly simple and so wonderfully lucrative that before it had run its course, he had removed from the citizens of Boston and surrounding hamlets a sum in excess of $15,000,000. And in 1920, $15,000,000 was real money.

Ponzi accepted money from his customers in return for an unsecured note for 150 percent of the deposit, payable in 90 days. For example, if someone gave Ponzi $100, he promised to return $150 in three months. If figured at straight interest, Ponzi was paying 200 percent a year. If compounded (if the investor reinvested the interest every quarter), the yearly interest was an astounding 406 percent.

Ponzi did not merely live up to the terms of his notes, he bettered them. Most notes were paid off in 45 days instead of 90. How was he doing this? He claimed that he had found a hole in the international monetary system that he was exploiting. The vast fortunes he was making for all those who believed in him were based on postal reply coupons. It seemed that the value of international postal reply coupons was fixed by treaty at a certain exchange rate; however, the actual value of the foreign currencies fluctuated daily. All that was necessary was for Ponzi's European agents to buy these coupons in countries where the rate fluctuation made them cheap and take them to countries where the current exchange rate made them more valuable—and his investors pocketed the difference.

The consummate swindler, Charles Ponzi, at the height of his success. (International News Photo.)

In fact, Ponzi was doing no such thing. The fluctuations in currency were so slight that Ponzi would have had to invest hundreds of millions of dollars in reply coupons to make the millions of dollars of profit he was paying back. And the countries involved did not print nearly enough coupons to satisfy such a demand. Had such a run on coupons actually happened, the various postal services would probably have just stopped issuing coupons until the situation was sorted out.

Ponzi was actually running a classic PETER TO PAUL SWINDLE in which he was paying off his investors with money from new investors. And "Peter" was pouring money into Ponzi's pockets at a much faster rate than "Paul" was taking it out. "Peter" had certainly caught the investing fever. The streets in front of Ponzi's little office at 27 School Street were packed with people impatiently waiting to give Ponzi their money. As the New York *Evening World* described it:

> Like a tidal wave, the passion for investment swept over Boston folk until it took more than half of Boston's police force to subdue the enthusiasm of a throng of prospective investors that overflowed from the banking offices, through the corridors, down the stairs and into the street, blocking traffic. . . .
>
> In his dingy little office, close by the old Revolutionary burying grounds, Ponzi doled out the notes and took in the money. In narrow corridors, up the stairway, at the doorways, with the air hot and dense from the crowds that gathered day by day, handsome women with jewels in their ears and the money-mad fever touched unkempt women with babies in their arms and children tugging at their skirts.
>
> . . . Lifetime savings were given away as if under the touch of an unseen hypnotist. Gaunt old maids gave their money away as if it were pest-ridden, boys in knickerbockers gladly turned over all their wealth. Widows in long black veils, stenographers, fruit peddlers in overalls, all kinds, young and old, rich and poor, some looking affluent, some downtrodden, jostled and pushed and sometimes fought to get a place near the magic entrance.

The Boston *Post* determined to investigate this phenomenon. But they proceeded cautiously. Ponzi was the most popular man in Boston, quite possibly the most popular man on the East Coast. There were some doubters, including newspapermen and public officials, but no one was willing to cast the first stone. After all, Ponzi was so rich, he must be doing something right. Then, as now, wealth provided insulation against retribution. Most people did not doubt—they wanted to believe. The *Post* reported that one afternoon, as Ponzi left the State House after appearing to answer some questions (which he did with magnificent aplomb), he was cheered by a large crowd:

> "You're the greatest Italian of them all," someone shouted.
>
> "No," Ponzi called back; "Columbus and Marconi. Columbus discovered America. Marconi discovered the wireless."
>
> "But you discovered money," called a voice.

So the *Post*, its curiosity piqued by the marvel that was Ponzi, investigated. On July 25, 1920, the first of a series of articles appeared doubting his veracity. Ponzi met his doubters more than halfway. He invited the district attorney and the U.S. attorney to send auditors to his offices. They did so, but the men they sent seemed unsure of what they were supposed to be doing. They poked and prodded, and they decided nothing, and Ponzi went on taking in money. As the *Post* continued to doubt, and a couple of other papers like the financial *Daily News Bureau* joined the slowly rising chorus, Ponzi agreed to stop accepting deposits until the audits were done. But he kept redeeming his notes freely for anyone who asked. So, after a brief run on his notes, people stopped asking and held onto their notes.

Ponzi explained to the investigators that he had "in the United States upward of five million dollars, and between eight million and nine million dollars in depositories abroad." When asked his plans, he revealed that he intended to start a different banking system. "Instead of giving the net profit entirely to the stockholders, the net profit should be divided equally between the stockholders and the depositors because the stockholders are taking the depositors' money and paying only five per cent," as he explained to the *Post*.

On August 2, the *Post* ran an article by Ponzi's former press agent, William H. McMasters, who was determined to bite the hand that had been feeding him. McMasters revealed that Ponzi was actually hopelessly in debt: The big pile of money in Ponzi's safe was more than balanced by the big pile of notes that he would have to redeem. As he put it:

> Ponzi has stopped operations for a week. He hasn't sent a cable abroad. He hasn't sent a dollar to New York or received a dollar from New York in spite of his claim that he is operating in millions, and he hasn't dug up a new dollar to meet the drain that must come to settle the $7,500,000 in notes outstanding, all of which must be paid in thirty-eight days.
>
> It would seem like a joke if there were not 25,000 noteholders involved in it, thousands of whom had put their last dollars into the scheme and think that because Ponzi hasn't been arrested he must be all right.

The next morning, Ponzi was met by a tremendous crowd at his office. He smiled and told them to line up. "I have one word to the public," he told the *Post* reporter, "let them come for their money, but let them come orderly. They will get it. I may run out of check-books, but I'll never run out of money." Ponzi rented a nearby tavern—the Bell-in-Hand in Pie Alley—to serve those waiting a free lunch of hot dogs, doughnuts and coffee. And he paid off everyone who came through the door. By evening the run was over. Many of those who had come to get their money changed their mind and left it with Ponzi. His self-assurance and determination had its effect.

Ponzi issued a statement to the press, in which he said he felt there were people deliberately working to sabotage his great schemes. "Should I be able to realize fully my dreams such a realization would mean the downfall of an autocratic clique which has been able to prey on the credulity of the people."

Newspapers throughout the country were evenly split between believers and doubters. Sometimes the same paper would be both believer and doubter on different days—or even different pages. The Rochester (New York) *Times-Union* straddled the fence, declaring: "Whether Ponzi's bubble bursts or not, the American people will have to take off their hats to a man as clever as he is." Their editorial writer could not grasp the concept that the whole thing might be merely a gigantic swindle. Some newspapers, while believing in Ponzi's truthfulness, objected to the "easy money" he was making for his investors on moral or ethical grounds.

On August 10, the Ponzi bubble burst. The *Post* reported that Ponzi was actually a Charles Ponsi, who had served 20 months in a Montreal prison for fraud and also served two years in the federal penitentiary in Atlanta for smuggling aliens. On the thirteenth, the federal investigators finished their audit. Ponzi's books showed assets of $1,593,000 against liabilities of $6,396,000. He was amazed. "I've been swindled," he declared. But the people were no longer prepared to believe. They finally saw their emperor's lack of garments. The Ponzi scheme to manipulate reply coupons had never been implemented. He just took money in with one hand and gave it back with the other. As Harold F. Wheeler wrote in the Boston *Post*:

> The money-making secret of the wondrous wizard was only a dream. His stories of how he doubled the amazing flood of dollars poured in upon him were fantastic lies. He never had any dealings in international postal orders save a few hundred dollars. He never had a scheme for manipulating foreign exchange.

He had no vast amounts of money in Europe, no army of foreign agents. . . .

Like Ponzi's stories of his financial "coups" are the tales he has told about his career. He made a romance out of his jail term in Canada by declaring it was a noble effort on his part to save his employer and three little children from disgrace when it was just a plain, ordinary case of theft induced by his love of luxury and fine clothes. He painted halos around his head, but the facts have shown only sordid swindles.

His bubbling vivacity, his boundless imagination, his smooth and ready tongue, coupled with a remarkable and winning charm of manner, his astute pretense of secrecy and mysterious hints of corrupt European governments ready to yield millions when approached in shady ways, carried him to heights of which in his wildest moments he never dreamed.

Ponzi was indicted on 68 counts by the State of Massachusetts and 86 counts by the federal government. His first trial was for using the mails to defraud. His defense of "financial dementia" was supported by the warden of the Atlanta penitentiary, who was quoted in the Boston *Transcript* as saying: "I don't think he has ever wanted to break the law, but he has an obsession for planning financial coups: he loves these things so well that he transgresses the law for the sake of putting them over."

This transgression cost him four years in a federal penitentiary. When he was released in 1924, he was tried in Massachusetts. His first trial there resulted in a hung jury, but in July 1925, a second trial convicted him. While he was free on appeal, he went to Florida, where he was convicted of spurious real estate dealings. He fled to Texas, but Massachusetts extradited him. When he got out of prison in 1934, he was deported to Italy. His story after that grows apocryphal. Some reports have him acting as a financial adviser to Mussolini, which is not altogether unbelievable, Mussolini would have liked Ponzi. By the end of World War II, he was in Brazil, where in January 1949, he died.

PORTRAIT PARLÉ

A French phrase for "spoken picture," *portrait parlé* is a system of describing individuals developed by ALPHONSE BERTILLON in the 1870s, and was adopted by police departments worldwide. Based on Bertillon's technique for identifying specific individuals, which he called anthropometry, and which depended on precise measurement of specific parts of the body, the *portrait parlé* allowed the police to communicate the description of a wanted person to a distant police department. Originally, the description was divided into four sections:

1. Color of left eye* hair, beard and skin.
2. Shape and size of various specific parts of the head.
3. General observations: body shape, carriage, voice and language, dress, observed social standing, etc.
4. Location and description of scars, birthmarks, tattoos, and other indelible marks.

As anthropometry fell into disuse, replaced by fingerprinting, *portrait parlé*, with its hundreds of precise measurements, has been also largely discarded. At present, the IDENTIFICATION OF INDIVIDUALS depends largely on fingerprints and standardized photographs, with a supplemental identification form used for recognizing or locating wanted criminals.

POULSATTER, Belle (1859–?)

See: BELLE GUNNESS

PRISONS

Toward the end of the eighteenth century, incarceration began replacing corporal punishment as

* An arbitrary choice.

the preferred method of judicial correction in the United States. This was largely due to the influence of the Quakers, who were repelled by the severity of corporal punishments and believed them ineffective. Reform groups tried to establish prisons as early as the last quarter of the seventeenth century, but the British government objected. The existing prisons, used for debtors and people awaiting trial, were little different from medieval dungeons.

The Society for Alleviating the Miseries of Public Prisons was founded in Philadelphia in 1787 by Benjamin Rush and other Quakers. Rush, a doctor and reformer, and one of the signers of the Declaration of Independence, felt that the humiliation of public punishment would only lead to more crime and that the jails then in existence were soul-destroying hellholes. The society, now called the Pennsylvania Prison Society, began by alleviating the miseries of the Walnut Street Jail in Philadelphia. By 1790, it had succeeded in removing the children from the jail, confining the men and women separately and separating the debtors from those awaiting trial for serious crimes.

By the beginning of the nineteenth century, there was general agreement that the whip, the stock, the branding iron and the ducking stool were ineffective tools of criminal reform and that what was needed was incarceration in which the prisoner could be exposed to good, wholesome work and reading or being read to from the Bible. In 1819, a prison was opened in Auburn, New York, to operate under what became known as the Auburn Plan. Prisoners worked together in prison shops during the day, under the watchful supervision of the guards, and retired at night to individual cells. These cells were placed back to back in several long tiers, and the whole cell block was encased in an exterior shell. Since the cells were to be used only for sleeping, they were just 3 feet 3 inches wide, 7 feet high and 7 feet deep. The prisoners were forbidden to talk to each other, even at work, and were marched to and from the shops in lockstep, their eyes looking down.

The Eastern State Penitentiary, which opened in Philadelphia, Pennsylvania, in 1829, used a different system, based on a Quaker idea of the curative power of isolation, which became known as the Pennsylvania Plan. The cells were considerably larger, about 8 by 12 feet, and had flush toilets and central heating because the inmates were kept in them in solitary confinement for their whole period of incarceration. The prisoners exercised in small, individual exercise yards behind each cell, like the dog runs in commercial kennels. It was arranged that prisoners with adjoining yards never exercised at the same time, so they would have no contact. The only visitors allowed were those approved by the Pennsylvania Prison Society, mostly clergymen, and the only literature allowed was the Bible. Prisoners were, however, allowed to work at tasks that could be performed individually in the cells, such as furniture making or hand weaving. This regimen of enforced isolation was supposed to restore self-esteem and prepare the convict to take his place in society as a reformed man. In actuality, this method drove a high percentage of the inmates insane.

In the 1870s, the idea of reform was introduced into penology, and the first "reformatories" were opened. New York's Elmira Reformatory was opened in 1876, and others followed. The experiment was tried on the younger prisoners, who were believed to be capable of reform. The prisoners were divided into three grades; they started in the middle grade and could go either up or down depending upon their behavior. Staying in the top grade was the key to parole.

The reform system gradually died, until by 1920, it was extinct. The prison guards were not given adequate training in the new system, and many of them would have been incapable of following it properly. Salaries for prison staffs were not high enough to secure competent people. The grading became based upon favoritism or influence.

In 1934, ALCATRAZ became the flagship of the federal penitentiary system. Designed to hold incorrigibles, it was purely punitive, with no hint of an attempt at rehabilitation, even though it had the highest ratio of guards to prisoners in any institution in the country: one guard for every three prisoners.

Overcrowding, harsh treatment, and primitive conditions have caused a series of prison riots over the years. Some of them have resulted in great loss of life and considerable damage, such as the 1930 riot at Ohio State Penitentiary, in which 300 prisoners died in a fire, and the 1971 Attica, New York, prison riot, during which 32 inmates and 11 guards were killed by the state police as they poured into the prison in an ill-conceived attempt to rescue guards who had been taken as hostages.

The United States, which regards itself as the most advanced and civilized country in the world, has the highest percentage of incarcerated citizens of any industrial country. *See also:* PUNISHMENT; SING SING

PRIVATE EYE

Private eye is a slang expression for private detective. A popular etymology of the term is that it came from the symbol of ALLAN PINKERTON's National Detective Agency: an eye surrounded by the motto "We Never Sleep." This may be, but it seems more probable that it came from the term "private investigator," since "P.I." is another slang term for that profession.

PROHIBITION

THE NATIONAL EXPERIMENT THAT FAILED

We wash our hands of the liquid foe,
The offspring of perdition,
And to the ballot yearly go
To vote for Prohibition;
For no man has a moral right
To deal out to another
A licensed curse to swell his purse
Regardless of his brother.
—National Temperance Almanac, 1878

The average self-respecting young man will shudder with disgust at the mere thought of hunting up a sneaking bootlegger.
—Cyclopedia of Temperance and Prohibition, 1891

At 12:01 A.M. on January 17, 1920, the Eighteenth Amendment to the Constitution of the United States became law, enacting Prohibition and the enforcement provisions of the VOLSTEAD ACT. It was the first attempt to impose a national ban upon the consumption of alcoholic beverages, but the country was no stranger to more limited prohibitions.

In the American colonies in the eighteenth century, spirituous drink was regarded as a good thing. "It sloweth age; it strengtheneth youth; it helpeth digestion; it cutteth the flegme; it abandoneth melancholie; it relisheth the heart; it lighteneth the mind . . . it keepeth the weason from stiffling, the stomach from wambling, and the heart from swelling," as a contemporary sage put it, according to J. C. Furnas in *The Late Demon Rum* (1965). But it was recognized that it was possible to have too much of a good thing. Drinking was acceptable, almost mandatory; public drunkenness was not. Habitual drunkards were put in the stocks or the whipping stools and could be sentenced to wear a scarlet letter "D" around their necks for up to a year. There were laws regulating when a tavern could be opened for business and for how long, and how many drinks a customer might have at one sitting.

The colony of Georgia, founded by James Oglethorpe in 1733, was an exception. Oglethorpe was determined that his settlers should be a sober, industrious group. Nothing stronger than beer was to be imbibed by the new Georgians. But the colonists had no sooner settled in than they began distilling rum, the brandy of the Americas, and even importing it from South Carolina. Entreaties from the English trustees of the Georgia colony for prohibition were ignored. The trustees passed a letter of prohibition: "As it appears by your letters that the sickness among the people is owing to the excessive drinking of rum punch, the Trustees do absolutely forbid their drinking, or even having any rum, and agree with you so entirely in your sentiments that they order all rum that shall be brought there to be immediately staved." This edict was ignored.

The trustees, annoyed at seeing their authority flouted even in this small way, appealed to the British Parliament and to King George II. Parliament passed and the King signed an act prohibiting the import or sale of rum in Georgia, which went into effect in 1735. It accomplished nothing. The colonists ignored the new regulations, and the colony had neither the funds nor the men to enforce them. Rumrunners from South Carolina landed their barrels in secluded coves or carried them by oxcart, horseback or on their own backs into the colony. Speakeasies were opened in the backs of shops and in private homes. In 1742, the trustees gave up prohibition in favor of licensed taverns. Even Oglethorpe admitted that there probably were not 12 men in the colony who would convict anyone of selling rum.

It was another 100 years before the temperance movement, forgetting the lesson of Georgia, gained enough strength to try again. This time it was the Maine Temperance Union, headed by reformer Neal Dow, that led the crusade. The union, after breaking away from the Maine Temperance Society because the society proposed the drinking of wine and beer, succeeded in banning the sale of alcoholic beverages in Portland in 1842. But, as in Georgia a hundred years before, the taverns closed and the speakeasies opened; often in the same location with the same proprietor.

Dow decided that the area was too small. Prohibition could never work in a city—it had to be at least a whole state. By 1850, Dow was mayor of Portland, and his man, John Hubbard, was governor of Maine. On June 2, 1851, an all-encompassing prohibition law was passed in Maine. The manufacture and sale of intoxicating liquors was strictly forbidden. Search and seizure warrants could be issued on the complaint of as few as three voters. The arresting officers were allowed to keep any fines imposed by the courts, a measure designed to make them more enthusiastic about enforcement. Dow gave the tavern owners two days to get rid of their stock of booze, and then he led a squad of enforcers into the shops and took axes to kegs containing thousands of dollars worth of whiskey and rum.

The temperance movement was now convinced that they were riding the crest of a wave. In Saratoga Springs, New York, a National Temperance Convention saw the success of the Maine law as the answer to their prayers. By 1855, an additional dozen states, from New Hampshire to the Midwest, had passed variants of the Maine law. Victory seemed to be within the grasp of the forces of temperance. But within a few years all of their successes, except for Maine, had been reversed. In some states, the courts ruled the laws unconstitutional; in other states the voters rebelled and forced the return of liquor.

In the 1870s, the women's crusade began that would eventually lead to national Prohibition. The national Women's Christian Temperance Union (WCTU), led by Frances Willard, was an organization of middle- and upper-class women who had a missionary zeal to do good. The people they wanted to do it to were the lower classes; especially lower-class men. And the good they wanted to do was to deprive them of their booze. The life of the lower classes was mean, brutish and short, not because of the low wages, long hours, horrible working conditions or lack of adequate food or housing, but because of liquor. Or so the Union professed to believe.

The WCTU worked hard to promote temperance among the young. They had laws passed that required schools to teach the effects of alcohol. "Scientific" experiments to show that alcohol was a poison were mandatory in the schools of 40 states. Tens of thousands of schoolchildren learned that if a worm is dropped in a bottle of alcohol, it dies.

Gradually the WCTU and the Anti-Saloon League worked to make Prohibition the law of the land. They had the moral high ground, since no one could dispute that drunkenness was a social evil and that some men spent their entire paychecks drinking instead of paying their rent or buying food for their children. In the 1880's plays like *The Drunkard* (written in 1884) and *Ten Nights in a Barroom* (1854) drew large audiences.

The WCTU and the league were one-issue political machines. It did not matter to them whether a political candidate was Republican or Democrat, Catholic or Protestant, liberal or conservative; what mattered was whether he was wet or dry. And gradually they elected drys, or men who were willing to be dry for their support. As Bill Severn tells it in *The End of the Roaring Twenties* (1969):

> When they entered an election battle, the League's agents would swarm into the area to bring every imaginable pressure to bear on candidates and officeholders. It would be saturated with literature, honeycombed with speakers and organized church by church and street by street. Quick to take full advantage of the needs of the moment, they shifted tactics, policies, and alliances according to local conditions. Some agents later boasted of false rumors they spread, of tricks they played, of lies they told and even of votes they bought to outwit those they considered too evil to be dealt with honestly. Convinced they were doing "Godly work" and that the end justified the means, many took the attitude that all was fair in any battle to "beat the Devil at his own game."

By 1914, the dry movement had enough votes in Congress to hold a slight majority when the Hobson bill—Alabama Representative Richmond P. Hobson's resolution to propose to the states a constitutional amendment banning the sale of liquor—was brought up on the floor of the House. But its rules required a two-thirds majority for the bill to pass. The House put forth a renewed effort during the elections of 1916, and its effort was rewarded. By now the war in Europe was in full swing. Although the United States had not entered it yet, it was clear that its sympathies lay on the side of Great Britain, and many of the brewers in the United States were Germans. The drys began a campaign to discredit beer-drinking as un-American. The brewers were pictured as spies, traitors and "murderous Huns." When America entered the war, the league stepped up its propaganda. The German troops were said to commit outrages against women and children while drunk on beer. And besides, making beer was un-American because the grain could be used to make bread to feed the troops.

On August 1, 1917, the Prohibition Amendment passed the Senate by a vote of 65 to 20. On December 18, 1917, it passed the House of Representatives by 282 to 128 and was submitted to the states for ratification. At one minute past midnight on January 17, 1920, it became the law of the land.

John F. Kramer, the country's first Prohibition commissioner, felt that the enforcement problems would be few, and his optimism was shared by the Department of Justice and most local police departments. "This law will be obeyed in cities large and small," Kramer declared. "There will not be any violations to speak of," the chief revenue agent in New York agreed. To take care of the few that might attempt to violate the law, a force of 1,500 Prohibition agents had been assembled to police the whole country.

The most prescient of the public figures was former President William Howard Taft. "The business of manufacturing alcohol, liquor and beer will go out of the hands of law-abiding members of the community, and will be transferred to the quasi-criminal class," he warned. "In the communities where the majority will not sympathize with a federal law's restrictions, a large number of federal officers will be needed for its enforcement."

By the end of the first dry day, the first speakeasies had opened in New York and Chicago. By the end of the first dry week, more than half a million dollars worth of liquor had been stolen from warehouses where it was being kept under government bond for medicinal use. By the end of the first dry month, criminal gangs were running booze in from Canada. By the end of the first dry year, the courts were clogged with Prohibition enforcement cases, and law enforcement officials were admitting that their best efforts were ineffective against the flow of liquor that was coming from all directions.

And now the hidden consequences of the Prohibition laws were becoming apparent to all: consequences similar to the events in Georgia 200 years before, but on a larger scale. The gangs in all major cities had organized and formed a vast crime confederation for the purpose of supplying the public with booze. The sounds of machine guns were heard in the streets, and occasional innocent bystanders were slaughtered as the gangs fought over territory. The major gang leaders—JOHNNY TORRIO and AL CAPONE in Chicago, LUCKY LUCIANO and DUTCH SCHULTZ in New York, Jack Dragna and BUGSY SIEGEL in Los Angeles—became public figures. Elected public officials and law enforcement officers were paid by the mobsters to turn a blind eye toward their bootlegging activities. And once they had done that, they discovered that they were effectively owned by the gangsters and were forced to provide protection for murder, extortion and a variety of allied sins.

The gangsters might have become liquor wholesalers, but they did not give up being gangsters. The violence was always there, close to the surface. Edward D. Sullivan, in *Rattling the Cup on Chicago Crime* (1929), described the scene:

> Beer is delivered by violence in Chicago. The owner of a speakeasy is a harried man. When he opens his place, it is usually after negotiation with a tough beer-running outfit whose promise of protection is satisfactory. The joint keeper would rather have good protection than good beer. Good beer may be important to his customers, but satisfactory protection is absolutely vital to himself. Once he begins negotiations with his beer suppliers, they do not solicit him. They tell him what they'll do and inform him what he'll do, as well. He will take a certain amount of beer at certain times and he'll like it and pay for it. Terms, cash.
>
> Things are all right until along comes the representative of an even tougher beer-running organization. He may introduce himself by spraying the bartender's teeth around the place. He leaves a message which the bartender will subsequently lisp to the owner, that a daily quota of another type of beer will be delivered and paid for beginning on a certain day.
>
> It will be seen that the owner of the joint, his bartender, and the brewery representative are in a tough business. They'd better be hard. In a case of this kind, the joint-keeper calls up his original beer supplier, tells him needle beer's oldest story, and the mob of that brewery takes over the joint and runs it for a few days. When the beer organization, which is trying to muscle in, arrives with its delivery, there is a scene reminiscent of the Fall of Port Arthur. The joint becomes the property of whoever wins the conflict but, in any case, the loser has the prerogative of dropping around at his convenience and taking a shot at the actual owner of the place. The beer business pays well if you can keep your health.

The noble experiment lasted for 13 years, a period that became known as the Roaring Twenties. The illegality of alcohol pervaded the whole era; in a perverse way it made drinking respectable. The literature and films of the 1920s are marked by the tremendous capacity of many of the main characters for alcoholic beverages. Prohibition was finally repealed in 1933, but the crime organizations created during that noble experiment are, for the most part, still with us.

GLOSSARY
OF PROHIBITION-RELATED TERMS

Bathtub Gin—Alcohol distilled in a bathtub and flavored with essence of juniper to make it smell like gin
Bootlegger—The booze supplier, either wholesale or retail
Drys—Those people who supported Prohibition
Hip Flask—A metal flask contoured to fit a hip pocket
Needled Beer—Beer that has had raw alcohol added to it
Rumrunner—Importer of distilled beverages
Speakeasy—Illegal bar
Volstead Act—The law empowering the Eighteenth (Prohibition) Amendment
Wets—Those people who favored legal drinking

PUERTO-RICAN NATIONALISTS

See: GRISELIO TORRESOLA; LOLITA LEBRON

PUNCH BOARD SCAM

The punch board was a staple item in candy stores, drugstores and dime stores across the country in the first half of the twentieth century. It was about 10 inches high by 8 inches wide and three-quarters of an inch thick, and it sat on the counter of the store by the cash register. The surface of the board was filled with over 1,000 round black dots, which could be "punched out" with a small wire kept by the board, to reveal a tightly-rolled piece of paper.

One of those punched-out pieces of paper would be a prize worth $10 cash, and two others would be worth $5 each. There would be a sprinkling of one-dollar prizes, and a dusting of "doll" prizes, small stuffed dolls worth a quarter or so.

The board cost the merchant $2, and the prizes totaled up to between $25 and $30. At a nickel a punch, the board made $50 for the proprietor—a nice $20 profit.

Some shopkeepers bought their punch cards only from dealers who would tell them where the big prizes were, so they could punch them out before their customers got them. But most were honest, or they learned that without word going around the neighborhood of an occasional $5 winner, people would lose interest in the boards.

In the punch board scam, the salesman was in collusion with a partner, who would show up at the merchant's store a couple of days after the board went up on the counter and would punch out one or more of the big prizes. It was a small but adequate way to make a dishonest living.

PUNISHMENT

My object all sublime
I shall achieve in time,
To let the punishment fit the crime,
The punishment fit the crime;

And make each pris'ner pent
Unwillingly represent
A source of innocent merriment,
Of innocent merriment!
—*William Schwenck Gilbert*

Every society has devised punishments for its criminals, and, with the passage of time, adjusted these punishments to make them more closely fit the crime.

In the colonial days, the authorities preferred punishment to penology. The stocks and ducking stool were favorites, along with public flogging and branding for the more serious offenses. The Quakers were influential in replacing corporal punishment with imprisonment, but the punishment soon followed into the prisons.

The penal institutions have never been able to reconcile their dual functions of punishing and rehabilitating the criminal, with public opinion fluctuating between the two. Punishment has usually been in favor because the prison guards think that it makes their charges easier to handle. There is, however, an unfortunate tendency for people with sadistic tendencies to take jobs as prison guards, and it is difficult, even today, to weed such people out.

The first warden of SING SING prison in New York, ELAM LYNDS, believed in punishment for the good of the soul. He kept prisoners confined in tiny solitary confinement cells for up to a year, without permitting them to speak to anyone. Those that survived the year had usually been driven insane. Lynds was also a fan of the whip and would whip any prisoner he caught talking in his cell. This model of penology was very popular at the turn of the twentieth century.

A common punishment in many prisons was, and still is, "the cooler": a small, bare cell without lights, windows, toilet or furniture, in which the prisoner is put in solitary confinement, without blankets and often without clothing.

In 1915, the New York State Prison Commission visited Blackwells Island (Welfare Island) Penitentiary and discovered, among other things, that a version of the Chinese Water Torture, called the water-drop cure, was in common use. This involved shaving the head of a troublesome prisoner and tying him to a chair placed under a tank of water. A small hole in the bottom of the tank would drip water on the man's head for as long as it took for him to plead for mercy. A day of this was enough to drive anybody completely insane.

Bank robber WILLIE SUTTON, in his autobiography, *Where the Money Was* (1976), describes the treatment in Dannemora, a New York State penal institution by the Canadian border, in the 1920s:

> The guards were . . . destined to work in the penal system from birth and they were the most sadistic people I ever came into contact with. The officers carried sticks with metal tips on them. You had to march everywhere in complete silence. (The whole prison was operated on a silent system, which meant that the inmates were allowed to talk only within certain specified areas.) The marching orders were given by tapping the stick on the ground. Two raps meant go. One rap meant stop. For no reason at all, you would get rapped sharply across the back. At the slightest provocation, they would pounce upon a prisoner, batter him to the ground, and beat him almost to death.
>
> Off in the corner was a small red brick building with twenty-two cells in it. That was the isolation block. The number of prisoners who "committed suicide" there by hanging themselves was truly remarkable. Especially when you consider that everything except the clothes on their backs had been taken away from them, and no other inmates were ever permitted near the place.

This sort of treatment has been outlawed in American prisons today, but it has been outlawed before and still it persisted. *See also:* PRISONS

PURVIS, Melvin (1903–1960)

THE ARCHETYPAL G-MAN, WHOSE BRAVERY, CAPABILITY AND HONESTY HELPED CREATE THE LEGEND OF THE FBI

An FBI special agent from 1927 to 1935, Melvin Purvis was in charge of the Chicago office during the halcyon years of the Depression and PROHIBITION, when bank robbers and bootleggers were the public heroes. Purvis was involved in several of the more memorable captures of the time, including that of Public Enemy Number One Verne Sankey, personally removing him from a barbershop where he was getting a shave. Purvis traded shots with BABY FACE NELSON and JOHN DILLINGER, killed PRETTY BOY FLOYD in a gun battle in a cornfield and was present when Dillinger was killed as he left a Chicago theater.

Purvis was proud of putting together a case against Chicago bootlegger Roger "The Terrible" Touhy and his gang for the 1933 kidnapping of millionaire brewer William Hamm and was shocked when a jury found them not guilty. It later developed that the kidnapping had actually been done by the BARKER-KARPIS GANG. Purvis then charged Touhy with kidnapping Jake "the Barber" Factor, a gangland ally of AL CAPONE. This time the case was solid, and Touhy was convicted and received a life sentence in an Illinois prison. Years later it was revealed that the kidnapping was a frame created by Capone to rid himself of Touhy's competition. Less than a month after Touhy was released from prison in 1959, he was gunned down on the front porch of his sister's house.

Purvis had the same thirst for publicity as did his boss, J. EDGAR HOOVER, and made pronouncements on behalf of the Chicago field office, making sure that his name was prominent in the news story. He was, however, a brave, honest and honorable man. When Anna Sage, the "Lady in Red" who turned in Dillinger, wanted a guarantee that she would get the reward money and that deportation proceedings that had been started against her would be dropped, Purvis gave his word. Sage received most of the reward money, but Hoover declined to honor Purvis's guarantee about the deportation, and she was subsequently deported. As a result, Purvis turned in his badge.

Purvis wrote his memoirs, *American Agent*, in which he managed not to mention Hoover by name at all. In World War II, Purvis served as a colonel in the U.S. Army War Crimes Office.

F.B.I. agent Melvin Purvis, who aided in the captures of such notable gangsters as "Baby Face" Nelson, John Dillinger, and "Pretty Boy" Floyd. (Dept. of Special Collections, University Research Library, UCLA.)

PURVIS, Will (1874–1943)

In 1893, Will Buckley, a member of a Mercer County, Mississippi, group called the White Caps (a group resembling the KU KLUX KLAN), was found shot to death. Bloodhounds followed a trail from the murdered man to a spot near the farm of Will Purvis, a 19-year-old local farmer. Jim Buckley, the murdered man's brother, identified Purvis as his brother's murderer. Purvis had joined the White Caps about three months before, and it was believed that he killed Buckley as a result of a dispute within the organization.

Purvis was tried for the killing, convicted and sentenced to be executed on February 7, 1894. Nearly 3,000 people gathered to watch the public hanging, many of whom were not convinced of the young man's guilt. When, on the first attempt, the knot proved to be poorly placed and Purvis survived the drop unharmed, the crowd took that as a sign from divine providence and refused to allow the execution to continue. Purvis was returned to his cell. A short time later, before a new execution could be scheduled, he escaped and stayed at large until 1896, when A. J. McLaurin took office as governor of Mississippi. Purvis surrendered when McLaurin promised to reduce his sentence to life imprisonment. In 1898, McLaurin pardoned Purvis and he was released.

In 1917, a one-time White Capper named Joe Beard confessed to the murder at a revival meeting, saying that he had to cleanse his soul before going to meet his maker. He said, in sufficient detail to make it clear that he was the actual murderer that he and another White Capper had been chosen by lot to execute Buckley.

In 1920, Purvis was awarded $5,000 compensation by the Mississippi Legislature "for a great wrong done you."

PYRAMID SCAMS

The pyramid scheme exists in many forms, some illegal, some quasi-legal and some legal. The pyramid letter is an advanced version of the chain letter, in which the person receiving the letter sends $10 to the person whose name heads a list of 10 names in the letter, and then crosses that name off, puts his name on the bottom and sends copies of the letter to ten of his closest friends. The force that operates this pyramid is moral 'suasion, greed, plus the letter's recounting of five horrible things that happened to people who broke the chain. If nobody breaks the chain, when the recipient's name reaches the top of the list he will receive ten billion dollars.

The pyramid schemes turn into scams when they charge the victim to get involved. Companies that purport to sell products, but actually concentrate on selling distributorships, have crossed the thin line from scheme to scam. The victim pays, say, $1,000 to become a salesman. He becomes a distributor by getting ten other people to pay $1,000, and gets $250 of each such payment, along with a piece of the profit of any product that the new salesmen happen to sell. Some large American corporations work in this fashion, but it is essentially a con game. The pyramid scam is a specialized version of the PETER TO PAUL SWINDLE.

R

RELES, Abe "Kid Twist" (1907–1941)

HE COULD SING, BUT HE COULDN'T FLY

One of the leaders of Brooklyn's MURDER, INCORPORATED under bosses ALBERT ANASTASIA and LOUIS "LEPKE" BUCHALTER, Abe Reles was personally involved in at least 30 Syndicate killings. The police had a rap sheet on him going back 16 years, listing 42 arrests for such things as assault, burglary, robbery and six separate counts of murder. He had been in jail briefly six times. When, in 1940, he was pulled in with some of his comrades for questioning in regard to several murders, nobody expected the pattern to be any different than before: stonewalling and waiting for his expensive lawyer to get him out. But, suddenly and startlingly, Reles decided to confess. Brooklyn Assistant District Attorney Burton B. Turkus, in charge of homicide cases under William O'Dwyer, Brooklyn's new district attorney, was astounded at what he heard and quickly called in his boss. They listened transfixed to Reles's saga of multiple murders during the past decade in an organization they had not known existed.

Once Reles started talking, he did not stop. The police put him in heavily guarded protective custody and only took him out to testify in the murder trials of his former friends. Reles's defection had a snowball effect; the mob bosses, to protect themselves, issued orders to kill anyone else who might be tempted to talk. The threat increased the body count in the New York area and drove a dozen or so hoods, who would never have otherwise opened their mouths, into the district attorney's office seeking protection. Such murderous characters as Allie Tannenbaum, Julie Cantalano, Blue Jaw Magoon and Joe "The Baker" Liberito turned state's evidence in hopes of staying alive.

Reles's testimony was responsible for putting PITTSBURGH PHIL and Buggsy Goldstein in the electric chair for the murder of Irving "Puggy" Feinstein, a minor gambler. He described the killing from the witness chair in great and horrendous detail. A part of his testimony is excerpted below:

> I put the radio on a little louder, because Puggy is making a noise. I go for the rope. I go back over to the couch with it, and Harry [Pittsburgh Phil] is saying, "The bastard bit me on the hand." Harry is like laying over Puggy, so he should not move. Buggsy is hitting him to make him quiet, pounding him. I give Harry one end of the rope and I hold the other end. Puggy is kicking and fighting. He is forcing his head down, so we can't get the rope under his throat. Buggsy holds his head up, so we can put the rope under. Then me and Harry exchange ends, cross them, so we can make a knot, a twist. Then we cross them once more. Then we rope around his throat again, to make two loops. Buggsy gets Puggy by the feet, and me and Harry get him by the head. We put him down on the floor. He is kicking. Harry starts finishing tying him up. I am turning him like, and Harry gets his feet tied up with the back of his neck. He ties him up like a little ball. His head is pushed down on his chest. His hands are in between. The rope is around his neck and under his feet. If he moves, the rope will tighten up around his throat more.
>
> Big Harry says, "We'd better burn this bum up, so nobody will know him. Go get some gas."

Reles's testimony aided in the conviction of a dozen or so hoodlums, including big boss Lepke Buchalter. At three o'clock in the morning of November 12, 1941, while Reles was being guarded by police on the sixth floor of the Half Moon hotel on Coney Island, he mysteriously went out of the window of room 623 and fell to his death. A knotted bedsheet was found dangling from the window. Whether he committed suicide, died while trying to escape or was murdered is not known. A police captain, who was informed of the incident, was heard to remark, as he was driven to the scene, "Well, the canary could sing—but he couldn't fly."

RELIGIOUS RIGHTS

The separation of church and state is guaranteed in the United States by the First Amendment to the Constitution, with this formula: "Congress shall make no law respecting an establishment of religion, or prohibiting the free exercise thereof; . . ." The interpretation of this statement has been the responsibility of the Supreme Court.

It is clear that all varieties of religious beliefs are protected under the First Amendment. It is in the exercise of these beliefs that religion and the state come into conflict. In 1879, the Supreme Court agreed that, despite their religious strictures, Mormon men were entitled to no more than one wife each. On the other hand, in 1943, it decided that the children of Jehovah's Witnesses could not be required to salute the American flag. Then it decided that Amish children could not be compelled to attend public school. The unemployment benefits of Seventh-Day Adventists who turned down jobs requiring them to work on Saturdays were protected in a 1960s decision.

Individuals were also protected from creeping religiosity. In 1961, the Supreme Court struck down a provision of the Maryland Constitution requiring a justice of the peace to take an oath that he believed in God. In 1963, Bible-reading exercises and prayer in public schools were deemed improper.

The basic formula was that an individual's right to religious freedom would prevail except when the government had a "compelling reason" to abridge or deny that right. A child in need of immediate medical attention for a life-threatening illness could not be deprived of that attention because of the religious views of the child's Christian Scientist parents. On the other hand, in line with the drug phobia of the country, Native Americans were forbidden the use of peyote in their religious ceremonies, even though it was a part of their ancient tradition.

RICCA, Paul "The Waiter" (1897–1972)

A good friend and chief lieutenant of AL CAPONE in the Chicago Syndicate, Paul Ricca gingerly and carefully followed the path to power after Capone went to prison. By 1940, he was the first among equals in the Syndicate hierarchy, his strength based on the respect given him by the other gang leaders, his known willingness to use violence to excess and a well-developed ability to know who to pay off and how to accomplish it.

Ricca was born in Italy where, at the age of 20, he spent two years in prison for murdering a man named Emelio Parrillo. When he was released, he killed the chief witness against him, Vincenzo Capasso, and fled to the United States. He was tried by the Italian government in absentia and sentenced to 25 years. He got his nickname "The Waiter," because that was the job he always cited when questioned by authorities as to his occupation.

Ricca and much of the rest of the Chicago Syndicate leadership went to prison in 1943 for a massive extortion directed against the motion picture industry. Sentenced to 10 years, they were released on parole after three years due to the intercession of attorney general Tom Clark. Rumors, never substantiated, flew around Chicago that Ricca had somehow "reached" Clark, and this accounted for the early release. By 1950, Ricca's power was so pronounced that the KEFAUVER COMMITTEE thought him to be "the national head of the Crime Syndicate," and the 1958 MCCLELLAN COMMITTEE thought he was "America's most important criminal."

Ricca had his citizenship removed in 1957 and was ordered deported in 1959. In an extraordinary delaying maneuver, Ricca succeeded in having the Italian government take away his Italian citizenship and refuse to accept him, even to serve out the years he owed an Italian prison for the old murder charge. The American government was still trying to find another country that would take him when he died in 1972.

RICO

One of the strongest legal weapons in the war against ORGANIZED CRIME, RICO, the Racketeer Influenced and Corrupt Organizations section of the Organized Crime Control Act of 1970, strengthened the hands of prosecutors going after the bosses of the major rackets. RICO made the commission of any two of a list of crimes over a 10-year period sufficient grounds to warrant conviction of involvement in "an ongoing rackets enterprise." It also made the planning of or even the discussion of a crime a criminal offense equal to the commission of the crime. This removed the insulation from the mob bosses, who never dirtied their hands but sent others out to do their killing.

Under RICO, an organization could be shown to be a "criminal enterprise" if its members engaged in a "pattern of racketeering," which was defined as committing two or more racketeering offenses within a period of ten years. It was now against the law to be a member of such a criminal enterprise. And membership could be shown by "association in fact." That is, formal membership or employment was unnecessary; constant association with the group and evident involvement with its activities was sufficient.

The penalties upon conviction of a RICO offense are heavy: up to twenty years in prison, a fine of up to $25,000 for each count, and confiscation of property or businesses obtained as a result of the illegal enterprise.

One of its most powerful and most controversial provisions allows lawmen to seize through forfeiture any property used in a crime. Although it permits drug lords and other master criminals to be deprived of the fruits of their illicit labors and provides law enforcement agencies with a subsidiary source of income and equipment, it is subject to easy abuse by those in authority. There are not enough safeguards built into the law to prevent overzealous or corrupt law enforcement officials from wrongfully seizing property. Already, cases are on record in which, for example, a man borrows a vehicle and uses it for a drug deal, unbeknownst to the owner, and then it is seized by the police and not returned, on the theory that the owner *should* have known about it. This action deprives the owner of the use of his vehicle, which may be a needed tool in his business, for a year or more and costs him a fortune in attorney fees before he gets it back—if he does get it back.

At the time when Congress passed the law, the United States felt besieged by crime, and something had to be done. As Senator John McClellan said at the House MCCLELLAN COMMITTEE hearings, "The public is demanding that we recognize that the right of society to be safe transcends the right of the criminal to be free. When the forces of right and peace clash against the forces of evil and violence, something has to give."

It was 10 years before federal prosecutors figured out how to use the new laws. As Stephan Fox explained in *Blood and Power* (1989): "the RICO law presented a brier patch of challenges. Instead of small, easy cases that led quickly to impressive numbers of indictments and convictions, RICO promised slow, complex investigations that might not succeed. But as Federal prosecutors figured out how to use the new law RICO investigations and prosecutions have struck at the heart of organized crime, bringing RICO indictments against Mafia leaders in Boston, Kansas City, New York, Philadelphia, and other cities. It was a RICO trial that finally put Gambino family boss JOHN GOTTI in prison."

The first federal prosecutor to effectively use the RICO law was Rudolph Giuliani, a U.S. attorney in New York City with a grudge against organized crime. A lot of hard work and RICO made him the most effective racket buster since THOMAS E. DEWEY. Giuliani's concept of a lawyer's duty was unusually strict. "I don't socialize with mob lawyers," he told a reporter in an interview. "When I was in private practice I wouldn't represent mob people. . . . Organized crime figures are illegitimate people who would go on being illegitimate people if I got them off."

RINTELEN, Franz von (1877–1949)

A captain in the German Navy, Franz von Rintelen served as an espionage agent in the United States in the days immediately preceding World War I. Arriving in New York City in 1915, von Rintelen set up an espionage and sabotage network throughout the East Coast. The company he founded, E. V. Gibbons, Inc., acted as a broker for munitions that were shipped across the Atlantic to the Allied countries. Von Rintelen thus caused the Allied powers to pay for their own destruction, as his cargoes were fitted with time bombs. Von Rintelen did not want to destroy the ships, but merely to start a fire in the hold, which would cause the cargo to be jettisoned or the ship to be abandoned.

Von Rintelen also founded the Labor National Peace Council, which attempted unsuccessfully to cause workers to boycott the armament industry. He hatched various schemes for blowing up American munitions plants, factories, bridges and other points of interest, although the United States was, technically anyway, still a nonbelligerent. Franz von Papen, the German military attaché, was not pleased by this activity, feeling that von Rintelen was going too far. He arranged for the captain to be recalled to Berlin.

By a strange twist of fate, the codebreakers of Room 40, the British Navy's deciphering service, intercepted and decrypted Berlin's message ordering von Rintelen's return. When the Dutch ship von Rintelen was on reached Southampton, he was taken off and interned by the British. In 1917, he was extradited to the United States, where he was tried for sabotage and put in the federal penitentiary in Atlanta, Georgia. When he was released from prison after the war, von Rintelen moved to Great Britain, where he became a naturalized citizen.

ROGER'S BARRACKS

Roger's Barracks was a well-known Chicago ROOKERY. *See also:* UNDER THE WILLOW

ROOKERY

THE SQUALID THIEVES' QUARTER WHERE POLICEMEN FEARED TO TREAD

Rookeries, dens of thieves in urban areas, were a product of economic and social forces. The nineteenth century was a period of exponential expansion in the size and populations of the great cities of Europe and the United States. Improved methods of farming and changes in land use were driving people off the farms, and the first stages of industrialization were providing low-paying jobs for them in the cities. This situation was exacerbated in the United States by the first great wave of immigration, which brought the huddled masses of Europe into the American cities.

City POLICE forces, which were barely emerging from the period of the night watch, were neither equipped with sufficient manpower nor experience enough to handle the tide of criminals that accompanied the law-abiding peasantry filling the cities. Police departments were also hampered by political control, and thus, were unprotected from the destructive influences of graft and corruption then prevalent in city politics.

In the worst slum areas of New York, Boston and Chicago, where the "rookeries" sprang up, were unbelievable miasmas of crime and corruption. Policemen, who would enter the slum areas only in groups of three or more, would not enter these rookeries at all, and whatever happened inside them happened, with dead bodies thrown into the adjoining streets to be collected by the authorities.

In New York City from the 1820s to the 1870s, the "Bloody Ould Sixth Ward" was one of the worst districts. In the heart of the sixth was "Five Points," a roughly triangular area formed by the intersection of Cross, Anthony, Little Water, Orange and Mulberry streets. Today, the boundaries of the area would be roughly north of Canal Street from Broadway to the Bowery (Third Avenue). Among the worst of the rookeries in Five Points were the Cow Bay tenements and a vast old building called the Old Brewery. Erected in 1792 as Coulter's Brewery, it produced some of the finest beer on the East Coast until Coulter moved away and the building was transformed into a tenement in 1837. It was five stories tall and was well described in Herbert Asbury's *The Gangs of New York* (1928):

> Around the building extended an alley, about three feet wide. . . . The northern path led into a great room called the Den of Thieves, in which more than seventy-five men, women and children, black and white, made their homes, without furniture or conveniences. Many of the women were prostitutes, and entertained their visitors in the Den. On the opposite side the passageway was known as Murderers' Alley, and was all that name implies. . . .
>
> The cellars of the Old Brewery were divided into some twenty rooms, which had previously been used for the machinery of the brewing plant, and there were about seventy-five other chambers above-ground, arranged in double rows along

Murderers' Alley and the passage leading to the Den of Thieves. During the period of its greatest renown the building housed more than 1,000 men, women and children. . . . [T]he house swarmed with thieves, murderers, pickpockets, beggars, harlots, and degenerates of every type. Fights were of almost constant occurrence, and there was scarcely an hour of the day or night when drunken orgies were not in progress; through the flimsy, clapboard walls could be heard the crashing thud of brickbat or iron bar, the shrieks of the unhappy victims, the wailing of starving children, and the frenzied cries of men and women, and sometimes boys and girls, writhing in the anguish of delirium tremens. Murders were frequent; it has been estimated that for almost fifteen years the Old Brewery averaged a murder a night, and the Cow Bay tenements almost as many. Few of the killers were ever punished, for unless the police came in great force they could not hope to leave the Old Brewery alive, and the inhabitants were very closed-mouthed.

Chicago earned the sobriquet of "the wickedest city in the United States" in the years right after the Civil War. It harbored a variety of establishments, such as John Ryan's Concert Saloon on South Clark Street, which gave bawdy shows under the guise of "elegant and chaste performances," and was a hangout for thieves. But the hard-core rookeries were the Chicago Patch on Chicago Avenue, controlled by an ancient harpy called Mother Klein; Conley's Patch at Adams and Franklin Streets, bossed by a gigantic black woman known as the Bengal Tigress whose rages were feared by the hardest malefactors; Under the Willow, also known as Roger's Barracks, run by the diminutive Roger Plant and his large wife; and Shinbone Alley, which harbored a large collection of black hoodlums since before the Civil War.

THE ROSENBERG CASE

See: Ethel and Julius Rosenberg

ROSENBERG, Ethel (1915–1953) and Julius (1918–1953)

THE HUSBAND AND WIFE SPIES WHOSE TRIAL AND EXECUTION STILL STIR THE CONSCIENCE OF THE NATION

In 1951, Julius and Ethel Rosenberg were tried for the crime of espionage. The trial and the Rosenbergs' subsequent conviction and execution became one of the great *causes célèbres* of this century. To this day, more than four decades after the

Alleged spies, Julius and Ethel Rosenberg, who were executed at Sing Sing in 1953. (Federal Bureau of Investigation.)

event, the dispute continues. Many people believe fervently that the Rosenbergs were guilty, were the indirect cause of the death of thousands of American boys and fully deserved execution. Others argue just as fervently that the Rosenbergs were innocent, were railroaded by a corrupt FBI and are martyrs to the cause of freedom.

The truth, as is so often the case, seems to lie somewhere in the middle. Measured opinion, given time to mature and access to reams of FBI documents released under the FREEDOM OF INFORMATION ACT, seems to fall as follows: The amount of damage the Rosenbergs did to the U.S. defense establishment was not severe, and there was certainly no compelling reason why they should have been the only people executed for espionage on behalf of a country with which we were not at war. But they were certainly guilty of espionage. In a recently published memoir, Nikita Khrushchev, premier of the Soviet Union in the 1950s, relates that Stalin once mentioned to him that the Soviet Union owed Julius and Ethel Rosenberg a debt of thanks for helping them develop the atomic bomb.

Julius was the son of Harry and Sophie Rosenberg, immigrants from Eastern Europe, who lived on New York City's Lower East Side. Harry worked as a sample maker in the garment industry, a well-paying and prestigious job within the immigrant community, and the family lived in the Lavanberg Homes, a well-maintained housing project that even had central heating.

At 16, Julius graduated from Seward Park High School (as had Ethel Greenglass a few years earlier) and, instead of studying for the rabbinate, as his father had hoped, entered the City College of New York, as an electrical engineering major. On campus he joined the Steinmetz Club, a branch of the Young Communist League (YCL), and soon became a staunch supporter of communism, well versed in the rhetoric and able to debate the opposition.

Ethel Greenglass was born on Manhattan's Lower East Side, the daughter of Barnet and Tessie Greenglass. Her father had a sewing machine repair shop on the ground floor of the tenement that their apartment was in at 64 Sheriff Street. Ethel was a strong-minded girl who usually accomplished what she set out to achieve. She graduated from Seward Park High School at the age of 15, after skipping several grades, and immediately found a job as a clerk, although in these first years of the Great Depression, there were thousands of applicants for every job. She was fond of amateur theatricals, sang with the Schola Cantorum, an amateur chorus which gave concerts at Carnegie Hall, and participated in amateur nights in vaudeville houses—usually singing "Ciribiribin" with a serious expression. The poverty of her childhood and the great contrast between rich and poor that was especially evident during the Depression turned Ethel into a convinced Communist, a belief that she shared with her younger brother David.

Ethel Greenglass married Julius Rosenberg in the summer of 1939, just after he graduated from CCNY. In 1940, Julius found a job with the U.S. Army Signal Corps as a civilian employee. By now, Julius and Ethel were both committed Communist party members; Julius was chairman of his local branch which held its monthly meetings at their apartment. In 1943, David Greenglass, Ethel's younger brother, was drafted into the army, and the Rosenbergs quit their membership in the Communist party.

There are several possible reasons for this decision. Julius's Signal Corps job was sensitive, and membership in the Communist party could (and subsequently did) get him in trouble on the job. Then again, Julius and Ethel were beginning to raise a family, and the added responsibility might have made them decide that they could not afford the time to devote to Communist party activities.

However, Julius had held the Signal Corps job for several years without worrying about his Communist party affiliation. Many people are able to raise families without giving up time-consuming hobbies.

It is known, based on evidence supplied by

defectors from Soviet Intelligence, that dropping out of the Communist party, unless one was kicked out for harboring subversive or original thoughts, was often, if not usually, the first step toward subsequent utilization as a Soviet agent. This was partly a smoke screen to cover the fledgling agent's Communist affiliation, and also to provide a shield of plausible deniability for the American Communist party if the prospective agent happened to be caught and previous affiliation was discovered.

The Rosenbergs' previous Communist affiliation did come up once, during a routine loyalty check, but Julius explained that his wife had signed a Communist party nominating petition merely because a friend had asked her to. "I am quite sure she is no Communist," Julius told the investigator. "We never discuss politics, but I am quite sure her views are quite similar to my own."

That was good enough for the investigator, and the matter was dropped. But four years later, in early 1945, the FBI forwarded proof that Julius had indeed been a card-carrying member of the Communist party and transmitted a copy of Julius's Communist party membership card to Army Intelligence. On the basis of this, Julius Rosenberg was dismissed from his Signal Corps job.

In 1944, Ethel's brother David, now a corporal in the United States Army, was assigned to work as a machinist at Los Alamos, New Mexico. Julius passed word by way of David's wife, Ruth, that as David was working to develop the atomic bomb, he could pass on invaluable information to the Russians. As David related later, until that time he had not realized that he was working on the atomic bomb. No one had told him—he had no need to know. How Julius knew is not recorded. Ruth was very hesitant, but David finally agreed to get involved. As Julius explained, the Russians had a right to know what their allies were doing. The Americans and British had no right to withhold this information from them. Apparently it made sense to David.

The first crack in the extensive Soviet spy *apparat* came in 1945, when Igor Gouzenko, a code clerk at the Soviet Embassy in Ottawa, Canada, defected to the West. In 1950, it effectively split open when Klaus Fuchs, a British atomic scientist, was shown to have been a Soviet spy throughout the war. The trail led from him to HARRY GOLD, to David Greenglass and, thus, to the Rosenbergs.

On March 6, 1951, the trial of Julius and Ethel Rosenberg and Morton Sobell, a college classmate of Julius, opened in the Federal Court House in Foley Square, in New York City. Judge Irving R. Kaufman, a justice for the Southern District of New York who had some previous experience with espionage cases, presided. The charge was conspiracy to commit acts of espionage contrary to the Espionage Act of 1917. Under the act, the maximum penalty was the death sentence.

The defendants pleaded not guilty. Emmanuel Bloch conducted the defense for Julius, while Bloch's father, Alexander, appeared for Ethel. Irving Saypol, the prosecuting attorney, charged that the defendants had "participated in a conspiracy against our country at the most critical hour in its history, in a time of war." He did not mention that, at that time, Soviet Russia was an ally of the United States.

"The evidence will reveal to you," the prosecutor continued, "how the Rosenbergs persuaded David Greenglass . . . to play the treacherous role of a modern Benedict Arnold while wearing the uniform of the United States Army. We will prove that the Rosenbergs devised and put into operation with the aid of Soviet nationals and Soviet agents in this country an elaborate scheme which enabled them, through Greenglass, to steal the one weapon which might well hold the key to the survival of this nation and the peace of the world—the atomic bomb."

Harry Gold testified against them, as did David and Ruth Greenglass, Ethel's brother and sister-in-law. Emmanuel Bloch made several decisions in the conduct of the defense that later consideration showed to be unwise. On the other hand, the FBI decided not to use evidence it was holding, based on decryptions of Soviet radio traffic, for fear it would compromise their methods of collection. The suppressed evidence showed that the defendants were indeed guilty.

It was not a good time to be convicted of anything connected with communism. The specter of the Red Menace hung over the land. American boys were fighting Communists in Korea. The Rosenbergs were ready scapegoats.

On March 29, the jury found the three defendants guilty. A week later, Judge Kaufman pronounced sentence. He began by stating, "Because of the seriousness of this case and the lack of precedents, I have refrained from asking the government for a recommendation. The responsibility is so great that I believe the court alone should assume this responsibility."

This was very noble, but not true. Kaufman solicited the views of the prosecution and of the Justice Department in Washington, as well as representatives of the Truman administration. The consensus was that it would be nice if Julius got the death penalty, Ethel got life and Morton Sobell got 15 years. The thought was that if Ethel was left in prison long enough, she might talk and reveal other Soviet spies.

The other possibility was that if Ethel also got the death penalty, it might pressure Julius into talking. And that is the bet that Judge Kaufman took. Or so many people think.

Julius and Ethel Rosenberg were each sentenced to death for their crimes. Morton Sobell got 30 years, with a recommendation that no parole be granted.

Immediately, public opinion began building against the sentences. At first, only the "progressive" papers and magazines protested, but gradually, a much wider segment of the public saw the death penalty as unjust. As always in such cases, a body of opinion rapidly arose that the Rosenbergs had been railroaded: not only were the sentences unjust, but the evidence against them had been manufactured by the FBI. But the government stood firm. In February 1952, the Circuit Court of Appeals rejected the Rosenbergs' appeal.

Nobel Prize winners Dr. Harold C. Urey and Professor Albert Einstein expressed doubt as to the guilt of the Rosenbergs and further stated that, regardless of their guilt, the death penalty was inappropriate. As Urey put it:

> Even if the verdict is correct, I am amazed at the unequal punishment for the same crime. For the very same conspiracy Ruth Greenglass was never brought to trial, though she admitted her guilt on the witness stand; David Greenglass got fifteen years; Morton Sobell and Harry Gold got thirty years, and Ethel and Julius Rosenberg got death. Only the last two took the witness stand and maintained their innocence.

The voices raised for clemency were numerous and worldwide. Pope Pius XII passed such a plea to the Department of Justice through the apostolic delegate in Washington, purely out of charity, "without being able to enter into the merits of the case."

The appeal process carried through into the Eisenhower administration. At the last moment, a stay of execution was granted by Justice William O. Douglas of the Supreme Court to consider a petition asserting that the case had been tried under the wrong law. With obscene haste, the attorney general applied to the Chief Justice of the Court to reconvene the Court and vacate the stay. He did. They did, Justices Douglas, Hugo Black, and Felix Frankfurter dissenting. The Rosenbergs were executed at eight o'clock (Julius) and eighteen (Ethel) in the evening of June 18, 1953 in the electric chair at Sing Sing prison in New York.

ROSS, Charles Brewster (1870–?)

THE VICTIM OF THE COUNTRY'S FIRST FAMOUS KIDNAPPING CASE

The first kidnapping in the United States to gain national attention was the abduction, on July 5,

Gustav Blair, 69, claimed to be kidnap victim Charlie Ross, who disappeared as a small child in 1939. One of many such claimants, he filed suit to make the estate recognize his claim. (Associated Press.)

1874, of Little Charlie Ross. Charlie and his six-year-old brother were taken into a buggy by two men and driven from their home in Philadelphia to a place about two hours to the north, where the brother was let out of the buggy, and Charlie was carried off.

Charlie's father, Christian K. Ross, immediately posted a $300 reward for the child's recovery or information regarding the abduction. The kidnappers sent Ross a letter demanding a $20,000 ransom, along with a threat to kill the child if the money was not forthcoming.

Newspapers across the country followed the progress of the case—which was very little—and wrote editorials denouncing the practice of kidnapping. According to the *New York Times* in an article on July 14:

> Must it, then, be accepted as true that any of us are liable to have our children stolen from the public streets and in open day? It is extremely unlikely that the child of any reader of this article will be stolen from him; but this Philadelphia business shows that any of us is liable to such a loss; for what may be done in one instance, and in one place, may be done in another instance and in another place. It seems that the crime can be committed with a considerable chance of impunity, and there are creatures ready and able to commit it upon sufficient inducement—that is prospect of gain. And the prospect of gain is, it must be confessed, very fair. In case of a stolen child, whose restoration is offered for a sum of money, how few parents, if the sum were within their reach, would hesitate to pay it? How few men would have the firmness—say rather the stoicism—to resist the pleadings of their own hearts, enforced by the cry of a frantic mother bereaved of her child? . . . Of perils by night we are careful enough, with our combination locks, burglar-alarms, and private watchmen; but that there are perils by day which also demand our serious attention this Philadelphia business is striking evidence.

Christian Ross tried to pay the ransom several times, but each time the kidnappers failed to show up. Then, two weeks after the kidnapping, the New York police received word from an informer that the kidnappers were William Mosher and Joseph Douglass. Both men had long criminal records and had recently escaped from a local jail, where they had been waiting to stand trial for burglary. The police began an intensive manhunt for the two, spurred on by the $20,000 reward being offered by the mayor and city fathers of Philadelphia. But they had no success until December 14, when Mosher and Douglass were apprehended trying to burglarize a home on Long Island. Mosher was shot and killed; Douglass was severely wounded but lived long enough to admit to the kidnapping, but not long enough to reveal the fate of Charlie.

Reports of sightings of Charlie Ross came in from all over the country and continued for 50 years after the event; but all of them proved false. The only person ever tried for the crime was William Westervelt, Mosher's brother-in-law, who was charged with aiding in the kidnapping, writing the ransom note and concealing the child. He was convicted and sentenced to a prison term of seven years and a fine of $1. But if he knew what happened to poor Charlie Ross, he never told.

ROTHSTEIN, Arnold (1882–1928)

GAMBLER, BOOKMAKER, AND BANKROLLER TO THE MOB, ROTHSTEIN OPERATED BEHIND A VEIL OF MYSTERY THAT HAS NEVER BEEN COMPLETELY PARTED

The man who became known as "The Big Bankroll" was the son of Abraham Rothstein, a silk and woolen merchant in Manhattan. Abraham was so well respected that he was asked to mediate a major dispute in the New York garment industry in 1919. He settled it successfully, and at a testimonial dinner given to him on that occasion, Governor Al Smith described him as "Abe the Just."

It is notable that Abraham's son Arnold was not mentioned at this dinner. Arnold was a gambler and had a reputation for being willing to gamble on anything. He also had a reputation for seldom losing. He loaned money for enterprises that promised a high profit, such as running booze from the Bahamas to the PROHIBITION-dry mainland. But first he would assure himself that the venture was a sound one. His judgment was so well respected that the knowledge that Rothstein was involved in a project gave it an air of solidity and legitimacy. This reputation sometimes inadvertently got him into trouble, as in the case of the WORLD SERIES OF 1919. Some gamblers had approached him in 1919 to get his imprimatur on a plan to fix the Chicago White Sox–Cincinnati Redlegs series, but he turned them down. "I don't want any part of it," he told them, explaining that he thought they would all be lynched if the plan was discovered. But the gamblers, afraid the deal would dissolve if Rothstein's refusal were known, wired their principals that The Big Bankroll had become a partner. This lie was to cost Rothstein many hours of testimony in various courtrooms over the years, but to balance that he probably made a few hundred thousand dollars betting on the series. Just because he wouldn't go along with the scheme didn't mean that he wouldn't bet on a sure thing if he knew about it.

Rothstein served as the mentor and bankroll for many up-and-coming gangsters, such as MEYER LANSKY, FRANK COSTELLO and LUCKY LUCIANO. Such notorious bootleggers as Waxey Gordon, DUTCH SCHULTZ and LEGS DIAMOND imported his liquor. Rothstein was an equal opportunity lender, who showed Lansky and Luciano that it was smarter to operate together than to fight over turf. It was Rothstein, contemporary wisdom has it, who first conceived of the idea of a national board of directors to oversee ORGANIZED CRIME.

Rothstein became a mythic figure during his lifetime, and the myth grew after his death. He was believed to have his finger in anything illegal or immoral that happened anywhere in the country. He seemed to collect nicknames, most of which he hated. In addition to "The Big Bankroll," he was also called "The Brain"—the one nickname he didn't hate—"Mr. Big," "The Man Uptown" and "The Fixer."

Rothstein enjoyed being the mysterious figure who stayed in the background and fixed things and controlled things, while others did the work, which is a fair description of what he did. In an interview with Zoe Beckley of the Brooklyn *Eagle*, he said: "The majority of the human race are dubs and dumbbells. They have rotten judgment and no brains and when you have learned to do things and how to size people up and dope out methods for yourself, they jump to the conclusion that you are crooked." When Edwin C. Hill of the New York *Sun* asked him how he made his money, Rothstein responded, "There are two million fools born for every intelligent man. That ought to answer you."

In 1920, the district attorney suspected Rothstein's involvement with professional gambler and con man NICKY ARNSTEIN in the theft of a large amount of liberty bonds. Arnstein was indicted and eventually convicted, but they could never prove a case against Rothstein. It is probable that neither of them were involved; Rothstein may have dealt in stolen bonds, but he probably did not have anything to do with stealing them; as for Nicky Arnstein, as his wife Fanny Brice said, "He couldn't mastermind his way out of a paper bag."

On November 4, 1928, Rothstein was sitting at his table in Lindy's restaurant, his office away from the office, when he received a call to go to the Park Central Hotel. When he got there, someone shot him and fled. Rothstein walked downstairs and collapsed. He died in the hospital a day later. In 1938, the New York *Herald Tribune*, in a retrospective editorial, opined, "Rothstein was a unique figure in the life of this city. No one has arisen since his death who resembles him very closely, which is probably all for the best."

RULOFF, Edward Howard (1819–1871)

AN EVIL MONOMANIAC WITH NO CONSCIENCE, RULOFF LIED AND STOLE AND MURDERED WHOMEVER GOT IN HIS WAY

Born in Hammond River, New Brunswick, Canada, with an oversized head and a thirst for knowledge with which to fill it, Edward Ruloffson soon became what he was to remain all his life: an intellectual giant and a moral imbecile. He had very few years of formal schooling, but he loved reading and would read anything and everything that passed under his hands. His mother, who was also an omnivorous reader, taught him a passing familiarity with Greek, Latin, the classics and other subjects popular with the erudite in her day.

The problem side of his character expressed itself when the 20-year-old Ruloffson was clerking for a local lawyer. The lawyer's home was burglarized, one of a series of burglaries in the community. A few days later, Ruloffson showed up at work wearing one of the lawyer's stolen suits. This misjudgment earned him two years in New Brunswick Prison.

Calling himself Edward Ruloff (or in some accounts, Rulloff), the large-headed young man, who now sported a thick black beard, appeared in Dryden, New York, in the summer of 1842. At first, he worked on a canal as a common laborer. But soon, hearing that a small private school in Dryden needed teachers for the new term, he applied for the job. He was soon teaching the children of Dryden's affluent citizens. By all accounts, Ruloff was an impressive teacher. He passed to his students his love of language, tracing for them the Greek and Latin roots of words, sometimes going back to the ancient Sanskrit or diverging into a discussion of Chinese pictographs or the roots of the alphabet. He also delved into biology, botany and zoology with his students, showing what seemed to be a profound knowledge of whatever subject he attacked.

In 1843, Professor Ruloff announced his engagement to Harriet Schutt, a 16-year-old girl, daughter of the family he was staying with and one of his students. Her relatives did not seem to think the age difference very important, but they did want to know more about the antecedents of this man who was about to become an in-law. Ruloff thought that was a great insult, telling them that his manifestly fine education should be proof enough of his being a gentleman, a ploy not altogether unfamiliar in the present day. Harriet's two brothers, William and Edward, were not convinced. But regardless of the brothers' opinions, Edward Ruloff and Harriet Schutt were married on December 31, 1843.

Immediately after the wedding, Professor Ruloff became Doctor Ruloff, giving up his teaching job and setting himself up as a botanical physician. Herbal medicine was beginning one of its periodic rebirths of popularity, and Ruloff rode the "natural healing" wave to success. He and his wife moved to Lansing, New York, near Ithaca, at the southern end of Lake Cayuga. His reputation spread, and he was soon traveling about the countryside, healing as he went. He was called to Ithaca to administer to the sick baby of his brother-in-law William, but the baby died, and so did its mother.

Harriet Ruloff gave birth to a baby girl in April 1845, and her mother came down from Dryden to assist. It was then that Harriet revealed to her mother that her relations with her husband were not all that she had hoped. He was moody and arrogant and had a bad temper. He would yell and even curse at her, and occasionally he would strike her for no apparent reason. One time when she was grinding pepper, he picked up the stone pestle and hit her over the head with it. The mother told one of Harriet's brothers, who came over and warned Ruloff to behave.

On June 23, Ruloff stopped at the house of a neighbor, Mr. Robertson, and asked a favor. He was going on an overnight trip, he said, and his wife was afraid to be alone. Mr. Robertson sent his daughter over to keep Mrs. Ruloff company. She later told of one curious incident: One time when Dr. Ruloff wanted to give the crying baby some medicine, his wife adamantly refused to let him approach the child.

The next day Ruloff reappeared at the Robertson home. He asked to borrow Robertson's horse and wagon. He explained in some detail that his wife's uncle had stopped to call on his way back to his home in Motts Corners. The uncle had offered to take Mrs. Ruloff and the baby back with him for a visit and had unloaded a large box of books to make room for them. Ruloff now wanted to take the box to Motts Corners and return with his wife and child. Robertson, a good neighbor, loaned his horse and wagon and even helped Ruloff load a large, heavy box into the back of the wagon. He remarked at the weight of the box.

Ruloff returned the wagon the day after and went home, but without his wife and child. They were, he explained, visiting relatives in Ohio. When word of this got back to the Schutts in Dryden, this caused some faint surprise. They had no relatives in Ohio, and as far as they knew, neither had Ruloff. The brothers went to see their brother-in-law, but by the time they arrived, he had gone. Edward followed, catching up with the doctor in Buffalo. Ruloff explained that he was on his way to join his wife and daughter, who were staying with a family named Dupuy in Madison, Ohio. He invited Edward to come along. Edward boarded the boat with Ruloff, but when they were under way, he realized that somehow Ruloff had again disappeared. Edward went as far as Madison, Ohio, and discovered that there was no Dupuy family there, and his sister was nowhere to be found. He returned as far as Cleveland, where he ran into Ruloff. This time Ruloff professed ignorance of Harriet's whereabouts. She had, he told Edward, disappeared.

Ruloff returned to Ithaca with his brother-in-law, apparently satisfied that his explanation was simple and unassailable. The local authorities disagreed, and he was arrested. Unfortunately, from the Schutts' point of view, it was impossible to try him for murder without some proof of death. The murder charge was dropped and one of simple abduction substituted. On that charge he was convicted and sentenced to 10 years in Auburn prison.

It was in the Auburn prison library that, having little else to do, Ruloff perfected his education. He had a love bordering on mania for philology, and he studied every language that he could find a text for. Those people who believed that education was the key to criminal reform brought him books, and before he matriculated from Auburn, he was fluent in Latin, Greek, French, German and Hebrew.

When he was released after 10 years, the people of the community had not forgotten him, and they were not satisfied that he had reformed. During the years he was in prison, someone had stumbled across the knowledge that at the time his wife and child disappeared someone had sold the bodies of a woman and child to the Geneva Medical College. They bore no marks of foul play, and they had long since been dissected by medical students, but the description of the woman fit that of Harriet. He was arraigned again, this time for murder.

Acting as his own attorney, Ruloff protested the charge, claiming that he could not be tried twice for the disappearance of his wife, under the double jeopardy clause of the Constitution. The judge agreed, and the charge of murdering his wife was dropped. Instead he was tried on a charge of murdering his daughter. He was convicted and sentenced to death. He appealed, claiming to be confident the decision would be reversed. But he decided not to wait for the reversal, and, on May 5, 1857, with the assistance of the sheriff's 18-year-old son, Albert Jarvis, he escaped from the jail.

Ruloff turned up at Allegheny College in Pennsylvania where, as Professor James Nelson, he impressed the academics with his knowledge of philology and various of the biological sciences. One night, for reasons of his own, he robbed a jewelry store. Forced to flee in midwinter, he next showed up in Jamestown, New York, with a case of frostbite, which forced the amputation of the big toe on his left foot, an operation which he performed on himself.

He next appeared teaching at a small school in Columbus, Ohio, which is where he was when a New York peace officer, Sheriff John Dennin, found him. He was extradited from Ohio and lodged again in an Ithaca jail. All of this time, Ruloff's appeal had been working its way through the judicial system, and now a decision was handed down. The trial court's finding was reversed in March 1859; the appeals court, noting that "absence in and of itself is not sufficient in a criminal case to establish death," ruled that the *CORPUS DELICTI* had not been proven.

When word of the decision was made public, a lynch mob gathered, stirred up partly by a poster which had been handed out, which read in part: "In the name of humanity, in the name of the relatives of the murdered wife, whose heartstrings have been lacerated by the fiend in human shape, in the name of the murdered wife and child, whose pale ghosts call to you from the silent tomb to do your duty, we ask you, shall the murderer go unpunished?"

The mob formed at the Clinton House in Ithaca and prepared to march on the jail. A battering ram was fashioned, and the mob was sauntering toward the jail when the Sheriff removed Ruloff to Auburn Prison. An attempt was made to try Ruloff for the murder of brother-in-law William's wife and child back in 1844, but when the bodies were exhumed, nothing could be found but a suspicious trace of copper, insufficient to support a murder indictment.

Now Ruloff's life truly became strange. He acquired two henchmen: Albert Jarvis, the sheriff's son, and William T. Dexter, a professional burglar whom he had met in Auburn. The trio, with Ruloff as the brains, went on a burglary spree in New England and New York. They specialized in removing bolts of silk and other expensive fabrics from warehouses and shops. At the same time, as Professor E. C. Howard, he taught English to immigrants in Hoboken, New Jersey, across the river from New York City. Meanwhile, as Professor Edouard Leurio, he worked on a scholarly philology tome, *Method in Formation of Language*, which would demonstrate the common origins of all languages. Ruloff was convinced this would be such an important work in the history of the human race that he would never have to work—or steal—again.

In 1867 "Professor Leurio" took his manuscript to the convention of the American Philological Association in Poughkeepsie, New York. The audience was very impressed with the erudition showed by the work and was convinced of its possible value. But when Ruloff-Leurio tried to get support to finance the publication of his work, he was informed that he would have to look elsewhere, there was no funding available for such a project.

Ruloff decided to fund the project himself, and he and his companions traveled to Binghamton, New York, to pay a midnight visit to the Halpert Brothers' Silk Shop. What they did not know was that two of the clerks, Gilbert Burrows and Fred Merrick, slept on the premises. Awakened by the sound of bolts of silk being removed, Burrows and Merrick emerged from the back and fought with the three thieves. Ruloff calmly shot both of the men, killing Merrick.

Aroused by the gunfire, a large number of the town's citizens formed into posses and searched the town. It was not until the next morning that they found any of the miscreants: Albert Jarvis and William Dexter, apparently beaten to death, were floating lifeless in the Susquehanna River.

The next night a constable heard suspicious noises in the vicinity of an outhouse behind some buildings near the railroad yards. The tall, respectable-looking elderly gentleman crouching by the outhouse gladly accompanied him back to the sheriff's office. The stranger explained that he was a scholar named Charles Augustus and had been ejected from a passing passenger train after a dispute with the conductor over a lost ticket. He added that he had to get to Ithaca to give a scholarly address that evening.

He was so convincing that the sheriff was about to have him escorted to the train station, when something clicked in the mind of one of the deputies. Law enforcement officers in those days were encouraged to spend their spare time studying "rogues' gallery" books full of the pictures and descriptions of known felons and memorizing what they read. The deputy noticed a depression in their guest's left shoe where a big toe should be. "Aren't you Ruloff?" he asked.

Ruloff admitted the identification, but he talked so convincingly of how he had been falsely accused in the past and how he only wanted to be left alone to pursue his philological studies, that if Burrows had not identified him as the man who had wounded him and killed his partner, he would have walked away.

In January 1871, Ruloff was convicted of murdering Merrick and sentenced to be hanged. He protested, citing his value to the world of philology and classical studies. A protest movement developed among the New York intelligentsia to save his life. On May 17, 1871, Edward Howard Ruloff was hanged by the neck until he was dead. A person who witnessed the execution reported that when they asked Ruloff if he wanted a minister to pray for him on the scaffold, he said no, but that if they wanted to have one up there to pray for the crowd, that was all right with him. His last words were: "Hurry it up. I want to be in Hell in time for dinner."

At that time, the study of the brain was very popular; its weight was considered a measure of the intrinsic intelligence of its user. The brains of famous literary figures, scientists, politicians and criminals were collected upon their deaths to be weighed and otherwise examined. Ruloff's brain was given to Cornell University. It was found to be seven ounces heavier than the average and five ounces more than that of Daniel Webster.

Ruloff was one of the more popular villains of the period, and a number of books purporting to tell the true story of his life and adventures were rapidly issued. *The Man of Two Lives* and *The Veil of Secrecy Removed: The Only True and Authentic History of Edward H. Ruloff* were published within months of his execution.

RUSSIAN MAFIA

In the 75 years of the Soviet Union's existence, capitalism was illegal. The buying of goods for resale, the lending of money at interest, the private ownership of property and hiring of workers were antithetical to communism and carried high penalties for those caught engaging in these practices. As a result a black market in goods and a criminal class that became known as the Russian Mafia developed.

During the past few decades, many Russians have immigrated to the United States. The Brighton Beach district of New York City became home to large numbers of these immigrants. Like previous immigrants they brought with them their own language, their own foods, their own customs and their own criminals. The Russian Mafia today, living in a land where their previous criminal activities are legal and encouraged, have combined entrepreneurial capitalism with a total disregard for U.S. laws and the police who attempt to enforce those laws. They have added to their capitalistic pursuits theft, extortion and selling "protection" to the Russian shopkeepers in their own neighborhood.

S

SACCO AND VANZETTI

TWO GENTLE ANARCHISTS CONVICTED AND EXECUTED FOR A CRIME THEY PROBABLY DID NOT COMMIT

On April 15, 1920, a five-man gang held up a shoe factory in South Braintree, Massachusetts, and escaped with the $15,776.51 payroll, killing the paymaster and a guard in the process. Two Italian anarchists, Nicola Sacco, a factory worker, and Bartolomeo Vanzetti, a fish peddler, were tried for the crime. The only possible connection they had with the events at South Braintree were that they both had pistols, and one of them—Sacco—looked something like one of the robbers. But neither anarchism nor Italian immigrants were popular in Massachusetts in the 1920s, and they were brought to trial. The courtroom was ringed with armed plainclothes guards to ward off the feared attack of gangs of other violent anarchists.

The prosecution based its case on two expert witnesses, ballistics experts who testified that the murder bullets came from the anarchists' guns. The first, Charles Van Amburgh, was later found to have doctored his testimony to fit the needs of the prosecution. In one subsequent case, it was shown that he gave false evidence to convict a man who was proved to be innocent. The second, police captain William Proctor, attempted to take Sacco's pistol apart on the stand, but did not know how. He later admitted in an affidavit that his statement that one of the murder bullets had markings "consistent with being fired by that pistol" merely meant that the bullet could have come from Sacco's gun, or many others, and that he personally did not believe that it had been fired by Sacco's gun. He further admitted that he had been heavily coached by the prosecution.

The judge and the jury of the case ignored several pertinent facts: A gang of MAFIA hoodlums led by THE MORELLI BROTHERS was robbing payrolls; this robbery was consistent with the others; and it could be demonstrated that neither Sacco nor Vanzetti could be members of this gang. Judge Webster Thayer, a model of judicial decorum, believed that he was supposed to convict, and he did everything in his power to convey that belief to the jury. Out of court he called the defendants "dago sons of bitches." On July 14, 1921, the jury found the two defendants guilty and Judge Thayer sentenced them to death. "Did you see what I did to those anarchist bastards?" he later asked a friend.

Governor Alvin Tufts Fuller of Massachusetts, not understanding what all the world-wide fuss regarding the trial was about, appointed a commission headed by Abbot Lawrence Lowell, president of Harvard University, to look into it. The Lowell Commission found everything in order, although it did comment on Judge Thayer's "grave breach of official decorum." They seemed to be more concerned that proprieties be observed in the courtroom than whether the defendants had received a fair trial.

On August 23, 1927, Nicola Sacco and Bartolomeo Vanzetti were electrocuted.

Years later, VINCENT TERESA revealed that he had been told by Butsey Morelli that Morelli and his brothers had committed the crime for which the two anarchists had been executed. "These two suckers took it on the chin for us," Butsey said. "That shows you how much justice there really is."

SAINT VALENTINE'S DAY MASSACRE

AS BUGS MORAN EXPLAINED: "ONLY CAPONE KILLS LIKE THAT."

On February 14, 1929, a Saint Valentine's Day that will live in infamy, the biggest gangland murder of the PROHIBITION years took place in a garage on Chicago's North Side. The main characters of the gang warfare, AL CAPONE, head of the Chicago Syndicate, and GEORGE "BUGS" MORAN, boss of the North Side Gang, were not on the scene. Capone was in Palm Beach, Florida, ostentatiously talking to the district attorney. Moran was across the street from the garage.

Seven men were in the garage at 2122 North Clark Street at ten o'clock that morning, waiting for a shipment of bootleg booze that was supposed to arrive any minute. They were members of the North Side Gang, DION O'BANION's old organization, which had been taken over by HYMIE WEISS when O'Banion was violently and suddenly removed from the scene. Bugs Moran assumed this authority when Weiss met a similar end. The North Side Gang had been in a long-standing feud with the Syndicate, headed first by JOHNNIE TORRIO and then by Al Capone, since the beginning of Prohibition a decade earlier.

Across the street, at the second-floor front window of 2119 North Clark Street, Phil and Harry Keywell, two brothers who were members of Detroit's Purple Gang and had been imported to Chicago just for this job, kept count of the men entering the garage, a North Side Gang headquarters. The supposed booze delivery was a setup to lure Moran into the garage. The object was to kill Moran and as many of his gang as they could catch in the garage. As the seventh man entered the garage, the Keywells compared his appearance with a picture of Bugs they had been given. They decided it was him. Phil went to a wall telephone and called the Circus Café, about a mile away, to give the okay.

At a garage next to the café, five men piled into an open car that looked suspiciously like a police car. Two of the men were wearing police uniforms. Three minutes later they pulled up in front of the North Clark Street garage and four of them got out, leaving the driver. The two in police uniforms entered the garage, clutching their revolvers. "O.K. You guys. Up against the wall," one of them barked.

Nobody knows what the seven men in the garage thought, but they must have assumed that it was a routine bust by some uniformed cops trying to make points with their bosses. Had they suspected anything else, they would not have gone so willingly to the slaughter. Meekly they lined up facing the wall.

The two men in civilian clothes came in behind the pseudo-cops and pulled submachine guns out from under their overcoats. Methodically they sprayed the wall with bullets; one man shot from left to right, aiming at the victims' heads, and the other sprayed from right to left, aiming at their backs and shoulders. They kept firing until their victims lay crumpled on the floor.

The seven victims were a pair of working gangsters, Pete and Frank Gusenberg; James Clark, whose real name was Albert Kashellek and who was Bugs Moran's brother-in-law; Adam Heyer, an ex-convict accountant and Moran's business manager; Johnny May, with a wife and six children, who worked as a $50-a-week mechanic at the garage; Dr. Reinhardt H. Schwimmer, an optometrist who was a gangster groupie and had dropped in to say hello to Bugs on his way to the office; and Albert R. Weinshank, proprietor of a local speakeasy. It was probably Weinshank whom the Keywell brothers had mistaken for Moran—they resembled each other.

Bugs Moran, the intended victim of the operation, was heading down North Clark Street toward the garage with two of his men, Willie Marks and Teddy Newbury, when the police car drew up to the garage. He saw the two supposed policemen get out and enter the garage and assumed it was a raid, so he prudently went into a coffee shop across the street to wait for the police to leave.

Mrs. Landesman, landlady of the building across the street, was attracted to the scene by the strange popping noises she heard. From her second-story window, she saw the attackers leave the garage. Two men in civilian clothes, she testified, came out with their hands up, escorted by two men in police uniforms holding guns on them. The four got into the car, which sped away. One of her boarders, C. L. McAllister, impelled by irresistible curiosity, went over to the garage to see what happened. A few seconds later he came out, his face ashen, and yelled up to Mrs. Landesman, "They're all dead men in there!" Mrs. Landesman called the police and, somewhat incoherently, told them what had happened. They sent a squad car.

Detective Clarence Sweeney, a five-year veteran policeman, was the first on the scene. He took one look at the carnage and then sent his partner back to notify the precinct.

Four corpses were on their backs, staring with sightless eyes at the ceiling. One man was kneeling, supported by an overturned chair, dead. Two were facedown. The whitewashed garage wall had been turned red with blood. A German shepherd belonging to one of the dead men was tied in a corner and it wouldn't stop howling.

Suddenly one of the men on the floor started crawling forward. Frank Gusenberg was not quite dead. Detective Sweeney knelt next to Gusenberg. "Frank—in the name of God, what happened?" he demanded. Gusenberg did not answer. He had 22 bullet wounds in him, but during the 90 minutes that he remained alive, he stubbornly refused to answer questions about the killings.

A reporter who came along with the police saw Bugs Moran standing outside the garage, staring at it, in the grip of some strange emotion. He professed to know nothing about it. But, when the reporter asked him who he thought did it, he spoke: "Only Capone kills like that," he said.

There was some concern at the time that the police might actually have been involved, but a forensic ballistics expert from New York, Major Calvin H. Goddard, was able to show that none of the bullets had come from any machine gun owned by the Chicago Police Department. Nobody was ever prosecuted for the murders, although those believed to have been directly involved died within a few years in gangland violence of one sort or another.

SCHEELE, Dr. Walter T.

THE GERMAN SPY IN WORLD WAR I WHO HELPED SINK OVER THIRTY SHIPS

A respected chemist and the president of the New Jersey Agricultural Chemical Company in the years before the First World War, Dr. Walter

Scheele was also a sleeper agent for Imperial Germany. He had been an agent in place in the United States since before the turn of the century, reporting to Berlin on the latest American discoveries in the fields of chemistry and explosives. At the start of the war in Europe, Scheele was on a $1,500-a-year retainer from the German government.

With the arrival of Captain FRANS VON RINTELEN in New York in 1915, Dr. Scheele was brought into more active use for the Fatherland, by devising a bomb which might be put aboard cargo vessels to destroy them while they were at sea. At that time, the United States was still at peace with Germany, and German attempts to blow up American shipping could only be regarded as piracy and gross violation of the law of nations. Nonetheless, Dr. Scheele devised such a bomb, and it was very successful. A lead tube was divided into two sections by a copper disk. One section held potassium chlorate; the other held sulfuric acid. The acid ate away the copper disk at a steady rate, and when it was penetrated and the two chemicals mixed, they exploded. The bombs could be timed by varying the thickness of the copper disk. If a strong fire was desired instead of an explosion, picric acid was substituted for the potassium chlorate, and the ends of the tubes were plugged with wax instead of solid plugs.

A German freighter, the S.S. *Friedrich der Grosse*, which was interned in the New York harbor, provided a secret workshop for manufacturing the bomb casings, which were then taken over to Scheele's laboratory at 1133 Clinton Street, Hoboken, New Jersey, to be filled. Because of their size and shape, the devices became known as "cigars" by those who made and used them. They were given to "friendly" longshoremen to place on board outgoing ships. They proved very effective.

Over the next two years, from 1915 until the entry of the United States into the war on April 6, 1917, the following ships had mysterious explosions or fires at sea:

The S.S. *Carlton*
The S.S. *Cressington Court*
The S.S. *Samland*
The S.S. *Strathway*
The S.S. *Minnehaha*
The S.S. *Touraine*
The S.S. *Lord Downshire*
The S.S. *Knutford*
The S.S. *Craigside*
The S.S. *Asuncion de Larringa*
The lighter *Dixie*
The S.S. *Rotterdam*
The S.S. *Santa Ana*
The S.S. *Rio Lages*
The S.S. *Euterpe*
The S.S. *Rochambeau*
The S.S. *Ancona*
The S.S. *Tynningham*
The S.S. *Inchmore*
The S.S. *Manchuria*
The S.S. *Sygna*
The S.S. *Ryndam*
The S.S. *Dalton*
The S.S. *Tennyson*
The S.S. *Livingston Court*
The S.S. *Carlton* (again)
The S.S. *California*
The S.S. *Kandahar*
The S.S. *Philadelphia*
The S.S. *Antilla*
The S.S. *Chicago*
The S.S. *Ponus*
The S.S. *Regina d'Italia*

On about 10 other ships, bombs were found and disarmed or thrown overboard before they could do any damage. How many ships were sunk in mid-ocean, and how many lives were lost due to this undeclared secret war cannot be determined. Scheele estimated that his bombs had destroyed cargoes worth more than $10 million in 36 different ships, even though no more than 25 percent of the bombs he gave out were actually planted onboard ships. The others, he said, were probably thrown overboard by the longshoremen who had been paid to plant them.

With the U.S. declaration of war on Germany, Scheele was ordered out of the country and fled to Cuba. Once there, he was virtually held a prisoner in the German community, allowed to go nowhere without an escort. In March 1918, Scheele was arrested by the Cuban police and quickly extradited to the United States.

When faced with a jail sentence in the United States, Scheele plea bargained for immunity, testifying freely about German weapons, including high explosives and poison gas formulae. It sounded so strange to the government attorneys that Thomas A. Edison and his chief chemist were brought in as experts to interview the German spy. The chemist pronounced Scheele "an eminent German chemist with unquestioned knowledge of the most important phases of contemporary chemical warfare methods and German commercial practice." *See also:* FEDERAL BUREAU OF INVESTIGATION

SCHRANK, John (1872–1943)

On October 14, 1912, New York saloon keeper John Schrank attended a Milwaukee, Wisconsin, political rally for ex-President Teddy Roosevelt, who was forming his Bull Moose party to try to regain the presidency. Roosevelt was preparing to address a large crowd outside his hotel when Schrank ran up and fired a shot at him at point-blank range. The shot penetrated a glasses case, a 50-page speech folded double and the ex-president's chest, lodging in his lung. Schrank was adjudged insane and spent the rest of his life in an insane asylum. Roosevelt cried, "It's all right boys—they haven't killed me yet!" and went on to give his speech, carrying the bullet inside of him for the rest of his life.

SCHULTZ, Dutch (1902–1935)

KING OF BOOZE AND NUMBERS DURING PROHIBITION, THE DUTCHMAN FINALLY WENT ONE STEP TOO FAR

With the start of PROHIBITION, the career of a Bronx bartender named Dutch Schultz was on the rise. Born Arthur Flegenheimer, he tended bar and committed minor offenses until he and his gang took over the beer distribution in the Bronx. Gradually, he extended his grasp until much of Manhattan was also receiving its booze from bootleggers supplied by Schultz. The territory was amicably divided between his gang and the MAFIA organization of LUCKY LUCIANO, who operated in lower Manhattan and Brooklyn.

Schultz expanded his operation in the early 1930s to include running the Harlem NUMBERS RACKET by organizing the black policy houses. Those who did not want to organize under Schultz's umbrella were either convinced or eliminated. He used his henchman OTTO "ABBADABBA" BERMAN, a human lightning calculator, to sway the odds in his favor by ensuring that no heavily played number was allowed to win. On the day that Greta Garbo returned to New York on the *Queen Mary*, for example, the numbers 714 ("Garbo" reduced to a three-digit number), 347 ("*Queen Mary*" similarly reduced), 294 (number in *Sister Lena's Dream Book* for your ship coming in) and 616 (the time the ship docked) were all played far more heavily than random chance would allow. Had one of those numbers actually come in, the strain of paying off at 600 to 1 would have strained the bank. This made Berman well worth the $10,000 a week that Schultz paid him.

Except for his extravagance in Berman's salary, Schultz was a parsimonious man. He was proud of never having paid over $2 for a shirt or $35 for a suit. "I think only queers wear silk shirts," he explained. He was also an erratic personality with a violent temper, which made him dangerous to his friends as well as his enemies. When he suspected his lieutenant "Bo" Weinberg of plotting against him, he personally set Weinberg's legs in cement and dropped him into the Hudson River without bothering to kill him first.

When THOMAS E. DEWEY was appointed special prosecutor by New York Governor Herbert Lehman, he targeted Schultz as his first major step in breaking the New York gangs. Schultz wanted to have Dewey killed, but the other crime bosses disagreed, feeling that it would bring too much heat on the whole organization. Schultz, however, told Luciano, MEYER LANSKY and the others that he was going ahead and having Dewey hit.

On the night of October 23, 1935, MURDER, INCORPORATED operative CHARLIE WORKMAN, a respected artist with the submachine gun, walked into the Palace Chop House and Tavern in Newark, New Jersey, and gunned down Schultz, Abbadabba Berman and two Schultz bodyguards. Schultz was taken to a hospital and died two days later. His voluminous last words were taken down in shorthand by an officer of the Newark Police Department but they revealed nothing of interest to the authorities.

SCHUSTER, Arnold (1928–1952)

THE INNOCENT YOUTH KILLED AT THE ORDER OF A MAD MOB BOSS

On Monday, February 18, 1952, WILLIE "THE ACTOR" SUTTON, a bank robber and jail-break artist whose exploits had become almost legendary, was captured by the police on a Brooklyn street while trying to replace the battery in his car. He had been spotted on the subway by Arnold Schuster, a young Coast Guard veteran who was then working as a pants presser in his father's tailor shop. A crime buff, who kept and studied wanted posters on notorious criminals, Schuster recognized Sutton from an FBI circular that showed six different versions of Sutton's ever-changing appearance. He followed Sutton off the subway and while Sutton was fixing his car, Schuster ran around the corner and flagged down a passing police car. Sutton was arrested.

On the evening of Saturday, March 8, 1952, Arnold Schuster was gunned down by a lone gunman as he walked back to his house from his father's tailor shop. The gunman, who had apparently lain in wait for Schuster in a darkened driveway several doors from his house, fired four bullets at the young man; one entered his brain from behind the left ear, one penetrated his lower abdomen, one passed through his nose and one singed his scalp. Schuster died instantly.

Sutton had been in custody during this time and was known to be almost excessively nonviolent for a bank robber. The only suspect in the case was a convict named Frederick Tenuto, who had escaped from Holmesburg Prison with Sutton. There was no evidence to show that Tenuto was anywhere near Brooklyn when Schuster was killed, but the newspapers, noting that Tenuto was known as "The Accommodation Killer," speculated that he had been doing Sutton a favor. "The Code of the Underworld," a concept right out of the pulp adventure magazines, was cited as Tenuto's motive.

The public, which had treated Sutton as a modern Robin Hood until then, turned against him because of Schuster's murder. The judge sentencing him for a robbery conviction a month after Schuster's killing gave him the maximum penalty, stating that were it not for Sutton's life of crime, "the chain of circumstances which led up to the death of the Schuster boy never would have happened."

Eleven years later, in October 1963, MAFIA turncoat JOSEPH VALACHI was testifying before the MCCLELLAN COMMITTEE as to how dangerous Mafia capo ALBERT ANASTASIA was. He related that Anastasia was watching the news on television when Schuster was shown as the man who had identified Willie Sutton. "I can't stand squealers!" he is supposed to have said. "Hit him!" Valachi testified that the henchman who went to do the job was, curiously enough, Frederick Tenuto.

Willie Sutton, in his book *Where the Money Was* (1976), puts his own slant on the story. Having spent a lot of time considering what happened to Schuster, he believed that Anastasia had ordered the hit. But he thought that identifying Tenuto was either faulty memory on Valachi's part or that Valachi had heard the story third or fourth hand. Tenuto, after all, was not one of Anastasia's hoods; he would have had to be imported. A more logical suspect was John "Chappy" Mazziotta, a member of Anastasia's crime family, who was actually tied to the sale of the murder weapon—a .38 caliber Smith & Wesson, one of a group which had been stolen from a U.S. Army shipment. The truth of the matter will probably never be known. Neither Tenuto nor Mazziotta have been seen since the day of Arnold Schuster's death.

Attorney Samuel Liebowitz confers with Heywood Patterson, Clarence Norris, and Roy Wright, three of the Scottsboro defendants case he argued on appeal. (International News Photo.)

SCOPES TRIAL

See: Clarence Darrow

SCOTTSBORO CASE

NINE NEGRO YOUTHS CONVICTED OF A RAPE THEY DID NOT COMMIT

In 1931, 12 black youths riding the rails got in a fight with 7 white youths in a freight car and tossed them off the train somewhere between Chattanooga and Stevenson, Alabama. Nobody was hurt, but one of the white youths reported the incident. The freight train was stopped at Paint Rock, Alabama, and nine of the black youths were rounded up by a posse of 70 white deputy sheriffs and taken to the Jackson County jail in Scottsboro. The other three evidently jumped off the train before it reached Paint Rock.

Also on the train were two white girls dressed in overalls: a 21-year-old prostitute named Victoria Price and a 17-year-old tramp named Ruby Bates. Victoria Price, afraid that she would be booked for vagrancy, told the authorities that she and Ruby had been gang-raped by the nine blacks, plus the three who had jumped from the train.

The two girls suddenly were transformed into the Flower of Southern Womanhood, and the black youths were nothing but savage beasts, one of whom, it was asserted, had bitten off one of Ruby Bates's breasts. Robert Leibowitz says in *The Defender* (1981):

> On March 31, 1931, the nine Negro boys were jointly indicted on a single true bill which charged them with having raped the two white

women—an offense punishable in Alabama by a sentence of from ten years in prison up to the death penalty. Moreover, in cases where a Negro was accused of assaulting a white woman sexually, conviction could be obtained on the uncorroborated word of his alleged victim, the presumption being that no white female would ever dream of bringing such a charge unless it was absolutely true. In this atmosphere the nine youths were arraigned that same day.

The trials, held 12 days later, were conducted under the constant threat of a lynch mob. Milus Moody, a 70-year-old attorney of Scottsboro, was appointed to defend the boys, but he just sat there and did nothing. Which he probably considered the wisest thing to do if he wanted to continue walking the streets of Scottsboro without getting lynched himself. The medical evidence indicated that, while neither of the girls was a virgin, neither of them had sexual intercourse on the day in question. They also showed no signs of the physical trauma they claimed to have gone through. "Guilty or not," the prosecutor told the jury, "let's get rid of these niggers." The jury found them guilty, and eight of the nine were sentenced to death. The youngest, Roy Wright, 13, from Chattanooga, came within a hairsbreadth of conviction: The jury stood 11 to 1 for a guilty verdict.

The case was taken in hand by the International Labor Defense (ILD), a Communist front organization which saw it as an opportunity to rally American blacks to their cause and to raise large amounts of money from the liberal North and from all over Europe for the Scottsboro boys' defense. Whatever their motives, they and the National Association for the Advancement of Colored People (NAACP) were the only groups willing to do anything to save the boys. The ILD appealed the case to the Alabama Supreme Court, which, on March 25, 1932, affirmed all the convictions but one: Eugene Williams was sent back for retrial as a juvenile. The only dissenter was the Chief Justice, C. J. Anderson, whose opinion read in part: "The record indicates that the appearance [of defense counsel] in the case was pro forma, rather than zealous and active . . . and strongly indicates that the defendants had not been accorded a fair trial as a result."

An appeal then went to the U.S. Supreme Court, which agreed with Justice Anderson and overturned the verdict, ordering new trials for all the defendants. The ILD asked New York attorney Samuel S. Leibowitz if he would take the case. After getting a written statement from the ILD that they would leave to him the management of the case, free of political interference, he agreed.

When Leibowitz went to Alabama, he was startled at the racial attitudes, which as a liberal northerner, he had not truly believed existed. He wrote that he talked to the local people about the case:

> The invariable reply was it didn't make any difference whether they were innocent or guilty. "We have to keep the niggers in their place and if we let these niggers go, it will not be safe for a white woman to walk the streets in any part of the South."

Leibowitz, the "New York Jew nigger-lover," as he was by then known, took a deep breath and took on the defense. By now Ruby Bates had renounced her original testimony, saying that Victoria Price had frightened her into it, and admitted that no rapes had taken place. Also, one of the white youths that had been kicked off the train came forward to refute much of Miss Price's testimony. It made no difference. In a series of new trials, the defendants were again convicted.

Leibowitz took the cases back to the U.S. Supreme Court after establishing in the local court that blacks had been systematically excluded from the juries. The prosecution did its best to deny this, although it could not show the name of one black on the jury lists. The Supreme Court, in a landmark decision, found that the exclusion of blacks from jury service was unconstitutional.

The trials began for the third time under intense public scrutiny from all over the world. The Alabama officials, realizing that their state was being made to look like an ignorant conclave of bigots around the world, dropped the charges against four defendants, while the remaining five were convicted. Within a few years four more had been paroled. The last Scottsboro boy, Haywood Patterson, escaped from prison and fled north. Two years later he stabbed a black man to death and was convicted of manslaughter in Michigan.

In 1976, one of the nine, Clarence Willie Norris, appealed to Alabama Governor George Wallace for a pardon. He had jumped parole in 1946 and eventually moved to New York. In 1977, pardon was granted, and he found himself something of a celebrity in Alabama when he returned to receive it.

SEALE, Arthur D. (1947–)

On April 29, 1992, Arthur Seale, a former Exxon security official, and his wife, Irene, kidnapped Exxon International executive Sidney J. Reso from his home in Morris Township, New Jersey. They waited in their van outside his house when he left for work in the morning, and as he stopped to pick up a newspaper on his driveway they drove the van in front of his car and leapt out. Seale waved a gun at the startled executive and grabbed him by the collar, pulling him into the van. In the excitement the handgun went off, wounding Reso in the arm. The Seales took Reso to a self-storage site, and locked him inside one of the self-store lockers.

Mrs. Reso, who had received the Seales' ransom notes demanding $18 million and signed "Warriors of the Rainbow," pleaded on television for her husband's life, telling of his serious medical problems. Reso died on May 3, and the Seales buried him in a shallow grave in the woods in southern New Jersey. They continued trying to collect the ransom.

On June 19, the Seales were arrested. On June 27, Irene confessed and led the police to Reso's grave. On September 8, Arthur Seale pleaded guilty to federal charges of attempted extortion, conspiracy to commit extortion, mail fraud and interstate travel to promote extortion. Pending state charges included kidnapping and felony murder.

SECRET BAND OF BROTHERS

The Secret Band of Brothers was a gang of hustlers and cardsharps that worked the Mississippi River in the early nineteenth century. Said to number as many as 1,000 members, the band was a collective enterprise, and members shared equally in all profits. Jonathan H. Green, who billed himself as the "Reformed Gambler," revealed the existence of this organization to the Louisville police in 1830. According to Green, the group was begun in 1798 by a con man named Goodrich in Hanging Rock, Virginia. *See also:* GAMBLING AND GAMBLERS

SECRET SERVICE

The U.S. Secret Service, a branch of the Treasury Department, was founded on July 5, 1865, for the purpose of strongly discouraging the production of counterfeit money. It was placed under the leadership of a one-time soldier, con man and spy named WILLIAM P. WOOD, who had shown good judgment and a sound sense of investigative technique in his just completed investigation into the assassination of President ABRAHAM LINCOLN.

The Secret Service was thus the first general investigative agency of the federal government. Until that time, the government hired investigators, such as ALLAN PINKERTON in Chicago, as the need arose. In 1901, after the assassination of President WILLIAM MCKINLEY, the job of protecting the person of the president was added to the other duties of the Secret Service. In 1968, protection was extended to include major presidential and vice-presidential candidates and, in 1971, to visiting heads of state and other foreign dignitaries. The service takes this job very seriously, and the White House Detail—the men guarding the president—have shown time after time that they are ready to lay down their lives to protect the president.

Until 1951, the Secret Service received its financing and authority from appropriations acts passed yearly by Congress. In 1951, the powers of the Secret Service were delineated in a permanent law, which had to be rewritten several times because of complaints from the Justice Department and its investigative branch, the FEDERAL BUREAU OF INVESTIGATION (FBI). FBI Director J. EDGAR HOOVER, protecting bureau jurisdiction, made sure that the phraseology of the new enabling law was as limiting as possible. The compromise bill authorized the Secret Service to "detect and arrest any person violating any laws of the United States directly concerning official matters administered by and under the direct control of the Treasury Department." But that was further amended at the insistence of the Justice Department. The final enabling legislation is in Title 18, U.S. Code, Section 3056 (as amended), and reads in part:

William J. Flynn, who moved from head of the Secret Service to head up the Bureau of Investigation, which later became the FBI. (Federal Bureau of Investigation.)

> Subject to the direction of the Secretary of the Treasury, the United States Secret Service, Treasury Department, is authorized to protect the person of the President of the United States and members of his immediate family, the President-elect, and the Vice President at his request; detect and arrest any person committing any offense against the laws of the United States relating to coins, obligations, and securities of the United States and of foreign governments.

Although its main mission, aside from presidential protection, has been the detection and suppression of COUNTERFEITING, the service has occasionally been involved in other activities, ranging from investigating land frauds and narcotics smugglers to fighting the KU KLUX KLAN and foreign spies.

The Secret Service's main foray into the field of counterintelligence occurred during World War I. At the request of President Woodrow Wilson, William J. Flynn, then chief of the Secret Service, opened a counterespionage unit in New York City with a staff of 10 agents. He also assigned agents in Washington, D.C., to keep watch on the German Embassy and to shadow certain Embassy officials on their daily rounds. The Secret Service's major coup came when, on Saturday, July 24, 1915, before the United States had entered the war, Dr. Heinrich Friedrich Albert, a commercial attaché of the German Embassy, left a leather briefcase on a New York City elevated train when he got off at the 50th Street Station. The Secret Service agent shadowing him grabbed the briefcase and exited by another door.

The documents in the case showed that Albert was the principal paymaster of the Imperial German spy *apparat*. The documents showed that he was prepared to pay for espionage, sabotage, subversion, propaganda and the preparation for an eventual German invasion of the United States—a country with whom Germany was at peace at the time. Publication of the translated documents in the New York *World* did much to sway public opinion away from the German cause. And when the translated Zimmermann Telegram was made public, it completed the job.

The Secret Service's major task has always been the suppression of counterfeiters. At the end of the Civil War, when it was estimated that one out of every two bills in circulation was counterfeit, the Secret Service determined to make the counterfeiting of U.S. currency, or other monetary documents, such a hazardous procedure that it would no longer be attempted. It has not succeeded completely in that impossible goal, but it has had some success.

At the turn of the century, the BLACK HAND extortion gangs were causing a lot of trouble for the police departments of major East Coast cities. Then, one MAFIA group in New York City, headed by Giuseppe Morello and Ignazio Lupo, known as "Lupo the Wolf," made the mistake of printing and passing counterfeit money. On February 19, 1910, seven of the eight Mafia counterfeiters drew sentences of 15 to 18 years and $1,000 fines. Morello drew a 25-year sentence. Lupo the Wolf was put away for 30 years.

Beginning in 1928, the service ran across another problem, when a quantity of $100 bills of exceptional quality began turning up, usually in major port cities, such as Houston, Galveston, or New York. They were copies of the large size bills, which were then being phased out and replaced by the smaller size that is still used today. But there were still a large quantity of the large bills in circulation. The paper and ink on these counterfeits were very good, and the plates were excellent. The Secret Service made a number of arrests and managed to stop the flow of bills but could not trace them to their source. In 1939, an article in the *Saturday Evening Post,* written by W. G. Krivitsky, cleared up the problem. Krivitsky, who claimed to have been a general in the Red Army, revealed that Joseph Stalin had authorized the counterfeiting of U.S. currency to pay for the industrial equipment required by his latest five-year plan. The Secret Service could not arrest Stalin, but at least it could now close the case.

A much smaller problem, but very frustrating to the agents assigned to it, was the counterfeiting career of retired New York building superintendent Edward Mueller, who printed his own $1 bills on a tiny press on top of his dresser at home. He passed a tiny amount of money—just enough for his own meager needs—but he proved impossible to catch. Known as MISTER 880 by the agents who looked for him, he had misspelled the president's name under his portrait, spelling it "WAHSINGTON." The agents took this as a personal affront. But by the time he was caught by a lucky accident in 1948, they had developed a secret fondness for him. He was sentenced to a year and a day in prison and a $1 fine.

In more recent times, the Secret Service have proved their mettle in protecting presidents, foiling an attempt upon the life of President Gerald Ford by Squeeky Fromme in 1975, and upon Ronald Reagan by JOHN HINCKLEY in 1981.

See also: ASSASSINATIONS; GRISELO TORRESOLA

SECRET SIX

In the 1920s, faced with a rising tide of crime in Chicago, which, like the rest of the country, was suffering from the unanticipated side-effects of PROHIBITION, and in particular the depredations of AL CAPONE and his fellow gangsters, a group of Chicago businessmen got together to discuss the problem. Among those at the meeting were Colonel Robert Isham Randolph, president of the Chicago Association of Commerce; Edward E. Gore, past president of the Chicago Crime Commission; and financier Samuel Insull. They proposed the creation of a fund to hire private detectives to gather evidence against the racketeers. Insull volunteered to match whatever the rest of the group raised. Eventually the fund exceeded $1,000,000.

Colonel Randolph called a press conference to announce the formation of what he called the "Committee of Courage." He would not tell the press who was involved, except to say that there were six leaders. The Chicago papers promptly dubbed the group the "Secret Six."

The detectives hired by the group did assemble evidence to show the public the extent of unlawful activity and to convict some lesser criminals, but it had little effect against the gang leaders. Still, the publicity probably helped convince people that the bootleggers were not necessarily their friends. In 1929, the ST. VALENTINE'S DAY MASSACRE turned public opinion in Chicago sharply against the gangsters.

In an ironic twist to the story, the financial empire of Samuel Insull, the Secret Six's chief benefactor, came crashing down in 1932, with a loss to investors of $785,000,000. Insull was tried twice on federal charges of using the mails to defraud and for embezzlement. He was acquitted from both charges.

SERIAL KILLERS

See: MASS MURDERERS

SHELL GAME

An ancient and dishonorable SHORT CON, whose name has become synonymous with "swindle," the shell game was described by Walter B. Gibson, in *The Bunko Book* (1946), as "the surest and simplest method ever devised to take away a man's money." In this regard, it may have some competition from THREE-CARD MONTE, but the proposition is essentially true.

The shell game can be found at carnivals, county fairs and any place where crowds of people congregate. Usually it is being played without the permission of the management, but sometimes the management or the local authorities are paid off. Despite its appearance as a form of gambling, it is a swindle, not a game. It is not merely that some dealers will cheat the player; the shell game is *never* played honestly.

Also called "the walnut shell and pea," "find the pea" and "thimble rig," the play of the game is simple. The game pieces are three walnut shells, a dried pea and a flat surface to put them on. The shells are called "the nuts" in the trade, and the operator is said to be "working the nuts." The pea is put under one shell by the operator, the three shells are moved about on the surface and the players bet on which shell conceals the pea.

The secret is that the pea is never under the shell. When placing the shell over the pea, the operator actually causes it to scoot out the back and into his waiting fingers; the motion is naturally covered by his hand. To make the move easier, most operators use a small piece of hard rubber to simulate the pea. Whichever shell the mark picks, he has to lose. The operator then turns over another shell, deftly dropping the pea at the same time. In the hands of a deft operator, the switch is invisible.

SHORT CONS

Short cons are CONFIDENCE GAMES involving few—usually no more than three—people aside from the mark (victim), and little or no specific preparation. They are also known as "against the wall" or "playing off the wall" and are called "bunco" by the police, who fight them with special units known as "bunco squads." There are endless variants of the classic cons, some of which have been in existence, with little change, for well over a century. A few of the more popular of the short cons are described here.

The Gold Brick Game. The mark (victim) is told that, for some reason, a third party is willing to sell a gold brick, or some other small, bulky item of high value, at way below its true value. The reasons are numerous: The party does not know that it is real gold; the party is a felon and will be arrested if the party tries to sell it to a dealer; the party is a miner whose partners do not know the party has the brick. The victim is shown a real gold brick. He or she is even allowed to test it. When the mark is convinced, he or she pays the money, the brick is packaged and he or she leaves with the brick.

In the classic version of this con, the package is exchanged for another, identical, package while the mark returns home. If the mark is from out of town, the exchange is made at the hotel. The story is told among old-time con men about the wise mark, who returned to his hotel room with the package containing the brick, knowing that the tricksters had the room next door. While they were still downstairs, he went to the room next door, found the substitute package and made the switch himself. When he came downstairs, the tricksters ran up and made the switch again, thus leaving the mark with the real gold brick. He rapidly left town.

The Back of the Truck. In this charming example of the unscrupulous cheating the gullible by appealing to their basic larceny, a truck pulls up to the corner of a business district during lunch hour or at closing time. The back of the truck is opened, and the driver or an associate, looking nervous, starts peddling expensive-looking merchandise from the tailgate. The presumption is that the merchandise was stolen, and that is why the prices are so low. The truth is that the merchandise is worthless, which is why the prices are so low.

The Hidden Value Hype. There are many versions of this old classic, which is still alive and exploited in every major city in the United States and in many small towns. Variants are the pedigreed dog con, the natural mink con, the rare coin con, the rare stamp con, the valuable violin con and the valuable antique con. One example will give the general idea.

In the valuable violin con, a friendly man goes into a bar or restaurant carrying a violin. He has a couple of drinks (or eats lunch), making friends with the proprietor. He goes back several times over the next few weeks, always carrying the violin. In conversation with the proprietor, he establishes that he would like to sell the violin if he could get his price, which is, say, $300. One day he leaves the violin with the proprietor to hold for him while he goes on an errand. While he is gone, a stranger comes into the establishment and sees and admires the violin. "I am something of an expert," he tells the proprietor, "and this is a very valuable instrument."

"How valuable?" the proprietor asks, his curiosity understandably piqued.

"I'd have to examine it carefully to tell you that," the expert says, "perhaps as much as ten thousand dollars." He pauses and then adds, "I'll give you a thousand dollars for it right now, if you'd like to sell it."

Thinking fast, the proprietor agrees to sell the valuable violin.

"Wonderful," the expert tells him. "I'll be back tomorrow noon with a certified check. Take good care of the violin!"

It is a rare proprietor indeed who tells the violin's owner about his good fortune. The average mark offers to buy the violin for $300, saying that his niece or nephew has decided to take music lessons. The expert, of course, never returns. And the mark has paid $300 for a $10 violin. *See also:* ADVERTISING CONS; MURPHY GAME; PUNCH BOARD SCAM; SHELL GAME; SPANISH PRISONER; THREE-CARD MONTE

SICKLES, Daniel E. (1825–1914)

MAD WITH JEALOUSY OR JUST MAD—CONGRESSMAN SICKLES INVOKED THE UNWRITTEN LAW

On the afternoon of Sunday, February 27, 1859, the Honorable Daniel Sickles, member of Congress from the Third District of New York, shot and killed Philip Barton Key, Esq., the U.S. district attorney, on a sidewalk in front of Sickles's house in Washington, D.C. Sickles had recently discovered that, during times when he was away, his wife was meeting Key in a house that had been rented by Key especially for that purpose.

Sickles, a New York attorney, married Teresa Bagioli, the daughter of a composer and music teacher, when he was 27 and she was 16. He had known her, so it was said, since she was a child. Shortly after the marriage, the two moved to London because Sickles was appointed secretary of the American Legation to Great Britain. When he returned to New York, he ran for Congress, won his seat, moved to Washington, and rented a house directly across from the White House on Presidents Square, soon to be renamed Lafayette Square. Sickles and his wife had, at the time of the murder, a five-year-old daughter named Laura.

Philip Barton Key, a Virginian and the son of Francis Scott Key, author of "The Star Spangled Banner," was 42 years old in 1859. Tall, handsome, a widower with four children, he was said to be "exceedingly popular among the gentler sex." Key was very social and was welcome at most of the important Washington gatherings, including those at Sickles's house. It was not long before Washington gossips noted that Key was welcome at Sickles's house when Sickles himself was away.

The events leading up to the murder were set in motion three days before, when Sickles was handed a letter by an unknown man as he was leaving the New Willard Hotel after a dance. It read:

Washington, Feb 24th, 1859

Hon. Daniel Sickles—

Dear Sir: With deep regret I inclose to your address these few lines, but an indispensable duty compels me to do so, seeing that you are greatly imposed upon.

There is a fellow, I may say, for he is not a gentleman, by any means, by the name of Philip Barton Key & I believe the district attorney who rents a house of a negro man by the name of Jno. A. Gray situated on 15th Street bt'w'n K and L streets for no other purpose than to meet your wife Mrs Sickles, he hangs a string out of the window as a signal to her that he is in and leaves the door unfastened and she walks in and sir I do assure you

With these few lines I leave the rest to you to imagine.

Most Respfly

Your friend R.P.G.

Immediately suspecting that these illiterate allegations were true, Sickles scouted out the house on 15th Street. There was such a house; it was rented by Key; and a heavily veiled woman did meet Key there. Sickles's last hope was that the woman was not Teresa.

Sickles called his friend and former clerk, a man named George Wooldridge, and, in an extended hysterical outburst, informed him of the letter and its allegations. It may be noted that Sickles was given to outbursts of wild hysteria and ranting whenever he discussed his wife's infidelity, but was amazingly calm and methodical in between the outbursts. He had Wooldridge rent a room opposite Key's rental house of assignation and peer through the blinds, watching all who came and went. While Sickles waited for word, he worked. He was due to address the House on the navy bill on Friday, and he prepared and delivered the speech with his usual clarity and force.

Wooldridge soon brought Sickles bad news. He had not recognized the veiled woman, but the hours she was at the house corresponded with the times Mrs. Sickles was away.

That evening Sickles confronted his wife with his suspicions. In the words of a contemporary account: "At first she strongly denied her guilt, but when asked by her husband whether on the previous Wednesday afternoon she had not entered the house on Fifteenth Street, in a certain particular dress, she was overcome by her feeling and exclaiming, 'I am betrayed and lost!' swooned away."

How the reporter came by this detail is not known, but the following events are certain. Sickles left his bedroom door ajar, so that the servants on the floor below could hear the tenor, if not the language, of the inquisition. First there was a loud argument, followed by an interval of silence, and then a period of intense sobbing, apparently by both husband and wife. After which, Sickles called two of the servants in to witness his wife's signature to a very curious document. As introduced at the trial it read:

> I have been in a house in Fifteenth Street, with Mr. Key. How many times I don't know. I believe the house belongs to a colored man. The house is unoccupied. Commenced going there the latter part of January. Have been in alone and with Mr. Key. Usually stayed an hour or more. There was a bed in the second story. I did what is usual for a wicked woman to do. The intimacy commenced this winter, when I came from New York, in that house—an intimacy of an improper kind. Have met half a dozen times or more, at different hours of the day. On Monday of this week, and wednesday also. Would arrange meetings when we met in the street and at parties. Never would speak to him when Mr. Sickles was at home; because I knew he did not like me to speak to him; did not see Mr. Key for some days after I got here. He then told me he had hired the house as a place where he and I could meet. I agreed to it. Had nothing to eat or drink there. The room is warmed by a wood fire. Mr. Key generally goes first. Have walked there together, say four times—I do not think more; was there on Wednesday last, between two & three. I went there alone. Laura was at Mrs. Hoover's. Mr. Key took and left her there at my request. From there I went to Fifteenth Street to meet Mr. Key; from there to the milk woman's. Immediately after Mr. Key left Laura at Mrs. Hoover's I met him in Fifteenth Street. Went in by the back gate. Went in the same bedroom, and there an improper interview was had. I undressed myself. Mr. Key undressed also. This occurred on Wednesday, 23rd of February, 1859. Mr. Key has kissed me in this house [Lafayette Square] a number of times. I do not deny that we have had connection in this house, last spring, a year ago, in the parlor, on the sofa. Mr. Sickles was sometimes out of town, and sometimes in the Capitol. I think the intimacy commenced in April or May, 1858. I did not think it safe to meet him in this house, because there are servants who might suspect something. As a general thing, have worn a black and white woolen plaid dress, and beaver hat trimmed with black velvet. Have worn a black silk dress there also, also a plaid silk dress, black velvet cloak trimmed with lace, and black velvet shawl trimmed with fringe. On Wednesday I either had on my brown dress, or black and white woolen dress, beaver hat and velvet shawl. I arranged with Mr. Key to go in the back way, after leaving Laura at Mrs. Hoover's. He met me at Mr. Douglas'. The arrangement to go in the back way was either made in the street or at Mr. Douglas', as we would be less likely to be seen. The house is in Fifteenth Street, between K and L Streets, on the left-hand side of the way; arranged the interview for Wednesday in the street, I think, on Monday. I went in the front door, it was open, occupied the same room, undressed myself, and he also; went to bed together. Mr. Key has ridden in Mr. Sickles' carriage and has called at his house without Mr. Sickles' knowledge, and after my being told not to invite him to do so, and against Mr. Sickles' repeated request.
>
> Teresa Bagioli.
>
> This is a true statement, written by myself, without any inducement held out by Mr. Sickles of forgiveness or reward, and without any menace from him. This I have written with my bedroom door open, and my maid and child in the adjoining room, at half past eight o'clock in the evening. Miss Ridgeley is in the house within call.
>
> Teresa Bagioli.
>
> Lafayette Square, Washington, D.C., Feb. 26, 1859.
>
> Mr. and Mrs. Pendleton dined here two weeks ago last thursday, with a large party. Mr. Key was

> also here, her brother, and at my suggestion he was invited, because he lived in the same house, and also because he had invited Mr. Sickles to dine with him, and Mr. Sickles wished to invite all those from whom he had received invitations; and Mr. Sickles said, "do as you choose."
>
> Teresa Bagioli.

After having induced his wife to write this amazing document, and having it witnessed, Sickles went to sleep. Teresa spent the night sitting on the floor of the governess's room, with her head resting on a chair.

When Sickles came downstairs the next morning, the servants observed that he had been weeping and was close to hysteria. He sent messages to Wooldridge and an old friend from New York named Butterworth to please join him, as he needed their advice. They came and listened to the story of his marital woes. Butterworth said the situation should be kept confidential, but Sickles told him it was too late for that: "The whole town knows of it! What would you do?"

"As a man of honor," Butterworth told him, "I have no advice to give you."

Sickles looked out the window at that moment—by now it was two in the afternoon—and observed Key walking by. It could have been a coincidence. It could have been that Sickles had been glancing out the window all day, waiting for Key to walk by. Key fluttered his handkerchief at an upstairs window.

Sickles and Butterworth left the house and went after Key. Butterworth reached him first and said something to him. The unsuspicious Key paused, giving Sickles enough time to reach him. Butterworth stepped back. Key saw Sickles and reached toward his chest. Perhaps he was reaching for the gun he habitually carried, but today he was unarmed.

"Key, you scoundrel! You have dishonored my home! You must die!" With these words, Sickles shot him in the groin. The first bullet did not kill Key. It would have, given a minute or two, but Sickles did not know that. Key threw an opera glass at Sickles, with no effect, and grappled with him, but was thrown off. Despite Key's cries of "Don't shoot! Don't shoot! Don't murder me!" Sickles fired again, this time hitting him in the chest. Key fell. Sickles approached the body and fired a third time, point-blank, into the prone body. Sickles stalked off with Butterworth. Key was carried into the nearby Cosmos Club, where, 15 minutes later, he died.

Sickles turned himself in to the attorney general and was taken to jail. The grand jury indicted him for murder, and trial was set for Monday, April 4. He had to spend the intervening month in jail, but as word of the events spread, Sickles became a popular hero. His predominant emotion through all of this seemed to be self-pity. A friend named Robert J. Walker, who saw Sickles just before he went to jail, recorded that Sickles

> advanced and took me by the hand. I think he then said, "A thousand thanks for coming to see me under these circumstances." He had scarcely repeated these words before I saw a great change in his appearance. He became very much convulsed indeed. He threw himself on the sofa, covering his face with his hands. He then broke into an agony of unnatural and unearthly sounds—something like a scream, interrupted by violent sobbing. From his convulsed appearance, he was in the act of writhing. His condition appeared to me to be very frightful, appalling me so much that I thought if it lasted much longer he must become insane. He was indulging in exclamations about dishonor having been brought to his house, his wife and child. He seemed particularly to dwell on the disgrace brought upon his child. Such an exhibition is sufficiently rare to deserve attention.

The trial lasted for 18 days. The indictment was against Mr. Sickles for the murder of Mr. Key, but the event also tried Mrs. Sickles for adultery. Her confession was read into evidence. The assumption was that it had driven Sickles insane, although it is clear from a reading of it that he dictated most of it to her. As Edward Hale Bierstadt noted in *Enter Murderers!* (1937):

> Whatever one may think of the woman who made this confession, there can be only one opinion of the man who forced it from her. Its morbid repetition and insistence on unnecessary detail; its crucifixion of Teresa, and its adulation, implied, of Sickles himself; these and more stamp it as Sickles' work and damn him in the stamping. Not only does it smack of the lawyer, but it reads far more like the answers of a witness undergoing a searching cross-examination than like a true confession. Sickles was sane enough to know exactly what he wanted to get on paper as evidence for a divorce, at any rate.

But the jury and the public were clearly on his side. The jury was out for an hour and ten minutes before bringing in a verdict of not guilty.

Within six months, Sickles did something unexpected that almost lost him all the public sympathy he had earned at the trial: He forgave his wife and took her back. The roar of disapproval was so great that he felt compelled to issue a public statement. It made him sound like a self-righteous prig, but it evidently satisfied the public.

When the Civil War broke out two years later, in 1861, Sickles joined a New York regiment as a colonel and was promoted to brigadier general within a year. He lost a leg at Gettysburg but survived the war to eventually serve as minister to Spain. Teresa died in New York three years after the murder, at the age of 25.

SIEGEL, Benjamin "Bugsy" (1905–1947)

THE HANDSOME, CHARISMATIC MOBSTER WHO INVENTED LAS VEGAS, AND WAS MURDERED FOR HIS TROUBLES

A handsome charismatic man who lived in a world of mayhem, murder and violent crime, Ben Siegel—never "Bugsy" to his face—was born in Brooklyn and grew up on the streets of New York City's Lower East Side. He received his nickname early because of a tendency toward erratic and violent behavior. While he was still a teenager, he became an executive in a PROHIBITION-related in-

Benjamin "Bugsy" Siegel, a ruthless killer, awaiting trial for murder in Los Angeles. (All Siegel photos, Dept. of Special Collections, University Research Library, UCLA.)

Siegel confers with his attorney, Jerry Geisler, who succeeded in winning a verdict of innocence.

dustry with his good friend MEYER LANSKY. The Bugs and Meyer mob supplied speakeasies on the Lower East Side with booze obtained by hijacking the shipments of the more traditional bootleggers.

By the 1930s, Bugs and Meyer had formed a relationship with the rising luminaries of the New York MAFIA—LUCKY LUCIANO, FRANK COSTELLO and their associates—that would shape the future of ORGANIZED CRIME in the United States for the next half century. Siegel and Lansky together were a formidable team. Siegel was the enforcer, and he had a talent for killing. Meyer was the brains, and before he died he became the brains behind all organized crime in America.

Siegel became bicoastal in the mid-1930s, maintaining a house in Los Angeles that he visited several times a year. By 1937, he had moved the focus of his activities to Los Angeles and used his East Coast clout to supplant Jack Dragna as the head of Los Angeles's organized crime activities. It was felt that Dragna, one of the old MUSTACHE PETES, was not making the most of the opportunities for illicit activities in Southern California, and Siegel was to remedy that.

Benny Siegel had been friendly with movie star George Raft since childhood, and soon, many more of the top figures of the motion picture industry welcomed him gladly into their homes. His suave good looks and the glamour of his underworld reputation made him attractive to the ladies of filmland, and his bedroom conquests are reputed to have included many of Hollywood's sexiest leading ladies.

In 1940, Siegel went to Las Vegas, a small Nevada town principally noted as a rest stop on the drive to Los Angeles, and saw great opportunity. Nevada was the only state where gambling was legal. Bugsy saw a giant, elaborate, expensive casino attracting gamblers from all over the coun-

Siegel displays his characteristic charm during a break in the trial.

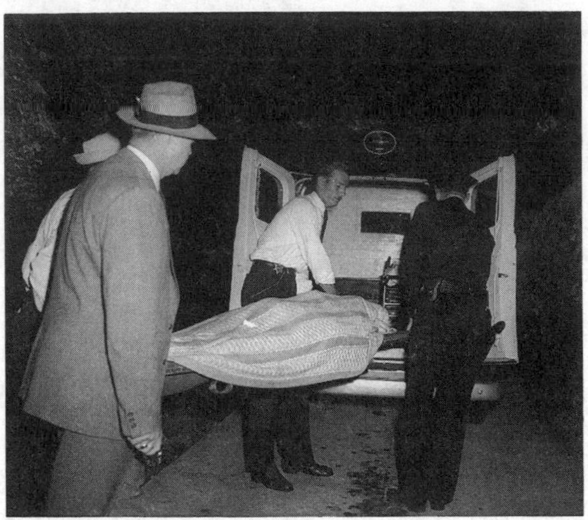

Siegel's body being loaded into the coroner's van after his murder in the Beverly Hills home of mistress Virginia Hill.

try. It would be very expensive to build, but it would be a steady money cow for the Syndicate. He talked a consortium of hoodlums into putting up $2 million and built the Flamingo, a gambling palace named after his girlfriend VIRGINIA HILL.

By the time the Flamingo opened, the $2 million budget had grown to $6 million in expenses, a sizable nut even for the ruling commission of organized crime. And to make matters worse, the Flamingo started by losing money. The mob bosses suspected Siegel of skimming and told him they wanted their money back. Siegel begged them to be patient a while longer and give him time to turn things around. By mid-1947, he had succeeded, and the Flamingo started to make money.

On June 20, 1947, Siegel was reading the newspaper in the living room of Virginia Hill's Beverly Hills home, which he was using while Virginia was in Europe, when a gunman fired two steel-jacketed bullets through the front window; both slugs hit him in the head. He was killed instantly. The crime was never solved.

SING SING

Constructed in 1825 near the village of Sing Sing, New York, which promptly changed its name to Ossining, Sing Sing prison was built by prisoners under the direction of its first warden ELAM LYNDS. Lynds remained its warden from its opening until 1845, when he was removed from office for malfeasance.

Sing Sing's most famous warden was Lewis E. Lawes, who instituted many reforms and was highly respected by the prisoners, the guards and outside penologists. Taking office on January 1, 1920, he found that the most difficult part of his job was officiating at the State of New York's executions, all of which were performed in Sing Sing's electric chair. When he took the job, he was in favor of capital punishment, but as the years passed, he changed his mind. By the time of his retirement in 1941, he was a bitter foe of the death penalty. In his book *Life and Death in Sing Sing* (1928), at the end of a chapter detailing his objections to legalized executions, he wrote:

> Capital punishment has never been and never can be anything but an uncertainty. It is a punishment for revenge, for retaliation, not for protection. We can have a punishment that is possible of application with both certainty and celerity, that presents an opportunity for individualization of treatment, and that is in accord with modern criminological methods. Can we not have the vision to see the possibilities of the future, the courage and faith to progress toward those possibilities?
>
> Bulwer Lytton truly said: "Society has erected the gallows at the end of the lane instead of guide posts and direction boards at the beginning."

Warden Lawes organized the Mutual Welfare League, a body of prisoners that, within limits, governed the prison. Elections to the league were held once a year, and there were two political parties, the Democratic party and the Cheese party. Lawes instituted a policy of allowing prisoners brief furloughs to attend funerals or visit dying relatives. He put them on their honor to return, and his faith was almost invariably rewarded. Lawes retired in 1941, after 21 years in office, and many of the reforms he instituted are still in force.

In his autobiography *Where the Money Was* (1976), WILLIE SUTTON described what it was like to be in Sing Sing in the 1930s:

> Upon my arrival, my head was shaved. Then they had me strip and turned me over to an inmate who was stirring a long stick around in a tub of blue ointment that gave off the smell of disinfectant. He smeared the stuff all over my head and around my private parts; I was being deloused. From there I was taken to the state shop and given an issue of clothing. A pair of dark gray prison suits . . . a coat, a cap, some heavy brogans, and, although it was summer, very coarse heavy underwear. . . .
>
> There was one long, dark, dreary cellblock to house the nine hundred inmates. One of those old-fashioned buildings with walls that were about ten feet thick. The windows were carved out of these massive walls, and very little sunlight penetrated into the block. The cell was so narrow that you had to walk in sideways and so small that the bed, which was more or less a flat iron latticework, was suspended from the wall on heavy chains. . . .
>
> A small bulb in the ceiling gave off a dim light. It would become even dimmer during an execution while the current was passing through the condemned man's body.

Other famous criminals who did time in Sing Sing or died in Sing Sing's electric chair are: JULIUS AND ETHEL ROSENBERG, FRANK ABBANDANDO, LUCKY LUCIANO, ALBERT ANASTASIA and RUTH SNYDER.

SIRICA, John J. (1904–1992)

John Sirica was the judge at the trial of the four original WATERGATE defendants, and it is probable that his relentless search for the truth was responsible for the gradual unraveling of the skein of lies surrounding the event and for the subsequent resignation of a sitting president.

Sirica spent his youth moving about the country with his family, as his father sought work in Ohio, California, Virginia, Florida and Washington. He worked his way through Georgetown University Law School, earning money by coaching boxing for the Knights of Columbus and sparring for Jack Britton, who had held the welterweight world's championship from 1919 to 1922. He also got to know the world's heavyweight champion, Jack Dempsey, and the two remained lifelong friends. Dempsey was the best man at Sirica's wedding.

When Sirica graduated from law school in 1926, he went to work as an assistant U.S. attorney in the District of Columbia. A few years later, he went into private practice. In 1957, he was appointed to a federal judgeship by President Dwight Eisenhower.

By the time of the burglary of the Democratic National Committee headquarters at the Watergate complex in 1972, Sirica was chief judge for the circuit. When the seven burglars came up for trial, he assigned himself the case.

By January 1973, four of the Watergate burglurs had pled guilty, and the putative ringleaders of the crime, G. Gordon Liddy and James W. McCord, Jr., had been found guilty. Determined to get to the bottom of this "third rate burglary," as a White House staffer characterized it, and find out who was covering up for whom, Sirica harshly sentenced Liddy and McCord, but let it be known that he would reconsider their stiff sentences if they would cooperate with the continuing investigation.

In March 1973, McCord wrote a lengthy document outlining the burglary and tracing the responsibility to the higher-ups in the administration. Judge Sirica made McCord's document public, and it was the information in that document that led to the revelation of the systematic high crimes and misdemeanors of the Nixon White House.

Some civil libertarians felt that Sirica went too far in using the judiciary as a weapon against the administration, but Sirica made it clear that he had not exceeded the authority of the court, even in principle. "I don't think we should sit up here like nincompoops," he commented. "The function of a trial court is to search for the truth."

Sirica presided over the trials of most of the Watergate defendants over the next two years, culminating with the trials and convictions of President Richard Nixon's top aides, H. R. Haldeman and John D. Ehrlichman, and former Attorney General John N. Mitchell.

In an interview with the *Los Angeles Times* years later, he said, "One of the most important lessons from Watergate is, when it appears there's a political scandal, instead of covering it up or dragging it out, you've got to bring it out into the open right away. I think our legislators and public officials have learned that."

Sirica suffered a heart attack in 1976 but continued on the bench, although with a reduced caseload. He wrote his memoirs of the Watergate events, *To Set the Record Straight,* in 1979. He retired from the bench in 1986.

SMITH, Edgar Herbert (1933–)

The 24-year-old boyfriend of 15-year-old Victoria Zielinski, Edgar Smith was questioned when Victoria disappeared from her Mahwah, New Jersey, home on March 4, 1957. The questioning turned serious when the girl's body was found in a sandpit in close proximity to a bloodstained pair of Smith's jeans. The girl had been viciously beaten to death. Despite his explanation that he loaned the pants to a friend, a jury found him guilty of murder, and he was sentenced to death.

Smith continued to protest his innocence, filing 14 appeals from his cell in Trenton Prison's Death Row. He was granted 13 stays of execution. For some reason, Smith became fixated on columnist William F. Buckley, sending him approximately 3,000 handwritten pages explaining his case and requesting help. Buckley was impressed by the correspondence and conducted a campaign with his column to win a new trial for Smith. With Buckley's help, Smith published a book, *Brief Against Death* (1968), which became a best-seller. He followed this with another book entitled *Reasonable Doubt* (1970).

In 1971, Buckley's pressure and Smith's pleas finally resulted in a new trial. Smith accepted a plea bargain, admitted to second-degree murder and was sentenced to 25 to 30 years. With time served, he was released on parole. Once out he again affirmed his innocence, saying that he had accepted the plea bargain as a means of getting out of jail because "I wanted to be free."

In October 1976, in San Diego, Smith assaulted a girl, Lefteriya Ozbun, in his car, taking her money and stabbing her when she attempted to escape. She finally broke free, falling onto the freeway from Smith's car, and Smith drove away. A week later, with the police hunting for him, Smith called his old friend Buckley from Las Vegas, Nevada. Buckley was out, so Smith left his phone number. When Buckley got the message, he called the FBI, who arrested Smith in a Las Vegas hotel room.

Smith was tried in San Diego for kidnapping, assault and attempted murder. He confessed to the charges and followed this by confessing to the murder of Victoria Zielinski 19 years before. She had refused to sleep with him, so he beat her to death with a baseball bat.

> "For the first time in my life, I recognized that the devil I had been looking at the last 43 years was me," Smith said on his way back to prison to serve a life sentence. "I recognized what I am, and I admitted it."

SMITH, Moe

See: IZZY AND MOE

SMITH ACT

The Smith Act was passed by the U.S. Congress on June 28, 1940, making it illegal, among other things:

1. To knowingly or willfully advocate, abet, advise or teach the duty, necessity, desirability, or propriety of overthrowing or destroying any government in the United States by force or violence or by the assassination of any officer of any such government.

2. With the intent to cause the overthrow or destruction of any government in the United States to print, publish, edit, issue, circulate, sell, distribute, or publicly display any written or printed matter advocating, advising, or teaching the duty, necessity, desirability, or propriety of overthrowing or destroying any government in the United States by force or violence.

3. To organize or help to organize any society, group, or assembly of persons who teach, advocate, or encourage the overthrow or destruction of any government in the United States by force or violence; or to be or become a member of, or affiliate with, any such society, group, or assembly of persons, knowing the purposes thereof.

The act was originally designed to combat fascist and Nazi subversion, the specter of which loomed large over the country in 1940. After World War II, it was re-aimed at "The Communist Menace," and many Communist agents, Communist sympathizers and innocent bystanders were jailed or otherwise persecuted under the broad umbrella of the provisions of the Smith Act. If one had years before committed the indiscretion of being a member of the Communist party in an excess of youthful idealism, it was almost impossible later to prove before a hostile House Un-American Activities Committee that one had not known the "purposes thereof."

SNYDER, Ruth Brown (1895–1928)

SHE TALKED HER LOVER INTO HELPING MURDER HER HUSBAND, AND GOT HER PICTURE TAKEN ON THE ELECTRIC CHAIR

Early in the morning of Sunday, March 20, 1927, the New York City police, responding to a call, rushed to 9327 222 Street, in Queens Village, the home of Albert Snyder, the 45-year-old art editor of *Motor Boating* magazine. They found Snyder tied up in his bed; he had been chloroformed, his skull had been smashed in with a sash weight and a picture wire had been wrapped tightly around his neck. There was a revolver next to him on the bed and three live cartridges on the floor. Snyder was quite dead. Judging by the rigidity of the body, he had been dead for some time. On another corner of the bed were a blue bandanna handkerchief and the corner of a page from an Italian newspaper.

His wife Ruth screamed when she saw the body. She had been knocked unconscious by two burglars, she told the police, and had awakened several hours later to find herself in the hallway, tied hand-and-foot and gagged. The crime took place shortly after Albert, Ruth and their nine-year-old daughter Lorraine arrived home after a late Saturday night whist party; she thought it was around 2:30 A.M. Two burglars, with "Italian-styled moustaches" had come into her room and knocked her on the head. When she came to she managed, despite her bonds, to crawl into her daughter's room and scratch at the door. Lorraine ran to the Mulhausens' house next door, and Mr. Mulhausen returned with her, loosened the wires around Mrs. Snyder's hands and feet and called the police.

Detective Inspector Arthur Carey, who responded to the homicide call, was immediately suspicious of Ruth's story. It was supposedly a burglary, yet nothing was missing but the money in Albert's wallet. Some jewelry that Ruth at first had claimed was missing turned up under her mattress. Then she suddenly remembered that she had put it there for safekeeping. Those who deal with murder know the patterns of different sorts of murders, and this did not fit any of the patterns. Burglars seldom murder householders, and when they do, they do not come equipped to do it in any of four different ways. The gun, the bandanna and the shred of newspaper seemed to Carey to have been artfully arranged on the bed—a stage setting in a bad melodrama. Aside from the missing jewelry, the search of the house also turned up a 5-pound sash weight that had traces of blood on it in a toolbox in the cellar, a bloody pillow slip in the laundry hamper and a tie pin with the initials "JG" on the bedroom floor.

The medical examiner, Dr. Archibald McNeaill, found that Albert had not been shot. He had been hit on the head with the sash weight, and the wound had bled copiously. The presence of cotton threads on Snyder's upper lip caused McNeaill to check for traces of chloroform, which he found. The two turns of picture wire around Snyder's neck actually killed him. Dr. McNeaill examined Mrs. Snyder and determined that she had not suffered any blow hard enough to knock her unconscious for five hours.

The investigators found a bottle of whiskey and a glass in the living room, but neither Mr. nor Mrs. Snyder nor their nine-year-old daughter had been drinking. This pointed to the presence of someone else in the house during the night. Inspector Carey noted that Mrs. Snyder had made a check out to an H. Judd Gray for $200, remembered the initials "JG" on the tie pin and searched for Mr. Gray.

Detective Chief Inspector Coughlan asked Ruth about her relations with her husband, and how he treated her. She explained:

"He was just the opposite to me. I am younger and like to have a good time. He likes to stay around the house and fix it up and dig in the grounds and feed the birds. I like to go out on parties and dances. He has never liked them."

But, she refused to admit to murdering her husband. She was indignant at the suggestion. The new insurance policy she had taken out on her husband's life was for only $1,000, she told them. Surely nobody could suspect her of killing Albert for $1,000. The detectives found that it was for $45,000, with double indemnity in case of violent death.

When her questioners brought up the name of Judd Gray, Ruth must have assumed that they knew a lot more than they did. She collapsed and confessed everything. Judd was a corset salesman who liked a good time. She had met him a little over six months before, and they had begun a hot and heavy affair almost at once. Judd was the ideal lover for her, as she was the ideal mistress for him. He called her "my queen" and kissed her feet. She began to fantasize how life could be for them if only her husband were out of the way.

She actually tried to kill Albert several times on her own; once with car exhaust and once with house gas, but he woke up in time on both occasions. Once she gave him bichloride of mercury, a violent poison, in a bottle of cough medicine. He got violently ill, but to her disappointment he did not die.

She broached the subject of her husband's death to Judd more than once, but he was repelled by the idea. She continued to mention it whenever they made love, but still he resisted. Finally he agreed, and they began plotting the murder. Unbelievably, they actually spent two months planning the ridiculous mishmash that ended in Albert's death.

On the night of the murder, Judd took a bus out to Queens Village and let himself into the empty house. He laid out the sash weight, the picture wire, the chloroform and some cotton and waited for the Snyders to return from the party. While he was waiting, he took several large glasses of whiskey to fortify himself for the task at hand. Shortly after 2:00 A.M., he heard the car pull up outside and hid himself. Ruth put her daughter to bed, slipped into her nightgown and then came to Judd while her husband was washing up in the bathroom. "I'll come back when he's asleep," she whispered, and then she returned to the bedroom to lie next to her husband until his steady breathing indicated that he was sleeping.

When she was sure Albert was asleep, Ruth went to fetch her lover, and they returned hand in hand. Judd brought in the various murder implements with his other hand. He gathered his courage by the side of the bed and struck at the sleeping Albert with the sash weight. Either he was overly nervous or fairly drunk because the first blow was a glancing one, which woke Albert. While Albert groggily fought with Judd, Ruth smacked him again with the sash weight. This time he was knocked out. The loving couple then chloroformed Albert and strangled him with the picture wire. They spent the next hour artfully arranging the bedroom to make it look like what they fancifully imagined a burglary-murder would look. Then Judd did a bad job of tying Ruth's hands and feet and left the house. Before he saw his inamorata again, he would be under arrest for murder.

During the trial, Ruth tried to affix most of the blame for the killing on Judd, but it did not stick. They were both convicted of first-degree murder, but it was clear in everyone's mind who the instigator was. On January 12, 1928, Ruth Snyder became the third woman to die in the electric chair at SING SING. New York *Daily News* photographer Thomas Howard, who witnessed the execution with a small camera strapped to his leg, managed to take a picture of Ruth in the electric chair as the switch was pulled. Judd Gray followed Ruth a few minutes later.

SON OF SAM

See: DAVID R. BERKOWITZ

SOUTHER, Glenn Michael (1957–1989)

Glenn Michael Souther was born in Hammond, Indiana, on January 30, 1957. After graduating from Greely High School in Cumberland Center, Maine, in 1975, he enlisted in the U.S. Navy at the age of 18. He served successively aboard the aircraft carrier *Nimitz* in the Mediterranean, on the headquarters staff for the Sixth Fleet in Italy and then at the headquarters of the Naval Air Training Command in Maryland. In 1982, when he left the navy, with the rank of petty officer first class, it was to attend Old Dominion University in Virginia. While at the university, he remained active in the naval reserve and worked as an intelligence analyst at the Norfolk, Virginia, Naval Intelligence Center. He apparently specialized in the interpretation of satellite photographs.

In May 1986, Souther graduated from Old Dominion with majors in sociology and modern language (Russian) and then suddenly disappeared. At the time he was the subject of an ongoing FBI espionage investigation.

On July 20, 1988, Souther surfaced in Moscow and thanked the Soviet Union for giving him political asylum. In a Soviet television program called "Camera on the World," he told of his unhappiness with the attitude of the United States toward the Soviet Union and his disillusionment with American nuclear arms policies.

At the time of his defection, navy officials said that any damage his espionage could have caused was of little importance. Over the next couple of years, they revised this opinion, finally deciding that, judging by what he had access to, he may have done major harm to the U.S. satellite surveillance program.

On Tuesday, June 27, 1989, the Soviet Union announced that Souther had died the previous Thursday of undisclosed causes. His obituary in *Krasnaya Zvezda* (Red Star), the Soviet military newspaper, referred to him as Mikhail Yevgenyevich Orlov, giving his American name in parentheses. It described him as an officer of the

KGB and said that "for a long time he performed important special assignments and made a major contribution to insuring the security of the Soviet Union."

SPANISH PRISONER

One of the oldest CONFIDENCE GAMES, the Spanish prisoner swindle dates back to before the Civil War and, in some variant or another, is still in use today. It is a SHORT CON, needing only one or two confederates, and is sometimes done without personal contact with the mark (victim) at all, but by a mass mailing of prisoner letters, continuing the action with whoever responds.

The premise is simple and clever. The mark meets an interesting stranger, in many cases a beautiful young girl. As they get to know each other, she tells him that she can see that he is a man to be trusted. He is delighted to discover this. She confides that her uncle is in a Spanish prison, unjustly convicted of a crime. This generic "Spanish prison" can, of course, be situated anywhere that current world events make logical. For a long time it was Spain, but now it could be Cuba, Argentina, Guatemala, Turkey, Iran or anywhere sufficiently remote and sinister sounding. Immediately after World War I, a rash of letters went out supposedly from Russian noblemen attempting to flee Bolshevik prisons with the Tsar's crown jewels. In the late 1930s, Jews in America received Spanish prisoner letters purporting to be from Jews in Nazi Germany.

The uncle is the possessor of a large fortune, a small part of which would be sufficient to bribe his jailers to let him escape—if he could get at it. But it is in a safety deposit box that can be opened only by the uncle, or in a trunk in customs that can be picked up only by the uncle or buried in a location only the uncle can retrieve.

If the mark is willing to put up the bribe money to help the uncle escape, the uncle would show his gratitude by splitting the vast fortune with the mark. The amount will be whatever the operators think the mark is good for; some marks have been taken for as much as $20,000.

If the mark puts up the money and seems convinced, the swindlers may be brazen enough to come back again, claiming that one more person remains to be bribed. And then they will disappear for good, leaving the mark to ponder how fortunate he was to look like a man who could be trusted. This may sound too simplistic for anyone to fall for, but if the tale is told properly, it can be quite convincing.

SPECK, Richard (1941–1991)

HE CAME TO BURGLARIZE AND STAYED TO KILL

On the evening of July 13, 1966, Richard Speck, a sometime seaman, garbageman and drifter with drinking and drug abuse problems and a long history of burglary, broke into an apartment in a nurses' dormitory for the South Chicago Community Hospital. Of the nine nurses sharing the apartment, six were present when he broke in. He tied them up, using a knife and a handgun to enforce his commands, and waited for the other three to return. When they arrived, he bound them also and put the nine together in a bedroom. Taking eight of them out one-by-one, he attempted to molest each of them without much success and then killed her. Three of them he stabbed to death, and five he strangled. Then, taking what money he could find, he left the apartment.

One girl, Corazon Amurao, hid under the bed and eluded Speck. Apparently, it was pure luck that he didn't find her. Terrified out of her mind, she stayed hidden through the night, not knowing whether Speck had left the apartment or not. It was not until 7:00 A.M. that she ventured out from under the bed to find her roommates dead on the floor.

A few days later Speck did a bad job of slashing his wrists in a Chicago flophouse, and was taken to the hospital. Detectives spotted him from Miss Amurao's description, and she identified him. He was convicted and sentenced to be electrocuted, but the sentence was voided by the Supreme Court's annulment of the death penalty in 1972. He was then resentenced to eight consecutive terms of 50 to 150 years, which, as law-and-order conservatives were fond of pointing out, made him eligible for parole in 1976. The eligibility, however, was merely a technicality, and there was no chance that any parole board would ever have released him. He died in prison on December 5, 1991, a day before his fiftieth birthday.

SPOONER, Bathsheba (1746–1778)

A REVOLUTIONARY WAR MURDERESS EXECUTED IN THE LAST PUBLIC HANGING IN THE STATE OF MASSACHUSETTS

When Bathsheba Ruggles was 18, her father, General Timothy Ruggles, gave her hand in marriage to Joshua Spooner, a wealthy landowner who had only two flaws as a husband: He was an ardent Revolutionary, while Bathsheba, like her father, was a staunch supporter of King George; and he was old enough to be her grandfather. Bathsheba also found her husband unable to fulfill those duties in the bedroom that a young, lusty wife has a right to expect. But she soon found a palliative for that, hoisting her skirts for the handsome young men that stopped at the Spooner mansion outside of Worcester, Massachusetts, on their way to fight on one side or the other of the Revolutionary War.

In 1777, when the war was in full swing, and Bathsheba was 31, Ezra Ross, a 16-year-old man who had been fighting for the revolutionary cause since Bunker Hill, staggered by the Spooner house. Bathsheba brought him in to feed him, which was the way she began with all of her gentleman suitors. But Ross collapsed from hunger and illness before he got past the dinner. Bathsheba put him to bed and nursed him back to health, waiting a full two weeks before suggesting other uses to which the bed could be put. He thought the idea a good one and spent some extra recuperative time with her before he went off to rejoin the war. A year and several campaigns later he returned.

When General Ruggles saw how the tides of war were turning, the ardent Tory fled to Nova Scotia, putting all of his large property holdings into Bathsheba's name before he left. Now the wisdom of marrying his daughter to the aged revolutionary was evident: The new government, which assuredly would have confiscated his property, would probably not touch the property of Mrs. Joshua Spooner.

Ezra Ross stayed with the Spooners, enjoying the bed and board of Bathsheba and the friendship of Joshua, who either did not know what was going on in his house or did not care. But Bathsheba, who regarded her husband as a nuisance sexually and politically, was determined to improve the situation. She tried to talk Ezra into slitting her husband's throat, but he was unable to go through with it. She then importuned him to poison her husband while the two were on a trip together.

While they were away, Bathsheba, suspecting that Ezra would not go through with the poisoning, made other plans. A pair of British prisoners of war had escaped from their incarceration at Rutland, Massachusetts, and they passed the Spooner mansion on their way to Canada. Bathsheba invited 30-year-old Sergeant James Buchanan and 27-year-old Private William Brooks into the house for a hot meal. She told them that her husband, an ardent revolutionary, was away, and that she, a fervent Tory, would let them stay until her husband returned. For two days she sounded them out, discovering that they both had been professional thieves before being drummed into the army and were not averse to making a few illicit pounds on their way to Canada.

She then told them of her troubles: a useless traitor of a husband who would be better off dead and a spineless jellyfish of a lover who seemed incapable of doing the job. Her husband's death, she gave them to understand, would be worth at least a thousand pounds to her.

It was as she feared; at the end of the trip she still had a living husband. The day after his return, he kicked the two British soldiers out of his house, confiding in a neighbor that he feared that they meant to rob him. The neighbor, Reuben Olds, who spoke to the two, later told the court that Sergeant Buchanan had replied, "It won't be healthy for [Spooner], for I would put him in the well for two coppers!" The two troopers got as far as nearby Cooley's Tavern before turning around and returning to hide in the Spooners' barn. They spent two weeks in the barn, screwing up their nerve for what had to be done. Bathsheba helped as much as she could, coming to the barn at night, bringing food and solace. Sergeant Buchanan finally agreed to the task and plotted for the three men to do it together.

On March 1, 1778, Joshua Spooner went, as was his custom, to spend a few hours at Cooley's Tavern. Buchanan, Brooks and Ross, fortified with ale supplied by Bathsheba, awaited his return. When he appeared, they did what they had to do and went into the house to tell the Widow Spooner. She seemed bewildered and ran around the house not knowing what to do. Finally she located her husband's money box and gave the perpetrators its contents: $243, promising them more as soon as she could find it. The trio dressed themselves in various articles of the defunct Mr. Spooner's clothing, took his watch and silver shoe buckles and left for Worcester.

The next morning Bathsheba affected surprise at her husband's absence and ran outside looking for him. When she could not find him, she sent their coachman, Alexander Cummings, to ride to the tavern and ask after his master.

Ephraim Cooley, proprietor of Cooley's Tavern and a good friend of Spooner's, rode back to the house. He found Spooner's hat in the snow, he found blood spots and finally, peering down the well, he found Spooner.

Buchanan, Brooks and Ross were frolicking in Brown's Tavern in Worcester when they were arrested. They had already attracted some attention, wearing Spooner's clothes, sporting silver shoe buckles with his initials and waving his watch around. When questioned, they freely confessed to the killing.

Bathsheba was brought to Worcester for a general confrontation. When she saw the trio, she sobbingly confessed that she had enticed them into committing the crime.

By the time the trial began on April 1, 1778, however, the quartet pled not guilty. The trial judge was William Cushing, chief justice of the Massachusetts Supreme Court, who would become an associate justice of the U.S. Supreme Court. They were prosecuted by Robert Treat Paine, one of the signers of the Declaration of Independence. Appearing for the defense was Levi Lincoln, who would become President Thomas Jefferson's attorney general and later decline an appointment to the Supreme Court.

Lincoln sensibly divided his defense. For the British soldiers, no defense was possible, and he offered none. He attempted to build a defense for Ezra Ross, noting that the lad, a hero of the Revolution, had been merely an onlooker and had been besotted with drink at the time, so his culpability in the murder was minimal, if indeed there was any.

For Bathsheba Spooner, Lincoln invented what at the time was a novel if not unique defense. She was, he maintained, insane at the time of the murder. He detailed for the jury her unsoundness of mind, pointing out how she had given the deadly trio the murdered man's "watch, buckles, waistcoat, breeches and shirts . . . to be worn in the eye of the world, where they were well known to be Spooner's clothes, and from their goodness of fashion might be known not to belong to the persons wearing them, being low and vulgar." She might just as well, he told the jury, "have written on their foreheads, in capitals, 'THE MURDERERS OF MR. SPOONER!' "

The jury were not convinced. All four were found guilty of murder and sentenced to be hanged on June 4, 1778. The three men, now heartily repentant, confessed their crime in detail, with Buchanan writing the confession, Ross signing it and Brooks affixing his mark. The part of Sergeant Buchanan's confession describing the event read as follows:

> Mr. Spooner was at length seen coming [from the tavern], and then was the time for the Devil to show his power over them who had forsaken God. William Brooks went out and stood within the small gate leading to the kitchen, and as Mr. Spooner came past him, he knocked him down with his hand. He strove to speak when down. Brooks took him by the throat and partly strangled him. Ross and Buchanan came out; Ross took Mr. Spooner's watch and gave it to Buchanan. Brooks and Ross took him up and put him into the well head first. Before they carried him away, I, Buchanan, pulled off his shoes: I was instantly struck with horror of conscience, as well I might. . . . Had we all been immediately struck dead, after the perpetration of so horrid a murder, and sent to hell, God would have been justified and we justly condemned.

Ross's parents, Jabez and Joanna Ross of Ipswich, petitioned the court for their son's life, pointing out his record of heroism during the war and describing how Ross had been "tempted by promises flattering to his situation, and seduced from both virtue and prudence, a child as he was, by a lewd, artful woman, but he too readily acceded to her measures, black as they were." It did no good; the court stood adamant.

Before the execution date the story took one last turn. Bathsheba notified the court that she was pregnant. If it were so, than by law and custom she could not be executed. The quartet were given a stay of execution while the court sent two male midwives and "twelve discreet lawful matrons" to verify her claim. They found that she was "not quick with child." Bathsheba protested, insisting on another examination. This time three men and three women examined her. All the men and one of the women declared in a letter to the court that she was, indeed, pregnant. Two of the women disagreed. Elizabeth Rice, one of the women from the first examination and a firm revolutionary, wrote the court that she was right and the others were wrong, that the Tory Mrs. Spooner was not pregnant.

A new date for execution was set. Bathsheba sent a letter to the court requesting:

> that my body be examined after I am executed by a committee of competent physicians, who will, perforce, belatedly substantiate my claims. . . . The midwives who examined me have taken into greater account my father's Royalist leanings than they have the stirrings in my body.

By some estimates more than 5,000 people crowded the streets of Worcester on July 2, 1778, to watch the hangings. As the four were led to the gallows, the men walking and Bathsheba following on a chaise, the sky darkened and a terrifying thunderstorm began, surrounding the proceedings with peals of thunder and bolts of lightning. There was some discussion as to exactly what aspect of the event God was commenting on with this display of atmospherics.

The last public execution in Massachusetts was over within the hour, and the four were pronounced dead. In accordance with her request, Mrs. Spooner's body was examined, and "a perfectly formed male fetus of five months" was discovered.

STAND-IN

A stand-in is a person paid to go to court in place of the defendant and, if necessary, serve the defendant's jail time. This practice has been used by different populations of criminals and in the first quarter of this century, was particularly popular among such ethnic groups as the Chinese and black communities, who profited from the Caucasian authorities' view that all ethnics look alike. The routine fingerprinting of suspects has all but eliminated the practice.

STEIN, Jules W. Arndt

See: NICKY ARNSTEIN

STEPHENSON, David C. (1891–?)

"Steve" Stephenson grew up in Texas and Oklahoma and served as an army officer in World War I. After the war, he showed up in Evansville, Indiana, and ran for Congress as a "wet" Democrat. He lost the election largely because of Anti-Saloon League opposition. Seeing the handwriting on the wall, he became a dry Republican and, just to be sure, joined the KU KLUX KLAN. By 1922, he was Kleagle of the state of Indiana. He built up a membership of over 50,000 Klansmen in the state and ran a slate of Klan candidates for statewide offices on the Republican ticket. His political workers, by appealing to the patriotism of the voters and beating up those opposed to them, swept the state. Citizens who complained had crosses burned in front of their houses; chronic complainers had their houses burned. By electing the judges, Stephenson and the Klan soon controlled the courts.

Stephenson, by now a Grand Dragon in the Klan, considered that he controlled the state, and it was his arrogance that destroyed him. On March 15, 1925, as he was leaving for Chicago, he decided that he wanted a 28-year-old spinster named Madge Oberholzer who worked at the State House. He had her kidnapped from in front of her house as she came home from a date and delivered to a train just as it was pulling out. Then he forced his favors on her in the lower berth of a Pullman car stateroom.

They left the train the next morning in Hammond, Indiana; Stephenson apparently amazed that Madge could not take a joke. Somehow Miss Oberholzer managed to get some bichloride of mercury tablets, and she swallowed six of them. Stephenson took her back to Indianapolis and put her in a loft above his garage, trying to talk her into marrying him before she died. She would have none of it, and Stephenson finally took her back to her home. There she lingered on long enough to tell the whole story to William H. Remy, the prosecuting attorney, and one of the few officials that Stephenson did not own.

Stephenson could not get out of standing trial, but he was successful in having the venue of the trial moved to Noblesville, Indiana—a small-town Klan stronghold. To his amazement, the Noblesville jury found him guilty of murder in the second degree, and the judge sentenced him to life imprisonment in the Michigan City penitentiary.

In 1927, seeing that the Klan could not get him out of prison, Stephenson released his files and dictated the story of the Klan, an amazing tale of lynchings, whippings, cross burnings, house burnings, murders and total subversion of the executive and judicial systems of the state. His testimony put a score of Republicans behind bars but did nothing to lessen his sentence. He was not released from prison on parole until 1950. He violated his parole by disappearing, was found working a linotype machine in Minneapolis and went back to prison. In 1956, he was released again and disappeared from public view.

STONO REBELLION

In the early morning hours of Sunday, September 9, 1739, a very carefully planned slave rebellion broke out in Stono, St. Paul's Parish, North Carolina. Somewhere between 20 and 30 slaves, reportedly encouraged by Spanish missionaries, determined to make their way down to St. Augustine, in Spanish Florida, where they would be free. They killed two clerks in Hutchenson's store, took all the weapons, powder and supplies they could carry and headed south. By the time they stopped for the night, they had burned several houses, induced 70 more slaves to join their march and killed 30 whites. The militia caught up with the rebels before morning and killed most of them, driving the rest into the woods. The fugitives were rounded up and executed, their heads cut off and put on mileposts through the area. As a result of this and uprisings the same year in St. John's Parish and in Stone Creek, South Carolina, the strictures against slaves were tightened further: They were forbidden to earn or keep money, to raise their own food or to move about freely. It was against the law to teach slaves to read. Slave owners were encouraged to treat slaves more humanely and exhorted to keep them under strict control.

As a result of the uprisings, white settlers tended to avoid the Carolinas, resulting in a population of more blacks than whites. This kept the level of white fear and the level of black repression high. *See also:* NAT TURNER; DENMARK VESEY

STOPA, Wanda (1899–1924)

SHE KILLED—AND DIED—FOR LOVE

On April 24, 1924, a month before the LEOPOLD AND LOEB CASE shocked Chicago, the city received a preliminary tremor when Wanda Stopa went after Vieva Dawley Smith with a .38 revolver. Stopa had risen from the slums of Chicago's Little Poland to become an assistant district attorney and, according to one of her professors, "one of the most brilliant women ever to be admitted to the local bar."

This was the middle of the Flapper era, and Wanda, craving excitement, flapped with the best of them. She spent her spare time in Towertown, which was then Chicago's arty bohemian section. In 1922, Wanda married Count Vladimir Glaskoff, a handsome, elegant man with courtly manners and no money. She shortly tired of her debonair husband and began spending time with Yeremya Kenley Smith, an advertising executive who possessed wealth, charm, sophistication, and an artistic soul. Perhaps she saw in him something of her father, who had been an artist before leaving Poland. The Glaskoffs had an understanding; Vladimir saw whom he wished, and Wanda spent her days away from the courtroom with Smith. She became convinced that Smith no longer loved his wife Vieva and would soon leave her for Wanda. Then Wanda would divorce Vladimir and they all would live happily ever after. She also, on her own, became addicted to morphine, which made her subject to fits of rage and depression.

Smith, as he declared firmly afterward, was amused by Wanda, loved her spirit for life and art, but had no intentions of leaving his wife. He told this to Wanda and was rewarded by fits of rage and depression. He decided to finance a stay in New York City for Wanda, hoping that the lure of Greenwich Village's shining bohemia would take her mind off her ideas of permanent cohabitation with him.

Stopa settled in the Village and gave parties. She spent Smith's money freely. She actually wrote a story and sold it to a magazine for a few hundred dollars. It was a murder mystery.

On the evening of Wednesday, April 23, 1924, Stopa threw a big party for her new friends. When the room was suitably awash with people who were suitably awash with Prohibition gin, she stood up and made an announcement. Life, she told them, crumbles like a handful of ashes. And she did not want ashes. "So now I'm going to my death. . . . Tomorrow I'm leaving here for Chicago and when I arrive I'm going to kill a woman—perhaps a man. But anyhow a woman. . . . Shoot her because she refused to give up the man I love. . . . I'll probably kill myself afterward."

The party guests enjoyed the joke, and the party continued while Wanda took two bags and caught a train for Chicago. The train arrived

Thursday morning, and Wanda took a cab from Union Station to Yeremya Kenley Smith's estate in Palos Park. Asking the cab driver to wait, she pulled her .38 and entered the house, hunting for Vieva Smith. She found her in the bedroom, lying in bed, getting over a bad case of influenza. Wanda went into the bedroom, waving her revolver and demanding that Vieva give Smith up to the course of true love. The caretaker of the Smith estate, 68-year-old Henry Manning, heard the excitement from the outside lawn and stepped up to the window to get a better view.

Vieva, who was too weak to get out of bed, told Wanda to stop being silly. "You're making yourself ridiculous," she said. "Kenley's tired of it and so am I."

This was perhaps not the wisest thing to tell the distraught, drug-ridden girl. Wanda did her best to aim the revolver and fired it, the bullet smacking into the wall a scant six inches from Vieva's head. Vieva staggered to her feet and fled through the window with Wanda chasing her, firing madly.

Manning jumped in front of the window to stop Wanda. She fired one more time, putting a bullet in the caretaker's head. By then Mrs. Smith was safely out of range, headed for a neighbor's house, Wanda put the .38 back in her purse and returned to the cab. She told the driver, an elderly man named Ernest T. Wood, who was too deaf to hear the excitement, to take her to Illinois Central Depot.

"Another Chicago girl went gunning today," was the headline in the *Chicago Tribune*. Police searched for Wanda in all the logical places, but she was nowhere to be found. Two days later, in Detroit, a guest in the Hotel Statler recognized her picture and called the police. When the detectives arrived, they checked the hotel register and found that she had signed in under her married name. They went up to her room to find her lying in bed with the house doctor ministering to her. Minutes later she was dead. Her body was removed to Little Poland, where the people gave her a star's funeral.

STRAUSS, Harry

See: PITTSBURGH PHIL

SUPREME COURT

The federal judiciary of the United States, one of the three coequal branches of government (with the executive and the legislative), is made up of district courts, in which cases are originated; appeals courts and the Supreme Court. There are also a few special courts such as Customs Courts, the Court of Claims (which hears claims against the federal government) and the Court of Customs and Patent Appeals, a specialized appellate court.

The Constitution of the United States provides that "the judicial Power of the United States, shall be vested in one supreme Court, and in such inferior Courts as the Congress may from time to time ordain and establish." This naming of the Supreme Court specifically, and vesting judicial power in it, is what constitutionally establishes it as a coequal branch of government. Early in its history, the Supreme Court asserted that the Constitution was the supreme law of the land and that the Supreme Court had the implied power to review lesser laws to see that they did not conflict with the Constitution. In *Marbury v. Madison* (1803), Chief Justice JOHN MARSHALL, writing for the majority, said:

> It is emphatically the province and duty of the judicial department to say what the law is. . . . So if a law be in opposition to the Constitution; if both the law and the Constitution apply to a particular case, so that the court must either decide the case conformably to the law, disregarding the Constitution, or conformably to the Constitution, disregarding the law; the court must determine which of these conflicting rules governs the case.

In 1925, Congress, by statute, specified the Supreme Court's appellate authority, which had been left vague in the Constitution. It gave the

Court almost complete discretionary control through the process of granting or denying writs of *certiorari*. The writ of *certiorari* (from the Latin meaning "to be informed") is a request for the Court to hear and review a case from a lower court. Four of the nine justices must vote in favor for a writ to be granted. It is the possibility of the Supreme Court granting *certiorari* more than anything else that has created prisons full of "jailhouse lawyers." And every once in a while the Supreme Court agrees to hear the case of some convict who had no other hope of ever walking under trees again.

Some prison administrations find the "jailhouse lawyer" threatening and discourage such activity. This is foolish and shortsighted, for whatever inconvenience it may cause to have a prisoner more aware of his rights, it is far more problematic to house hundreds of society's most violent members who have been deprived of hope.

The Supreme Court on average agrees to hear less than 5 percent of the writs sent by prisoners. As former Chief Justice Fred M. Vinson explained, "To remain effective, the Supreme Court must continue to decide only those cases which present questions whose resolutions will have immediate importance far beyond the particular facts and parties involved." And it tries its best to resolve the cases on constitutional grounds, regardless of the judges' personal feelings about the wisdom or folly of the laws involved. In *Griswold v. Connecticut* (1965), for example, the Court overturned a Connecticut law forbidding the use of birth control devices and the dissemination of information on such devices. The Court cited the right of marital privacy in the majority decision. But Justice Potter Stewart, in his dissenting opinion, showed what he thought the philosophy of the Court should be: "I think this is an uncommonly silly law. As a practical matter, the law is obviously unenforceable. . . . As a philosophical matter, I believe the use of contraceptives in the relationship of marriage should be left to personal and private choice. . . . But we are not asked in this case to say whether we think this law is unwise, or even asinine. We are asked to hold that it violates the United States Constitution, and that I cannot do."

The Court through the years has had a tremendous impact on criminal law and on police procedure involving the treatment of suspects. In *Wolf v. Colorado* (1949), the Court ruled that state prosecutors may continue using evidence gained through illegal search and seizure, even though the so-called exclusionary rule declared that unconstitutional on the federal level. But then, in *Mapp v. Ohio* (1961), the Court reversed itself and decided that the exclusionary rule must apply to states as well as to federal courts.

On March 18, 1963, in *Gideon v. Wainwright,* the Court ruled that indigent defendants are entitled to legal counsel in all criminal cases, and if the defendant cannot afford one, the state must provide counsel.

On June 13, 1966, in *Miranda v. Arizona,* the Court ruled that a criminal suspect must be informed of his or her rights before being questioned, basing its decision on the FIFTH AMENDMENT guarantee against self-incrimination. The MIRANDA RULE along with the *Gideon* decision had a profound effect on the process of criminal justice. Now, as soon as the police determine that someone is a suspect in a criminal case, they must read the suspect his or her rights and ensure that they are understood. From that point, if the suspect asks for a lawyer, one must be provided, and the questioning of the suspect cannot be continued until the lawyer is present.

In a unanimous decision on April 7, 1969, the Court ruled as unconstitutional laws that prohibited the reading or viewing of obscene material in the privacy of one's home. "Our whole constitutional heritage rebels at the thought of giving the government the power to control men's minds," said Justice Thurgood Marshall. But the right to privacy extended only so far in the minds of a majority of justices in 1976, when the Court upheld, by a vote of six to three, a lower court ruling allowing states to outlaw homosexual acts, even if committed in private by consenting adults. This reversed a 10-year trend toward expanding safeguards of privacy.

In *Furman v. Georgia,* June 29, 1972, the Court held that the death penalty can constitute cruel and unusual punishment, thus violating the Eighth Amendment. This effectively stopped executions in the United States. But four years later, on July 2, 1976, the Court ruled by a 7 to 2 vote that the death penalty is not inherently unconstitutional. It took the states a decade to rewrite their CAPITAL PUNISHMENT laws in ways that the Court agreed were constitutional. The states then resumed executions.

In recent years, the Court has begun a drift away from the extreme liberal rulings protecting the rights of the accused. Improperly obtained evidence can now be used, if the officers obtaining it acted in "good faith" and did not know, for example, that their search warrant was not valid. But the bedrock decisions of *Mapp v. Ohio, Gideon v. Wainwright* and *Miranda v. Arizona* are still in place protecting the accused from the excesses of the law.

SUTTON, Willie "The Actor" (1901–1980)

HE ROBBED BANKS BECAUSE "THAT'S WHERE THE MONEY IS."

Sutton began his life of crime before his teen years and was an accomplished burglar by the time he was 20. In 1926, he was caught in one of his burglaries and drew a four-year sentence to Sing Sing. When he was released, he concentrated on robbing banks, using a variety of disguises that gave him his nickname of "The Actor."

In committing his robberies, and in evading the police, Sutton dyed and bleached his hair, darkened his face, grew a mustache, shaved his mustache and otherwise altered his appearance. He dressed as a policeman, a bank guard, a postman, a messenger boy and a window washer, and he planned each of his jobs with meticulous care.

Sutton became something of a folk hero, as well as several other bank robbers during the 1930s. But unlike JOHN DILLINGER or BONNIE AND CLYDE, Sutton went out of his way not to harm anyone. His legend was enhanced by his uncanny record of escaping from prison. He escaped from New York's SING SING prison and Pennsylvania's Holmesburg Prison. When asked by a reporter why he robbed banks, he replied with a phrase that has become part of American folklore, "Because that's where the money is."

In 1952, Sutton, who was on the FBI's TEN MOST WANTED list, was spotted on the street by ARNOLD SCHUSTER, a crime buff who studied photographs of wanted men. Schuster notified the police, and Sutton was arrested. When Schuster was shot to death a few days later, it had a profound effect on Sutton's life. Although Sutton played no part in the crime, the public could not believe that he was not somehow involved. As Sutton put it in his autobiography, *Where the Money Was* (1976): "With the murder of Arnold Schuster, the public's attitude toward me turned completely around. They had viewed me as a little guy who had outwitted the authorities without hurting anybody, and there was now a young man, a Coast Guard veteran, who had been gunned down in the street, gangster-style, because he had tried to be a good citizen. I could understand their attitude very well. I felt the same way myself."

The judge also felt that way. In sentencing the 51-year-old Sutton to 60 years to life for outstanding charges, he said, "If Sutton were not the miserable character that he is, the chain of circumstances which led up to the death of the Schuster boy never would have happened. . . . These sentences ought to be sufficient to insure that Sutton is sealed off for life in a place where he can no longer bring misery and death, either directly or indirectly, to the public."

Sutton commented:

Arnold Schuster haunts me. He haunted me for purely selfish reasons while I was at Attica, but, above and beyond that, there is a wrenching philosophical point involved. I had been born thirty years before Schuster, and the fact of my being born, and being who I was, had resulted in his death. Throughout my career I had plotted and planned my jobs to make sure that I would not have to hurt anybody, and now, after it was over and I was sitting in jail, a good-looking, promising young man had been killed because of me.

The laughter of the gods.

After becoming an expert jailhouse lawyer, Sutton was released from prison in 1969 after serving a total of 33 years. Deciding that he was too old for bank robbery, he became a security consultant to bankers.

SYMBIONESE LIBERATION ARMY

See: Patricia Campbell Hearst

SYNDICATE, THE

See: Mafia

T

TAMMANY HALL

FOR TWO CENTURIES NEW YORK'S TAMMANY HALL ARTFULLY COMBINED POLITICS WITH GRAFT

In the year 1789, the Constitution of the United States went into effect and the ancient and puissant Society of Saint Tammany was founded in New York, thus establishing one of those systems of checks and balances that distinguish American democracy. Tammany was the Democratic political machine in New York City, and for nearly 200 years, it ran the city. A few times during that period, it even ran the state.

Like other city machines, it was a mixed evil. It gave political jobs to its friends and municipal contracts to its supporters, but it also enfranchised the poor. The power base of the city machine were the immigrants coming to America by the thousands every month. They took their new citizenship seriously and voted for the candidates that assured them of jobs and food and coal in the winter.

Richard Croker, a rising young politician of the last century, related that in the 1870s the Tammany philosophy was "Be kind to those in trouble; look after the sick in your district; see that the widows have food and coal and that the men have jobs; and the orphan children clothes; mourn with those that mourn and rejoice with them that rejoice."

But occasionally greed displaced reason, and Tammany saw the city of New York as a vast, rich trough from which to feed. The period from 1865 to 1872, when William Marcy Tweed was boss of Tammany Hall, was one such time. John T. Hoffman was governor of New York State and A. Oakley Hall was Mayor of New York City, and the Tweed Ring stole roughly one dollar for every two expended by the city. Tammany men held every city and state office, a Tammany district attorney sold justice to the highest bidder, and Tammany-employed gangsters discouraged dissent. Cartoonist Thomas Nast created a classic cartoon showing Boss Tweed and his henchmen as vultures peering down at New York City, with the caption "Let us prey."

Eventually a reform movement developed,

headed by Samuel Jones Tilden, who was subsequently elected governor of New York and was the Democratic candidate for president of the United States in 1876. (Tilden received more popular votes than Republican candidate Rutherford B. Hayes, but Hayes received one more electoral vote and was elected president.) Since the police were owned by Tweed and Tammany, the reformers used ALLAN PINKERTON'S men and other private detective agencies to gather information. The election of 1871 put in an entirely new Board of Aldermen, as well as a few honest judges and prosecutors, much to the surprise of Tweed and his cohorts, who did not realize the extent to which the public was fed up with paying up to 100 times the actual value for the city's goods, for substandard schools and hospitals and for absent city services. It was considered a great victory for the people. The *New York Times,* under a headline that read "New York Redeemed," said:

> The victory we have won is priceless, not only from what it gives us now, but because it will revive every man's faith in the ultimate triumph of truth and justice—because it will teach scheming politicians that the voice of the people is supreme, and that immortal principles on which this Government is founded, although they may be momentarily stifled by dishonest factions, will constantly rise triumphant, while the men who assailed them will pass away to everlasting infamy.

The principals of the Tweed Ring were indicted for massive theft from the public coffers. It was estimated that Tweed alone had taken over $12,000,000 in illegal money. Out of power and reading the handwriting on the wall, the Tweed Ring had scattered around the world, and it took some time to round them up and bring them to trial.

The first trial ended in a hung jury—it was later shown that several of the jurors had been bribed. During the second trial, each juror was watched by two policemen and a private detective, each of whom reported separately so that their reports could be compared.

Tweed was convicted and sentenced to 12 years in prison. A higher court reduced his sentence, and he was released in 1875. The city promptly sued him for the money he had stolen, and he was thrown back in jail when he could not come up with the bail money. He escaped from jail and fled, first to Cuba and then to Spain. By a curious twist, he was recognized in Spain by someone who could not speak English, but had seen a Thomas Nast cartoon of him, and returned to New York. He ended his life in jail in 1878.

The Tweed Ring may have been disbanded, but Tammany merely regrouped and went on. There was a saying at Tammany that reformers were never re-elected, so they just tucked in their belts and waited for better times. By the 1920s, Tammany once again controlled the city. By 1930, they were getting careless again, and the city was once more becoming aware of the tyranny of greed. On March 7, 1931, at a dinner of the Inner Circle, a club made up of New York newspaper reporters who worked the City Hall beat and their friends, the entertainment included the following song:

> Tammany Hall's a patriotic outfit,
> Tammany Hall's an old society;
> Fourth of July they always wave the flag, boys,
> But never will they waive immunity.
> Tammany Hall like Robin Hood professes
> To take things from the rich and give the poor
> Tammany Hall gets just a bit confused sometimes
> And takes from both to give to Tammany Hall.
> Tammany Hall will give you high position,
> Tammany Hall will give you judge or cop,
> Tammany Hall will even stand behind you
> When everyone's agreed that you're a flop.
> Tammany Hall appoints the city workers—
> They loaf six days and on the seventh rest—
> Tammany Hall will give you almost anything
> But Oh, what you must give to Tammany Hall.

The district leaders controlled the graft in Tammany at this time. PROHIBITION ruled the land, and bootleggers such as DUTCH SCHULTZ and LUCKY LUCIANO paid for protection. The money, handled by a district leader such as Jimmie Hines, the "Honest Blacksmith," was then distributed to the police captains, judges, and city officials who received a cut.

Jimmie Hines, an exemplar of the Tammany potentate, enjoyed a career that would have been disallowed in fiction. From a humble beginning in a blacksmith shop, he had risen to a position of awesome power. He was the district leader of the Monongahela Democratic Club of the Eleventh Assembly District, and his sphere of influence included almost everywhere that Tammany operated. He controlled judges, the district attorney, and that most practical of all things to control, the New York City Police Department, thanks to the Tammany system of "honest" graft and political patronage—in Tammany terms, an "honest" public official is one who stays bought.

Hines was the natural protector of anyone, big or small, who might have dealings with the law. He could fix a pushcart license violation or a numbers arrest with equal ease, and hardly ever accepted a donation for fixing a pushcart violation. In 1935, when Special Prosecutor THOMAS A. DEWEY was looking into the activities of Dutch Schultz, it originally looked as though Hines was the Tammany "fixer" for the Dutchman. But after Schultz was murdered, when his henchmen were being gathered by Dewey for trial for gambling, extortion and allied arts, Dewey realized that Hines was not so much Dutch's bag man, but something more like Dutch's partner, or maybe his boss.

At Hines's trial, he was represented by Lloyd Paul Stryker, a talented criminal lawyer whose book *The Art of Advocacy* (1954) is useful reading for trial lawyers today. A parade of numbers bankers, gangsters, madams, accountants, lawyers and other gangland characters was called to give evidence. A gentleman named Williams, a Harlem policy banker, decided for some reason to change his testimony between the time Dewey talked to him and the time he took the stand. He stuck firmly to his new story, although he had failed to carefully consider all its ramifications. Even Hines seemed fascinated to discover that, according to Williams's testimony, he could write but he could not read.

There were two trials. The first ended in a mistrial, over a technicality, and the second convicted Hines. He was sentenced to 4 to 8 years in prison.

With the end of Prohibition and the removal of Jimmie Hines, the high water mark of Tammany Hall had come and gone. The last effective Tammany mayor left office in the 1960s, but by then, the Tammany Tiger had lost most of its teeth. But the Tammany legacy is with New York City yet: Contracts with city unions for employees who do little and are paid much; schools built in the 1930s where students occasionally fall through the walls when the substandard plaster crumbles; subway stations still standing vacant because there never was a subway out to where the station was built. William Marcy Tweed and Jimmie Hines look down from somewhere high above New York City's City Hall, which cost only ten times what it should have to build, and the sounds of their laughter can be faintly heard. *See also:* NUMBERS RACKET

TATE-LaBIANCA MURDERS

See: CHARLES MANSON

TEACH, Edward (?–1718)

BETTER KNOWN AS BLACKBEARD THE PIRATE

Most official documents called him Teach or Thatch, although he was also known as Tache, Tatch and Tash, and there is a possibility that he was born with the name of Hyde. It has also been suggested that he was born Edward Drummond in Bristol, England. He called himself Edward Teach. But whatever his true name, it was under the name of Blackbeard the Pirate that he terrorized the Atlantic seacoast from Virginia to Florida beginning in 1716 and continuing until his death.

Teach had served as a deckhand on English privateers since his youth. His first command came when the notorious Captain Benjamin Hornigold, noting Teach's natural leadership abilities, as well as his impressive size and physique, took him from the deck crew of his privateer, the *Ranger,* and put him in charge of 70 men on a six-gun sloop.

Late in the year 1716, the *Ranger* took a French ship, the *Concorde*, as prize, and Teach asked Hornigold if he could take the *Concorde,* a well-built, speedy brigantine, and those men who would sail with him, and go off "a-pyrating" on his own. Hornigold agreed, and Teach set about creating his own legend.

When they reached Nassau, Hornigold and Teach and their men were made aware of a royal pardon that had been offered to any of the freebooters who would give up the life of piracy. Hornigold and almost 100 of his men accepted. Teach refused and took a crew out on the *Concorde,* now mounting 40 guns and rechristened the *Queen Anne's Revenge*.

It was always the pirates' concept to so frighten their quarry that they would put up little or no resistance. Teach, now that he was master of the *Queen Anne's Revenge,* carried this to an art form. He began calling himself Blackbeard. He grew his beard long and put it into little braids, each tied off with a colored ribbon. As one eighteenth-century writer described it, he had a "large quantity of hair which, like a frightful meteor, covered his whole face, and frightened America more than any comet that has appeared there for a long time." Before a battle, he adorned himself with a triple brace of pistols, a number of daggers and a broad cutlass and tied slow-burning fuses into his beard to wreathe his face in smoke. Those who opposed him felt that they were fighting the Devil himself.

In short order, he captured the *Great Allan,* a large English merchantman, and several smaller prizes and fought off the Royal Navy frigate *Scarborough* in a long and bloody naval battle. His reputation now established, he began to attract other pirate captains and crews to his side. His policy toward his men was to keep them drunk and happy and sufficiently afraid of him not to create trouble when they were sober. As he recorded once in his journal:

> such a Day—Rum all out—Our Company somewhat sober—a damn Confusion amongst us! Rogues a'plotting—great talk of separation—so I look'd sharp for a Prize.

And in the next entry:

> took one with a great deal of Liquor on Board, so, kept the Company hot, damned hot, then all Things went well again.

Part of Teach's method of maintaining discipline was to make the idea of going against him as unattractive as possible. To this end, he fostered the idea that he was a madman of superhuman abilities, who kept himself barely under control. It probably was not all acting. He once invited several members of his crew down into the hold, where they were closed in with pots of burning brimstone to see what Hell would be like. After the sulfur fumes had driven the other men onto the deck, he strolled out after them, grinning broadly. Another time he suggested that they all hang themselves to see who could swing the longest without choking to death. The crew declined the suggestion.

One evening Teach was drinking in his cabin with his gunner and mate when he suddenly cocked a brace of pistols, blew out the candle, crossed his hands under the table and fired both pistols. The gunner, Israel Hands, was hit in the kneecap and lamed for life. When asked why he did this to his friend, Teach is reputed to have replied that if he did not kill one of them now and then they would forget who he was.

In May 1717, Teach and the *Queen Anne's Revenge* teamed up with Stede Bonnet and his ship *Revenge*. Teach was the senior partner by virtue of intimidation; Bonnet was scared to death of him. In January 1718, Teach and Bonnet landed at Bath in North Carolina and arranged a capitulation to North Carolina Governor Charles Eden, accepting the amnesty offer King George I had made to all pirates who changed their ways. But the acceptance was a sham, and it is generally thought that Teach was secretly making a deal with Eden to arrange a safe port for a share in the spoils. While there, pardons in hand, they refitted for the next voyage and then set out to sea. For a while, they made Bath their home port, the local citizens finding the arrangement profitable to all concerned.

They captured the *Protestant Caesar* out of Boston and the *Adventure* off Turneffe Island and a number of small sloops in the Bay of Honduras. Many men in the crews were induced to join the pirate crews, which was not uncommon in this period, when deckhands on merchant ships and ships of war were normally so brutalized by those in command over them that the life of a pirate seemed a welcome relief, even with the threat of the gibbet for an ending.

With Teach now in command of a small fleet of ships and some 400 men, he began a systematic assault against shipping in the West Indies. Havana, Cuba, and various inlets in North Carolina were used to refit and to dispose of their booty. The merchants of the North Carolina towns, like the merchants of other North American seacoast towns during this period, would take any goods offered without inquiring too closely as to their provenance.

Teach and his small fleet were off of Charleston, South Carolina, in May 1718. They intercepted the shipping coming to and from Charleston harbor, and soon were in possession of eight or ten ships of various sizes, some with rich cargoes. Their presence offshore paralyzed shipping in the harbor and made the townsfolk nervous. In early June, Teach sent Richards, one of his captains, into Charleston with a demand for medical supplies. He threatened to kill several hostages including Samuel Wragg, a member of Governor Johnson's council, and Wragg's four-year-old son, unless the demand was met within two days.

The governor's council met while Richards strutted around town acting bold and fearless and every bit the pirate and making the burghers even more nervous. After a day's deliberation, the council capitulated and sent Richards back to his ship with the requested medicinals. Teach kept his word and released the hostages, after stripping them, searching them and relieving them of all their valuables, including £6,000 found on Samuel Wragg.

The British sent two warships, H.M.S. *Pearl* and *Lyme*, to hunt for Teach's flotilla. They caught up with him on November 22, at Ocracoke Inlet in the James River. As the draft was too shallow for the warships, Lieutenant Robert Maynard, first officer of the *Pearl,* took in a party of men in oared sloops. Teach cut his anchor cable in his haste to escape to the sea, but his ship ran aground. He fired his ship's guns at the approaching sloops, killing and wounding a fair number, but Maynard and his men boarded moments later. Teach fought furiously, taking several shots, before Maynard killed him with his cutlass.

The head of the notorious Blackbeard was severed from his body and hung at the end of the bowsprit as a cautionary exhibition while the ship sailed back to Bath. It was discovered that the timing of Teach's removal was fortuitous, as he had begun fortifying an island at Ocracoke Inlet, with the idea of making it a general safe haven for pirates. A letter found on the *Revenge* after Teach's death, written by North Carolina's Customs Chief Tobias Knight, strongly suggested that both Knight and Governor Eden abetted

Teach's predatory voyages. Knight was indicted and tried by North Carolina's provincial council, but he successfully blamed it all on Governor Eden, who was too sick to stand trial and died a few months later.

Israel Hands, the gunner that Teach had crippled, was pardoned and sent to England, where he became a model for one of the characters in Robert Louis Stevenson's *Treasure Island*.

In his book *Captains Outrageous* (1961), Neville Williams says of Teach:

> Considering that he was operating for less than two years it is remarkable that Blackbeard made such a hold on the popular imagination in his own day and since, for he was not a very successful pirate, nor a very daring one; his seamanship was inferior to that of the general run of pirate captains and he was little more than a brilliant showman.

TEAPOT DOME SCANDAL

See: OHIO GANG

TEN MOST WANTED

The FBI's Ten Most Wanted Fugitives list was created in 1950 with the cooperation of the International News Service (INS), a publicity device that served the double purpose of promoting the bureau and raising public awareness of the most dangerous fugitives in their midst. The INS sent the photographs to newspapers around the country, which used them from time to time, with sometimes impressive results. In 1953, an issue of the *Saturday Evening Post* ran a story about the list, complete with photographs and a warning to "call the nearest office of the FBI if you see one of these men." As a direct result of the article, three of the ten were arrested within the month.

Appearing on the list is an honor that most criminals would gladly forgo. Several have commented upon capture that they knew their days were numbered when their names appeared on the list. The average time between a name appearing on the list and the apprehension of the suspect is five months. The list is usually held to 10 names, but there have been exceptions, as when James Earl Ray's name was added after the assassination of Dr. Martin Luther King without waiting for a space to open up. From 1969 to 1970, the list expanded to 16 to make room for members of various New Left radical groups wanted for sabotage, bank robbery, murder and other forms of social protest. They tended to stay on the list much longer than average because of their extensive underground support network, a fact which also raised the average.

To give an idea of the sort of offenses that the FBI considers serious, some of the people on the list have been the following:

William Raymond Nesbit—Put on in 1950 for a jewel robbery and for blowing up his partner in a dynamite and black powder blast that broke windows five miles away. Put in prison for murder, he escaped and was recaptured in a cave by the Mississippi River, when a couple of boys recognized him from a newspaper reproduction of his "wanted" poster.

Joseph Levy—A bad check artist, Levy was put on in 1953 for "hanging paper" all over the country. His favorite ploy was to buy expensive gifts for then Vice President Nixon and pocket the change. He was apprehended as his name was being added to the list, so his stay on was one of the shortest on record.

Joseph Corbett—Added in 1960 for the kidnapping and murder of brewery owner Adolph Coors, III. After being chased all over the country, Corbett was finally caught in Vancouver, Canada. He was convicted of murder, and received a life sentence.

Richard Laurence Marquette—Put on in 1961 for a particularly grisly axe murder. Parts of his victim's body were found in his refrigerator, and parts were distributed on his Portland neighbors' lawns. He was the first person to cause the FBI to expand their list to 11 names. He was captured, convicted and received a life sentence.

George Zavada—Put on in 1964 for masterminding a series of bank robberies in California. He was wounded in a gun battle with federal agents and went to prison, where he died a year later of natural causes.

Jack Clouser—Put on in 1964 and stayed on for more than 10 years. Known as the "Florida Fox," Clouser, a former Orlando police officer, escaped from a mental institution where he had been sent after being convicted of kidnapping, robbery and assault. He sent taunting letters to various law enforcement officials, including J. EDGAR HOOVER, during the decade he was free. On August 22, 1974, he voluntarily surrendered, saying he was tired of running.

LESLIE DOUGLAS ASHLEY—One of the few transvestites to make the ten most wanted, he was put on the list in 1965 after escaping from a mental hospital. Ashley was charged with a particularly brutal murder. After about two weeks on the list he was captured by the FBI while working as "Bobo the Clown" in a carnival in Atlanta.

There have been seven women on the list in its first 40 years:

Maria Arrington—Placed on list in May 1969 after escaping from a Florida prison and threatening to kill the judge who had sentenced her to death. Rearrested in New Orleans in December 1971.

Angela Davis—Purchased guns used in a bloody Marin County, California, courtroom jailbreak. Placed on list in August 1970 and captured two months later. Tried and acquitted for murder, kidnapping and unlawful flight.

Bernardine Dohrn—Indicted for conspiracy to incite riots and to carry explosives across state lines and placed on the list in October 1970. Taken off the list in 1973.

Ruth Eisemann-Schier—Put on the list in 1968, the first woman to receive that honor. She was involved in a kidnapping in Georgia. She was captured in 1969 in Oklahoma.

Katherine Ann Power and Susan Saxe—Brandeis University radicals put on the list in 1970. Power drove the getaway car while Saxe robbed a Philadelphia bank with three ex-convicts, a robbery that resulted in the murder of a policeman. Saxe was arrested in 1975. Power was dropped from the list in 1984.

Donna Jean Wilmott—Put on in May 1987 for allegedly trying to free a radical friend from Leavenworth Penitentiary.

TERESA, Vincent Charles "Fat Vinnie" (1930–)

The number three man in the New England MAFIA, or so he described himself, Vincent Teresa turned informer when the Mob cheated him and treated his wife and children badly while he was in prison. The information he supplied to state and federal agencies was on a much higher level and more elaborately detailed than that of fellow informant JOSEPH VALACHI. Valachi was only a lowly soldier in the Mafia, but Vinnie Teresa had a higher rank.

The evidence supplied by Teresa in the late 1960s solved crimes and cleared up murders from Massachusetts to the Bahamas and led to the indictment and usually the conviction of over 50 Mafia dons. He spoke of stock swindles, fixed horse races, crooked casinos, union and business infiltration and murder. He testified against MEYER LANSKY, which must have required considerable courage even if he was in a witness protection program. The Mob put a price tag of half a million dollars on his head.

In the book he wrote with Thomas C. Renner, *My Life in the Mafia* (1973), Teresa described the estimated $150 million he had produced for the Mob, taking over $10 million as his share. He also described the way money flowed through his fingers; when it was so easy to make, he never worried about saving any of it.

Teresa and his family have had to relocate in the witness protection program several times, as testimony he gave at later trials would reveal a current identity. Once he blew it himself, when he was indicted for smuggling exotic and endangered birds and reptiles into this country.

TEXAS RANGERS

The oldest state police in the United States by several decades, the Texas Rangers was founded by the provisional government of the Texas Republic in 1835. Three ranger companies were put under the direction of the military authorities and used for border patrol functions along the Mexican border. Gradually police work replaced military duties, and by the 1860s, the rangers were primarily a police force. Disbanded briefly after the Civil War, the rangers were reorganized in 1874. From then until the end of the century, they fought outlaws, creating the legend that persists to this day. It was during this period that the almost certainly apocryphal story of the Lone Ranger was first told. The legend is that a town mayor, seeing that a major riot was brewing, telegraphed the rangers for assistance. The next day, the train pulled into the station and a single lawman detrained. "Where are the rest of your men?" the mayor asked.

"Hell," the ranger replied, "you've only got one riot, ain't you?"

In the first decades of the twentieth century, the rangers almost ruined their earlier reputation, becoming racist, chauvinist, antilabor, violent and highly politicized. They shot Mexican or black suspects in preference to arresting them, and sometimes after they had arrested them. In 1919, a Texas State Representative charged that the rangers had practically waged war against Mexicans during World War I, routing, arresting, beating and killing them by the hundreds. It was an extreme example of the wave of xenophobia engulfing the country, especially along the Mexican border. In what became known as the Ponvenir Massacre, Ranger Captain J. M. Fox, along with eight of his men and four deputized civilians, tortured 25 Mexican men and murdered 15 others in cold blood in the town of Ponvenir in December 1917. As a result of the bad press, Captain Fox and his men were fired from the rangers. They were never prosecuted.

In the early 1930s, the new governor of Texas was a woman known as Ma Ferguson, and she brought Texas politics to a new low. She fired all but one of the rangers because she thought they favored her opponent. The new crew that she hired to replace them were totally corrupt and vicious.

Her successor reversed the process and professionalized the rangers under the Texas Department of Public Safety. They were given back their independence a few years later. They have remained an efficient if reactionary organization. In the 1960s and 1970s, there were serious union complaints that the rangers' zeal in strikebreaking exceeded their authority, and this view was upheld by the Supreme Court in a 1967 case involving general mayhem committed by rangers against two striking melon pickers.

TEXAS TOWER MASSACRE

See: CHARLES WHITMAN

THATCH, Edward

See: EDWARD TEACH

THAW, Harry Kendall (1872–1947)

IN THE GRIP OF AN OBSESSION, HE KILLED THE MAN WHO "DESPOILED" HIS WIFE

Eldest son of William Thaw, who had built up a sizable fortune in the railroad and coke trade in Pittsburgh in the years after the Civil War, Harry Thaw achieved a brief moment of fame when he murdered architect Stanford White in the roof theater of New York's Madison Square Garden in 1906.

It was a crime of passion, but Harry Thaw had strange passions. His wife, the beautiful Evelyn Nesbit, once had an affair with White, and the fact preyed on Thaw's mind until he went mad with jealousy and shot the architect. Some said he was mad to begin with.

Before Evelyn Nesbit's sixteenth birthday, she had posed for Charles Dana Gibson, the artist

Harry K. Thaw, who murdered Stanford White in fury over his wife's prior relationship with the noted architect. (Collection of the author.)

Evelyn Nesbit, who graduated from the chorus line of the Floradora Review to become Stanford White's mistress and then Harry Thaw's wife. (Collection of the author.)

who created the "Gibson Girl," an image that defined the modern girl of the *fin de siècle* era. Gibson called his portrait of Evelyn "The Eternal Question." Coming from a small town in Pennsylvania to appear in musical reviews on Broadway, Evelyn had been featured in the show *Floradora* when White met her, and she became his mistress. White was one of the most important architects of the day, having designed New York's Washington Square Arch and the Columbia University Library among many other structures. He also had a taste for young, beautiful women.

Evelyn left White to go with Thaw, but as far as is known they parted amicably. It was shown that she even went to White for advice and assistance after they had separated. If her story on the witness stand belied this, if it alleged dastardly behavior on the part of White, it must be remembered that she was trying to save her husband and that there were certain things that a young lady just did not admit in 1906.

Thaw had been cut off by his father when he married Evelyn, but his mother, who had her own money, gave him $80,000 so that he could maintain his life style. He had certain strange habits that did not come out at the trial, but that were soon common knowledge among New York's journalists, who did not dare print such things. Apparently, he would invite showgirls to an apartment he maintained in a brothel and whip them for his own amusement. When he married 19-year-old Evelyn Nesbit early in 1906, he beat her on the boat during their honeymoon cruise to make her tell him all about her affair with White. He insisted on details, and Evelyn made them up to keep her new, strange husband happy. By the time they returned from their honeymoon, Thaw had an insane fixation on White, whom he fondly imagined had "despoiled" his young bride.

On June 25, 1906, a musical comedy called *Mam'zelle Champagne* was opening on the roof terrace of the old Madison Square Garden, a building that had been designed by Stanford White. The roof garden was set up as a supper club theater, and the audience sat at tables rather than regular theater seats. Thaw arrived with Evelyn and two friends. They had to pass White, who was sitting alone, to get to their table. Thaw glared at the back of White's head as they passed, but the architect was engrossed in the show and did not notice. Thaw made it a point to pass back and forth behind White several times over the next hour, glaring at White and working himself into a state of rage. On the last pass, Thaw suddenly pulled a revolver and shot White three times, killing him instantly. Thaw then immediately surrendered himself to a uniformed fireman who was standing by the door. "He ruined my life," Thaw explained. Or possibly, "He ruined my wife." There was some discussion as to which he actually said.

Thaw had his meals catered from Delmonico's Restaurant while he waited in the Tombs, New York City's prison, for his trial to start. The prestigious law firm that Thaw asked to lead his defense, Black, Olcott, Gruber and Bonynge, wanted to plead Thaw insane, but neither Thaw nor his mother would permit his sanity to be questioned. Thaw wanted to use the "unwritten Law" as his defense. His lawyers patiently explained to Thaw that the "unwritten Law" was not a legal defense, and even if it were, it only applied to catching your spouse in bed with someone, not to avenging acts committed before you even met her. Thaw was adamant. Black, Olcott, Gruber and Bonynge were replaced.

Delphin Delmas, a flamboyant trial lawyer, was then hired for the defense. District Attorney Travers Jerome handled the prosecution. Delmas presented a carefully designed defense, asserting that, although Thaw was insane at the moment he committed the crime, he was no longer insane and could not be held responsible. The plea of temporary insanity has since become a staple in a defense attorney's arsenal, but it was novel when Delmas used it.

Evelyn Nesbit was the defense's strongest witness. She described her seduction at the hands of sex-starved Stanford White, and the strange sex games that they played. He had, she claimed, drugged her one evening. And when she awakened from the drug, she was no longer a virgin. He had a red velvet swing in his studio, which he used to have young girls dressed in frilly frocks swing on while he watched. Evelyn told the jury how she had described her seduction to Thaw, and how he had gotten more and more upset. He could not leave the subject alone but kept making her return to it and add detail after detail, and his obsession grew into murder.

The first trial ended in a hopelessly deadlocked jury. The jury in the second trial found Thaw "not guilty because of insanity at the time of the act."

Thaw thought that meant that he was free, but District Attorney Jerome had him committed to the New York State Asylum for the Criminally Insane at Mattewan. There were several lunacy hearings after that, financed by his mother's money, but at each one, Thaw was still found to be insane. He escaped once to Canada, but the Canadians returned him to Vermont, and he was arrested in New Hampshire. In 1915, he was judged to be sane and released from the asylum. In 1917, he was convicted of horsewhipping a boy and was confined again until 1924. From then until he died in 1947, he managed to stay out of trouble. He wrote a maudlin book called *The Traitor* (1926) describing his life with Evelyn and justifying his killing of White, but his family suppressed it for 20 years.

Evelyn Nesbit divorced Thaw shortly after the trial, announcing that "Harry Thaw has turned out to be a degenerate scoundrel. He hid behind my skirts through two dirty trials and I won't stand for it." She went back to vaudeville at $3,500 a week and married her stage partner, then she divorced him and disappeared from view. She reappeared from time to time, performing in a vaudeville or nightclub act.

THIMBLE RIG

See: SHELL GAME

THREE-CARD MONTE

A CONFIDENCE GAME masquerading under the guise of a game of chance, three-card monte has been separating marks (victims) from their money for well over 100 years. Also known as "Find the Lady," the game is played with two neutral cards, often aces or tens, and a queen. The dealer, or "spieler," has one or two confederates, or "shills," who make the game look lively and appear to win enough to encourage the suckers. There also may be a couple of lookouts to give the spieler a chance to collapse the game if the police or other busybodies try to interfere with the action.

In the play of the game, the spieler holds two cards in one hand and the third in the other, shows the queen to the players and then throws the cards one after the other onto the table and invites bets as to the location of the queen. To the mark, it looks as though the queen is easy to spot, but the mark is wrong. When one of the shills bets, the queen is where he says it is, but when the mark bets, the queen has mysteriously moved. Just when the mark is about to give up, the spieler will turn away for a second, and one of the shills will seize the moment to put a crimp in a corner of the queen. He will then wink at the mark, as though to say "we are all in this together against the spieler." The unobservant spieler appears not to notice this byplay, and the mark will then bet heavily, thinking he cannot lose. But when he turns the crimped card over, somehow it is no longer the queen. It is not merely a question of some dealers cheating when they play. Like the shell game, there is no honest version of three-card monte. Some monte spielers were notorious for their deftness with the pasteboards. In his classic book *Gambling and Gambling Devices*, first published in 1912, John Philip Quinn relates:

> Probably the king of the monte men was a man known in sporting circles as "Canada Bill." He was recognized as a general "all round confidence operator," and so distrustful were those who knew him

of appearances which he put forth that on the occasion of his funeral, as the coffin was being lowered into the grave, one of his friends offered to bet $1,000 to $500 that "Bill was not in the box." The offer found no takers, for the reason, as one of his acquaintances says, "that he had known Bill to squeeze through tighter holes than that." It was reported some years before his death that he had offered one of the Trunk Lines of Railroad a premium of $25,000 per annum to be allowed to practice confidence games on its trains without molestation, on the condition that he would not attempt to victimize any class of passengers except preachers.

TIGER WOMAN

See: CLARA PHILLIPS

TOPPAN, Jane (1857–1938)

"Everybody trusted me. It was so easy. I felt strange when I watched them die. I was all excited and my blood seemed to sweep madly through my veins. It was the only pleasure I had."

So reads part of the confession of Jane Toppan, who was considered one of the better nurses in Lowell, Massachusetts, and was in great demand among doctors. True, many of her patients died, but medicine was not so far advanced at the end of the nineteenth century for that to be strange. People who required nursing were sick, and sick people died.

Toppan practiced nursing for over two decades, at one time holding the position of head nurse at Massachusetts General Hospital until her supervisors discovered that her nursing certificate was forged. She killed her patients with a mixture of morphine and atropine, gradually increasing the dose until they went into convulsions and died. She apparently was sexually stimulated by watching them die; she certainly did not get anything else from the murders. The doctors did not catch on because their patients, after all, were very sick, and because the morphine poisoning, which contracts the pupil of the eye, was balanced by the atropine poisoning, which dilates the pupil of the eye.

Eventually caught because of prescriptions she forged, she tried to commit suicide with her own poison. Under the impression that she was dying, she freely confessed to over 30 killings. But the poison failed in her case, and she lived to stand trial on June 25, 1902. The defense tried to plead her as insane, but she fought this idea. Although she did tell the court: "This is my ambition—to have killed more people—more helpless people—than any man or woman has ever killed."

Toppan finally allowed her lawyers to plea bargain, and the prosecution agreed to accept a verdict of not guilty by reason of insanity, provided that she be held at the Taunton, Massachusetts, State Hospital for the Criminally Insane for the rest of her life with no possibility of release. She died in Taunton 36 years later. Her final body count was estimated to be over 100 patients.

TORRESOLA, Griselio (?–1950)

On November 1, 1950, two Puerto-Rican nationalists, Griselio Torresola and his comrade Oscar Collazo, attempted to assassinate President Harry Truman at Blair House, where the president was living while the White House was being renovated. A White House guard named Leslie Coffelt was killed when he put himself between the assassins and the president. Torresola was killed and Collazo wounded. President Truman was unharmed. Collazo was sentenced to life imprisonment. Four years later, a related attempt was made against the House of Representatives by LOLITA LEBRON and three male companions. *See also:* ASSASSINATIONS

TORRIO, John (1882–1957)

THE NEW YORK GANGSTER WHO BUILT A CRIME EMPIRE IN CHICAGO

Johnnie Torrio grew up on New York City's Lower East Side, having come over from Italy at the age of two. He joined the FIVE POINTS GANG in his early teens and soon became one of gang leader Paul Kelly's henchmen. By the time he was 20, he had taken over a Brooklyn division of the Five Pointers known as the James Street Gang, which included such future luminaries as AL CAPONE and CHARLEY "LUCKY" LUCIANO.

In 1909, Torrio's uncle, Big Jim Colosimo, who ran a string of whorehouses in Chicago, needed some young muscle and thought of his Brooklyn nephew. Torrio helped out Big Jim and, by 1915, had moved to Chicago. Big Jim rewarded Torrio for his help by giving him a couple of brothels to run as his own. Torrio upgraded them and made them more profitable than they ever had been under Big Jim. In 1919, he brought Al Capone out from Brooklyn to help him as a chauffeur, bodyguard, muscle man and general factotum.

When PROHIBITION began in 1920, Torrio realized that rumrunning and bootlegging were the up-and-coming professions, and he wanted to stake out his piece of the action, but Big Jim was not interested in expansion. He was already a millionaire many times over, and he had a new girlfriend who was taking up most of his time. Big Jim would not acquiesce, and he would not step aside. Consequently, Torrio imported a hit man from his old gang in New York named FRANKIE YALE and while Torrio and Capone went off to establish alibis, Yale emerged from his hiding place in the hatcheck room and gunned down Colosimo by the front door of his own bar.

Torrio proceeded to build on the organization that Colosimo had established, bringing it into bootlegging, rumrunning and the illicit manufacturing of beer and a variety of distilled beverages. He held a sit-down (meeting) with the leaders of the other Chicago gangs and pointed out that there was enough spoils to go around, and that it would be more profitable to peacefully divide up the city and environs between them than to fight over territory. The ethnicity of the gangs did not matter; Irish, Polish, Jewish, even Neapolitan: a division of the spoils of the VOLSTEAD ACT outlawing drink would more than make up for the pleasures lost in eschewing ethnic or territorial strife. Torrio was founding the Chicago branch of the MAFIA, which would become known as "The Syndicate."

Most of the other gangs went along with his scheme, either seeing its wisdom or fearing the long arm of Torrio's enforcer, Al Capone. The only hold out of consequence was DION O'BANION's North Side Gang. His were the ways of the transgressor: he accepted those parts of the agreement favorable to his gang and ignored those parts that he chose to ignore. It created friction and occasional conflict and threatened the harmony of the arrangement.

After a couple of years of bickering, O'Banion announced that he was ready and willing to retire. If Torrio would buy his Seiben Brewery for $500,000, O'Banion would quit the rackets and spend his time raising flowers. It was a good price for the brewery, and Torrio snapped it up. A week after the transfer, the Seiben Brewery was raided by federal Prohibition agents, who broke up or confiscated the entire contents of the building. Torrio had been suckered by O'Banion, who had received advance warning of the impending raid.

Torrio did not appreciate the joke and was determined to have the last laugh. He called his friend Frankie Yale in New York and asked for another favor. On November 10, 1924, Yale, along with two local hoods, Albert Anselmi and John Scalise, shot O'Banion to death in the Irish mobster's own flower shop. HYMIE WEISS, who took O'Banion's place as head of the North Side

Gang, vowed vengeance. Torrio was ambushed in front of his apartment building on January 24, 1925, and taken to the hospital, not expected to survive. He had been hit in the arm, chest and stomach by a shotgun slug and four pistol bullets. Capone guarded the hospital with dozens of mobsters while Torrio fought for his life.

Torrio did survive the assassination attempt, but he did a lot of thinking in the hospital. He decided that the game was no longer worth the playing, and when he got out, he turned the Syndicate over to Capone. "It's all yours, Al, I've retired," he announced. He returned to Brooklyn after roaming around the Mediterranean for a couple of years and became one of the grand old men of the Mafia, consulted for policy decisions, but uninvolved in the day-to-day running of the Mob. It is said that he was consulted in the DUTCH SCHULTZ problem, when it was decided to remove the Dutchman before he could carry out his plan to kill Special Prosecutor THOMAS E. DEWEY.

TURNER, Nat (1800–1831)

LEADER OF AMERICA'S MOST FAMOUS SLAVE REVOLT

It is certainly true that the institution of slavery enslaves the master as surely as it enslaves the slave. In ancient Sparta, the Helots, probably the descendants of the original inhabitants who had been conquered by the oncoming Spartans, were held as slaves. The entire male population of Spartans were forced to train as warriors and remain constantly on the alert because the Helots disliked being slaves. A tyrannical secret police scrutinized both Spartan and Helot, ever alert for slave revolts. Nonetheless, slave revolts happened.

In the slaveholding states of the United States, the white masters were in constant fear of an uprising by their black slaves. The STONO REBELLION of 1739, although quashed, had set a precedent that the slaveholders did not like to think about. In Santo Domingo in the 1790s, slaves led by Toussaint L'Ouverture had successfully rebelled, and before the fighting was over, 60,000 people had died. With these models before them, the Southern slaveholders lived in a constant state of anticipatory fright. They did their best to minimize this fear by not publicizing any of the revolts or uprisings that did happen, but this merely served to foment constant rumors and magnify small events.

By the 1820s, conspiracies to escape or to revolt were firmly rooted among the Southern slaves, and a corresponding revolt paranoia kept the Southern whites in thrall. The well-planned revolt by a slave group in Charleston, South Carolina, headed by DENMARK VESEY, although unsuccessful, raised the fever on both sides.

In the summer of 1831, a slave preacher named Nat Turner began carefully planning his revolt. As a child, Turner had been recognized as exceptionally bright, although at his birth, his mother had been frightened by the strange bumps on his forehead and thought of killing him. Turner's master taught him to read, a practice that was frowned upon, if not illegal, and had the slave boy read selections from the Bible to amuse his guests. Turner became fascinated by the Bible and became a slave preacher. Through prayer and fasting, he convinced himself that the Lord had chosen him to lead his people to freedom. In his confession, taken before he was hanged, he said that in 1828 the Spirit had appeared to him and told him that "the Serpent was loosened, and Christ had laid down the yoke He had borne for the sins of men, and that I should take it on and fight against the Serpent, for the time was fast approaching when the first should be last and the last should be first."

Turner slowly gathered a group of disciples around him, choosing only field hands because he felt that house servants were untrustworthy—it was a house servant who had betrayed the plans of Denmark Vesey nine years before.

On August 22, 1831, Turner began the action by going with six fellow slaves into the house of his owner, Joseph Travis, where they murdered Travis and his wife. After this, more than 70 of his followers began a revolt that turned into a two-day riot and slaughter of their slave masters. White men, women and children were hacked to death and decapitated. By the end of their rampage, Turner and his men had murdered 57 whites.

By the second day, 2,000 militiamen and 800 federal troops were after the rebels. Most were caught or killed within hours. Turner escaped into the woods, where he hid for a month before he was caught. In the hunt, the white posse slaughtered blacks indiscriminately, killing more than 100 slaves, many of whom had nothing to do with the rebellion. Of the 55 prisoners taken, 17, including Turner, were hanged.

TWEED RING

See: TAMMANY HALL

UALE, Frank

See: FRANKIE YALE

UNIONE SICILIANO

L'Unione Siciliano was a Sicilian-American fraternal organization in the United States, founded around the turn of the twentieth century. It was quickly taken over as a cover organization by the MAFIA elements in the American Italian community and used as a front for protection rackets aimed mostly at Italian shopkeepers.

UNITED STATES BUREAU OF INVESTIGATION

The name of the Justice Department's investigative body from July 1, 1932, until it became the FEDERAL BUREAU OF INVESTIGATION on July 1, 1935, under President Franklin D. Roosevelt.

UNTOUCHABLES

See: ELIOT NESS

V

VALACHI, Joseph M. (1903–1971)

THE GANGLAND INFORMER WHO CONVINCED THE FBI THAT THERE REALLY WAS A MAFIA

A low-level soldier, or "button man," in the VITO GENOVESE crime family, Joseph Valachi suddenly attained national prominence in 1963 when he testified at the Senate Permanent Investigations Subcommittee, headed by Senator John L. McClellan, revealing the secrets of an organization he called *La Cosa Nostra* (literally, "this thing of ours"). Valachi, in prison on drug charges, had "rolled over," offering to tell all he knew about the MAFIA and the crimes committed by its members over the previous 30 years in return for protection. He suspected that his old boss, Vito Genovese, then in the federal penitentiary in Atlanta with him, had put a contract out on him. Deciding that this was the truth when Genovese gave him the "kiss of death," Valachi determined to stay alive. He killed Joe Saupp, a fellow prisoner whom he mistakenly thought was Joe DiPalermo, the man he believed had the contract on him. He thus found himself caught between the authorities, who would prosecute him for the murder of Saupp, and Genovese. The only way to stay alive was to give the authorities enough information to make himself valuable to them, so they would not prosecute him on the murder charge, which, after all, was self-defense, even if he did kill the wrong man.

Valachi was a member of Salvatore Maranzano's family at the beginning of the CASTELLAMMARESE WAR, and he described the details of this dispute from the soldier's point of view. Not privy to the planning and secret maneuvering of the lieutenants, which ended with the two bosses dead and the formation of a national crime organization, he described what it looked like to the men in the trenches, how they tried to stay abreast of the winds of change, so they would not find themselves blown in the wrong direction. Valachi heard and believed the story of the so-called Night of the Sicilian Vespers, when 30 or 40 of the old-time MUSTACHE PETES were supposedly murdered. He related it to the senators,

Joseph Valachi talks and fascinated senators learn about the inner workings of "La Cosa Nostra." (Collection of the author)

and it took some research to determine that it never happened.

His stories of the inner workings of the crime commission are second-hand and untrustworthy, but his stories of life as a low-level Mafia soldier are shocking and eye-opening. He told of a number of murders he had been involved in, describing them in every particular. Not very well educated, he nonetheless had an eye for detail and an ability to convey the sense and feeling of his accounts.

When he started to talk, the Mafia seriously tried to kill him. Genovese had, indeed, ordered his death, but Genovese was thought to be slowly going mad, and Valachi could probably have talked his way out of that one, had he managed to stay alive in prison. But now there was a contract out on him, offering $100,000 for his death.

Valachi did not directly send anyone to prison or the electric chair, as had ABE "KID TWIST" RELES 23 years before, but his testimony, going out over national television, gave a picture of ORGANIZED CRIME so detailed that few could still believe that the Mafia was a myth and that the talk about organized crime was just a way for police chiefs to get larger appropriations for their forces. He had a number of the names wrong when he talked about ancient crimes, the result of second-hand information and, possibly a faulty memory, but nobody could doubt the import, and the impact, of the mass of information that he revealed. After his testimony, he gave extensive interviews to journalist Peter Maas, who put them all together in *The Valachi Papers*, which was a best-seller when it appeared in 1968.

VALENTINE, Lewis J. (1882–1946)

A tough, honest, intelligent cop, Lewis Valentine joined the New York City police force in 1903 and rose from patrolman to police commissioner in 31 years. The rise was not steady, however, as during several of New York's more colorful administrations, honesty was not the most admired virtue in a cop. After 10 years on the force, he was promoted to sergeant and made a "shoo-fly," as members of the special squad that investigated reports of police wrongdoing were called. Then came a series of falls from grace, as TAMMANY HALL administrations came in, and promotions, as reform mayors were elected. Finally in 1934, when Fiorello La Guardia was mayor, Valentine was made police commissioner. He was determined to break the control of the gangs in New York. He made it clear to his men that his policy would be to promote the man who arrested gangsters and demote the man who was friendly with them. And heaven help any man caught taking graft. His tactics were considered a little rough by many civil libertarians, but his attitude resurrected a moribund police department. When La Guardia called Valentine into his office to face some civil rights fans who were complaining about his tactics, the mayor told him, "Lewie, these people claim you violate the Constitution." "So do the gangsters," Valentine replied and that ended the conversation.

By 1945, Valentine had earned such respect in office that all three major mayoral candidates made it a point of stating that they would keep him on his job. But he decided that it was time to retire. His voice became known nationwide after he retired when he did a series of introductions to episodes of the "Gangbusters" radio program. He went to Japan for much of the year 1946 at the behest of General Douglas MacArthur to reorganize the Japanese police. After returning home, he wrote his autobiography, published as *Night Stick*.

VEROTTA, Giuseppi (1915–1921)

Giuseppi Verotta was a kidnap victim of the BLACK HAND.

VESEY, Denmark (1767–1822)

Denmark Vesey had bought his own freedom around 1800 from his master for $600 after he won $1,500 in a lottery. By 1820, he was a skilled and well-paid carpenter in Charleston, South

Carolina who owned $8,000 worth of property and had as much respect as a free black could expect in a white, slave-owning society. But there were worse indignities than low social status. His wife and children were slaves, and he had to have their master's permission in order to visit them. Vesey grew to regard the situation as intolerable. Twenty years before, the blacks in Santo Domingo, led by Toussaint L'Ouverture, had overthrown their masters and set up their own country, successfully resisting the efforts of the European powers to retake the island several times.

Vesey became convinced that the blacks of South Carolina should be free and that it was possible if led by someone as skillful as L'Ouverture. Slowly, over the next two years, he recruited his people and made his plans. A capable, intelligent, charismatic leader, he was able to train his lieutenants in secrecy and spread the word selectively in the slave community. Some were trained as blacksmiths to forge weapons, some could handle boats, others horses and wagons. One group developed make-up, wigs, beards, and clothing so that selected agents could pass as whites during the crucial moments at the beginning of the rebellion.

Unfortunately, the secret finally leaked out, and the son of one of the rebels told the authorities. In June 1822, one of Vesey's networks of slaves was arrested and tortured. They held out long enough for most of the conspirators to escape, but Vesey and his top lieutenant Peter Poyas were arrested. They consistently denied everything, but to no avail. A total of 130 blacks and four whites were brought to trial. Vesey and Poyas and 33 other blacks were hanged. The four whites who were involved were fined and given jail sentences. Regulations concerning blacks were tightened, and the punishments for black recalcitrance were increased.

See also: STONO REBELLION; NAT TURNER

VOLSTEAD ACT

The Volstead Act was passed by Congress on October 28, 1919, and established national PROHIBITION as well as the provisions for enforcing the Eighteenth Amendment to the Constitution through the Commissioner of Internal Revenue.

VON BÜLOW, Claus (1926–)

HIS STEPCHILDREN ACCUSED HIM OF TRYING TO MURDER HIS RICH WIFE— THE SECOND JURY DISAGREED

Claus Cecil Borberg was born in Copenhagen, Denmark, on August 11, 1926, son of Svend and Jonna Borberg. Svend was a successful playwright and drama critic, and Jonna a beautiful, vivacious woman, was the daughter of Fritz Bülow, who was both a successful businessman and a respected public official. When Claus was four his mother divorced Svend and went back to her family name of Bülow. Claus attended several boarding schools as a boy, and was still in school when the Germans invaded Denmark in 1940. At the end of the school year he was smuggled out of Nazi-occupied Denmark and joined his mother in London. At the age of 16, after six months cramming for the entrance examinations, he began his studies at Cambridge. In 1946 he became the youngest person to ever graduate from Cambridge with a degree in law. He practiced law for a few years and then went to work for Billionaire oilman J. Paul Getty as an administrative assistant.

Martha Crawford was born six weeks prematurely in a Pullman car on September 1, 1931. Her father, 71-year-old George Crawford, an immensely rich Pennsylvania natural gas magnate, was trying to rush his wife, Annie Laurie, to a New York hospital to give birth, but they didn't make it. Known as Sunny by all who knew her, except for one family friend who persisted in calling her "Choo Choo," Martha grew up surrounded by all the luxury and privilege of extreme wealth. She married Prince Alfred "Alfie" von Auersperg in 1957, when she was 25, and he a few years younger. There were two children by this union: Prince Alexander "Alex" and Princess Annie Laurie "Ala." The marriage lasted for eight years and broke up reasonably amicably.

In 1966 Bülow married Sunny von Auersperg. Shortly thereafter, at Sunny's request, he added the "von" to his name. His ancestry entitled him to use it, but until he married Sunny he had never felt the need. Although his career had remunerated him extremely well, putting him into the upper middle class, his income was vanishingly small alongside of Sunny's inherited wealth, which was well into the tens of millions of dollars. In 1967 the von Bülows had a daughter, whom they named Cosima. Among their several residences, they took a 20-room house in Newport, Rhode Island which a previous owner had named Clarendon Court. The house had been built for a railroad magnate in 1904, and in 1950 it had appeared in the Bing Crosby–Grace Kelly film *High Society* as the rich girl's mansion. They purchased it partly because Sunny's mother already owned a house nearby. Sunny and Claus completely redecorated the house and became active members of Newport society.

On the morning of December 27, 1979, while the von Bülows were staying at their Newport cottage, Sunny's maid, Maria Schrallhammer, tried to wake up her mistress at eight, but was unable to do so. Claus told Maria that Sunny had been up all night, and had imbibed a few drinks, and to let her sleep it off. But as the day wore on and her mistress remained comatose, Maria became increasingly worried and, according to her account, pestered Claus to call a doctor.

At around two o'clock Claus called Dr. Janis Gailitis, a local physician who had treated Sunny before, and left a message with his service. The doctor called back around three. Von Bülow described his wife's symptoms, telling Dr. Gailitis that Sunny had awakened a couple of times, but had gone back to sleep, a story that Maria didn't believe was true. He also described Sunny's drinking problem to the doctor; a problem that the loyal maid refused to believe her mistress suffered from. Gailitis told Claus to watch for any changes in Sunny's breathing and, if such a change occurred, to call him immediately. At around six in the evening, when Sunny's breathing developed a rattling sound, Claus called Dr. Gailitis. The doctor arrived just in time to clear Sunny's mouth of vomit and administer cardiopulmonary resuscitation, thus, with the subsequent aid of a fire department rescue team oxygen mask, saving her life. She was taken to the hospital, her husband riding beside her in the ambulance.

Sunny regained consciousness the next day and recovered completely within a couple of days. The medical tests she was given were not able to attach any specific cause to the incident. They did find that she had abnormally low blood sugar, a fact which would later seem to gain much importance. Maria, who had her suspicions about the incident, resolved to keep a close watch on her mistress, especially when Mr. von Bülow was around.

One year later, on the morning of December 21, 1980, again while staying at the Newport mansion, Sunny von Bülow was found lying unconscious on the bathroom floor. She was rushed by ambulance to Newport Hospital emergency room, where she went into cardiac arrest and was only saved by the frantic efforts of the on-duty physicians. The next day, when Sunny did not recover from her deep coma, she was transferred to the Peter Bent Brigham Hospital in Boston, since renamed the Brigham and Women's Hospital. There a series of blood and urine tests were performed, which found nothing significant beyond very low blood sugar level and a trace of barbiturate. And still, despite the lack of any evident cause, Sunny remained comatose; a silent reminder to the staff that, for all that can now be achieved in medicine, there still remains a vast dark uncharted region for which no chart is given.

As time passed and Sunny failed to regain consciousness, Prince Alex and Princess Ala listened to Maria's suspicions about their stepfather and allowed themselves to become convinced that he had, at the very least, behaved in an unhusbandly manner toward his wife. If Claus was guilty of trying to murder Sunny, they certainly didn't want him inheriting any of her sizable fortune should she die. (Their subsequent behavior suggests that they didn't want Claus inheriting any of their mother's money whether he was guilty or not.) They chose not to tell their fears to the police, preferring to take control of the investigation themselves. They hired Richard Kuh, a former District Attorney of Manhattan now in private practice, to conduct an inquiry into the circumstances surrounding Sunny's two comas.

Keeping the investigation secret from Claus, Kuh interrogated the two von Auersperg children and the maid, Maria, and hired a private detective to gather additional evidence. Maria told of seeing a small black bag in Claus's possession, which contained bottles of pills, and Prince Alex and the private eye conducted a search of the Newport house. They found the bag, and in it, among other things, several hypodermic needles, one of which was caked with some dried substance. They gave the various powders and pills in the bag, along with the suspicious needle, to Dr. Richard Stock, the family physician. He had the residue on the needle analyzed, and the report came back that it was mostly insulin, along with traces of amobarbital and Valium.

On February 1, 1982, over a year after Sunny von Bülow lapsed into an irreversible coma, Claus von Bülow was put on trial in a Newport, Rhode Island, courthouse for the attempted murder of his wife. An impressive body of circumstantial evidence had been marshalled against him, much of it collected, not by the police, but by the private agents of his stepchildren. The medical story of the two comas was told, along with expert evidence that the most probable cause for Sunny's condition was an injection of insulin. Maria testified about the black bag, and claimed to have seen a bottle of insulin in it before Sunny fell into the second coma. She had, she said, shown the bag to Prince Alex and asked him, "For what insulin?" As Sunny was not a diabetic, he had no answer.

It was revealed that Claus had a mistress, Alexandra Isles, who testified against him. He had promised to divorce his wife and marry her, she swore, but he seemed incapable of telling Sunny, getting to the brink several times but backing away each time. She said Claus called her when Sunny went into the coma. When asked whether she still thought the charges against Claus were, as she had at first characterized them, "a pack of nonsense," she replied that she didn't know. Claus, in a gentlemanly gesture, requested that his attorneys not cross-examine her.

Claus von Bülow was convicted on two counts of assault with intent to commit murder on March 16, 1982, after the jury had deliberated for 37 hours. On May 7 he was sentenced to 30 years in prison, but was permitted to stay free on $1 million bail pending his appeal.

Von Bülow then approached Harvard Law Professor Alan Dershowitz and asked him to handle the appeal. Dershowitz, who only took cases that interested him, and who initially assumed that von Bülow was guilty, agreed to meet and talk with von Bülow. Two points about the case especially interested him. The first was a constitutional issue: the black bag, found by the stepchildren's hired investigator, was admitted into evidence even though had it been found by a policeman, searching without a warrant, it would have been inadmissible. As Dershowitz put it in his book *Reversal of Fortune* (1986), "The constitutional issue posed by this private search whose fruits were then turned over to the police and public prosecutors was an important one. A wealthy family's hiring its own private police—who are not bound by the Bill of Rights—raised a profound civil liberties issue which had long interested me." The other point was the question of the notes attorney Kuh had kept when he examined the witnesses at the start of his investigation. The trial judge had ruled that he didn't have to produce them, but Kuh himself had used them to question the testimony of defense witnesses. If Kuh, siding with the prosecution, had access to the notes, shouldn't the defense have the same access?

Dershowitz agreed to handle the appeal, and, on examining the evidence, did not find it nearly as convincing as the jury had. The brief he filed with the Rhode Island Supreme Court was 100 pages long. Along with the extensive legal arguments, it suggested something that is usually neither plausible nor relevant in a criminal appeal: that there was a strong possibility that Claus von Bülow was, in fact, innocent. The prosecution in turn filed a 101-page brief affirming their belief that von Bülow was guilty as sin.

On April 27, 1984, the state Supreme Court reversed the conviction of Claus von Bülow. After thinking it over, the prosecutor's office refiled the charges, and on April 25, 1985, the second trial commenced.

The state Supreme Court had decided in favor of Dershowitz's notion that the defense should have access to the notes attorney Kuh had made when the von Auerspergs' investigation began. Despite Kuh's insistence that the notes contained nothing that could possibly help the defense, Dershowitz and his crew of investigators found several suggestive areas of inquiry in the handwritten documents. The Auersperg children had first discussed buying Claus off to renounce his interest in the estate, before they had settled upon the expedient of having him convicted of attempted murder. Neither Prince Alexander nor the maid, Maria, had made any mention of finding either insulin or hypodermic needles in the black bag at the preliminary interview. Maria had actually made a detailed list of what she saw in the bag: Valium, and unmarked bottles of powder, liquid and pills. Sometime between then and when the private detective, with Prince Alex's help, searched the bag, the needles and a bottle of insulin had miraculously appeared. The notes showed that it was not until January 20, 1981, when the medical tests showed the possibility of excessive insulin in the comatose Sunny that Maria suddenly claimed to remember seeing them there earlier.

Further, there was the matter of the insulin-caked needle. A hypodermic needle that has actually been used to inject some liquid into someone will not be caked on the outside with that liquid. The act of injecting—thrusting the needle through the skin and then pulling it back out—will serve to wipe the tip of the needle clean of anything on it.

The prosecution built up essentially the same case as they had in the first trial. But this time the defense was much more effective, aided by the Kuh papers and expert testimony that the high insulin readings in Sunny's blood tests were almost certainly faulty, and could not be relied on. On July 10, 1985, the second jury found Claus von Bülow not guilty on both counts of attempted murder.

Dershowitz points out in his book that Thomas Noguchi, the chief medical examiner for Los Angeles, wrote that there is a medical condition called islet cell hyperplasia, in which the insulin-producing cells of the pancreas multiply abnormally, that might have caused Sunny's condition. What actually happened to Sunny von Bülow, tragic accident, rare medical condition, or attempted suicide, will probably never be known; but despite the combined efforts of the state of Rhode Island and one of America's richest families to convince them otherwise, the jury in the second trial decided that Claus von Bülow was not involved.

WALKER, John Anthony, Jr. (1937–)

HE MADE HIS FAMILY INTO SPIES AND SOLD HIS COUNTRY'S SECRETS FOR 17 YEARS

Head of what has been described as "the Walker Family Spy Ring," retired Chief Warrant Officer John Walker, U.S.N., was an active spy for the KGB for 17 years before he was arrested by the FBI. It is believed that his activities did more harm to the United States than those of any other spy apprehended since the end of World War II.

Walker and his older brother Arthur were born and grew up in Scranton, Pennsylvania. They attended Saint Patrick's Catholic high school and both were altar boys in their church. Arthur was a good, well-behaved student. John was rebellious and resentful of authority. Arthur enlisted in the navy. John committed a burglary and was caught and put on probation. Arthur spoke to the judge, who agreed to lift the probation if John joined the navy.

Walker enlisted on October 25, 1955, and discovered to his surprise that, although he still resented authority, he liked the navy. A clever person could manipulate the system, once he learned how it worked, and Walker was clever. He served as a radioman on board a submarine tender and then on board a World War II–type diesel submarine. He married 19-year-old Barbara Crowley in 1957, and they had four children, three girls and a boy, over the next six years. After a short while, he was working on the large nuclear submarines. By 1965, Walker was a warrant officer, an impressive achievement for someone who had enlisted without graduating from high school.

In 1968, Walker was communications watch officer at the navy base in Norfolk, Virginia. One day in January he drove to Washington, D.C., parked his car downtown and took a taxi to within a couple of blocks of the Soviet Embassy. He walked by the embassy building several times, perhaps to build up his courage, before going in and asking to speak to "someone in security." The Soviets had a new spy; one who was unbelievably well placed and who would prove to be unbelievably productive.

Later that year, his wife Barbara discovered his secret. They argued about what he was doing, but he intimidated her into silence with threats of what it would do to the family if he were discovered. It was a silence that she found increasingly more difficult to keep.

Over the next few years, Walker became the head of an espionage group that included his brother, Arthur, and a shipmate named Jerry A. Whitworth. They supplied thousands of documents to the Soviets, leaving them stuffed into paper bags full of garbage in dead drops all around Washington. The KGB rewarded them with paper bags full of money.

In 1976, Barbara divorced John, but she still kept silent about his treason, for fear of what his arrest would do to their children. She became a heavy drinker so that she could sleep nights. By this time, Walker had left the navy and started his own business, a private detective agency. The KGB approved, realizing what a splendid cover that made for a spy. In 1978, Walker tried to get his daughter Laura, who had joined the army, to spy for him, but she refused. In 1982, Michael Walker, John's son, joined the navy. Shortly after, he began collecting secret documents for his father.

On November 23, 1984, Barbara Walker called the FBI. It took her a while to convince them that she was serious and not merely a vengeful ex-wife. At the time, she did not know that her son Michael was already trapped by his father's web of intrigue. The FBI began to build a case against Walker, setting up Operation Windflyer to gather evidence and determine who else was involved. On May 20, 1985, they arrested Walker after following him to a dead drop and picking up a paper bag full of classified documents that he left for his Soviet handler. Two days later, his son Michael was arrested on board the aircraft carrier *Nimitz*. Within the next two weeks, Arthur Walker and Jerry Whitworth were also arrested.

It turned out that Whitworth had written several letters to the FBI in 1984, calling himself RUS and offering to expose a 20-year-old spy ring in return for immunity from prosecution. In his first letter he said:

> I have been involved in espionage for several years, specifically I've passed along Top Secret Cryptographic Keylists for military communications. Tech Manuals for same, Intelligence Messages, and etc.
>
> I didn't know that the info was being passed to the USSR until after I had been involved a few years and since then I've been remorseful and wished to be free.

The FBI had communicated with RUS by classified ads, as he suggested, but he never gathered the courage to turn himself in. Now he was under arrest and it was too late.

The harm that the Walker spy ring did to the United States was immense. By passing along great quantities of cryptologic material, they enabled the Soviets to break into and read many of the code systems used by the military, yielding access to its deepest secrets. Just as a partial list, for nearly 15 years, the Soviets must have known the locations of American nuclear submarines while on patrol, the plans for bombings and other military actions during the war in Vietnam, technical manuals on many American cryptologic systems, the capabilities of the U.S. missile submarine fleet and much of its equipment, and how successful the U.S. Navy was in antisubmarine warfare. A defector from the KGB, General Vitaly Yurchenko, stated that the Walker family spy ring was the greatest coup in the history of the KGB.

In 1985 Arthur Walker was sentenced to three life terms in prison. John and Michael Walker pled guilty in a plea bargain that allowed Michael to avoid a life sentence. John received a life sentence, but would be eligible for parole in 10 years. Michael received a 25-year sentence and would be eligible for parole in a little over eight years. In return, Walker agreed to co-operate in an extensive two-year debriefing and to testify in Jerry Whitworth's trial. Whitworth was found guilty of seven counts of espionage and four counts of tax evasion. He was sentenced to 365 years in prison and fined $410,000.

WATERGATE

THE "THIRD-RATE BURGLARY" THAT BROUGHT DOWN A PRESIDENT

In the early morning hours of June 17, 1972, five men, were apprehended by the District of Columbia police department after breaking into the headquarters of the Democratic National Committee at the Watergate complex. The five were soon identified as working for CREEP, the Committee to Reelect the President, and their leader, James McCord, was the security chief of CREEP. As CREEP was controlled by people close to President Richard Nixon, there was media speculation as to how high up the authorization for the break-in had come from, and just what the burglars hoped to find.

In short order the five original burglars were joined by E. Howard Hunt and G. Gordon Liddy, more senior members of CREEP, as defendants in the case. They all maintained a stoic silence in regard to the events of that night up to the day of sentencing. It later became known that Nixon, through his chief aides John Erlichman and Robert Haldeman, had authorized payment of "hush money" to the seven defendants, but the conspiracy of silence worked well enough to prevent the Watergate break-in, "that third-rate burglary," as Haldeman described it, from influencing the results of the 1972 presidential election, in which Nixon beat Democrat Senator George McGovern by an overwhelming landslide.

In March, 1973, the conspiracy began to unravel when James McCord, in a letter to Judge John Sirica who was trying the Watergate case, claimed the direct involvement of CREEP chairman John Mitchell, who had resigned as Attorney General of the United States to head Nixon's reelection campaign. As the revelations unfolded a group of those close to the President, including aides Haldeman and Erlichman, resigned, and FBI director L. Patrick Gray admitted to a specially convened Senate Watergate Committee that he had destroyed Watergate evidence at the direct request of Nixon aides. In June, 1973 John Dean, who had resigned as the President's counsel, testified to the committee that Nixon had himself authorized the payment of hush money.

The burglary itself could have been accepted, if not condoned, as an act of stupidity in the midst of a highly partisan campaign. But Nixon's refusal to admit any wrongdoing, and a consistent and ongoing effort to cover up the facts, brought his presidency to ruin. When the existence of tape recordings of the President's talks to his aides was revealed to the Senate committee by Alexander Butterfield, a junior member of the White House staff, the whole situation began to unravel. Special Prosecutor Archibald Cox tried to get the tapes, and Attorney General Elliot Richardson was promptly ordered by Nixon to fire Cox. Rather than obey the order, both Richardson and his assistant William D. Ruckelshaus resigned. The order was passed down to Solicitor General Robert Bork, who, on October 20, carried out what became known as "the Saturday Night Massacre." This highly unpopular act for the first time brought forth rumblings of impeachment from the congress.

Nixon did turn some of the tapes over to the new special prosecutor, Leon Jaworski, but when one of them was revealed to have a mysterious 18-minute gap on it, the public reaction was worse than anything said during that 18 minutes could have caused. Jaworski refused to be satisfied with the few tapes he had been given, and continued to press for the rest of them. The Senate Watergate committee also wanted the tapes. Nixon refused to hand them over, claiming executive privilege.

On March 1, 1974, Haldeman, Erlichman, Mitchell, and four others were indicted for conspiring to obstruct justice in the Watergate break-in. On July 24 the Supreme Court, in a unanimous decision, ordered Nixon to turn over the tapes. On July 27 the House Judiciary Committee approved the first two articles of impeachment against President Nixon. A third charge was added three days later. The charges embraced obstruction of justice, violation of the oath of office, misusing federal agencies, including the FBI, the CIA, and the IRS, and ignoring subpoenas issued by the House of Representatives.

When his closest remaining aides, including presidential Chief of Staff, General Alexander Haig listened to the tapes that were about to be turned over to the special prosecutor, and heard verification of the charges from the president's own lips, they became convinced that, if he was impeached, he would be found guilty. On August 8, 1974, President Nixon announced his resignation, effective noon the next day.

WEBSTER, Dr. John White (1791–1850)

THE HARVARD PROFESSOR CONVICTED OF MURDER

Sometime in the last quarter of the nineteenth century, an attorney named Ben Butler was heatedly cross-examining a witness in a Massachusetts courtroom. The judge leaned forward to remind Butler that the witness was, after all, a Harvard professor. "Yes, I know, your honor," Butler replied. "We hanged one the other day."

The man to cast this stain upon a great university, from which it took half a century to recover, was Dr. John White Webster, graduate of the Harvard Medical School, who had been the holder of the Erving Chair of Chemistry and Mineralogy at Harvard since 1827. In 1849, he bludgeoned to death fellow Harvard professor Dr. George Parkman.

In the early afternoon of Friday, November 23, 1849, Dr. Parkman, a tall, lean elderly man with a remarkably white set of false teeth, was seen striding toward the Medical College wearing a black frock coat and trousers, a purple silk vest, black stock and high hat. He was never seen again. As he was a prominent, important and easily recognizable man, his disappearance caused quite a stir. He had given the university the land upon which the Medical College now stood; he had endowed the Parkman Chair of Anatomy, then being occupied by Dr. Oliver Wendell Holmes. He could not be allowed to simply vanish.

Twenty-eight thousand handbills were printed and distributed, offering a reward of $3,000 for the doctor alive, or $1,000 for proof of his death. The police began an earnest hunt for a young tough who had robbed the doctor a few months previously.

On Sunday, two days after the disappearance, Professor John White Webster appeared at the Parkman home with the information that he had seen Parkman at the college on the afternoon in question. He had paid Parkman $483 "and some cents" toward an outstanding debt, whereupon Parkman had hurriedly departed. This added to the theory that Parkman had been assaulted for his money. But what had happened to him?

On Tuesday, for no discernible reason, Webster gave a large turkey to Ephraim Littlefield, the janitor at the Medical College. It was two days before Thanksgiving, but in his seven years at the College, Littlefield had never received a present from Webster. Instead of making him grateful, it made him suspicious. He remembered a conversation he had overheard between Webster and Parkman the day before Parkman's disappearance. Parkman had appeared in Webster's laboratory and thundered, "Doctor Webster, are you ready for me tonight?"

"No, Doctor," Webster had answered, "I am not ready tonight."

"Doctor Webster, something must be accomplished tomorrow!" Parkman had replied, shaking his fist at Dr. Webster and exiting.

Littlefield did not understand the import of that conversation, but he became convinced that Webster had something to hide and that he was hiding it in his basement vault at the Medical College. Littlefield determined to find out. He brought a variety of hammers, sledges, crowbars, chisels and drills into his basement apartment at the Medical College, and began knocking a hole in the wall leading to Webster's vault. It took him two days to break through. "I held my light forward, and the first thing I saw was the pelvis of a man and two parts of a leg. I knew this was no place for such things."

The police agreed and placed Dr. Webster under arrest. The usually sedate Boston *Evening Transcript* treated the detention of a Harvard professor with unabashed hyperbole:

> In the streets, in the market place, at every turn, men greet each other with pale, eager looks, and the inquiry, "Can it be true?" And then the

> terrible reply, "The circumstances begin to gather weight against him," is wrung forth; the agitated listener can only vent his sickening sense of horror, in some such expression as that of Hamlet—*O, horrible! O, horrible! most horrible!*

Dr. Webster, protesting his innocence with every step, was brought to trial on March 19, 1850. The evidence against him was all circumstantial, as the body parts in his vault could not be identified, but their cumulative weight was ponderous. He owed Dr. Parkman money, and as security for the loan, he had given Parkman a lien on much of his personal property, including a valuable cabinet containing mineral samples. But without telling Parkman, he had then sold the cabinet. Parkman, understandably miffed, was demanding payment on the note. Webster, who lived far beyond his salary as a Harvard professor, could not pay. Several people had heard angry words between them. It was testified that the body parts that were found, to whomever they had originally belonged, had been dissected by a professional hand. And, most damning of all, Dr. Nathan C. Keep, Parkman's dentist, identified a set of false teeth found in Webster's stove as those he had made for Parkman.

The defense pointed out that it was not unusual for a medical doctor, particularly one in a teaching hospital, to have body parts somewhere about. This was something that the public had long suspected. The bodies, it was asserted, were those of paupers who had died and had their corpses donated to science. The public was not convinced of this. Many notable Bostonians were brought forward to speak of Dr. Webster's good character. Among them were Oliver Wendell Holmes; Jared Sparks, president of Harvard College and John Gorham Palfrey, a former member of Congress and editor of the *North American Review*. Holmes had also spoken for the prosecution in the matter of the dissection of the body.

After a 10-day trial, the jury was out for a bit over three hours before returning a verdict of guilty. Dr. Webster protested his innocence until shortly before his execution and then confessed in great detail.

Dr. Parkman had arrived at Webster's front door demanding his money. When Webster said that he could not pay, Dr. Parkman began shaking his fist and cursing. Webster, in a fury, picked up a stick and hit Parkman over the head. Parkman fell. Webster tried to revive him but discovered that he was dead. He locked the doors, dismembered the body in a laboratory sink and distributed it about the premises.

On August 30, 1850, Dr. John White Webster became the first Harvard professor to be hanged by the neck until he was dead. As President Jared Sparks remarked, "Our professors do not often commit murder."

WEISS, Hymie (1898–1926)

CHICAGO GANGSTER AND ENEMY OF AL CAPONE

Born in Poland as Earl Wajciechowski, Weiss came to the United States with his parents, who settled in Chicago and Americanized their name. Weiss began running with DION O'BANION's North Side Gang while still in his teens and soon became O'Banion's right-hand man. He developed a reputation for cool-headed intelligence and cold-blooded murder. When O'Banion was murdered in his own flower shop in a feud with JOHNNIE TORRIO and AL CAPONE, Weiss took over the leadership of the North Side Gang and swore revenge. GEORGE "BUGS" MORAN, a longtime O'Banion henchman, was his second-in-command.

Weiss attempted to eliminate Torrio and Capone several times, once shooting up Capone's limousine and then attacking Torrio's limousine. In the first attack, they wounded the driver, and in the second, they killed the driver and a dog; but the principals remained unharmed. The third time, Weiss and Bugs Moran nailed Torrio as he was leaving his house; Weiss firing a sawed-off shotgun and Moran an army forty-five. Torrio was nearly killed and decided while in the hospital that this was a good time to retire from active participation in the rackets.

With one down, Weiss now focused on Capone. On September 26, 1926, 10 cars drove slowly past the Hawthorne Inn in Cicero, Illinois. As the cars approached, four or five blank shots were fired, designed to pull Capone outside to see what was happening. Then, after a 10-second pause, a symphony of shotgun, machine gun and pistol shots filled the night air. Over 1,000 rounds were fired in something under 30 seconds; a rate of fire approaching that of an infantry platoon in battle. The windows of every shop on the block were knocked out, and over 30 cars were riddled with bullets. Louis Barko, a Capone bodyguard, was hit in the shoulder, and Mrs. Clyde Freeman, the wife of a race horse owner from Louisiana, was hit in the eye by glass shards from her windshield; her husband was parking their car when the fusillade began.

Capone paid $10,000 for a series of operations to save Mrs. Freeman's sight and determined to get Weiss once and for all. On October 11, 1926, 23 months after O'Banion's slaying, 21 months after Torrio's enforced retirement, and three weeks to the day after the restaurant attack, he struck. As Weiss crossed the street to his State Street office, which was on the floor above O'Banion's flower shop, he was hit with machine gun and shotgun fire coming from two windows across the street. He was killed instantly. Patrick Murray, a member of his gang, was also killed; wounded were Sam Peller, Weiss's driver; W. W. O'Brien, a lawyer trying a case Weiss was interested in; and Benjamin Jacobs, an investigator for O'Brien.

The Holy Name Cathedral, which was an accidental target of the gunman, was hit repeatedly in the cornerstone. The inscription on it, taken from St. Paul's epistle to the Philippians, originally read: "At the name of Jesus every knee should bow in heaven and on earth." Machine gun bullets did a selective job of erasure on the inscription, leaving it reading:

Every Knee Should
Heaven And On
Earth.

Weiss received a gangland funeral, almost as big as that he gave for Dion O'Banion.

WHITE, Stanford (1853–1906)

Distinguished American architect and son of Richard Grant White, a noted essayist and critic, Stanford White was murdered by HARRY KENDALL THAW in the roof theater of Madison Square Garden in New York City, a building that he had designed.

WHITE SLAVERY

The term *white slavery* was used for a person who is held "as though in slavery." It especially applies to girls being held in brothels against their wills and forced into prostitution. The White Slave Traffic Act of 1910, commonly known as the MANN ACT, was passed to prevent the interstate trafficking of such women. Other forms of involuntary servitude that do not involve prostitution are called peonage and are prohibited by the Thirteenth Amendment to the Constitution.

WHITMAN, Charles (1941–1966)

THE TEXAS TOWER SNIPER WHO KILLED 16 PEOPLE BEFORE HE WAS STOPPED

On August 1, 1966, at about 11:30 A.M., Charles Whitman, an ex-Marine who was a student at the University of Texas in Austin, lugged a rifle, a carbine, two pistols and close to 1,000 rounds of ammunition, along with a footlocker full of supplies, up to the top of the 27-story tower on the university campus, which gives a panoramic view of the school and all surrounding it. On his way to the top, he killed a receptionist, Edna Townsley, who was working at the reception desk and two tourists who just happened to be there.

Once on the tower's observation deck, he took the rifle and shot everyone he could see, littering the campus with dead and wounded and fending off all attempts to dislodge him for over an hour and a half. The sniping attack was televised, holding all of Austin hypnotized in front of their sets until it ended. The police cordoned the area off with over 100 officers. They tried sharpshooters and firing at him from a low-flying plane, with no success. Finally, police officer Ramiro Martinez headed a frontal assault on the observation deck from the floor below. Martinez was wounded, and Whitman was killed. The final count of his sniping victims was 16 dead and 30 wounded.

The police then discovered that he had prepared for his morning's escapade by typing a note at home that read in part: "I don't quite understand what is compelling me to type this note. I have been to a psychiatrist. I have been having fears and violent impulses. I've had some tremendous headaches in the past. I am prepared to die. After my death, I wish an autopsy on me to be performed to see if there's any mental disorder." He added that he was going to kill his wife, Kathy. There was a postscript that read: "I have just killed my mother. If there's a heaven, she's going there. If there's not a heaven, she's out of her pain and misery." Whitman's wife Kathy was in bed, stabbed to death. They went to his mother's house and found her also, stabbed and shot to death.

The psychiatrist that Whitman visited about two months before, Dr. Maurice Heatly, had in his notes the observation: "At one point [Whitman] said he was thinking about going up on the tower with a deer rifle and start shooting people." Among the items that Whitman had taken to the observation deck with him were sandwiches, bottles of water, fruit cocktail, a roll of toilet paper and a bottle of Mennen spray deodorant.

The autopsy, performed at his request, found that he had a tumor in the hypothalamus, which is not known to cause homicidal mania.

WILD BUNCH

See: HOLE IN THE WALL GANG

WIRETAP

The earliest form of electronic eavesdropping, and one that gains in popularity and sophistication with each passing year, is the clandestine interception of telephone calls. In 1916, the Thompson Committee, a U.S. Senate committee investigating public utilities, was told by an official of the New York Telephone Company that the New York City police routinely tapped telephone wires—and had been doing so since 1895.

Although in the United States wiretapping was officially outlawed by the attorney general as early as 1924, it was routinely used as a weapon in the continuing war against bootleggers during PROHIBITION. In 1934 the Federal Communications Act prohibited the interception or disclosure of interstate telephone communications, which meant that wiretap evidence could not be used in court. But there was nothing to stop wiretapping to develop other evidence that *could* be used in court.

The FBI, which at first had resisted the use of wiretap, used it heavily in the 1930s. And in the 1940s, when the bureau was put in charge of counterespionage, the tapping of the telephones of private citizens became endemic. President Franklin Roosevelt's attorney general, Robert Jackson, declared in 1940 that the FBI was to watch those who, because of supposed sympathies with "foreign dictators," were "a likely source of federal law violation." After that, every president accepted, or even extended, this wiretapping authority for 25 years, until Attorney General Nicholas Katzenbach declared, and President Lyndon Johnson affirmed, that the federal use of wiretap was to be limited to national security cases and to be done only with the prior approval of the attorney general.

Wiretap is a legal tool of police forces in most states, but only with a warrant signed by a judge, who has to be shown "probable cause" why the police believe that this invasion of privacy will uncover evidence of a specific crime.

WOOD, William P.

The first head of the U.S. SECRET SERVICE, William Wood was a man who craved excitement. During the Mexican-American War, Wood led a company of irregular "marauders." During the Civil War, he spied for the North, spending much of his time behind enemy lines. Sometimes he posed as a Confederate soldier, sometimes as a returning Confederate spy, and sometimes he merely allowed himself to be captured, confident of his ability to escape. President Abraham Lincoln asked Wood to investigate stories that Union prisoners of war were being starved in their Southern prisons. He did so and reported that the stories were true.

When he was appointed keeper of the Old Capitol Prison, Wood assigned some men to act as Southern sympathizers and offer to smuggle mail for the prisoners back home to Richmond. After a while, he had a regular mail service operating, carefully steaming each letter open and reading it before sending it on.

Wood's iconoclastic behavior constantly got him in trouble with higher authorities. One time, he arranged for a prisoner exchange with some Confederate prison camps. When the steamer he and his prisoners were on was stopped by federal troops because Wood did not have the proper authority to conduct the exchange, Wood armed his prisoners, overpowered the federals and went on his way. General Dix of the Union Army complained to Secretary of War Edwin M. Stanton that Wood refused to obey orders.

Among the criminals that were taking advantage of the confusion of war to ply their trade were an army of counterfeiters. It was a time when, by some estimates, half the money in circulation was counterfeit. Wood was enlisted in the fight against counterfeiters and quickly rounded up a few dozen. His efforts in this direction were sidetracked by the assassination of President Lincoln; Wood was one of the chief investigators who pieced together the story of what actually happened.

One of Lincoln's last acts was to approve the idea of creating a federal force to combat counterfeiting. After his death, the plan was carried through, and on July 5, 1865, William P. Wood was sworn in as the first chief of the newly created Secret Service, with the mission of restoring confidence in the currency of the United States. When he resigned on May 5, 1869, the task was well in hand. It was not until the assassination of President William McKinley in 1901 that the job of guarding the president was added to the other Secret Service duties.

WORKMAN, Charlie "the Bug" (1908—)

MURDER INCORPORATED'S ACE EMPLOYEE

The second oldest of Samuel and Anna Workman's seven children, Charlie Workman grew up with his three brothers and three sisters in a tenement on New York City's Lower East Side. Charlie, always the trouble maker and always in trouble, quit school in the ninth grade. He saw no reason to go on to high school when a smart, tough kid could do so well on the streets. By the time he was eighteen his curly hair and good looks had earned him the nickname of "Handsome Charlie," and his coolness and toughness had earned him the respect of the less than honest members of his community.

Charlie's first arrest, in 1926, was for grabbing a package of cotton thread from the back of a truck making deliveries in New York's garment district. He was convicted for stealing the 12 dollars worth of thread, and received a suspended sentence. A few months later he was back in trouble with the police for shooting a man in the head in an argument over money. The case was dropped when the man, who was not seriously hurt, refused to identify Workman as his assailant. These two early brushes with the law established the dual foci around which Workman's life would revolve. His illicit dealings in the garment district grew over the years from petty theft to union racketeering and major extortions, and his penchant for shooting people soon made him a respected member of LOUIS "LEPKE" BUCHALTER's Brooklyn mob—that group of wiseguys who hung out in Midnight Rose's Brownsville candy story and received their orders from Lepke chieftain ALBERT ANASTASIA. This was the organization that *New York World-Telegram* reporter Harry Feeney would soon make infamous as "MURDER, INCORPORATED."

It was Buchalter who gave Workman his lasting MONIKER, saying he was so gutsy he was bugs; and so Workman became "Charlie the Bug" thereafter. He and the other aces of Murder, Inc., men like ABE "KID TWIST" RELES, Harry "Pittsburgh Phil" Strauss, FRANK "DASHER" ABBANDANDO, and Martin "Buggsy" Goldstein, performed "hits"—contract killings—for mob bosses all over the country. For these services the Syndicate paid Workman a flat $125 a week, at a time when the unemployment rate was still over twenty percent and the average salaried employee earned less than $25 a week. Lepke's contract killers were encouraged to supplement their salaries with all they could steal from their victims.

Workman was highly regarded in his chosen vocation. Fellow Murder, Inc. alumnus Allie "Tick Tock" Tannenbaum described Charlie the Bug as "one of the best killers in the country." In October 1935 he was given the most important assignment of his career, one that showed the confidence the mob bosses had in the quality of his work: the murder of mob boss DUTCH SCHULTZ.

Schultz, it seems, was plotting the murder of New York's racket-busting special prosecutor THOMAS E. DEWEY. His fellow gang bosses disagreed, and at a big sit-down (meeting) they told him so. It was bad policy to kill cops, prosecutors or reporters. Dewey was going after Schultz, gathering evidence to bring an indictment against him for crimes connected with bootlegging, gambling, prostitution, and Schultz's various other activities. CHARLEY "LUCKY" LUCIANO, MEYER LANSKY, FRANK COSTELLO, JOE ADONIS, and the other East Coast gang leaders at the sit-down decided that it was smarter to eliminate the witnesses than to go after the prosecutor. Schultz stormed out of the meeting, telling them that they could do what they wanted to, but he was going to get Dewey.

Shortly thereafter Charlie Workman was given the contract on Schultz. He usually worked alone, but this time he took Emmanual "Mendy" Weiss, to act as a back-up, and a driver known only as "Piggy." He and Mendy entered the dining room of the Palace Chop House and Tavern, 12 East Street, Newark, New Jersey, at about quarter past ten on the evening of October 23, 1935. Workman immediately pulled his .38 revolver and headed past the 60-foot length of bar toward the table at the rear. Weiss pulled the sawed-off shotgun from under his overcoat and encouraged the customers and staff toward the front of the room to think of their own safety instead of doing anything silly. Then he came on behind Workman.

Sitting around the rear table were OTTO "ABBADABBA" BERMAN, a mathematics wizard who worked for Schultz, and two Schultz bodyguards; Bernard "Lulu" Rosenkrantz and Abe "Misfit" Landau. Schultz himself had just gone to the bathroom seconds before Workman entered the Chop House. Workman started shooting as soon as he was in range, and he was a crack shot. The two bodyguards managed to get their .45's out, but they were too badly damaged too quickly to do any effective shooting. All three were down within seconds, with anywhere from three to five shots in them.

Workman continued on to the men's room, switching his empty .38 for the .45 stuck in his belt, looking for Schultz. He found Schultz at the urinal and fired twice. One shot went into the wall, the second went into Schultz. It passed through his large intestine, gall bladder and liver before coming out the other side and dropping to the floor. Schultz also dropped to the floor.

As Workman made his way out of the restaurant, the two bodyguards, unbelievably, staggered after him shooting. Too weak and blinded by pain to aim, they managed to shoot up the bar in their attempt to get Workman. Landau actually made it to the street before he collapsed.

Workman was seriously annoyed to discover that his two companions had left the scene in the getaway car before he emerged from the bar. He was forced to run off into the night before the police arrived, and had to walk several miles to find a train station to get back to New York.

All four of Workman's victims died, Schultz lingering the longest, mumbling disjointed phrases through his pain and delirium. His words were taken down by a police stenographer hoping they'd provide some information, about Murder, Inc., but they didn't. Before Schultz became delirious he told police that he didn't recognize his assailant, and it may have been true, although Workman claimed to have worked for Schultz on several occasions.

The murder remained unsolved until 1940, when Abe Reles, to save his own skin, began spilling his guts to District Attorney William O'Dwyer. He told of things the authorities had never dreamed of, including the existence of the murder mob operating out of Midnight Rose's candy story. A few months later Allie "Tick Tock" Tannenbaum was provided with similar motivation, and reached a similar conclusion. Based on evidence supplied by Reles, O'Dwyer began digging up bodies that had been planted by Tannenbaum. By the third body, Tannenbaum was talking his head off to save his skin.

In June, 1941, six years after Dutch Schultz ceased his existence, Charlie Workman was extradited to New Jersey to stand trial for the murder. His imaginative defense was that he had been driving a hearse at the time for a New York City mortician. Halfway through the trial, when his alibi collapsed because the mortician confirming it was shown to be perjuring himself, Workman withdrew his innocent plea, and had his lawyer plead *non vult* (*Non vult contendere*, literally "he will not contest"), a plea used in criminal cases in which the defendant does not contest the charge, although not admitting guilt. (In practice it allows the court to treat the defendant as though he had pled guilty.)

The judge sentenced Charlie Workman to life at hard labor and sent him to Trenton State Prison. In 1944 Mendy Weiss went to the electric chair at SING SING along with Lepke Buchalter and fellow hit man Louis Capone (no relation to Big Al) for an unrelated killing. In 1952 Workman, who was a model prisoner, was transferred to the Rahway State Prison Farm, a medium-security prison. In 1964, after 22 years and 9 months in prison, he was paroled. He ended his days as a notions salesman in the garment district, a job he seemed to enjoy. When asked about the old days he would not respond, except to say that his current life was better.

WORLD SERIES of 1919

THE YEAR THE WHITE SOX FIXED THE SERIES

It is one of the sporting legends of the United States that the baseball World Series of 1919, between the Chicago White Sox and Cincinnati Redlegs, was fixed, and that ARNOLD ROTHSTEIN, famed New York gambler, did the fixing in what has become known as the "Black Sox Scandal."

The facts, as we know them, are more complex. The White Sox were owned by Charles Comiskey, a great baseball fan and one of the founders of the American League. One of his cardinal beliefs was that baseball players should not be paid large salaries. Most of the other team owners shared this philosophy, but Comiskey carried it to extremes. After all, under baseball's reserve clause, a player, once signed, was bound to the team that had signed him. As Comiskey put it, "If they don't play for me, they can't play for anyone." Most of his players were paid the big-league minimum of $2,500 a year, slightly better than the salary of a well-paid workman. To some of his top players, Comiskey generously gave as much as $4,500.

Thirty years before, professional baseball players, suffering under the reserve clause and an attempt to introduce "productivity grades," in which a player would be paid according to his playing record, revolted and quit the major league teams en masse, forming a Players' League, which immediately attracted wide support from the fans. The owners, to protect their lucrative franchises, fought the new league with all their power. They found willing allies in other big businessmen, who were afraid that the idea of workers controlling their means of production might spread. The new teams found it impossible to get bank loans or to raise money, and their games were not reviewed in the newspapers. The league quickly folded.

Despite Comiskey's tight-fisted policy, his team was doing very well during the 1919 season. The players asked the team manager William "Kid" Gleason to go to Comiskey and try to get them raises. Comiskey said no.

Late in the season, as it became clear that the White Sox were going to win the American League pennant, several of the players hit upon the idea of enhancing their salaries by throwing the World Series. The ringleaders were Chick Gandil, the first baseman, and Eddie Cicotte, the team's leading pitcher. They took their scheme to Joe "Sport" Sullivan, a big-time Boston gambler.

Their proposition was that, for a payment of $10,000 a player, they would ensure that the White Sox lost the series. They told Sullivan that it would take eight to ten men to ensure losing and that they would recruit the required extra men. Therefore, the price for the fix was set at a round $100,000, payable in advance.

Sullivan thought the idea was sound, but he did not have the necessary $100,000. However, that presented no serious problem. Arnold Rothstein of New York dealt with that sort of money every day before breakfast. "I'll talk to A.R.," Sullivan promised.

Cicotte and Gandil returned to Chicago and presented their proposal to a select group of their teammates. Enlisted in the plot were "Shoeless Joe" Jackson, left field; Oscar "Happy" Felsch, center field; Claude Williams, pitcher; Charles "Swede" Risbergand, shortstop; George "Buck" Weaver, third base; and Fred McMullin, utility infield. In Shoeless Joe they had the second best hitter in the league, beaten only by Ty Cobb, and in Claude Williams, the team's second-best pitcher. The group included five of the team's eight regular starters and its two best pitchers.

As World Series starting time approached, and no word had come back from Sport Sullivan, Cicotte spoke to Bill Burns, a former baseball player and known heavy gambler who had made a fortune in oil. Burns liked the idea but was unwilling to commit $100,000 of his own money to the scheme. He said he would try to arrange it through Rothstein, whom he did not know personally, but whom he could arrange to meet through mutual connections.

Burns called William Maharg, a Philadelphia gambler and former boxer, and invited him to meet Burns at the Ansonia Hotel in New York. As Maharg later testified: "He said a group of the most prominent players of the White Sox would be willing to throw the coming World Series if a syndicate of gamblers would give them a hundred thousand dollars the morning of the first game. . . . I saw some gamblers in Philadelphia. They told me it was too big a proposition for them to handle, and they recommended me to Arnold Rothstein, a well-known and wealthy New York gambler."

Burns and Maharg went to see Rothstein in the Astor Hotel. Rothstein had already been approached by Sullivan and declined to get involved, saying, "It's too raw. Besides, you can't get away with it." He told the same thing to Burns and Maharg.

Burns then went to another gambler named Abe Attell, an ex-featherweight boxing champion, who claimed that he could fix things up with Rothstein. Attell said that Rothstein had refused to deal with them because he did not know them, but he knew Attell. And now the deal was on.

On the morning of the first day of the series, Burns and Maharg went to Attell to pick up the $100,000 to pass on to the players. Attell said that they needed to keep the money to place the bets and came up with a counter-proposal. He suggested that he would pay $20,000 on the evening of each day that the White Sox lost. That year the first team to win five games won the series, so it would have come out the same.

The White Sox lost the first game, and Burns and Maharg went to get the first installment. Attell now said that he would pay it all at the end of the series. He never paid.

The Cincinnati Redlegs won the series 5–3. Word was out on the street that the series had been fixed and that Rothstein had fixed it. Ban Johnson, president of the American League heard the word even before the series was over and hired private detectives to investigate. On the basis of the investigation, he made a public statement that the series had been fixed, and "the man behind the fixing of the series was Arnold Rothstein."

Rothstein denied it. "There is not a word of truth in the report that I had anything to do with the World Series of last fall. I do not know if it was fixed," he said. "My only connection was to refuse to do business with some men who said they could fix it."

A grand jury investigation was started in Chicago. Three of the players, Cicotte, Jackson and Williams, confessed to the grand jury. Two more, Gandil and Felsch, confessed to the newspapers. The remaining three either denied involvement or stood mute.

Rothstein voluntarily appeared before the grand jury. He was tired of hearing his name connected to such a botched operation.

> The whole thing started when Attell and some other cheap gamblers decided to frame the Series and make a killing. The world knows I was asked in on the deal and my friends know how I turned it down flat. I don't doubt that Attell used my name to put it over. That's been done by smarter men than Abe. But I wasn't in on it, wouldn't have gone into it under any circumstances and didn't bet a cent on the Series after I found out what was under way. My idea was that whatever way things turned out, it would be a crooked Series anyhow and that only a sucker would bet on it.

During the course of the next year, the signed confessions of the three ball players, along with the official minutes of the grand jury hearings, disappeared. When the case was tried in a Chicago courtroom in September 1920, Attell was nowhere to be found; he had fled to Canada and could not be extradited. The three ball players took the FIFTH AMENDMENT on the stand, a relatively new ploy popularized by William J. Fallon, Rothstein's favorite attorney. The only remaining witness was Maharg, and since he was one of the conspirators, his testimony had to be corroborated or it could not be entered as evidence. The judge was forced to dismiss the case.

When the case was being heard by the grand jury, a group of young boys waited outside the courtroom to see the ball players, their heroes, emerge. Shoeless Joe Jackson came out and one of the small boys came up to him. "Say it ain't so, Joe!" the boy demanded.

"I'm afraid it is," Shoeless Joe told him.

X, Malcolm (1925–1965)

THE CHARISMATIC BLACK LEADER ASSASSINATED AT THE HEIGHT OF HIS INFLUENCE

Malcolm X, a Black Muslim leader who had been born Malcolm Little, in Omaha, Nebraska, was a powerful speaker and a charismatic leader. He had become a follower of the Black Muslim movement in 1950, while in prison on a burglary charge. When he was released in 1952, he became a minister of the sect and a trusted aide of Muslim leader Elijah Muhammad. By the early 1960s, he had risen to a position of leadership within the Nation of Islam, the Muslim separatist movement. The Nation believed that blacks and whites could not live together and advocated establishing a separate state for blacks. They believed in defending themselves vigorously, by force if necessary, an ideology that pleased their black supporters and frightened whites. Malcolm X became a favorite of black audiences and the bugaboo of fearful Whites because of his powerful speaking against the white institutions that kept blacks in the cycle of poverty and economic and political subjugation.

In 1963, angered by Malcolm X's distress at the assassination of President John F. Kennedy, and possibly seeing him as a potential rival, Elijah Muhammad suspended him from the Nation. Malcolm used the time to study his Muslim faith and visit Mecca. When he returned to the United States he formed the Organization for Afro-American Unity and announced his vision of Islam, in which blacks and whites could live in harmony side by side. This created a serious schism within the Black Muslim movement, which led to sectarian violence. In 1964, Malcolm X's autobiography (written with the aid of Alex Haley) was published. It presented a strong, articulate story of growing up black in America.

On February 21, 1965, Malcolm X was preparing to speak to a rally of his supporters in the Audubon Ballroom in Manhattan, when three men rushed onto the stage. One of them, Talmadge Hayer, shot and killed Malcolm X with a shotgun at close range. Hayer was grabbed by Malcolm's bodyguards, but somehow the other two escaped. The 22-year-old Hayer confessed but refused to name his accomplices. The police picked up two men, Norman 3X Butler and Thomas 15X Johnson, but Hayer flatly denied that they were involved. Supporters of Malcolm X also doubted whether they were the culprits since, as well-known supporters of Elijah Muhammad, they would have had a hard time gaining entrance to the hall, much less making their way to the stage. Nonetheless, they were convicted.

Y

YALE, Frankie (1885–1928)

Born Frank Uale in Brooklyn, New York, Yale was a partner with JOHNNIE TORRIO in the notorious Five Points Gang and was a master extortionist and murderer before his twenty-first birthday. By the early 1920s, he ran the *UNIONE SICILIANO* as a front for extorting money from Italian shopkeepers.

Torrio and AL CAPONE sent for Yale when someone important had to be killed in Chicago. He is believed to have been responsible for the murders of BIG JIM COLOSIMO and DION O'BANION.

In 1928, Capone discovered that Yale had been double-crossing him, hijacking liquor destined for Capone speakeasies and then selling it back to Capone. On July 1, 1928, a black sedan pulled alongside of Yale's car on 44th Street in Brooklyn, and Yale died in a hail of gunfire. One of the weapons used, a Thompson submachine gun, was traced back to a Chicago gun dealer named Peter von Frantizius, who had made a lot of money supplying money to the Capone organization.

Yale had the biggest funeral of any gangster in New York City up to that time.

YOUNGBLOOD, Herbert (1899–1934)

On Saturday, March 3, 1934, JOHN DILLINGER, noted bank robber and escape artist, used a smuggled gun to escape from the jail at Crown Point, Indiana. He took with him Herbert Youngblood, a black man being held on a murder charge, and two hostages. They escaped in the sheriff's car, letting the hostages out when they were well away from town.

Two weeks later, on Friday, March 16, Youngblood was in a gun battle with three deputy sheriffs in a Port Huron, Michigan, tobacco store. He killed one of the sheriffs and wounded the other two, but they managed to get six bullets into him. In his dying statement, he told the lawmen that he had been with Dillinger the day before. This centered the search for Dillinger in Northern Michigan and across the Canadian border.

Despite the popular myth that dying men do not lie, Youngblood's dying statement was not true; he had actually separated from Dillinger some time before, and at the time Dillinger was with his girlfriend in St. Paul, Minnesota. Perhaps Youngblood was doing Dillinger one last favor, or perhaps he just had a sense of humor.

YOUNGER BROTHERS

RUTHLESS BANKROBBERS AND KILLERS WHO ROAMED THE OLD WEST

Cole Younger (1844–1916)
Jim Younger (1848–1902)
John Younger (1851–1874)
Bob Younger (1853–1889)

Henry and Bersheba Younger had a family of eight sons and six daughters in the years before the Civil War. Of them, four of the sons and all the daughters were decent, respectable folk, and therefore, we know little about them. But the four remaining brothers, Cole, Jim, John and Bob, entered the romantic pages of Western history, although there was nothing of the romantic about them. All four served with Quantrill's Raiders during the Civil War. Bob Younger was only 12 when he joined in the attack on Lawrence, Kansas. Quantrill and his band practiced raping and looting under the guise of warfare, and when the war ended, many of them found it hard to quit the practice.

In 1866, the Younger brothers joined with Frank and Jesse James and formed a gang for the purpose of robbing banks and trains. Over the next 10 years, they robbed scores of banks and killed at least a dozen people. In 1874, John Younger was killed when he and Jim got in a fight with three lawmen, during which two of the lawmen also were killed. On September 7, 1876, the gang robbed the First National Bank of Northfield, Minnesota. The citizens of Northfield, perhaps fed up with having their bank robbed, assaulted the robbers on their way out of town, killing two of them and then forming a posse to follow the rest. The James brothers split off from the Youngers and managed to get away. On September 21, the posse caught up with the Youngers and another gang member named Charlie Pitts and a gun battle ensued. Pitts died, and the Youngers were so wounded that nobody expected them to live. Cole Younger, with 22 bullets in him, managed to stand up in the wagon and bow to a group of women as they arrived in town. All three brothers survived and were sentenced to life in prison. Bob died of tuberculosis in prison, and Jim and Cole were finally released in 1901. Jim committed suicide a year later.

In 1903, Cole Younger and Frank James, living legends of a past time, toured in a Wild West show. Cole wrote his autobiography, *The Story of Cole Younger*, which solidified his and his brothers' place in American myth. *See also:* JAMES BROTHERS

YUMA PENITENTIARY

Opened in 1826 in Yuma, Arizona Territory, Yuma Penitentiary was an example of one of the more severe versions of penology. The prisoners were worked all day and chained to the floor in their cells all night. The conditions, and the guards, were exceptionally brutal. Escape attempts were so common that Yuma became the first prison to set up Gatling guns around the perimeter. It was closed at the beginning of this century and is now a museum.

Z

ZANGARA, Joseph (1900–1933)

A man with an anarchistic turn of mind and a marksmanship medal from the Italian Army, Joseph Zangara emptied his pistol into a car carrying President Franklin D. Roosevelt and Chicago Mayor Anton J. Cermak on a Miami, Florida, street on February 15, 1933. He killed Cermak and wounded several bystanders, but missed Roosevelt entirely. This led to the theory that Zangara was actually a hit man sent by the Italian MAFIA to rub out Cermak, who had declared war on AL CAPONE and his mob in Chicago. If so, it was a secret he took with him to the electric chair.

ZENGER, John Peter (1697–1746)

Born in Germany, John Peter Zenger came to America in 1710. In 1735, while he was the editor of a newspaper called the *New York Weekly Journal*, the newly appointed royal governor of New York, William Crosby, got in a dispute over money with some Dutch merchants. Crosby took the case directly to the Justices of the Supreme Court, probably because he was reasonably sure that a jury would rule against him. As he could both appoint and fire the Supreme Court justices, he thought he could control their decisions. To Crosby's surprise, Chief Justice Morris ruled against him. Crosby promptly removed Morris.

Zenger published editorials in the *Weekly Journal* condemning Crosby's high-handed behavior. Crosby promptly had Zenger arrested and thrown into prison. Zenger was then tried for seditious libel. Andrew Hamilton, a well-respected lawyer from Pennsylvania, told the court that he was going to defend Zenger against the charge of libel by proving that the statements in Zenger's editorials were true. The judge ruled that truth was not a defense against a libel charge, but the jury disagreed. Facing the anger of both the judge and Governor Crosby, it refused to convict Zenger and discharged him.

This case helped establish two basic tenets of American democracy: (1) truth is an absolute defense against libel, and (2) freedom of the press is fundamental to a free society.

ZODIAC

CALIFORNIA'S SERIAL KILLER HAS NEVER BEEN CAUGHT

A Northern California mass murderer in the "Jack the Ripper" mode, the killer who called himself Zodiac sent letters to the newspapers during a series of murders in the late 1960s. Several of them were in the form of cryptograms, which he defied the authorities to solve, claiming that clues to his identity were concealed in the messages. One of them was broken by a local high-school teacher, but it did not contain any usable clue to Zodiac's identity.

The first murders known to be by Zodiac were of 17-year-old David Faraday and his 16-year-old girlfriend, Bettilou Jensen, who were sitting in Faraday's parked car on a road outside of Vallejo, California, when he struck. He shot David three times in the head with a .22 caliber pistol before the boy could move. Bettilou leapt from the car screaming and ran off down the road. Zodiac killed her with five bullets in the back. This was on December 10, 1968.

On July 4, 1969, Zodiac attacked another young couple in their car, which was parked in a public park outside of Vallejo. The girl was killed. The 19-year-old boy survived four gunshots but was unable to give a good description of their assailant, since Zodiac had shone a powerful flashlight in their faces.

One month later, on August 4, Zodiac wrote a gloating letter to the San Francisco newspapers, daring the police to catch him. He subsequently killed Cecelia Shepard, her multiple stab wounds forming the rough shape of a cross in her back. When he killed a cab driver and took a piece of his victim's bloody shirt away with him, he was seen leaving the scene. The witnesses described a young, white male with short reddish-brown hair, wearing thick eyeglasses.

The Zodiac's murder spree ended by 1971, and he was never heard from again. Letters claiming to be from Zodiac eventually claimed that he had taken more than 30 victims, to use them all as slaves in the afterlife. The police total was six.

Glossary of Legal Definitions

The laws of each state and criminal jurisdiction define crimes in slightly different ways. But there are some basic understandings of what actions constitute what crimes. Here is a list of the basic definitions of various criminal activities and of legal terms used in their prosecution.

ABET—To encourage, incite or assist another to commit a crime.

ABSCOND—To hide or flee in order to prevent the legal process.

ACQUIT—To find a defendant not guilty of a crime.

ADMISSION—A statement made by a person that may be used in evidence against him or her.

ADULTERY—Sexual intercourse between two people, at least one of whom is married to someone else.

AFFIDAVIT—A statement sworn to before a notary public or other person with the legal authority to administer an oath.

AGGRAVATED ASSAULT—A particularly fierce or reprehensible assault; an assault resulting in serious bodily injury; an assault committed intentionally while committing another crime.

ALIBI—A defense in which it is claimed that the accused could not have committed the crime because he or she was elsewhere at the time.

ANTITRUST—A federal statutory crime; violating laws intended to promote free competition in the marketplace. The two most important antitrust laws are the Sherman Act, which protects the rights of individuals to compete freely and makes illegal any contract, combination or conspiracy in restraint of trade, and the Clayton Act, which addresses some of the vagueness in the Sherman Act.

APPEAL—A complaint to a superior court about the actions of an inferior court.

ARRAIGNMENT—The process of charging a defendant and taking his or her plea.

ARREST—Depriving a person of his or her liberty by legal authority. An arrest must be based upon probable cause that the person has committed an offense. A person can be detained by police authorities for some length of time, usually 48 hours, on suspicion, without making a formal arrest but must be either released or arrested after this time.

ARSON—Willfully or maliciously burning or attempting to burn any property.

ASSAULT—Intentionally inflicting or attempting or threatening to inflict bodily harm. If it is merely an attempt, it must be accompanied by the apparent willingness and ability to carry out the threat to complete the offense.

AUTOPSY—The dissection and medical investigation of a corpse to determine the cause of death.

BAIL—The sum of money held by the court to be defaulted if a defendant neglects to appear for trial.

BATTERY—The unlawful infliction of force or physical harm, however slight, by one person upon another.

BLACKMAIL—The extortion of money or other things of value from someone by threatening bodily harm or by threatening to expose real or fictitious immoral conduct or criminal activity.

BRIBERY—Paying or offering to pay money or provide something else of value to a public official, police officer, judge, witness or government employee to unlawfully influence their actions.

BURGLARY—Breaking and entering another's property with intent to steal. In common law, it was the act of breaking into a dwelling place during the hours of darkness. It has been extended to cover daylight hours, but in some jurisdictions, the time of day is still relevant to the seriousness of the crime, with burglary after dark carrying a stiffer penalty than burglary during the day.

CAPITAL OFFENSE—A criminal act punishable by death. In the United States, capital offenses are usually limited to murder and treason in time of war. In some states, under what are known as the "little Lindbergh laws," kidnapping is also a capital offense.

CHURNING—The buying and selling of securities by a stockbroker for the purpose of generating commissions without regard to his or her clients' needs.

CIRCUMSTANTIAL EVIDENCE—The provable facts surrounding an event from which the circumstances of the event can be inferred by a process of logic.

COMMON LAW—The body of law originating in England that is based upon judicial precedent rather than statute. It is more flexible than statute law, since it grows and changes with the passage of time, as new events demand new interpretations.

COMPOUNDING A FELONY—Allowing a felon to escape punishment by refusing to aid in the prosecution or abetting in the felon's escape in return for a reward. A victim who offers to refuse to prosecute if a burglar returns the stolen goods is compounding a felony.

CONFESSION—A voluntary statement admitting to the commission of a crime.

CONFIDENCE GAME—An illegal stratagem for taking money away from victims by first gaining their confidence and then knowingly misleading them as to the facts upon which they will base a decision to invest or otherwise dispose of their money.

CONSPIRACY—An agreement by two or more persons to commit an unlawful act or to use unlawful means to commit an act not in itself unlawful. The conspiracy itself is illegal even if the act is not committed.

CORPORAL PUNISHMENT—Physical punishment upon the body of the felon, such as whipping. Currently out of favor as cruel and unusual.

CORPUS DELICTI—Latin phrase meaning "the body of the crime." Often misunderstood to mean the corpse in a murder case, it actually refers to the proof that a crime has been committed. In a murder case, it is helpful to have the corpse to establish the *corpus delicti*, as without one, it is usually difficult to prove that the victim has actually been murdered.

COUNTERFEITING—Manufacturing representations of or altering money, stamps or other negotiable instruments of the United States or any other government. The crime also includes the passing of such manufactured or altered instruments.

COURT-MARTIAL (PLURAL: COURTS-MARTIAL)—Military courts constituted for trying and punishing military crimes, such as crimes committed on a military base or crimes committed by a member of the military while in uniform or acting in a military capacity or purely military offenses such as desertion or conduct unbecoming an officer.

DEFENDANT—In a criminal trial, the person accused of the crime.

DISTRICT ATTORNEY—The officer of a governmental authority, such as a city, county or state, charged with prosecuting those accused of crimes. The district attorney may have many assistants, depending on the size of the district.

DOUBLE JEOPARDY—A doctrine arising from the Fifth Amendment to the Constitution of the United States which forbids a person accused of a crime from being "twice put in jeopardy of life or limb." A fundamental tenet of U.S. law, it provides that a defendant cannot be tried twice for the same crime, whatever the outcome of the first trial. An exception is made in the case of a mistrial granted through necessity.

EMBEZZLEMENT—Not a crime under common law, but one created by statute, this is the fraudulent appropriation of property by one to whom it has been entrusted or by one into whose hands it has passed lawfully, such as a bank teller handling the bank's money.

ENTRAPMENT—The use by the police or other government agency of an *agent provocateur* to induce a person to commit a crime that he or she would not otherwise have committed for the purpose of arresting him or her.

EXTORTION—Originally, under common law, the taking of money by a public official as an excessive or unauthorized fee. Now, the illegal taking of money by threats or other forms of fear and coercion, but not including direct robbery.

FELONY—Generally, a crime punishable by imprisonment for more than one year or by death. The original common law felonies were arson, burglary, larceny, mayhem, murder, rape and robbery.

FENCE—A knowing receiver of stolen property.

FIFTH AMENDMENT—Part of the Bill of Rights, the Fifth Amendment to the Constitution of the United States provides that no person can be tried for a major crime unless an indictment has been issued by a grand jury, that no defendant of a criminal trial can be put in double jeopardy, that no person can be required to testify against himself, that neither life, liberty nor property can be taken without due process of law and that private property cannot be taken by the government without compensating the owner for its loss. A defendant can "take the Fifth" if he or she declines to testify because the testimony might be self-incriminating.

FORGERY—Creating or altering a document or other writing for fraudulent purposes. Also the creating of false evidence.

FRAUD—Depriving a person of property or legal rights by unlawful deception, concealment or misrepresentation.

FRUIT OF THE POISONOUS TREE DOCTRINE—A rule of evidence stating that evidence obtained as either the direct or indirect result of an illegal act on the part of a government official cannot be used against the defendant in a criminal trial. This doctrine, obviously needed to prevent excesses of police zeal, is slowly being relaxed as the Supreme Court gets more conservative.

GRAND JURY—A group of people sworn to inquire into crimes at the behest of the state's attorney and bring indictments against those reasonably accused of the crimes.

GRAND LARCENY—*see* Larceny.

HABEAS CORPUS—Latin phrase meaning "you have the body." Known as the Great Writ, the writ of habeas corpus is used to invoke a judicial determination as to whether the detention of an individual is legal. Thus it tends to prevent people being detained by police authority without being properly charged with a crime. It is also the writ which is used by federal courts to determine whether a conviction in a state court has followed due process of law.

HOMICIDE—*see* Murder.

ILLEGAL—Against the law. Subjecting one to trial

and, on conviction, to imprisonment, fines or sanctions.

INDICTMENT—A formal accusation submitted by the district attorney or other public prosecutor under oath to a grand jury charging one or more persons with a crime. If the grand jury determines that a crime has been committed and that there is probable cause to assume that the person or persons named in the indictment committed the crime, they pass out a true bill, and the district attorney can then take the case to trial.

INQUEST—A trial, often without a jury, by a coroner to determine the cause of death in any case where the deceased has been killed, or has died suddenly or in suspicious circumstances or in prison. It is a trial of the facts rather than of a person.

INSANITY—The legal understanding of insanity in a criminal trial is "that degree or quantity of mental disorder which relieves one of the criminal responsibility for his actions." There are three standards generally used to determine whether a criminal defendant can be regraded as legally insane: The M'Naghten Rule, formulated in eighteenth-century Great Britain, holds that a person is not responsible for criminal acts if, as a result of mental disease or defect, he or she did not understand his or her action or that it was wrong, or that he or she was under a delusion that, if true, would be an adequate defense for the action. The first major modification of M'Naghten was the Durham Rule, adopted by the District of Columbia Court of Appeals in 1954. It holds that, "an accused is not criminally responsible if his unlawful act was the product of mental disease or mental defect. This was further modified by the test proposed by the American Law Institute's Model Penal Code of 1962 (known as the ALI Test). A combination of the two preceding rules, the ALI Test holds that "a person is not responsible for criminal conduct if at the time of such conduct as a result of mental disease or defect he lacks substantial capacity either to appreciate the criminality of his conduct or to conform his conduct to the requirements of law." However, it specifically excludes repeated criminal conduct, as such, from being a sign of mental defect. A finding of insanity precludes finding a defendant guilty of a crime. Because of this, and fears that a criminally insane person could more easily get out of confinement from an asylum than from a prison, it has been suggested, and adopted in some jurisdictions, that the finding of "not guilty by reason of insanity" be replaced by "guilty but insane."

JURY—A group of (usually 12) people called and sworn to hear and judge the facts of the issue in a trial.

KIDNAPPING—Unlawfully taking and carrying away a person against that person's will.

LARCENY—Taking the property of another unlawfully and depriving the owner of its use. It is commonly divided into grand larceny and petty larceny (originally "petit larceny") by the dollar value of the items so taken. The amount varies from state to state, and in some states, automobile theft or larceny by extortion becomes grand larceny regardless of the dollar value involved.

LIBEL—False and malicious publication of material with the intention of defaming a living person. Normally a tort, not a criminal act. If the material is spoken rather than written, the offense is slander.

MANN ACT—The White Slave Traffic Act. A federal statute prohibiting the transportation of a woman in interstate commerce for the purpose of prostitution or any other immoral purpose. Originally intended to prevent the organized movements of prostitutes, it has been used in the past to harass unmarried couples who drive across state lines and stop at a hotel overnight.

MANSLAUGHTER—The unlawful killing of another person without malice or premeditation. Considered less serious than murder, where the element of malice is present, it is usually divided into voluntary and involuntary manslaughter. Voluntary manslaughter is the intentional killing of another individual in the heat of passion, without forethought, such as in a fight. Involuntary manslaughter, also called negligent manslaughter or criminally negligent homicide, is the killing of someone through recklessness or negligence, such as the reckless driving of an automobile.

MISDEMEANOR—A criminal offense less than a felony, usually one punishable by a small fine or a jail sentence of under one year.

MURDER—Unlawful homicide with malice aforethought. As opposed to manslaughter, where the element of malice is missing. It is divided into two classes: first-degree murder, which is the willful, deliberate and premeditated killing of a human being, and second-degree murder, in which the element of premeditation is missing. Felony murder, a killing during the commission of a felony, or as a result of a felony, is regarded as first-degree murder.

PARDON—The relief of someone from further punishment for a criminal act. The power of pardon is vested in the chief executive: the president, or the governors of the various states. It is limitless except, in some state constitutions, in cases of treason or a judgment on impeachment.

PAROLE—A conditional release from prison which reserves the right to return the parolee to prison if any of the conditions of the parole are violated.

PERJURY—Knowingly making false statements while under oath.

PETTY LARCENY—*see* Larceny.

POSSE COMITATUS—Latin phrase meaning "to be able to be an attendant." A person called upon to aid a sheriff in effecting an arrest. While not an officer, a person acting as *posse comitatus* has, for the duration of such action, the same protection under the law for his actions as the sheriff who called him.

POST MORTEM—Latin phrase meaning "after death." The examination of a body to determine the cause of death. To satisfy the law in particular instances, this may or may not include an autopsy.

PROBATION—A condition in which a person found guilty of a crime is sentenced to supervised release rather than imprisonment. If the person violates the terms of probation, he or she can be put in prison to serve out the remainder of his or her sentence.

PUBLIC DEFENDER—An attorney working for the local government who represents anyone accused of a crime who cannot afford to hire his or her own attorney.

RACKETEERING—An organized conspiracy to commit extortion or other crime.

RAPE—Sexual assault. Unlawful sexual intercourse with a person by force or threat without his or her consent. Statutory rape is the crime of having sexual intercourse with a female under the age of consent, an age set by state law, which varies from 11 to 18 years.

ROBBERY—The felonious taking of anything of value from another by force or the threat of force.

SEARCH WARRANT—A written authority issued by a judge directing police authorities to search a specified premises for a specified object or objects. The Fourth Amendment of the Constitution of the United States requires that police searches be conducted only after a warrant is obtained and that warrants may be issued only upon the show of probable cause that the specified object is at the specified location.

SLANDER—Spoken statements that are untrue and that tend to defame another. Truth is regarded as an absolute defense against a charge of slander. This is usually a tort, subjecting the slanderer to lawsuit rather than a criminal offense. If the statements are written rather than spoken, they are libel.

TREASON—Under the United States Constitution, treason is the crime of levying war against the United States or adhering to its enemies and giving them aid and comfort. It takes two witnesses to an act of treason, or a confession in open court, to obtain a conviction. It is a capital offense, but usually a prison sentence is given if the act is committed during peacetime. The only exceptions to this were the executions of Julius and Ethel Rosenberg.

VENUE—The geographical area in which the crime is committed; the governmental subdivision in which the accused will be tried.

VERDICT—The finding of a jury, regarding the guilt or innocence of a person standing trial.

Chronology

1701—(May 21) Pirate captain WILLIAM KIDD is hanged in London.

1718—(November 22) EDWARD TEACH, better known as "Blackbeard the Pirate," is killed in a swordfight by Lieutenant Robert Maynard, of H.M.S. *Pearl*.

1739—(September 9) The slave rebellion in STONO, North Carolina, results in the death of three score whites and over a hundred slaves.

1775—DOCTOR BENJAMIN CHURCH of Boston is arrested for treason against the Continental Congress.

1778—BATHSHEBA SPOONER kills her husband with the aid of her lover and three passing British deserters.

1786—12-year-old HANNAH OCUISH kills 6-year-old Eunice Bolles in a fight over some strawberries. She is hanged.

1807—Ex-vice president AARON BURR is tried for treason. He is acquitted.

1850—ALLAN PINKERTON founds the Pinkerton's National Detective Agency.

—(August 30) Harvard Professor, JOHN WHITE WEBSTER, is hanged for the murder of Harvard Professor George Parkmann.

1859—(February 27) DANIEL SICKLES, a member of Congress, murders Philip Barton Key, United States District Attorney and son of the composer of the National Anthem, in front of the White House in Washington, D.C., for having an affair with his wife.

1866—(May) The KU KLUX KLAN is founded in Pulaski, Tennessee.

1871—(May 17) EDWARD HOWARD RULOFF, a brilliant sociopathic killer, is hanged in New York. His brain, donated to Cornell University, is found to be seven ounces heavier than the average.

1875—"Hanging Judge" ISAAC PARKER becomes a Judge on the Arkansas circuit.

1881—(October 26) Wyatt Earp and his brothers have a gunfight with the Clanton clan in Tombstone, Arizona's O.K. Corral. (*see* EARP BROTHERS)

1882—(April 3) Bank robber Jesse James is murdered for the reward by fellow bank robber Bob Ford. (*see* JAMES BROTHERS)

1892—(August 4) Andrew Borden and his wife Abby are murdered in their home. Andrew's daughter LIZZIE BORDEN will be accused of the crime, tried and acquitted.

1896—(May 7) HERMAN WEBSTER MUDGETT, builder of Chicago's infamous murder castle, who killed over 100 people before he was caught, is hanged.

1900—(February 1) THE EVERLEIGH CLUB, Chicago's most luxurious bordello, opens for business.

1906—(June 25) HARRY KENDALL THAW kills architect Stanford White in a jealous fit over White's previous relationship with Thaw's wife, the beautiful Evelyn Nesbit.

1919—AL CAPONE moves to Chicago to help his old friend JOHNNY TORRIO.

1920—(January 17) PROHIBITION becomes the law of the land.

1922—(September 16) The Reverend Edward

Hall and choir singer Eleanor Mills are found shot to death in a field outside New Brunswick, New Jersey. (*see* HALL-MILLS CASE)

1924—(May 10) J. EDGAR HOOVER is appointed head of the Bureau of Investigation, which will become the F.B.I.

—(May 21) LEOPOLD & LOEB murder 14-year old Bobby Franks in Chicago.

1925—CLARENCE DARROW defends John T. Scopes in a Tennessee courtroom for the crime of teaching evolution. Scopes is convicted.

1926—(June 23) After disappearing for a month, Evangelist AIMEE SEMPLE MCPHERSON, reappears with a tale of having been kidnapped. It soon becomes clear that she actually ran off with Kenneth Ormiston, who ran the Temple radio station.

1927—(August 23) Anarchists Nicola Sacco and Bartolomeo Vanzetti are executed in Massachusetts for a murder they almost certainly did not commit. (*see* SACCO AND VANZETTI)

1928—ELIOT NESS becomes head of a special prohibition enforcement unit in Chicago that became famous as "the Untouchables."

—(November 4) ARNOLD ROTHSTEIN, "The Big Bank Roll," is murdered in New York's Park Central hotel.

1929—(February 14) The SAINT VALENTINE'S DAY MASSACRE takes place in a Chicago garage.

—(March 9) In a true locked-room mystery, laundry man ISADOR FINK is found shot dead in his small New York shop with all the windows and doors closed and locked from inside.

1931—(March 31) In what will become known as the SCOTTSBORO CASE, nine negro boys are indicted for raping two white women in Alabama. Although it quickly becomes clear that they are innocent, it will take years to get them out of prison.

1932—(March 1) The baby son of Charles and Annie Morrow Lindbergh is kidnapped from his crib at their New Jersey home. (*see* LINDBERGH KIDNAPPING)

1934—(January 1) ALCATRAZ Federal Penitentiary, the "escape proof" prison in San Francisco Bay, opens for business.

—(July 22) Bank robber, JOHN DILLINGER, is gunned down by the F.B.I.

1935—(January 26) MA BARKER is killed in a gunfight with the F.B.I. (*see also* BARKER-KARPIS GANG)

—(October 23) Ganglord DUTCH SCHULTZ is gunned down in a New Jersey tavern by MURDER INCORPORATED hitman CHARLIE "THE BUG" WORKMAN.

1936—(April 3) Carpenter Bruno Richard Hauptmann dies in the electric chair in Trenton, New Jersey for the kidnapping of the Lindbergh baby. (*see* LINDBERGH KIDNAPPING)

—(May 1) Bank robber, ALVIN KARPIS, surrenders to FBI chief J. EDGAR HOOVER.

—(June 7) Prosecutor THOMAS E. DEWEY wins a conviction against CHARLIE "LUCKY" LUCIANO for sixty two counts of compulsory prostitution and sends Luciano to prison.

1939—(August 6) New York Supreme Court Justice JOSEPH CRATER disappears.

1940—ABE "KID TWIST" RELES reveals to the astounded authorities the existence of MURDER, INCORPORATED.

1944—(March 4) LOUIS "LEPKE" BUCHALTER, head of MURDER, INCORPORATED, dies in the electric chair at Sing Sing.

1947—(June 20) BENJAMIN "BUGSY" SIEGEL, the man who found Las Vegas for the mob, is murdered in the house of his girl friend VIRGINIA HILL in Beverly Hills.

1948—COLONEL RUDOLF ABEL, Soviet spymaster, enters the United States.

—WHITTAKER CHAMBERS accuses ALGER HISS of treason.

1952—(February 18) Bank robber, WILLIE "THE ACTOR" SUTTON, is spotted on a New York street by crime buff ARNOLD SCHUSTER, and arrested by the police. Schuster is murdered on March 8 at the direction of Mafia boss, ALBERT ANASTASIA, who "can't stand squealers."

1953—(June 18) ETHEL AND JULIUS ROSENBERG are executed for treason in New York's SING SING prison.

1957—(June 21) COLONEL RUDOLF ABEL is arrested by the F.B.I.

—(November 14) Mafia bosses from all over the United States meet at the Apalachin, New York home of Joseph Barbara for a conference. (*see* APALACHIN CONFERENCE)

1962—(June 14) ALBERT DESALVO, the Boston Strangler, kills his first victim.

1963—JOSEPH VALACHI, a button man in the Genovese crime family, tells the McClellan committee all about the MAFIA.

1965—(February 21) Black Muslim leader, MALCOLM X, is murdered in the Audubon Ballroom in New York City.

1966—(August 1) Ex-marine CHARLIE WHITMAN climbs to the top of a tower at the University of Texas in Austin and begins shooting people on the ground below.

1967—The SUPREME COURT declares the death penalty unconstitutional under existing statutes. There will be no executions in the United States for the next nine years until the States re-write the statutes. During this time the average annual number of murders in the United States neither increases nor decreases. (*see* CAPITAL PUNISHMENT)

1969—(August 9) CHARLES MANSON sends members of his cult to the Los Angeles house of Terry Melcher to kill everyone inside. They murder actress, Sharon Tate, who was renting the house, and three of her friends.

1973—(August 7) Elmer Henley Jr. shoots mass murderer DEAN CORLL and reveals Corll's torture chamber to the police.

—(October 10) SPIRO AGNEW resigns the vice-presidency of the United States to avoid bribery charges.

1974—(February 5) PATRICIA CAMPBELL HEARST is kidnapped from her Berkeley, California apartment.

1975—(July 30) Teamster ex-president, JAMES HOFFA, leaves the Manchus Red Fox restaurant in Detroit and is seen no more.

1976—(July 15) Three men wearing stocking masks kidnap a school bus full of children outside of CHOWCHILLA, California. (*see* CHOWCHILLA KIDNAPPING)

1977—(August 10) "Son of Sam killer DAVID BERKOWITZ is arrested in New York as he approaches his car.

1978—(February 15) Serial killer TED BUNDY is caught in Florida driving a stolen car. He will be convicted of multiple murders and executed on January 24, 1989.

—(December 21) "Killer Clown" JOHN WAYNE GACY is arrested on a drug charge. Within hours the police will begin finding some of the many bodies buried under his house.

1982—(February 1) CLAUS VON BÜLOW goes on trial in Newport, Rhode Island, for the attempted murder of his wife Sunny.

1989—(January 24) After spending close to 10 years in Florida's death row, mass murderer THEODORE BUNDY goes to the electric chair.

1991—(July 22) Flagged down in the street by an hysterical Tracy Edwards, two Milwaukee policemen enter the apartment of JEFFREY DAHMER to find, among other macabre momentoes, a severed human head in the refrigerator.

1992—(April 2) Mafia boss JOHN GOTTI, "The Teflon Don," is found guilty by a Federal jury in New York, of fourteen counts ranging from tax evasion to murder, and sent to prison for life.

—(May 20) 17-year-old AMY FISHER is arrested for the attempted murder of her lover's wife, Mary Jo Buttafuoco.

Selected Bibliography

GENERAL

Alderman, Ellen & Kennedy, Caroline, *In Our Defense*, New York, William Morrow, 1991

Alix, Ernest Kahlar, *Ransom Kidnapping in America, 1874–1974*, Carbondale and Edwardsville, Southern University Press, 1978

Asbury, Herbert, *Gem of the Prairie*, New York, Knopf, 1940

Ashton-Wolfe, H., *The Forgotten Clue*, New York, Houghton Mifflin, 1930

Browning, Frank & Gerassi, John, *The American Way of Crime*, New York, G.P. Putnam's Sons, 1980

Cooper, Courtney Ryley, *Designs in Scarlet*, New York, Little, Brown & Co., 1939

Corey, Herbert, *Farewell, Mr. Gangster!*, New York, D. Appleton-Century Company, 1936

Hooton, Earnest Albert, *Crime and the Man*, Cambridge, Mass., Harvard U. Press, 1939

Israel, Jerold H. & LaFave, Wayne R., *Criminal Procedure: Constitutional Limit*, New York, West Pub. Co. pb. 1975

Kavanagh, Marcus, *The Criminal and His Allies*, New York, Bobbs-Merrill, 1928

Kerner Commission, *The Kerner Report* [*on Civil Disorders*], New York, Pantheon, 1968

Leibowitz, Robert, *The Defender: The Life And Career of Samuel S. Leibowitz*, New York, Prentice Hall, 1981

Leighton, Isabel (ed.), *The Aspirin Age 1919–1941*, New York, Simon & Schuster, 1949

Sullivan, Edward D., *Rattling the Cup on Chicago Crime*, New York, Vanguard Press, 1929

Train, Arthur, *Courts and Criminals*, New York, Charles Scribner's Sons, 1926

——— *My Day In Court*, New York, Charles Scribner's Sons, 1938

——— *The Prisoner at the Bar*, New York, Charles Scribner's Sons, 1926

——— *True Stories of Crime*, New York, Charles Scribner's Sons, 1908

Wolf, Marvin J. & Mader, Katherine, *Fallen Angels: Chronicles of L.A. Crime and Mystery*, New York, Facts on File, 1986

Wolsey, Serge G., *Call House Madam*, San Francisco, Martin Tudordale, 1942

CON GAMES, FRAUDS & SWINDLES

Asbury, Herbert, *Sucker's Progress*, New York, Dodd, Mead, 1938

Gentry, Curt, *The Vulnerable Americans*, New York, Doubleday, 1966

Gibson, Walter B., *The Bunko Book*, New York, Sidney H. Radner, 1946

Klein, Alexander, *The Double Dealers*, New York, Lippincott, 1958

——— *Grand Deception*, New York, Lippincott, 1955

Koschitz, *Koschitz's Manual of Useful Information*, Kansas City, MO., McClintock & Koschitz, 1894

MacDonald, John C., *Crime Is a Business*, Stanford, Stanford U. Press, 1939

Nash, Jay Robert, *Hustlers and Con Men*, New York, M. Evans, 1976

Rudensky, Morris (Red) & Riley, Don, *The Gonif*, Blue Earth, Minn., The Piper Company, 1970

Robertson, Frank G. & Harris, Beth Kay, *Soapy Smith, King of the Con Men*, New York, Hastings House, 1961

CRIMINALISTICS

Bridges, B.C. (rev. by Charles E. O'Hara), *Practical Fingerprinting*, New York, Funk & Wagnalls, 1942/1963

Browne, Douglas G. and Brock, Alan, *Fingerprints: Fifty Years of Scientific Crime Detection*, New York, Dutton, 1954

Federal Bureau of Investigation, *Fingerprint Identification*, U.S. Government Printing Office, 1991

Federal Bureau of Investigation, *Handbook of Forensic Science*, U.S. Government Printing Office, 1975

Helpern, Milton, M.D., with Bernard Knight, M.D., *Autopsy*, New York, St. Martins Press, 1977

Houts, Marshall, *Where Death Delights*, New York, Coward-McCann, 1967

Inbau, Fred E., *Lie Detection and Criminal Interrogation* (Second Edition), Baltimore, The Williams & Wilkins Co., 1948

Lewis, Alfred Allan, *The Evidence Never Lies*, New York, Dell, 1984

Soderman, Harry and O'Connell, John J., *Modern Criminal Investigation*, New York, Funk & Wagnalls, 1935

Soderman, Harry and O'Connell, John J., *Modern Criminal Investigation* (fourth edition), New York, Funk & Wagnalls, 1952

Thorwald, Jürgen, *Crime and Science*, New York, Harcourt, Brace & World, 1967

CRIMINOLOGY

Clark, Ramsey, *Crime in America*, New York, Simon & Schuster, 1970

Clinard, Marshall B., *Sociology of Deviant Behavior*, New York, Holt Rinehart & Winston, 1974

Forer, Lois G., *Criminals and Victims*, New York, W.W. Norton, 1980

Jeffery, C.R., *Criminal Responsibility and Mental Disease*, Springfield, Illinois, Charles C. Thomas, 1967

Katzenbach, Nicholas *et al, The Challenge of Crime in a Free Society: A Report by the President's Commission on Law Enforcement and Administration of Justice*, New York, Avon, 1968

Reid, Sue Titus, *Crime and Criminology, 2nd Ed.*, New York, Holt, Rinehart & Winston, 1979

ESPIONAGE

Bernikow, Louise, *Abel*, London, Hodder and Stoughton, 1970

Bryan, George S., *The Spy In America*, Philadelphia, Lippincott, 1943

Chambers, Whittaker, *Witness*, New York, Random House, 1952

Flexner, James Thomas, *The Traitor and the Spy*, New York, Harcourt, Brace, 1953

Hiss, Alger, *In The Court Of Public Opinion*, New York, Knopf, 1957

Hyde, H. Montgomery, *The Atom Bomb Spies*, New York, Atheneum, 1980

Khokhlov, Nikolai, *In The Name Of Conscience*, New York, David McKay Co., 1959

Pilat, Oliver, *The Atom Spies*, New York, G.P. Putnam's Sons, 1952

Rosenberg, Julius and Ethel, *The Testament of Ethel and Julius Rosenberg*, New York, Cameron & Kahn, 1954

Schneir, Walter and Miriam, *Invitation to an Inquest* (extended reprint), New York, Pantheon, 1983

MURDER AND KIDNAPPING

Alix, Ernest Kahlar, *Ransom Kidnapping in America 1874–1974 / The Creation of a Capital Crime*, Carbondale, Southern Illinois University Press, 1978

Ambler, Eric, *The Ability to Kill*, New York, Curtis, 1956

Bierstadt, Edward Hale, *Enter Murderers!*, New York, Garden City Publishing Co., Inc., 1937

Busch, Francis X., *They Escaped the Hangman*, New York, Bobbs-Merrill Company, 1953

DeFord, Miriam Allen, *Murderers Sane & Mad*, New York, Abelard-Schuman, 1965

Dershowitz, Alan M., *Reversal of Fortune*, New York, Random House, 1986

Dobkins, J. Dwight & Hendricks, Robert J. *Winnie Ruth Judd: The Trunk Murders*, New York, Grosset & Dunlap, 1973

Higdon, Hal, *The Crime Of The Century: The Leopold And Loeb Case*, New York, Putnam, 1975

Holmes, Paul, *The Sheppard Murder Case*, New York, David McKay, 1961

Hynd, Alan, *Murder, Mayhem and Mystery*, New York, A.S. Barnes & Co., 1958

Langford, Gerald, *The Murder of Stanford White*, New York, Bobbs-Merrill, 1962

McKernan, Maureen, *The Amazing Crime and Trial of Leopold and Loeb*, New York, Signet, 1957

Nash, Jay Robert, *Murder, America*, London, Harrap London, 1981

Packer, Peter and Thomas, Bob, *The Massie Case*, New York, Bantam Books, 1966

Samuels, Charles and Louise, *The Girl in the House of Hate*, New York, Gold Medal, 1953

Scaduto, Anthony, *Scapegoat: The Lonesome Death of Bruno Richard Hauptmann*, New York, Putnam, 1976

Thaw, Harry K., *The Traitor*, Philadelphia, Dorrance & Co., 1926

Waller, George, *Kidnap: The Story of the Lindbergh Case*, New York, Dial Press, 1961

Wright, William, *The Von Bülow Affair*, New York, Delacourt Press, 1983

MASS MURDERERS AND SERIAL KILLERS

Abrahamsen, Dr. David, *Confessions of Son of Sam*, New York, Columbia University Press, 1985

Davis, Don, *The Milwaukee Murders*, New York, St. Martins, 1991

Frank, Gerald, *The Boston Strangler*, New York, New American Library, 1986

Larsen, Richard W., *Bundy: The Deliberate Stranger*, New York, Pocket, 1980

Sullivan, Terry w/ Maiken, Peter T., *Killer Clown: The John Wayne Gacy Murders*, New York, Pinnacle, 1983

ORGANIZED CRIME

Asbury, Herbert, *The Gangs of New York*, New York, Alfred A. Knopf, Inc., 1928

Balsamo, William & Carpozi, George, Jr., *Under the Clock*, Far Hills, N.J., New Horizon Press, 1988

Bonanno, Joseph, with Sergio Lalli, *A Man of Honor* (Autobiography), New York, Simon & Schuster, 1983

Chalmers, David M., *Hooded Americanism*, New York, Doubleday, 1965

Conklin, John E. (ed), *The Crime Establishment*, New York, Prentice Hall, 1973

Fox, Stephen, *Blood and Power: Organized Crime in Twentieth-Century America*, New York, William Morrow, 1989

Gage, Nicholas (ed.), *Mafia, USA*, New York, Playboy Press, 1972

Goode, James, *Wiretap: Listening in on America's Mafia*, New York, Fireside (Simon & Schuster), 1988

Gosch, Martin A. & Hammer, Richard, *The Last*

Testament of Lucky Luciano, New York, Little, Brown and Co., 1974

Horan, James D., *The Mob's Man*, London, Rob ert Hale, Ltd., 1960

Jennings, Dean, *We Only Kill Each Other: The Life and Bad Times of Bugsy Siegel*, New York, Prentice Hall, 1967

Katcher, Leo, *The Big Bankroll*, New Rochelle, N.Y., Arlington House, 1958

Kwitny, Jonathan, *Vicious Circles*, New York, W.W. Norton, 1979

Martin, Raymond V., *Revolt In the Mafia*, New York, Duel, Sloan and Pearce, 1963

Maas, Peter, *The Valachi Papers*, New York, Putnam, 1968

Monaco, Richard & Bascom, Lionel, Rubouts: *Mob Murders in America*, New York, Avon, 1991

Mustain, Gene & Capeci, Jerry, *Mob Star: The Story of John Gotti*, New York, Dell, 1989

O'Brien, Joseph F. & Kurins, Andris, *Boss of Bosses*, New York, Dell, 1992

O'Neill, Gerard & Lehr, Dich, *The Underboss*, New York, St. Martin's, 1989

Pasley, Fred, *Al Capone: The Biography of a Self-Made Man*, New York, Garden City, 1930

Pileggi, Nicholas, *Wiseguy: The Story of Henry Hill*, New York, Simon & Schuster, 1985

Sondern, Frederic, Jr., *Brotherhood of Evil: The Mafia*, New York, Farrar, Straus, 1959

Talese, Gay, *Honor Thy Father*, New York, World, 1971

Teresa, Vincent Charles (with Thomas C. Renner), *My Life in the Mafia*, New York, Doubleday & Co., 1973

Tyler, Gus (ed.), *Organized Crime in America*, Ann Arbor, U. of Michigan Press, 1962

OUTLAWS, CROOKS AND ROBBERS

Behn, Noel, *Big Stick-up at Brinks!*, New York, Warner, 1978

Black, Jack, *You Can't Win*, New York, Macmillan, 1926

Booth, Ernest, *Stealing Through Life*, New York, Knopf, 1929

DeFord, Miriam Allen, *The Real Bonnie & Clyde*, New York, Ace, 1968

Hickey, Neil, *The Gentleman was a Thief*, New York, Holt, Rinehart, 1961

Jackson, Bruce, *A Thief's Primer*, New York, Macmillan, 1969

Johnson, Ray, *Too Dangerous To Be At Large*, New York, Quadrangle/The New York Times Book Co., 1975

Maurer, David W., *Whiz Mob*, New Haven, Conn., College & University Press, 1955

Preece, Harold, *The Dalton Gang*, New York, Hastings House, 1963

Rosberg, Robert, *Game of Thieves*, New York, Everest House, 1981

Sutton, Willie with Edward Linn, *Where the Money Was*, New York, Viking, 1976

Toland, John, *The Dillinger Days*, New York, Random House, 1963

PENOLOGY

Lamott, Kenneth, *Chronicles of San Quentin*, New York, David McKay, 1961

Lawes, Lewis E., *Life and Death in Sing Sing*, New York, Doubleday, 1928

——— *Twenty Thousand Years in Sing Sing*, New York, Blue Ribbon, 1932

Maguire, Kathleen & Flanagan, Timothy J. (eds), *Sourcebook of Criminal Justice Statistics 1990*, Washington, D.C., U.S. Department of Justice, Bureau of Justice Statistics, USGPO, 1991

Robinson, Louis N., *Penology in the United States*, Philadelphia, The John C. Winston Company, 1921

POLICE AND THE LAW

Bowen, Walter S. and Neal, Harry Edward, *The United States Secret Service*, New York, Chilton, 1960

Branham, Vernon & Kutash, Samuel (Eds), *Encyclopedia of Criminology*, New York, Philosophical Library, 1949

Carey, Arthur A., *Memoirs of a Murder Man*, New York, Doubleday, Doran and Company, 1930

Cook, Fred J., *The FBI Nobody Knows*, New York, Macmillan, 1964

Daley, Robert, *Target Blue: An Insiders View of the N.Y.P.D.*, New York, Delacourt, 1973

Danforth, Harold R. and Horan, James D., *The D.A.'s Man*, New York, Crown, 1957

Hills, Stuart L., *Crime, Power, and Morality*, Scranton, Chandler, 1971

Horan, James D. & Swiggett, Howard, *The Pinkerton Story*, New York, Putnam's, 1951

Lewis, Anthony, *Gideon's Trumpet*, New York, Random House, 1964

McWatters, George S., *Knots Untied: or Ways and By-Ways in the Hidden Life of American Detectives*, Hartford, J.B. Burr and Hyde, 1871

Pinkerton, Allan, *Thirty Years a Detective*, New York, G.W. Dillingham Co., 1883

Rachlin, Harvey, *The Making Of a Cop*, New York, Pocket Books, 1991

Reynolds, Quentin, *Courtroom*, New York, Farrar, Straus and Co., 1950

______ *Headquarters*, New York, Harper, 1955

Rubinstein, Jonathan, *City Police*, New York, Farrar, Straus, 1973

Smith, Bruce (rev by Bruce Smith Jr.), *Police Systems in the United States*, New York, Harper & Row, 1940

Söderman, Harry, *Policeman's Lot*, New York, Funk & Wagnalls, 1956

Stead, Philip John (Ed), *Pioneers in Policing*, Montclair, N.J., Patterson Smith, 1977

Sullivan, John L., *Introduction to Police Science*, New York, McGraw-Hill, 1966

Sullivan, Mary, *My Double Life*, New York, Farrar & Rinehart, 1938

Sullivan, William, *The Bureau: My Thirty Years in Hoover's FBI*, New York, W. W. Norton & Co., 1979

Tully, Andrew, *Treasury Agent: The Inside Story*, New York, Simon and Schuster, 1958

Ungar, Sanford J., *FBI*, Boston, Little, Brown & Co., 1975

Vallee, Walter & McNear, Robert, *The Night Chief*, South Bend, Indiana, Regnery/Gateway, 1980

Wilkie, Don (as told to Mark Lee Luther), *American Secret Service Agent*, New York, Frederick A. Stokes Co., 1934

Willemse, Captain Cornelius W., *Behind the Green Lights*, Knopf, 1931

POLITICS AND CRIME

Callow, Alexander B., Jr., *The Tweed Ring*, New York, Oxford U. Press, 1965

Lavine, Emanuel H., *"Gimme" or How Politicians Get Rich*, New York, Vanguard, 1931

LeBrun, George P. (as told to Edward D. Radin), *It's Time to Tell*, New York, William Morrow, 1962

Lynch, Denis T., *"Boss" Tweed*, New York, Boni and Liveright, 1927

MacKaye, Milton, *The Tin Box Parade*, New York, Robert M. McBride & Co., 1934

Northrop, William B. & John B., *The Insolence of Office: The Story of the Seabury Investigations*, New York, Putnam's, 1932

Ornitz, Samuel, *Haunch Paunch and Jowl*, New York, Garden City Publishing Co., Inc., 1923

PROHIBITION

Furnas, J.C., *The Life and Times of The Late Demon Rum*, New York, Capricorn Books, 1965

Lyle, John H., *The Dry and Lawless Years*, Englewood Cliffs, N.J., Prentice-Hall, 1960

Severn, Bill, *The End of the Roaring Twenties: Prohibition and Repeal*, New York, Julian Messner, 1969

Taylor, Robert Lewis, *Vessel of Wrath: The Life and Times of Carry Nation*, New York, New American Library, 1966

Topic Index

Entries on individuals and subjects are arranged alphabetically in this volume. For entries on the following topics, see the entries listed below.